ENCOUNTERS

AMERICAN TRANSNATIONALISM

Perspectives from the Sheldon Museum of Art

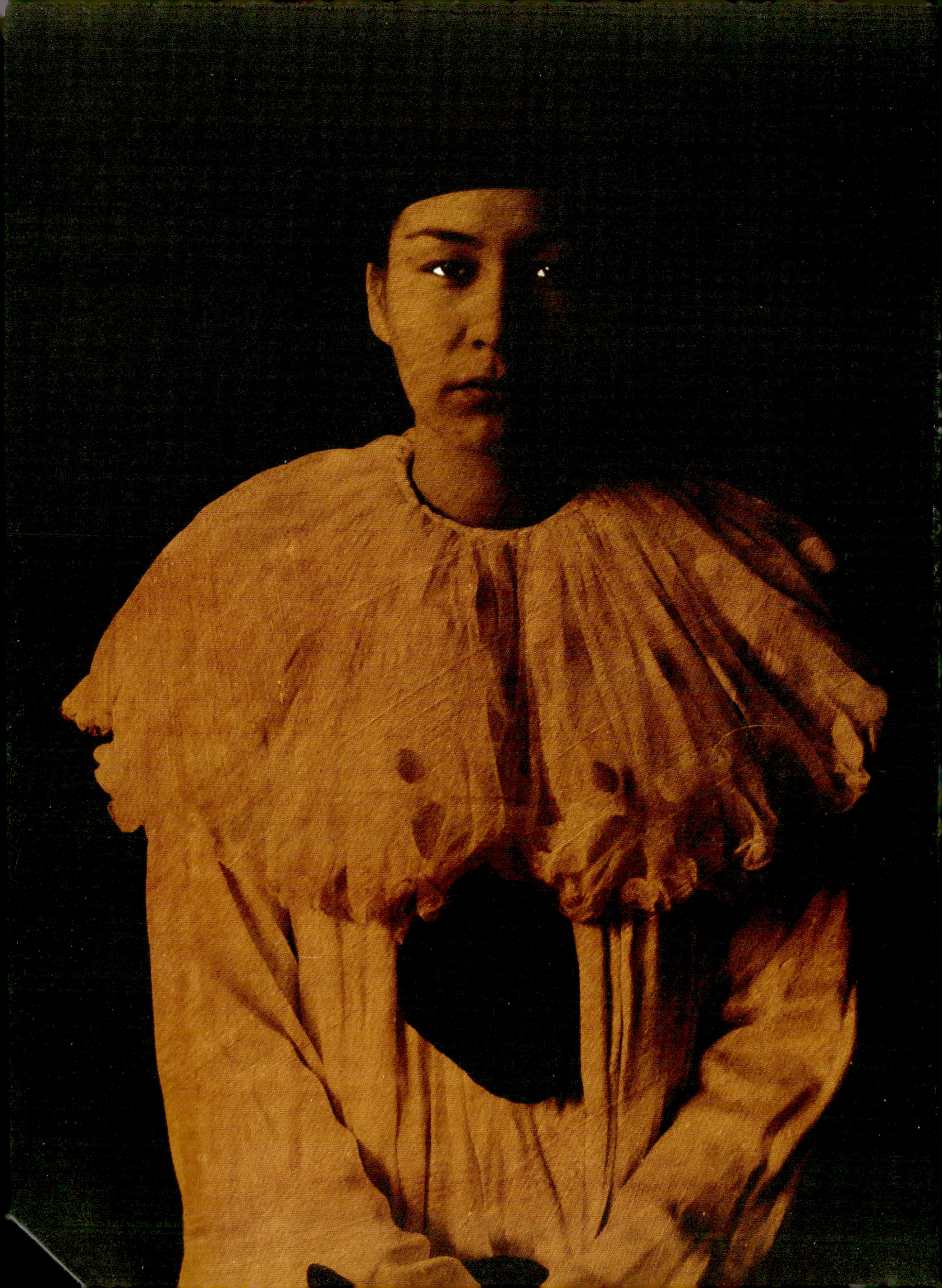

ENCOUNTERS

Photography from the Sheldon Museum of Art

EDITED BY BRANDON K. RUUD

With contributions by

Brandon K. Ruud	Jorge Daniel Veneciano
Britt Salvesen	Janet L. Farber
Gregory Nosan	Ashley Hussman
Zeynep Çelik	Robert G. O'Meally
Sarah Feit	Sharon L. Kennedy
Keith F. Davis	

University of Nebraska Press | Lincoln and London

Encounters: Photography from the Sheldon Museum of Art was published in conjunction with an exhibition organized by the Sheldon Museum of Art, University of Nebraska-Lincoln, and presented from February 1 to April 28, 2013.

Support for this exhibition and publication is generously provided by the Office of the President of the University of Nebraska, James B. Milliken, and the Robert Mapplethorpe Foundation.

Project coordinated by Gregory Nosan

Photo research by Ashley Hussman, Laura Mohr, and Jaclyn Siemers

Photographs of works in the collection of the Sheldon Museum of Art by John Nollendorfs, Edson Rumbaugh, and John Spence, coordinated by Genevieve Ellerbee

Library of Congress Cataloging-in-Publication Data

Sheldon Museum of Art.

   Encounters / photography from the Sheldon Museum of Art ; edited by Brandon K. Ruud ; with contributions by Brandon K. Ruud, Britt Salvesen, Gregory Nosan, Zeynep Çelik, Sarah Feit, Keith F. Davis, Jorge Daniel Veneciano, Janet L. Farber, Ashley Hussman, Robert G. O'Meally, Sharon L. Kennedy.

   pages   cm. — (American transnationalism : perspectives from the Sheldon Museum of Art)

"Published in conjunction with an exhibition organized by the Sheldon Museum of Art, University of Nebraska Lincoln, and presented from February 1 to April 28, 2013."

Includes bibliographical references and index.

   ISBN 978-0-8032-4518-1 (pbk. : alk. paper)

1. Travel photography—Exhibitions. 2. Photographs—Nebraska—Lincoln—Exhibitions. 3. Sheldon Museum of Art—Exhibitions. I. Ruud, Brandon K., 1968– editor of compilation. II. University of Nebraska-Lincoln. III. Title.

   TR790S496 2013   770.74'78282—dc23   2012027330

Designed and set in Neutraface and Minion Pro by A. Shahan.

Front cover: Lalla Essaydi. *Les femmes du Maroc, # 25 A,* 2006 (cat. 6).

Back cover: Lalla Essaydi. *Les femmes du Maroc, # 25 B,* 2006 (cat. 6).

p. ii: Luis González Palma. *Milagros,* 1993 (cat. 22). **p. vi:** Frederick Sommer. *Smoke on Glass,* 1965 (cat. 85). **p. viii:** Yinka Shonibare. *The Sleep of Reason Produces Monsters (America),* 2006 (cat. 25). **p. x:** Ruth Bernhard. *Two Forms,* 1965 (cat. 107). **p. xii:** Jean Pascal Sébah and Policarpe Joaillier. *A Turkish Woman in Street Dress,* 1894 (cat. 3). **p. 56:** Richard Misrach. *Desert Fire #1, Burning Palms,* 1983 (cat. 43). **p. 96:** Danny Lyon. *Uptown, Chicago, July 1965,* 1965 (cat. 50). **p. 118:** Imogen Cunningham. *Wood beyond the World,* 1912 (cat. 56). **p. 138:** André Kertész. *Satiric Dancer,* 1926 (cat. 72). **p. 190:** Artist Unknown. *Portrait of Mother and Daughter,* 1850s (cat. 90). **p. 236:** Renée Cox. *Mother of Us All,* 2004 (cat. 23). **p. 238:** Eugène Atget. *Men's Fashions* (p. 208). **p. 240:** Minor White. *Juniper, Lake Tenaya, California,* 1964 (cat. 40).

CONTENTS

Acknowledgments   vii

Introduction: *Photography in Transnational Light*
by Jorge Daniel Veneciano   ix

BETWEEN AND ACROSS CULTURES   1

NATURE AND THE BUILT ENVIRONMENT   57

RITES OF PASSAGE   97

RELIGION AND SPIRITUALITY   119

TRADITION AND MODERNITY   139

GENDER, IDENTITY, AND SEXUALITY   191

Contributors   237

Illustration Credits   239

Index of Artists and Works   241

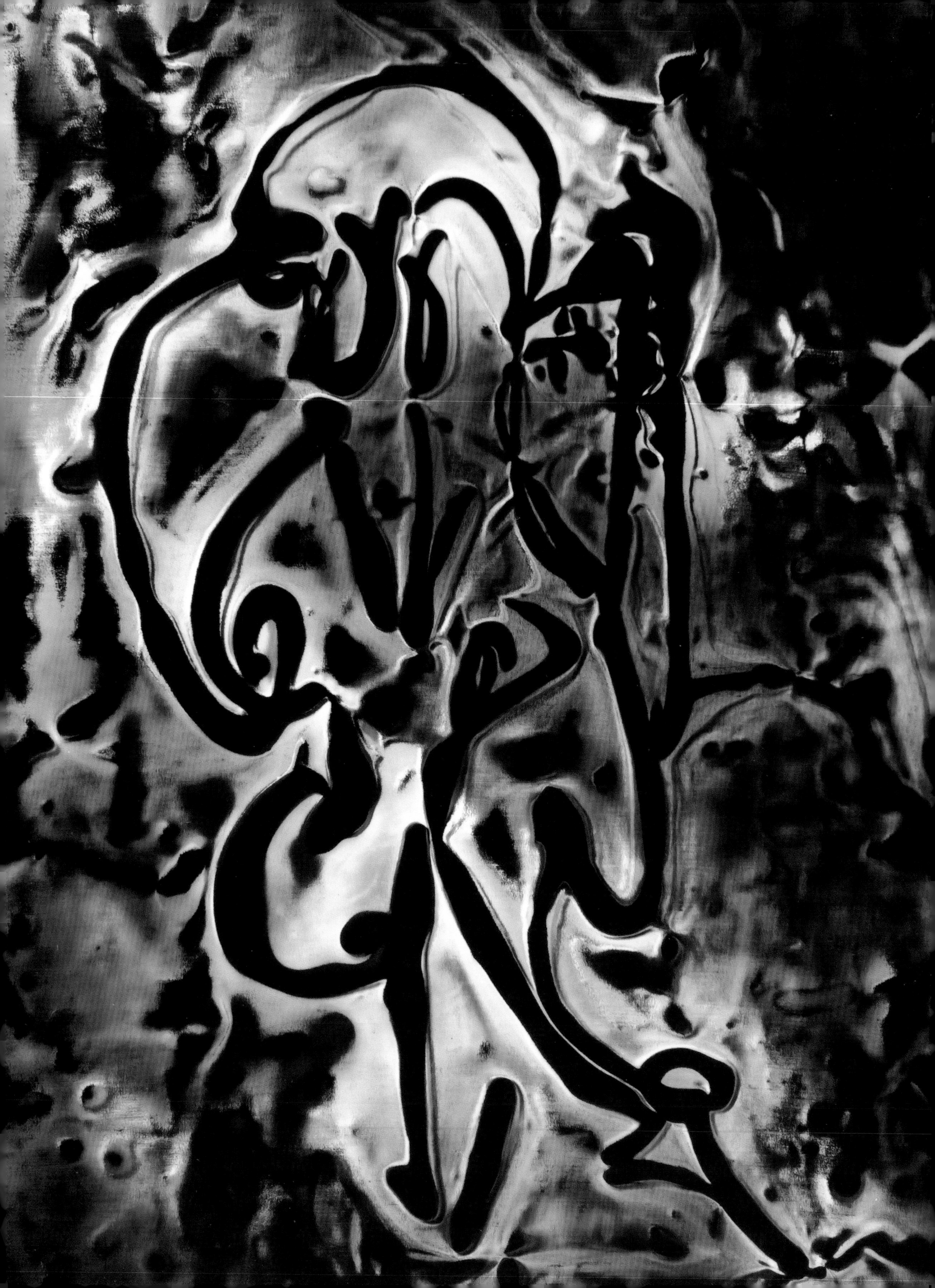

Brandon K. Ruud

This project is the first major monograph to explore the Sheldon Museum of Art's extensive photography collection—which numbers over two thousand objects—in more than three decades. A substantial undertaking, it could only have been accomplished with the help of skilled individuals both within and beyond our institution. John Nollendorfs, Edson Rumbaugh, and John Spence lent their expertise in photographing the images, and associate registrar Genevieve Ellerbee coordinated all aspects of imaging, assisted by former collections assistant Laura Mohr. Object research was initially led by assistant curator of education Sarah Feit with the strong support of graduate interns Lindsay Andrews and Jaclyn Siemers, each of whom was indispensable to the task.

I am extremely grateful to the catalog authors for their contributions, which make this book immeasurably richer. Zeynep Çelik, Keith Davis, Janet L. Farber, Sarah Feit, Ashley Hussman, Gregory Nosan, Robert G. O'Meally, Britt Salvesen, Jorge Daniel Veneciano, and Sharon Kennedy all brought invaluable expertise and insights to the project, and it has been my pleasure to work with—and learn from—each and every one of them. Many thanks also go to our partners at the University of Nebraska Press, including Donna Shear, who championed the idea of launching a series of Sheldon publications; Bridget Barry, who coordinated our joint efforts with a steady hand; and Andrea Shahan, who designed this publication with her characteristic brilliance. Their colleagues Ann Baker, Courtney Ochsner, and Joeth Zucco contributed to this project's success in innumerable ways as well. The Sheldon's collaboration with the press was suggested and enthusiastically championed by the museum's director, Jorge Daniel Veneciano; I thank him for his confidence and look forward to the next publication in this series. A project of this magnitude also requires substantial financial support, and for their generosity, I am grateful to University of Nebraska president, James B. Milliken, and the Robert Mapplethorpe Foundation for helping to make this endeavor a reality.

Finally, I am thankful for the assistance of two people in particular: curatorial assistant Ashley Hussman and director of education and publications Gregory Nosan. Ashley joined the Sheldon staff in the fall of 2011 as the project was well underway, but she quickly stepped in and skillfully managed many of its most challenging aspects, including researching objects, obtaining copyright and licensing permissions, and verifying inscriptions. Her abundant talents are on display in the two entries she contributed. In addition to bringing his love of language and sharp attention to detail to the editing process, Greg was a helpful partner in the catalog's development, offering a receptive ear and a keen knowledge of art-book production. His skills as a scholar and writer are amply demonstrated in his essays for this volume.

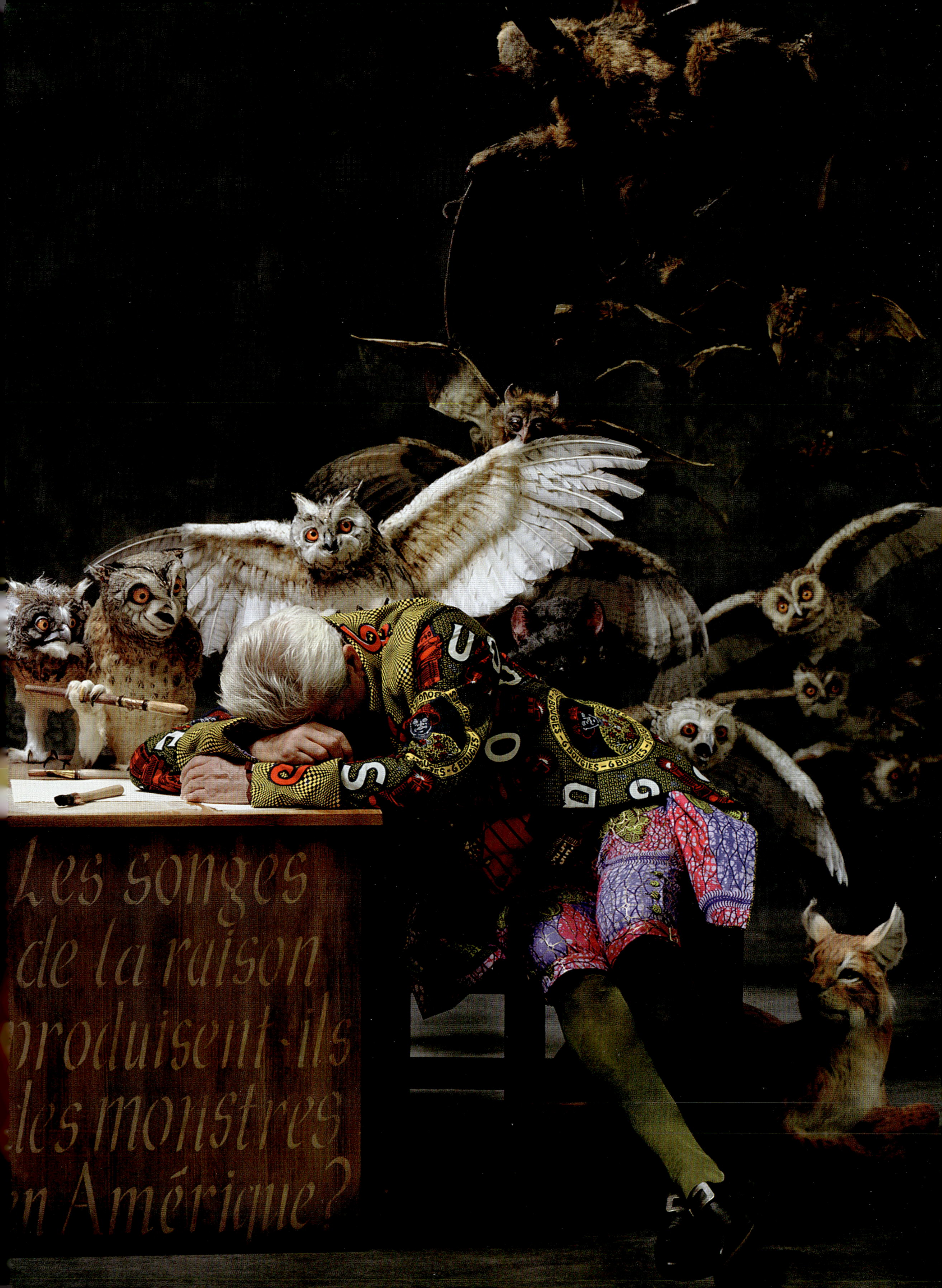

Les songes
de la raison
produisent-ils
les monstres
n Amérique?

Jorge Daniel Veneciano

This volume offers a transnational study of the photography collection at the Sheldon Museum of Art. Though our holdings emphasize American art, this area is international in scope, spanning over 175 years of the medium's history and containing prints by canonical figures as diverse as Julia Margaret Cameron and James VanDerZee and contemporary artists as challenging as Lalla Essaydi, Catherine Opie, and Yinka Shonibare. This survey presents a wide selection of more than one hundred photographs and develops new transnational methods of research to the study of museum collections.

The transnational study of art, at its most basic, cuts across national boundaries to trace aesthetic and cultural influences. It makes good sense as an approach because reality always overflows the containers we design for it. Nations, for instance, are made by people yet comprise children, men, and women of different cultural tastes, regional dialects, religions, and skin colors. We pursue scholarly integrity as an ideal, therefore, not by superimposing sameness on national culture but by acknowledging the cultural confluences that build a nation. Applied to the United States, transnational study gives us richer ways of describing the *pluribus* to the *unum* we call America.

In this project, instead of regarding culture as a unity, we think about cultures in dialogue—that is, we think about encounters as being articulated from different vantage points. As negotiations with difference, encounters often produce by-products, hybrids, liminal states that are not easily slotted into fixed categories. This is the ambivalent space, for example, of polylingual, "hyphenated" Americans.

Yet this publication takes us beyond any stable notion of transnational study. We turn the concept of encounters into a metaphor for analyzing exchanges that occur on a scale smaller than that of nations. This is our advance on the idea of transnationalism: not only do we use it to learn about national cultures in contact with one another, but we also hold it up, as a mirror, to explore encounters internal to the United States—between European Americans and indigenous peoples, between recent immigrants and assimilated populations, and even between explorers and the sublime lands of the New World.

We take the spirit of encounters as posing challenges to thinking in terms of singularity and apply this challenge to the individual as well as the state. As individuals we experience the in-betweenness of changes and growth against the backdrop of social expectations. These are personal encounters—with the uncertainties between adolescence and maturity, for example, or between individuality and conformity. We can even look at the acculturation of sexuality and gender as ongoing encounters between what it means to be men and women, with all the possibilities in between and outside these boxes. Religion and spiritualism answer our encounters with the unknown. This is transnationalism turned inward, expanding rather than becoming another fixed category. These metaphoric applications of transnational study appear as six sections in this volume, each organized as schools of images and scholarship in dialogue.

Finally, photography is perhaps the most transnational of visual media in the sense that it fosters encounters as no other medium does. Their perceived aptitude for recording the likeness of things in time and space makes photographic prints ideal instruments for cultural encounters. Their durability and portability allow them to convey their content over time and space. This facility revolutionized our worldview. The world began shrinking measurably as visual evidence of far-flung places and peoples became increasingly accessible.

As an educational institution, the Sheldon Museum of Art strives to make sense of photography's revolutionizing worldview by introducing innovative ways of interpreting the artifacts in its collection and in the world around us.

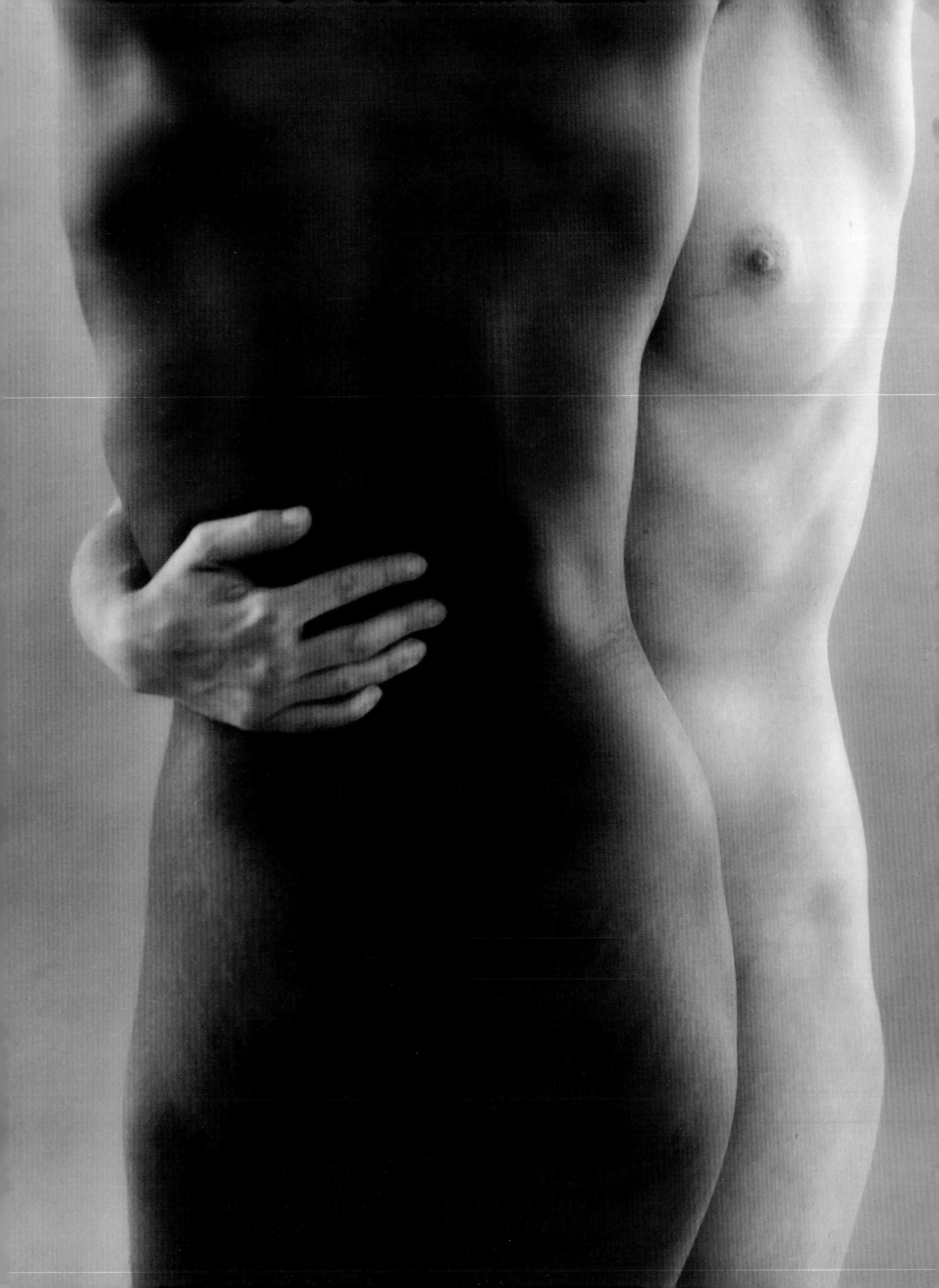

ENCOUNTERS

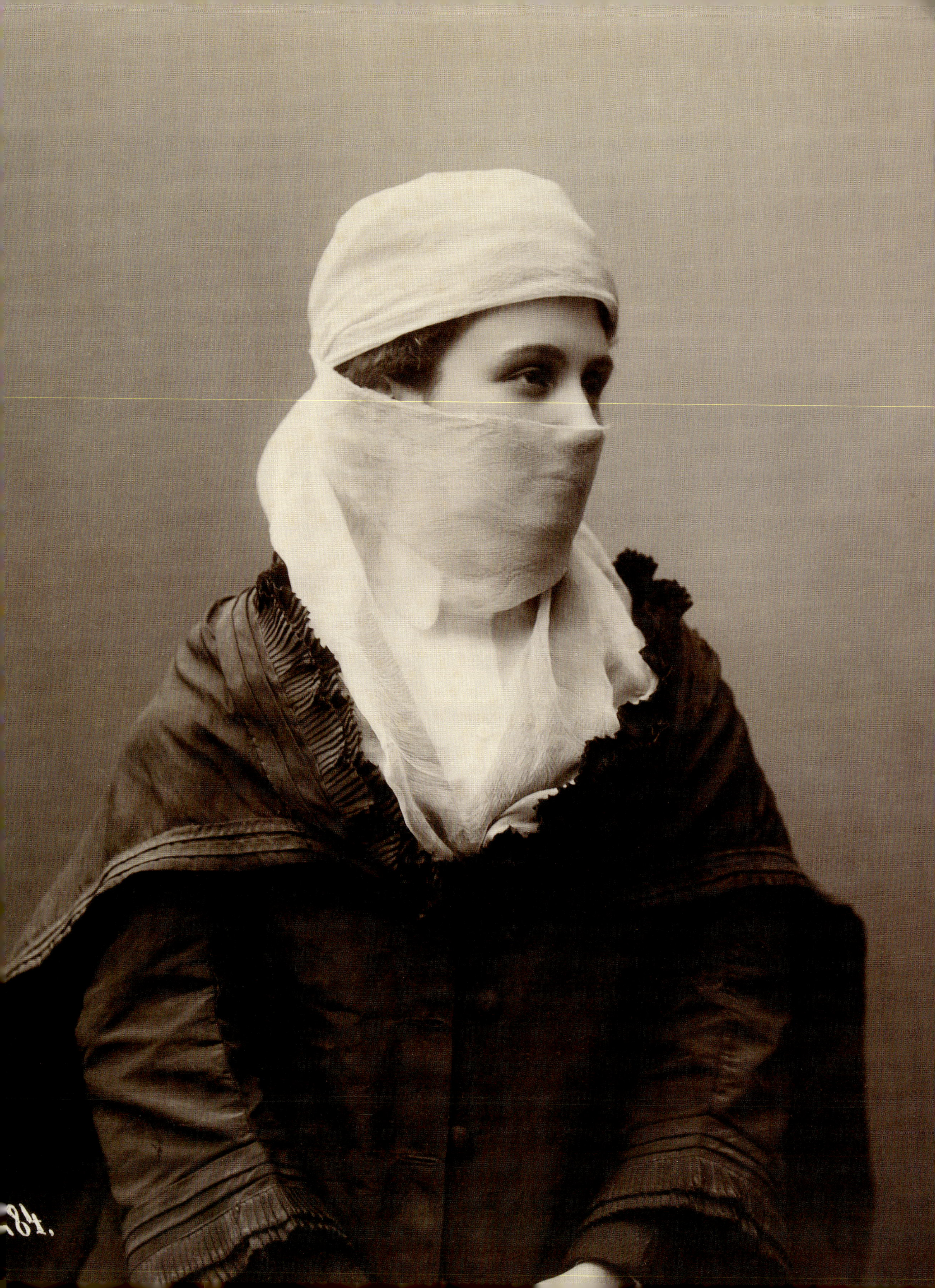
84.

BETWEEN AND ACROSS CULTURES

For centuries, artist-explorers made drawings and watercolors to depict the places and people they encountered, frequently publishing these works in magnificent volumes intended for educated, cosmopolitan audiences. In the nineteenth century, photography revolutionized the creation and transmission of such images. As tourism transformed itself from an exclusive province of the elite into an increasingly middle-class pursuit, travelers sought ways to document and record their foreign experiences on their own. At the same time, large photography firms capitalized on these new consumers, producing, distributing, and selling small mounted pictures that could be placed in albums and exchanged as *cartes de visite*, images that were traded between acquaintances and collected enthusiastically.

These widely circulating photographs helped establish popular ideas about the cultures being depicted and, in many instances, reiterated stereotypes about subjugated peoples that were already firmly part of the American and European consciousness. Such is the case with the images in this volume taken by the Middle Eastern firms of Félix Bonfils and Jean Pascal Sébah (cats. 5 and 10; 3, 4, and 91). The Sheldon's collection is surprisingly rich in these early tourist photographs, which represent cultures from Europe to the Middle East to Asia. The museum's holdings also contain works by contemporary artists such as Lalla Essaydi (cat. 6) and Yinka Shonibare (cat. 25). These artists specifically address the issues of cultural identity set down by their late nineteenth-century predecessors, exploring the experience of colonialism and diasporas and charting the complex network of aesthetic and cultural influences that informs their art.

By exposing themselves to alien societies, many nineteenth- and twentieth-century travelers were searching for a sense of national identity and personal rejuvenation. This dynamic was not limited to foreign tourism, however: photographers also looked to "primitive" cultures that existed within their own countries. Rapid industrialization and mechanization led numerous artists to seek examples of rustic simplicity as an antidote to the perceived ills of modern life. American photographers saw these qualities in Native Americans, and John Anderson and Charles Fletcher Lummis (cats. 14 and 12), among others, depicted indigenous populations in an attempt to salvage what they thought were vanishing cultures. At the same time, the influx of immigrants gave rise to concerns about fair labor practices, housing, and unemployment, and photographers such as Lewis Hine took to the streets in order to capture immigrants' distressing conditions. Alfred Stieglitz's iconic photograph *The Steerage* (cat. 15) shows the reverse of the American Dream: huddled masses not flocking to the United States but fleeing from it.

These cultural diasporas became the concern of other contemporary photographers who not only documented the phenomenon but also investigated ways to question the complex, multilayered nature of migrations, whether they were chosen or forced. In his work, for example, Tseng Kwong Chi investigated what it means to be a foreign visitor in another country, photographing himself dressed in the national uniform of Chinese Communism while standing next to famous American landmarks (cat. 20); Carrie Mae Weems explores issues of authority and power in the creation of the African diaspora on both sides of the Atlantic (cat. 21); and Renée Cox revisits her Jamaican heritage, embodying the historical figure of Queen Nanny of the Maroons, the leader of a slave rebellion on the island (cat. 23).

1

Artist Unknown

Basket and Broom Peddler, late nineteenth century
Albumen print with hand coloring
Image and sheet: 19.7 × 26.7 cm (7 ¾ × 10 ½ in)
University of Nebraska, Anna R. and Frank M. Hall
Charitable Trust, H-2278

In 1854 American commodore Matthew Perry forced Japan to resume international trade after over two centuries of cultural isolation. A little over a decade later, to help finance the country's industrialization, Japan's pro-Western Meiji government encouraged further contact and trade, particularly in its highly prized art. For European and American consumers who were looking to escape the perceived ills of their own rapidly developing industrial economies, this loosening of borders and opening of exchange ushered in a craze for all things Japanese. For them, Japan came to represent a fantasy world free from the degradations of mechanization and mass production. As Japanism spread, artists and writers in particular responded to the possibilities of Japanese art and design.[1] They absorbed and reinterpreted Asian aesthetic approaches in their own art, embracing the use of flattened pictorial space, harmonies of light and dark, skewed perspectives, and stylized vegetal motifs.

Western travelers also took advantage of the newly porous national boundaries. In the mid-nineteenth century, they visited Japan mainly on business, diplomatic, and scientific ventures. Later in the century, however, they came as tourists, cameras in hand. On the one hand, this new technology represented a method of capturing Japanese culture through a Western lens; on the other, it seemed to be an advancement that was out of step with the traditional society that visitors sought. Perhaps because of their perceived detachment from the commercialism of modern consumer culture, Japanese merchants and street vendors drew particular attention and admiration from tourists, finding themselves the frequent topic of essays and guidebooks.[2] Douglas Sladen, for example, wrote an article for the British general-interest magazine *Windsor* in 1896, describing at length the clothing and wares of Japanese street vendors. He featured several photographs in the piece and employed a language that was both objective and poetic: "He wears the outer and inner kimonos—the latter held in by a cotton crêpe sash at the waist—breeches, leggings of stout blue cotton wrapped around his legs after the manner of the Sardinians, who used to make London streets hideous with their bagpipes, thick *tabi*, and the rope sandals secured by tying round the insteps and ankles. He only has the coarser kind of baskets. The Japanese excel in the manufacture of all kinds of them."[3]

Photographers also used street vendors as a favorite subject, perhaps because it allowed them to showcase some of the crafts prized by foreigners and build an understandable narrative around them. This image is typical of Japanese photographs produced at the end of the nineteenth century, and the inscription at bottom right suggests that it was created specifically for an English-speaking tourist market.[4] The three figures stand posed almost equidistant from each other, creating a visual triangle and performing a drama sketched out by the photographer. While the merchant looks suspiciously at the camera, the woman at center holds one of his baskets delicately in both hands, presenting it to the viewer, while her compatriot at left demonstrates one of the long-handled wooden ladles for sale. The hand tinting—a common feature of Japanese photographs at the time—adds rosy hues to the baskets, ropes, and even the tearoom sign at the upper left, while vivid splashes of red and purple accent the women's lips and clothing. **BKR**

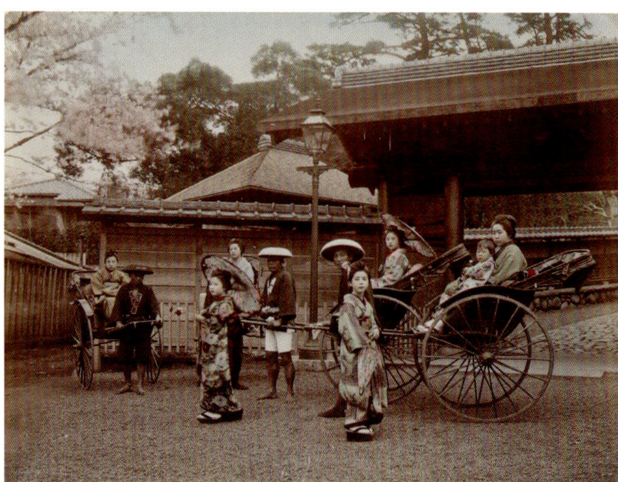

Artist Unknown. *Untitled (Street Scene in Kyoto)*, late nineteenth century. Albumen print with hand coloring; 21 × 27.3 cm (8 ¼ × 10 ¾ in). University of Nebraska, Anna R. and Frank M. Hall Charitable Trust, H-2276.

1. For more on Japanism, see Ellen E. Roberts, "The Spell of Japan Was upon Them: Japanism and the Arts and Crafts Movement," in *Apostles of Beauty: Arts and Crafts from Britain to Chicago*, ed. Judith A. Barter et al., exhibition catalog (Chicago: Art Institute of Chicago; New Haven CT: Yale University Press, 2009), 45–82. 2. For a typical example, see Edward S. Morse, *Japan: Day by Day*, 1877, 1878–79, 1882–83, 2 vols. (Boston: Houghton Mifflin, 1917), 119–21. 3. Douglas Sladen, "How the Japanese Live," *Windsor Magazine* 3 (January–June 1896): 73. 4. For more on Japanese photographs from this period, see Terry Bennett, *Photography in Japan, 1853–1912* (Tokyo: Tuttle Publishing, 2006), esp. 194 and 208, figs. 262 and 287.

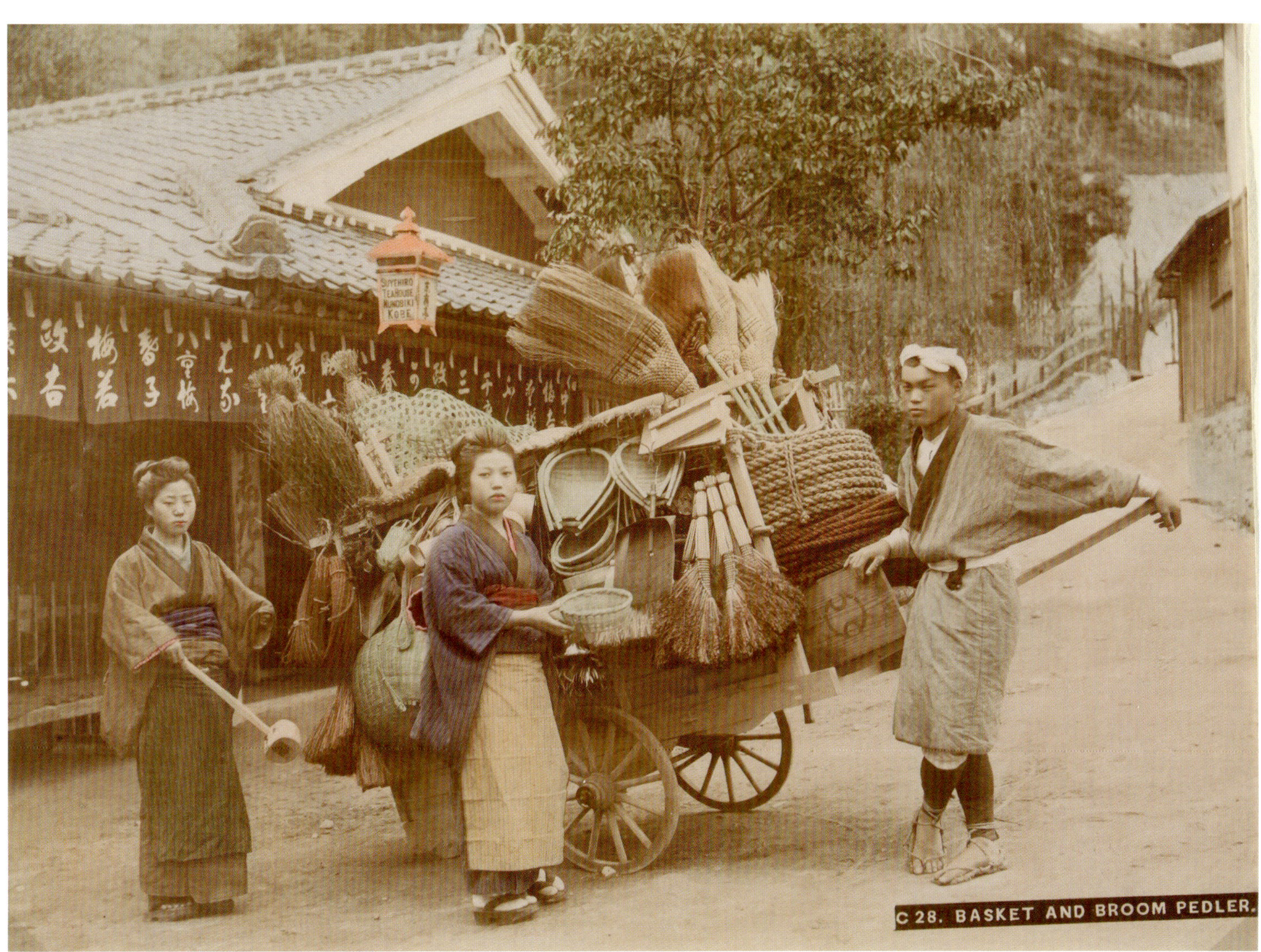

C 28. BASKET AND BROOM PEDLER.

2

Arnold Genthe

American, born Germany, 1869–1942

*Paying New Year's Calls, Chinatown,
San Francisco*, c. 1900
Gelatin silver print
Image: 34.1 × 23.3 cm (13 7/16 × 9 3/16 in); mount: 45.7 ×
35.6 cm (18 × 14 in)
Signed, on mount, lower left, in pencil:
Arnold Genthe / N.Y.
University of Nebraska, Anna R. and Frank M. Hall
Charitable Trust, H-2030

Shortly after he immigrated to the United States in 1895, Arnold Genthe secured a job as a tutor to the children of a wealthy San Francisco family with German connections. During his spare time, he trolled the city's streets with his Baedeker guidebook, teaching himself photography with a small camera to satisfy his desire for artistic images of his new surroundings. In particular, he became fascinated with Chinatown (otherwise known as the Tangenbru district). The area, constructed during California's gold rush, had grown to twelve square blocks and become the physical and spiritual home of tens of thousands of Chinese, who were segregated as a result of racist hostility.[1] Between 1896 and 1906, Genthe repeatedly visited the district, publishing many of his photographs in the 1908 volume *Pictures of Old Chinatown* with accompanying text by the journalist Will Irwin. Genthe took most of these pictures surreptitiously, hiding in doorways or behind buildings to capture his subjects, whom he described as having a "deep-seated superstition" of the camera, which they called a "black devil box."[2] In truth, numerous formal portraits of Asian Americans from the time correct this assumption and instead suggest that their aversion to the camera was less a result of unfamiliarity than of Genthe's own voyeuristic prying.

Genthe's attitude toward his subjects informed his romantic opinion of Chinatown, which to him represented an exotic excursion, equally appealing for its alien charms and its hidden dangers. In his memoir, he described open streets where "dark-clad silent figures of the men" and "children in gay costume" thronged among shop windows decorated with "brocades and embroideries, bronzes and porcelains" and festooned with "gilt signs inscribed in the picturesque Chinese characters." At the same time, there existed a dangerous underworld where in "dark alleys and courtyards . . . drug addicts and suspicious characters" pursued "their insidious ways."[3] Genthe's photographs highlight this impression, with the majority devoted to children in holiday costume, giving the impression that this was their everyday dress.

In addition to his choice of subjects, Genthe's selective editing and manipulation of his compositions also reinforced his romantic artistic vision. As Emma J. Teng has argued, the photographer "tended to crop his published compositions fairly tightly around the central figures, thus eliminating panoramic street views" and "leading the viewer to wonder what lies just beyond the field of vision": "By the tight controlling of space, the use of dramatic shadows, and the focus on architectural detail rather than entire buildings, Genthe recreates visually the mysterious and sinister atmosphere of the Chinatown cityscape."[4]

The surroundings in *Paying New Year's Calls*, which is cropped to focus exclusively on the adult and child, disappear in a ghostly pictorialist haze, and the figures exist apart from any context. A nitrate negative housed at the Library of Congress, however, reveals a much wider expanse of street, showing late nineteenth-century brownstones with fire escapes, large sidewalks, a crisscross of telephone wires, and a series of streetcar tracks over which the pair step. Rather than depicting Chinatown as distant, foreign, and remote, Genthe's original negative clearly shows the district to be part of San Francisco's urban fabric, as open and accessible by foot, rail, and telephone as any other place in the city. **BKR**

1. For more on the history of San Francisco's Chinatown and racism in California, see John Kuo Wei Tchen, *Genthe's Photographs of San Francisco's Old Chinatown* (New York: Dover Publications, 1984), 3–9; and Emma J. Teng, "Artifacts of a Lost City: Arnold Genthe's Pictures of Old Chinatown and Its Intertexts," in *Re/collecting Early Asian America: Essays in Cultural History*, ed. Josephine Lee, Imogene L. Lim, and Yuko Matsukawa (Philadelphia: Temple University Press, 2002), 56–57. **2.** Arnold Genthe, *As I Remember* (New York: Arno Press, 1979), 34. **3.** Genthe, *As I Remember*, 32–33. **4.** Teng, "Artifacts of a Lost City," 65–67.

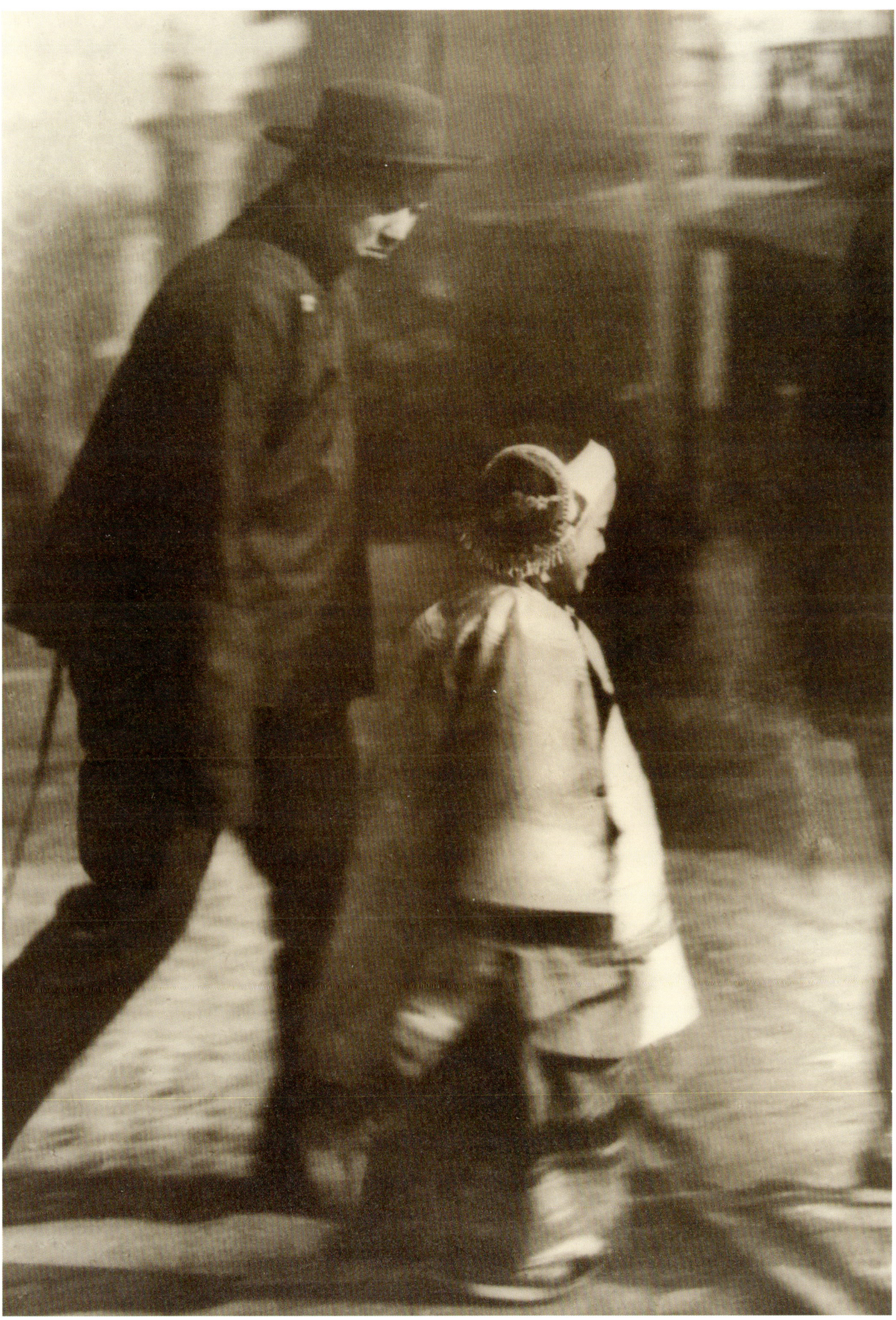

Jean Pascal Sébah
Turkish, 1872–1947

Policarpe Joaillier
French, active 1888–1908

A Turkish Woman in Street Dress, 1894
Albumen print
Image and sheet: 25.4 × 21 cm (10 × 8 ¼ in)
Printed, in image, lower left: *N. 784.*
University of Nebraska, Anna R. and Frank M. Hall
Charitable Trust, H-2285

The story of the Sébah studio is linked to the nineteenth-century market for travel photography, which recorded a steady growth from the 1860s onward. Established in Istanbul in 1857 by Pascal Sébah, who was the son of a Syrian Catholic father and an Armenian mother, the studio responded to the demands and desires of foreign tourists with photographs of the city's favorite sites and a range of local people (in the French convention of *scènes et types*) as well as with personal shots taken in the studio against "typical" backdrops. The studio's phenomenal success in the Ottoman capital led Pascal Sébah to open another studio in Cairo in 1873, where he catered to similar clients.[1] That same year, he engaged in an important project under the leadership of Osman Hamdi, a prominent Ottoman intellectual and painter and later the director of the Imperial Museum in Istanbul, to provide a catalog of costumes with the understanding that this ethnographic study would display the "variety in unity" of the human landscape throughout the empire.[2] Prepared on the occasion of the Universal Exposition in Vienna, *Les costumes populaires de la Turquie en 1873* won Sébah a gold medal.

Upon Pascal Sébah's death, the studio was taken over by his son Jean Pascal, who started a partnership with French photographer Policarpe Joaillier in 1890. Responding to the growing demands of the tourism industry, the studio of Sébah and Joaillier thrived by producing not only affordable and highly popular *cartes de visite* but also, in the early twentieth century, postcards.

This photograph of a Turkish woman in street dress was taken in the studio of Sébah and Joaillier and dates from the 1890s.[3] It belongs to the tradition of the photographs in *Les costumes populaires* in that the neutral background emphasizes the clothing and is very closely related to two images from that book: *The Turkish Woman of Constantinople* and *The Muslim Woman of Rhodes.*[4] In all three images, the garb is the same: dark outdoor clothing; a double-layered cloak with the top layer wrapped around the shoulders; and a white *ferace*, a head cover that partially conceals the face. The difference is in the framing: in the photographs of the women of Constantinople and Rhodes, the subjects are presented full-length and with two other figures in the consistent format of *Les costumes*, which gives the book an encyclopedic tone; the Sheldon photograph is a portrait.

The studio of Sébah and Joaillier issued several photographs like this, testifying to the favorable reception of a respectful and seemingly documentary representation of Muslim women. However, this was not the only type of depiction of Muslim women—or even the most popular—circulated among foreigners. More frequent were photographs of reclining odalisques in harem interiors, complete with a recognizable catalog of Oriental paraphernalia: hookahs, mother-of-pearl tables, rugs and screens, and decorative elements such as arches and wooden lattice windows (see, e.g., cat. 7). Such sexualized photographs, with their links to Orientalist painting, belong to a prominent genre in nineteenth-century visual culture and have proven to be an enduring phenomenon, extending to the present day and evoking intriguing responses.[5] *A Turkish Woman in Street Dress* opposes such imagined, fantasized representations and derives from a broader Ottoman trend toward ethnography that is epitomized not only in *Les costumes* but also in many of Osman Hamdi's paintings, which show the women of Istanbul in public places. **ZÇ**

1. For general information on the Sébah studio, see Engin Özendeş, *From Sébah and Joaillier to Foto Sabah: Orientalism in Photography* (Istanbul: Yapı Kredi Kültür Sanat Yayıncılık Ticaret ve Sanayi A. Ş., 1999). **2.** Osman Hamdi Bey and Marie de Launay, *Les costumes populaires de la Turquie en 1873* (Constantinople: Imprimerie du Levant Times and Shipping Gazette, 1873). **3.** For the accepted title of the Sheldon's photograph, see Özendeş, *From Sébah and Joaillier*, 12. **4.** For reproductions of these two photographs, see Hamdi Bey and de Launay, *Les costumes populaires*, plates 4, 6. **5.** For one such response, see the entry in this volume on Lalla Essaydi's *Les femmes du Maroc* (cat. 6).

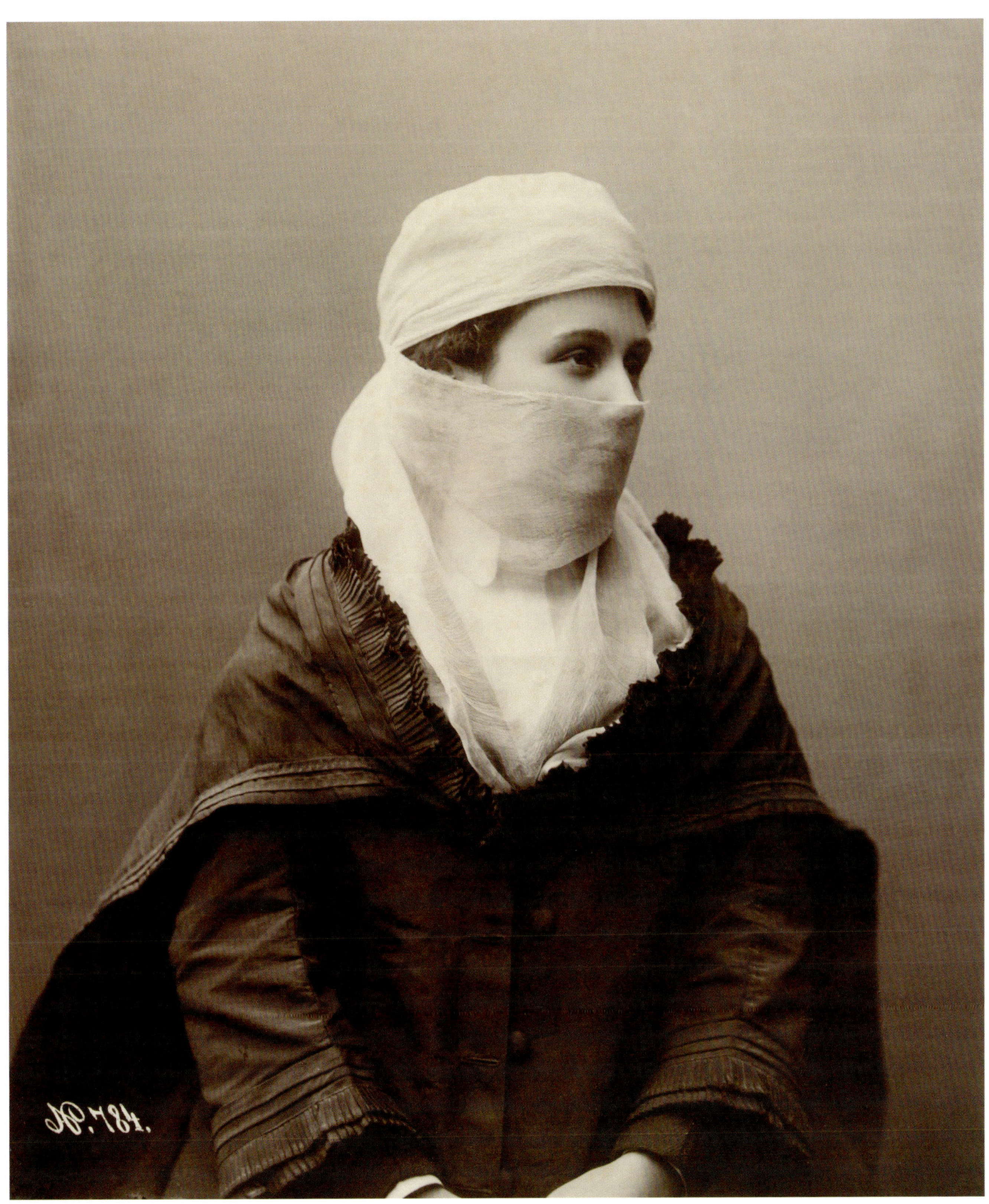

№ 784.

4

Jean Pascal Sébah
Turkish, 1872–1947

Policarpe Joaillier
French, active 1888–1908

Yuksek-Kaldirim, c. 1900
Albumen print
Image and sheet: 26.5 × 21 cm (10 7/16 × 8 1/4 in)
Printed, in image, lower left: *204. Yuksek-Kaldirim.*;
lower right: *Sébah & Joaillier*
University of Nebraska, Anna R. and Frank M. Hall
Charitable Trust, H-2261

This photograph, which dates from the 1890s, shows one of Istanbul's most popular sites.[1] Loosely translated from Turkish as "high steps," Yüksek Kaldırım is the shortest pedestrian route between the waterfront in the Galata Quarter to Pera on the hill, two very busy areas of the city. By the mid-nineteenth century, the cobblestone street would have been clogged daily with an average of forty thousand people. While a short subway line immediately to the west was built in 1875, the thoroughfare maintained its intense traffic in part due to the various commercial activities lining it.[2] In the late nineteenth century, a zone of banking establishments had developed to the west (left) of the passageway, drawing even more activity to the neighborhood. The signs glimpsed on the photograph include a bookstore, a children's clothing store, a hotel, and a shop specializing in electric bells. Written in Turkish in Arabic letters and in French, these signs testify to the presence of an ethnically mixed population.

The diverse crowd is also captured in the photographer's frame: modern Ottoman men in European clothes and fezes, European men and women, monks in long robes, Muslim women, children, street sellers, porters carrying immense loads, and even the infamous stray dogs of Constantinople. If all kinds of people passed through Yüksek Kaldırım, the neighborhood itself was home to Armenians, Greeks, and Jews and, in the aftermath of the Crimean War, to British, French, and Italians. Fragments of their residential life are revealed by means of an open window, wooden shutters, potted plants on tiny roof terraces and balconies, and drying laundry. The architecture offers as lively a medley as the people. The scene is dominated by the Galata Tower on the hill, the lonely remainder of Genoese fortifications built in the fourteenth century and demolished in 1865 to make way for new streets. The rest of the built fabric flaunts a European tone, with stripped-down neoclassical details. The topography and the high density give the overall settlement an idiosyncratic character, with facades overlooking the buildings below and bay windows maximizing light, air, and views.

The photograph reflects the cosmopolitan face of the Ottoman capital at the end of the nineteenth century and preserves the urban image of one of its most important nodes. Today, Yüksek Kaldırım is still there, still heavily loaded with pedestrian traffic and many shops, now specializing in electronics and musical instruments. The cobblestone steps have been replaced by asphalt, and the Galata Tower has been restored and fitted with a conical dome. However, it is the residential profile that has changed most radically. After a long derelict period beginning in the mid-1920s, during the past two decades the neighborhood has undergone a gentrification process and is becoming home to a financially comfortable, urbane, well-educated, and relatively young sector of Turkish society. **ZÇ**

1. For a discussion of the Sébah studio, see *A Turkish Woman in Street Dress* (cat. 3). **2.** Peter Oberling, "The Istanbul Tünel," *Archivum Ottomanicum* 4 (1972): 220; and Zeynep Çelik, *The Remaking of Istanbul: Portrait of an Ottoman City in the Nineteenth Century* (Seattle: University of Washington Press, 1986), 96–98.

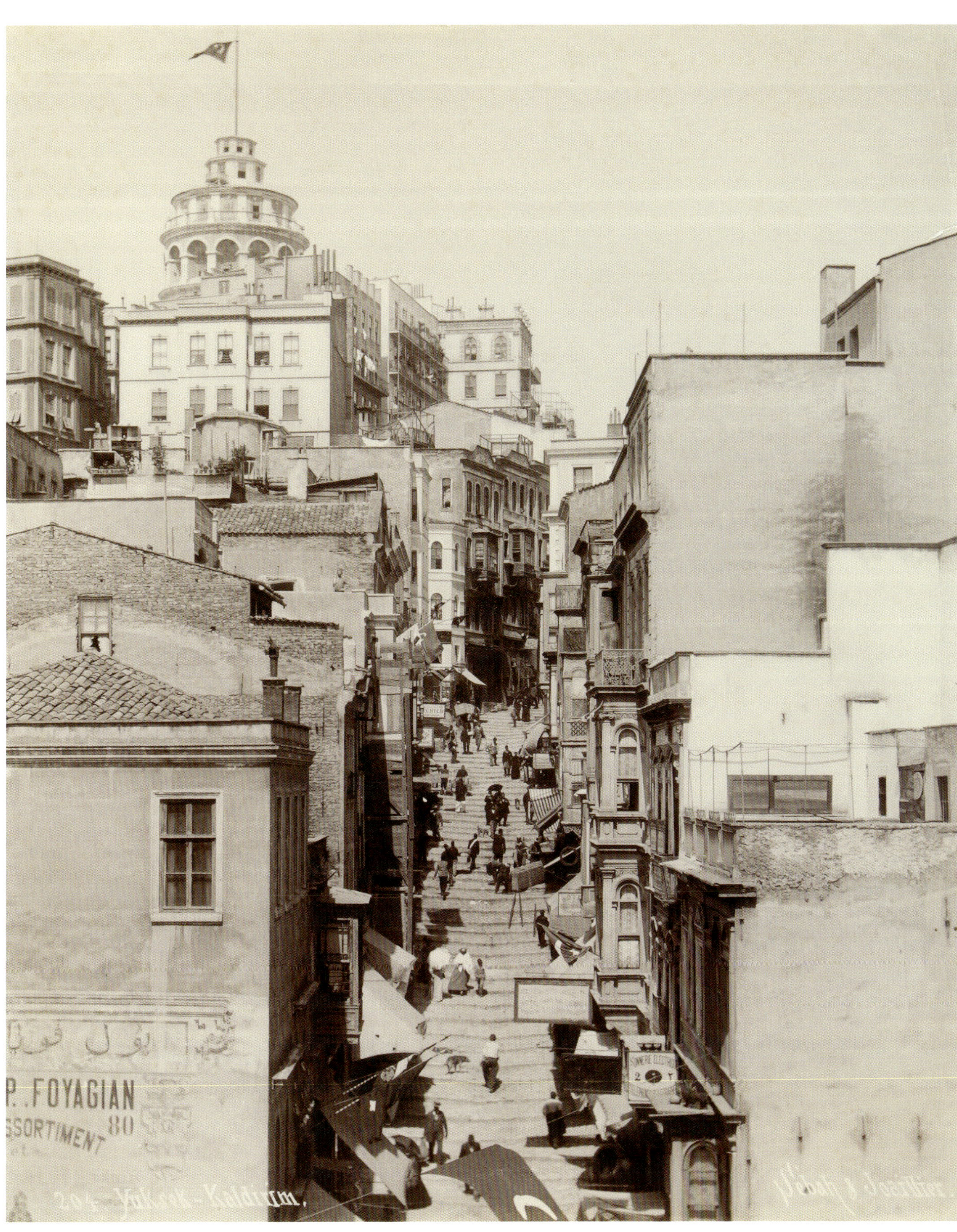
بول فوي
P. FOYAGIAN
SSORTIMENT 80
204 Yuksek-Kaldirim.
Sébah & Joaillier

5

Félix Bonfils

French, 1831–1885

Egyptian Women in Street Costume, undated
Albumen print
Image and sheet: 28.1 × 21.6 cm (11 1/16 × 8 1/2 in)
Printed, in image, lower left: *572 Femmes égyptiennes, costume de sortie*; lower right: *Bonfils*
University of Nebraska, Anna R. and Frank M. Hall Charitable Trust, H-2274

Viewing it [the veil] as a disguise for whatever is attractive or graceful in the person and adornments of the wearer, we should not find fault with it for being itself deficient in grace: we must remark, however, that, in one respect, it fails in accomplishing its main purpose; displaying the eyes, which are almost always beautiful; making them to appear still more so by concealing the other features, which are seldom of equal beauty; and often causing the stranger to imagine a defective face perfectly charming.

EDWARD WILLIAM LANE, *An Account of the Manners and Customs of the Modern Egyptians*

Published in 1836, Edward William Lane's *An Account of the Manners and Customs of the Modern Egyptians* described everything from the country's architecture, clothing, and costume to information on daily life.[1] The above passage from Lane's book only begins to suggest how potent and prominent the fantasy of the beautiful, mysteriously veiled woman became in nineteenth-century written and visual descriptions of the East. Orientalist images of women were frequently sexualized, regardless of whether the sitters were well covered or barely dressed and meant to evoke a harem scene.[2]

Egyptian Women in Street Costume is representative of many of Félix Bonfils's portraits. The proprietor of an established photography studio since the 1860s, Bonfils was based in Beirut but traveled throughout the Middle East taking pictures.[3] In this image, two veiled women, both wearing the metal *burguoung* over their noses, are distinguished by their color of dress. While Bonfils's subjects included architecture and street scenes, it is in his studio portraits that a sense of repetition becomes most apparent, as he frequently recycled background images and props. The same clumps of hazy trees and scattered rocks can be seen in portraits set in Egypt and Palestine, for example.[4]

Lane's and Bonfils's portrayals of the veiled women they encountered contrast powerfully with Jean Pascal Sébah's more overtly eroticized *Fellahine* (cat. 91). All three women are shown wearing the *burguoung*, yet the similarities in dress and comportment end there: Bonfils's figures are stoic and stiff, while Sébah's playful, scantily clad Egyptian peasant woman seems to smile behind her veil.[5] Both images, however, were constructed with generalized props: the rocks, trees, and painted backdrop in the Bonfils, a water jug and screen in the Sébah. This generic quality can be seen to characterize the women as well: operating together, the figure of the public, virtuous woman and the private, wanton one served to create and reinforce European fantasies of the Middle East.   SF

1. Edward William Lane, *An Account of the Manners and Customs of the Modern Egyptians* (London: Ward, Lock and Company, 1890). http://www.dspace.rice.edu/jsp/xml/1911/9176/71/LanMa1890.tei-timea.html.   2. For more information on the general nature of Orientalist images of women, see Sébah's *Fellahine* (cat. 91) and *A Turkish Woman in Street Dress* (cat. 3).   3. For background on the Bonfils studio, see cat. 10.   4. For other Bonfils images, see the Library of Congress Website (http://hdl.loc.gov/loc.pnp/cph.3b16510).   5. See Sébah's *Fellahine* (cat. 91).

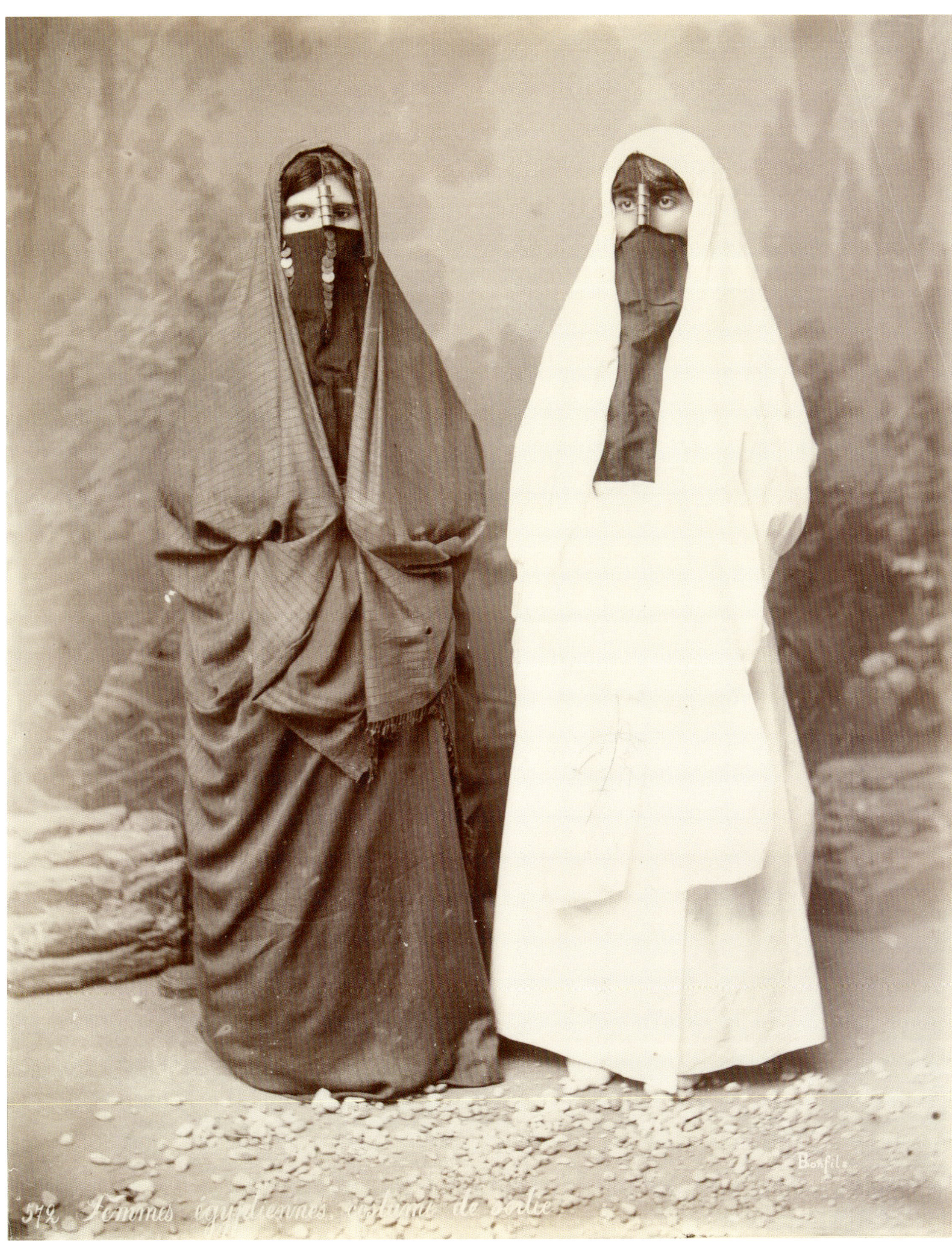
572 Femmes égyptiennes, costume de sortie
Bonfils

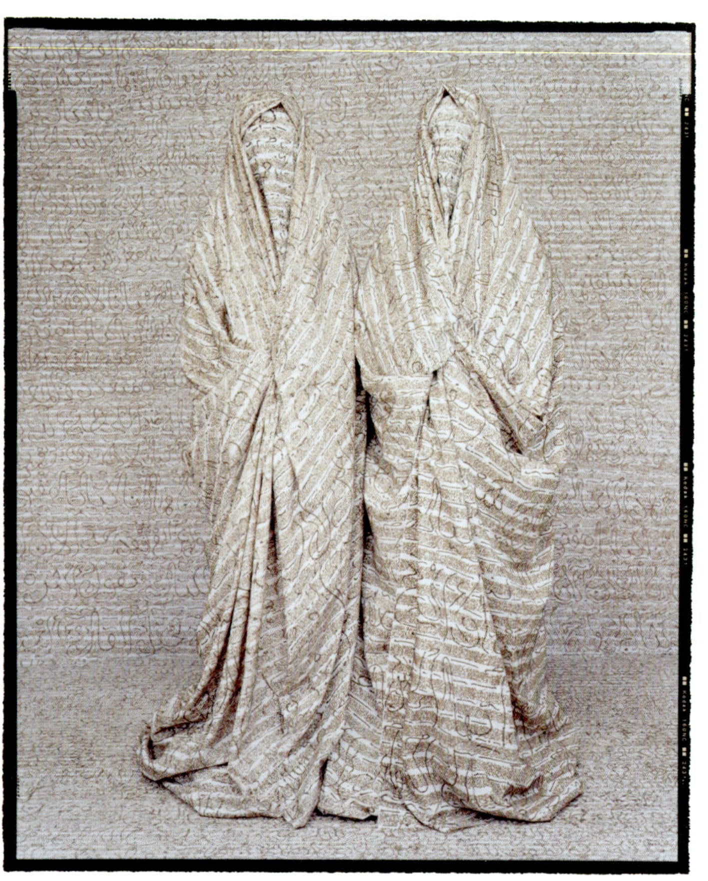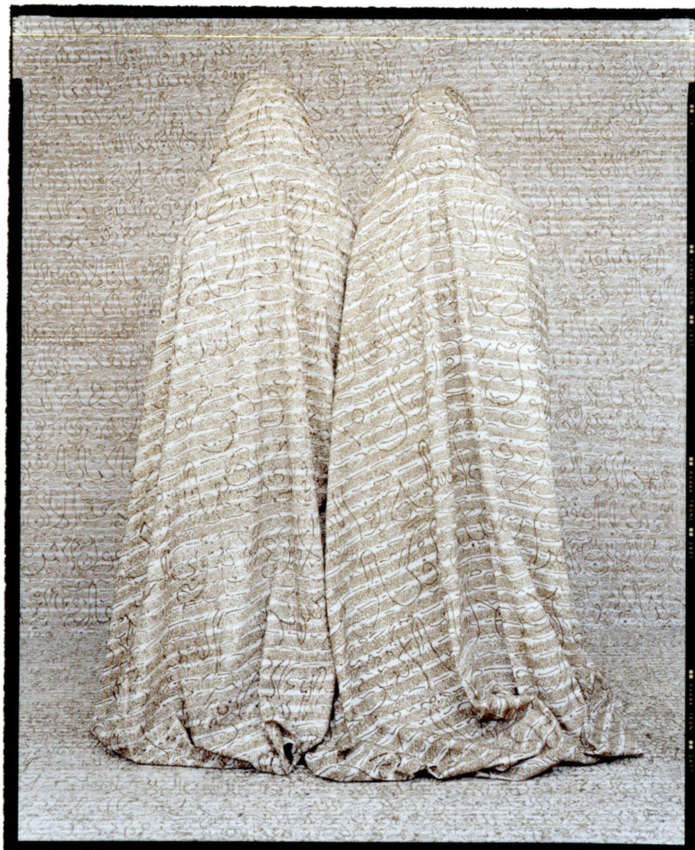

6

Lalla Essaydi

Moroccan, born 1956

Les femmes du Maroc, #25, A and B, 2006
Chromogenic print mounted on aluminum
Image: 137.2 × 110.5 cm (54 × 43 ½ in); mount: 152.4 ×
121.9 cm (60 × 48 in)
University of Nebraska, Robert E. Schweser and
Fern Beardsley Schweser Acquisition Fund, through
the University of Nebraska Foundation, U-5612.1–2

Lalla Essaydi's arresting, life-size photographs, which address issues of culture, diaspora, gender, and space, are a deliberate response to the romantic, sexualized images of Middle Eastern women created for nineteenth-century tourist postcards and souvenir albums. The title of this series, *Les femmes du Maroc* (The women of Morocco), references the region's French colonial past and the type of photographs created by mainly European studios such as Bonfils, Sébah, and the Zangaki brothers, examples of which appear in this catalog (cats. 7 and 91). Considering her work, the artist has remarked, "I want the viewer to become aware of Orientalism as a projection of the sexual fantasies of Western male artists, in other words, as a voyeuristic tradition, which involves peering into, and distorting private space."[1] Essaydi, however, is not interested merely in critiquing Arab or Western society; instead, she wants to engage "with cultural patterns, in order to get beyond stereotypes and convey my own experience as an Arab woman."[2]

Born in Marrakesh, Essaydi began to dissect these stereotypes and explore Arab cultural identity when she relocated to Boston, where she received her artistic training at Tufts University and the School of the Museum of Fine Arts. In her early *Converging Territories* series, she took photographs in her abandoned childhood home in Morocco, using a room where men confined women for days at a time when they challenged patriarchal authority. The artist regards such spaces as a "locus of memory"—a specific architectural setting that enables her to both incorporate her own biography and address Eastern and Western gender distinctions.

The male-dominated public spaces of meeting halls, offices, and streets, for example, stand in stark contrast to the private domestic sphere of women. While Essaydi's female subjects are metaphorically and physically confined by the spaces they inhabit, they dress in street clothes, presenting themselves as they would in public; in the process, they mock nineteenth-century photographs that depict scantily clad yet veiled women lounging seductively in private rooms.

For *Les femmes du Maroc,* the artist constructed her photographs in a Boston studio, continuing to incorporate her training as a painter into her works by applying henna calligraphy on the floors, furniture, and walls as well as on the garments of her subjects.[3] The calligraphic text, which can take Essaydi months to paint, is integral to Islamic art and religion, where it is associated with male pursuits. Henna, however, is a distinctly feminine material: Moroccan women use it to decorate their hands and feet during significant rites of passage such as weddings and childbirth. The calligraphy provides, in Essaydi's words, a "record of personal experience" and denotes an "absence of any specificity of place."[4] For her models, the artist employs Moroccan women who, like herself, now live in the West; part of the Arab diaspora, they are strongly etched with their original cultural identity. **BKR**

1. Quoted in Lindsey Moore, "Minding the Gap: Migrations, Diaspora, Exile and Return in Women's Visual Media," in *Contemporary Art in the Middle East,* ed. Paul Sloman (London: Black Dog Publishing, 2009), 78. **2.** See Amanda Carlson, *Lalla Essaydi: Converging Territories* (New York: Powerhouse Books, 2005), 27. **3.** For more on painting's influence on Essaydi's work, see Ray Waterhouse, "Lalla Essaydi: An Interview," *Journal of Contemporary African Art* 24 (2009): 145. **4.** See Carlson, *Lalla Essaydi,* 27.

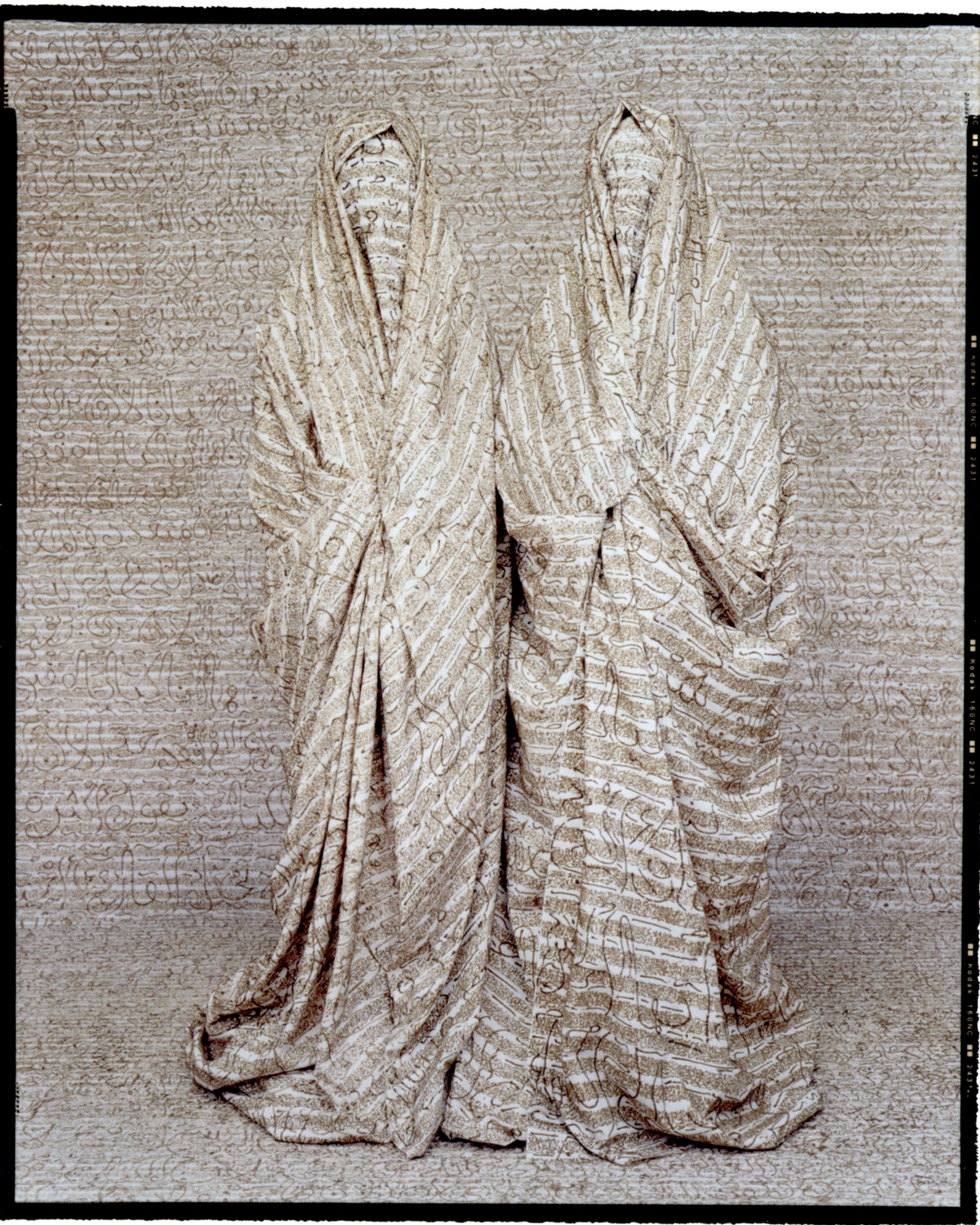

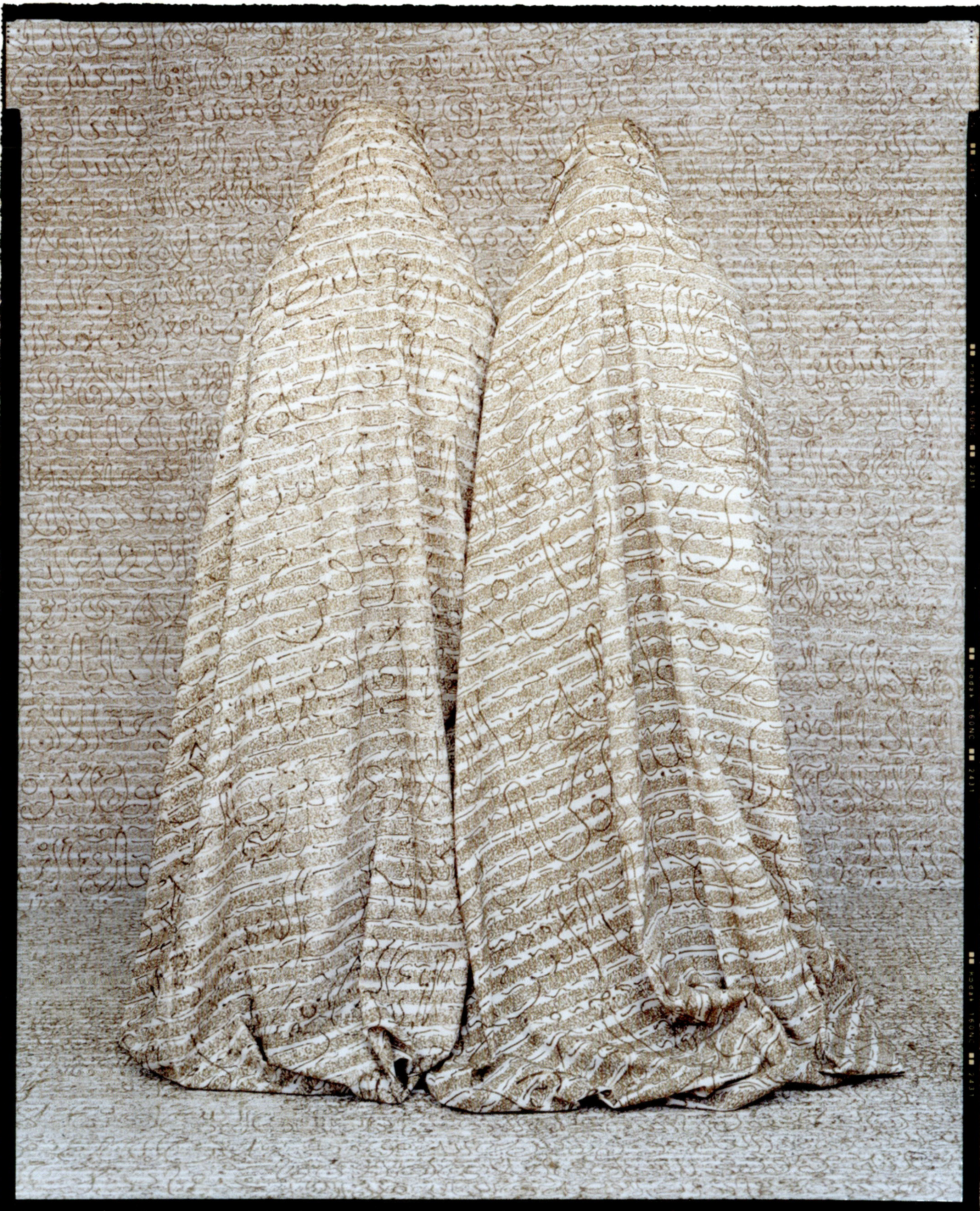

Adelphoi Zangaki (Zangaki Brothers, Constantine [?] and G.)

Greek, active 1860–1889

Femme turque, undated
Albumen print
Image and sheet: 21.9 × 27.9 cm (8 5/8 × 11 in)
Printed, in image, lower left: *Zangaki*; lower right:
791 Femme Turque
University of Nebraska, Anna R. and Frank M. Hall
Charitable Trust, H-2268

Around the time this photograph was taken, Ottoman intellectuals were beginning to critically scrutinize the image of the Turkish woman as represented in European visual discourse. Ahmed Midhat summarized the formula:

[This] lovable person lies negligently on a sofa. One of her slippers, embroidered with pearls, is on the floor, while the other is on the top of her toes. Since her garments are intended to ornament rather than to conceal [her body], her breasts are covered by fabrics as thin and transparent as a dream. . . . In her mouth is the black end of the pipe of a *narghile*, curving like a snake. . . . This is the Eastern woman Europe depicted until now. . . . What a misconception.[1]

Fatma Aliye Hanım, a prominent writer, deconstructed the authenticity of scenes such as this, which were intended for European viewers. She stated that such photographs did not depict Turkish women but rather Christian ones who posed as Orientals. Fatma Aliye Hanım then took stock of the details of these types of photographs: the head scarf is the Arabian *kaffiyeh*; the vest and the pants are Albanian; the chair in the foreground is from Damascus; and the cup on it is from India. She added sarcastically that she could not identify the ethnic identity of the odalisque reclining languidly and smoking a narghile.[2]

Although widespread among local intellectuals, this perspective did nothing to discourage the ever-growing popularity of such imaginary scenes, which were constructed for the tourist market, disseminated through photograph albums and postcards, featured in travel literature, and circulated in periodicals like *L'illustration* and the *Illustrated London News*. *Femme turque* (Turkish woman) was produced by the studio of the Zangaki brothers, who maintained ateliers in Cairo and at Port Said, at the entrance to the Suez Canal. Of Greek origin, the brothers enjoyed great commercial success, practicing from the 1860s to the 1890s, and they prospered with the opening of the canal and the increasing popularity of Egypt as a tourist destination.[3] Their photographs covered a wide range of topics, from general views of Cairo to monuments of Egypt from different periods of its rich history as well as the canal itself and the new settlements alongside it. One of the Zangakis' particular specialties was images of people; often classified as *types et scènes*, these suggested events from everyday life.

Femme turque belongs to this latter category and embodies the fallacies that Ahmed Midhat and Fatma Aliye Hanım were challenging. Shot in the studio, the reclining woman replicates the innumerable odalisques in her relaxed pose, smoking a narghile. Her setting and her clothes are a hodgepodge of various established signs that denote Turkishness, even though they do not carry any ethnographic value. The collage displays some amusing inconsistencies. For example, the cushions and the coffee table are generically Middle Eastern, but the architectural background is neoclassical—albeit highly ornate and Orientalized. Cramming as many references as possible into one image, the photographers have even included a veil, here curiously worn in private during the leisure activity of smoking rather than in public, as was the custom. **ZÇ**

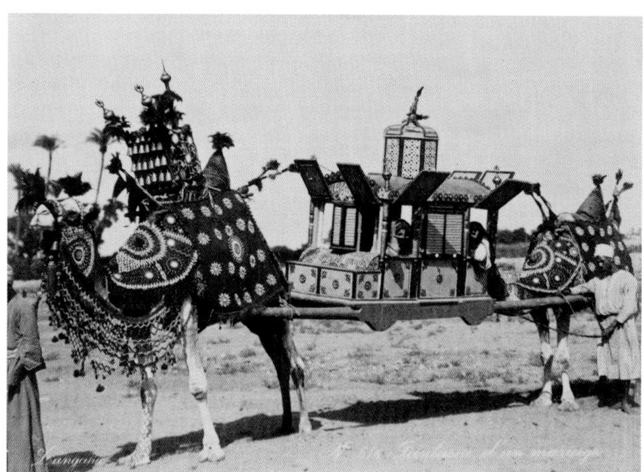

Adelphoi Zangaki (Zangaki Brothers, Constantine [?] and G.). *Fantasia d'un mariage*, undated. Albumen print; 21.3 × 27.5 cm (8 3/8 × 10 13/16 in). University of Nebraska, Anna R. and Frank M. Hall Charitable Trust, H-2264.

1. Ahmed Midhat Efendi, *Avrupa'da bir Cevalan* (Istanbul: Tercüman-ı Hakikat, 1890), 164–65. 2. Fatma Aliye Hanım, *Nisvan-ı Islam*, ed. Mübeccel Kızıltan (1893; repr., Istanbul: Mutlu Yayıncılık, 1993), 134–37. For a detailed analysis of Fatma Aliye Hanım's book, see Zeynep Çelik, "Speaking Back to Orientalist Discourse at the World's Columbian Exposition," in *Noble Dreams, Wicked Pleasures: Orientalism in America, 1870–1930*, ed. Holly Edwards, exhibition catalog (Williamstown MA: Sterling and Francine Clark Art Institute; Princeton NJ: Princeton University Press, 2000), 92–96. 3. On the Zangaki brothers, see Paul E. Chevedden, *The Photographic Heritage of the Middle East: An Exhibition of Early Photographs of Egypt, Palestine, Syria, Turkey, Greece, and Iran, 1849–1893* (Malibu CA: Undena Publications, 1981), 28.

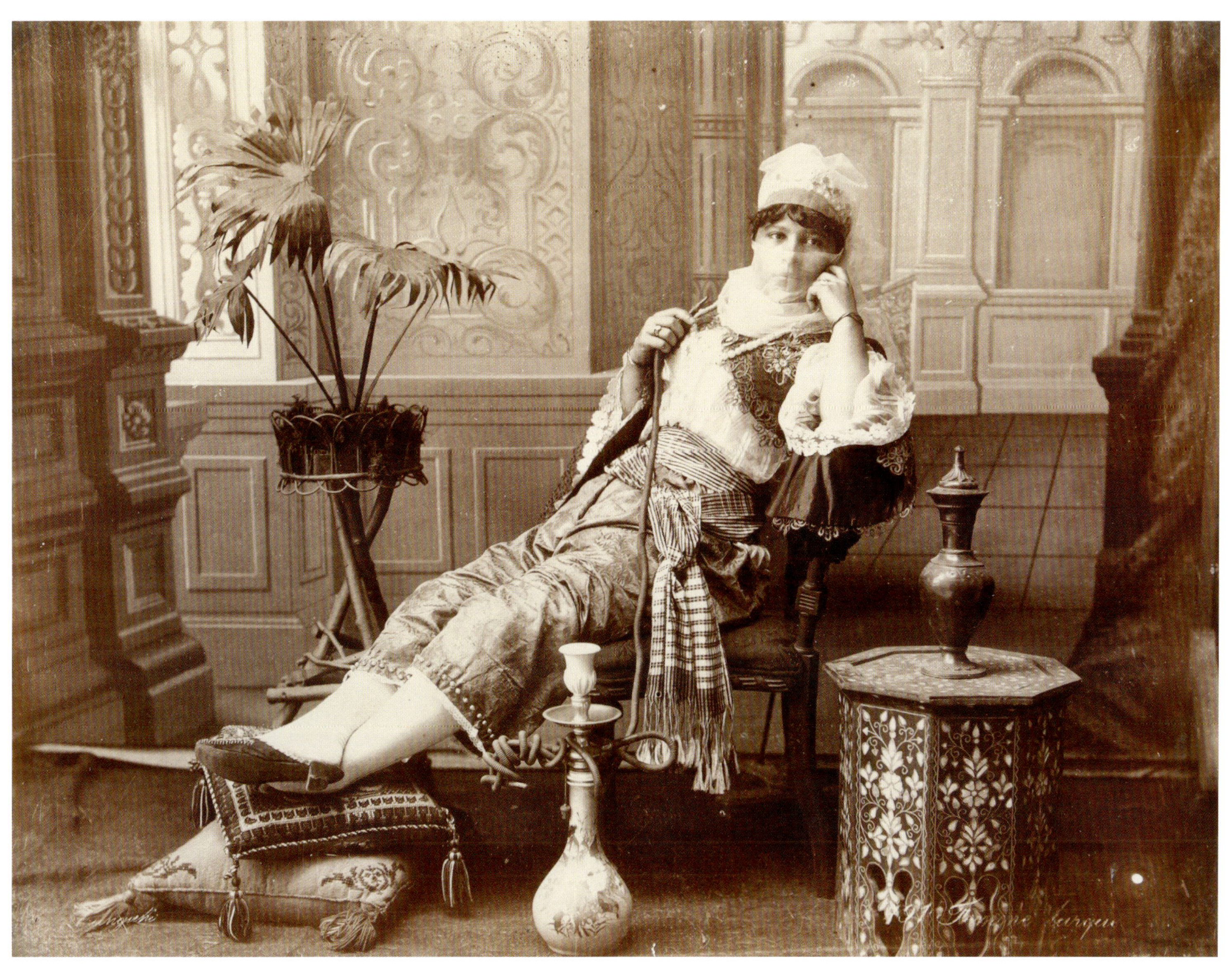

8

Señán y González
Spanish, active c. 1900

Granada, Alhambra, Door of Justice, c. 1895
Albumen print
Image: 25.4 × 20.3 cm (10 × 8 in); sheet: 26.4 × 20.3 cm
(10 ⅜ × 8 in)
Printed, in image, lower center: *3 Granada.—Alhambra.*
Puerta de Justicia. Señán y González, ftg.
University of Nebraska, Anna R. and Frank M. Hall
Charitable Trust, H-2279

Although early nineteenth-century Spain was economically behind other European countries, as tourism expanded beyond elite audiences and became a possibility for the growing middle class, the country became a magnet for travelers in search of romantic history and picturesque scenes. The ultimate destination for casual tourists and creative artists alike was Andalucía, which lured them with "the seductive powers of the Moorish architecture, the flamenco, bullfights and bandits."[1] For European visitors raised on the *Arabian Nights,* the palace and fortress complex of the Alhambra in Granada became an iconic symbol for the region, serving as a link to Spain's Islamic past and fulfilling numerous Orientalist visions from the convenience of the tourists' own continent. Perhaps attracted in part by the country's preindustrial character, the first foreign travelers to photograph the Alhambra in the 1840s and 1850s were mainly from Britain and France. In a trend that continued into the later part of the century, they sought to record not only the ruined towers and walls but also the profound changes the building underwent through repeated remodeling.

Andalucía was home to several photography firms that capitalized on sites such as the Alhambra. One such establishment was Señán y González, which went by several different names during its existence. Little is known about the company other than that the lead photographer was Rafael Señán, a native of Granada. Based in Seville, he specialized in photographic series of the Alhambra that were often marketed and published by competing firms in collections of albums and as postcards.[2] In the main, Señán y González produced countless albumen prints of the Alhambra, including exterior views of doorways and portals; interior scenes of courtyards, patios, and bas-relief sculptures; and picturesque images of gypsies posed against elaborately carved capitals and window frames embellished with Arabic script.[3]

This photograph depicts the Puerta de la Justicia, or Door of Justice, one of the main entrances to the Alhambra, which was commissioned in 1348 by Sultan Yusuf I. Framed by a massive horseshoe archway and surmounted by a square tower, the space was originally used as an informal courtroom. Rather than reveal the full scope of the architecture, this image shows the main interior door in tight detail. The crumbling repairs and the overgrown shrubbery that has taken hold in the cracked brickwork reveal the frayed condition of the palace by the end of the nineteenth century; the potted plants lining the wall at left and the introduction of a modern gas lamp at right suggest more prosaic functions. At right, just above the typical arched doorway, is an elegant fragment of plasterwork decorated with stylized vegetal patterns, perhaps the only reminder of the building's original history and use. **BKR**

1. David Balsells, *De París a Cádiz: Calotipia y colodión,* exhibition catalog (Barcelona: Museu Nacional d'Arte de Catalunya, 2004), 225. **2.** For a very brief biography of Señán, see Balsells, *De París a Cádiz,* 246; and Antonio Jesus González, *Postales andaluzas: Rafael Señán y la fotografía turística, 1864–1911* (Cajasur: Monte de Piedad y Caja de Ahorros de Córdoba, 2009), 28–31. **3.** For additional examples of the company's work, see González, *Postales andaluzas;* and Marie-Loup Sougez, *Images in Time: A Century of Photography at the Alhambra, 1840–1940* (Madrid: T. F. Editores, 2011), 74, 125, 160, 169.

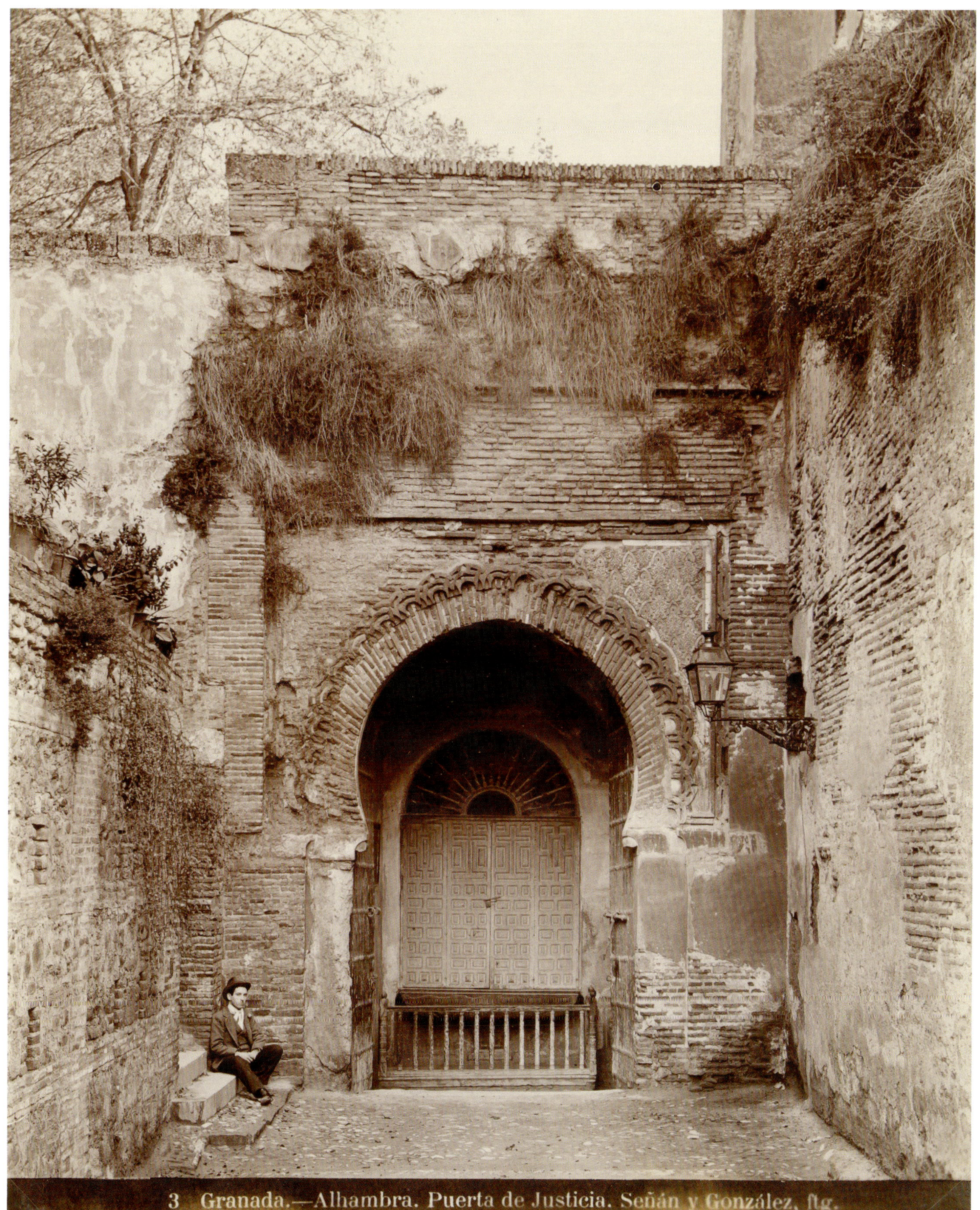

3 Granada.—Alhambra. Puerta de Justicia. Señán y González, ftg.

James Robertson

English, 1813–1888

Felice (Felix) Beato

English, born Italy, 1832–1909

Constantinople, c. 1855
Albumen print
Image: 24.3 × 27.3 cm (9 9/16 × 10 3/4 in); sheet: 37.8 ×
45.6 cm (14 7/8 × 17 15/16 in)
Signed, in image, lower right, in black ink: *Robertson*
University of Nebraska, Anna R. and Frank M. Hall
Charitable Trust, H-1291

Even by the time of the invention of the daguerreotype in 1839, Istanbul already occupied a prominent place in European cultural productions of the "Orient." Foreign artists had painted many views of Istanbul that were inspired by the natural beauties and the built forms of the city, fueled by fantasies about the lands of Islam and responding to the rapidly shifting role of the Ottoman Empire in international politics. Photography picked up on this genre, turning the Ottoman capital into a favorite site for European photographers as early as the 1850s, the decade that corresponds to the most productive period of James Robertson's career. The photographs of Istanbul taken by Robertson and his partner, Felice Beato, were disseminated widely at the time through publications and exhibitions; Robertson and Beato enjoyed, for example, considerable commercial success with their photographic album, *Views of Constantinople*, in 1853.[1]

Robertson's forty-year tenure in Istanbul, which was interrupted by trips around the Mediterranean and possibly to India, started in the early 1840s with his appointment as the superintendent and chief engraver to the imperial mint. His interest in photography seems to date from 1850, the year he began a partnership with Beato. The Crimean War (1853–56) opened a new chapter in their career, and their images of Sevastopol and Balaklava from 1855 established them as pioneering war photographers.[2] Even though the pair is best known as the photographers of the Crimean War, the photographs they took around the eastern Mediterranean region, but especially of Istanbul, have an important place in the history of photography.

Istanbul's geography yielded to the city's depiction in general views such as these, which look across the water, from hilltops, or from two strategically located towers, the Galata

Tower in Pera and the Beyazit Tower in the vicinity of the Süleymaniye Complex. *Constantinople* is shot from the Beyazit Tower, toward the northeast. In the horizon are the entrance of the Bosporus and the hills of the Asian shore. To the left, the Galata Bridge connects the two sides of the Golden Horn. While Galata (at the end of the bridge) and Pera (on the hill above Galata) are only distinguishable by the density of their built fabrics—including the crowded shoreline and a few mosques identified by their minarets—the fragment of Istanbul from Beyazit to Eminönü is revealed in sharp detail in the foreground. At the foot of the bridge is the Valide Sultan Mosque (1663), framed by the much lower, L-shaped Egyptian Market (or Spice Market), which was built as part of the mosque complex under the patronage of mother sultan (the mother of the ruling sultan) Turhan Hatice (1628–83). The commercial zone is dotted by *hans*, compounds of shops and workshops organized around courtyards. Among these, the Büyük Valide Han (1651) is partially visible at right. Built by Kösem Mehpeyker Sultan (1589–1651), another mother sultan, it stands out for its large scale and, together with the Valide Sultan Mosque and its market complex, etches the memory of the Ottoman era known as the "sultanate of women" onto the urban fabric.[3] The wooden houses, with their pitched tile roofs, large eaves, and bay windows, define a residential neighborhood adjacent to the commercial one. The minarets enhance the panoramic view with vertical elements, while the boats in the harbor pull the gaze toward the horizon.

Robertson and Beato's photograph documents Istanbul on the eve of a series of major transformations. In the aftermath of a massive fire in 1865, which demolished much of the neighborhood in the foreground, straight, wide, and modern streets were introduced. Other urban renovation incentives in the second half of the nineteenth century would demolish the crowded shores of Galata and replace them with spacious stone embankments, and the Galata Bridge would be rebuilt.[4] Subsequent urban reforms brought more radical changes, leaving intact only the topography and the major monuments. Robertson and Beato's photograph is an invaluable document that reconstructs the city before the modernization projects. ZÇ

1. "Photographic Notes," *Journal of the Birmingham Photographic Society*, February 1, 1858, 34. 2. For general information on the career of James Robertson, see B. A. Henisch, "James Robertson of Constantinople," *History of Photography* 8, no. 4 (October–December 1984): 299–313; and B. A. and H. K. Henisch, "Robertson of Constantinople," *Image* 17, no. 3 (September 1974): 1–11. 3. For female royal patronage of architecture in the seventeenth century, see Leslie Peirce, *The Imperial Harem: Women and Sovereignty in the Ottoman Empire* (New York: Oxford University Press, 1993); and Lucienne Thys-Şenocak, *Ottoman Women Builders: The Architectural Patronage of Hadice Turhan Sultan* (Aldershot UK: Ashgate, 2007). 4. For transformations to the urban fabric of Istanbul, see Zeynep Çelik, *The Remaking of Istanbul: Portrait of an Ottoman City in the Nineteenth Century* (Seattle: University of Washington Press, 1986), esp. chap. 3.

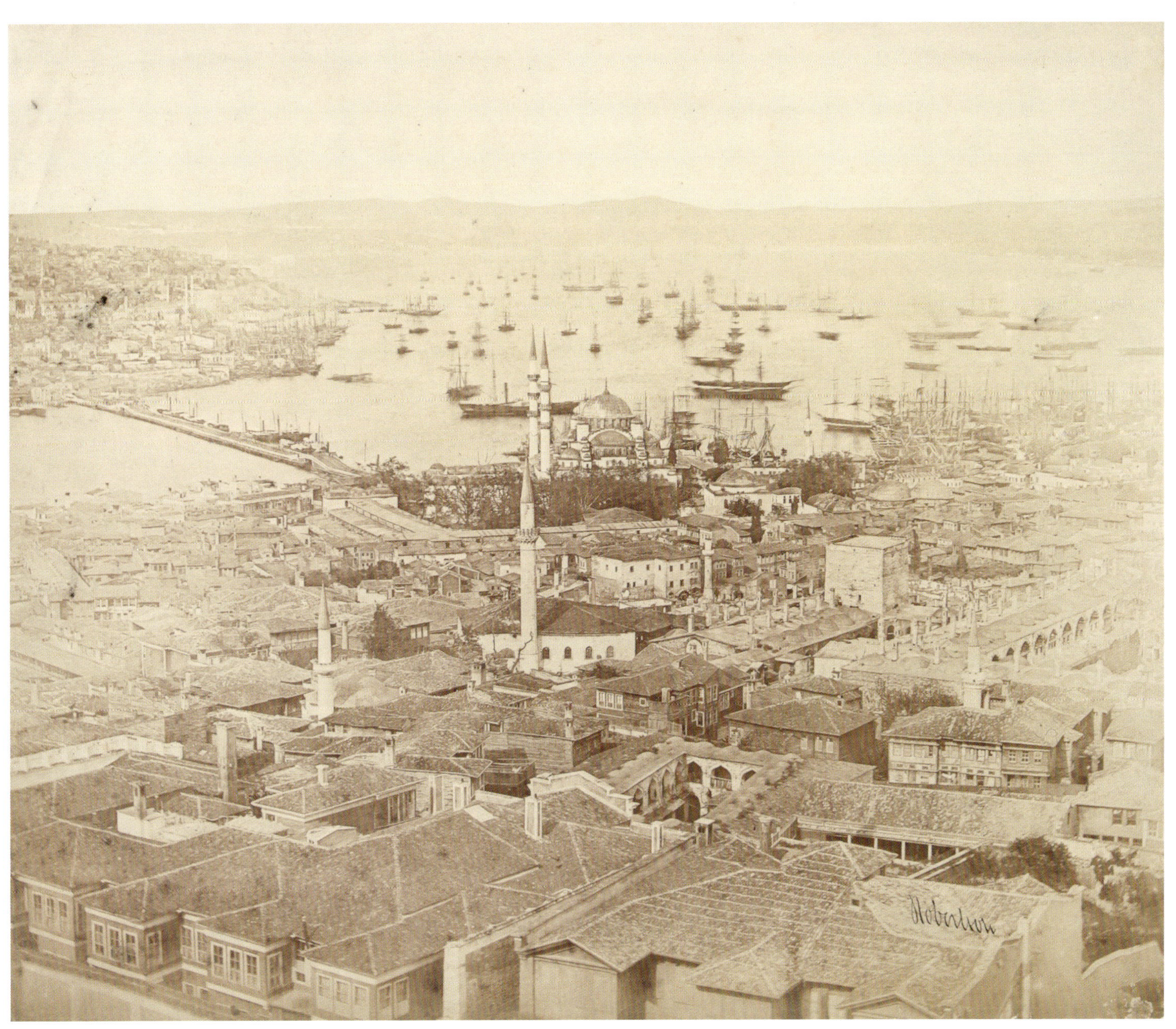

10

Félix Bonfils
French, 1831–1885

Cairo Seen from Mokkatam, c. 1870s
Albumen print
Image and sheet: 28.1 × 21.6 cm (11 1/16 × 8 1/2 in)
Printed, in image, lower left: *Caire près du Mokkatam.*
44.; lower right: *Bonfils*
University of Nebraska, Anna R. and Frank M. Hall
Charitable Trust, H-2273

Our firm was founded in the Orient in 1865. Our employees are constantly traveling in order to renew our negatives in accordance with every latest development in photographic art. Thus our views are known throughout the whole world and justly appreciated for their perfect execution and their permanence.

Please do not confuse our prints with those of other firms. Always demand the *Marque de Garantie*: our name in white at the bottom of each view.

From a mid-1880s Bonfils catalog

In these statements, which attempt to distinguish his firm from rival studios, Félix Bonfils assured potential customers of the high quality of his images. One of many photographic ateliers that appeared in response to the Western demand for images of the East, Bonfils's was particularly prolific. In 1871, for instance, his output comprised 591 negatives and 15,000 prints of Egypt, Greece, Palestine, and Syria. Subject matter included architecture, portraits, and scenes of daily life, and titles were often given in French.[1]

In this view of Cairo, the presence of the mosque of Muhammad ع Ali would instantly have labeled the city as "foreign" to a Western viewer. Taken as a distant panorama from the Mokkatam Hills, a vantage point beyond the city walls, the image documents the mosque's dominating presence. It also seems to serve as a reminder of the photographer's status as an outsider: this was a town and a country not his own.

Born in 1831 in Alès, France, Bonfils first traveled to Lebanon at the age of twenty-nine, when he took part in a French military expedition under Gen. Beaufort d'Hautpoul. After returning to France for several years, he, along with his wife and two children, moved to Beirut. As the opening quote suggests, Félix was not the only photographer to take pictures under the Bonfils name. In addition to serving as studio assistants, both his wife, Lydie, and his son Adrien occasionally took images themselves. In 1878 Adrien became the chief photographer, with his father moving over to manage the business aspect of the studio. Adrien continued to run the firm under the name Photographie Bonfils until 1894, when he sold the business.

Bonfils, like many photographers, took images of popular tourist sites such as the monumental mosque of Muhammad ع Ali, which is located in the citadel of Cairo. Governor from 1805 to 1848, Muhammad ع Ali is often called the "founder of modern Egypt." Under his leadership, the country developed firmer ties with Europe and expanded its military and agricultural systems, often at the cost of both the peasants and the Mamluks, Egypt's longtime ruling class.[2] The mosque, begun in 1828, exhibits a complex, varied lexicon of architectural features that give voice to a moment of change in Egyptian culture. Its large central dome and smaller half-domes are clearly Ottoman in appearance, but the structure also contains some European influences, including a clock tower donated by the French. The building was created by a crew of Egyptian stonemasons and craftsmen from Istanbul and Europe.[3] The largest of its day, the mosque can be considered a statement of Muhammad ع Ali's might as he pushed against the boundaries of the Ottoman Empire and eagerly positioned Egypt as a modern power. **SF**

1. The mid-1880s Bonfils catalog is quoted and described in Carney E. S. Gavin, *The Image of the East* (Chicago: University of Chicago Press, 1982), 16, 19. **2.** Khaled Fahmy, "The Era of Muhammad ع Ali Pasha 1805–1848," in *The Cambridge History of Egypt*, ed. M. W. Dalley (Cambridge: Cambridge University Press, 1998), 139–79. **3.** Muhammad ع Ali challenged the Ottoman sultan with aspects of the mosque's architecture. For example, while the presence of multiple minarets was supposed to be limited exclusively to Ottoman royalty, his mosque includes two. Mohammad Al-Asad, "The Mosque of Muhammad ع Ali in Cairo," *Muqarnas* 9 (1992): 39–55.

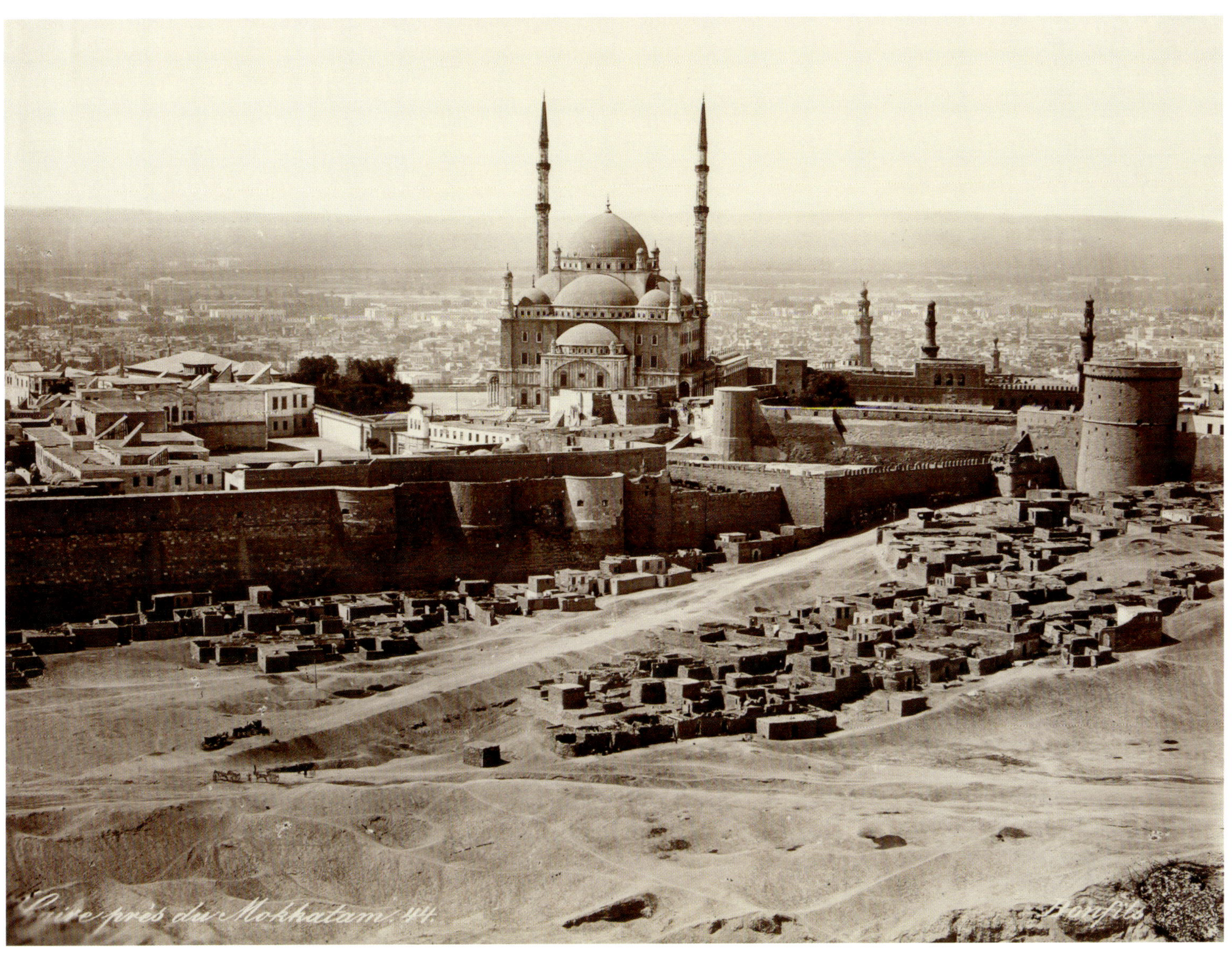

Prise près du Mokhatam. 44.

Alvin Langdon Coburn

English, born America, 1882–1966

The Sphinx, London Embankment, 1905; published 1909
Photogravure
Image: 21.6 × 15.6 cm (8 ½ × 6 ⅛ in); sheet: 22.2 × 16.5 cm
(8 ¾ × 6 ½ in)
University of Nebraska, Anna R. and Frank M. Hall
Charitable Trust, H-2736

Born in Boston, Alvin Langdon Coburn absorbed that city's cultural atmosphere, including its passion for Asian art and its experiments with mystical spirituality. His tutelage under F. Holland Day and summers spent at Arthur Wesley Dow's Ipswich, Massachusetts, school informed his early work. Dow's Japanese-inspired theories of balanced asymmetry, harmony of line, spare compositions, and *notan*—a Japanese word meaning the balance between light and dark—exercised particular influence over the artist.[1] Coburn also studied with Gertrude Käsebier (cat. 46), who formed the Photo-Secessionists along with Alfred Stieglitz (cat. 15), Edward Steichen (cat. 95), and Clarence White (cat. 69); Coburn joined the group in 1902. Two years later, he traveled to Britain on assignment to photograph the country's leading artistic luminaries, and these writers, including G. K. Chesterton, George Bernard Shaw, and H. G. Wells, remained important collaborators and influences for the next several decades.

Inspired by both literary precedents and the city's status as a powerful symbol of the modern age, Coburn proposed a series of photographic essays on major American and European metropolises, including Boston, London, New York, and Paris, with text by important writers. An adept craftsman, the artist prepared by studying photogravure at London's Bolt Court Technical School and in 1909 installed two copperplate photogravure presses in his home along the river Thames. In October of that year, he published *London*, which featured twenty plates along with text by author and Liberal Party politician Hilaire Belloc.[2]

Among these plates was *The Sphinx, London Embankment*, which shows one of a pair of bronze statues that line the shores of the Thames near the Houses of Parliament. The sphinxes flank Cleopatra's Needle, an ancient Egyptian obelisk carved during the reign of Thutmose III (c. 1479–1425 BCE) and given to the city of London in 1819 by Muhammad ʿAli, Egypt's Turkish governor (cat. 10).[3] Coburn's photograph—shot from the river's edge, toward the steps of the embankment—completely elides the obelisk. Instead, it focuses on its enigmatic guardian and the leafless winter trees, using foreground shadows and the deliberately blurred building in the background to add an aura of mystery. Critic and poet Arthur Symons, the planned author of Coburn's original book on London, may have inspired the photograph's moody tone: "Below, the Embankment curves towards Cleopatra's Needle: you see the curve of the wall, as the lamps light it, leaving the obelisk in shadow, and falling faintly on the grey mud in the river. Just that corner has a mysterious air. . . . I know not what makes it quite so tragic and melancholy."[4] Although these statues may have been overlooked by the Londoners who passed by them daily, the sphinx was a potent figure for both Freemasons and symbolist artists, exactly the circles in which Coburn traveled. Portals, stairways, steps, and rivers were familiar, frequently illustrated Masonic symbols, and the sphinx traditionally admonished Egyptian priests not to share sacred information with the uninitiated, a strict principle of Freemasonry.[5] **BKR**

1. For Coburn's early career and study under Dow, see Nancy Newhall, "Alvin Langdon Coburn: The Youngest Star," in *Alvin Langdon Coburn: Photographs, 1900–1924*, ed. Karl Steinorth, exhibition catalog (Rochester NY: International Museum of Photography at George Eastman House; Zurich: Edition Stemmle, 1998), 23–45; and Alexandra Munroe, ed., *The Third Mind: American Artists Contemplate Asia, 1860–1989*, exhibition catalog (New York: Guggenheim Museum, 2009), 402. 2. In 1914 Coburn privately printed another publication with the same title; in it he featured ten new photographs of the city and a text by G. K. Chesterton. For a history of Coburn's printing projects, see Sheila J. Foster, Manfred Heiting, and Rachel Stuhlman, *Imaging Paradise: The Richard and Ronay Menschel Library at George Eastman House, Rochester* (Rochester NY: George Eastman House; Göttingen: Steidl, 2007), 219–25. 3. It was not until 1878 that the obelisk was finally erected in its present location. 4. Arthur Symons, *London: A Book of Aspects* (London: Privately printed, 1909), 4–5. 5. See Mike Weaver, *Alvin Langdon Coburn: Symbolist Photographer, 1882–1966; Beyond the Craft*, exhibition catalog (New York: Aperture/George Eastman House, 1986), 54–57; and Nicholas Freeman, *Conceiving the City: London, Literature, and Art, 1870–1914* (Oxford: Oxford University Press, 2007), 189–91.

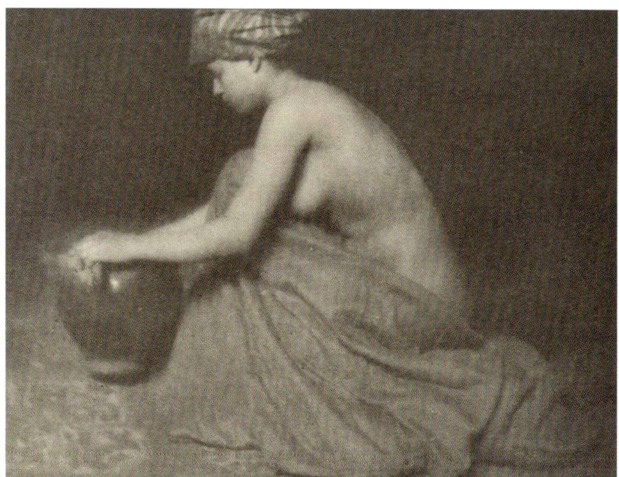

Alvin Langdon Coburn. *The Water Carrier*, 1913. Photogravure; 10.5 × 12.1 cm (4 ⅛ × 4 ¾ in). University of Nebraska, gift of Del Zogg, U-3730.

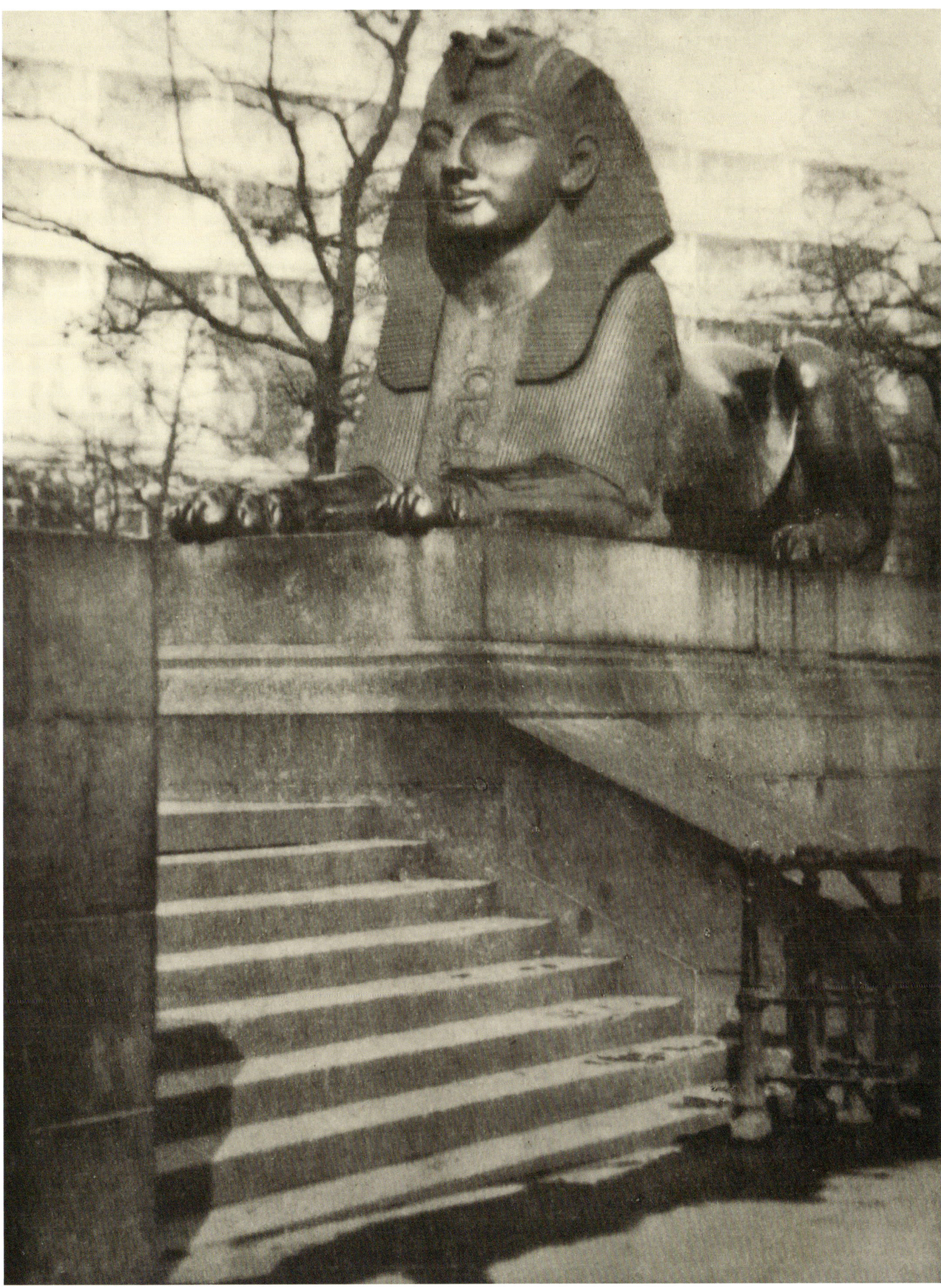

Charles Fletcher Lummis

American, 1859–1928

Pueblo of Taos, Old Church and North House, 1889;
published 1891
Cyanotype
Image: 11.1 × 17.5 cm (4 3/8 × 6 7/8 in); sheet: 12.7 × 20.5 cm
(5 × 8 1/16 in)
Printed, in image, bottom center, in white: *703. / TAOS,
N.M. / OLD CHURCH / N. HOUSE*
University of Nebraska, Anna R. and Frank M. Hall
Charitable Trust, H-2060

Charles Fletcher Lummis began his career as a journalist, initially taking up photography as an adjunct to his reportage. In 1884 he struck an extraordinary bargain with the newspaper publisher Harrison Gray Otis: he agreed to walk 3,500 miles from his home in Ohio to California, writing a letter a week for the *Los Angeles Times*.[1] The success of this stunt secured him a job with Otis's newspaper. Four years later, however, he became partially paralyzed from a stroke. Seeking a place to convalesce, Lummis chose New Mexico based on his transcontinental experience, moving to San Mateo and then settling in Isleta Pueblo, thirteen miles south of Albuquerque. Fully intending to return to the *Times*, he kept comprehensive journals and produced a series of popular books, including a compendium of his journey through the United States. In addition, Lummis bought a small camera to help him document the people and places of the desert Southwest. The difficulty and impediments of developing photographs in such a remote location led him to experiment with printing in cyanotype, a chemical process based on light exposure that results in a distinctive blue color.[2]

In this photograph of the Taos Pueblo north of Santa Fe, Lummis focused on the ruins of the San Geronimo Chapel with the Hlauuma, or North House, featured in the left middle ground. The original chapel of this name was first built in 1619 and later destroyed in the Pueblo Revolt of 1680. Although reconstructed, it once again suffered extensive damage during the United States' war with Mexico in 1847; a new church on a different site was completed three years later. During its nearly 250-year history, the old San Geronimo Chapel symbolized the confrontations and negotiations that occurred during Spanish colonization and the United States' subsequent imperial ambitions. The indigenous Tiwa-speaking people revolted against and later adapted Spanish culture and religious practices, then commingled with Anglo-Americans through trade and settlement.

Lummis first published *Pueblo of Taos* in *A New Mexico David* (1891), a heavily biased, quasi-fictional account of Spanish colonial adventures and exploits. He used this photograph to illustrate his biography of Manuel Chaves, a Spanish-descended colonel who engaged in several wars against indigenous peoples.[3] Lummis's writing on Chaves follows a narrative of victimization in which innocent, persecuted settlers are forced from the land or attacked by savage Indians only to bravely and gallantly resecure their birthright.[4] Indeed, as Sherry L. Smith has argued, Lummis's primitivist excursions led him to associate Native Americans with "boyish impulses," while he endowed the Spanish with noble qualities, investing them with a masculine authenticity and potency that he imagined as an antidote to the feminizing artificiality of the civilized East Coast.[5] He did, however, make an exception for the Pueblo Indians, a community he described as "the most peaceful and best-governed in North America."[6] He accorded special respect to their sedentary farming culture, their participation through production and trade in the capitalist economy, and their ability to integrate into—and thus survive within—white society. **BKR**

1. For biographical treatments of Lummis, see Karen Current, *Photography and the Old West*, exhibition catalog (Fort Worth TX: Amon Carter Museum of Western Art; New York: Harry N. Abrams, 1978), 228–33; for an anecdotal overview of his life, see Turbesé Lummis Fiske and Keith Lummis, *Charles F. Lummis: The Man and His West* (Norman: University of Oklahoma Press, 1975). **2.** Lummis described the complexity of developing his images: "in an adobe room with a big basin bowl for a sink, no outlet except the outside door, no running water" (Current, *Photography*, 230). **3.** For this story and a reproduction of the photograph, see Charles F. Lummis, *A New Mexico David and Other Stories and Sketches of the Southwest* (New York: Charles Scribner's Sons, 1891), 190–217. **4.** For a discussion of this ideology as it pertains to the settlement of the American West, see Patricia Nelson Limerick, *The Legacy of Conquest: The Unbroken Past of the American West* (New York: W. W. Norton and Company, 1987), 35–54. **5.** Sherry L. Smith, *Reimagining Indians: Native Americans through Anglo Eyes, 1880–1940* (Oxford: Oxford University Press, 2000), 119, 128–29, 132. **6.** Charles F. Lummis, *Mesa, Cañon and Pueblo: Our Wonderland of the Southwest* (New York: Century Company, 1925), 308.

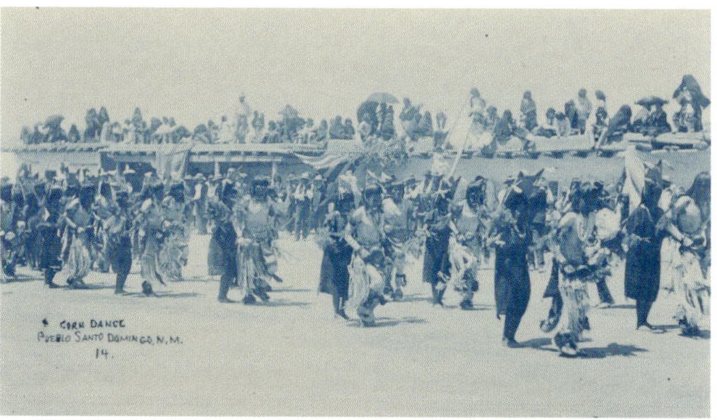

Charles Fletcher Lummis. *Pueblo Santo Domingo, Corn Dance*, 1888. Cyanotype; 11.1 × 18.8 cm (4 3/8 × 7 3/8 in). University of Nebraska, Anna R. and Frank M. Hall Charitable Trust, H-2056.

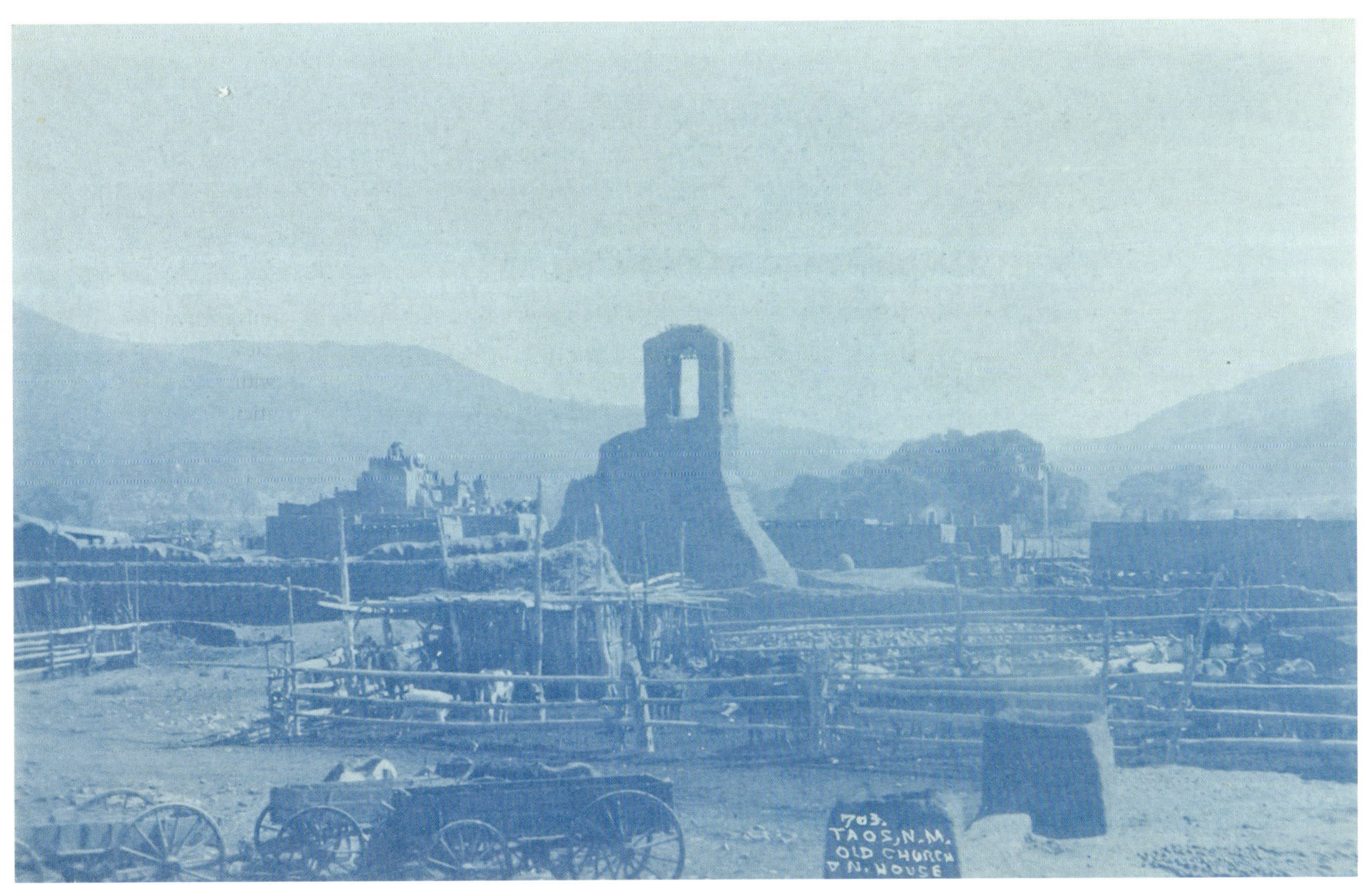
703.
TAOS, N.M.
OLD CHURCH
& N. HOUSE

William R. Cross
American, active 1870s–1890s

Bailey, Dix and Mead
(Joshua Bradford Bailey, George P. Dix, and
John L. Mead)
American, firm active 1881–82

Steps, 1882
Albumen print
Image: 15.2 × 10.2 cm (6 × 4 in); sheet: 16.5 × 10.8 cm
(6½ × 4¼ in)
Printed, bottom center: *Copyright, 1882, by Bailey,
Dix & Mead*; on verso, upper center: *STEPS*; middle
center: [description of image]; lower center:
Address, BAILEY, DIX & MEAD, Fort Randall, D. T.
University of Nebraska, gift of the Doan Family
Foundation, Fort Dodge, Iowa, U-5609

Issued in 1882, this jarring yet poignant image of a Nez Perce Indian nicknamed "Steps" was part of a series that was meant to demonstrate American military superiority, offering assurance that the Plains Indian Wars were coming to a close and the frontier was safe for white settlement. The occasion was the surrender of Sitting Bull at Fort Buford in present-day North Dakota on July 19, 1881; he had returned from four years of exile in Saskatchewan following his victory at the Battle of Little Big Horn. The military eventually transferred Sitting Bull and his Lakota Sioux followers to Fort Randall, on the present-day South Dakota and Nebraska borders. Understanding the popular appetite for images of the frontier wars, three local entrepreneurs—Joshua Bradford Bailey, George P. Dix, and John L. Mead—commissioned William R. Cross to photograph the prisoners and other participants and issue the images as a series of stereoscopic prints. A commercial photographer, Cross traveled through the Nebraska and Dakota territories, typically stationing himself at

military forts and producing images of dress parades, formal portraits, and photographs of the surrounding landscape. During a period at Fort Niobrara, he established a studio where he was assisted by the young John Anderson (cat. 14).[1]

The twenty-four photographs in Cross's series construct a clear narrative of Native American defeat and U.S. military dominance. At the same time, the text that accompanied this particular photograph made it clear that the army was not responsible for wounding Steps: his injuries were the result of his own poor decision to disobey the government and eventually ally himself with Sitting Bull: "No. 3. STEPS. A Nes [sic] Perce Indian, who escaped from his band, while surrounded in the bad lands of Nebraska, by Gen'l Miles in 1878. He then joined Sitting Bull's band of Uncapapa Souix [sic] Indians in the British possessions and has followed their fortunes ever since. He lost his feet above the ankles, also his right hand by being frozen, having been caught in one of the severe snow storms, 21 years ago."[2]

To highlight Steps's and Sitting Bull's defeat and surrender, the photographer intentionally captured Steps in a subservient pose, kneeling with his left hand raised, forced to show his missing limbs to the camera. **BKR**

1. For more on William R. Cross's travels and his experience with Anderson, see John A. Anderson, Henry W. Hamilton, and Jean Tyree Hamilton, *The Sioux of the Rosebud: A History in Pictures*, Civilization of the American Indian 111 (Norman: University of Oklahoma Press, 1971), 4. **2.** This inscription is printed on the back of the photograph. For a transcription, see University Art Museum, University of Minnesota, *American Identities: Cabinet Card Portraits, 1870–1910; from the Doan Family Collection*, exhibition catalog (Minneapolis: University Art Museum, University of Minnesota, 1985), 24.

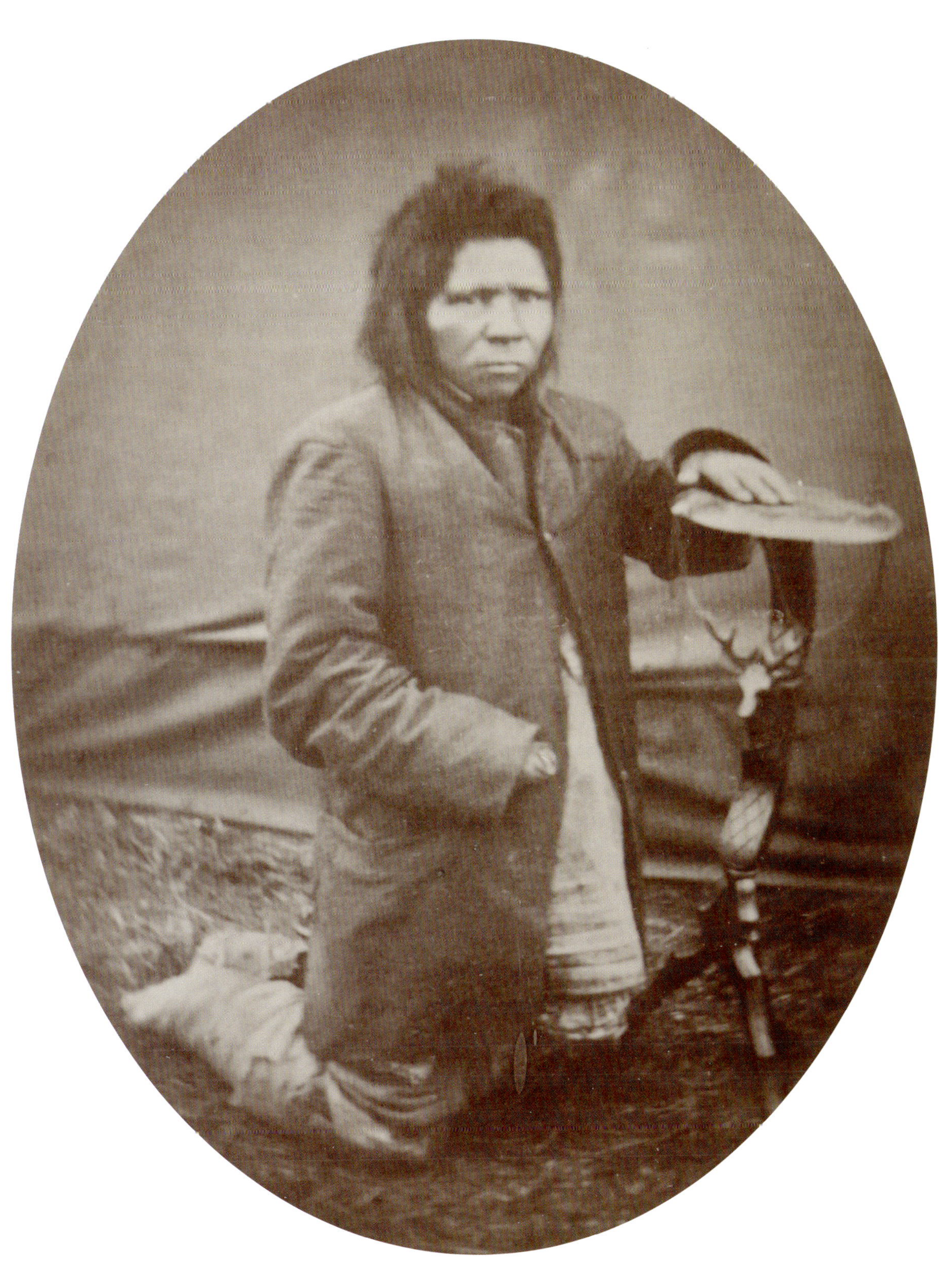

John A. Anderson

American, born Sweden, 1869–1948

Jordan's Trading Post, 1893
Gelatin silver print
Image: 18.7 × 23 cm (7 3/8 × 9 1/16 in); sheet: 27.9 × 35.6 cm
(11 × 14 in)
University of Nebraska, gift of Mid-America Arts Alliance,
U-1953

Born in Sweden, John A. Anderson immigrated to the United States with his family in 1870; after a short stint in Pennsylvania, they settled on an eighty-acre homestead near Fort Niobrara, outside Valentine, Nebraska. This experience had a formative impact on Anderson, determining the subjects and themes that would become the focus of his artwork. Like many turn-of-the-century photographers—perhaps most notably here James VanDerZee (cat. 57)—Anderson was self-taught, purchasing his first camera in 1885 from savings he earned as a carpenter. His early images revolved around the sand hills of his Nebraska home, the Badlands of South Dakota, and the army station at Fort Niobrara. In 1889, for ex-

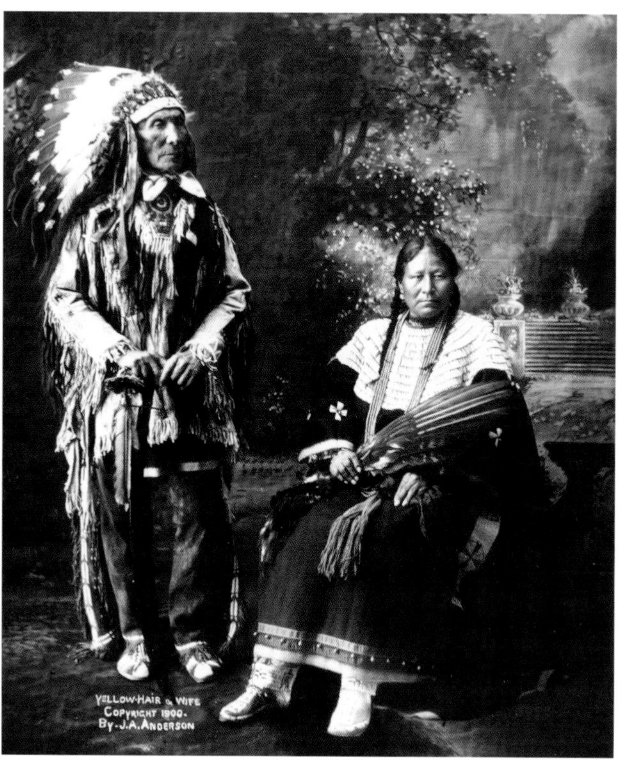

John A. Anderson. *Yellow Hair and His Wife, Plenty Horse*, 1900. Gelatin silver print; 21.8 × 17.5 cm (8 9/16 × 6 7/8 in). University of Nebraska, gift of Mid-America Arts Alliance, U-1960.

ample, at the request of Gen. George Crook, he served as the official photographer for the Crook Treaty Commission during discussions at the Rosebud Reservation in South Dakota. Anderson also studied and apprenticed with itinerant photographers who visited the fort; this led him to purchase a scenic backdrop and open his own studio. There he concentrated on making formal portraits, often of Native Americans from the nearby reservations, who appeared in ceremonial clothing.[1]

Beginning in the early 1890s, Anderson began working for Col. Charles P. Jordan, a licensed trader on the Rosebud Reservation, which was home to the Sicangu Oyate (also known as the Brulé Sioux Nation) and the Rosebud Sioux, a branch of the Lakota people. In 1893 he purchased a share in the Jordan Trading Post, which later became the Jordan Mercantile Company.[2] These establishments were sites of cross-cultural relations where African Americans, European Americans, and Native Americans met and mingled; international goods were sold; and local crafts and products were shipped to urban markets.

Anderson's photograph of the Jordan Trading Post reflects some of these transnational interactions. The young African American male fourth from the left, for example, was from Rapid City, South Dakota, and taken to Rosebud to be trained as a jockey by Tom Flood, the mustachioed man who hovers over him just to the right.[3] Next, on the right side of the photograph, sits Reuben Quick Bear, a Sioux from Wyoming who was forcibly relocated to South Dakota when the government opened the reservation. Quick Bear was removed again in the late 1870s to attend the Carlisle Indian Industrial School, an institution in central Pennsylvania whose mission was to assimilate Native American children into white society by transforming their ethnic identity. As a result of this education, contemporaries described Quick Bear as contributing "in various ways to both the society of his own people and that of whites"; he was elected county commissioner, served as a postmaster and an official on the Indian agency, and owned the Blackpipe Trading Post.[4] Anderson continued his association with the people and places in and around Rosebud for the next forty-two years before relocating to Rapid City and then California. **BKR**

1. For a history of Anderson's early photography and training, see John A. Anderson, Henry W. Hamilton, and Jean Tyree Hamilton, *The Sioux of the Rosebud: A History in Pictures*, Civilization of the American Indian 111 (Norman: University of Oklahoma Press, 1971), 4–5; and Don Doll and Jim Alinder, eds., *Crying for a Vision: A Rosebud Sioux Triology, 1886–1976* (Dobbs Ferry NY: Morgan and Morgan, 1976), n.p. 2. For more on Anderson's involvement in the Jordan Trading Post, see Anderson, Hamilton, and Hamilton, *The Sioux of the Rosebud*, 7–8. 3. For this identification, see Anderson, Hamilton, and Hamilton, *The Sioux of the Rosebud*, 119, plate 81. 4. "History of Mellette County," in *Mellette County, 1911–1961* (White River SD: Mellette County Centennial Committee, 1961).

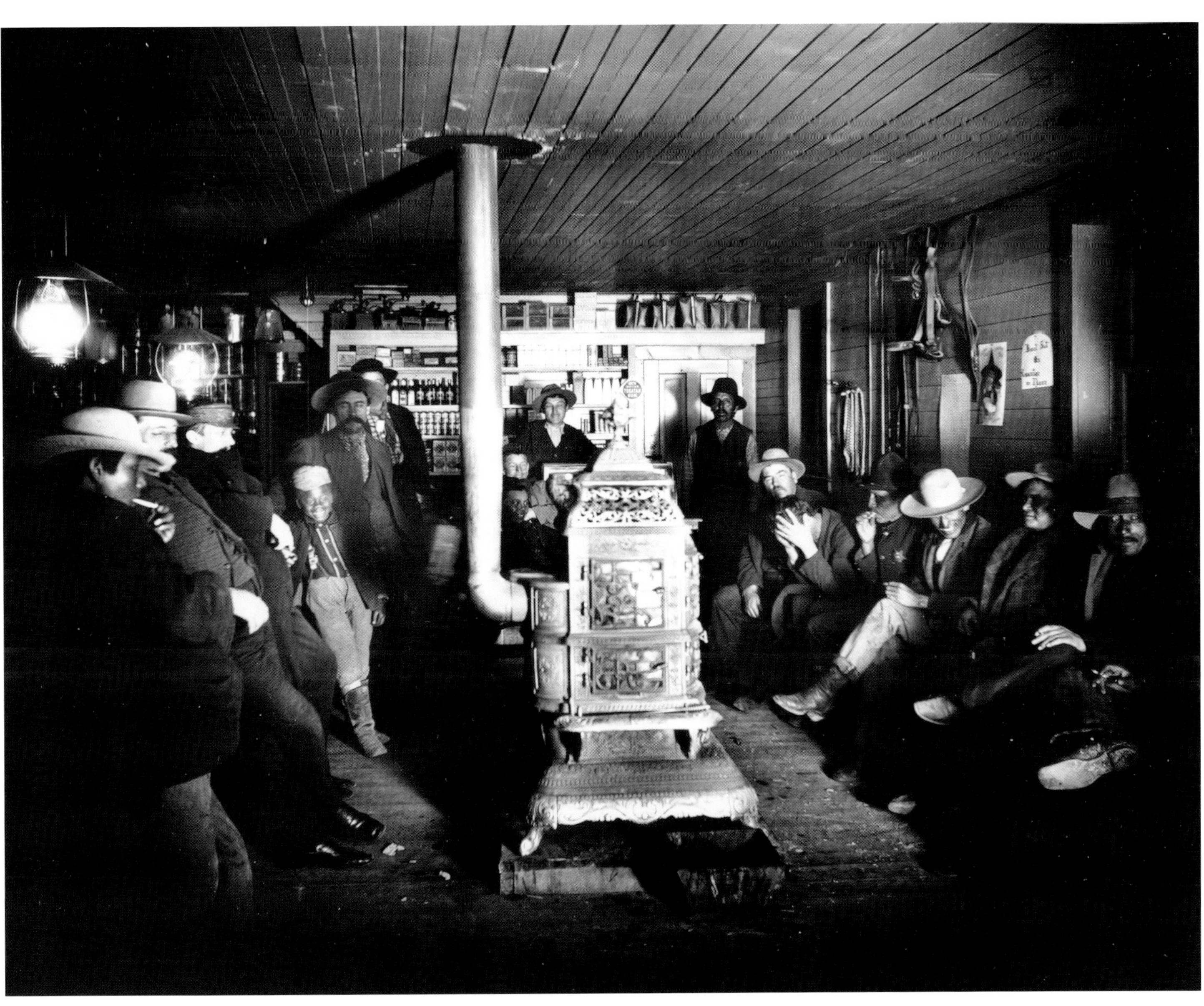

Alfred Stieglitz

American, 1864–1946

The Steerage, 1907; printed 1913 (or earlier)
Photogravure
Image: 33.3 × 26.5 cm (13 1/8 × 10 7/16 in); sheet: 43.2 ×
32.1 cm (17 × 12 5/8 in)
University of Nebraska, gift of Lawrence Reger, U-642

Dubbed the "midwife to ideas," Alfred Stieglitz was one of the leading promoters of modernism during the first half of the twentieth century, exhibiting and mentoring the greatest American artists of the day: Charles Demuth, Arthur Dove, Marsden Hartley, and his future wife, Georgia O'Keeffe, to name only a few.[1] Through his galleries—291, the Intimate Gallery, and An American Place among them—and his journal *Camera Work*, Stieglitz was a tireless supporter not only of modernism but of photography as well. His first venture in this arena was the Little Galleries of the Photo-Secession, named for a group of independent Munich photographers and the circle of like-minded Americans that Stieglitz spearheaded, including Alvin Langdon Coburn (cat. 11), Gertrude Käsebier (cat. 46), and Edward Steichen (cat. 95).[2] Stieglitz and his colleagues' initial goals were to advance photography as a fine art, marrying individual artistic vision with pictorialist techniques such as darkroom experimentation and the use of soft-focus lenses.

To advance the Photo-Secessionist agenda, Stieglitz began publication of *Camera Work* in 1903. The magazine featured articles and editorials by Stieglitz and cover designs by Steichen along with high-quality, full-page photogravures by members of the group; Käsebier, in fact, was the subject of the first issue, which featured several of her images. Stieglitz published this picture in the October 1911 issue of *Camera Work*, which, by then, was losing readership because of its decreasing coverage of photography and increasing support of the European avant-garde.[3] Changes in photographic styles, evidenced in works such as this, also may account for the decline in circulation.

The inspiration for *The Steerage* came to Stieglitz during a 1907 transatlantic voyage to Europe, where he planned to absorb the latest photographic trends and study autochrome, an early color process. Although from a privileged background,

Stieglitz expressed distaste for the upper classes and especially the newly rich; this inspired him to stroll the ship's decks to see the steerage passengers. Here, he captured men, women, and children crowding the ship's bow. Hanging laundry, staring out to sea, and looking up at the first-class deck, they exist as an interesting counterpart to the masses of immigrants who made the reverse trip to America at the time. Although Stieglitz forgot about the image and did not publish it until years later, at the time it represented a strict departure from his moody, soft-focus pictorialism and announced a new interest in straightforward, documentary photography. Nonetheless, it retains many of the artistic principles Stieglitz advocated: the asymmetrical composition and compressed pictorial space, for example, owe a debt to Japanese woodblock prints, which were popular among artists of the time.[4] For his part, Stieglitz described *The Steerage* in terms that revealed his increasing interest in European modernism. "To me," he later stated, "it is a study in mathematical lines, in balance, in a pattern of light and shade."[5] **BKR**

1. For more on Stieglitz's role as a gallerist, see Sarah Greenough, *Modern Art and America: Alfred Stieglitz and His New York Galleries*, exhibition catalog (Washington DC: National Gallery of Art; Boston: Bulfinch Press, 2000). The nickname "midwife to ideas" comes from an artwork by Stieglitz's friend, Marius de Zayas; for this as well as a recent treatment of his gallery activity, see Lisa Mintz Messinger, ed., *Stieglitz and His Artists: Matisse to O'Keeffe*, exhibition catalog (New York: Metropolitan Museum of Art; New Haven CT: Yale University Press, 2011), 223, no. 224. **2.** The Little Galleries were opened in 1905 and later renamed 291 after their location on New York's Fifth Avenue. **3.** For a complete list of the artworks that appeared in that journal, see Alfred Stieglitz and Marianne Fulton Margolis, eds., *Camera Work: A Pictorial Guide* (New York: Dover Publications, 1978); *The Steerage* appears on page 100. **4.** For Stieglitz's experience with Japanese art, see Alexandra Munroe, ed., *The Third Mind: American Artists Contemplate Asia, 1860–1989*, exhibition catalog (New York: Guggenheim Museum, 2009), 420. **5.** *Outlook*, February 20, 1924, quoted in Malcolm Daniel, *Stieglitz, Steichen, Strand: Masterworks from the Metropolitan Museum of Art*, exhibition catalog (New York: Metropolitan Museum of Art; New Haven CT: Yale University Press, 2010), 21.

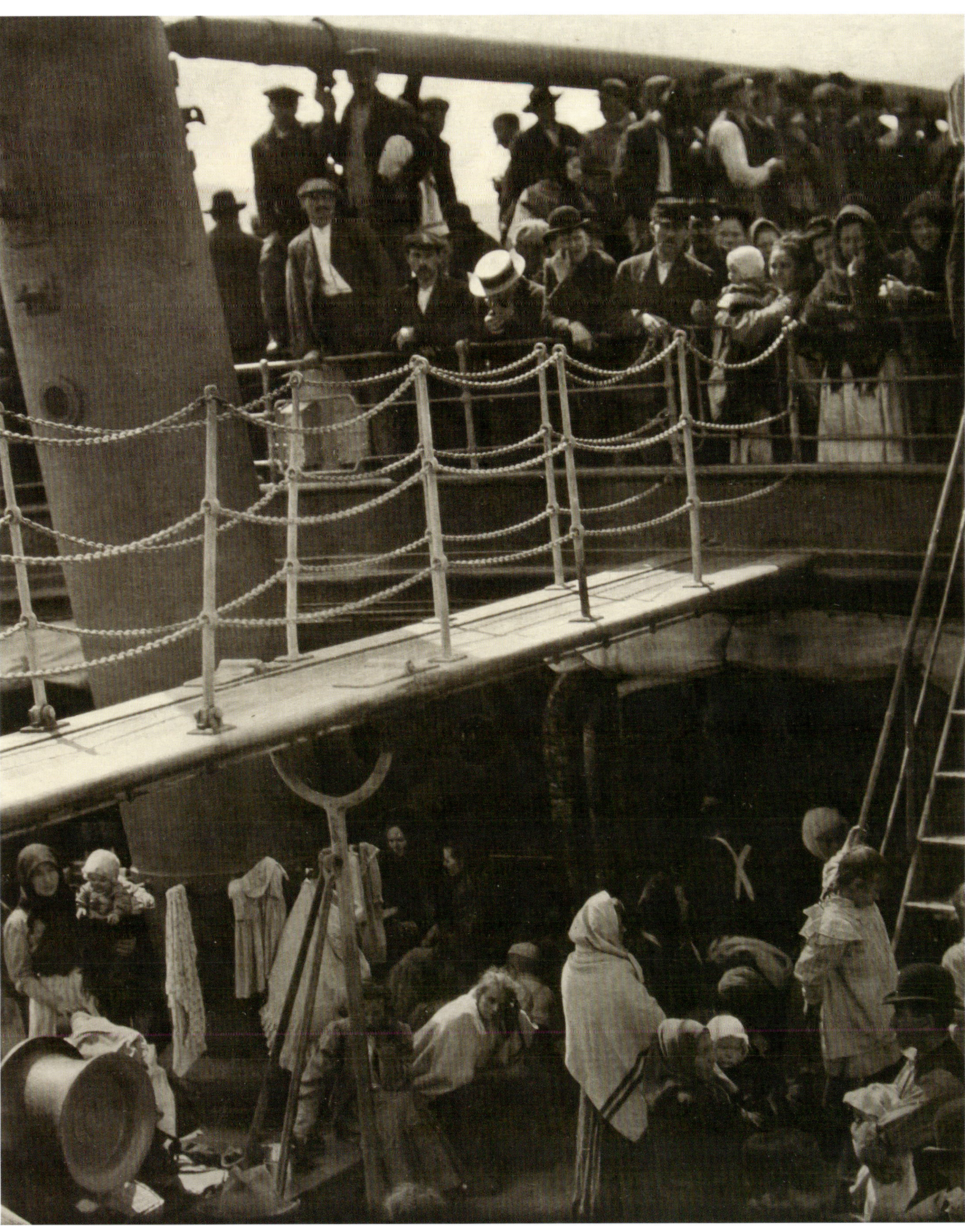

Lewis Hine

American, 1874–1940

Slovak Mother—Ellis Island, 1905
Gelatin silver print
Image: 17.8 × 13 cm (7 × 5 ⅛ in); sheet: 25.2 × 20.3 cm
(9 ¹⁵/₁₆ × 8 in)
University of Nebraska, gift of Del Zogg, U-3792

Toward the end of his life, Lewis Hine credited his passion for documenting children and human labor to his own youth and upbringing: "After Grammar-school . . . my education was transferred for seven years to the manual side of factory, store, and bank. Here I lived behind the scenes in the life of the worker, gaining an understanding that increased through the years."[1] Hine went on to study sociology at the University of Chicago, which boasted several progressive reformers on its faculty, and the city itself exercised equal influence—at that time, it was one of the epicenters of American industrialization and socialist agitation. It was at the invitation of Illinois Normal School professor Frank Manny that Hine relocated to New York to teach at the Fieldston School for Ethical Culture; Manny also encouraged Hine to take up photography as an adjunct to his teaching and graduate studies at New York University.

Because of his background, education, and interests, Hine prized photography's documentary power over its aesthetic potential, viewing it is as an agent of social change. As such, he dismissed the contemporaneous Photo-Secession and its emphasis on artistic compositions and experimental techniques as bourgeois hobbyism. For him, photography's artistic promise rested with its ability to expand perceptions about the outside world and embody the progressive ideals that he valued. Hine thus sought out projects and subjects that accorded with his reform agenda, including a series for Jane Addams's Hull House, a settlement residence for immigrants and workers in Chicago; New York tenements for the National Child Labor Committee; and the Pittsburgh Survey, a pioneering sociological study of the living and working conditions of a large industrial city. Among his first efforts at documenting social conditions was a photographic study of immigrants at Ellis Island that he took with his students between 1903 and 1906.

Hine's desire to capture the customs center coincided with a new public interest in immigration; each day nearly five thousand people poured through the facility, and it came, in a sense, to represent the country's larger transition from an agrarian to an industrial economy. For the artist, the experience also presented an opportunity to "capture and record some of the most picturesque of what many of our friends were talking about."[2] Here, he photographed a young Slovak woman in a waiting area, holding what might amount to all of her worldly belongings on her back and in her hands. Hine identified the subject's ethnicity and imagined her role in the family unit in a caption on the back of the photograph ("Slovak Mother"); otherwise, she is alone, stoically shouldering the burden of her voyage and new circumstances. Hine published *Slovak Mother* years later in the social-reform journal *Charities and the Commons* (later titled the *Survey*). In the accompanying article, the editors cropped and decontextualized the image, giving it the title *Jill Came Stumbling After.*[3] **BKR**

1. Lewis Hine, "Fifty Years of Preparation," in Guggenheim Fellowship application, October 1940, Roy E. Stryker Papers, National Archives, Washington DC, quoted in Alan Trachtenberg et al., *America and Lewis Hine: Photographs, 1904–1940,* exhibition catalog (New York: Brooklyn Museum of Art/Aperture, 1977), 120. **2.** Trachtenberg et al., *America and Lewis Hine,* 122. **3.** For a reproduction of the image as it appeared in the article, see Kate Sampsell-Willmann, *Lewis Hine as Social Critic* (Oxford: University of Mississippi Press, 2009), 43, fig. 1.4.

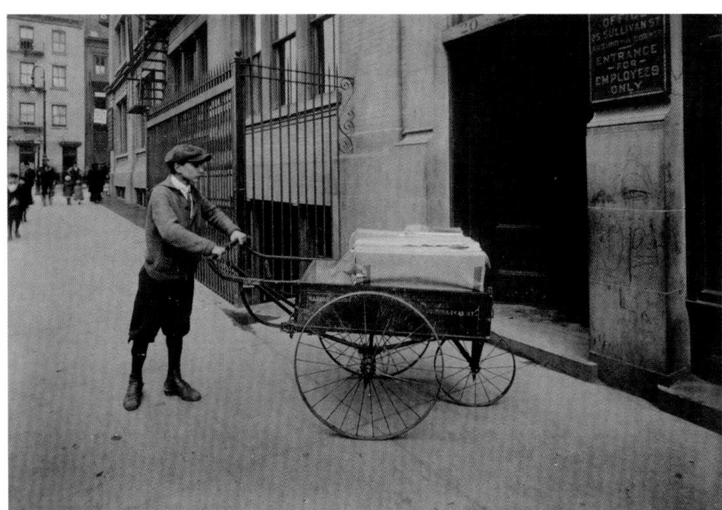

Lewis Hine. *Sullivan's Delivery Boy, South Carolina,* 1908. Gelatin silver print; 12.1 × 17.1 cm (4 ¾ × 6 ¾ in). University of Nebraska, Anna R. and Frank M. Hall Charitable Trust, H-2035.

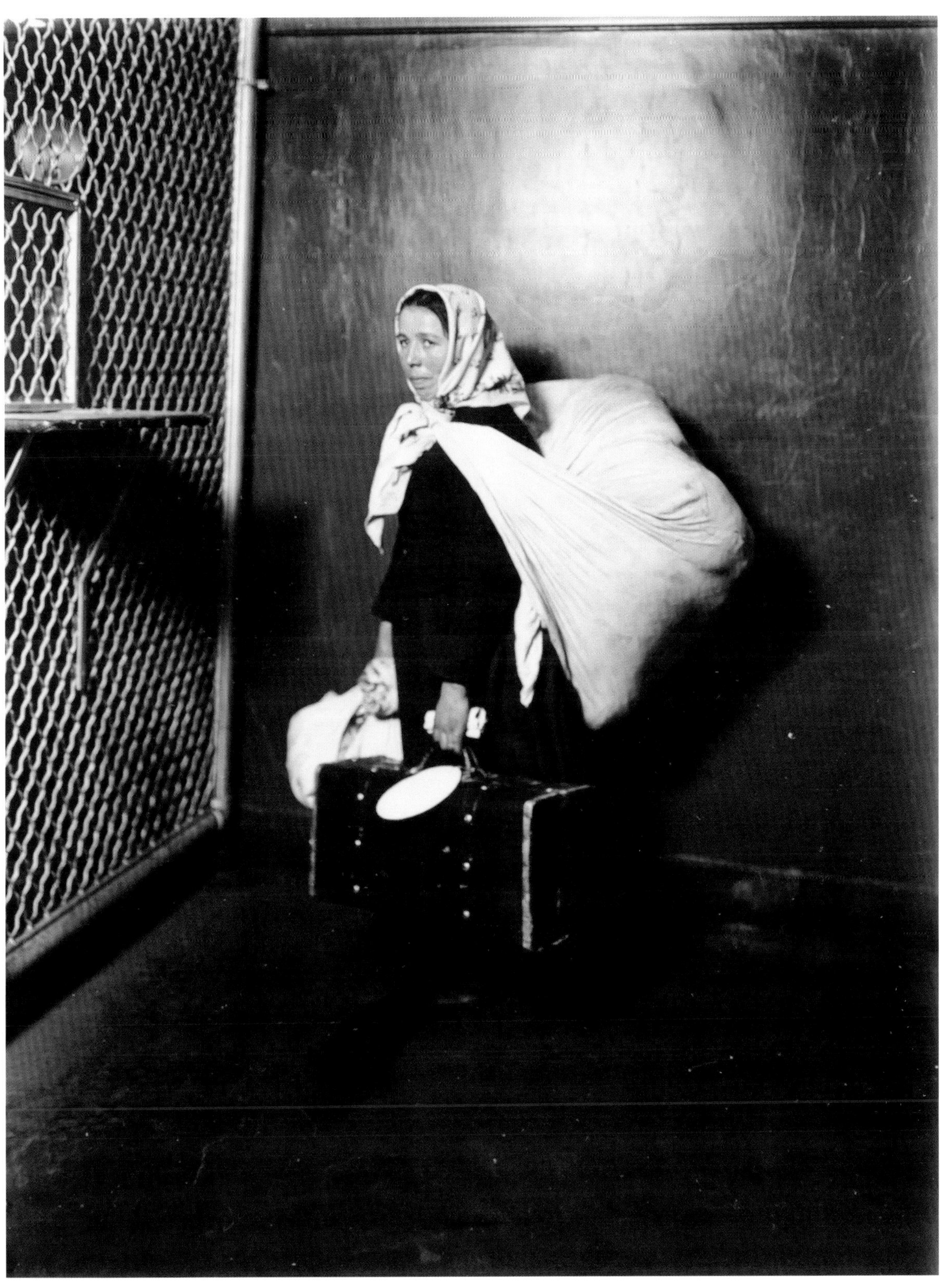

Dorothea Lange

American, 1895–1965

The General Strike, San Francisco, 1934; printed c. 1965
Gelatin silver print
Image and sheet: 31.4 × 25.7 cm (12 3/8 × 10 1/8 in)
Signed, in image, upper right, in black ink: *Dorothea Lange*
University of Nebraska, Anna R. and Frank M. Hall Charitable Trust, H-1067

Dorothea Lange trained with Arnold Genthe (cats. 2 and 96) in his portrait studio after he relocated to New York City and then with Clarence White (cat. 69) at Columbia University. After a brief stint at a teacher's college and an attempt to travel around the world to further develop her photography skills, the Hoboken native found herself stranded in San Francisco. There she quickly established a portrait studio; married her first husband, painter Maynard Dixon; and eventually developed relationships with a group of like-minded photographers, including Ansel Adams (cat. 35), Imogen Cunningham (cats. 56 and 103), and Edward Weston (cat. 58). Lange did not officially join their collective, f64, which advocated "pure photography" in opposition to the pictorialist practice of aligning the medium with painting and etching. Nonetheless, the group's members exercised considerable influence over her technique and choice of subject: by the early years of the Great Depression, she had abandoned society portraiture in favor of gritty street scenes.

Lange later confessed that this shift in focus and tone was swift, but she offered differing explanations as to its cause. In the 1950s, she asserted that her epiphany occurred in the Sierra Nevada in 1929: "With the thunder bursting and the wind whistling it came to me that what I had to do was to take pictures and concentrate upon people, only people. All kinds of people, people who paid me and people who didn't."[1] In a subsequent interview, however, she spoke of how in 1933 she watched an unemployed man from the upstairs window of her studio and decided to take her camera into the street, declaring, "I better make this happen."[2] Equally influential was Lange's budding relationship with Paul Taylor, an agricultural economist and professor at the University of California, Berkeley, who became her second husband in 1935. The artist made this photograph while working with Taylor, who was covering the General Strike of 1934 for *Survey Graphic*, an illustrated supplement to the *Survey*, the social-reform journal that employed several photographers, including Lewis Hine (cat. 16). The strike began with a work stoppage by nonunionized longshoremen, gaining traction when they were joined by thousands of "unemployed and under-employed unionists . . . ready for aggressive action."[3] The results were bloody, with destructive police violence that left two picketers shot dead.

Lange's photograph, in contrast, captures a calmer moment amid the chaos and hostility. The strikers and their supporters form an almost orderly line behind an unruffled policeman whose large build, pressed suit, and composure serve as the clear focus for the camera. *The General Strike* provides a telling antidote to Genthe's soft-focus, romanticized views of San Francisco's Chinatown of a generation earlier. While the strikers here are all white men, the nature of the action and the image speak to the internationalism of the American economy and the union movement during the 1930s. While the picketer at extreme left aligns his economic interests with the Soviet Union against Japanese imperialism, other signs imply more global participation and interests, suggesting that the site of this event was in the city's Chinatown district.[4] **BKR**

1. Quoted in Milton Meltzer, *Dorothea Lange: A Photographer's Life* (Syracuse NY: Syracuse University Press, 2000), 64. 2. Quoted in Meltzer, *Dorothea Lange*, 69–70. 3. The quote is from the article Paul Taylor authored with Norman Leon Gold for *Survey Graphic* in September 1934; see Jan Goggans, *California on the Breadlines: Dorothea Lange, Paul Taylor, and the Making of a New Deal Narrative* (Berkeley: University of California Press, 2010), 88–92. 4. The photograph has also been titled *Street Demonstration, Chinatown, San Francisco, California*; see Pierre Borhan et al., *Dorothea Lange: The Heart and Mind of a Photographer* (Boston: Little, Brown, 2002), 79.

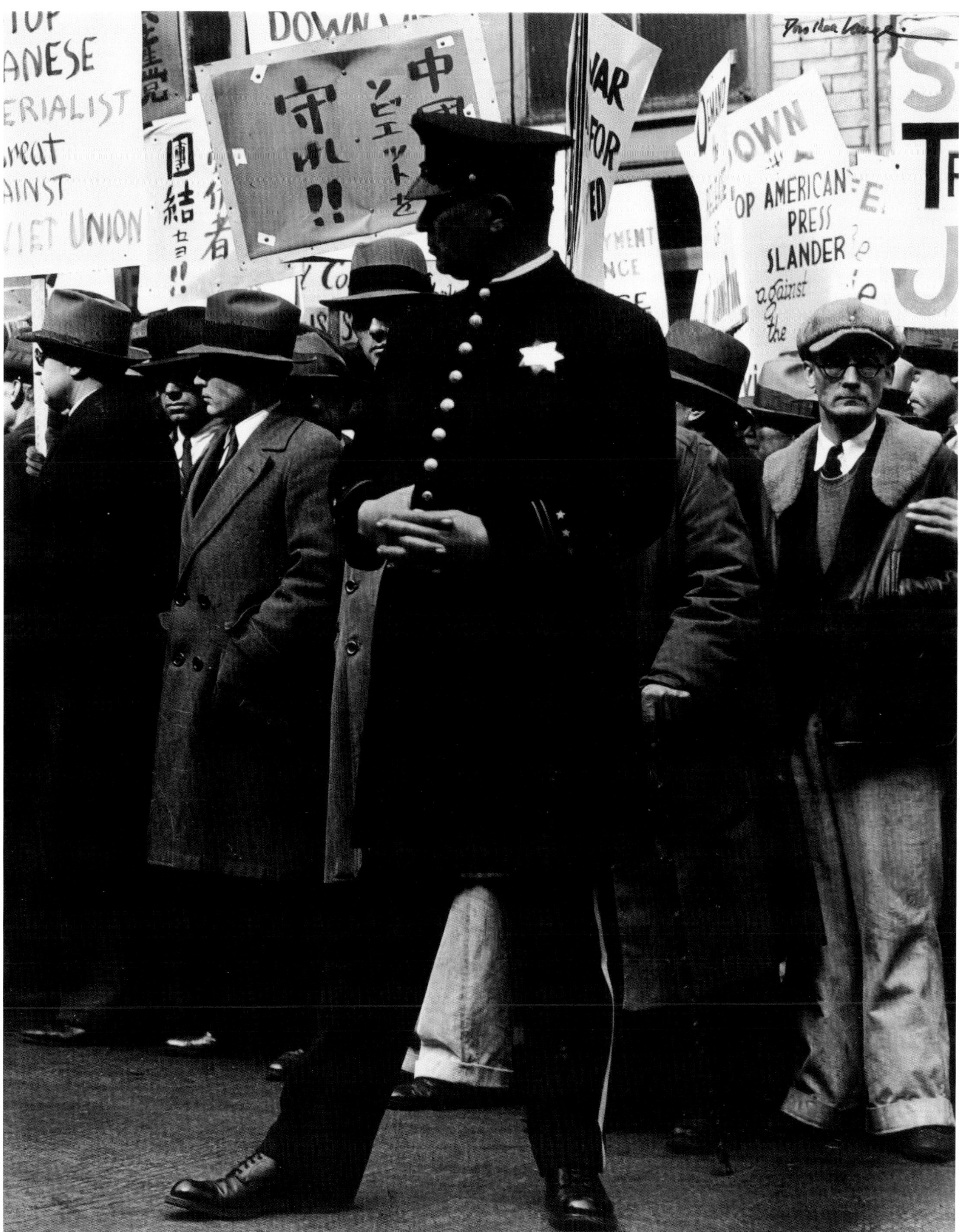
TOP
ANESE
ERIALIST
reat
ainst
VIET UNION
DOWN
中國
守れ!!
ソビエットを
団結せ!!
WAR
FOR
OWN
OP AMERICAN
PRESS
SLANDER
against
the
S
T
J
Dorothea Lange

18

Aaron Siskind

American, 1903–1991

Uruapan 11, Mexico, 1955
Gelatin silver print
Image and sheet: 37.1 × 48.9 cm (14 5/8 × 19 1/4 in)
University of Nebraska, Anna R. and Frank M. Hall
Charitable Trust, H-618

The son of Russian Jewish immigrants, Aaron Siskind grew up in New York City. As a young man, he was interested in art, literature, music, and progressive politics. After receiving a degree in English in 1926 from the City College of New York, he taught for twenty-three years in the city's public schools. From 1951 until his retirement in 1976, he was a renowned and influential professor of photography, first at the Institute of Design in Chicago and then at the Rhode Island School of Design.

Siskind's interest in photography was part of his larger investigation of politics and art. In the 1930s, he became involved in the New York Workers' Film and Photo League, which focused on progressive social causes such as civil rights and issues of labor and housing. The Photo League hosted classes, exhibitions, and lectures, all with an emphasis on documentary fact gathering and political advocacy. Siskind was deeply involved in the group's projects from 1936 to 1940. In this same period, his interest in contemporary art deepened, resulting in personal friendships with some of the young painters later celebrated as abstract expressionists, including Willem de Kooning, Adolph Gottlieb, Franz Kline, and Barnett Newman.

In the early 1940s, Siskind's core concern—a humanism at once visceral and cerebral—remained constant, while the nature of his work changed radically, moving from factual records of people and places to quasi-abstract renderings of detritus, graffiti, and found objects. This stylistic shift was prompted by a personal quest for a fresh, purified way of seeing. Siskind focused on discarded things, the casual, accidental, or automatic gesture, and the effects of time and decay, revealing in them the mute traces of past human actions and a relentless entropy.

For Siskind, form became a new kind of content. Instead of recording people and places with poignant stories, he evoked emotions directly in an abstract vocabulary of pictorial tensions and relationships. This was a distinctly prelinguistic artistic realm: the power of his pictures was emotional and intuitive, not a matter of traditional narrative.

Made during a 1955 trip to Mexico, *Uruapan 11* is characteristic of Siskind's mature approach. This work is ambiguous in scale: the image exerts itself as a coherent picture, first and foremost, rather than a simple description of the physical world. The primary subject is human mark making: what appear to be painted letters that have themselves been painted over. This apparent combination of assertion and negation, message and erasure, is poignant, suggesting a kind of existential futility or cosmic yin-yang duality. In purely visual terms, these marks reveal a family resemblance to abstract expressionist paintings of the era. Ironically, perhaps, part of Siskind's inimitable genius lay in his evocation of the creative energies of an ageless, nameless Everyman—anonymous and omnipresent marks echoing the avant-garde art of his day. Finally, his treatment of space is astute. In acknowledging the photograph as an intrinsically two-dimensional graphic creation, the artist focused repeatedly on subjects such as painted walls, which were themselves flat. In works such as this one, however, Siskind extended that awareness by including a sliver of sky (with evidence of a tree) at the top of the frame. The result is a compelling play between two and three dimensions, darkness and light, culture and nature, closure and openness.

From the most inconsequential things, Siskind created an art that was sublimely expansive: visceral and philosophical, personal and universal. **KFD**

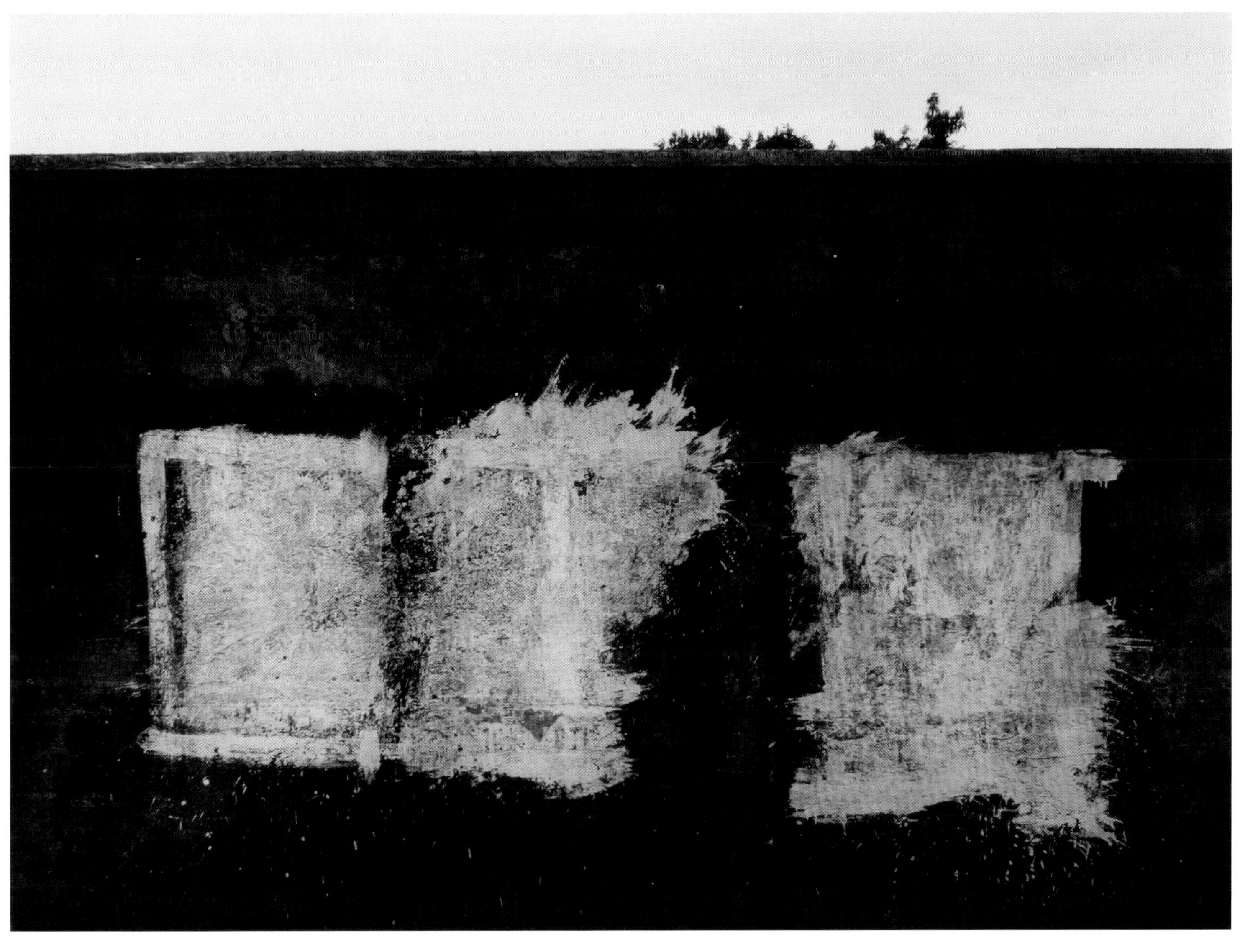

Graciela Iturbide

Mexican, born 1942

El gallo, Juchitán, 1986
Gelatin silver print
Image: 47.6 × 32.9 cm (18 ¾ × 13 in); sheet: 50.8 ×
40.6 cm (20 × 16 in)
Signed, lower right, in black ink: *Graciela Iturbide*
University of Nebraska, Olga N. Sheldon Acquisition
Trust, U-5495

Although drawn to art and visual culture, Graciela Iturbide was initially unsure of her direction and enrolled at the National Autonomous University in her native Mexico City to study filmmaking and screenwriting. While there, she took an advanced course in photography with Manuel Álvarez Bravo (cat. 79), who asked her to become his apprentice, thus determining the future direction of her life and profession. Although Álvarez Bravo refused to give Iturbide any technical training, he strongly encouraged her interest in documenting daily life in Mexico, a subject she has pursued throughout her career.

In 1979 Iturbide was one of a group of artists invited to participate in an exhibition in the town of Juchitán de Zaragoza, which is located on the Tehuantepec Isthmus along Mexico's southern Pacific coast. During the twentieth century, the region exercised considerable influence on both foreign and Mexican artists, including Henri Cartier-Bresson (cat. 73), Frida Kahlo, Tina Modotti, and, most importantly in this case, Emilio Amero (cat. 47), who created a photographic portfolio of the nearby town of Tehuantepec. Artists were drawn to the area largely because of its large population of mestizos of Huaves and Zapotec descent who maintained local customs and practices, serving as a symbol of Mexico's national identity and past. Fascinated by Juchitán's folkways and people, Iturbide returned for extended periods over the next six years, studying Zapotec culture and accumulating hundreds of negatives. Eventually, on the advice of a friend, she created a photographic essay titled *Juchitán de las mujeres*, which many critics consider her masterwork. Iturbide later credited the women of the area for their influence: "In Juchitán I went to the market, I stayed with the women, those strong, fat, politicized, liberated, marvelous women. I discovered the world of women. I was able to stay with them all the time, and they gave me a certain kind of protection. Of course, being a woman made access to their daily life and traditions easier for me."[1]

In addition to its reputation for a matriarchal culture, Juchitán possessed a preindustrial agricultural life and livestock economy that also attracted Iturbide, who cited its residents' "close proximity to animals" as an important aspect of her work at the time.[2] The beautifully structured *El gallo* demonstrates this closeness. Here, a young boy playfully nuzzles a rooster's wings against his cheeks, peering through them at the viewer with a mischievous glint in his eyes. The downy white feathers stand out strongly against the darkness of the boy's skin, while the gray of his shirt and the wall in the background create superbly complex intermediate tones. At left, the thrust of a second rooster—head cocked, talons bared, accompanied by flying feathers and chicken feed—adds energy and vitality to the composition as well as another element of humor. At the same time, the birds' struggle suggests both their ultimate fate and the difficulty of working with animals, further evidenced by the stained, torn hem of the boy's shirt. **BKR**

1. Graciela Iturbide, interview by Fabienne Bardu, 2006, in *Graciela Iturbide: Eyes to Fly With*, by Fabienne Bardu and Alejandro Castellanos (Austin: University of Texas Press, 2006), 10. **2.** Bardu and Castellanos, *Graciela Iturbide*, 11; for more on the region's influence on Iturbide and its transition to a livestock economy, see Roberto Tejada and Alfredo López Austin, *Images of the Spirit: Photographs by Graciela Iturbide*, exhibition catalog (New York: Aperture, 1996), 13.

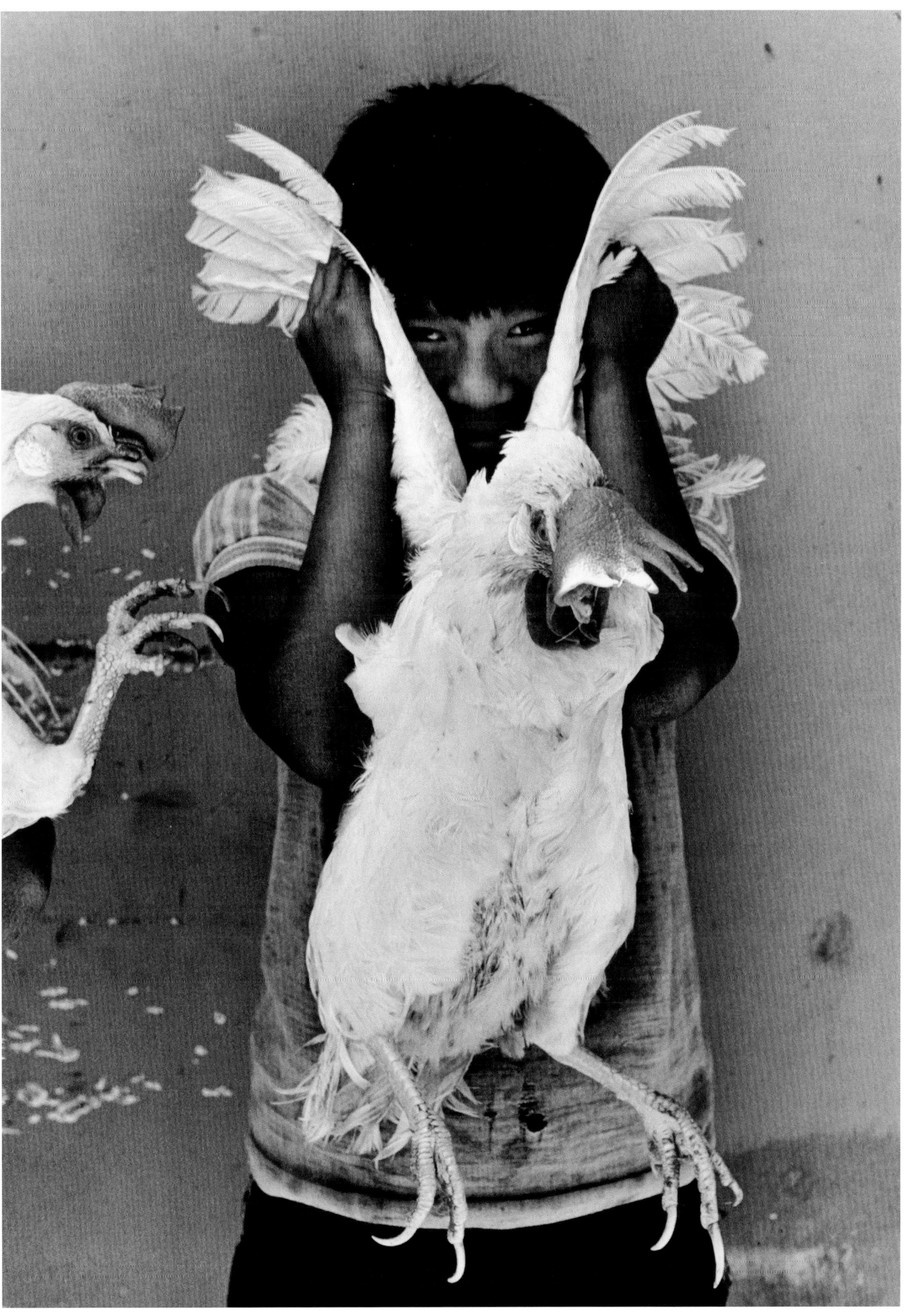

Tseng Kwong Chi

American, born Hong Kong, 1950–1990

New York, New York (from the series *Expeditionary Self-Portrait*), 1979; printed 2001
Gelatin silver print
Image: 37.8 × 38.1 cm (14 7/8 × 15 in); sheet: 50.2 × 40.6 cm (19 3/4 × 16 in)
On verso, middle center: artist's estate stamp with handwritten inscriptions; in black ink: 6/25 *New York, NY 1979* / *Printed 2001*
University of Nebraska, Robert E. Schweser and Fern Beardsley Schweser Acquisition Fund, through the University of Nebraska Foundation, U-5404

Tseng Kwong Chi was born in Hong Kong, where he studied traditional Chinese calligraphy and painting. At age sixteen, he moved with his family to Canada and later continued his art studies in Paris. In 1979 Tseng settled in New York City and quickly became a central figure in the vibrant East Village art scene, which also included Jean-Michel Basquiat, Keith Haring, Kenny Scharf, Julian Schnabel, and Andy Warhol. Participating in and documenting performances and parties, he created an archive of the restless downtown energy of the 1980s.[1]

Extroverted, cosmopolitan, and urbane by nature, Tseng took on a very different persona in his most famous series of photographs, perhaps in order to reflect on the contradictions inherent to his own identity. Donning a secondhand Mao suit, a plastic identity badge, and mirrored sunglasses, he attended a gala at the Metropolitan Museum of Art. The distinctive uniform of the Chinese Revolution granted him both authority and anonymity; he became an "embodiment of cultural difference."[2]

This provocative doppelgänger opened up new conceptual possibilities for Tseng. During his childhood in China, he had developed a fascination with the legend of Mao Zedong's Long March (1934–35), endlessly reiterated for propagandistic purposes. Later, living in the West, he became aware of the many contrasts between Eastern and Western cultural attitudes. Tourism, both literal and metaphorical, became his means of revealing these contrasts.

Initially titled *East Meets West*, Tseng's *Expeditionary Self-Portrait* series was produced between 1979 and 1989. Numbering over one hundred images, it documents Tseng's personal Grand Tour of sites in Europe and America. The artist himself appears in each photograph, wearing his Mao ensemble and posing with monuments, whether natural or human-made, sacred or commercial. Each composition is different, figure and setting harmonized. *New York, New York* is a particularly dramatic example, taken from a worm's-eye view. Tseng occupies the left foreground, while the twin towers of the World Trade Center loom behind him, silhouetted against a sky so underexposed that it appears black in the print. The mirrored lenses of his sunglasses are visual analogues to the reflective surfaces of the skyscrapers, just as his upright posture conforms to their rectitude.

Tseng described himself as "an inquisitive traveler, a witness of my time and an ambiguous ambassador."[3] As a constructed representative of the Chinese presence in America, he knowingly triggered reactions of curiosity and fear. In 1979, when Tseng made this photograph, President Richard Nixon's 1972 trip to China was still in recent collective memory, as was the inauguration of the World Trade Center just one year later. Tseng died of AIDS-related illness in 1990. He did not witness the terrorist attacks of September 11, 2001, which destroyed the World Trade Center, and China's rise to economic power, which has changed Western perspectives on Asia—epochal occurrences that have irrevocably altered our interpretation of this image. Even so, Tseng presciently captured the complex symbolic potential of the architecture and of racial difference. **BS**

1. See Marvin J. Taylor, ed., *The Downtown Book: The New York Art Scene, 1974–1984*, exhibition catalog (New York: Grey Art Gallery and the Fales Library and Special Collections, New York University; Princeton NJ: Princeton University Press, 2006). **2.** Dan Cameron, "Alone Again, Naturally," in *Tseng Kwong Chi: Self-Portraits, 1979–1989*, ed. Dan Cameron et al., exhibition catalog (New York: Paul Kasmin Gallery, 2008), 10. **3.** Lilly Wei, "From Here to Eternity," in *Tseng Kwong Chi*, 9.

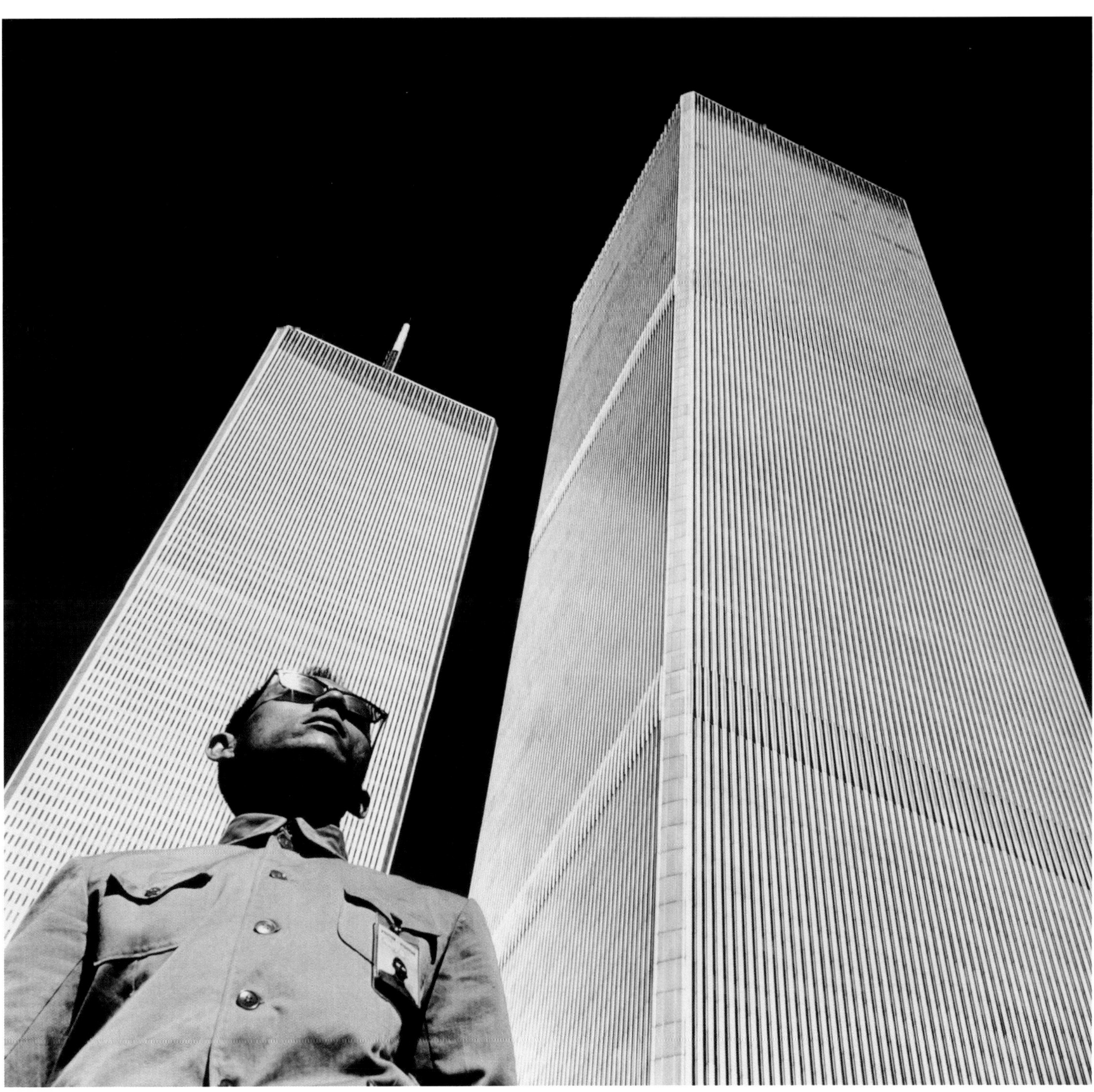

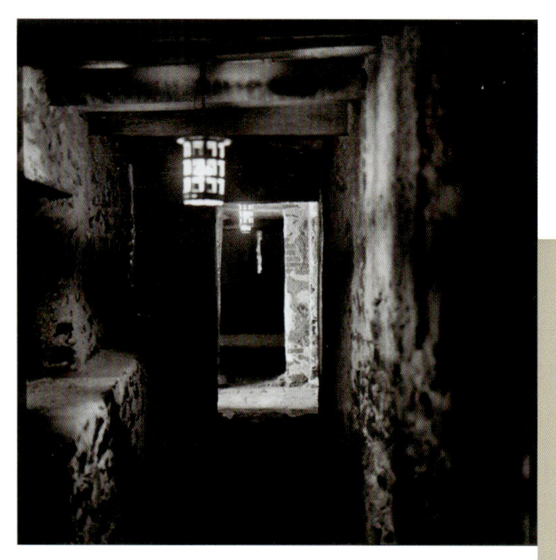

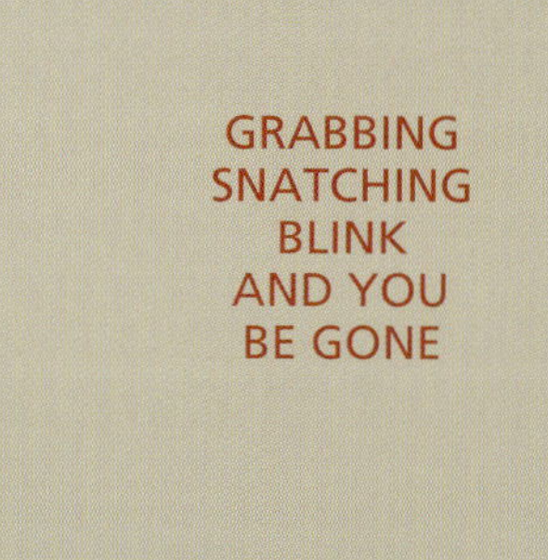

GRABBING
SNATCHING
BLINK
AND YOU
BE GONE

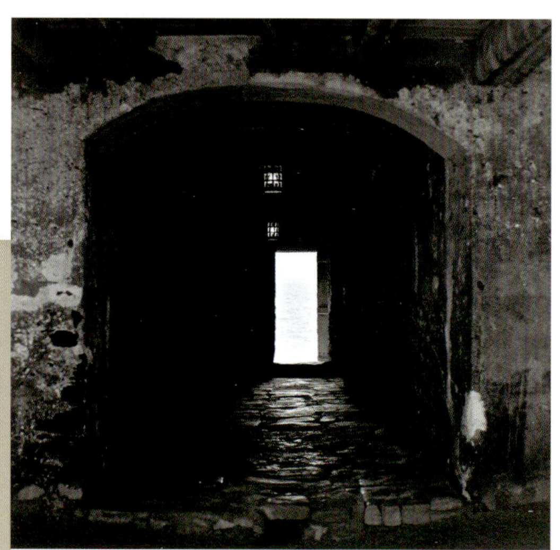

21

Carrie Mae Weems
American, born 1953

Grabbing Snatching Blink and You Be Gone (from the
series *Slave Coast*), 1993
Gelatin silver print
Image and sheet: 50.2 × 50.2 cm (19 3/4 × 19 3/4 in)
University of Nebraska, gift of an anonymous donor
by exchange, U-5002 1–3

Over the last three decades, Carrie Mae Weems has created
a body of work that explores themes of cultural, ethnic, and
sexual identity, often through the lens of history. From the
very beginning of her career, however, the artist saw these
subjects as smaller parts of an overarching interest in authority and social control: "I've been interested in the idea
of power and the consequences of power; relationships are
made and articulated through power. It's assumed that autobiography is key, because I so often use myself, my own experience—limited as it is at times—as the starting point. But
I use myself simply as a vehicle for approaching the question
of power, and following where that leads me to and through.
It's never about me; it's always about something larger."[1]

To convey these power dynamics, Weems uses both images and words. Storytelling is an essential aspect of her art,
which is why she frequently works serially and sequentially,
interspersing her photographs with textual elements. In addition, she often threads her projects together, regularly connecting each one in a conversation with those that precede
or follow it. In her *Sea Island* series (1991–92), for example,
Weems photographed the home of the Gullah people on the
barrier islands of Georgia and South Carolina, questioning
Africa's role in shaping the culture and society of African
Americans.[2] To extend this dialogue on the African diaspora, the artist toured western Africa and, as a result, produced three bodies of work: *Africa*, *Slave Coast*, and *Landed
in Africa*. In these series, the artist documented the architectural and cultural artifacts of the slave trade, creating richly
toned prints whose beauty is often at odds with the horror
of their subject.

Photographs from *Slave Coast* show the interior of the
House of Slaves, a memorial and museum on Gorée Island
off the coast of the Senagalese capital, Dakar. Built as a home
in the late eighteenth century and reopened as a historical
site and monument in 1962, Gorée raises issues of history and
remembrance even as scholars continue to debate its exact
significance in the Atlantic slave trade.[3] For many Africans,
Americans, and Europeans, however, Gorée has come to
symbolize the slave trade, and hundreds of thousands make
yearly pilgrimages to better understand the human costs of
this era in our history. These are perhaps most sharply revealed in the house's Door of No Return, the final threshold
that kidnapped West Africans passed through before being
herded onto ships. Weems reinforced the abruptness of that
abduction by juxtaposing her photograph with the text *Grabbing Snatching Blink and You Be Gone*, which contradicts
the almost quiet emptiness of the image. The vacant halls,
however, evoke a sense of emotional absence and symbolize the disappearance of millions of Africans during the period while the grim, threatening holding facility possesses
a haunting and timeless presence. To the artist, the site also
serves as a productive point of connection to Africa's many
places and peoples. **BKR**

1. Carrie Mae Weems, interview by Dawoud Bey, 2009, *BOMB Magazine* 108
(Summer 2009), accessed January 15, 2012, http://bombsite.com/issues/108/
articles/3307. **2.** For an overview of Weems's career and examples from
many of her earlier projects, see Thomas Piché Jr. and Thelma Golden,
Carrie Mae Weems: Recent Work, 1992–1998 (New York: George Braziller,
1998). **3.** For a brief overview of this debate, see Howard W. French, "The
Evil That Was Done Senegal: A Guided Tour," *New York Times*, March 6, 1998.

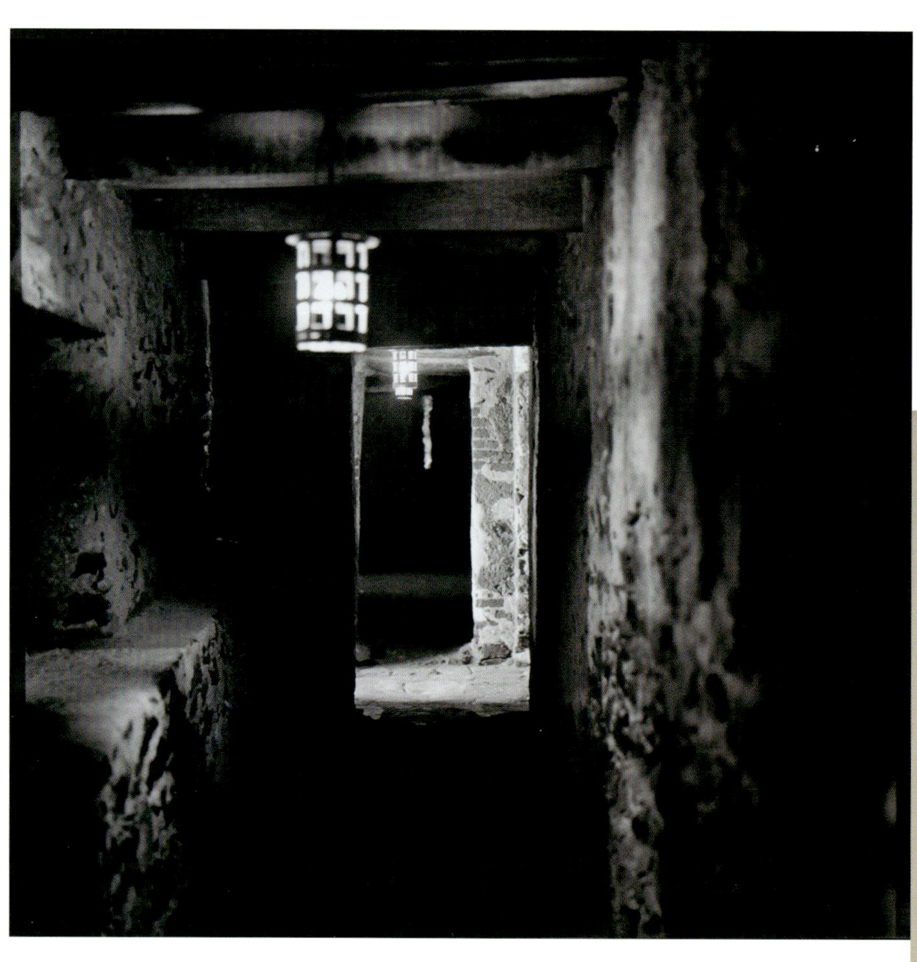

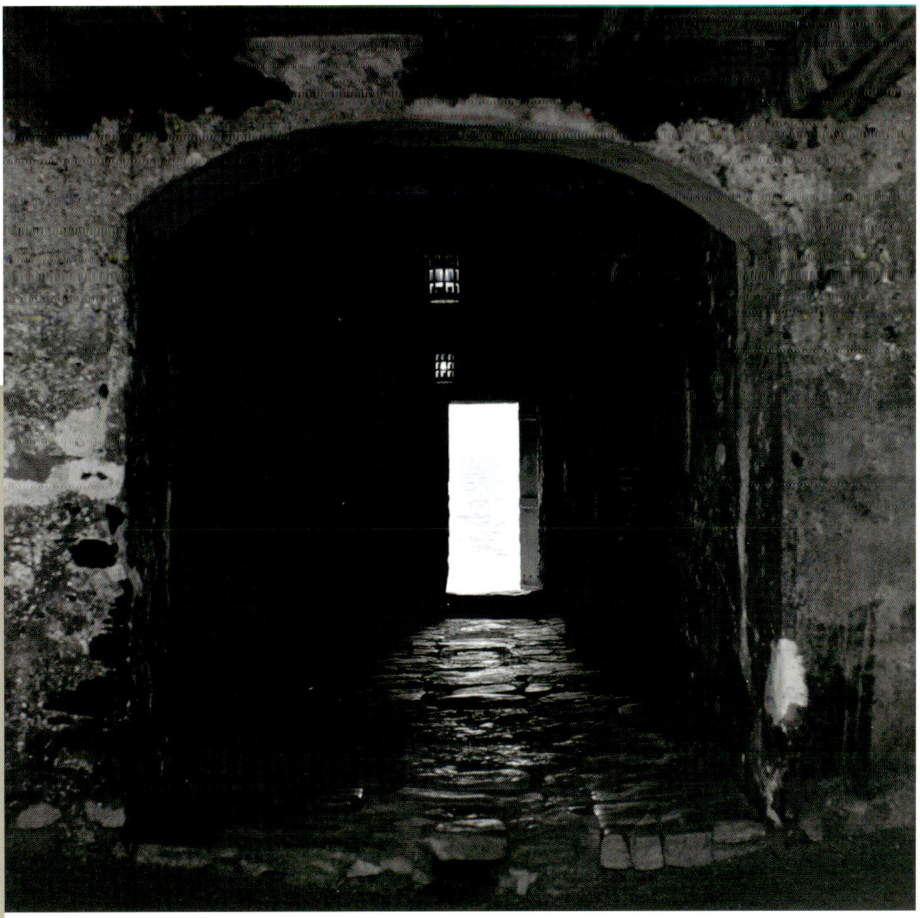

GRABBING
SNATCHING
BLINK
AND YOU
BE GONE

22

Luis González Palma
Guatemalan, born 1957

Milagros, 1993
Sepia-toned gelatin silver print with collage
Image and sheet: 50.2 × 27.3 cm (19 ¾ × 10 ¾ in)
Inscribed, on verso, middle center, in pencil: *González /
"Milagros" / 1993 / 9/10*
University of Nebraska, Anna R. and Frank M. Hall
Charitable Trust, H-3026

Luis González Palma has been described as a "thoroughly modern artist with the soul of a baroque painter."[1] Indeed, his strange, enigmatic images explore the convergence of Guatemala's ancient Mayan roots and colonial experience. The directness and immediacy of his portraits, for example, invite viewers to examine their subjects with scientific intensity and scrutiny. In addition, the artist often mixes image and text, provoking comparisons to fieldwork on non-Western societies; in this photograph, for instance, handwritten words appear on lined paper in the corner. At the same time, González Palma is not interested in exploring or duplicating ethnographic documents or folkloric customs from the distant or recent past but rather in engaging with the themes of cultural mythology, ethnicity, and social history that have created the contemporary Guatemalan state.[2]

The title of this image, *Milagros*, can refer to the votive offerings—flowers, notes, photographs, rosaries—that are found on the altars of Latin American churches, an expression of gratitude for a saint's intercession. The figure's static pose and eerily glowing eyes endow it with a supernatural energy; this, along with the sepia tone of the photograph, creates the feeling of a carved wooden sculpture found in a colonial cathedral. In addition, the elaborately textured costume resembles the hand-sewn clothing made for those statues, which renders them more lifelike and spiritually accessible. At the same time, the artist has asserted that he named the piece after Peruvian photographer Milagros de la Torre, whose combination of insouciance and melancholy might have been captured in the figure's grim visage and harlequin costume.

Unsurprisingly, theatricality is part of the artist's aesthetic agenda. Working exclusively in the studio, González Palma emphasizes the artificial qualities of his subjects' surroundings, supplying his sitters—Guatemalans of Mayan descent—with complicated, symbolically loaded costumes: a mask of a crescent moon with a face, a headdress made of feathers, a wreath of twigs, or, in this case, a harlequin suit.

As a final finish to his work, the photographer also defaces, distresses, paints, scratches, and tears his prints in expressionistic gestures, most evident in this image on the subject's richly starched collar. This act—along with the sepia tone—not only gives his images an antique quality but also links his process to one of his influences, the photographer Joel-Peter Witkin (cat. 63). In González Palma's words, the "sensation of antique coloring, the dark color of the earth, and the faces colored with history" reveal the "universal persistence of both beauty and pain."[3] Pain is an enduring premise of the artist's work, a shroud that we acquire when we are born and that is with us until we die, a constant reminder of Guatemala's bloody revolution. **BKR**

1. Peter Hay Halpert, "Luis González Palma: A Thoroughly Modern Artist with the Soul of a Baroque Painter," *Art and Antiques* 15 (December 1992): 81. **2.** A. D. Coleman, "Letter from New York, #37," *PhotoMetro* 103 (November 1992): 31. **3.** Quoted in David Travis, "The Persistence of Beauty, the Persistence of Pain: Photographs by Luis González Palma," essay for the Stephen Cohen Gallery, 1992, curatorial files, Sheldon Museum of Art.

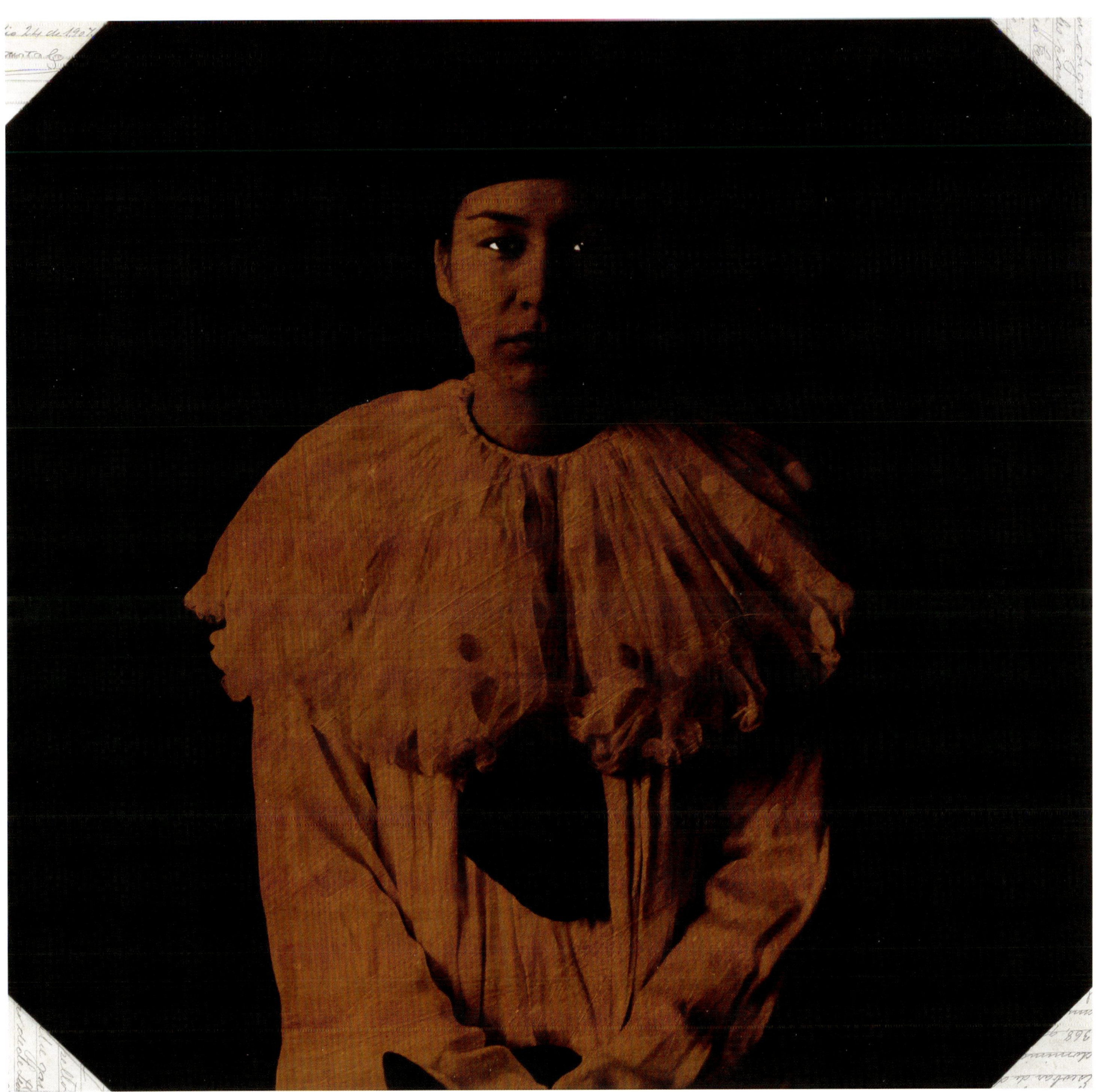

23

Renée Cox
American, born Jamaica, 1960

Mother of Us All, 2004
Digital inkjet print on watercolor paper
Image: 92.7 × 114.3 cm (36 1/2 × 45 in); sheet: 111.8 × 132.7 cm
(44 × 52 1/4 in)
Inscribed, on verso, lower center, in pencil: *Renée Cox
04*; lower right: *COXR-0120 AP1*
Sheldon Art Association, purchased with funds from the
Sheldon Forum, S-870

Though Renée Cox was born in Colgate, Jamaica, her family moved to Queens, New York, when she was an infant. At age ten, she was sent to an Anglican boarding school in Jamaica in anticipation of her family's plan to move back home. In the course of that year's experience, she learned of the story of Queen Nanny of the Maroons, an eighteenth-century resistance fighter against the island's British colonizers—and inspiration for the work *Mother of Us All*. Perhaps unconsciously absorbing and reflecting the lessons and spirit of Queen Nanny, the young Cox put up her own resistance to her family's plans to return to Jamaica. She convinced them to stay in New York, where they settled in the suburb of Scarsdale.

The ideal of a strong black woman, fighting for freedom, would run through Cox's photographic series, with the artist herself playing the heroic figure. If it seems a self-absorbed course of art making, as it has for some critics, it may be because the history of art was built on images of white heroic men and permissive women. They make up the unconscious of art—what we take for granted—against which Cox delivers her self-conscious responses.

In the early 1990s, for example, the artist began a series of self-portraits titled *Yo Mama*, deploying the expression from a type of joke or insult exchanged originally among African American urban male youth, always at the expense of the other's mother. Cox appropriated the verbal affront as her own, turning it, to some extent, against the viewer. The most audacious image in the series is *Yo Mama's Last Supper* (after Leonardo), in which all the apostles are black men and Cox stands naked in the central seat at the table—Christ's place.

Cox later re-created herself as "Rajé," a female superhero who wears a spandex leotard in the Jamaican colors and liberates the likes of Aunt Jemima and Uncle Ben from their cardboard-box plantations. Those were fantasy heroes. However, the themes of "mama," Jamaica, and liberator come together in Cox's 2004 series *Queen Nanny of the Maroons*, which is based on the historical figure who, in Jamaica, is elevated to mythic stature. (The Maroons were runaway slaves who fled first from the Spanish colonizers, then from the British, establishing independent settlements in the country's remote highlands.)

Having begun her photographic essay on the lives of Jamaican highland peoples, descendants of the Maroons, the artist recognized that the central motivating figure, Queen Nanny, was missing from the series and yet everywhere present in spirit. Figures like Queen Nanny remain submerged, not written into history, because, as Cox understands it, history gets written by the colonizers.[1] She therefore inserted herself into photographic vignettes, moments in the life of a resistance fighter who, in contrast to history's heroes, is a woman and a person of African origin. In that sense, she is "mother of us all," certainly to Jamaicans. Beyond that, she is like Eugène Delacroix's *Liberty Leading the People*, a figure of democratic unity. *Mother of Us All* portrays a contemporary avatar of Queen Nanny, a woman of steadfast composure, with her children, who range in attitudes of readiness for the lives ahead of them. They look at us and await our response to their existence. **JDV**

1. Renée Cox, interview by Nicole Plett, October 21, 2008, transcript, Institute for Women and Art, Rutgers University, New Brunswick, New Jersey.

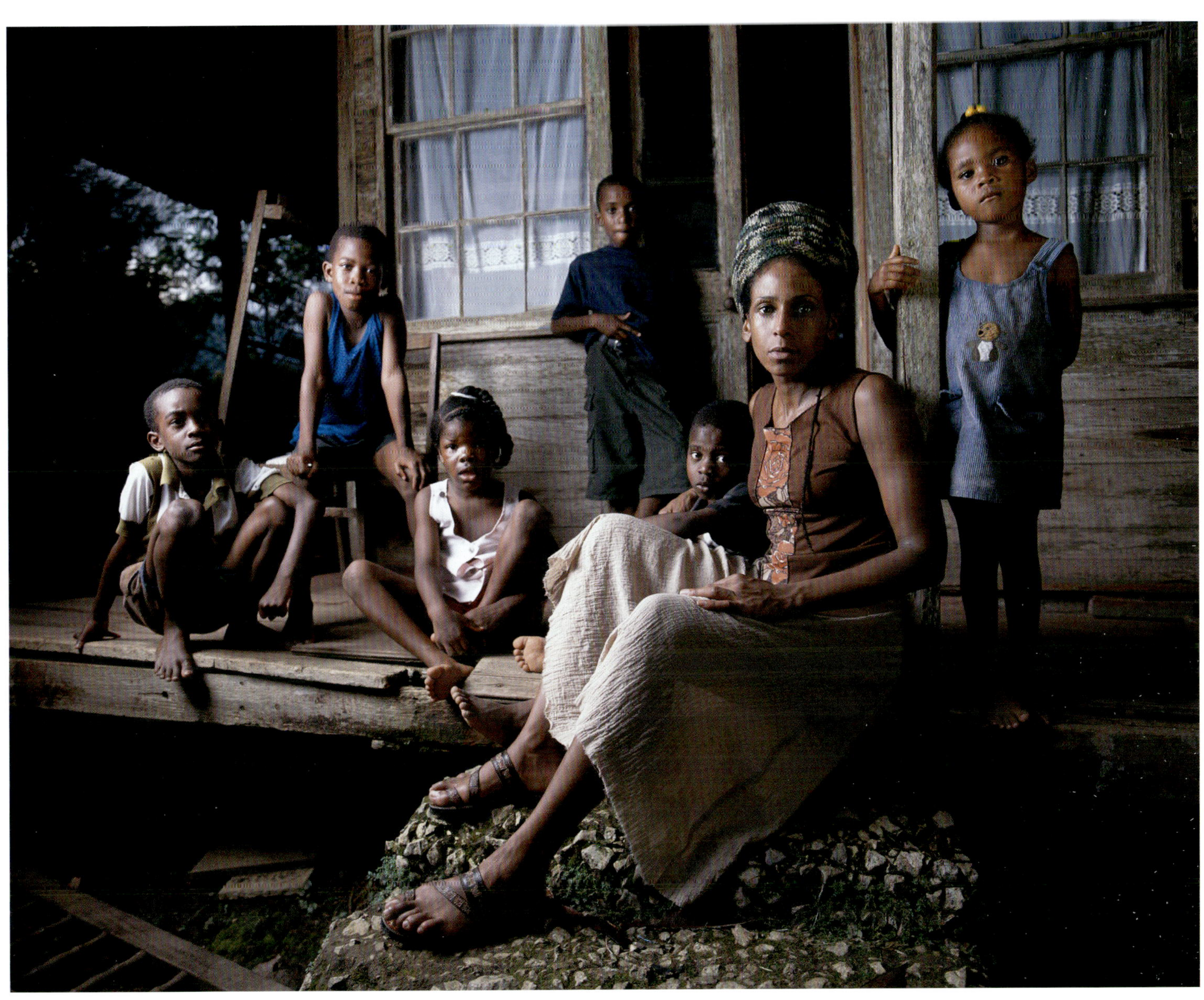

24

Binh Danh

American, born Vietnam, 1977

Vivian Nguyen, Environmental Studies, UNL, Class of 2014, 2011
Archival pigment print
Image and sheet: 101.6 × 76.2 cm (40 × 30 in)
University of Nebraska, gift of the artist, U-5663

Binh Danh was two years old when his family arrived in the United States from a Vietnamese refugee camp in Malaysia. Until 1999, when he visited Vietnam, his home country, again, its history and his connection to it existed only in his imagination. Photographs from his grandparents and visual documents of the Vietnam War provided a way for him to access his place of birth. These images and his experience of displacement inspired Danh to explore Vietnamese American history and identity through photography.

In graduate school, Danh invented a printing process using chlorophyll, which allowed him to print images on organic materials such as leaves and grasses, which he subsequently embedded in resin. "I am using these tools of science," he explained, "to help me articulate complex concepts—as science for me is truth and knowledge, and history is about preservation."[1]

Beginning in 1975, Lincoln and Omaha, Nebraska, became significant resettlement areas for families displaced by the Vietnam War. In 2011 the Sheldon Museum of Art invited Danh to create what became a portrait of Lincoln's Vietnamese community. The exhibition, entitled *Viet Nam, Nebraska*, invited public dialogue about what it means to be Vietnamese American. According to Danh, it promoted the idea of planting Vietnam into the soil of an adopted land. He photographed people of different generations and religions, new arrivals, and those who came in 1975.

Vivian Nguyen, Environmental Studies, UNL, Class of 2014 is from a series of photographs taken of University of Nebraska–Lincoln students. Describing this work, the artist stated, "I believe most of these students were born here in the United States or arrived as children and therefore do not have a connection to Viet Nam. As young adults in this country, they are trying to develop an identity."[2] Focusing on this negotiation, Danh explores how the Asian body fits into the landscape of a place. The portrait, which captures an environmental studies student in dance costume on a campus lawn, offers an image of complexity, a picture of shifting contexts and newfound mobility.

Assuming a confident stance, Nguyen looks directly at her viewer, challenging any perception of shyness or invisibility that might be associated with her gender and ethnicity. Through such portraits, Danh is interested in capturing changes in history. Many first-generation immigrants and refugees want to preserve their ethnic heritage and traditions. According to the artist, "They carry their cultural tools with them, using them to remake the landscape into something familiar."[3] With his camera, Binh Danh creates an open-ended narrative of the Vietnamese American community and writes a new chapter in its history. **SLK**

1. Binh Danh, interview by Boreth Ly, quoted in *Bihn Danh: In the Eclipse of Angkor*, exhibition catalog (Roanoke VA: Eleanor D. Wilson Museum at Hollins University, 2009), 11. **2.** Binh Danh, interview by Sharon Kennedy, in *Viet Nam, Nebraska: Photographs by Binh Danh*, gallery guide (Lincoln NE: Sheldon Museum of Art, August 2011). **3.** Kennedy, *Viet Nam, Nebraska*.

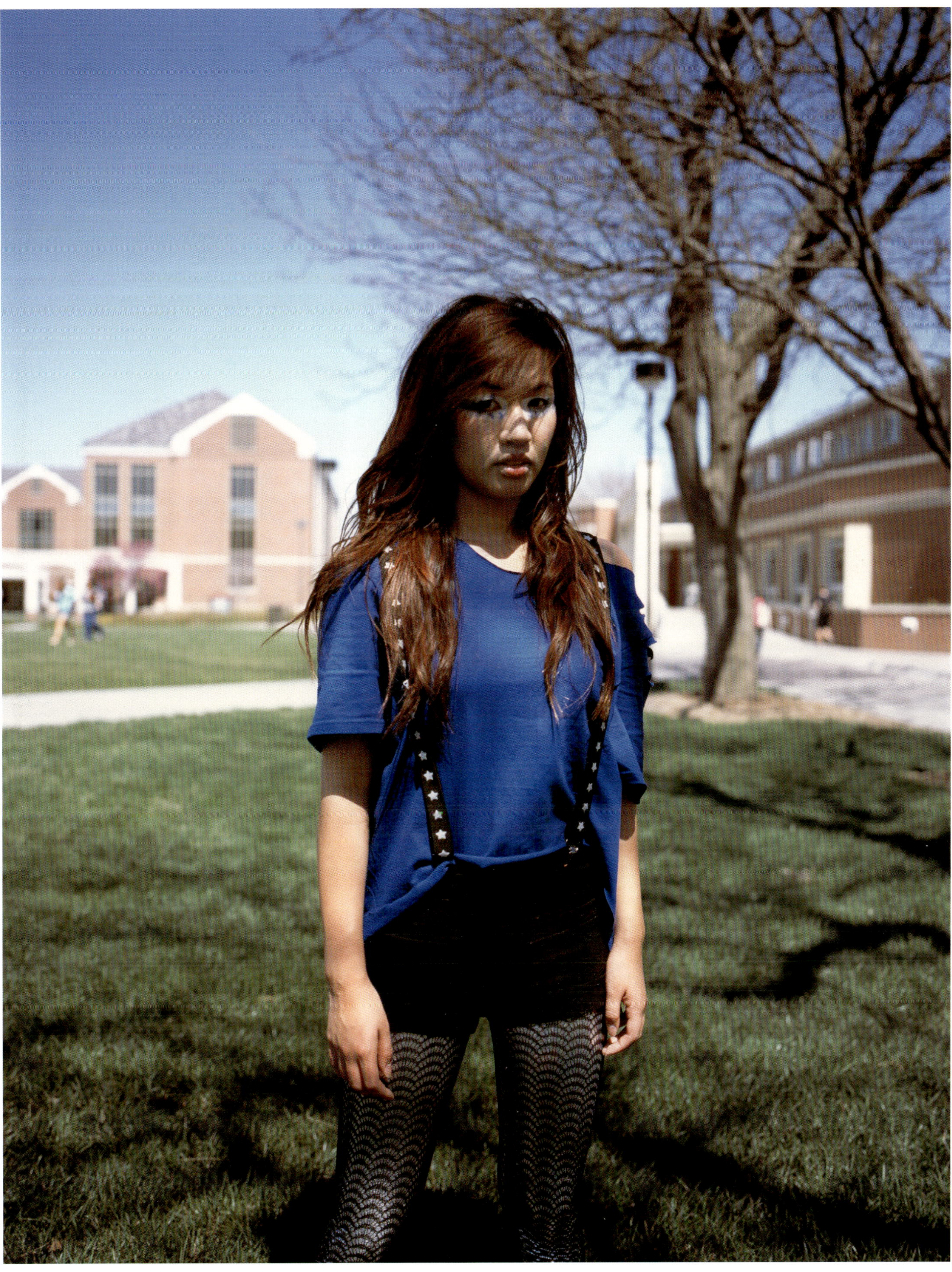

25

Yinka Shonibare
English, born 1962

The Sleep of Reason Produces Monsters (America), 2006
Chromogenic print mounted on aluminum
Image and sheet: 182.9 × 125.7 cm (72 × 49 ½ in)
University of Nebraska, Robert E. Schweser and
Fern Beardsley Schweser Acquisition Fund, through
the University of Nebraska Foundation, U-5639

Hairy ghoulishness is about to pounce on sartorial elegance in this nightmarish tableau by Yinka Shonibare. The difference between taste and monstrosity dissolves in the image, which suggests that one may produce the other. Titled *The Sleep of Reason Produces Monsters (America)*, it reprises Francisco Goya's famous etching of the same title. The style, color, and taste exhibited by the sleeping subject suggest a late eighteenth-century man, embodiment of the Enlightenment and the Age of Reason. To what extent, the work invites us to consider, does his taste—a result of judgment and reason—give rise to a parallel world of monsters that it would otherwise mask? Is the monstrous merely the nighttime of reason?

Yinka Shonibare, an installation artist, filmmaker, photographer, and painter, was born in the United Kingdom to Nigerian parents and raised in Lagos, Nigeria, until age seventeen, when he relocated to London to study art. Achieving many successes and international acclaim, he was made a Member of the Order of the British Empire (MBE) in 2005.

Shonibare seems to relish his title with both pride and irony, naming a recent exhibition and book *Yinka Shonibare, mbe*. The exhibition featured the series *The Sleep of Reason Produces Monsters* (2008), which comprises five photographic prints, each a variation implicating a different continent or continents (Africa, America, Asia, Australia, and Europe). The Sheldon acquired the American print for its transnational reverberations. The colorful fabrics, a trademark of Shonibare's artwork, were originally invented by colonial era Dutch textile printers, made popular thereafter in West Africa, and now purchased in London. This image neatly conjures the African–European–American triangle of trade routes that created and built the New World. In this sense, the work is about the dreams and reasons that motivated the Americas into being.

The English title of the series translates the Spanish wording that appears in the original Goya etching: *El sueño de la razón produce monstruos*.[1] Goya's print may be read as a critique of reason or a celebration of the romantic sublime, notions also applicable to Shonibare's series. The latter, however, alters Goya's work significantly. For example, Goya's statement is declarative: "The dream of reason produces monsters." An opinion is rendered. Shonibare's text, however, changes the statement's mode from declarative to interrogative in the French translation on the side of the desk. It now reads: "Do the dreams of reason produce monsters in America?" Instead of pronouncing on reason, Shonibare interrogates it—not abstractly, as would a philosopher, but in the historical, geopolitical terms relevant to continents' colonization. He puts into question the use of reason that went into that colonizing, asking us to consider its dark side. Can we imagine the monstrousness reason might produce? We can. We've learned about it from reading history, though history prefers to reproduce reason rather than question it.

Poststructuralist advances in feminist theory, psychoanalysis, and the postcolonial critique of the Enlightenment inform Shonibare's work as ways of questioning history. Photography assists as a staging rather than recording medium to underscore the work's questioning strategies. The thread running through these discourses is that of problematizing accepted wisdom. Shonibare's American print effectively transcribes Goya's uncanny prescience in the terms of our times. **JDV**

1. One of Goya's 1797 preparatory drawings for this 1799-issued print bears the inscription *El autor soñando* (The author/artist dreaming), which renders unambiguous Goya's use of the word *sueño* as "dream," not "sleep," as is often translated for the 1799 print. The drawings also show that the dreamer is himself a nightmare-haunted artist.

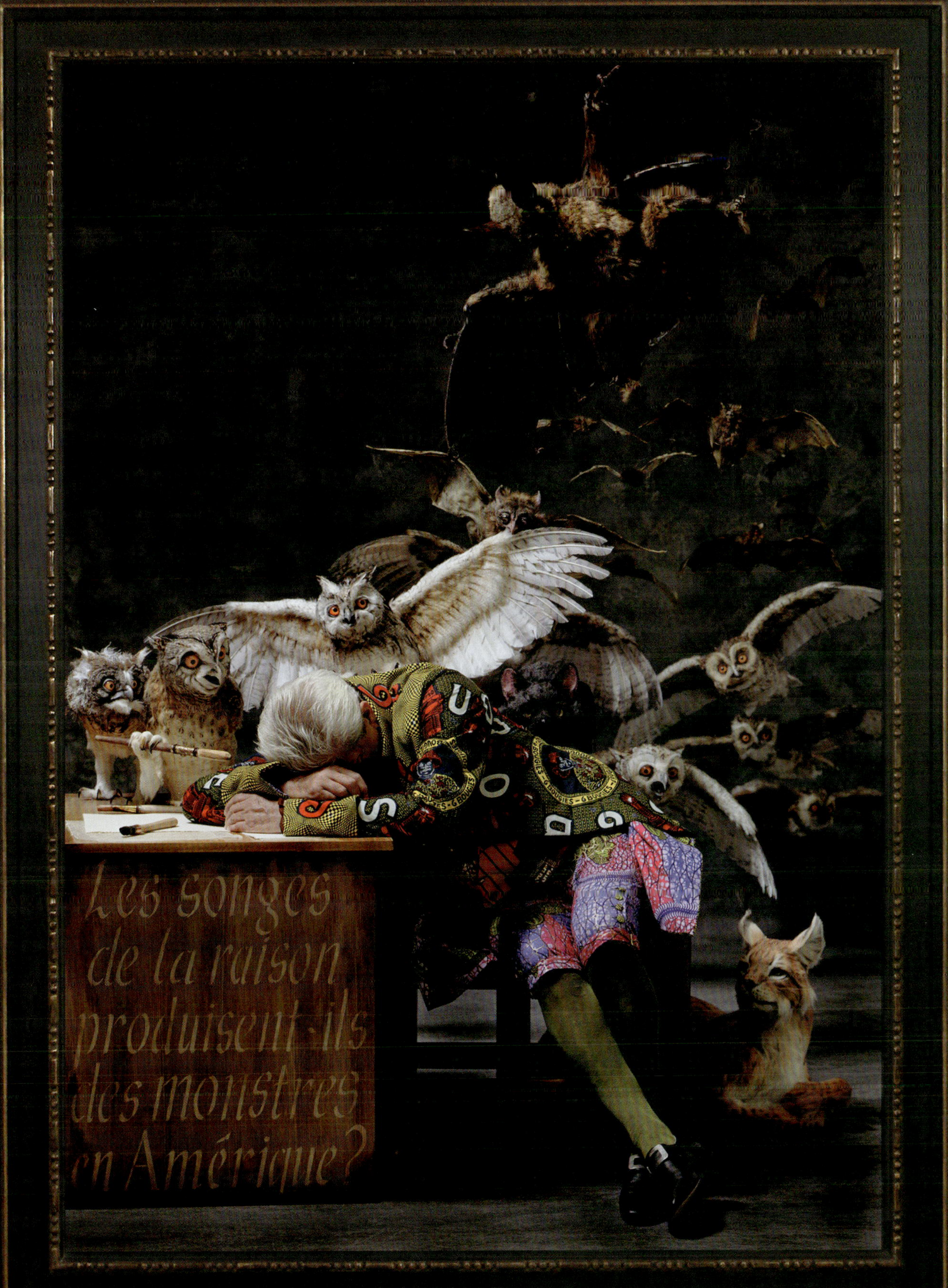

Les songes
de la raison
produisent-ils
des monstres
en Amérique?

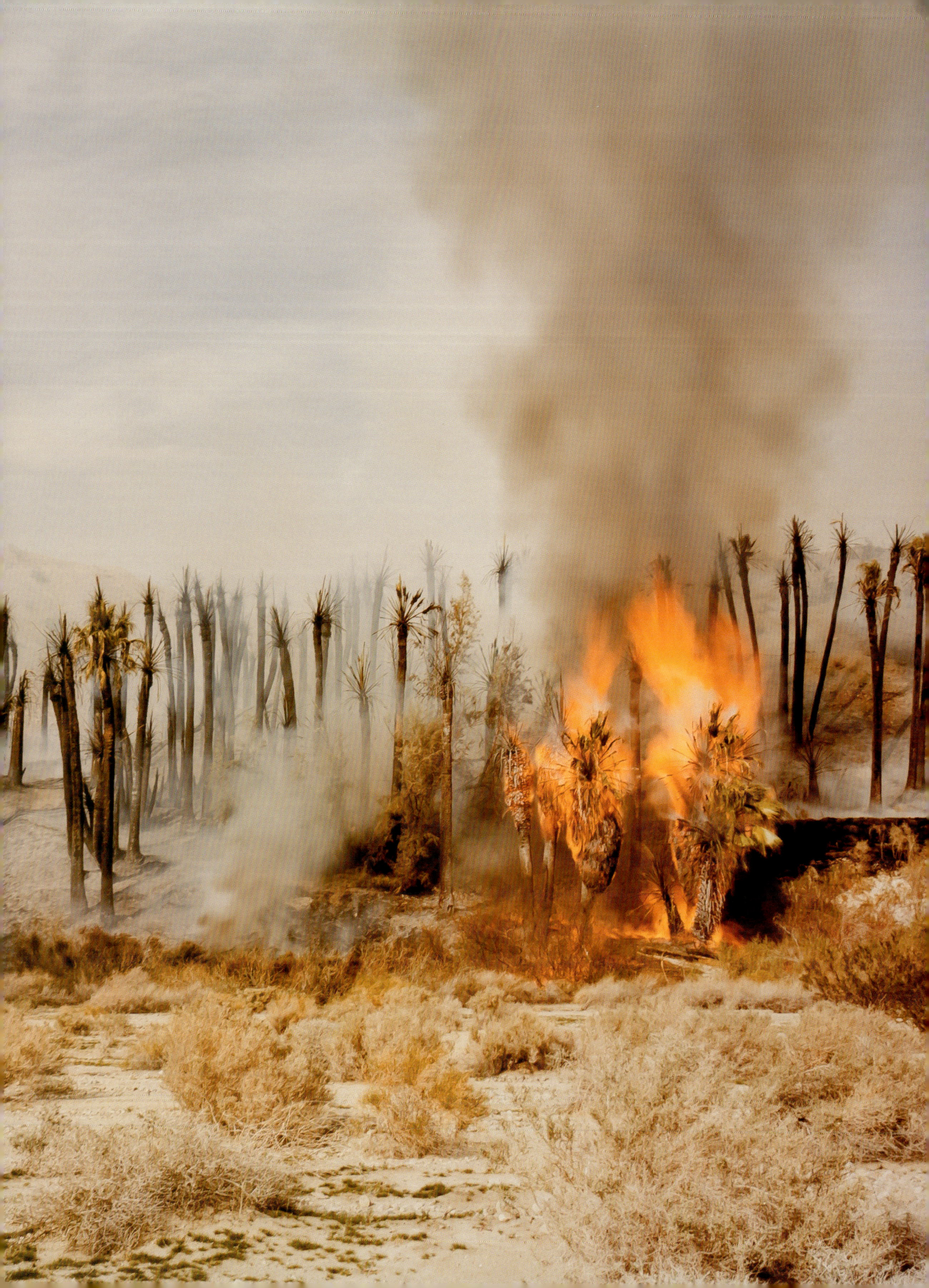

While concern about the environment might seem to be a particularly contemporary phenomenon, nineteenth-century photographers also expressed a keen interest in nature, documenting its pristine qualities and recording the changes wrought by time and human intervention. Many American practitioners worked on commission, joining government expeditions to document the unspoiled frontier. As the transcontinental railroad encouraged tourism to even the most remote locations, photographers also created stunning panoramas and stereoscopic views for souvenirs. While some of these artists chose to create formal studies of lines, patterns, and shapes in nature, others acted as advocates for the preservation of the wilderness.

Still other photographers chose to focus on the aspects of landscape that could be mastered and controlled, using their images to celebrate new technological marvels that demonstrated humanity's ability to alter and manage the environment in the service of commerce. Bridges, canals, dams, and power plants represent the most dramatic and obvious forms of these labors and were themselves the products of transnational cooperation for the people who engineered and constructed them (cats. 28, 36, 37, and 42). Other interventions into the landscape, though, appear more imaginative than physical. In his images of rural England, for example, Francis Bedford celebrated the viewer's ability to transform nature by encountering it through the lens of picturesque aesthetics (cat. 27). The artist's visits to the countryside, however—like those of the tourists who purchased his prints—were made possible by the new technology of rail travel.

Contemporary photographers have frequently turned their attention to the consequences of these incursions. Richard Misrach made this his life's work, starting in the late 1970s, recording the effects of human settlement on the desert Southwest (opposite and cat. 43), while Terry Evans, inspired by the diverse ecology of the midwestern prairie, has attempted to gauge such destructiveness across the globe (cat. 37). Most recently, artists such as Dana Fritz (cat. 44) have begun to question traditional distinctions between nature and culture, seeing the dichotomy of wilderness and civilization as a false one, given our millennia-long intervention in the natural environment.

The frontier and the metropolis have long been construed as binary opposites: preservation of the natural landscape is set against the needs of an urban economy, and rural simplicity is seen as the antithesis of cosmopolitan culture. Some photographers have transgressed these constructed antagonisms, however. Isaiah West Taber showed the merger of society and the natural world in his tourist view of the Yosemite Valley (cat. 31), for example, and Harry Callahan found a place for nature within the urban fabric, even in its most diminished or cultivated form (cat. 38). While some photographers focused exclusively on wild landscapes, others made urban ones their métier. Driven by the early twentieth-century city's rapid development and reputation as the site and source of modernity, photographers like Berenice Abbott (cat. 34) and Herbert Seligmann (cat. 33) showcased its architectural excitements, rapid rhythms, and dramatic alterations.

The built environments of cities are, of course, both products of and theaters for transnational encounters. The nineteenth-century views of Cairo by Félix Bonfils (cat. 10) and an Istanbul shopping district by the firm of Sébah and Joaillier (cat. 4) dramatize not only the international language of architecture but also the fluid mix of ethnicities and identities in cosmopolitan cities. In the latter scene, Europeans, Turks, and Arabs of various religions mix with children, shop owners, and street vendors in a neighborhood that was itself home to a great range of nationalities over time—Armenians, Greeks, and Jews gave way to British, French, and Italians in a movement that underscores the international fabric from which great cities are made.

26

Francis Frith and Company

English, 1822–1898; firm active 1860–1971

Village 1906, Alfington, 1906
Collotype
Image and sheet: 14.3 × 20.6 cm (5 ⅝ × 8 ⅛ in)
Printed, in image, lower center: 56678; inscribed, on
verso, in black ink: © F. Frith & Co. Ltd Reigate 56678
University of Nebraska, Anna R. and Frank M. Hall
Charitable Trust, H-2145

Originally a businessman and entrepreneur, Francis Frith
accumulated a small fortune in dry goods and printing at a
young age, which allowed him to satisfy his great passion:
travel. Although he was perhaps an accomplished amateur
photographer prior to his first journey abroad, it was the
pictures that he took while visiting Africa and the Middle
East during the late 1850s that solidified his reputation. During these excursions, Frith documented the landscape, the
people, and especially the ruins of Beirut, Egypt, Jerusalem,
Palestine, and Syria in photographs that he first exhibited in
1857 and later published in albums.[1] His attitude toward the
medium as an art form, however, was complicated. Writing
for the *Art Journal* in 1859, he recognized the camera's "mechanical character, and the rapidity with which its results are
produced," adding that its "truthfulness is the greatest charm
of its results."[2] Directness was, in fact, Frith's main aesthetic

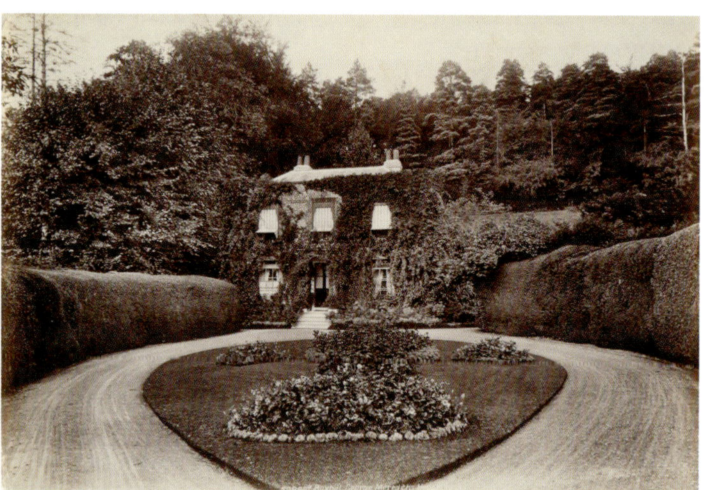

Francis Frith and Company. *George Meredith's House at
Boxhill, Surrey,* undated. Albumen print; 14.3 × 20.6 cm (5 ⅝
× 8 ⅛ in). University of Nebraska, Anna R. and Frank M. Hall
Charitable Trust, H-2146.

objective, and he condemned those of his colleagues "who
would willfully blur or distort a subject in the name of art."[3]
At the same time, he stressed discernment in selecting the
subject and final composition: "The student should bear in
mind that what he is to aim at is not the production of a large
number of 'good' pictures, but, if possible, of ONE which shall
satisfy the requirements of his judgment and taste."[4]

After his final trip to Africa and the Middle East in 1859,
Frith married, settled in Surrey, and embarked on an ambitious project: an encyclopedic photographic essay of every
town and village in Great Britain. To accomplish this goal, he
hired several staff photographers and assistants, who worked
under his supervision and according to his specifications;
his two sons eventually joined the business and continued
the project well into the twentieth century. By the time of
Frith's death, his firm had amassed twenty-six thousand images, and today the archives hold some three hundred thousand photographs of approximately four thousand locations
throughout the British Isles.[5] Frith's goal was not to publish
or sell photographic prints but rather to enter the lucrative
postcard trade, satisfying the Victorian demand for picturesque country scenes, rugged mountain vistas, and views of
faraway places. His postcards were printed by the thousands
in Germany and retailed at newsagents, stationers, and to-
bacconists; by 1890 Francis Frith and Company had grown
into the world's largest photographic publisher, with over two
thousand outlets in Europe.[6]

This image, taken by one of the firm's staff photographers
in 1906, depicts Alfington, a small village in Devon. Scenes
like this one, with its thatch-roofed houses, tranquil stream,
and horse-drawn carriage, presented viewers with a comfortable, nostalgic view of a bygone era—an antidote, perhaps,
to their own experience of rapid industrialization and ur-
banization. Francis Frith and Company's photographs also
provide an indispensable record of changing demographics
and social patterns at the turn of the century, when agriculture and rural populations were in continuous decline. **BKR**

1. For a concise history of Frith's travels through the Middle East as well as
several examples of his photographs from the time, see Engin Çizgen, *Photography in the Ottoman Empire: 1839–1919* (Istanbul: Haset Kitabevi, 1987),
100–102. **2.** Francis Frith, "The Art of Photography," *Art Journal* 5 (1859), in
The Art of Photography: 1839–1989, ed. Mike Weaver, exhibition catalog (New
Haven CT: Yale University Press, 1989), 135. **3.** Quoted in Philip Ziegler, *Britain Then and Now: The Francis Frith Collection* (London: Weidenfeld and
Nicholson, 1999), 10. **4.** Frith, "The Art of Photography," 136. **5.** Undated
letter from the Francis Frith Collection, curatorial files, Sheldon Museum
of Art. Maureen Anderson, writing for the Francis Frith Collection, placed
the number at seven thousand; see Maureen Anderson, *Francis Frith's England in the 1880s* (Salisbury: Frith Book Company, 2001), 9. **6.** For the most
detailed account of Frith's life and the firm of Francis Frith and Company,
see Bill Jay, *Victorian Cameraman: Francis Frith's Views of Rural England,
1850–1898* (Newton Abbot UK: David and Charles, 1973).

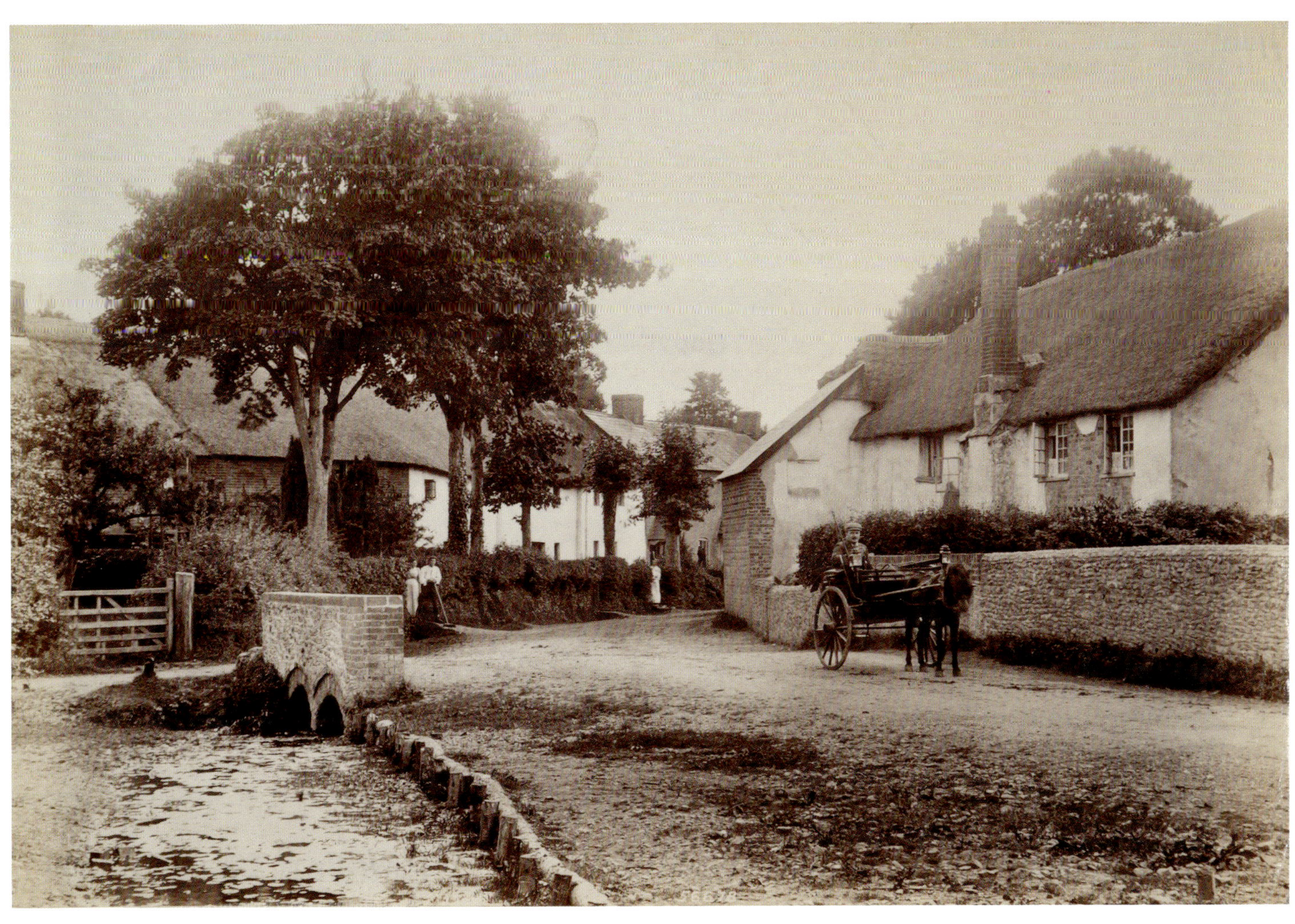

27

Francis Bedford
English, 1816–1894

Ludlow Castle from the River, c. 1860s
Albumen print
Image and sheet: 19.7 × 28.6 cm (7 ¾ × 11 ¼ in)
Printed, lower left: *Bedford. 1782.*; lower right: *Ludlow Castle, from the River.*
University of Nebraska, Anna R. and Frank M. Hall Charitable Trust, H-2810

Like that of William Henry Fox Talbot, Calvert Jones, and many pioneering photographers of the previous generation, Francis Bedford's work was eased by financial independence and informed by previous training—in his case, as a lithographer and painter of architectural subjects. The son of a successful London architect and artist, he achieved a measure of early notoriety himself, showing his work at the Royal Academy and publishing over 150 lithographs in the sumptuous catalog of the industrial arts featured at the Great Exhibition of 1851.[1]

In the 1850s and 1860s, Bedford embraced the new medium with zeal, exhibiting landscapes at the recently created Photographic Society; recording important objects from the royal collection; and traveling to Germany at Queen Victoria's request to take views of Coburg, the hometown of her husband, Prince Albert. In fact, it is for his travels within Britain—and far beyond it—that Bedford is best known. In 1862 he accompanied the young Albert Edward, Prince of Wales, on an educational expedition to Egypt, Greece, Lebanon, Palestine, and Turkey that is regarded as the first royal tour with a professional photographer. Extensively covered in the press, the trip was perhaps meant to offer the rakish prince a *"close and not unpleasing proximity to the religious lessons" the Holy Land had to teach.*[2] It gave Bedford access to sites and vantage points that were normally off-limits, allowing him to use his knowledge of buildings and formal composition to create cityscapes, landscapes, and architectural studies that earned tremendous praise upon his return to London.[3]

If Victorian viewers were fascinated by such exotic images, they were equally smitten with pictures of their own cultural and natural treasures. Bedford happily accommodated them in this line as well: both before and after his voyage to the East, he traveled the British countryside producing views like *Ludlow Castle from the River* that he exhibited, sold to the public, and supplied as book illustrations. In the process, he established himself as possibly the nation's most practiced and celebrated outdoor photographer. The artist focused in particular on regions—in this case, Shropshire—that were popular with middle-class tourists, whose numbers were growing prodigiously in the 1860s. Coming by rail from cities and suburbs, these new audiences approached recreation as something that ought to be intellectually, morally, and physically improving. Like aristocratic travelers a century earlier, they encountered the natural world with guidebooks in hand, ready to absorb information on the best spot to view the landscape and even what to feel as they did so.[4]

As a tourist destination and photographic subject, Ludlow Castle would have been triply appealing. First, it was a source of national pride, rich in bloody history and literary associations: begun by the Normans in the eleventh century, the structure served as a center of power in the borderlands between England and Wales for more than six hundred years. Second, it was an overgrown ruin, with all the romantic appeal that implied; it was praised as "the very perfection of decay," and visitors would have been tempted to luxuriate in its tattered beauty, meditating on the transitory nature of earthly things.[5] Third, it had long been celebrated as an object of picturesque beauty. Here, Bedford combined architecture and landscape in a flawless image that would have allowed its owners to relive their aesthetic and emotional response to Ludlow Castle in their own parlors. Framing the castle with lush vegetation on either side, the sky above, and its own reflection in the glassy river Teme below, Bedford gave tourists not just a keepsake but a moment in which past and present, nature and culture are held in a state of silent balance. **GN**

1. This was Matthew Digby Wyatt, *The Industrial Arts of the Nineteenth Century* (London: Day and Son, 1851). For more on Bedford's biography and career, see Stephanie Spencer, *Francis Bedford, Landscape Photography and Nineteenth-Century British Culture: The Artist as Entrepreneur* (Farnham UK: Ashgate, 2011); and Spencer, "Francis Bedford, 1816–1894," in *Commercial Aesthetics: Nineteenth Century British Photographs by Francis Bedford, Francis Frith, James Valentine, and George Washington Wilson*, exhibition catalog (Saint Louis MO: Saint Louis Valley Community College, 1992), 25–26. 2. "Return of the Prince of Wales from the Holy Land," *Illustrated London News*, June 21, 1862, 624, quoted in Linda Wheatley-Irving, "Holy Land Photographs and Their Worlds: Francis Bedford and the 'Tour in the East,'" *Jerusalem Quarterly* 31 (Summer 2007): 79–96. 3. These photographs were published lavishly in Francis Bedford and W. M. Thompson, *Photographic Pictures Made by Mr. Francis Bedford during the Tour in the East* (London: Day and Sons, 1863) and in a smaller format three years later. 4. See Stephanie Spencer, "Tourism and Photography," in *Commercial Aesthetics*, 9–15. 5. Daniel Defoe, *A Tour through the Whole Island of Great Britain*, ed. Philip Nicholas Furbank, W. R. Owens, and Anthony J. Coulson (New Haven CT: Yale University Press, 1991), 188.

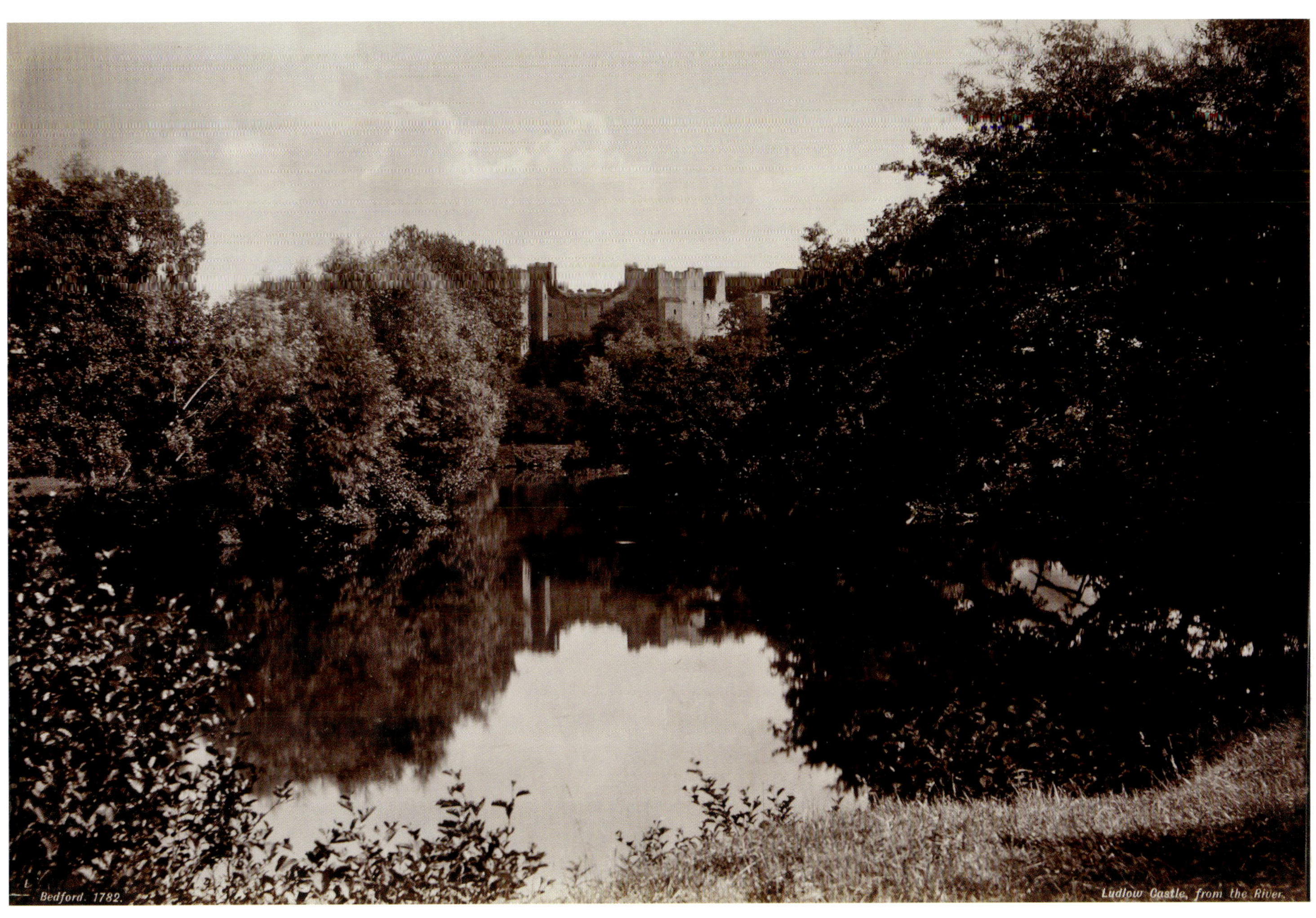
Bedford. 1782.
Ludlow Castle, from the River.

28

Artist Unknown

French

View of the Corinth Canal, after 1893
Salted paper print
Image and sheet: 21.9 × 28.9 cm (8 5/8 × 11 3/8 in)
Printed, in image, lower left: *18 Vue du Canal de Corinthe*
University of Nebraska, gift of Jon Nelson, U-4049

This image of the Corinth Canal is part of a long-standing photographic tradition of recording wonders of engineering such as bridges and dams (see below) and, in the process, human dominance over the earth. A man-made waterway that connects the Corinthian and Saronic Gulfs with the Aegean Sea, the canal cuts through the narrow Isthmus of Corinth and separates the Peloponnesian Peninsula from the Greek mainland. While the dream of uniting the two gulfs had its genesis in classical antiquity—attempts were even made to create such a waterway during the Roman Empire—construction did not begin on the present canal until 1881, inspired largely by the successful opening and operation of the Suez Canal in 1869. Commissioned by the Greek government and initially developed and engineered by a French firm, the project was hampered almost immediately by financial and geological problems that eventually bankrupted the original builders. When it was finally completed and opened in 1893, the canal's narrowness and frequent landslides from the sedimentary rocks on its steep walls caused navigational problems, and it failed to attract the level of traffic anticipated by its operators. It quickly became almost obsolete and of little economic consequence, but then, as now, it was appealing as an attraction in its own right.

The canal's reputation as a tourist spot is evidenced not only by this trade photograph, which was marketed to sightseers and vacationers who visited the site, but by the attention that travel writers devoted to the waterway even before its official opening. An American traveler writing for the *Nation* in 1891, for example, informed the magazine's readers of the canal's majesty as well as its difficult, laborious construction: "Here we were at the entrance of one of the most stupendous works of the nineteenth century, or of any century. Twelve hundred men are now employed upon it. These are Armenians, Italians, and Montenegrins. The canal will be finished within three years, and it will admit the largest merchant ships now in use in the Mediterranean and will enable any two of them to pass at any point."[1]

This image, created by a French firm, contradicts the author's starry-eyed assessment of the channel yet supports its reputation as a tourist magnet. The photographer's position close to the water demonstrates the narrowness of the canal, which possesses only enough room to allow a small vessel to pass through, navigated by a small group of men at the right. At the same time, a set of stairs and a viewing deck on the left permit tourists to negotiate the canal's steep walls to experience its glory and wave to passing ships. Despite its unfulfilled potential, the Corinth Canal stands as a symbol of the nineteenth century's ambitions for its transportation infrastructure as well as of humanity's aspiration to alter and change the natural landscape in the service of international commerce and trade. **BKR**

1. Horace White, "The Corinth Canal," *Nation,* July 2, 1891, 8–9.

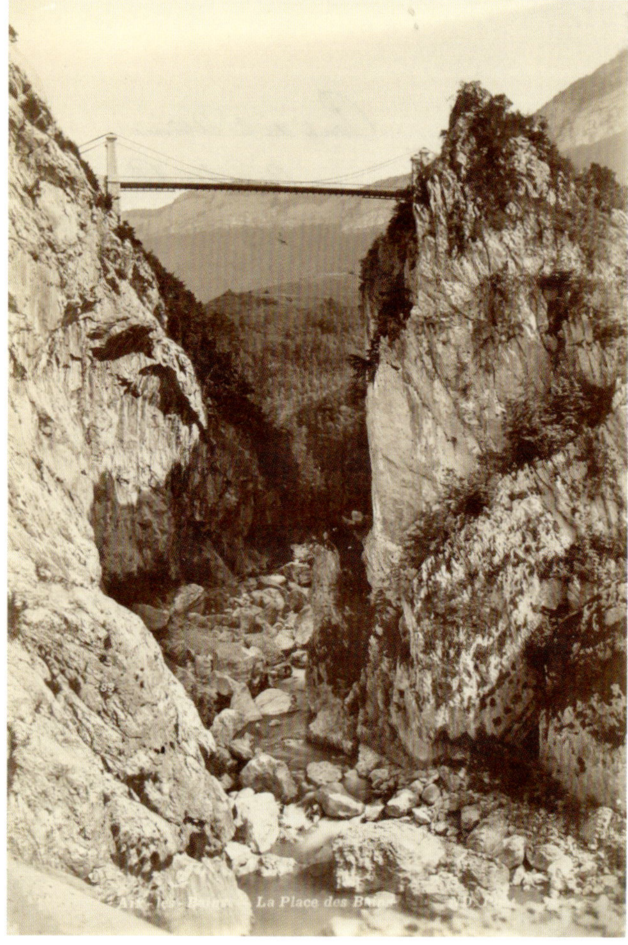

Artist Unknown. *Aix-les-Bains–La Place des Bains,* nineteenth century. Albumen print; 18.4 × 10.6 cm (7 1/4 × 4 3/16 in). University of Nebraska, gift of Jon Nelson, U-3960.

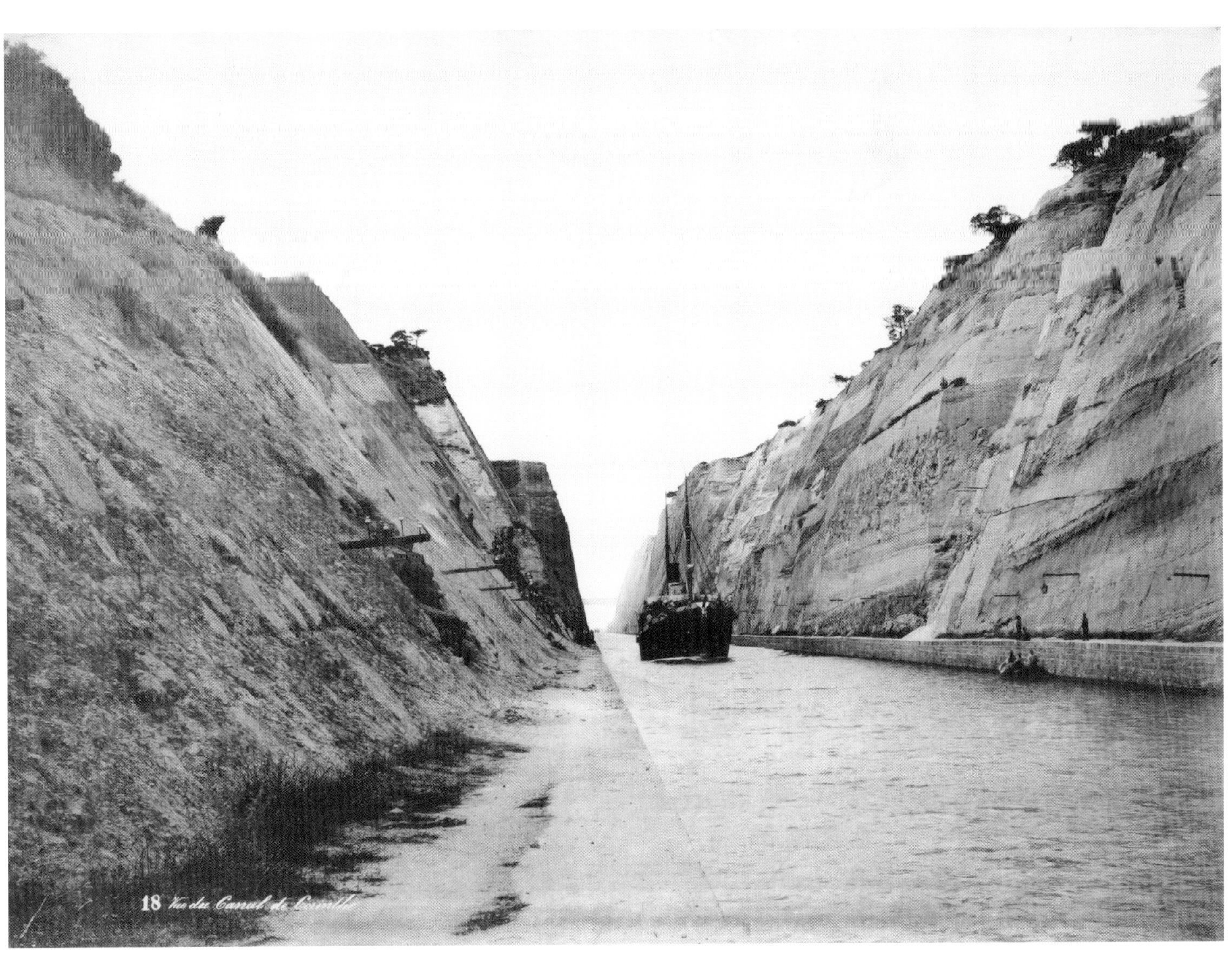
18 Vue du Canal de Corinthe

29

William Henry Jackson

American, 1843–1942

Pike's Peak from the Garden of the Gods, c. 1873
Albumen print
Image: 14.9 × 24.9 cm (5 7/8 × 9 13/16 in); mount: 35.6 ×
43.2 cm (14 × 17 in)
Inscribed, in image, in white: *3082. PIKE'S PEAK FROM
THE GARDEN OF THE GODS. WHJ & Co*; on mount,
lower center, in black ink: *Gate-way at the Garden
of the Gods, Nr Manitou*
University of Nebraska, Anna R. and Frank M. Hall
Charitable Trust, H-2036

William Henry Jackson initially headed west in 1866 after participating in the Civil War, abandoning his dreams of becoming a painter. Traveling with his brother Edward, he settled briefly in Omaha, where they took up photography and specialized in images of the region's Native Americans. In 1869 the Union Pacific Railroad commissioned Jackson to document the scenery along various western routes to promote tourism and settlement. Based on the success of these photographs, Jackson accompanied a government survey the following year through the Rocky Mountains to the Yellowstone River. A year later, he joined geologist Ferdinand V. Hayden on an expedition into the Yellowstone territory of northwestern Wyoming; this was the first federally funded venture to explore and record the region's geological features. Hayden's survey consisted of some fifty participants, including not only Jackson as the official photographer but also painter Thomas Moran. The following year, Hayden's report from an earlier expedition—along with Jackson's impressive photographs and Moran's dramatic paintings—helped persuade Congress to establish Yellowstone as the first national park in the United States and also encouraged westward expansion to the American frontier.

For his part, Jackson published a descriptive catalog of his photographs from this period beginning in 1874, detailing his process and providing explanatory notes on locations. His remarks on images of Pike's Peak and the Garden of the Gods reveal that the region was already a popular tourist destination and a source of curiosity two decades previously: "It has many picturesque features, and is sure to engage the attention of the traveler. Along its north face, and extending behind it, are Cheyenne and Bear Canons, extremely wild and rugged, and picturesque gorges. About three miles away, is the old town of Colorado City, built in 1859, during the first days of the 'Pike's Peak' excitement. Although brushing up and improving under the influence of the influx of summer tourists, yet it is being overshadowed by more pretentious rivals."[1]

Although he benefited from its construction through awards and commissions, Jackson lamented the arrival of the railroad and, with it, pioneers, travelers, and tourists. He later fondly recalled his experience shooting the region before the advent of full civilization: "I went off with Jim Stevenson in one of our ambulances to photograph the Pikes Peak region. That side trip was my introduction to the country below Denver, and, apart from valuable additions to my growing collection of negatives, it was important to me in that it was just about the last chance anyone had to see the 'old' Colorado, for the Denver Pacific was just coming in."[2]

Jackson made several views of the geological formations at the Garden of the Gods and the distant Pike's Peak in the background, including some that feature tourists in the foreground or the occasional horse and buggy in the middle distance.[3] In this photograph, he eschewed any of those elements, instead creating a picturesque, unspoiled view, concentrating on the irregular rock configurations and the majestic mountain in the distance. Nonetheless, the series of grooved tracks that wind their way through the area suggest a path well trodden by both explorers and sightseers. In fact, as Thomas G. Andrews has acknowledged, an absence of established train routes and a fear of attacks by Native Americans restricted white travelers to the most heavily developed areas, and roads and paths were already a routine feature of the western landscape.[4] **BKR**

1. Department of the Interior, *The Photographs of the U.S. Geological Survey of the Territories, for the Years 1869 to 1875, Inclusive*, 2nd ed. (Washington DC: Government Printing Office, 1875), 55–56. 2. William Henry Jackson, *Time Exposure: The Autobiography of William Henry Jackson* (1940; repr., New York: Cooper Square Publishers, 1970), 192. 3. For a selection of these images in the collections of the Denver Public and Princeton University Libraries, see http://digital.denverlibrary.org/cdm4/item_viewer.php?CISOROOT=/p15330coll21&CISOPTR=6885&DMSCALE=25&DMWIDTH=600&DMHEIGHT=600&DMX=0&DMY=208&DMMODE=viewer&DMTEXT=&REC=10&DMTHUMB=1&DMROTATE=0 and http://pudl.princeton.edu/sheetreader.php?obj=jw827b96f#page/1/mode/2up. 4. Thomas G. Andrews, "'Made by Toile'? Tourism, Labor, and the Construction of the Colorado Landscape, 1858–1917," *Journal of American History* 92, no. 3 (December 2005): 843.

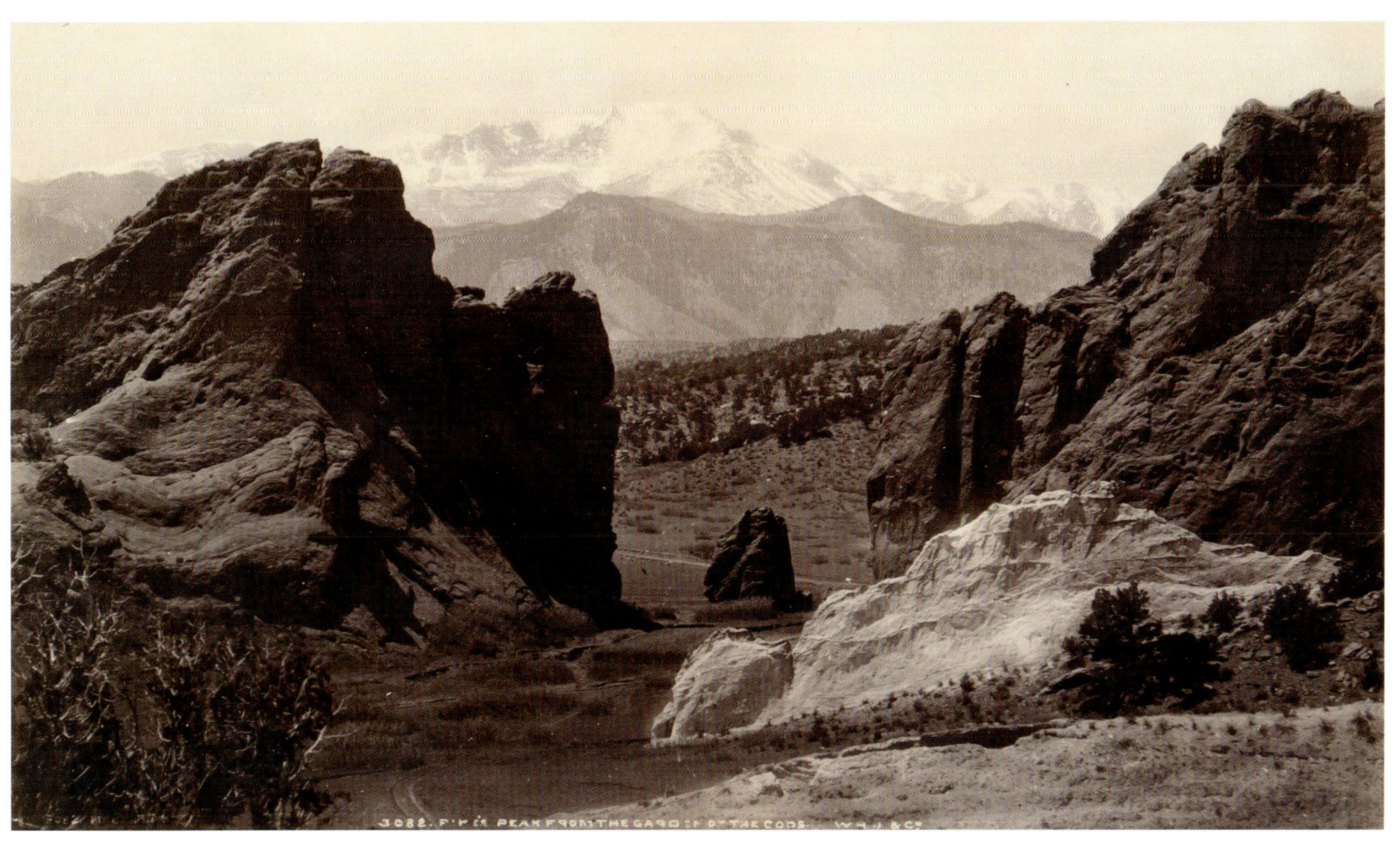
3088. PIKE'S PEAK FROM THE GARDEN OF THE GODS.   W.H.J. & Co.

30

Edward Sheriff Curtis

American, 1868–1952

Part of Columbia Glacier, Prince William Sound, 1899;
published 1901
Photogravure
Image: 11.3 × 17.3 cm (4 7/16 × 6 13/16 in); sheet: 15.9 × 24.6 cm
(6 1/4 × 9 11/16 in)
Printed, lower left: *PHOTOGRAPH BY CURTIS*; lower
center: *PART OF COLUMBIA GLACIER, PRINCE WILLIAM
SOUND*; lower right: *GILBO & CO*
University of Nebraska, gift of Albert Mikuta, U-1900

In 1899 Edward Sheriff Curtis accompanied an expedition
to Alaska funded by New York railroad magnate Edward R.
Harriman under the auspices of the Washington Academy of
Sciences. The goal of the enterprise was to catalog the fauna,
flora, landscape, and people of the Alaska coastline from its
southern panhandle to Prince William Sound. The expedition included several distinguished artists, ethnographers,
naturalists, and scientists, including George Bird Grinnell,
Clinton Hart Merriam, John Muir, and Robert Swain Gif-
ford. Their multivolume report contained forty-six of Curtis's
photographs from the voyage—as well as several illustrations
after his images—reproduced by the firm of Gilbo and Company in photogravure, including this photograph of Columbia Glacier originally taken on June 26, 1899.

Merriam's introduction to the first volume of the report,
which appeared in 1901, demonstrated special concern about
the region's glaciers—not only their discovery and size but,

perhaps surprisingly, their growth, reduction, and future dimensions: "A number of glaciers not previously known, as
well as many others which had been vaguely or imperfectly
known, were mapped, photographed, and described, and
much evidence was gathered of changes that have occurred
in their length and size. In many instances it was possible
to compare their condition and extent in 1899 with earlier
records, so as to discover and measure the changes; and in
all cases their relation to neighboring features were photographed or otherwise recorded, so that future changes may
be readily determined."[1]

In his narrative of the expedition, John Burroughs described Columbia Glacier—named by the Harriman Expedition participants after Columbia University—in more romantic language:

Prince William Sound is shaped like a great spider: an open irregular body of water eighty miles or more across, fringed by
numerous arms and inlets that reach far in amid the mountains.
In the afternoon we reached its head and saw another palisade of
shattered ice, about two hundred feet high and four miles long,
barring our way. We named this the Columbia Glacier. Its front
was quite as imposing as that of the Muir, but it was less active;
apparently no large blue bergs are born out of its depth, for the
reason, doubtless, that its depth is not great.[2]

Born in Wisconsin, Curtis apprenticed to a photographer
in Minnesota before he and his family relocated to Seattle.
There he specialized in portraits of Native Americans and
photographs of Washington's topography; it was his photography of Mount Rainier, in fact, that brought him to the
attention of Grinnell and led to his invitation to join the
Harriman Expedition. Curtis's Alaskan work, as well as that
for subsequent expeditions, led to a commission from finan-
cier J. P. Morgan to produce an encyclopedic series on Native Americans. Curtis's stated goal was to document indigenous life before traditional ways disappeared. Nonetheless,
in the over forty thousand photographs he took, Curtis employed techniques that were more pictorialist than scientific,
utilizing dramatic lighting, theatrical angles, and staged re-
creations, editing out or removing elements that did not fit
his vision of Native American life. **BKR**

1. Clinton Hart Merriam, introduction to *Narrative, Glaciers, Natives*, vol. 1
of *Alaska*, by John Burroughs, John Muir, and George Bird Grinnell (New
York: Doubleday, Page and Company, 1901), xxvii. **2.** John Burroughs, "Alaska:
Narrative of the Expedition," in Burroughs, Muir, and Grinnell, *Narrative,
Glaciers, Natives*, 67.

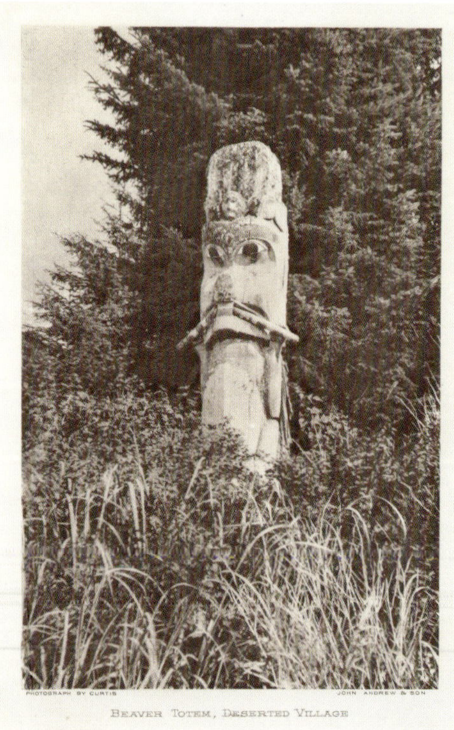

Edward Sheriff Curtis. *Beaver Totem, Deserted Village*, 1899.
Photogravure; 42.7 × 11 cm (16 13/16 × 4 5/16 in). University of Nebraska, gift of Albert Mikuta, U-1901.

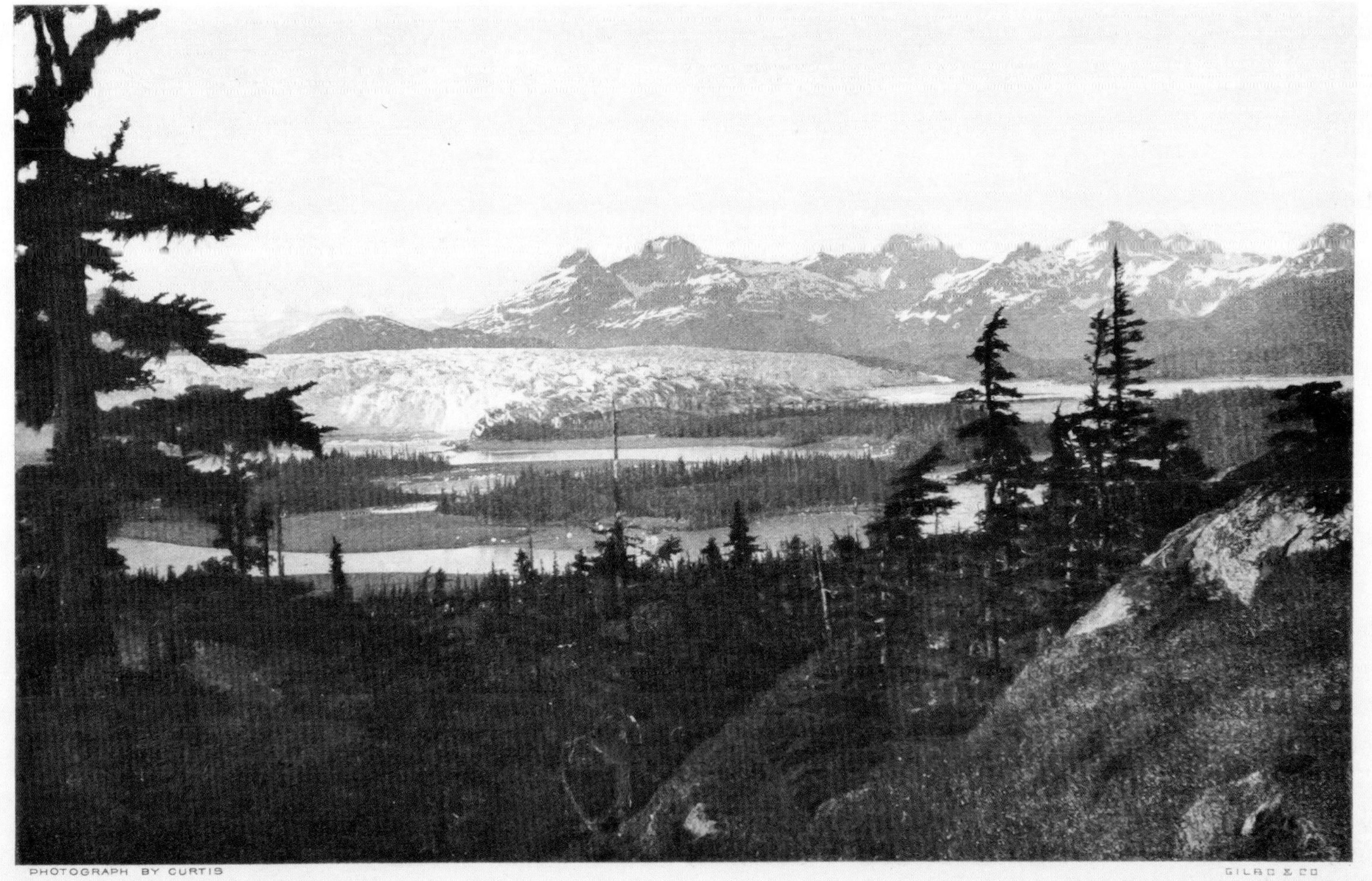

Part of Columbia Glacier, Prince William Sound

31

Isaiah West Taber

American, 1830–1912

Sentinel Rock and Sentinel Falls, 1871–1906
Albumen print
Image: 19.1 × 12.2 cm (7 1/2 × 4 13/16 in); sheet: 19.4 × 12.2 cm
(7 5/8 × 4 13/16 in)
Printed, lower center: *B 969 Sentin Rock and
"Sentinel Falls.["] Taber Photo., San Franc*
University of Nebraska, Anna R. and Frank M. Hall
Charitable Trust, H-2571

Isaiah West Taber initially traveled westward in 1850 to find his fortune during the California gold rush, and it was this entrepreneurial spirit that eventually led him to photography. After his failure to strike gold, Taber returned east, where he launched a dental practice and experimented with photographic techniques, establishing himself two years later as an ambrotypist.[1] The photographic firm of Bradley and Rulofson lured Taber back to California in 1864, and he opened his own studio in San Francisco in 1871. He visited the Yosemite Valley shortly after his arrival, but he specialized in photographic portraiture, and his income and reputation rested with the substantial inventory of images of the West by other photographers that he sold to a burgeoning tourist market.[2] Taber's real success came in the mid-1870s with the bankruptcy of Carleton Watkins, perhaps California's premier photographer at the time: he purchased the contents of Watkins's gallery, and for several decades marketed, published, reprinted, and sold Watkins's images of the Yosemite Valley until the San Francisco earthquake and fire of 1906 destroyed his own inventory.[3]

By the time that Taber printed and published this small card, the Yosemite region had already become a popular tourist destination, largely based on its impressive granite formations such as Sentinel Rock and its surrounding falls as well as the quixotically named Three Brothers (see above). Travel to the region soared beginning in the 1850s largely through the efforts of James Mason Hutchings, creator of *Hutchings' California Magazine*. In his writings, Hutchings described the region in hyperbolic terms; using a rhetoric at once spiritual and capitalistic, he praised California as both a place for "religious veneration" and an American Eden replete with "mineral and agricultural products" and "wonderful resources and commercial advantages."[4]

By the 1860s, developers had constructed a number of inns and lodges in Yosemite, among them Leidig's Hotel, which is silhouetted against the prominent Sentinel Rock in this image. The hotel was built and operated by the Leidig

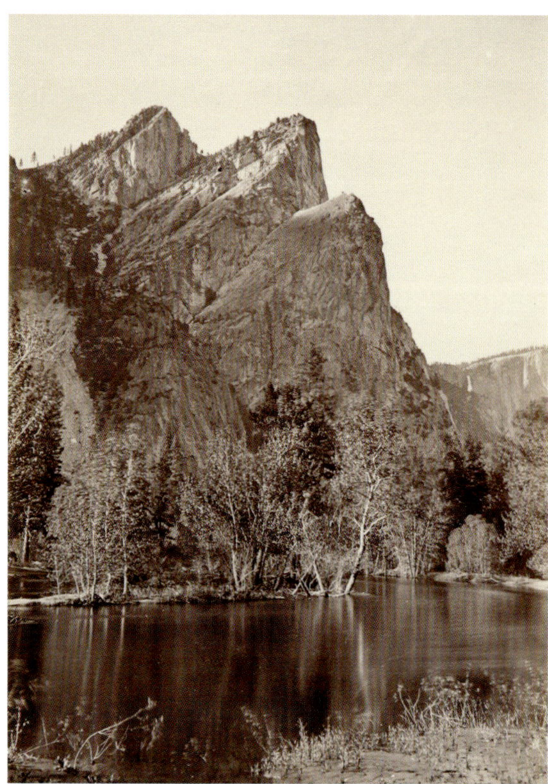

Isaiah West Taber. *Three Brothers, Yosemite Valley*, undated. Albumen print; 19.4 × 12.2 cm (7 5/8 × 4 13/16 in). University of Nebraska, Anna R. and Frank M. Hall Charitable Trust, H-2572.

family from 1869 to 1888 and earned a respectable reputation based on its access to and stunning views of Yosemite's natural wonders. An 1876 visitor, for instance, described its attractions as follows: "This house stands in the shadow of Sentinel Rock, and faces the great Yosemite Fall; is surrounded with porches, making a pleasant place to sit and contemplate the magnificence of the commanding scenery."[5] Taber's photograph also suggests the importance of tourism in the region's development, as it focuses as much on Leidig's Hotel as on the formation in the background. It would have reminded viewers that the inn provided creature comforts and a simulacrum of home even as it allowed tourists to experience the glories of America's natural wilds.[6] The family's arrival in the Yosemite area also heralded one of the more common milestones associated with Anglo-American settlement: later historians touted their son Charles as "the first white boy to be born in the Valley."[7] **BKR**

1. For a biography and chronology of Taber's life, see Linda Bonnett and Wayne Bonnett, *Taber: A Photographic Legacy* (Sausalito CA: Windgate Press, 2004), 154–61. 2. For the souvenir trade in art in California, see Kate Nearpass Ogden, "Sublime Vistas and Scenic Backdrops: Nineteenth-Century Painters and Photographers at Yosemite," *California History* 69, no. 2 (Summer 1990): 148–49. 3. For similar views of Sentinel Rock by Watkins, see Weston Naef and Christine Hult-Lewis, *Carleton Watkins: The Complete Mammoth Photographs* (Los Angeles: Getty Publications, 2011), 82–83, cats. 180–82. 4. "Our Introduction" and "The Yo-Ham-I-Ie Valley," *Hutchings' California Magazine* 1, no. 1 (July 1856): 1, 2. 5. Caroline M. Churchill, Leidig's Hotel guestbook, 1876, quoted in *One-Hundred Years in Yosemite*, by C. P. Russell (Stanford CA: Stanford University Press, 1932), 112. 6. Visitors raved equally about the quality of the hotel's food and the coziness of its beds. Russell, *One-Hundred Years.* 7. Russell, *One-Hundred Years.*

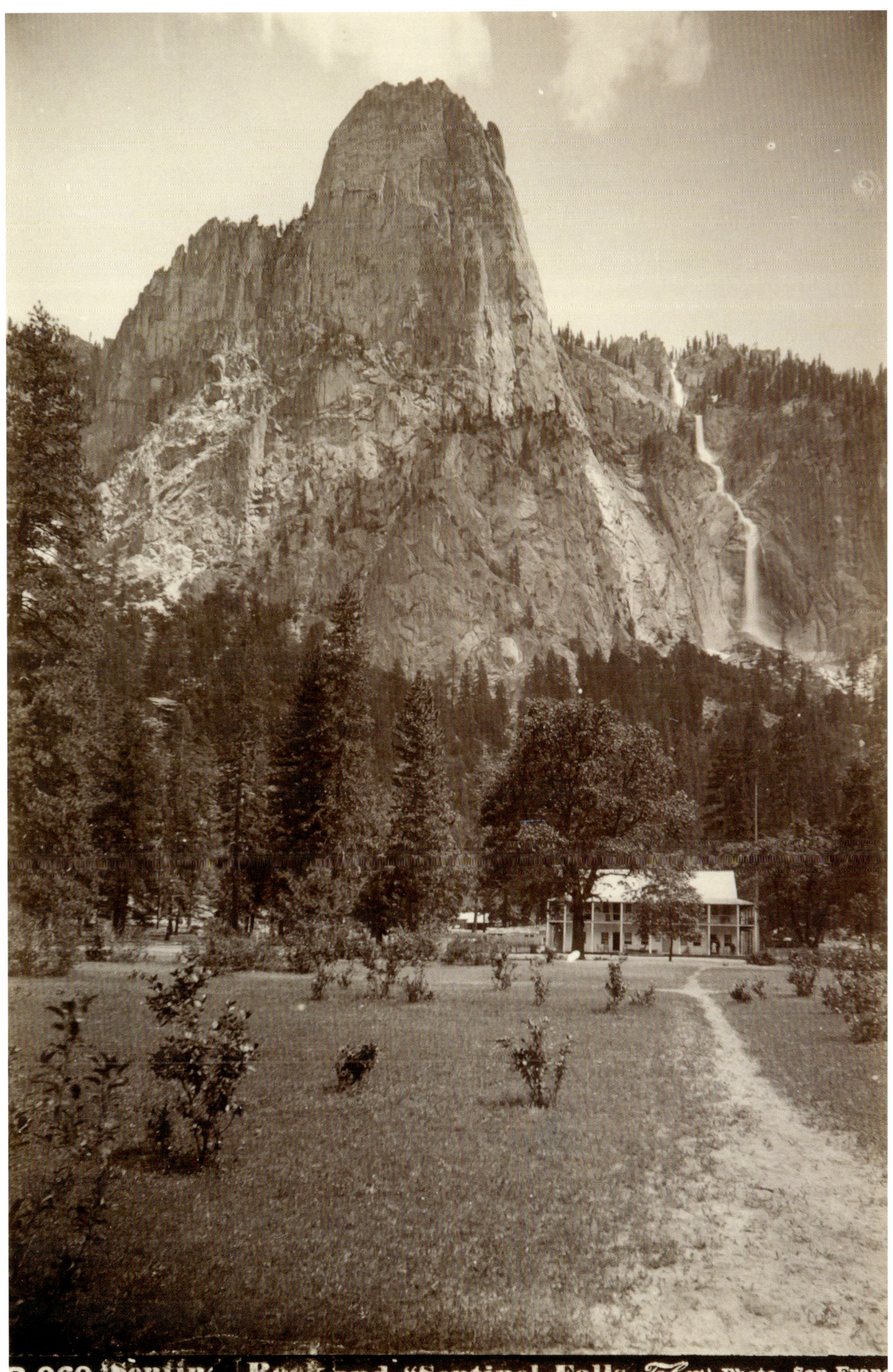
B 969 "Sentinel" Rock and "Sentinel Falls. Taber Photo., San Franc

32

Laura Gilpin

American, 1891–1979

The White House, Canyon de Chelly, 1930
Gelatin silver print
Image and sheet: 35.6 × 28 cm (14 × 11 in)
Nebraska Art Association, purchased with the aid of
funds from the National Endowment for the Arts, N-472

A westerner by birth, Laura Gilpin spent most of her life in and around the desert Southwest and devoted much of her career to documenting the region's people and places. Her parents introduced her to photography through the gift of a Brownie, a low-cost snapshot camera first unveiled by Eastman Kodak in 1900. In 1916, when pictorialism was at its height, she began studies at the Clarence White School of Photography in New York. Gilpin eventually abandoned her teacher's enigmatic, soft-focus approach in favor of more sharpened images, but she later claimed that the White School instilled in her an appreciation for design and problem solving. "Mr. White," she recalled, "would give us design problems, like taking three objects and making one of the first importance, one of second, and one of third. White against white, and dark against dark, a problem in rectangles. . . . Design is the foundation for everything."[1]

Gilpin's lifelong interest in capturing and understanding elements of design is amply illustrated in *The White House,* her perfectly composed image of an ancient Puebloan ruin in northeastern Arizona. The delicate striations that mark the upper cliff walls possess subtle nuances within their tones and also create a pleasing harmony between dark and light. The inward-curving rock formations, which culminate in a natural cave, produce a striking balance with the built structures at the center of the composition. The black-and-white streaks at the top are both neutralized and emphasized by the strong glare of the bright, natural light at the lower portion of the print, the "white against white" that White taught Gilpin to develop and control.

The area of northeastern Arizona where Gilpin took this photograph is one of the longest continuously inhabited sites in North America, much admired for the ruins built by ancient Puebloan peoples and populated by the Navajo. (The name *de Chelly,* in fact, is a French bastardization of the Navajo word for "canyon," *tséyi'.*) The American military explored the Four Corners region in the mid-nineteenth century, and in the following decades, it was documented by the Bureau of American Ethnology and promoted as a tourist destination. By the early 1900s, it had become a magnet for photographers, including Edward Sheriff Curtis and Ansel Adams, who took a similar view of the White House a decade later from another angle.[2] Gilpin first visited the ruins at Betatakin Canyon and the nearby Canyon de Chelly in 1930 with her friend and lifelong companion, Elizabeth Forster, a professional nurse who cared for the ailing photographer after she returned to her hometown of Colorado Springs in 1917. Gilpin's original goal was to create a series of lantern slides of southwestern archaeological sites, but after Forster accepted a nursing position at the local Red Rock settlement the following year, Gilpin made several trips to visit her friend, always with her camera and tripod in tow. She began a project of photographing Navajo life with the intention of creating prints for exhibitions and a possible publication, a project that did not reach fruition until almost forty years later.[3] **BKR**

1. Laura Gilpin, interview by Paul Hill and Thomas Cooper, March 1975, in *Dialogue with Photography* (New York: Farrar, Straus and Giroux, 1979), 284. **2.** For the 1894–95 report, see Cosmos Mindeleff, "The Cliff Ruins of Canyon de Chelly, Arizona," in *Sixteenth Annual Report of the Bureau of American Ethnology, 1894–95* (Washington DC: Government Printing Office, 1897), 73–198, plates 41–63, figs. 1–83. **3.** For a review of these photographs and projects as well as the couple's history in the area, see Martha A. Sandweiss, *Laura Gilpin: An Enduring Grace,* exhibition catalog (Fort Worth TX: Amon Carter Museum, 1986), 51–58.

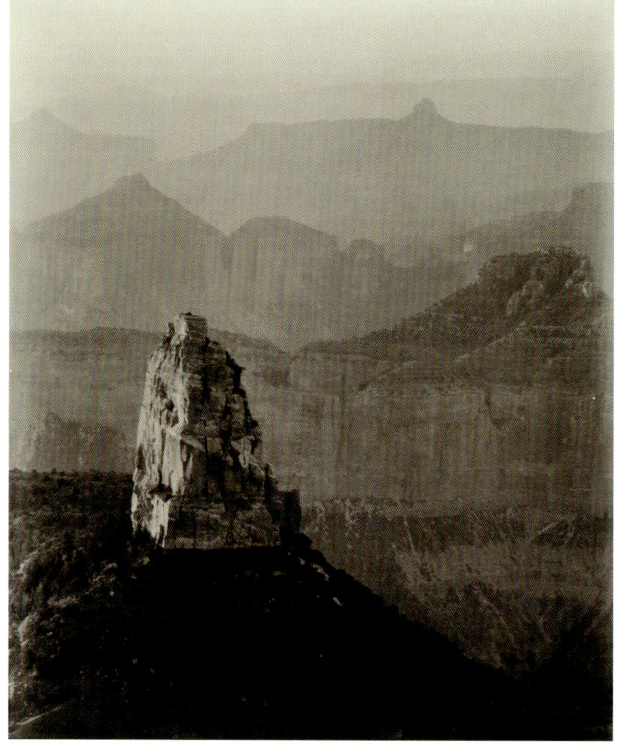

Laura Gilpin. *Sunrise at the Grand Canyon,* 1930. Platinum print; 24.1 × 19.7 cm (9 1/2 × 7 3/4 in). Nebraska Art Association, purchased with the aid of funds from the National Endowment for the Arts, N-465.

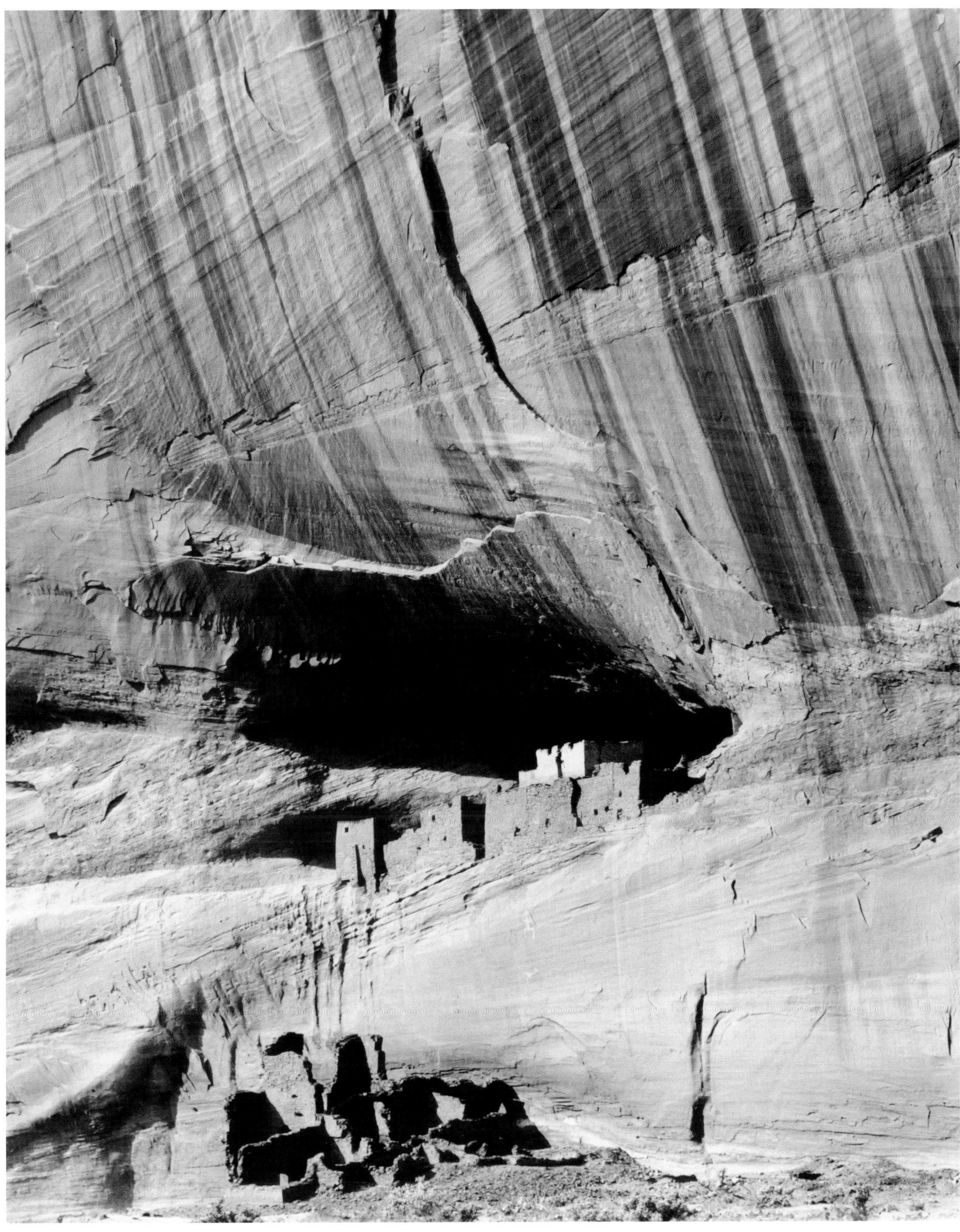

33

Herbert J. Seligmann

American, 1891–1984

New York, Skyline, c. 1930
Gelatin silver print
Image: 7.6 × 10.2 cm (3 × 4 in); sheet: 7.9 × 10.5 cm
(3⅛ × 4⅛ in)
University of Nebraska, Anna R. and Frank M. Hall
Charitable Trust, H-2423

Author and journalist Herbert Seligmann was a prolific writer, producing books and articles on a wide range of topics from literary criticism and a biography of D. H. Lawrence to political commentary on the American invasion of Haiti and the rise of Nazism. After his 1914 graduation from Harvard University, Seligmann began contributing essays to some of the country's most esteemed magazines and journals, including the *New Republic*, the *New York Evening Post*, the *New York Globe*, and the *New York Tribune*. He also published several books on civil rights—*The Negro Faces America* and *Race against Man*—as well as two volumes of poetry and collected essays. One of Seligmann's contemporaries described him as possessing the "rare faculty of ascertaining with nicety the quality, force and timbre of the novel or painting, the symphony or personality, to which he has been exposed, and crystallizing it coolly in a sentence or a phrase."[1]

The writer's first love, however, was art, and he produced a rich body of criticism and essays on the subject for the *Nation* as well as editing a volume of the letters of artist John Marin. Seligmann, like Marin, was a friend and disciple of the photographer Alfred Stieglitz (cat. 15), devoting several essays to his work and many others to that of the artists Stieglitz championed. In a 1934 essay on Stieglitz, Seligmann lauded his efforts to elevate photography to a fine art in the "stale cultural barbarism" of America: "In the midst of such a society Stieglitz conducted his world-wide battle to achieve the recognition of photography as an art equivalent to the other accepted arts. In America, the serious, devoted, and accomplished workers whom Stieglitz inspired and led, fought and broke the exhibition system. . . . As an individual worker Stieglitz had from the outset deepened and enriched the resources of the medium."[2]

Perhaps inspired by his sympathy for Stieglitz's mission and a fondness for his artwork, Seligmann first began to experiment with photography himself immediately following World War I, when he traveled through Europe as publicity director for the American Jewish Joint Distribution Committee. As might be expected given his mission and position, Seligmann's photographs from this period are portraits of Jews taken in central and western European countries; Seligmann went on to use photography as a tool for his reportage in the 1920s, taking pictures in Haiti as well as the Adirondacks and the western United States. He also continued to pursue the medium as a sideline, and during the 1930s, he took several pictures of New York's streets and skyscrapers. Here, the photographer focused on the Manhattan skyline looking downtown. Flanked by the East River on the left and a wide street on the right, the composition is an exercise in geometry: the verticals of the city's skyscrapers are contrasted with the strong horizontals of Brooklyn Bridge and the wharfs and warehouses that dot the river. As emblems of modernity, the bridge and the office towers serve to demonstrate America's advanced engineering skills, while the ships with their billowing smokestacks and the cars at right evoke the speed of the modern city. **BKR**

1. Paul Rosenfeld, *Men Seen: Twenty-Four Modern Authors* (New York: Dial Press, 1925), 237. 2. Herbert Seligmann, "291: A Vision through Photography," in *America and Alfred Stieglitz: A Collective Portrait*, ed. Waldo Frank et al. (New York: Doubleday, 1934), 58.

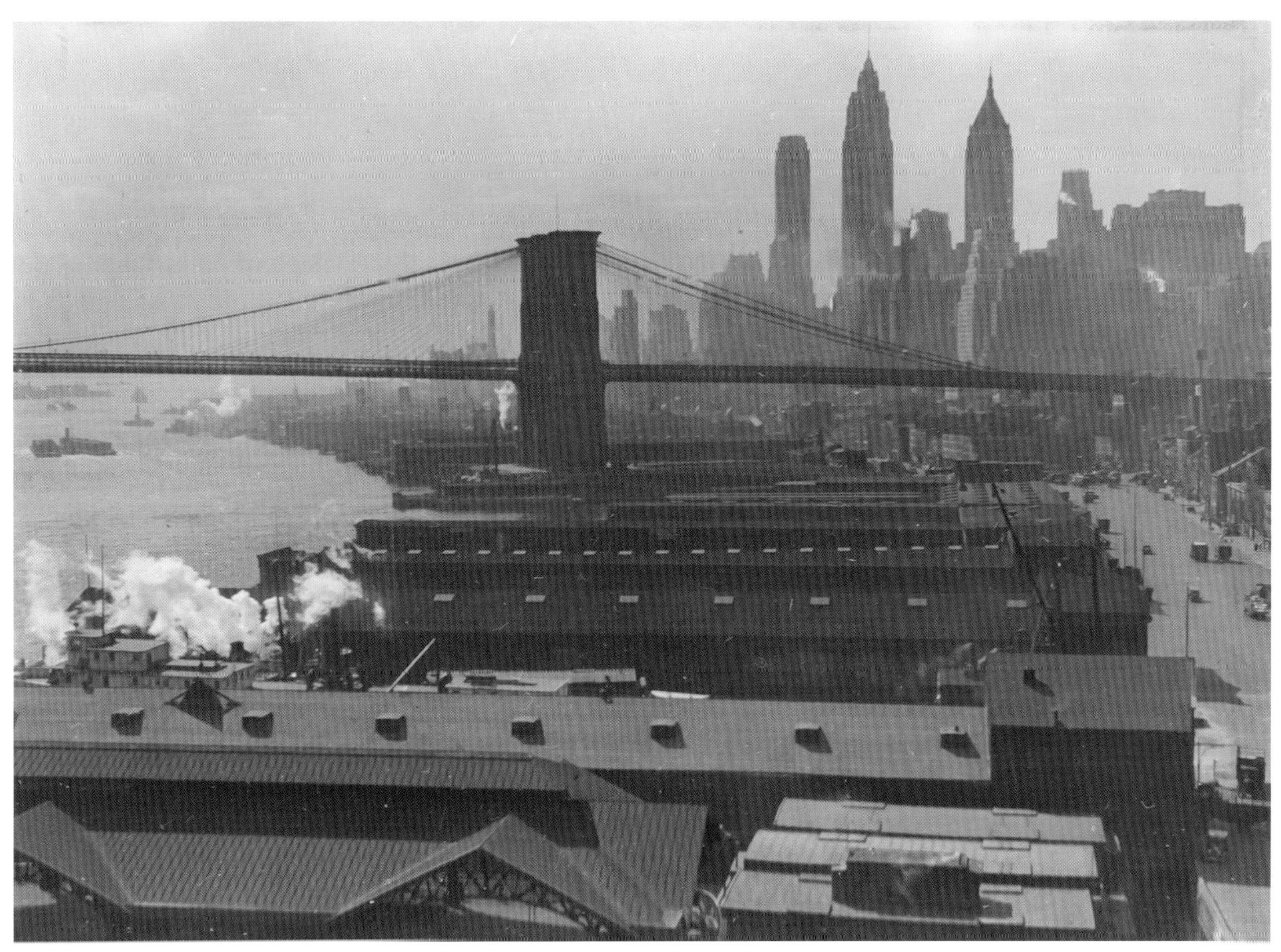

Berenice Abbott

American, 1898–1991

Cliff and Ferry Streets, 1935
Gelatin silver print
Image and sheet: 22 × 8.6 cm (8 5/8 × 3 3/8 in)
University of Nebraska, allocation of the
U.S. government, Federal Art Project of the
Works Progress Administration, U-1856

After dropping out of college in her home state of Ohio, Berenice Abbott moved to New York in 1918 with the intention of becoming a journalist. An introduction to the bohemian residents of the city's Greenwich Village district, however, altered her goals, and in 1921 she moved to Paris, where she studied sculpture for two years. From 1923 to 1925, Abbott worked as a darkroom assistant to surrealist painter and photographer Man Ray, later writing that she "took to photography like a duck to water."[1] After establishing her own studio in Paris in 1927, she specialized in photographic portraits of artistic and intellectual luminaries, including Jean Cocteau, James Joyce, and Eugène Atget (cat. 99). Atget's documentary images of Paris's recognizable back alleys, monuments, and streets influenced Abbott considerably, prompting her to shift focus from portraiture to cityscapes; she purchased much of the older artist's collection after his death, describing Atget's photographs as opening a "new world . . . in the realm of creative expression."[2]

Writing in 1932 on the occasion of Abbott's first exhibition of cityscapes, distinguished critic Edward Alden Jewell made deliberate reference to Atget's impact: "Miss Abbott's present exhibition . . . deals [with] the New York scene. The moment you enter the gallery you realize that this is New York caught in the tradition of the famous French photographer, Eugène Atget. Then you realize that it was Miss Abbott who, a few seasons ago, purchased and brought to this country the Atget collection. . . . It is only fair to note that, particularly in views of skyscraper developments, the American photographer succeeds in asserting her own personality, her own artistic credo."[3]

After she returned to New York in 1929, Abbott made the city her premier subject, capturing its varied aspects during a period of rapid change. Although she initially worked on her own initiative, by 1935 she received support from the Federal Art Project of the Works Progress Administration, a government program established to assist artists during the Great Depression; she eventually amassed some 302 images of the city.[4] Here, in the early morning of November 29, 1935, Abbott photographed the corners of Cliff and Ferry Streets, an intersection close to the East River a few blocks from the Manhattan terminus of the Brooklyn Bridge.[5] The changing nature of this urban environment is evidenced by a guidebook that only a couple of decades earlier discussed the district's history as the site of several tanneries.[6] In Abbott's photograph, cars line the narrow, winding thoroughfare; a lit streetlamp is visible at the right and a wooden sign for Mac Lac Shellac at the left; while an already obsolete horse-drawn carriage winds its way toward the viewer. The dark, shadowy streetscape contrasts with the sunlit, towering American International Building, which, during the Great Depression, served as an emblem of the nation's modernity, ingenuity, and engineering prowess. **BKR**

1. Quoted in Julia Van Haaften, ed., *Berenice Abbott, Photographer: A Modern Vision*, exhibition catalog (New York: New York Public Library, 1989), 11. 2. Berenice Abbott, "Eugène Atget," in *Photography: Essays and Images*, ed. Beaumont Newhall (New York: Museum of Modern Art, 1980), 235–37. 3. Edward Alden Jewell, "Photographs by Miss Abbott," *New York Times*, September 29, 1932. 4. Abbott exhibited many of these photographs in the 1937 show *Changing New York*, produced under the auspices of the Federal Art Project; she subsequently published several examples in a book of the same title. See Berenice Abbott and Elizabeth McCausland, *Changing New York* (New York: E. P. Dutton, 1939; repr., Dover Publications, 1973, as *New York in the Thirties*). 5. Today the intersection no longer exists but is a series of residential towers. 6. Frank Bergen Kelley, *Historical Guide to the City of New York* (New York: Frederick A. Stokes, 1909), 63–64.

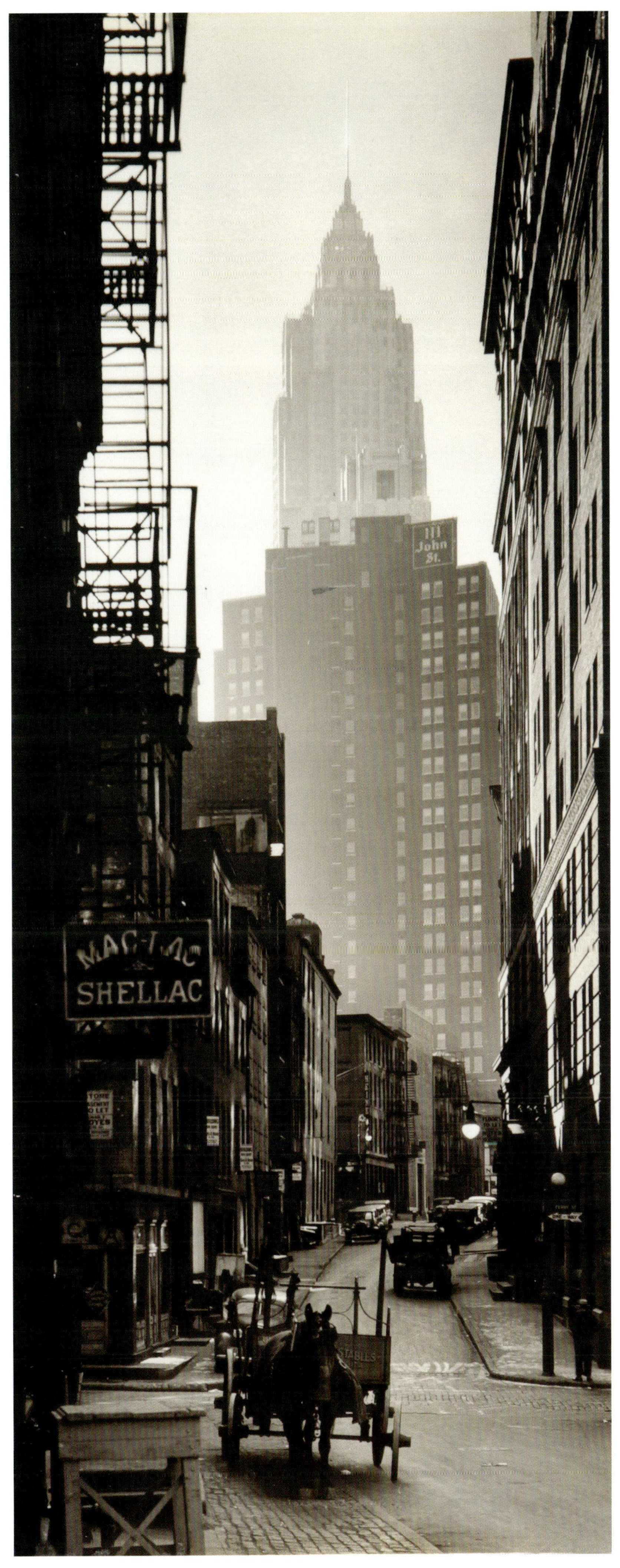

MAC-LAC
SHELLAC
111
John
St.

Ansel Adams

American, 1902–1984

Zabriskie Point, Death Valley National Monument, California, c. 1942
Gelatin silver print
Image: 23.5 × 19.1 cm (9 ¼ × 7 ½ in); mount: 31.4 × 26.7 cm (12 ⅜ × 10 ½ in)
Signed, on mount, lower right, in pencil: *Ansel Adams*
University of Nebraska, Anna R. and Frank M. Hall Charitable Trust, H-509

Ansel Adams is perhaps one of America's best-known photographers, admired for his now-iconic landscapes of national parks and western scenery. The year 1916 represented a milestone for the artist, bringing him two experiences that would influence the direction of his life and career. First, he made his initial visit to Yosemite, a place where he would spend considerable time until his death; and second, with the trip as an occasion, his parents gave him a Kodak No. 1 Box Brownie camera. Shortly afterward, he joined the Sierra Club, an organization that shaped him considerably; Adams published his first photographs and writings in the group's 1922 bulletin and, six years later, presented his first one-person exhibition at its San Francisco headquarters. He went on to become a director of the club, which instilled in him a love for the country's natural wonders and a sense of duty in preserving them; it also determined the course of his assignments and supplied the subjects that became staples of his photographic output.

In September 1941 Harold Ickes, secretary of the interior, commissioned Adams to photograph the country's national parks, Native American reservations, and other locations under the Department of the Interior's jurisdiction for use as mural-sized prints to decorate its new headquarters. In his selection of Adams, Ickes was inspired not only by the dramatic changes to the American landscape brought by the agricultural catastrophes of the 1920s and 1930s—and the government's responses to them—but by the artist's own conscientious efforts at preserving the wilderness.[1] Over the following year, the photographer traveled through several states and eventually presented the government with over two hundred prints; at the same time, he took images for his own use and worked on other commissions. Although Ickes's project was ended by America's entry into World War II, it enabled Adams to create some of his most famous and enduring photographs. During this period in the early 1940s, for instance, he made *Moonrise over Hernandez, New Mexico* (below), an image that took on mythical proportions through the artist's increasingly rhapsodic descriptions; he called it "one of my best."[2]

Adams offered three prints of the Death Valley area to the Interior Department, all of them panoramic views of the basin with mountains in the distance. By contrast, *Zabriskie Point, Death Valley National Monument, California* shows an area of the southern California desert near the Nevada border in detail and sharp focus. The landscape's distinctive ridges are the result of sediment deposits from the formation and subsequent erosion of Furnace Creek Lake over millions of years. These natural features, with their idiosyncratic patterning and strong contrasts of light and dark, surely appealed to Adams's artistic sensibilities. But his environmental concerns must have also played a part in his choice of subject and composition: Zabriskie Point was named after Christian Brevoort Zabriskie, a longtime employee of and eventual general manager and vice president for the Pacific Coast Borax Company, which had large mining operations in the area for several years. **BKR**

1. For this commission, see Jonathan Spaulding, "The Natural Scene and the Social Good: The Artistic Education of Ansel Adams," *Pacific Historical Review* 60, no. 1 (February 1991): 33–34; and Spaulding, "Yosemite and Ansel Adams: Art, Commerce, and Western Tourism," *Pacific Historical Review* 65, no. 4 (November 1996): 628–29. **2.** Ansel Adams to David McAlpin, January 10, 1943, in *Ansel Adams: Letters, 1916–1984*, ed. Mary Street Alinder and Andrea Gray Stillman (Boston: Little, Brown and Company, 2001), 145.

Ansel Adams. *Moonrise over Hernandez, New Mexico*, 1941; printed c. 1955. Gelatin silver print; 26.7 × 34.1 cm (10 ½ × 13 ⁷⁄₁₆ in). University of Nebraska, gift of Beaumont Newhall, U-3508.

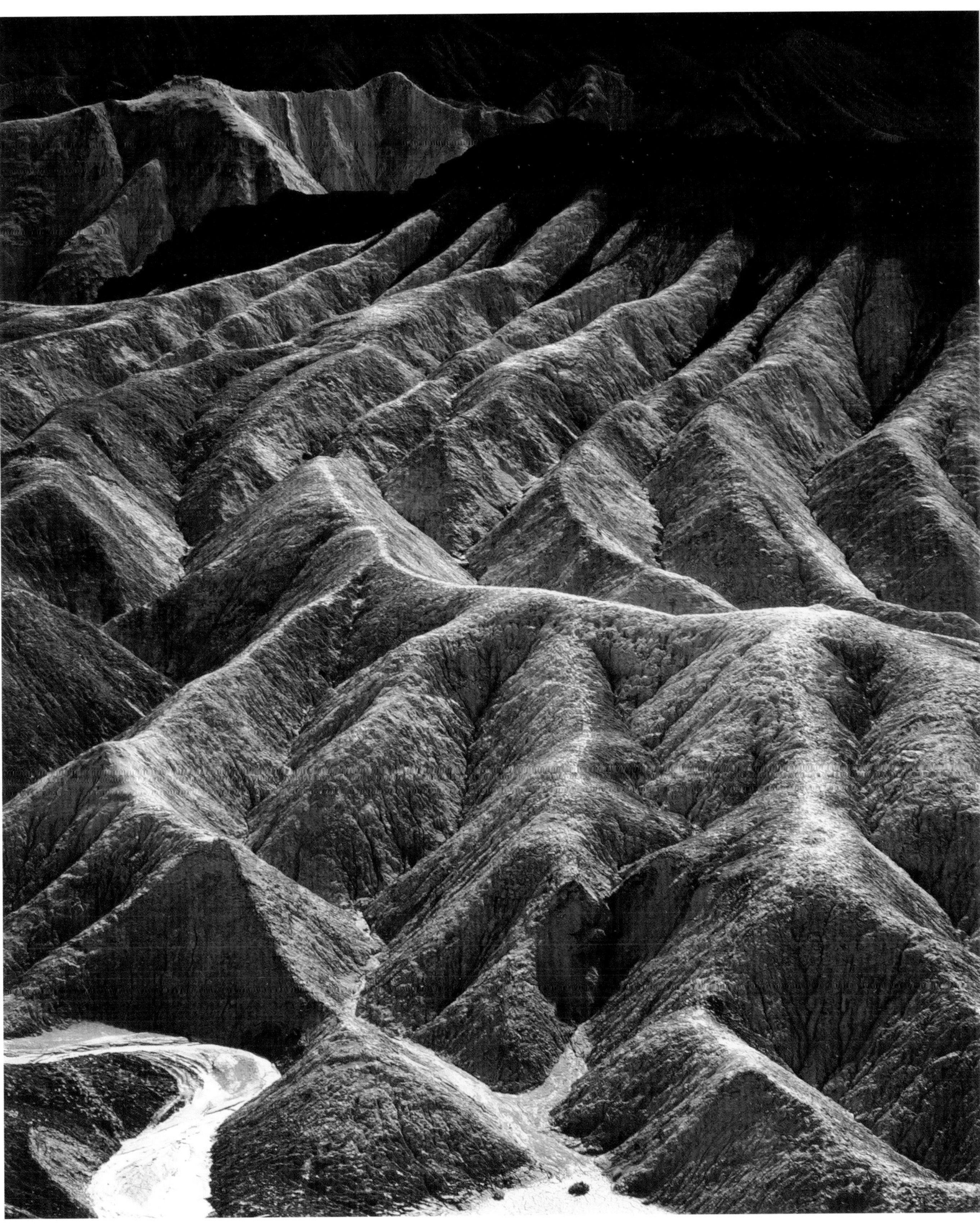

36

Margaret Bourke-White
American, 1904–1971

Steel Lines, Fort Peck, Montana, 1936
Gelatin silver print
Image and sheet: 27.8 × 35.6 cm (10 15/16 × 14 in)
University of Nebraska, Anna R. and Frank M. Hall
Charitable Trust, H-2152

Printed in the inaugural issue of *Life* magazine, this image exemplifies the might of modern architecture in the first half of the twentieth century. Widely known for her industrial subjects, Margaret Bourke-White was the ideal photographer to document the New Deal era. Trained at Columbia University with famed photography teacher Clarence H. White (cat. 69), she moved in 1927 to Cleveland, Ohio, where she began to take photographs of the area's steel mills and skyscrapers. Her pioneering photographic essays appeared in some of the major magazines of the day, including *Fortune*, *Life*, and *Time*.

Pictorialist images romanticizing industry first became prevalent in the early 1900s, produced by noted photographers including Alvin Langdon Coburn, Edward Steichen, and Alfred Stieglitz (see cats. 11, 95, and 15).[1] During the 1930s, such industrial scenes took on a renewed importance in response to the Great Depression and also suggested themselves as a way to represent American modernism. At the same time, large-scale dam projects such as the one at Fork Peck, Montana, became symbols of government building initiatives and progress in the face of economic uncertainty, serving as monuments to humanity's power to control its environment.[2]

Life took notice of the new construction out west when it dispatched Bourke-White to document the project and the town that sprang up around it. The Fort Peck Dam, named after an 1860s trading post, stemmed from the Public Works Administration. Begun in 1933, it took seven years to complete and is one of the largest hydraulically filled dams in the world. At its peak, the project employed over ten thousand workers in eastern Montana. The dam not only provided much-needed work but also generated boom towns and an influx of forty thousand people into the area.[3] In the editorial introduction to *Life*'s first issue, Bourke-White's work was described as "a human document of American frontier life, which, to them [the editors] at least, was a revelation."[4]

Included in the story "Franklin Roosevelt's Wild West," the images documented daily occurrences in both the towns and the new construction projects. *Steel Lines, Fort Peck, Montana* records the power of machines and workers acting together. Taken looking up at the structure, the image shows how human experience is intertwined with the large-scale industrial work. At first glance, the men appear as part of the giant construction, climbing and standing in and around it. Small in scale compared to the massive steel lines, they interrupt the geometric pattern of radiating spokes and circles.

Some images in Bourke-White's photo essay document "wild frontier life" in the form of portraits depicting daily living and drunken fun. Yet while life in the towns may have been rowdy, this sense of freedom did not extend to the land. *Steel Lines* suggests an attempt to tame or control the landscape. Literally used to help exert control over the flow of water, figuratively the steel lines and the view of them that Bourke-White provides remove any sense of the frontier's vast natural landscape. **SF**

1. Melissa A. McEuen, *Seeing America: Women Photographers between the Wars* (Lexington: University Press of Kentucky, 2000), 205. **2.** Richard Guy Wilson, "Machine-Age Iconography in the American West: The Design of the Hoover Dam," *Pacific Historical Review* 54, no. 4 (1985): 463–93. **3.** For a history of the Fort Peck Dam, see Fredric L. Quivik, "New Deal Oasis on the High Plains," *Montana: The Magazine of Western History* 54, no. 4 (2004): 69–74. **4.** Introduction to the first issue of *Life*, November 23, 1936, 3.

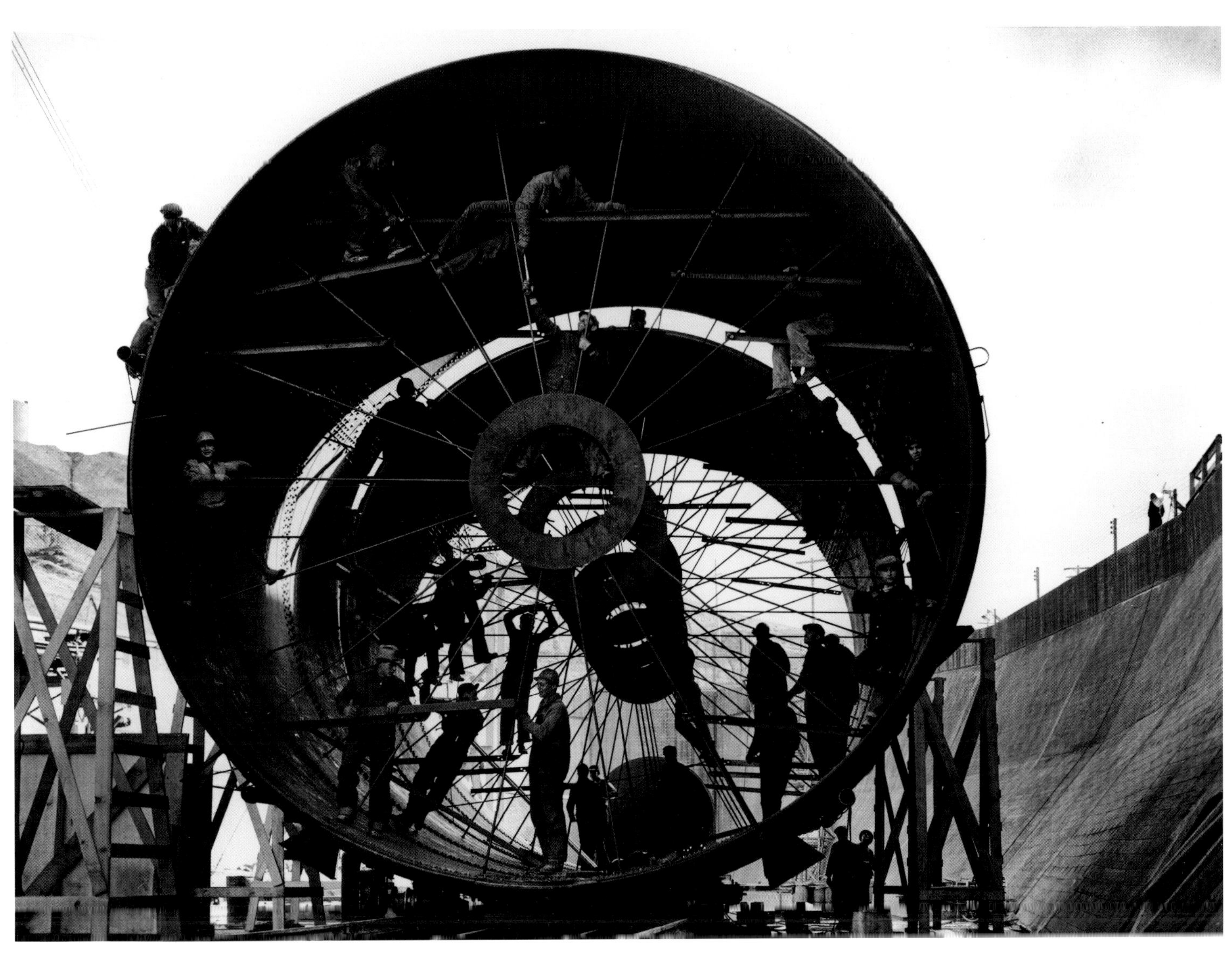

37

Terry Evans
American, born 1944

Dam near Hyderabad, 1979
Ektacolor print
Image: 22.9 × 22.9 cm (9 × 9 in); sheet: 35.6 × 27.9 cm
(14 × 11 in)
Inscribed, on verso, lower left, in black ink: *dam near
Hyderabad*; lower center: *Oct. 1979*; lower right:
Terry Evans
University of Nebraska, gift of the artist, U-3004

Trained in art at the University of Kansas, Terry Evans practiced black-and-white portrait photography for nearly ten years when, in 1978, she received a commission that changed the direction of her career. The Land Institute in Salina, Kansas, where Evans was living at the time, asked her to survey the work of professors and students on a virgin prairie. This encounter with the prairie's rich ecological diversity forced her to reconsider her choice of subjects, and since then she has produced a significant body of work devoted to the world's landscape and ecology, documenting its great variety but also its subtle and dramatic changes. For over thirty years, Evans has recorded the tall grass prairies of the Great Plains, the glaciers of Greenland, and fauna specimens at Chicago's Field Museum of Natural History as well as producing an aerial pictorial of that city. In all these works, she has followed the simple dictate of using her camera to capture reality. "I want my photographs to be clear and factual," she explained. "I don't want them to be romantic interpretations but instead an expression of what's really there."[1]

Even as she rethought her subjects, the artist also began reexperimenting with color photography, a process that she had given up years earlier due to dissatisfaction with the results. Evans approached her photographs of the prairie in terms of pattern more than color, but after several successful trials, she was finally satisfied with the full range of "harmony and beauty." For her, "Color became a consuming way to work."[2]

Immediately after she had received her commission from the Land Institute, Evans made a trip to Asia, visiting China and India and approaching the landscape of those countries in the same way she had just been experiencing that of the prairie, obtaining beautiful shots of converging ground and sky. During her visit to India, the photographer visited the Nagarjuna Sagar Dam, the subject of this image. Opened in 1967 during the government of Indira Gandhi, the structure is located approximately one hundred miles southeast of Hyderabad on the Krishna River and is the world's tallest masonry dam. Rather than focusing on engineering marvels or the technological wonder of the structure itself, as Margaret Bourke-White had done at the Fort Peck Dam two generations earlier (cat. 36), Evans instead draws our attention to its effects: the flooding of the ancient Buddhist settlement of Nagarjunakonda upon the dam's release. **BKR**

1. Quoted in Linda Ulrich, "Photos Show 'What's Really There,'" *Lincoln Sunday Journal and Star*, November 16, 1980. **2.** Ulrich, "Photos Show."

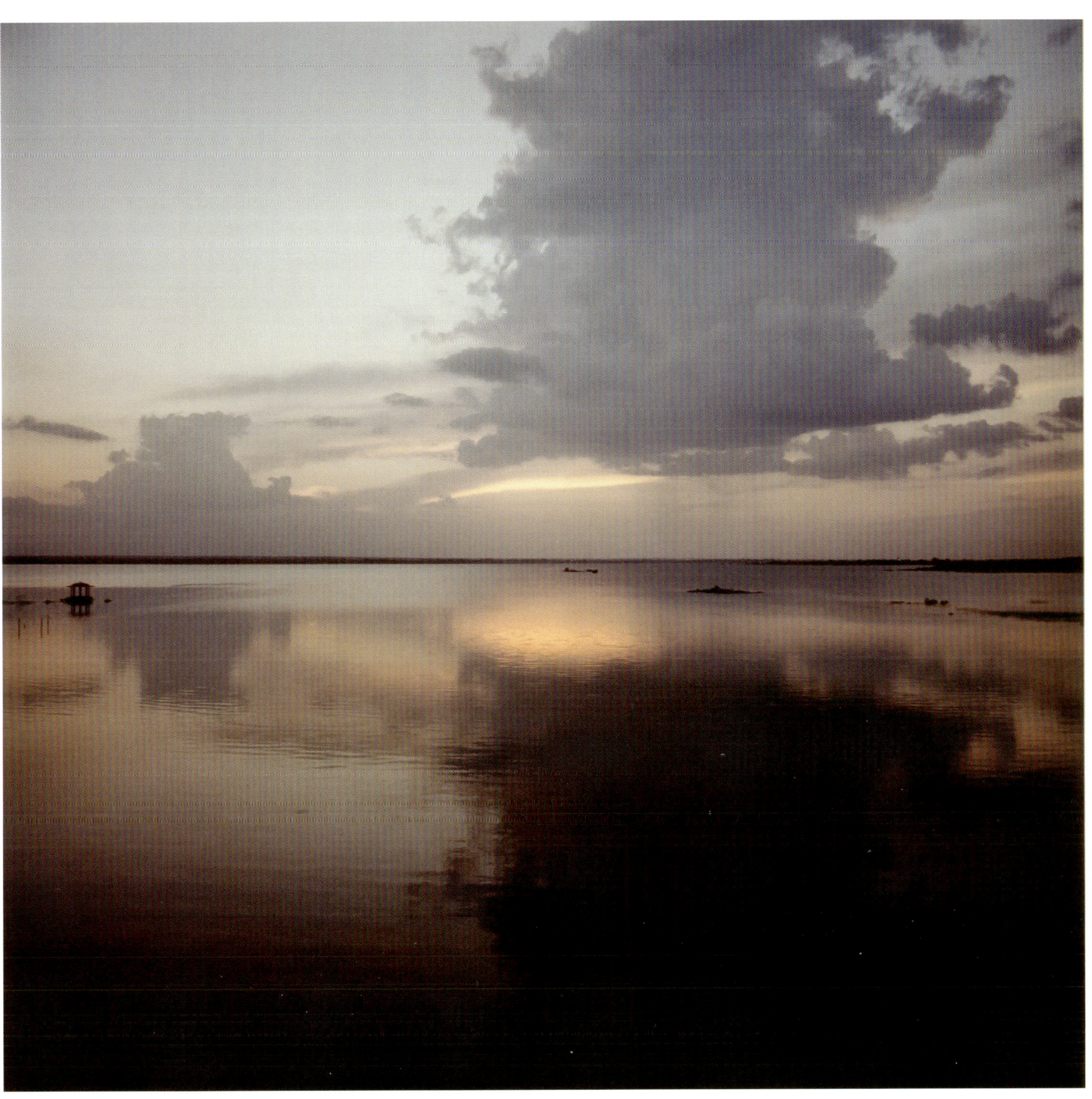

38

Harry Callahan

American, 1912–1999

Chicago (#101 from *Photographs: Harry Callahan*),
c. 1950
Gelatin silver print
Image: 19.1 × 24.1 cm (7 1/2 × 9 1/2 in); mount: 36.8 × 40.6 cm
(14 1/2 × 16 in)
Signed, on mount, lower right, in pencil: *Harry Callahan*
University of Nebraska, Anna R. and Frank M. Hall
Charitable Trust, H-1055

Harry Callahan took up photography in Detroit in the early 1940s. He quickly discovered a fascination with camera vision, and he was fortunate to encounter some individuals who helped foster his talent. First, he met Arthur Siegel, a successful commercial photographer who had completed a course of study at the New Bauhaus (later the Institute of Design) in Chicago a few years previously. In a lecture at the Chrysler Camera Club, Siegel illustrated Bauhaus principles of design and experimentation with his own works, which feature effects such as multiple exposure, solarization, and tilted viewpoints.

While Siegel's approach was intellectually stimulating, Callahan responded equally strongly to the example of Ansel Adams (cat. 35), whom Siegel invited to conduct a workshop in Detroit in the summer of 1941. Adams, widely respected for his skill in the darkroom and a tireless advocate for the medium, instilled in Callahan a dedication to craft and a belief in the expressive capacities of photography. Based on these formative influences, Callahan embarked on a self-directed, wholly unprogrammatic course of study. Five years later, in 1946, Siegel invited him to join the faculty at the Institute of Design, and thus Callahan began a thirty-year career in teaching.

Although he had no experience as an instructor, Callahan enjoyed the institute's ethos of freedom and exploration.[1] Just as he led students through various problem-solving exercises, in his own work he applied new techniques to favorite subjects, giving himself assignments in the field and in the darkroom. Sometimes these efforts stalled, and at other times they succeeded; often a fluke, mistake, or chance observation would take him in an unanticipated direction.

On a winter day in 1950, the artist set out for a walk along Lake Shore Drive with his 8 × 10-inch camera and tripod—something he had done dozens of times before, usually with no fixed goal or destination in mind. Again repeating a familiar routine, he set up his camera and tripod facing the direction of Lake Michigan. Under a dark cloth, he could see the scene upside down in the camera's ground-glass back: an elegant frieze of six leafless trees with the horizontal lines of the shore and water visible beyond.

The resulting negative is a perfect exposure, capturing the varied textures of the trees' bark, the granular snow, the slight ripples on the water's surface, and the wisps of cloud in the sky as well as the tonal gradation from white through gray to black. However meticulously detailed, the resulting test prints were, by Callahan's account, "dull."[2] Convinced of the image's potential, he persisted in the darkroom, exaggerating the contrast of light and dark and suppressing textural detail with strategic under- and overexposure so the trees read as opaque silhouettes against a pale, ethereal background. The entire composition flattens, taking on the rhythmic, ornamental aspect of a multipanel Japanese screen. Although printed by contact and thus only 7½ × 9½ inches in size, *Chicago* is expansive, infused with crisp air and cold light. In keeping with its atmosphere of hushed observation, this photograph captures a moment of discovery and transformation. **BS**

1. For more on the Institute of Design, see David Travis and Elizabeth Siegel, eds., *Taken by Design: Photographs from the Institute of Design, 1937–1971*, exhibition catalog (Chicago: Art Institute of Chicago and University of Chicago Press, 2002). 2. Quoted in *Callahan in New England*, interview by Diana L. Johnson, exhibition catalog (Providence RI: David Winton Bell Gallery, List Art Center, Brown University, 1994), 7.

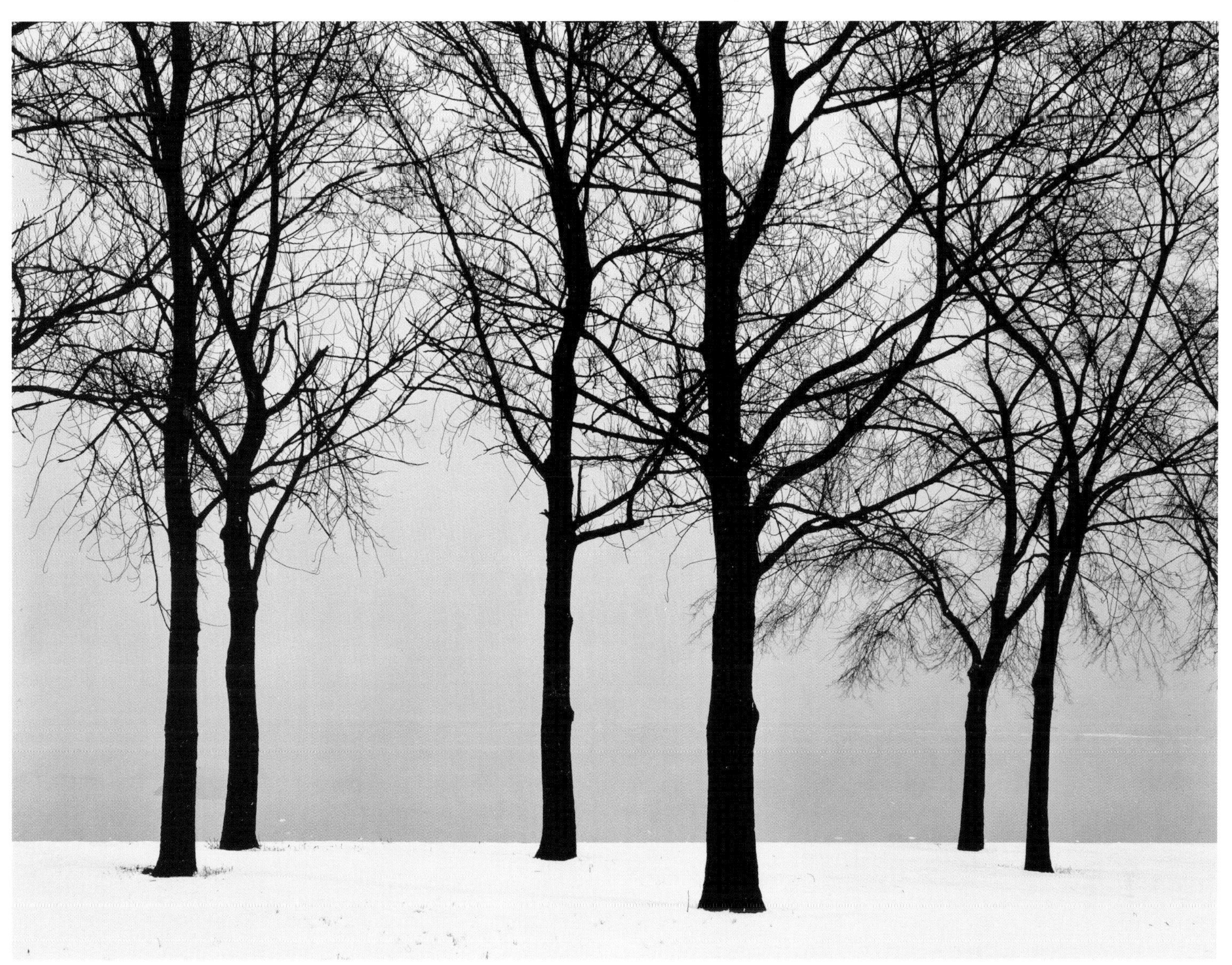

39

O. Winston Link

American, 1914–2001

Bringing in the Cows on the Norvel Ryan Farm, as Train No. 3 Passes [Cow 13, Shawsville, Virginia], 1955; printed 1987
Gelatin silver print
Image: 49.2 × 39.8 cm (19 3/8 × 15 11/16 in); sheet: 50.8 × 40.6 cm (20 × 16 in)
Inscribed, on verso, in pencil: *Printed by / O. Winston Link / 2-87*
University of Nebraska, gift of Natasha Nicholson and Tom Garver in honor of Eva and George Neubert, U-5389

O. Winston Link's photographic legacy rests, essentially, on one body of work. Between 1955 and 1960, he undertook a personal project to capture the waning years of the American steam railroad. Link was enough of a train enthusiast to be fascinated by the specifics of power, size, and speed. But he was also compelled by a decidedly romantic idée fixe of creating images that would describe a harmonious relationship between the iron horse and small-town America, whose landscape and commerce it had helped transform over the course of 150 years.

In January 1955, Link, a New York–based industrial photographer, was on freelance assignment at Westinghouse in Staunton, Virginia. While there, he took a late-day trip to nearby Waynesboro, whose train station was on the Shenandoah Valley Line of the Norfolk & Western Railway. Watching trains arriving in majestic clouds of smoke against inky skies awoke Link's muse. He returned the next evening with his camera, determined to begin shooting the steaming behemoths at night, as the darkness seemed to cloak them in added mystery and magic.

Using his experience in the advertising trade, the artist quickly sought permission from Norfolk & Western to record their trains. Granted nearly unfettered access to linemen, rail yards, and stations, he was even able to slightly adjust timetables and ask conductors for a second pass-by to yield the best possible outcome. Link's wartime expertise with radio-controlled night photography enabled him to design the special flash reflectors and power supplies that were necessary to make stop-motion images of locomotives moving at sixty miles per hour. To achieve his desired effect, he carefully planned and staged all aspects of the composition and equipment placement.

In the resulting series, which comprises some 2,400 negatives, Link created a vivid vision of a nearly Rockwellian good life into which the network of the rails was uniquely knit. The photographs, shot largely on black-and-white film, are characterized by intense contrasts and gradations of tone, underpinned by a clean, precisionist aesthetic emphasizing strong lines of architecture and machinery. Link's strategic staging and synchronized flash techniques also enhance the delineation of objects, as if viewing a diorama. Many images concentrate on the statuesque presence of the engine, snorting smoke heavily into the night air. Perhaps his most iconic tableaux are the more theatrical setups in which he charmed local citizens into posing as drive-in moviegoers, porch dwellers, and swimmers as trains huffed by in the background. Though Link was not overtly sentimental, his aim to document a swiftly passing era often produced scenes that tread the line between verism and nostalgia. Read from a greater historical distance and through the filter of a postmodern sensibility, his works appear self-aware, ironic, and surreal.

Taken in the first year of the series, *Bringing in the Cows on the Norvel Ryan Farm* exemplifies Link's method of directed image making. By focusing on the routine of father and son tending their dairy herd, on the barn and soaring silo, the photographer depicts agrarian life punctuated by the rhythms of the rails. By juxtaposing the two activities, Link suggests the degree to which they are intertwined, even as he contrasts the plodding slowness of the former with the hurtling speed of the latter. Yet he is known to have asked Ryan to delay his nightly practice to fit the schedule of the passenger train Pocahontas, seen racing by in the background on raised tracks as an apparition veiled in steam.[1] The result is an image steeped in classic Americana, of time stopped in its tracks if only for a moment. **JLF**

1. "Photograph Record, no. 2002.07.02," O. Winston Link Museum, accessed December 23, 2011, http://linkmuseum.pastperfect-online.com/37479cgi/mweb.exe?request=record;id=9179F729-F8D4-4168-84FB-566219332816;type=102.

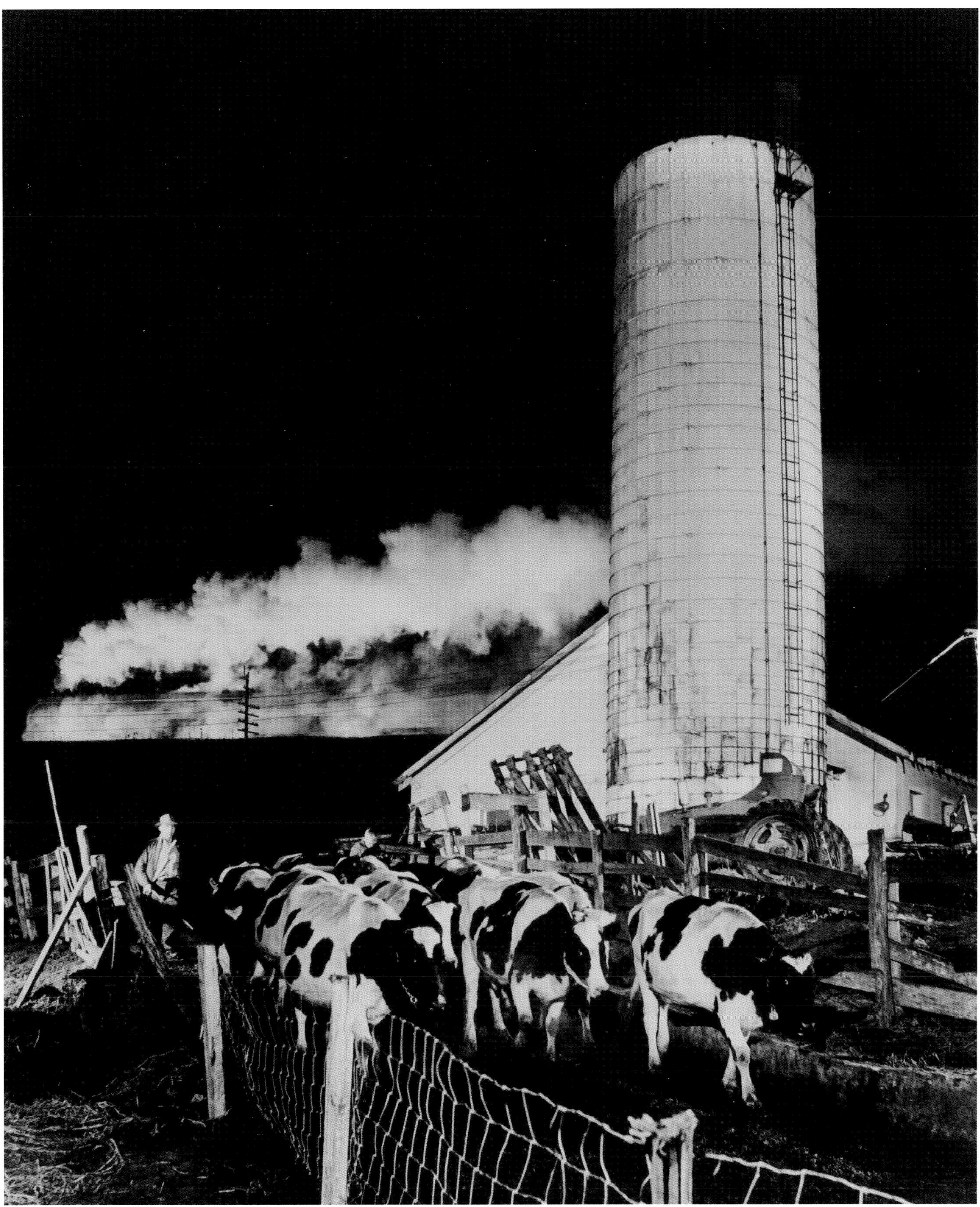

Minor White

American, 1908–1976

Juniper, Lake Tenaya, California, 1964
Gelatin silver print
Image: 28.3 × 23.2 cm (11 1/8 × 9 1/8 in); mount: 48.6 ×
40.3 cm (19 1/8 × 15 7/8 in)
Inscribed, on mount, lower left, in pencil: *1964*;
lower right: *Minor White*
University of Nebraska, Anna R. and Frank M. Hall
Charitable Trust, H-1132

Minor White was equally influential as an educator and writer as a photographer, devoting much of his career to teaching and cofounding the photography journal *Aperture* along with Ansel Adams and Dorothea Lange (cats. 35 and 78), among others, and serving as the magazine's editor until the year before his death. White came to photography while living in Oregon in the late 1930s, but his first real education took place after World War II while studying art history at Columbia University. There, White's introduction to Adams as well as other leading photographers such as Edward Weston (cat. 58) jumpstarted his career, but it was his personal introduction to Alfred Stieglitz's ideas that would provide him with a lifelong aesthetic challenge; later in life, he explained that Stieglitz "filled a hole there somehow."[1]

Throughout his career, White advanced and expanded on the theory of equivalents that Stieglitz (cat. 15) first developed through his photographs of clouds in the 1920s. Stieglitz endowed these works, which are considered some of the first intentionally abstract photographs, with poetic associations through titles like *Music* and *Songs of the Sky*, a quality that likely appealed to White's sensibility and his early experiments with poetry and the sonnet form.[2] In addition, Stieglitz placed special significance on the ambiguous sequencing of his photographs of clouds, creating artificial associations and often mixing different images into series and sets. He further subverted traditional exhibition orientation by hanging the photographs sideways or upside down, thus "destabilizing [the viewer's] relationship with nature in order to have you . . . think more about the feeling that the cloud formation evokes" than about the subject itself.[3] This idea of manipulating the photographic sequence beyond its order in the film roll had an equal impact on White's photographic process, and he often treated his and other artists' series in the same manner.

White's equivalents were often photographs of more mundane subjects, decontextualized architectural elements such as barns, doorways, and peeling paint: objects usually considered ordinary but made unique through their framing and the quality of light in which White photographed them. Through this project, for the photographer, these equivalents thus became imbued with greater significance, a feeling or emotionally symbolic impression that carried a sense of recognition with the viewer. Nature held a special significance for White and was a frequent subject of his work during his periods in Oregon and California (where he moved at Adams's invitation in 1948) and even after he returned to the East Coast in 1953. White used these fragmented images of natural elements—such as the section of a juniper tree here—and of rocks, sky, and water to explore his transcendental philosophies, preaching that his images would yield "specific suggestive powers that can direct the viewer into a specific and known feeling, state, or place within himself."[4] In this regard, White may have been directing his energies toward a resolution of his bisexuality, feelings that tormented him through much of his life, when such orientations were less socially acceptable. **BKR**

1. Minor White, interview by Paul Hill and Thomas Cooper, November 1975, in *Dialogue with Photography* (New York: Farrar, Straus and Giroux, 1979), 359. **2.** White went on to produce a portfolio of thirteen prints in the fall of 1947 that he titled *Song without Words*, an obvious homage to Stieglitz; see John Pultz, "Equivalence, Symbolism, and Minor White's Way into the Language of Photography," *Record of the Art Museum, Princeton University* 39, no. 1/2 (1980): 28–39. **3.** Sarah Greenough et al., *In Focus: Alfred Stieglitz: Photographs from the J. Paul Getty Museum* (Los Angeles: J. Paul Getty Trust, 1995), 132. **4.** Minor White, "Equivalence: The Perennial Trend," *PSA Journal* 29, no. 7 (1963): 17–21, reprinted in *Photographers on Photography*, ed. Nathan Lyons (Englewood Cliffs NJ: Prentice-Hall, 1966), 112.

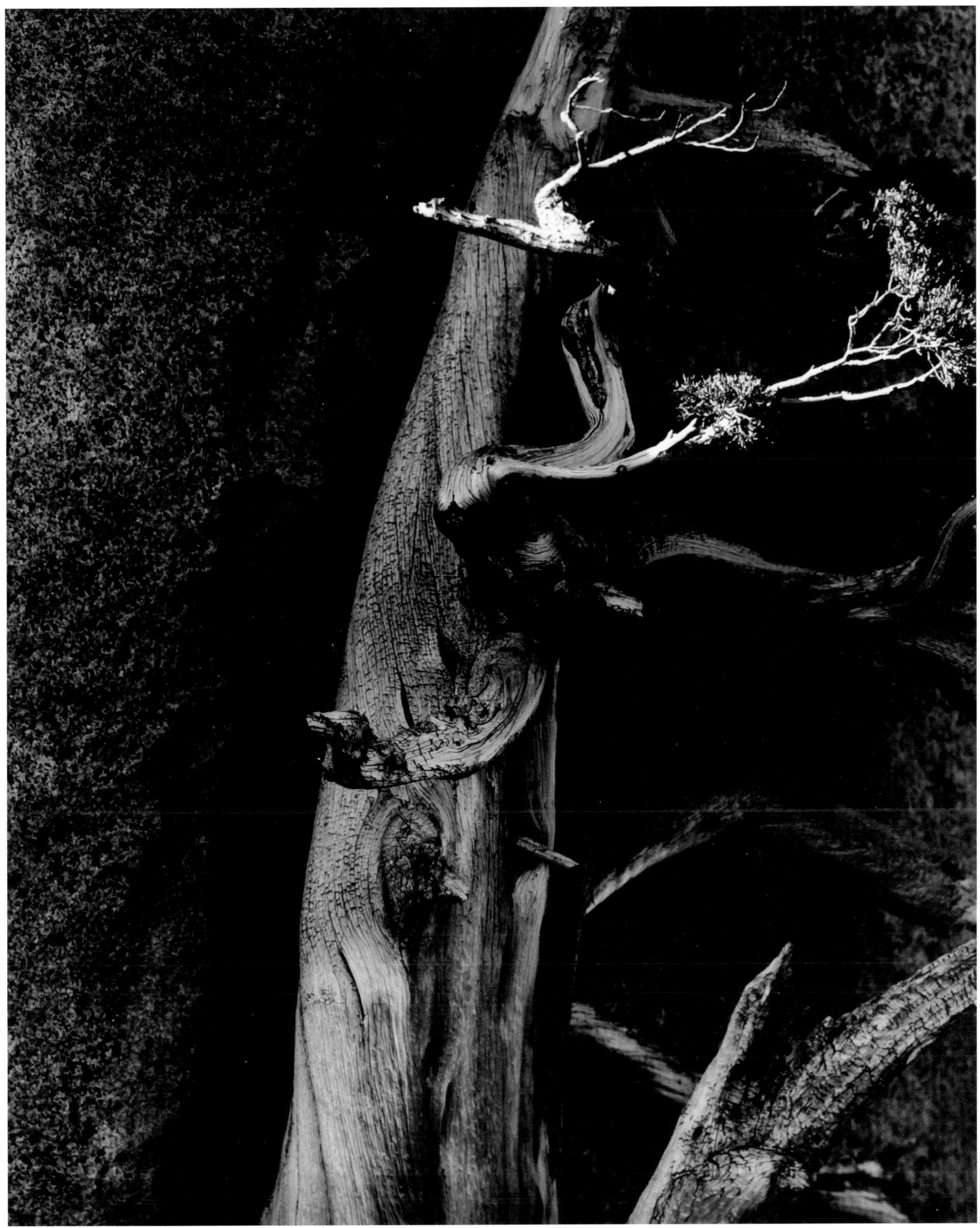

41

Mark Klett

American, born 1952

*Looking through the Snow Tunnel above Goat Lake,
Sawtooth Range, Idaho*, 1981
Gelatin silver print with silver ink
Image and sheet: 40.6 × 50.8 cm (16 × 20 in)
Inscribed, in image, along the bottom, in silver ink:
*Looking through the snow tunnel above Goat Lake:
Sawtooth Range, Idaho 8/9/81*; on verso, lower left,
in pencil: © *1981*; lower center: *Mark Klett*
University of Nebraska, Anna R. and Frank M. Hall
Charitable Trust, H-2723

Mark Klett views the land through the prism of time and culture. He refuses a timeless, Platonic standpoint, choosing instead to acknowledge his own presence in the scenes he records and the layers of history (and representations) they have accumulated. With both wit and grace, his landscape photographs acknowledge and pay homage to the achievements of his predecessors. Klett was trained to look analytically at the landscape: he received his BS in geology from Saint Lawrence University in Canton, New York. For three summers after graduation, he did fieldwork for the U.S. Geological Survey, assessing potential coal deposits in Montana and Wyoming. He was good at this work, but his truest interest lay in art. He received his MFA from the Visual Studies Workshop in Rochester and headed west to teach at Colorado Mountain College.

Klett's interest in engaging the history of landscape depiction was stimulated by the shared enthusiasm of his colleagues in Colorado, Ellen Manchester and JoAnn Verburg. The result was the Rephotographic Survey Project (RSP). Beginning in 1977, the RSP team found the exact vantage points used by William Henry Jackson (cat. 29), Timothy O'Sullivan, and other leading nineteenth-century photographers and made exactly matching modern views. The results spoke both to changes in the land over a century and to the interpretive choices of those earlier photographers. Through a simple but rigorous methodology, the RSP established a fascinating dialogue between past and present, representation and experience.[1]

This conceptual process also informs Klett's work outside the RSP. The artist is particularly intrigued by O'Sullivan, whose photographs from the 1860s and early 1870s often include evidence of his own presence: his campsite, dark tent, traveling companions, or wagon. O'Sullivan's images are both factual and self-reflexive: he depicts his surroundings while foregrounding his own place in the landscape. This union of objective and subjective inclinations lies at the heart of Klett's art. Characteristically, *Looking through the Snow Tunnel* incorporates signs of its own making, which include the uneven margins of the black-and-white Polaroid negative and the diaristic title written in silver ink on the print's surface. Like O'Sullivan, Klett included his traveling companions in the view—here, a friend with his dog. The ordinariness of these figures is both telling and deliberate; while O'Sullivan was part of a scientific team in little-known territory, Klett is a modern-day traveler, hiker, and artist.

Extending O'Sullivan's example, Klett finds his own way to emphasize the photographic act. By looking outward from the recesses of an ice cave, he suggests the fundamental components of the picture-making process: a landscape view that passes through an aperture and is captured in a darkened imaging chamber (or camera obscura). The resulting image embraces both the pleasures of a fleeting moment and an entire rich history of representation. **KFD**

1. See Mark Klett et al., *Second View: The Rephotographic Survey* (Albuquerque: University of New Mexico Press, 1984); and Klett and Kyle Bajakian, *Third Views, Second Sights: A Rephotographic Survey of the American West* (Santa Fe: Museum of New Mexico Press, 2004).

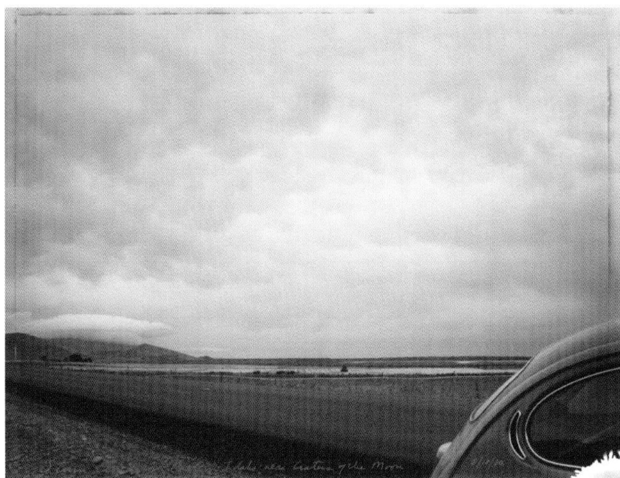

Mark Klett. *Storm Clouds over Eastern Idaho: Near Craters of the Moon*, 1980. Gelatin silver print; 40.8 × 50.5 cm (16 1/16 × 19 7/8 in). University of Nebraska, Olga N. Sheldon Acquisition Trust, U-3880.11.

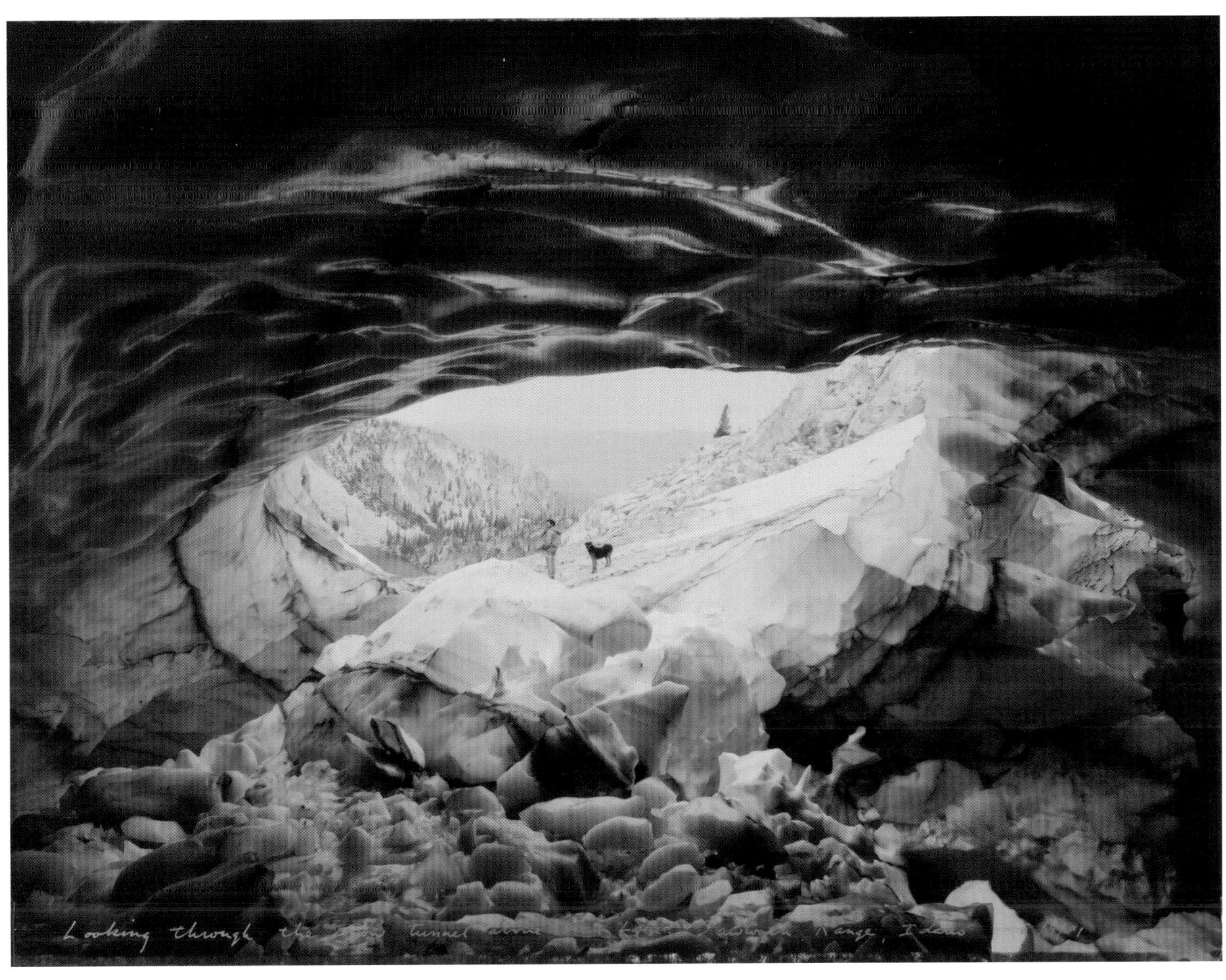
Looking through the ice tunnel across the Sawtooth Range, Idaho

42

John Pfahl

American, born 1939

Four Corners Power Plant (morning), Farmington, New Mexico (from the series *Power Places*) 1982; printed 2011
Digital print
Image: 33 × 45.7 cm (13 × 18 in); sheet: 43.2 × 55.9 cm (17 × 22 in)
Inscribed, on verso, lower center, in black ink: *Four Corners Power Plant (morning), Farmington, New Mexico 6/15 © Pfahl October 1982*
University of Nebraska, Anna R. and Frank M. Hall Charitable Trust, H-2593

Throughout his career, John Pfahl has chosen landscape as his primary subject. He holds a personal attachment to place, and, for him, the term *landscape* encompasses both nature and the human impact on it. His innovations in the genre have been significant.

Pfahl learned the techniques of photography—including the color darkroom—as an undergraduate at Syracuse University. He then worked in commercial journalism and advertising, which made him realize he wanted to pursue the medium as a fine artist. He perfected his color technique after returning to Syracuse for an MFA in 1966.

In addition to honing his darkroom skills, Pfahl also studied photography's history and contemporary developments, availing himself of the collections and community around the George Eastman House and the Visual Studies Workshop in Rochester. He admired the canonical landscapes of Ansel Adams (cat. 35), Eliot Porter, and other leading figures, but by the 1970s, this tradition seemed to have reached a dead end. Inspired by the alternative applications of photography put forward by conceptual artists in the 1960s, Pfahl first made a name for himself with a series called *Altered Landscapes* (1974–78), in which he quoted classic compositions but inserted objects and markings so as to cause confusion between the perspectival image of the world and the flat surface of the print.[1]

With his next project, *Power Places*, the artist returned to straight photography and raised the stakes to consider the impact of humankind on the environment. From 1981 to 1984 he traveled the country to capture coal, hydroelectric, and nuclear power plants; oil refineries; solar and wind stations; and so forth.[2] These pictures show the structures in the context of the landscape. Since many of them are located in remote areas of incredible beauty, they can acquire a luster and naturalness that mask their destructive potential. The 1979 partial meltdown of a nuclear power plant in Three Mile Island, near Harrisburg, Pennsylvania, is perhaps the most terrifying example . . . , and likely on Pfahl's mind as he assembled his series shortly thereafter.

The facility depicted in *Four Corners Power Plant* is one of the nation's largest coal-fired generating stations, opened in 1963 and still operating today. Built on Navajo land in northwestern New Mexico, it supplies power to Arizona, California, New Mexico, and Texas. In a pair of photographs, one taken in the morning and the other in the evening, Pfahl celebrates the beauty of the high desert. Yet this landscape has been damaged by the plant's emissions: ozone and mercury pollute the region's air and water.

Ironically, state regulators have long been unable to mitigate these effects because of the plant's location. Traditional Native American beliefs about the sanctity of the land have been sadly compromised by the contemporary need for jobs. This conflict between environmental preservation and technological progress dates back to the Industrial Revolution. As Pfahl suggests, neither impulse is wholly good or evil; the artist's task is to pay attention and to act when imbalances begin to develop. **BS**

1. *Altered Landscapes: The Photographs of John Pfahl*, introduction by Peter C. Bunnell (San Francisco: Friends of Photography in association with Robert Freidus Gallery, 1981). **2.** Kathleen McCarthy Gauss, *John Pfahl: Power Places*, exhibition catalog (Los Angeles: Los Angeles County Museum of Art, 1985), 74.

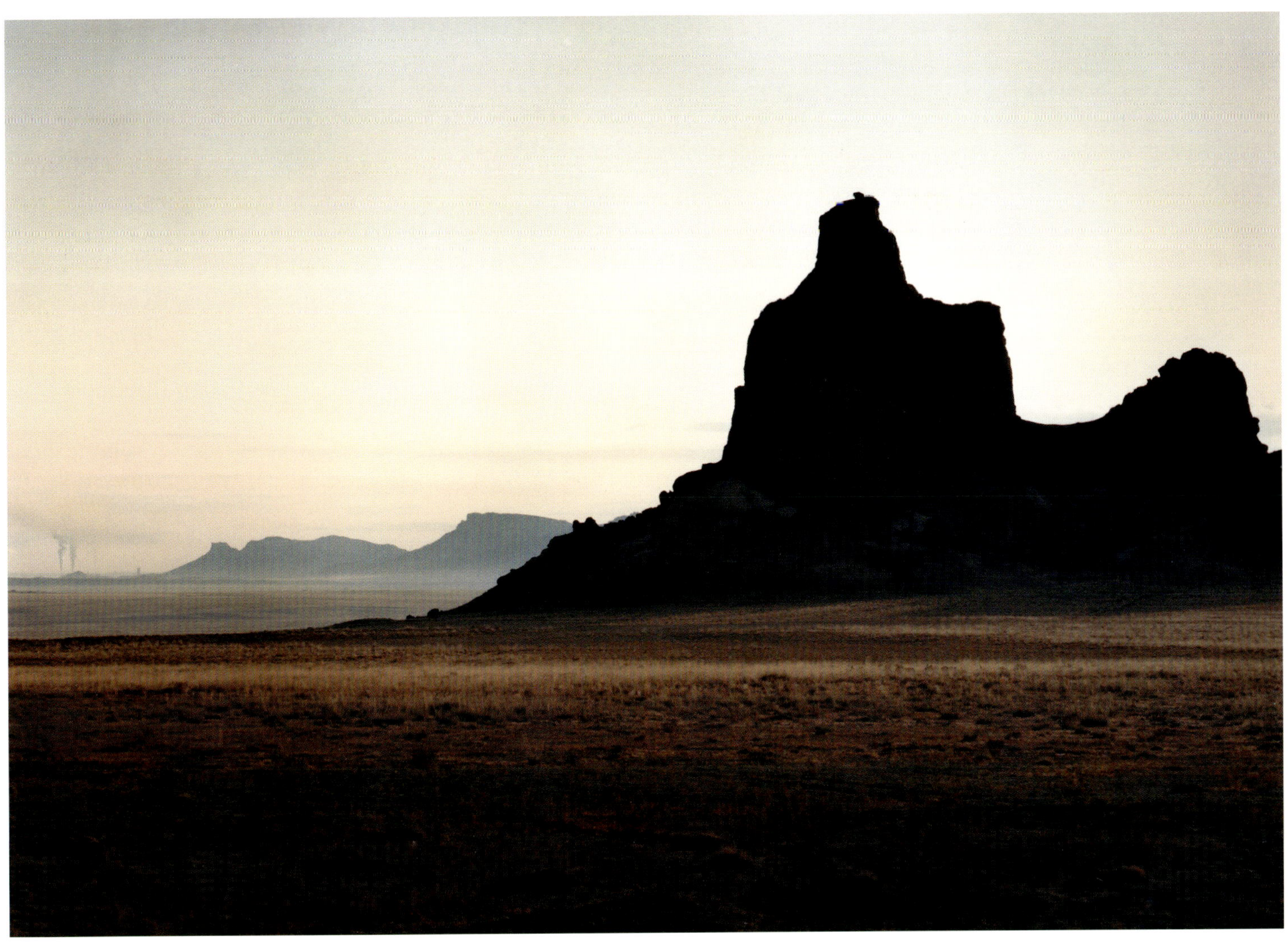

43

Richard Misrach

American, born 1949

Desert Fire #1, Burning Palms (from "The Fires"
in the series *Desert Cantos*), 1983
Ektacolor chromogenic print
Image: 46.4 × 58.4 cm (18 ¼ × 23 in); sheet: 50.8 × 61 cm
(20 × 24 in)
Inscribed, lower left, in black ink: *#5 DESERT FIRE #1
(Burning Palms)*; lower right: © *Richard Misrach 1983*
University of Nebraska, Anna R. and Frank M. Hall
Charitable Trust, H-2616

Richard Misrach was one of the leaders in the revival of color photography in the 1970s, most famed for his landscapes of the desert Southwest. In this regard, he is an heir to previous generations of landscape photographers who attempted not only to celebrate and showcase the American landscape but also to document its changes through both human intervention and natural disasters. Unlike Ansel Adams, William Henry Jackson, and Isaiah West Taber (cats. 35, 29, and 31), however, Misrach did not seek out the grandest, most sublime, or most frequently traveled sites; instead, he gravitated toward the quieter, lesser-known areas of southeastern California, northwestern Utah, and Nevada. A California native, Misrach explains his fascination with the American desert as the "strange sensation of being a small figure in a vast landscape. . . . It's the heat, the feel of the earth, the rich solitude and the silence, and the remarkable scale of everything that makes being there so deeply fulfilling."[1]

In 1979 Misrach began his expansive project of recording the destruction of the desert landscape, continuing the undertaking for several decades. He considers each of his desert photographs as independent yet part of a larger, greater effort that he divided into thematic groupings that he documented and numbered as they were completed. The series takes its name from the *canto*, a term that refers to a subsection of an extended song or poem; every one of Misrach's cantos might address a distinct subject, be produced over a different amount of time, and contain its own number of works. By 1992 the artist had completed fourteen fully defined cantos, each addressing a particular aspect of the landscape. "The Highway" and "The Terrain," for example, deal with transportation infrastructure, including freeways and railroads;

"The Flood" shows towns inundated by California's Salton Sea; "The Event" addresses entertainment and tourism, as onlookers watch a car race; and both "The War (Bravo 20)" and "Project W-47 (The Secret)" document the surreal, war-scarred landscapes of abandoned nuclear test fields.

Desert Fire #1, Burning Palms is the first photograph in "The Fires," a canto that deals with the effects of the scorched desert and the difficulty of extinguishing blazes in an arid climate. The image combines both of Misrach's lifelong interests: it is a symbol of environmental destruction, whether human-made or natural, and also a striking exploration of various tonal values. The flaming palms just to the right of center are among the most lurid colors in the artist's oeuvre, while the muted, subtle tones of the desert foreground and the horizon blend together and shift in the light, continuing the inquiry into the relationship of ground and sky that characterizes a number of the *Desert Cantos*.[2] Misrach himself has acknowledged that his earliest cantos, including "The Fires," are less overtly political than his later ones, functioning as "more or less aesthetic metaphors."[3] Nonetheless, the unsettling effects of environmental damage are present in both overt and less obvious ways. As Reyner Banham has pointed out in relation to Misrach's work, the art of landscape photography itself is a "pollution of . . . virgin purity" in which "human artifacts . . . can be as durable as metal or glass, and as threatening to fragile ecologies."[4] **BKR**

1. Richard Misrach, interview by Melissa Harris, March 1992, in *Violent Legacies: Three Cantos*, by Richard Misrach (New York: Aperture, 1992), 84. 2. For examination of Misrach's photographs, see Kathleen McCarthy Gauss, *New American Photography*, exhibition catalog (Los Angeles: Los Angeles County Museum of Art, 1985), 29. 3. Misrach, *Violent Legacies*, 90. 4. Reyner Banham, "The Man-Mauled Desert," in *Desert Cantos*, by Richard Misrach and Reyner Banham (Albuquerque: University of New Mexico Press, 1987), 5.

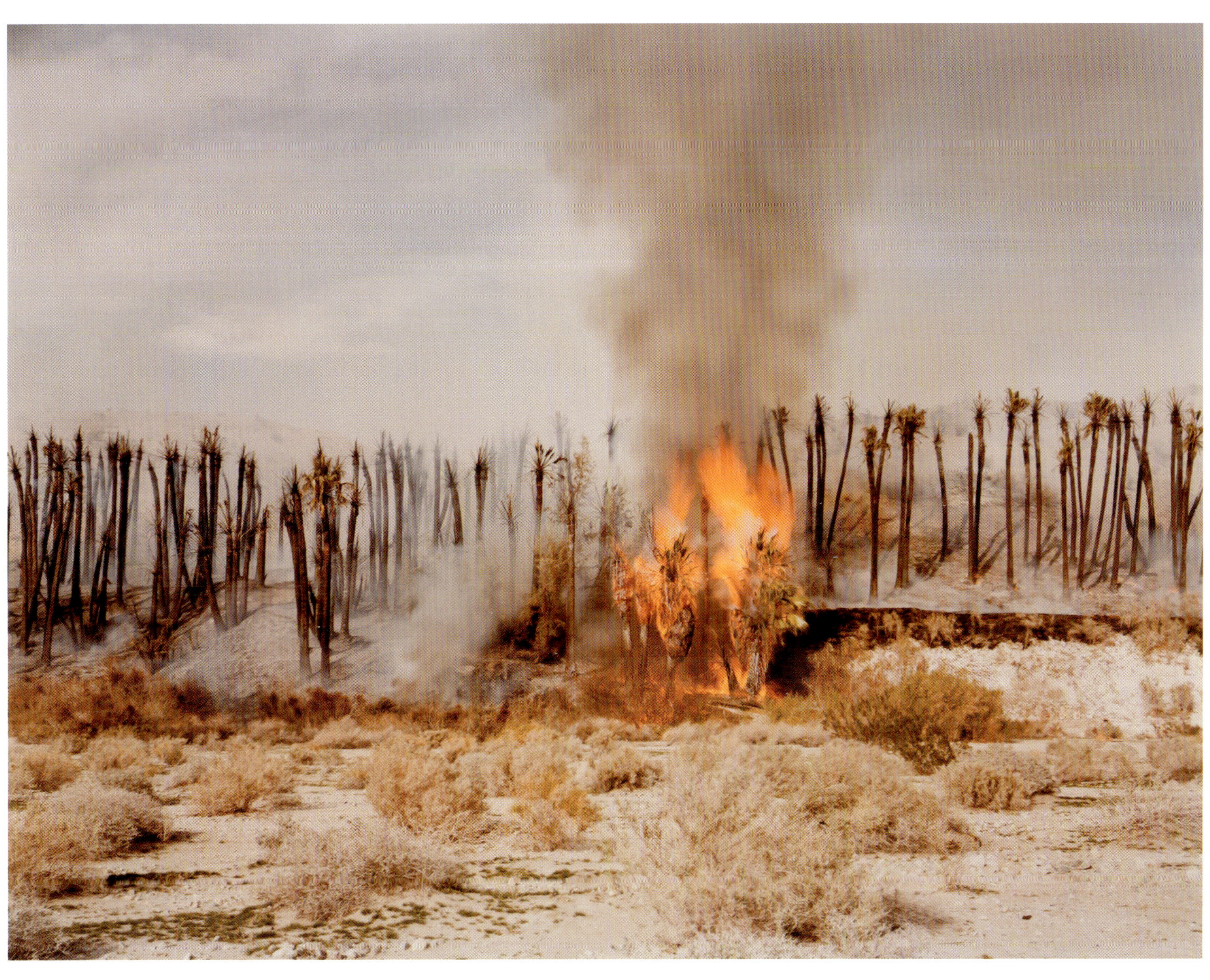

44

Dana Fritz

American, born 1970

Painted Leaves and Dripping Moss, Lied Jungle
(from the series *Terraria Gigantica*), 2007
Archival pigment print
Image: 40.6 × 61 cm (16 × 24 in); sheet: 43.2 × 63.5 cm
(17 × 25 in)
Inscribed, on verso, lower left, in pencil: *"Painted Leaves
and Dripping Moss, Lied Jungle,"* 2007;
lower center: 3/3; lower right: *Dana B Fritz*
University of Nebraska, gift of the artist, U-5618

Dana Fritz cites her childhood on her grandparents' farm
and in her parents' garden as formative experiences: "I was
never the kid . . . climbing trees or jumping in the river, but
I could tell when I was on the farm that land was being used
differently. My experience with nature was always controlled
by culture—it was structured, delineated."[1] Equally inspiring
was her time spent studying with renowned photographer
Mark Klett (cat. 41) at Arizona State University and her subsequent investigation of desert plants and the historic uses
of vegetation. This interest in the intersection of nature and
culture and what it tells us about society has been at the heart
of the artist's work from her early series *Garden Views*, in
which she photographed formal gardens—themselves controlled and miniaturized natural environments—in Europe,
Japan, and the United States.

In her recent series *Terraria Gigantica*, Fritz extended this
dialogue about artifice and truth by photographing and researching three of the world's largest indoor landscape complexes: Biosphere 2 outside of Tucson; the Lied Jungle and
the Desert Dome at Omaha's Henry Doorly Zoo; and the
Eden Project in Cornwall, England. While she originally intended to depict people interacting with these settings, her
examination of all three spaces led her to appreciate their distinct missions and historical roles. Each, for example, may be
seen as the offspring of a particular idea current at the time
of its creation. The Lied Jungle is an immersion landscape
intended to unite animals and visitors within a simulated

natural habitat; Biosphere 2 is the product of the space race
and the dream of intergalactic colonization; and the Eden
Project aims to redevelop and preserve nature, a reflection
of our contemporary concern with conservation. All sites are
now focused on education and research. Despite the fact that
these creations are closed, environmentally controlled systems, the artist has grown to reject the dichotomy between
humanity and nature, arguing that our interventions have
altered the planet to the extent that "using 'wilderness' as the
reference point for nature is not useful to move forward."[2]

Fritz divides her photographs from the *Terraria Gigantica* series into three different types—vistas, thresholds, and
fragments—that intersect but also present a definite trajectory, reflecting the overall ideas and purposes of the locations
she explores. Vistas represent the larger view of the environment with a clear reference to place (see below); thresholds—which include the majority of Fritz's images—refer to
liminal spaces that reveal the intersection of the artificial
and the natural; and fragments capture small, detailed areas
that often elide context.[3] In *Painted Leaves*, the artist photographed a corner of the Lied Jungle where moss, dripping
down a concrete wall, breaks the illusion of the atmospheric
painted landscape in the background; at right, the intrusion
of the balcony with its decaled glass also interrupts the magical spell of the exotic rain forest. **BKR**

1. Quoted in Debora Kuan, "It's a Living: Dana Fritz," *Photo District News*,
April 1, 2008; for the online edition, see http://www.pdnonline.com/pdn/
pdnedu/Its-A-Living-Dana—346.shtml. **2.** "Phototalks: Dana Fritz," interview
by Steve Bisson, January 14, 2011, *Urbanautica*, http://www.urbanautica.com/
post/2742824122/fritz-phototalks. **3.** Dana Fritz, interview by Brandon K.
Ruud, November 29, 2011, transcript, curatorial files, Sheldon Museum of Art.

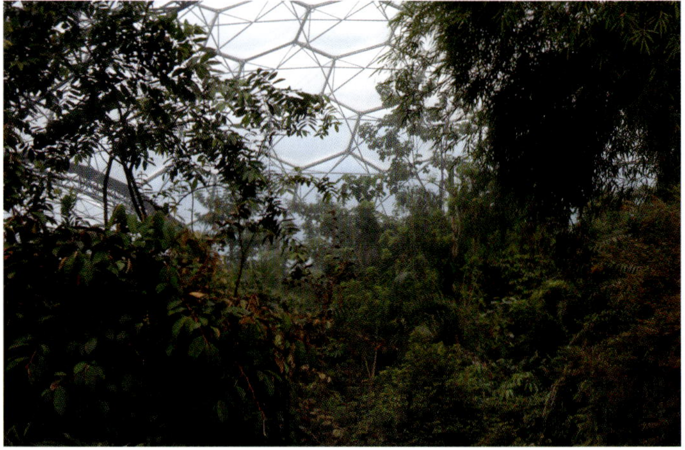

Dana Fritz. *Humid Tropics, Eden Project*, 2009. Archival pigment print; 40.6 × 61 cm (16 × 24 in). University of Nebraska,
gift of the artist, U-5619

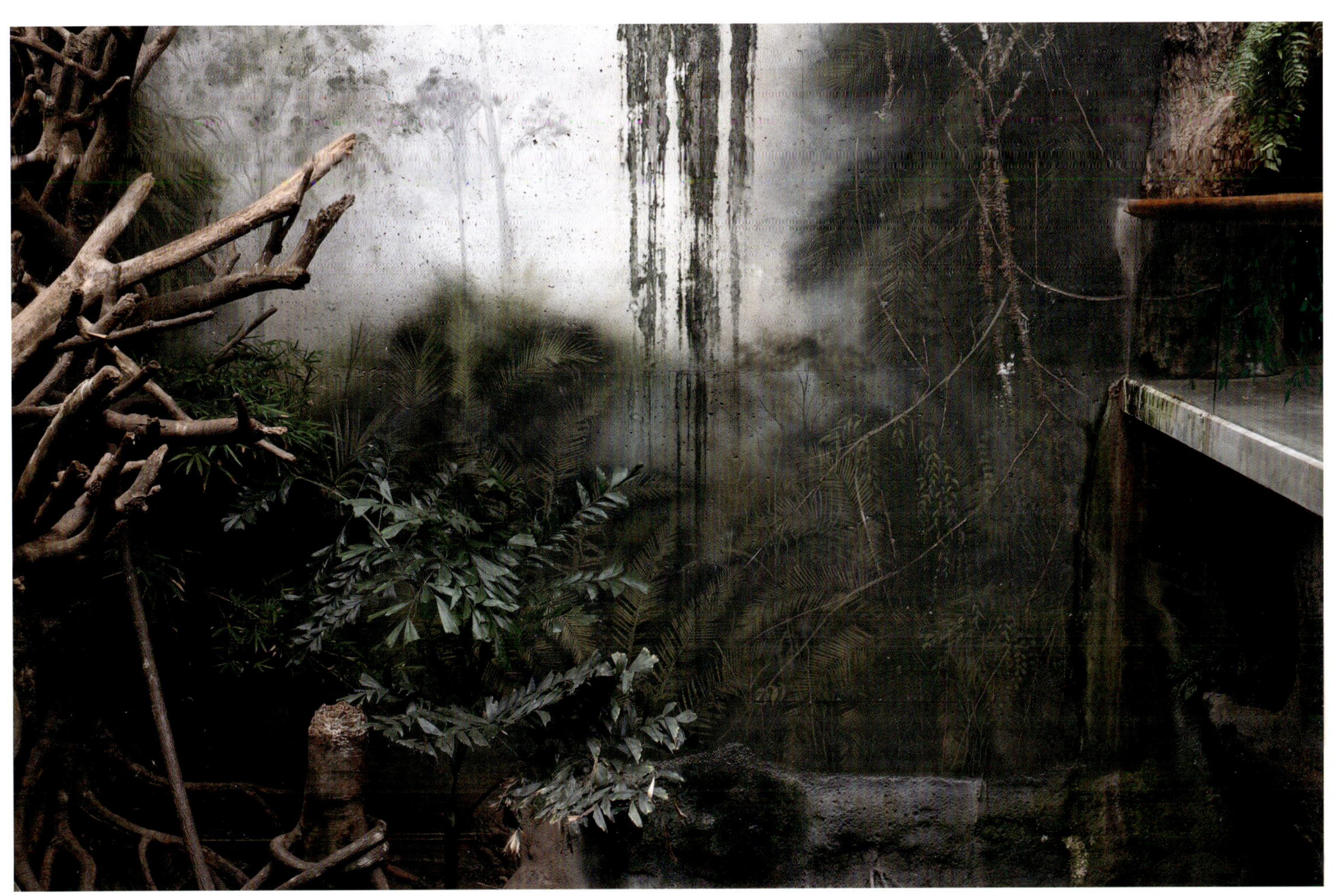

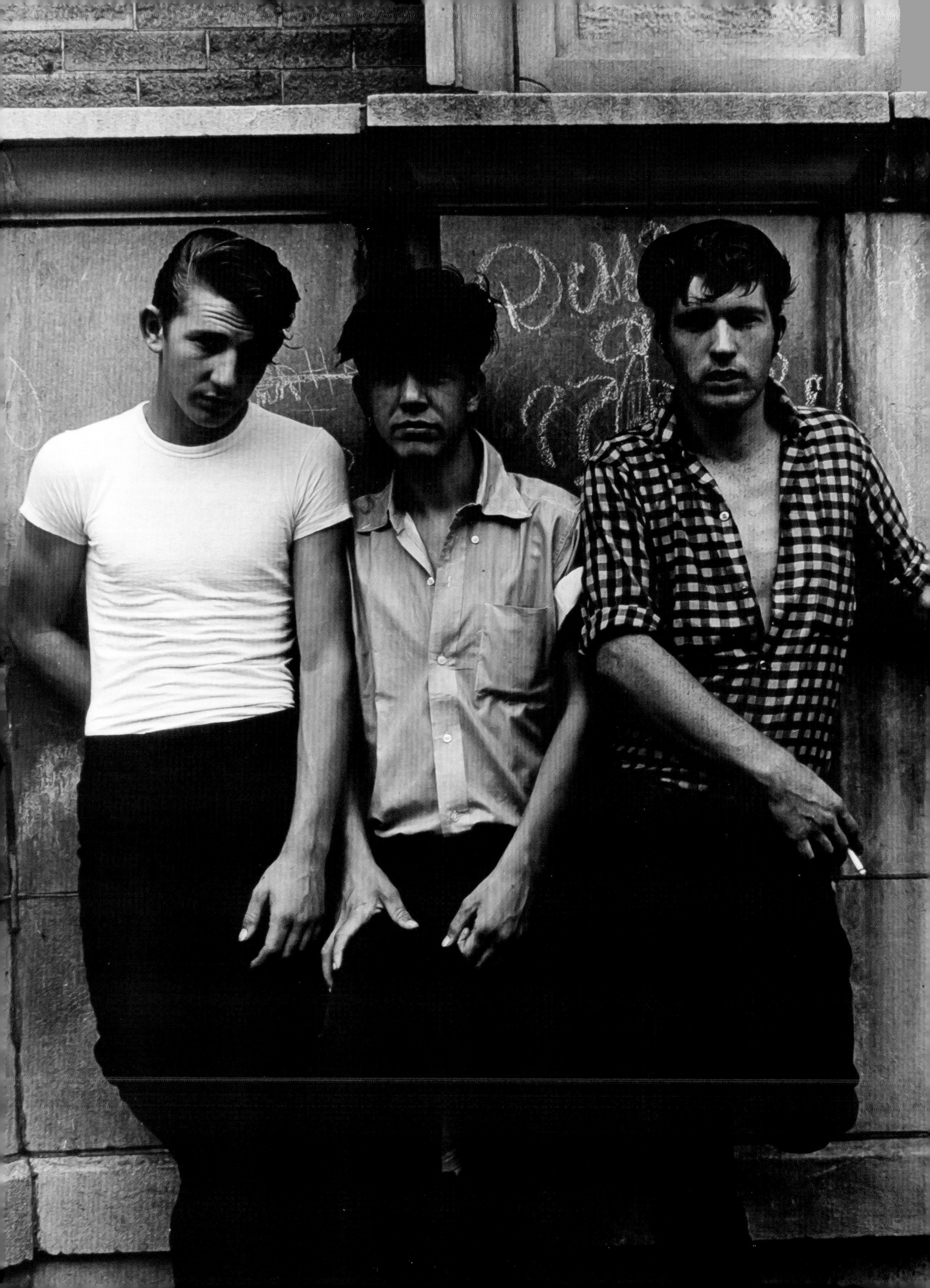

RITES OF PASSAGE

Ritual events and personal milestones are themselves encounters that mark our transition from one stage of life to another. Since many of these rites are personal, photography's wide use makes it especially well poised to document and share them, providing evidence along the way of both private and public transformations. In some cases, these moments can seem routine—even monotonous—but, placed within their own cultural contexts, they offer glimpses into the mores and values of their particular time and place.

Emilio Amero's dancing bride (cat. 47), for example, seems at first glance to take part in a ritual common to many societies. Yet her performance is specific to her culture and location, and the artist's motivation was largely to capture and convey a special sense of Mexican national identity. In another example, Lauren Greenfield's photograph of a young woman recovering from a recent rhinoplasty (cat. 52) shows a minor medical procedure as an important rite in terms of the subject's Los Angeles home, her social milieu, and her own self-worth. At the same time, Roy DeCarava's *Graduation* (cat. 48) challenges and subverts traditional ideas and images associated with such occasions, highlighting—like Greenfield's photograph—the roles class, race, and socioeconomic status play in the meaning of our rituals and traditions.

Adolescence itself is a rite of passage, filled with a bewildering number of firsts that mark the passage of time, changing us and moving us to life's next phase. Indeed, it is often regarded as a liminal stage, a gray area between childhood and adulthood, a time of innocence that is also fraught with peril. Perhaps no society understood this better—and expressed it so exhaustively in photographs—than Victorian England. Aroused by dreams of a preindustrial age, artists and ideologues created a cult of innocence evoked, as critic John Ruskin put it, by "the large eyes of children, in perpetual wonder."[1] Julia Margaret Cameron's photograph of Alice Liddell as Alethea (cat. 45) speaks to this obsession. The inspiration for Lewis Carroll's *Alice* books, the subject sported a biography that underscores the perceived dangers of childhood; so does Cameron's image, which positions Liddell amid vines and flowers, themselves symbols of the cycle of life, of emergence and extinction.

Diane Arbus's photograph of a young boy with a toy hand grenade (cat. 49) affirms the instability of childhood innocence for a contemporary American audience. Playacting and mimicking adult behavior are familiar routines, but in Arbus's hands, the boy's grenade and hostile expression remind us of the all-too-quick transition to maturity. Similarly, the candy cigarette in the hands of Sally Mann's young daughter Jessie (cat. 53) raises similar issues about the appropriate age and time for that particular journey. Only around seven years old when the photograph was taken, the girl startles us with her worldliness, provoking even the most jaded viewers among us to want to throw their arms around her, protecting her innocence and continuing the work of the Victorians. At the same time, in Danny Lyon's photograph of young men posturing and preening, working hard to prove their rebelliousness (opposite and cat. 50), a half-smoked cigarette becomes a marker of a successful transition to manhood. In Arbus's and Mann's photographs, these props are only plastic and candy; they gain their emotional and visual power by foreshadowing the link between adulthood and self-destruction that Lyon's image makes explicit.

1. John Ruskin, *The Fall*, vol. 3 of *The Stones of Venice* (London: Smith, Elder and Company, 1853), 52, quoted in Maria Morris Hambourg, "Picturing Victorian Britain," in *The Waking Dream: Photography's First Century*, by Hambourg et al., exhibition catalog (New York: Metropolitan Museum of Art/Harry N. Abrams, 1993), 6.

45

Julia Margaret Cameron
English, born India, 1815–1879

Alethea, 1872
Albumen print
Image: 32.4 × 23.2 cm (12 3/4 × 9 1/8 in); sheet: 46.5 × 35.9 cm (18 5/16 × 14 1/8 in)
Inscribed, on mount, lower center, in pen: *Alathea* [*sic*]; lower right: *Study of Alice Liddell*
University of Nebraska, Anna R. and Frank M. Hall Charitable Trust, H-1288

By the time she took this image in the early 1870s, Julia Margaret Cameron had established herself as a professional artistic photographer, actively advancing her career in an effort to support her family's diminishing finances. She took inspiration from legendary and religious figures as well as Old Master paintings and Pre-Raphaelite art and literature; her models were family, friends, and neighbors who visited her home on the Isle of Wight. The model for *Alethea* was Alice Liddell, who has long been regarded as the inspiration for Charles Dodgson's *Alice's Adventures in Wonderland*, published in 1865 under the pseudonym Lewis Carroll. Liddell, in fact, was accustomed to posing for the camera from a young age: Dodgson photographed her in various sentimental guises in the late 1850s and early 1860s, when he was tutoring at Oxford and became a close friend of her family.[1] In the early 1870s, the Liddells began renting a house near the Camerons' home, Dembola Lodge. Their Oxford connections gave them easy entrée into the Camerons' cultivated social circles, and Alice's experience in front of the camera—not to mention her fabled childhood—likely made her an ideal subject for Cameron's artfully staged photographs.

Scholars have proposed several identifications for the allegorical figure Liddell impersonates here. In ancient Greek, *alethea* means "true" or "truthfulness," a word whose resonances would have been appreciated by Cameron and her circle of friends. Alice's father, Henry George Liddell, the dean of Christ Church and vice chancellor of Oxford University, himself contributed to the 1843 Greek-English lexicon; that book lists *alethea* as "true, sincere, truthful, frank, honest, real, and actual," suggesting the term's many emphatic meanings for Cameron's Victorian audience.[2] Others have equated Alethea with Pomona, the Roman goddess of abundance and fruitfulness; the same year she took this photograph, Cameron made a frontal, half-length view of Liddell as Pomona surrounded by similar plants and vines.[3] In that image, however, Liddell is imposing and striking, gazing directly at the viewer with her hand on her hip. Here, conversely, she is wistful and slightly obscured, the tendrils of her hair blending in with the trailing flora against which she is silhouetted. Taken together, these two views evoke nature's cyclical routine, from emergence to profusion to demise. They may also refer to the twenty-year-old Liddell's own transition to womanhood from the precarious, often dangerous state of childhood outlined in Dodgson's books. **BKR**

1. For examples of some of these photographs, see Graham Ovendon, *Pre-Raphaelite Photography* (London: Academy Editions, 1972), 73–74, 87, plates 56–57, 73. **2.** Sylvia Wolf, "Alethea," in *Julia Margaret Cameron's Women*, by Sylvia Wolf et al., exhibition catalog (Chicago: Art Institute of Chicago; New Haven CT: Yale University Press, 1998), 228. **3.** Jeremy Howard, *Whisper of the Muse: The World of Julia Margaret Cameron*, exhibition catalog (London: Colnaghi, 1990), 92. For reproductions of Cameron's *Pomona*, see Mike Weaver, *Julia Margaret Cameron, 1815–1879* (Boston: Little, Brown, 1984), 123; and Wolf et al., *Julia Margaret Cameron's Women*, cat. 9.

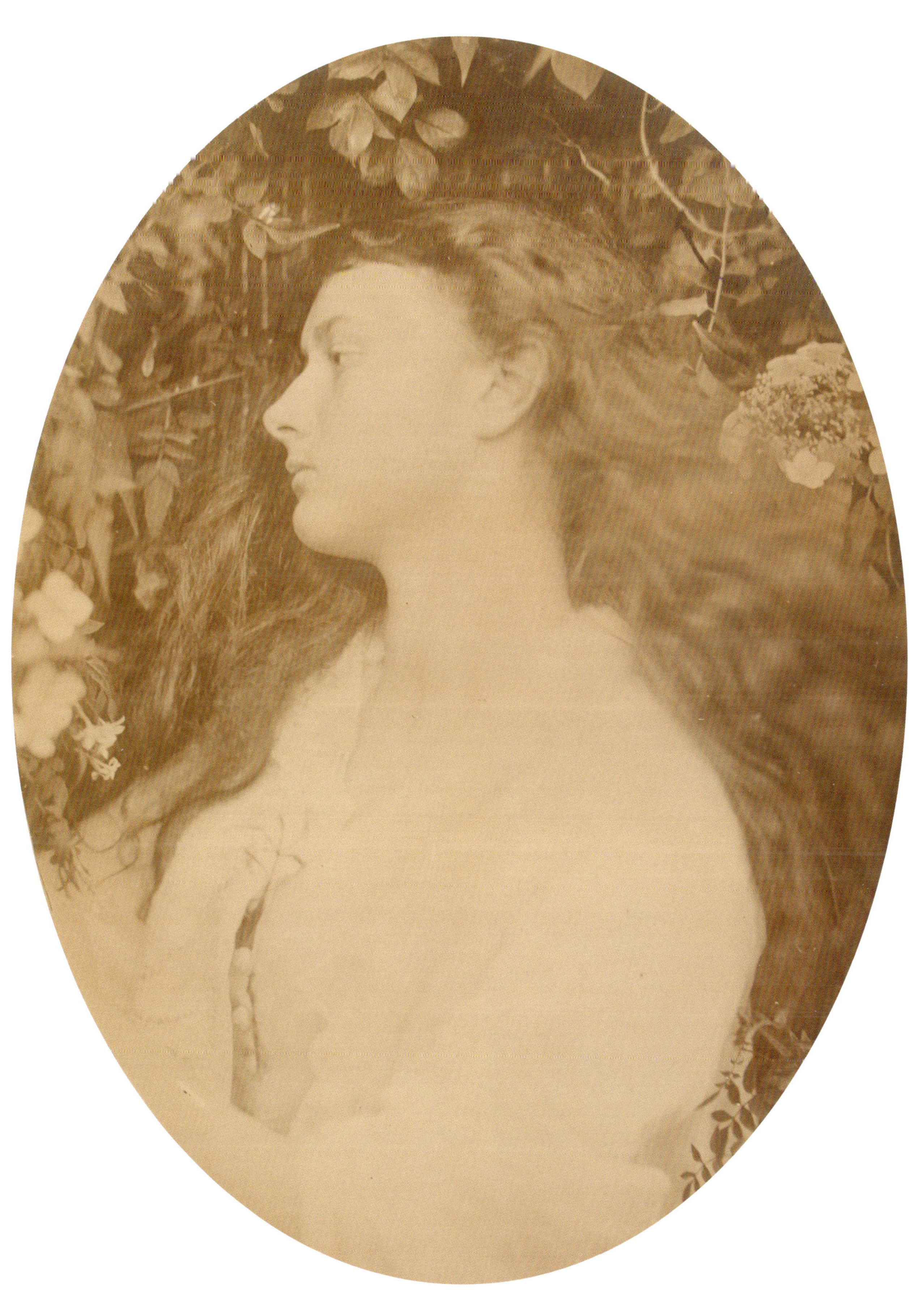

46

Gertrude Käsebier

American, 1852–1934

Sunshine in the House (The Clarence White Family in Maine), 1913
Gelatin silver print toned with gum bichromate
Image: 34.3 × 26.7 cm (13 1/2 × 10 1/2 in); sheet: 35.6 × 27.9 cm (14 × 11 in)
University of Nebraska, Anna R. and Frank M. Hall Charitable Trust, H-1295

Gertrude Käsebier, who did not begin studying art until after she had raised three children, used it as a means of escaping her loveless marriage and achieving a measure of autonomy. She initially trained in painting and drawing with Arthur Wesley Dow at Brooklyn's Pratt Institute, embracing his Japanese-inspired philosophy of flattened, asymmetrical pictorial space. Käsebier abandoned painting for photography but applied Dow's methods to her pictures and, in the early years of the twentieth century, became a founder and active member of the Photo-Secession. Led primarily by Alfred Stieglitz (cat. 15), the group promoted photography as a fine art and advanced the tenets of pictorialism, which sought to embrace the same artistic principles as painting and etching.

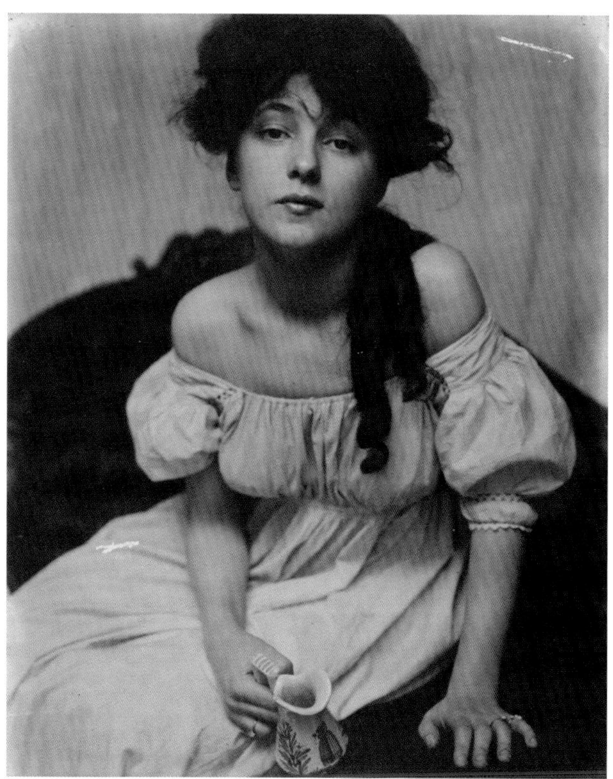

Gertrude Käsebier. *Portrait (Miss N.)*, 1902, printed 1967. Gelatin silver print toned with gum bichromate; 34.1 × 26.8 cm (13 7/16 × 10 9/16 in). University of Nebraska, Anna R. and Frank M. Hall Charitable Trust, H-1294.

Like many female photographers of the time, Käsebier became highly praised for her images of women, especially those that celebrated the virtues of motherhood. This reaction was perhaps a response to the modernity and mechanization of the camera itself. Indeed, in a 1907 article tellingly titled "Photography as an Emotional Art," critic Mary Fanton Roberts, writing under the name Giles Edgerton, emphasized Käsebier's intuition and artistry over her intellect: "Of the usual expressions of technical methods and the usual studio talk Mrs. Käsebier cares nothing, and knows but little. Her interest is not centered in the mechanical end. She knows it, and uses it with supreme skill, but with the unconscious skill with which a musician plays or a great painter wields the brush."[1] Dismissing any interest Käsebier might have had in form, Roberts went on to commend the artist's sensitivity to her subjects—especially the "quality of world sympathy" that Roberts believed expressed itself most "sincerely and convincingly" in Käsebier's "photographs of Motherhood."[2]

Despite these pronouncements, Käsebier's *Sunshine in the House (The Clarence White Family in Maine)* is a masterpiece of composition and form as well as of artistic sensitivity. Here, she posed photographer Clarence White, his wife, Jane, and their three children in the home of F. Holland Day, another noted practitioner of the art. Sun shines through the doorway and window, illuminating some individuals and throwing others into shadow. A diagonal sunbeam on the floor leads the viewer's eye into the composition, contrasting the strong vertical lines of the door and window with the horizontal ones of the ceiling beams; the sunbeam also acts as a symbolic barrier separating the two older sons from their younger brother and parents.[3] Despite the group dynamics in play, Jane is the clear focus: light strikes her face and upper body as she shifts her head toward the viewer. Her emotional distance from her family, who engage one another through eye contact or touch, introduces a narrative element and psychological depth to the work; we notice the papers in her hand and wonder whether they are the source of her detachment. **BKR**

1. Giles Edgerton [Mary Fanton Roberts], "Photography as an Emotional Art: A Study of the Work of Gertrude Käsebier," *Craftsman* 12, no. 1 (April 1907): 90. **2.** Edgerton, "Photography." **3.** Barbara L. Michaels, *Gertrude Käsebier: The Photographer and Her Photographs* (New York: Harry N. Abrams, 1992), 148.

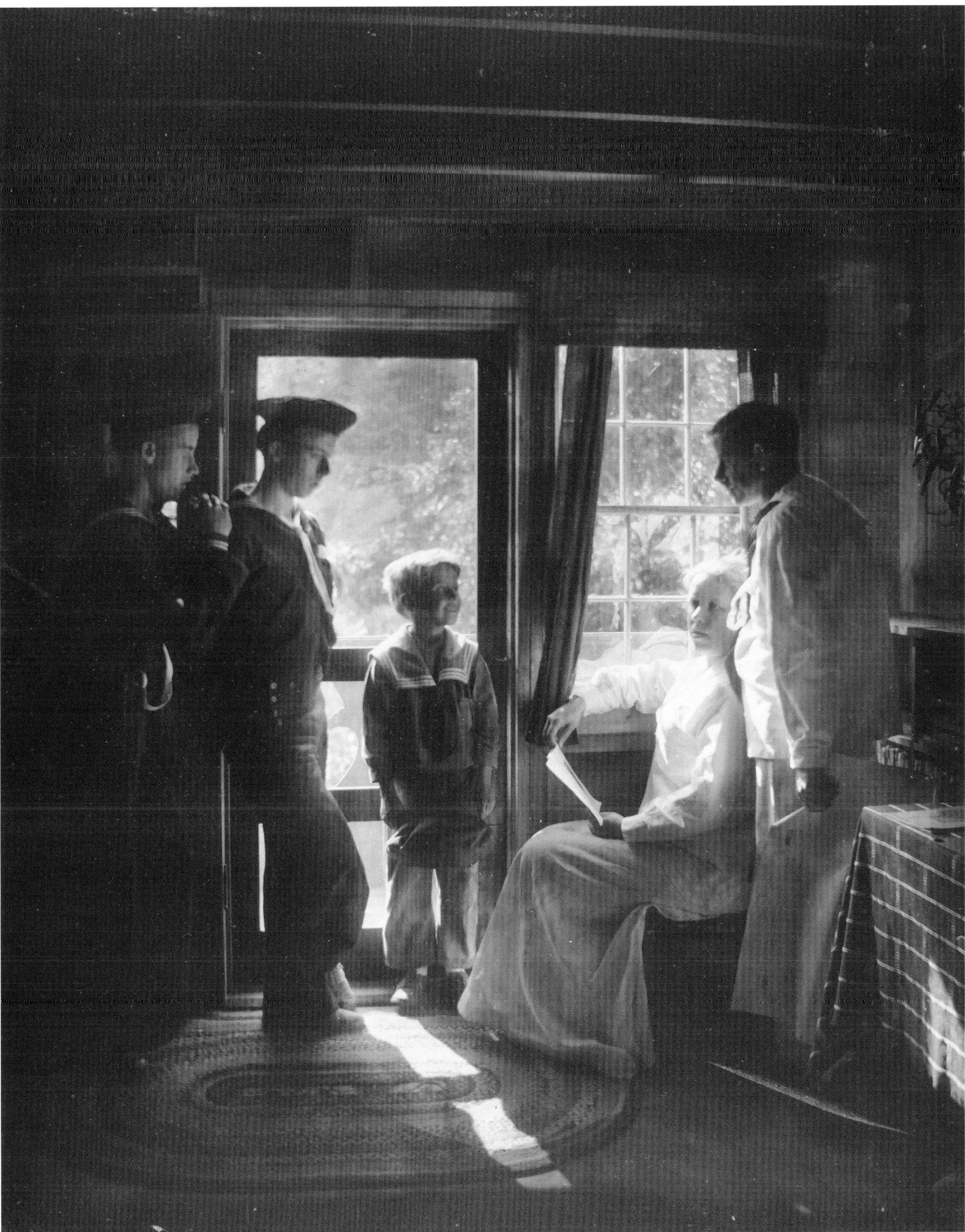

47

Emilio Amero

American, born Mexico, 1901–1976

Bride Dancing the Zandunga (from the portfolio *Amero Picture Book*), 1940
Gelatin silver print
Image and sheet: 34.1 × 26.8 cm (13 7/16 × 10 9/16 in)
University of Nebraska, University Collection, U-1713.20

Emilio Amero was among the generation of Mexican artists who came of age during the revolution and later benefited from the country's efforts at rebuilding national unity through mural commissions for public buildings. Although he worked alongside such famous artists as José Clemente Orozco and Diego Rivera, Amero also profited from the shared interest in mural decoration that was developing between Mexico and the United States, and he resided north of the border for extended periods during the 1920s and 1930s. Accomplished in diverse art forms, he was particularly drawn to the graphic possibilities of printmaking, and while working and studying lithography in New York during the late 1920s, he produced a series of photograms, his first serious experience with the medium.[1] Thereafter, photography remained a staple of his output and an important adjunct to his work, and he produced a range of images that included not only experimental, abstracted pieces like the photograms but also films and classic, timeless pictures like this one.

In 1938, after returning to Mexico from his second stay in the United States, Amero began traveling extensively throughout the country, particularly in its southern portions, camera in hand. During this period, his goal was to publish a portfolio of his work, but the photographs perhaps served as a memento and final farewell to his home country as well: the artist may have been planning his return to the United States at this time, and when the University of Washington offered him a teaching position in 1940, he seized the opportunity.[2] Nonetheless, during this transition, Amero produced maquettes for his project, and New York's Weyhe Gallery printed and sold a limited edition of the portfolio that same year. The collection contained thirty images that, in formal terms, represented a return to more established photographic conventions, featuring mainly bust- and half-length portraits as well as pictures of regional crafts, foods, and traditions.

Like his contemporary Manuel Álvarez Bravo (cat. 79) and other Mexican artists after the revolution, Amero searched for a visual idiom in which to articulate his country's national identity. Here, a young bride performs the Zandunga, an indigenous folk dance common at weddings in the southern Pacific region of Tehuantepec in the present-day state of Oaxaca. The performance itself is a mixture of eroticism and melancholy that Amero captures brilliantly in the bride's unexpectedly grim expression. The subject was popular at the time, as artists often found the quintessence of Mexican culture in its native customs; Rivera painted several versions of the subject throughout the 1920s and 1930s.[3] An American promoter of Mexican folk culture described the dance as a "simple waltz step," with the women flirtatiously raising their skirts toward the men "without deigning to look at their partners."[4] Amero caught the bride in such a pose but decontextualized the dance by focusing on her to the exclusion of her partner, making the viewer the second participant in this pas de deux. **BKR**

1. For more on the photogram technique, see cat. 82. **2.** Ariel Zúñiga, *Emilio Amero: Un modernista liminal/A Liminal Modernist* (Mexico City: Albedrió, 2008), 72. **3.** For two examples by the artist, see Anna Indych-López, *Muralism without Walls: Rivera, Orozco, and Siqueiros in the United States, 1927–1940* (Pittsburgh: University of Pittsburgh Press, 2008), 106–7, figs. 58, 59. **4.** Frances Toor, quoted in Indych-López, *Muralism without Walls*, 108.

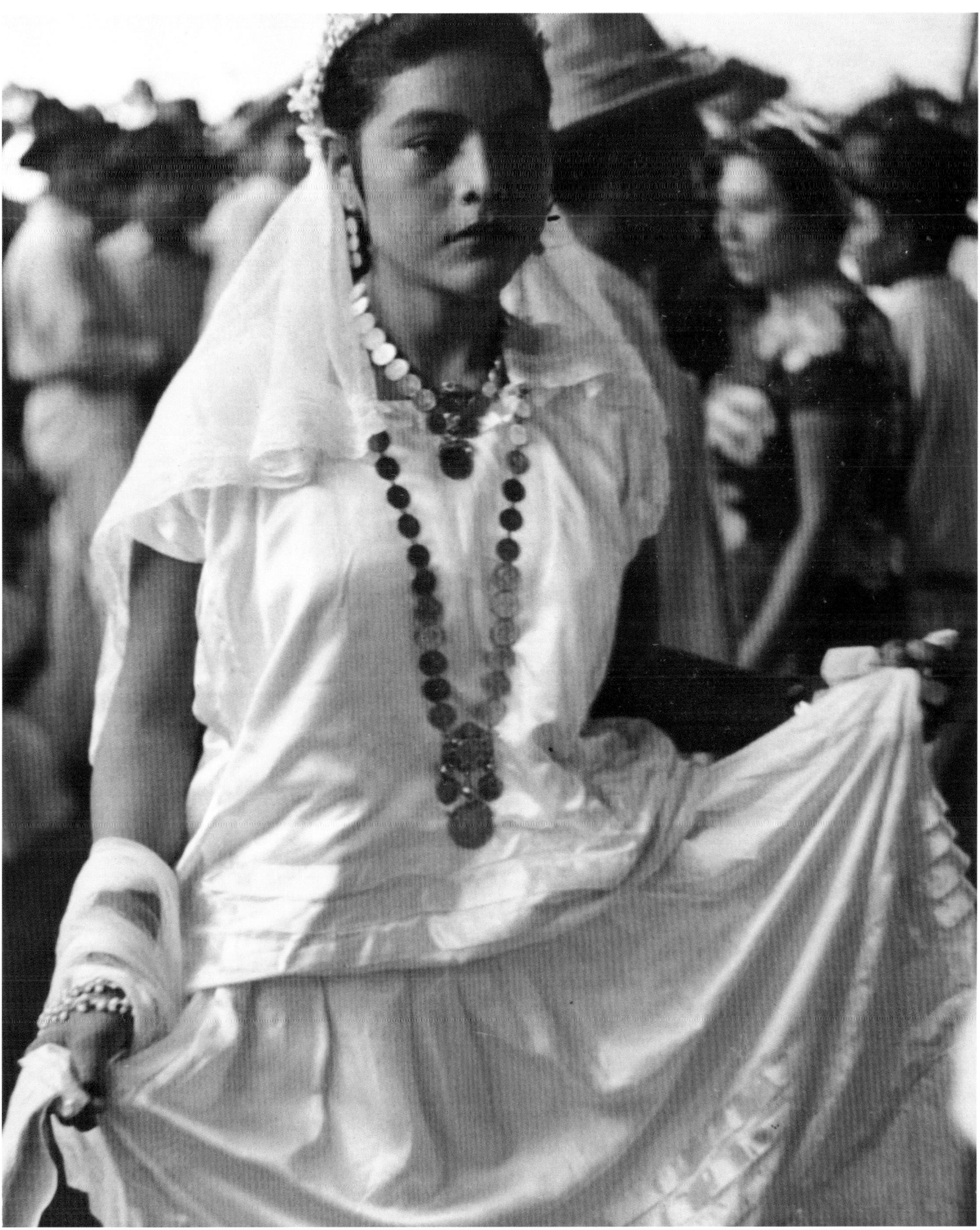

48

Roy DeCarava

American, 1919–2009

Graduation, 1949
Gelatin silver print
Image and sheet: 24 × 34.3 cm (9 7/16 × 13 1/2 in)
University of Nebraska, Catherine M. Johnsen
Acquisition Fund, U-689

Roy DeCarava decided to be an artist as a young man and, after attending art classes in his native Harlem, found work as a commercial illustrator. Many of his early photographs were intended to support his work in serigraphy, but he increasingly found himself drawn to the medium and by the late 1940s had devoted himself to it with what Peter Galassi termed a "clarity of artistic purpose."[1] *Graduation* dates to this time in DeCarava's life. Many of the photographs that he produced during this fertile period, including *Graduation*, were featured in *The Sweet Flypaper of Life*, a 1955 collaboration in which playwright and poet Langston Hughes supplied the text. Although critics praised the book upon its debut, the project was a disappointment for the photographer, mainly because of Hughes's fictional interpretations of DeCarava's images. DeCarava later recalled, "Langston did not want to know any facts about the persons I had photographed on the streets. He told me he knew them already."[2] Hughes, in fact, ignored the title and context of this picture, writing in the book, "It's nice to see young folks all dressed up going somewhere—maybe to a party."[3]

Graduation—a rite of passage for many American teenagers—evokes promises of a new life and, with it, a fresh start. In this piece, such hopes are overcast by the grim surroundings of the young woman, who lifts the hem of her dress as she navigates a ruined inner-city street littered with debris. In the foreground, a discarded newspaper bears a headline on South Korea, acknowledging the increasing hostility in the region and forecasting the impending conflict. New York's changing demographics as well as dramatic alterations to America's living patterns more generally are represented by the advertisements the young woman views skeptically. At extreme right is a sparkling new billboard promoting the 1950 Chevrolet Bel Air, a hardtop model that masqueraded as a convertible. The billboard reflects the new mobility enjoyed by postwar suburbanites, and DeCarava's astute eye recognized that its content—a car driving away to an unseen, heavenly horizon—as well as its position in respect to the young woman serve as a metaphor for the white middle class's flight from the cities. At the same time, the image implicitly guarantees that carefree suburban leisure is an attainable goal. By contrast, the smaller, Spanish-language broadside next to it screams "the shout of a woman in the night," alluding to the dangerous street on which the young woman finds herself.

DeCarava's composition is a masterpiece of artistic control and structure, particularly in its play of light and dark. The subject herself is a study in these tonal distinctions: her skin contrasts with the glaring, vivid white of her dress and gloves, and her figure creates a strong, attenuated shadow against the daylight. Additional shadows crisscross the photograph, from the immediate foreground to the middleground building and then to the tenement in the left background. The natural daylight creates a strong diagonal that forces the viewer's attention rightward, stressing and underlining the promises and the realities of the pasted advertisements on the side of the brick building. **BKR**

1. Peter Galassi, *Roy DeCarava: A Retrospective*, exhibition catalog (New York: Museum of Modern Art/Harry N. Abrams, 1996), 17. **2.** Quoted in Erina Duganne, *The Self in Black and White: Race and Subjectivity in Postwar American Photography* (Hanover NH: Dartmouth College Press/University Press of New England, 2010), 147. **3.** Duganne, *The Self in Black and White*.

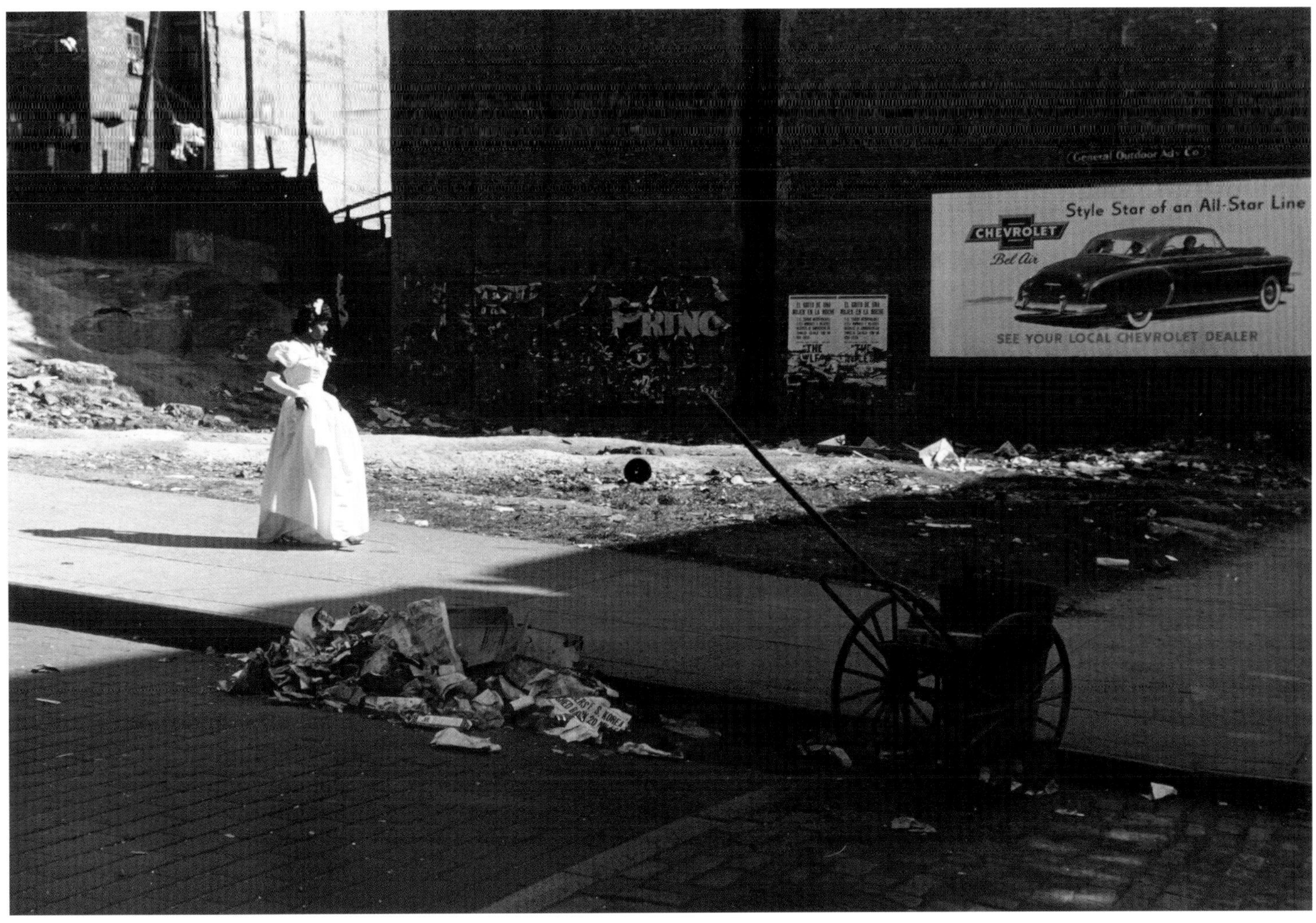
General Outdoor Adv. Co.
Style Star of an All-Star Line
CHEVROLET
Bel Air
SEE YOUR LOCAL CHEVROLET DEALER
PRINC

49

Diane Arbus

American, 1923–1971

*Child with a Toy Hand Grenade in Central Park,
N.Y.C.*, 1962
Gelatin silver print
Image: 37.8 × 37.5 cm (14 7⁄8 × 14 3⁄4 in); sheet: 53 × 40.6 cm
(20 7⁄8 × 16 in)
Stamped, on verso, upper left: *Not to be reproduced in
any way without written permission of Doon Arbus*; upper
right: artist's estate's stamp with handwritten inscriptions
University of Nebraska, Anna R. and Frank M. Hall
Charitable Trust, H-2155

Born into wealth and privilege, Diane Arbus later recounted
that her interest in distinguishing between appearance and
reality in self-presentation was a result of her parents' striving for upward mobility. "It was a front," she recalled. "My
father was a frontal person. A front had to be maintained."[1]
The artist later added that everybody "has the thing where
they need to look one way but they come out looking another way" and that the camera was "recalcitrant," resolved "to
do one thing" while "you may want to do something else."[2]
Arbus's enduring, mesmerizing images are a result of her
uncanny ability to detect and capture such qualities—what
she called "flaws"—in subjects of differing backgrounds, lifestyles, and socioeconomic statuses.

Like Paul Strand (cats. 59 and 60), Arbus was educated
at New York's Fieldston School for Ethical Culture, and she
nursed her interest in photography through visits to Alfred
Stieglitz's An American Place gallery in the early 1940s. It was
her friendship and study with photographer Lisette Model
beginning in the late 1950s, however, that encouraged and
solidified her choice of subjects, what Model called a singular
achievement in depicting "people who are discriminated."[3]

James Goodwin has also credited Arbus's equipment and
technique as partly responsible for the special relationship
between the artist and the people she photographed: beginning in 1962, she switched to the twin-lens Rolleiflex camera, which produces a large negative and thus greater clarity
and detail. Because the Rolleiflex was held at chest or waist
level, Arbus was free to engage and interact with her subjects
directly, free of the intermediary of the camera's viewfinder.[4]

According to the contact sheet from the session for *Child
with a Toy Hand Grenade*, Arbus experimented with several
locations and positions as she moved around her subject. The
addition of the hand grenade, however, alters the dynamic
and mood of the photograph dramatically. Here, Arbus beautifully evoked the tensions between boyhood fascination with
war and the actual horrors of battle; juxtaposing the child's
aggressive stare and posture with his juvenile romper and the
sylvan setting, she reminds viewers of the fragile boundaries
between childhood and adulthood, between monkey business and violence. **BKR**

1. Interview with Studs Terkel, December 1969, quoted in *Diane Arbus: A
Biography*, by Patricia Bosworth (New York: Avon, 1984), 324. Although Bosworth's unauthorized biography is dismissed by critics and scholars, the
interview is documented. **2.** Diane Arbus, *Diane Arbus*, exhibition catalog
(Millerton NY: Aperture, 1972), n.p. **3.** Quoted in James Goodwin, *Modern
American Grotesque: Literature and Photography* (Columbus: Ohio State
University Press, 2009), 147. **4.** Goodwin, *Modern American Grotesque*, 155,
158.

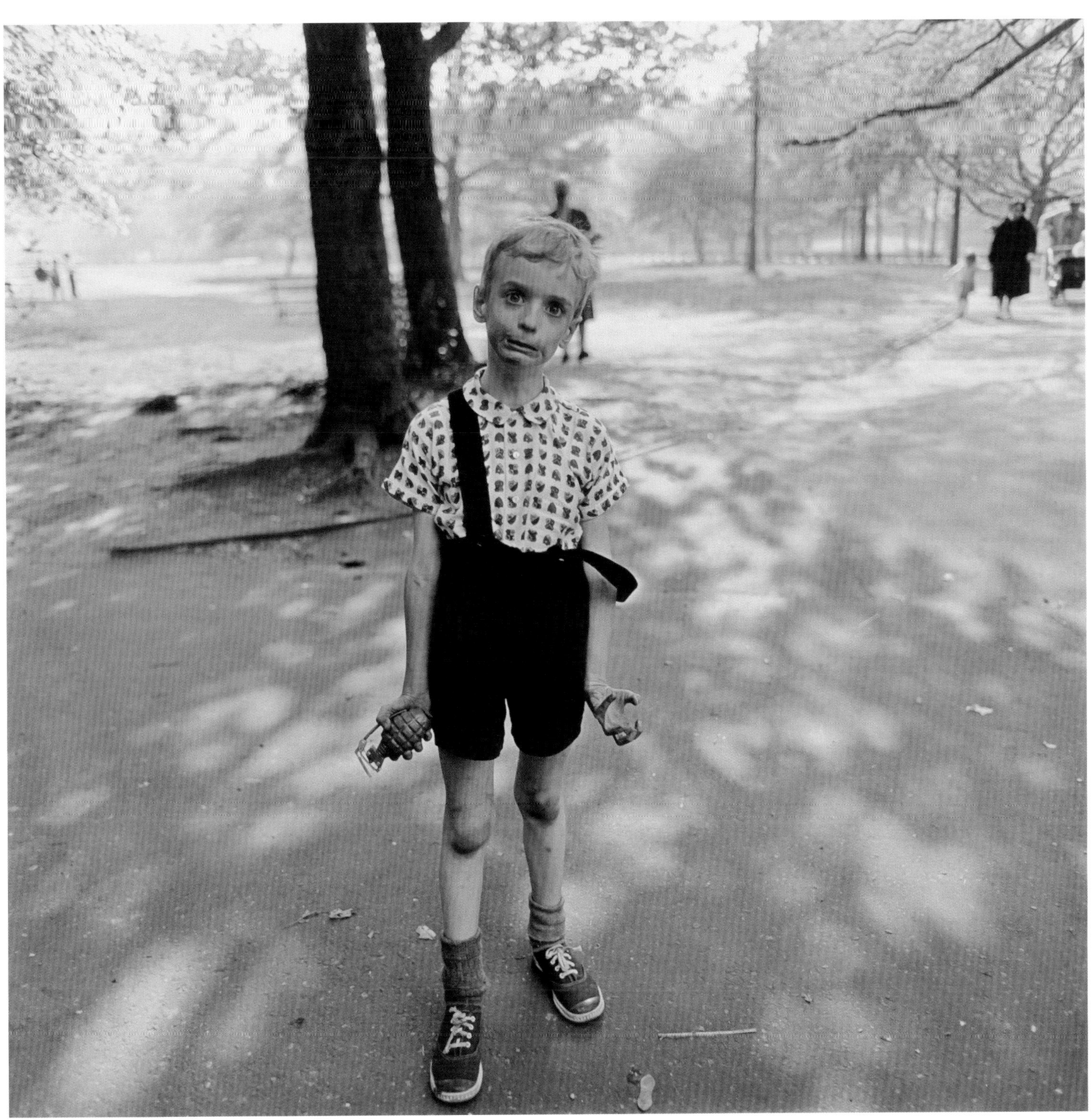

50

Danny Lyon
American, born 1943

Uptown, Chicago, July 1965, 1965
Gelatin silver print
Image: 15.1 × 15.1 cm (5 15/16 × 5 5/16 in); mount: 22.9 ×
25.4 cm (9 × 10 in)
Inscribed, on verso, on mount, lower right, in blue ink:
UPTOWN, CHICAGO *July 1965* / *Danny Lyon*
University of Nebraska, Anna R. and Frank M. Hall
Charitable Trust, H-1016

In a 1992 exhibition at New York's Museum of Modern Art, curators described Danny Lyon as one of the "young rebel[s] in American photography," classifying him with a group of artists in the 1950s, 1960s, and 1970s who "recorded the lives of young people who defied conventional social values in their struggle to define themselves."[1] During a postwar period that brought both prosperity and conformity, photographers such as Lyon focused on the disenfranchised and rebellious, showing a different side of American teenage life than was often seen on movie and television screens. While these artists practiced the objective observation of photojournalism, they also insinuated themselves into the lives of their subjects, achieving a remarkable level of candor and frankness as a result. They also, in many cases, personified the very ideals they sought to document.

Lyon's outsider biography parallels his aesthetic and personal objectives. The artist first began practicing photography while a history major at the University of Chicago. His enthusiasm and passion for motorcycling led to his first major project, a study of motorcyclists in the 1968 collection *The Bikeriders*. He made the photographic essay between 1963 and 1967, focusing on the Chicago Outlaws Motorcycle Club, a group that he belonged to and rode with across the country. Like many such clubs in post–World War II America, the Chicago Outlaws celebrated freedom, nonconformity to mainstream culture, and, above all, loyalty to the group. According to Lyon, the photographs were "an attempt to record and glorify the life of the American bikerider."[2]

In this photograph, taken during the same period, Lyon depicted a trio of young men against a graffiti-scarred apartment building in Chicago's Uptown neighborhood. In the mid-1960s, Uptown itself was an affront to postwar conventions and values. Originally settled by German and Swedish immigrants, during the 1910s and 1920s it became the city's leisure hot spot, boasting tony beachside hotels, glitzy theaters, and opulent ballrooms. By the 1950s, however, rezoning and the rerouting of Lake Shore Drive had altered the area's fortunes, and it became a destination for Chicago's poor, home to Appalachian, Japanese, and Native American newcomers seeking work in the city's factories.[3]

The subjects of Lyon's photograph embody Uptown's rough edges during this period. The glowering young men stare at and posture for the camera even as they lower their heads and seek refuge behind long, tousled bangs. They defiantly challenge the viewer with their open, unbuttoned tops and T-shirts; relaxed, insolent postures; and, in one case, a lit cigarette. At the same time, they close in on themselves, tucking in their shoulders and using their arms—or each other—as defenses against the outside world. Through his attention to these subtle nuances, Lyon skillfully captured the edgy, awkward rebelliousness of being a teenager. The image is also, of course, somewhat of an illusion—"a collaboration," as one scholar put it, "of an idealistic artist and subjects who project themselves by particular costume and conduct."[4] **BKR**

1. Edward Robinson, "The Young Rebel in American Photography, 1950–1970," *MOMA* 12 (Summer 1992): 20. The group included such artists as Larry Clark, Bruce Davidson, Robert Frank, and Gale Gedny. 2. Danny Lyon, *The Bikeriders* (New York: Macmillan, 1968), ix. 3. Amanda Seligman, "Uptown," in *The Encyclopedia of Chicago*, ed. James R. Grossman, Ann Durkin Keating, and Janice L. Reiff (Chicago: University of Chicago Press, 2004), 847–48. 4. Robinson, "The Young Rebel," 21.

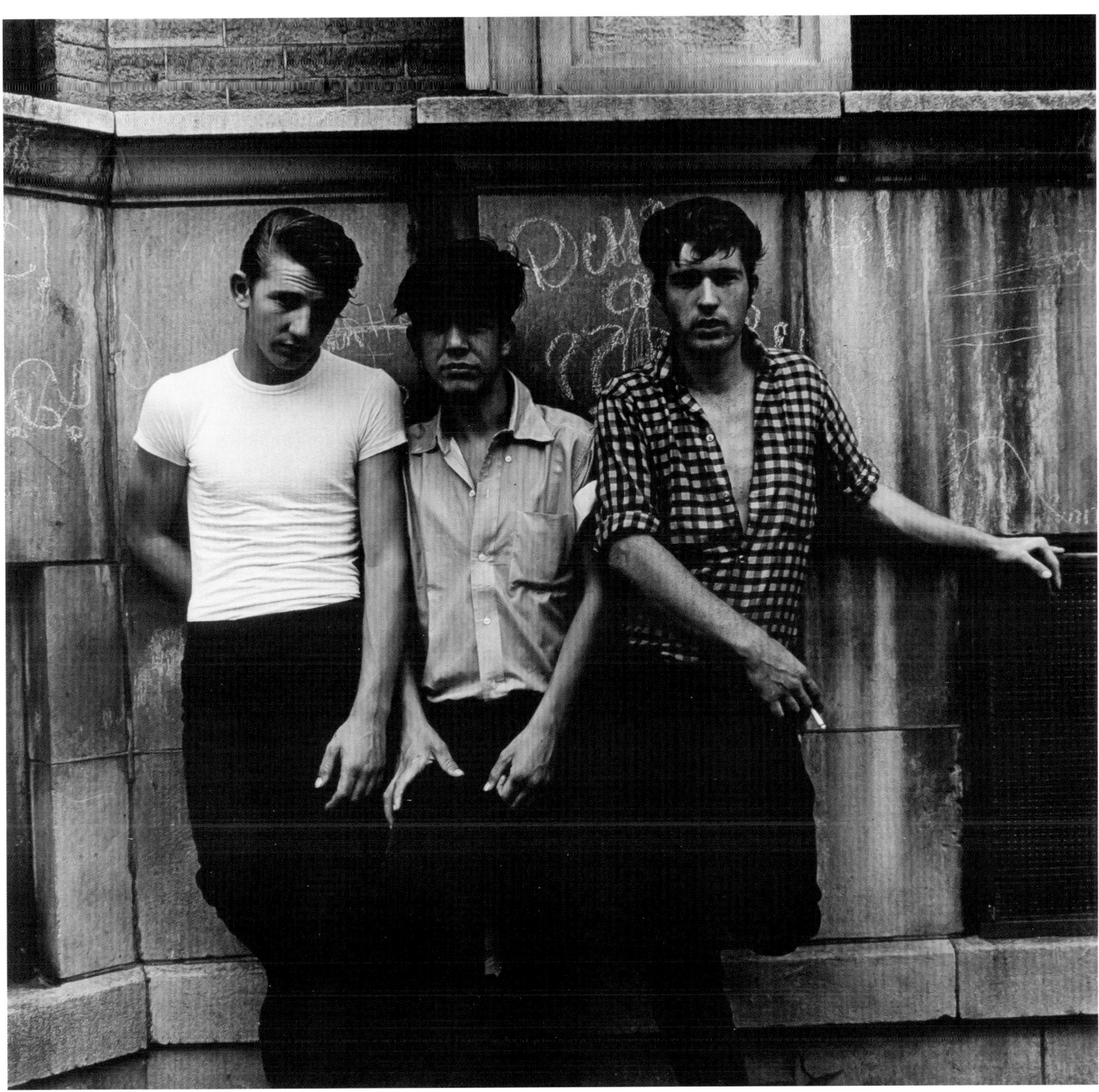

51

Starr Ockenga

American, born 1938

Mother and Daughter, early 1980s
Gelatin silver print
Image: 21 × 31.1 cm (8 ¼ × 12 ¼ in); sheet: 27.3 × 35.2 cm
(10 ¾ × 13 ⅞ in)
University of Nebraska, Anna R. and Frank M. Hall
Charitable Trust, H-2047

Starr Ockenga studied photography with Harry Callahan (cats. 38 and 83) and Aaron Siskind (cat. 18) at the Rhode Island School of Design. While it could be argued that her entire professional output explores the theme of domesticity, her early photographs, taken just a few years after her graduation, concentrated on familial relationships, especially those between parents and children. In the majority of these works, some or all of the participants appear in the nude—a way for the artist to investigate, as she explained it, "the colors of flesh, its subtle variations of hue" in black-and-white photography.[1] Ockenga often shot these portraits of her friends in her own home, creating a makeshift studio and relying on her own furnishings as props. In her selection, the photographer chose objects that would subtly accentuate the variations of hue she was attempting to capture.

Here, Ockenga staged the image to present a subtle diversity of whites, from the whitewashed corner of the room to the milky skin of her subjects. Only the floral brocade curtain at right and the finely netted grain of the mother's bra offer textural contrasts, while the pair's dark hair and eyes dramatically offset the stark whiteness. Ockenga's nudes were initially met with condemnation. Some critics and reviewers raised questions about the exploitive nature of her images of pubescent and prepubescent girls, foreshadowing similar criticism of nudes by Sally Mann (cat. 53) a decade later. Others questioned the sincerity of the artist's insistence that all bodies are beautiful, especially since all her models were young and attractive.[2]

Ockenga's studies of her friends and family, however, have deeper implications for the artist: "I became intrigued with signals in relationships, with the extent to which simple gestures can uncover complexities of feeling, with the emotional and physical webs a person creates with loved ones."[3]

In this work, the tender gestures between the two women dramatize the mother-daughter relationship the title proclaims. As the daughter reaches her right arm around her mother, she is drawn closer, bringing her head to rest on her mother's shoulder as she shifts her right hip and raises her left side. In creating the image, Ockenga was influenced by similar themes in works by Mary Cassatt a century earlier, in which, she remarked, "relationships are described through the subjects' intimate gestures."[4] While the mother's covered breasts and the large flower situated in her bodice suggest feminine maturity, her daughter's exposed bosom symbolizes youthful suppleness and fecundity. The artist readily acknowledges that the unadulterated white of the photograph only reinforces the young woman's purity and virginity, qualities associated with youth.[5] For Ockenga, however, childhood and pubescence also have darker associations, and through the study of photography, she hoped to capture not only "pure exuberance" but also the "more mysterious nature of fantasy" and the "inner consciousness" of children.[6] **BKR**

1. Quoted in "Starr Ockenga," *Center Quarterly* 4, no. 4 (1983): 8. **2.** Estelle Jussim, "Starr Ockenga's Nudes: Some Notes on the Genre," *Massachusetts Review* 24, no. 1 (Spring 1983): 98. **3.** Jussim, "Starr Ockenga's Nudes." **4.** Jussim, "Starr Ockenga's Nudes." **5.** Jussim, "Starr Ockenga's Nudes," 103. **6.** "Starr Ockenga," 8.

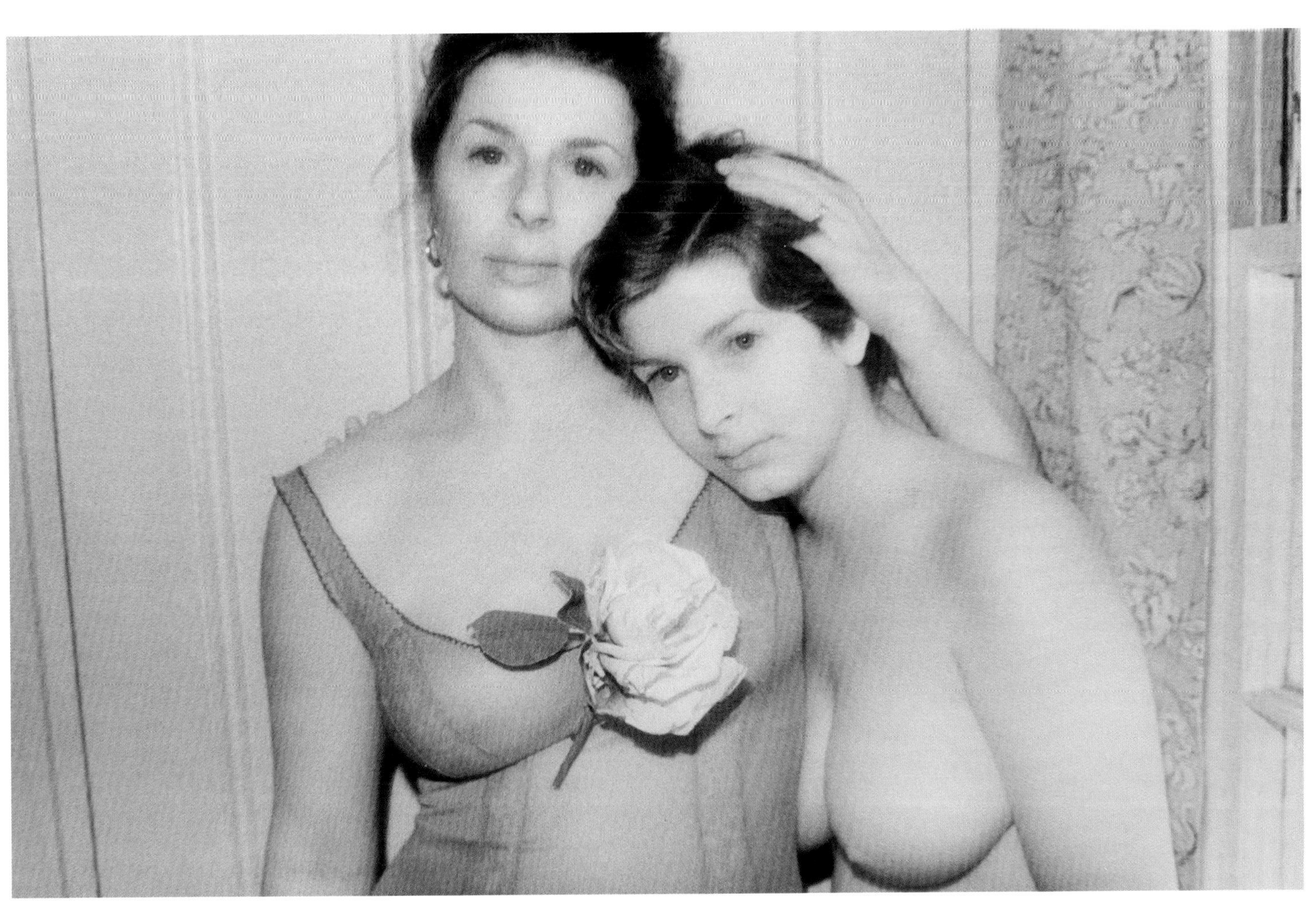

52

Lauren Greenfield

American, born 1966

Lindsey at a Fourth of July Party Three Days after Her Surgery, Calabasas, 1993
Cibachrome print
Image: 32.9 × 49.5 cm (12 15/16 × 19 1/2 in); sheet: 40.6 × 50.8 cm (16 × 20 in)
Inscribed, on verso, lower left, in black ink: *Lauren Greenfield 1993 2/25*
University of Nebraska, James E. M. and Helen Thomson Acquisition Trust, U-4949

Long before photographer Lauren Greenfield explored American values regarding beauty, materialism, and success, her vision had been shaped by her native Los Angeles, epicenter of popular and celebrity culture. After graduating from Harvard University in 1987 with a degree in visual anthropology and photographic and film studies, Greenfield soon began international assignment photography for *National Geographic* but quickly found that her position as a cultural outsider did not result in the kind of honest, informed storytelling that was her goal. To harness the spirit of metropolitan American life, she returned to her home city in 1992.

First, Greenfield visited her alma mater, the private Crossroads School in Santa Monica, where she began to explore the face of privileged adolescence. Her quest took her into overstuffed bedrooms, to lavish proms and party crews, to model shoots and music-video tapings. There she observed materially centered, youth-obsessed teens who were catapulted into an adult world by proximity to Hollywood. Her subjects were astute and well aware of their relationships to conspicuous consumption—from the right look to the right friends—and of the status it conferred. As her project expanded across Los Angeles, Greenfield found that these same influences held sway across all economic lines, bound up with such homogenizing forces as media and hip-hop culture.

The resulting body of work became the groundbreaking 1997 publication and exhibition *Fast Forward: Growing Up in the Shadow of Hollywood*. The photographs display Greenfield's reportorial bent and preference for spontaneous, non-directed image making with 35mm color film. Their powerful documentary qualities reinforce the truth of events and surroundings, stripping bare any illusion of adolescence as innocent, sheltered, or uncomplicated. That the artist gave her subjects a voice—their narratives appear alongside her photographs—is further testament to the underlying objectivity of her portrayals. *Fast Forward* was instantly lauded as a revealing and often uncomfortable record of adulthood in the making.

Part of the *Fast Forward* series, *Lindsey at a Fourth of July Party Three Days after Her Surgery, Calabasas* is a striking example of Greenfield's uncluttered visual narratives. It depicts a smiling young woman, nose bandaged, taking part in a casual celebration. She is neatly dressed and groomed, proud to be seen by comrades and camera only days after a cosmetic procedure once shyly explained as a necessary medical correction. Lindsey's text describes years of self-consciousness about her weight and appearance, recounting her envy as friends routinely had everything from nose jobs to breast implants. Having waited, at her parents' insistence, until her eighteenth birthday to have the surgery, she reveals the results of her achievement under Greenfield's sharp, decoding gaze. This is Lindsey's personal Independence Day, wrapped in the blue and white bunting of her dress and bandages, seated next to bobbing red and white balloons.

Despite recording Lindsey's personal elation, such a photograph intentionally poses questions regarding cosmetic surgery for teens and about a society whose ideals of beauty and perfection can have such early and far-reaching consequences. Those important discussions, Greenfield feels, are left open for the viewer. She has continued to confront such issues in her subsequent work, including the photographic and film projects *Girl Culture* and *Thin*. In the project *Kids + Money*, she revisited Los Angeles to investigate the expanding role of consumerism in childhood. And her 2012 documentary, *The Queen of Versailles*, profiles a family whose pursuit of an opulent American Dream is transformed by the recession into a cautionary tale. All deftly display Greenfield's ability to expose the complexities within the familiar. **JLF**

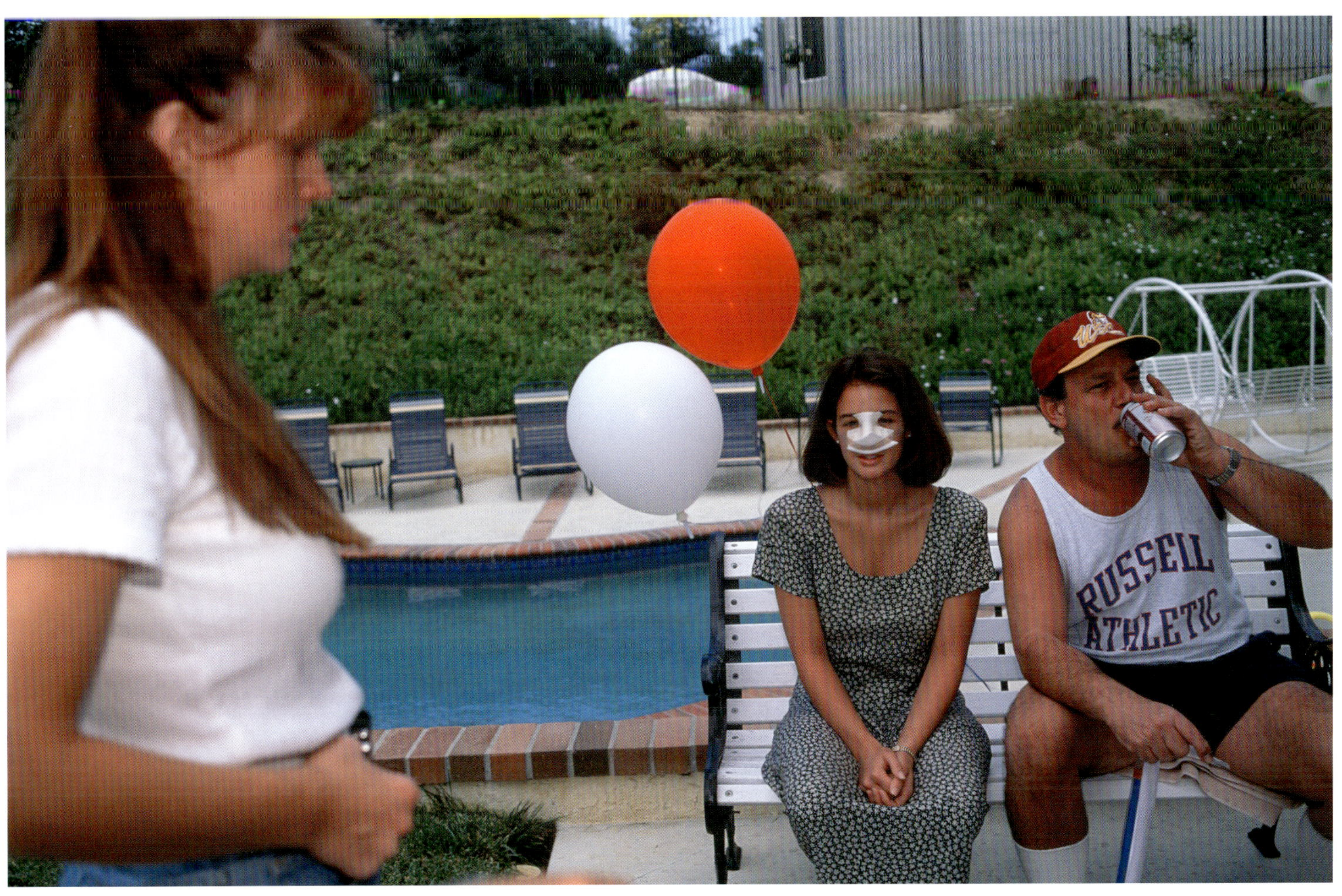

53

Sally Mann
American, born 1951

Candy Cigarette (from the series *Immediate Family*), 1989
Gelatin silver print
Image and sheet: 19.7 × 24.7 cm (7 3/4 × 9 3/4 in)
Inscribed, on verso, lower left, in pencil: *25 20 × 24 / ed. 25 16 × 20 / 25 8 × 10*; lower right: *Candy Cigarette / 7/25 © 1989 / Sally Mann*
University of Nebraska, Robert E. Schweser and Fern Beardsley Schweser Acquisition Fund, through the University of Nebraska Foundation, U-5654

Sally Mann has used the pastoral setting of her native Lexington, Virginia, and her family home as both a backdrop and an inspiration for her work, from her early landscapes to portraits of her children, and her latest nudes. The artist has been exploring the theme of young girls on the verge of womanhood for several decades, beginning in the mid-1980s with the series *At Twelve*, for which she photographed preteens in rural Rockbridge County, Virginia. A more recent series, *Immediate Family*, resulted from the demands of family and motherhood: unable to devote time to working on location, Mann started shooting her three children at home, documenting their evolution and maturation. Her schedule revolved around the rhythms of domesticity and children's seasonal schedules: while working on *Immediate Family*, she spent most of the year in the darkroom and photographed only in the summer, when her children were most active outdoors.[1]

In this photograph, Mann's oldest daughter, Jessie, stands at the center, staring directly and defiantly at the camera, crossing her right arm against her waist and holding a candy cigarette between the fingers of her raised hand. Her flowing blonde hair, knowing look, and thrust pelvis give her the appearance of someone far beyond her years. Her younger sister Virginia, arms akimbo, turns her back to view a figure on stilts in the background. This latter element, which introduces a touch of diaphanous white against the twilight sky, gives the photograph an otherworldly, surreal quality, yet Mann herself regards this image and others from the series as deeply familiar: "Some are fiction, some are fantastic, but most are of ordinary things every parent has seen— a wet bed, a bloody nose, candy cigarettes. They dress up, they pout and posture, they paint their bodies, they dive like otters in the dark river."[2] The artist's self-conscious addition of the candy cigarette, however, has contributed to an ongoing debate about the nature of Mann's images of her children, particularly the nudes; about her own role as maternal protector; and about her children's consent in the creative process. As art and cultural critic Richard B. Woodward suggested in his profile on the artist, "By posing Jessie with a candy cigarette and Virginia in Lolita glasses . . . Mann gives them props whose dark associations they can't begin to understand. Rather than preserving their innocence, the photographs seem to accelerate their maturity by relying on the knowingness of the viewer."[3]

Despite the allegations of exploitation that embroiled Mann in the culture wars when *Immediate Family* first debuted in the early 1990s, the artist regards the photographs as an "intense collaboration" with her children that resulted in "typical family pictures." "We are spinning a story," Mann explained, "of what it is to grow up. It is a complicated story and sometimes we try to take on grand themes: anger, love, death, sensuality, and beauty. But we tell it all without fear and without shame."[4] **BKR**

1. Richard B. Woodward, "The Disturbing Photography of Sally Mann," *New York Times Magazine*, September 27, 1992, 33. **2.** Sally Mann, introduction to *Immediate Family*, by Sally Mann and Price Reynolds (New York: Aperture, 1992), n.p. **3.** Woodward, "The Disturbing Photography," 35. **4.** Quoted in Katherine A. Bussard, *So the Story Goes: Photographs by Tina Barney, Philip Lorca di Corcia, Nan Goldin, Sally Mann, and Larry Sultan*, exhibition catalog (Chicago: Art Institute of Chicago; New Haven CT: Yale University Press, 2006), 79.

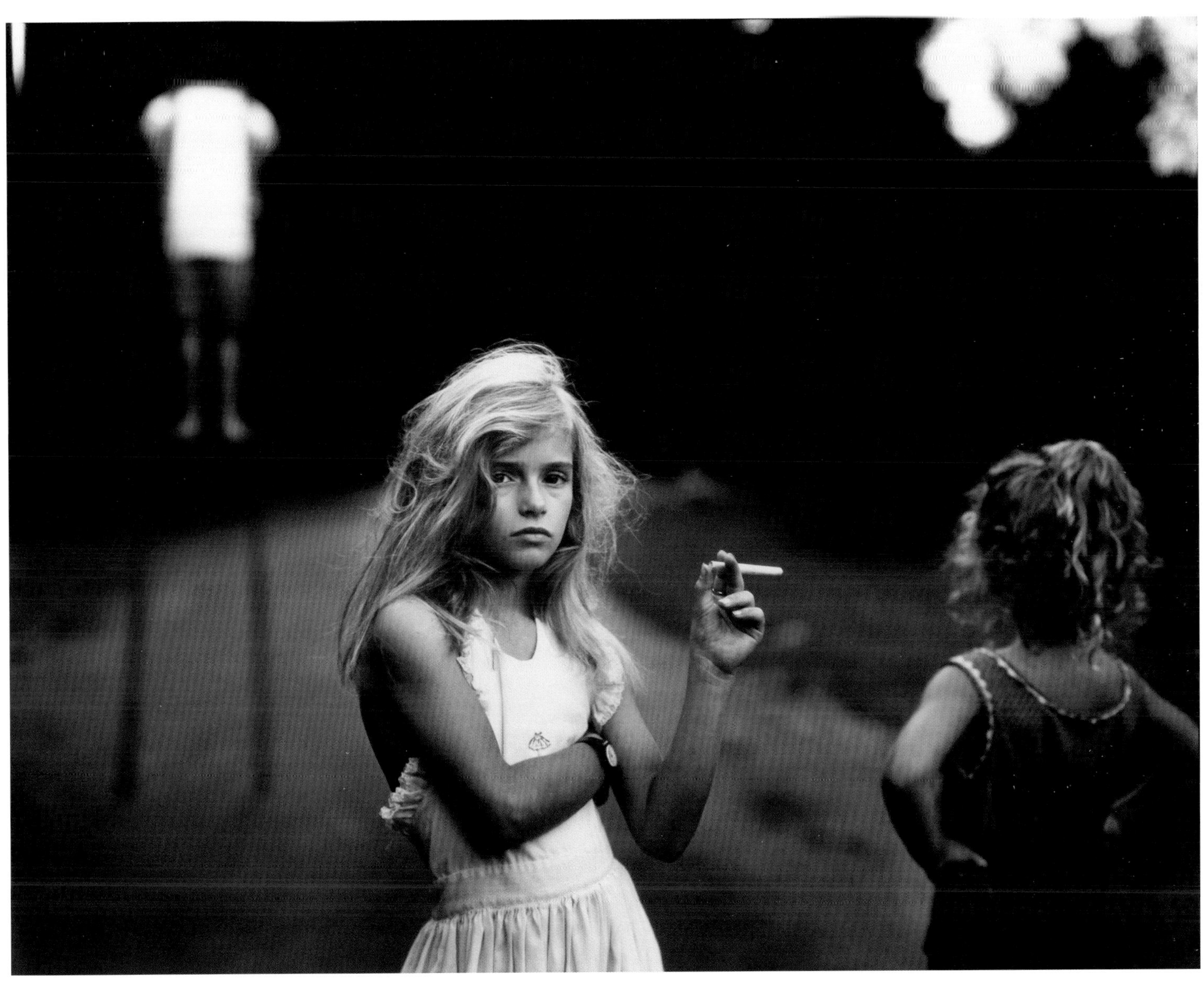

54

Alec Soth
American, born 1969

The Flechs, 2006
Chromogenic print
Image: 101.6 × 127 cm (40 × 50 in); sheet: 121.9 × 147.3
(48 × 58 in)
Printed, on verso, lower center: *The Flechs edition 6/7
2006*; signed, in black ink: *Alec Soth*
Nebraska Art Association, purchased with donations
from the Sheldon Forum, N-841

Alec Soth is one of the most intelligent artists to depict the American social landscape of our time. He comes from the Midwest and respects regional identity without trafficking in clichés. Perhaps for this reason, his photographs can seem both ordinary and exotic.

Soth owes a debt to such great predecessors as Walker Evans (cat. 101), Robert Frank, and Dorothea Lange (cat. 78) and to a certain extent thinks of himself as carrying on the documentary tradition established during the middle third of the twentieth century. At the same time, he recognizes that photography's role in the art market and in society has changed and grown. Soth came of age in an era of postmodern loss of confidence in veracity and representation, but he nevertheless believes in direct experience and personal narrative.

His particular mode of honest observation clearly struck a chord. His 2004 book *Sleeping by the Mississippi* earned critical acclaim, and he appeared in the Whitney Biennial that same year.[1] Using the most traditional equipment—an 8 × 10-inch box camera—Soth deliberately slows down, stops to look, and encourages us to imagine the chain of events that led up to the deceptively simple scene captured in the photograph.

In 2006, following the success of *Sleeping by the Mississippi*, Soth published NIAGARA. Although both projects address iconic North American waterways, the artist approached them differently. The earlier series accumulated in the course of meandering road trips; the later one came out of an exploration of a single site and its melodramatic

mythology. Soth approached the subject from a number of angles. Portraits of newlyweds, images of handwritten letters, and interior views of motel rooms all have a kind of defiant normalcy. The individuals depicted in and implied by these scenes seem oblivious to the natural glory of Niagara Falls, as does Soth. Yet tacitly, all are aware that the falls brought them to this point in their lives, and each has some sort of faith in the site's redemptive potential.

All of this is intuited, not spelled out. Typically, Soth does not crowd the frame with incidental detail. *The Flechs* is exemplary in this regard. Six children are arranged in an orderly row, the tallest at the center; a man stands at left and a woman at right. Given the adults' formal clothing, the girls' matching pink dresses, and the bouquets of flowers, we infer this is one of Niagara's many wedding parties. The mood, however, is not carefree. Aaron and Nicole Flech have just exchanged vows in the presence of their children from previous marriages. There were no guests and no photographer (other than Soth) at the ceremony, which was held in a hotel chapel.[2] Responsibility and a bit of apprehension seem to hover over the newly consolidated family as they face the stranger with the large, old-fashioned camera. But moods are constantly changing, as the falls continually churn. In another portrait of the Flechs, taken moments before or after and included in NIAGARA, the adults smile contentedly and the children giggle. No single picture, Soth reminds us, can tell the whole story. **BS**

1. Alec Soth, *Sleeping by the Mississippi* (Göttingen: Steidl, 2004); and Chrissie Iles, Shamim M. Momim, and Debra Singer, *Whitney Biennial 2004* (New York: Whitney Museum of American Art, 2004). **2.** We know this from Soth's handwritten notes, taken at the site and reproduced in NIAGARA (Göttingen: Steidl, 2006), 99.

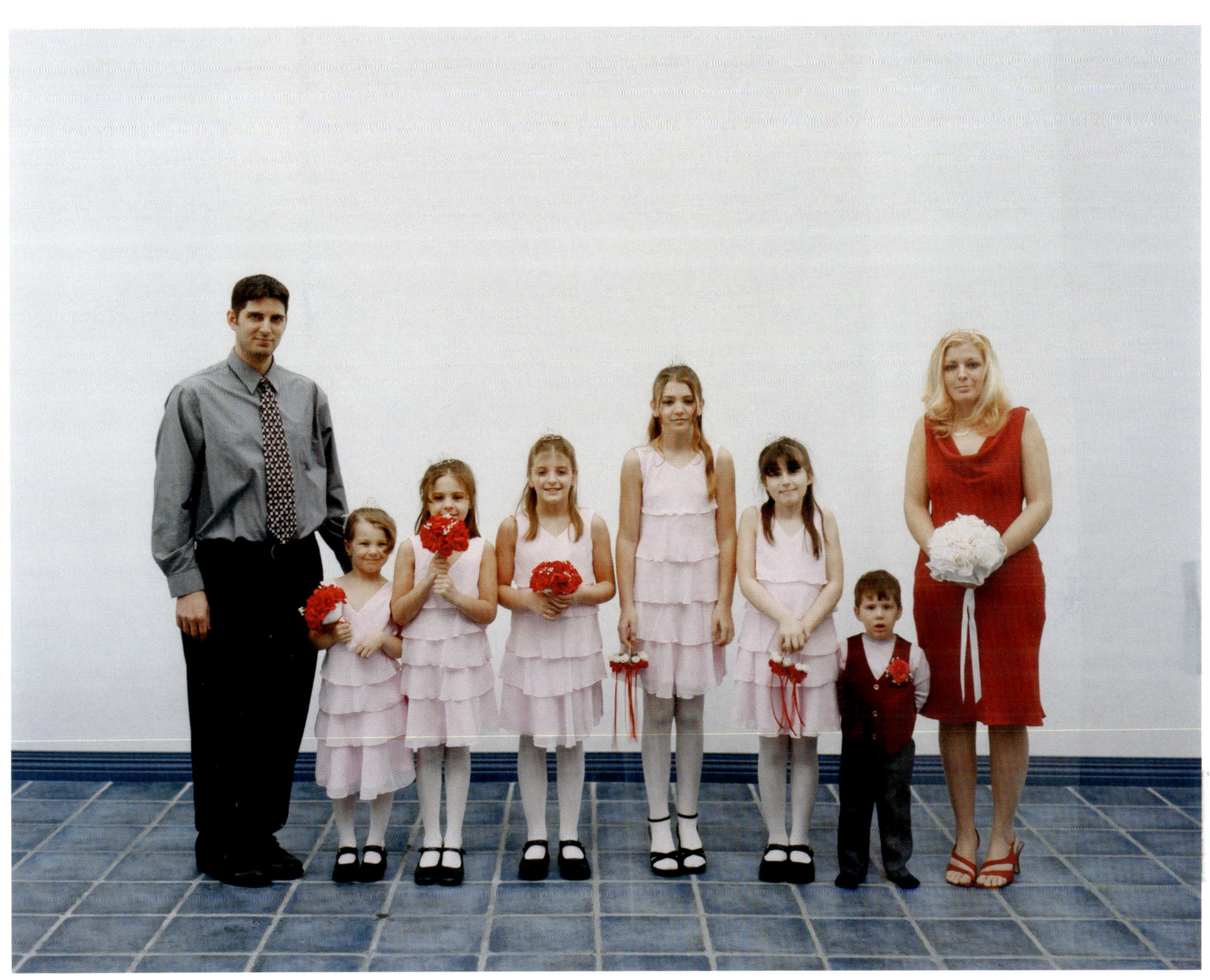

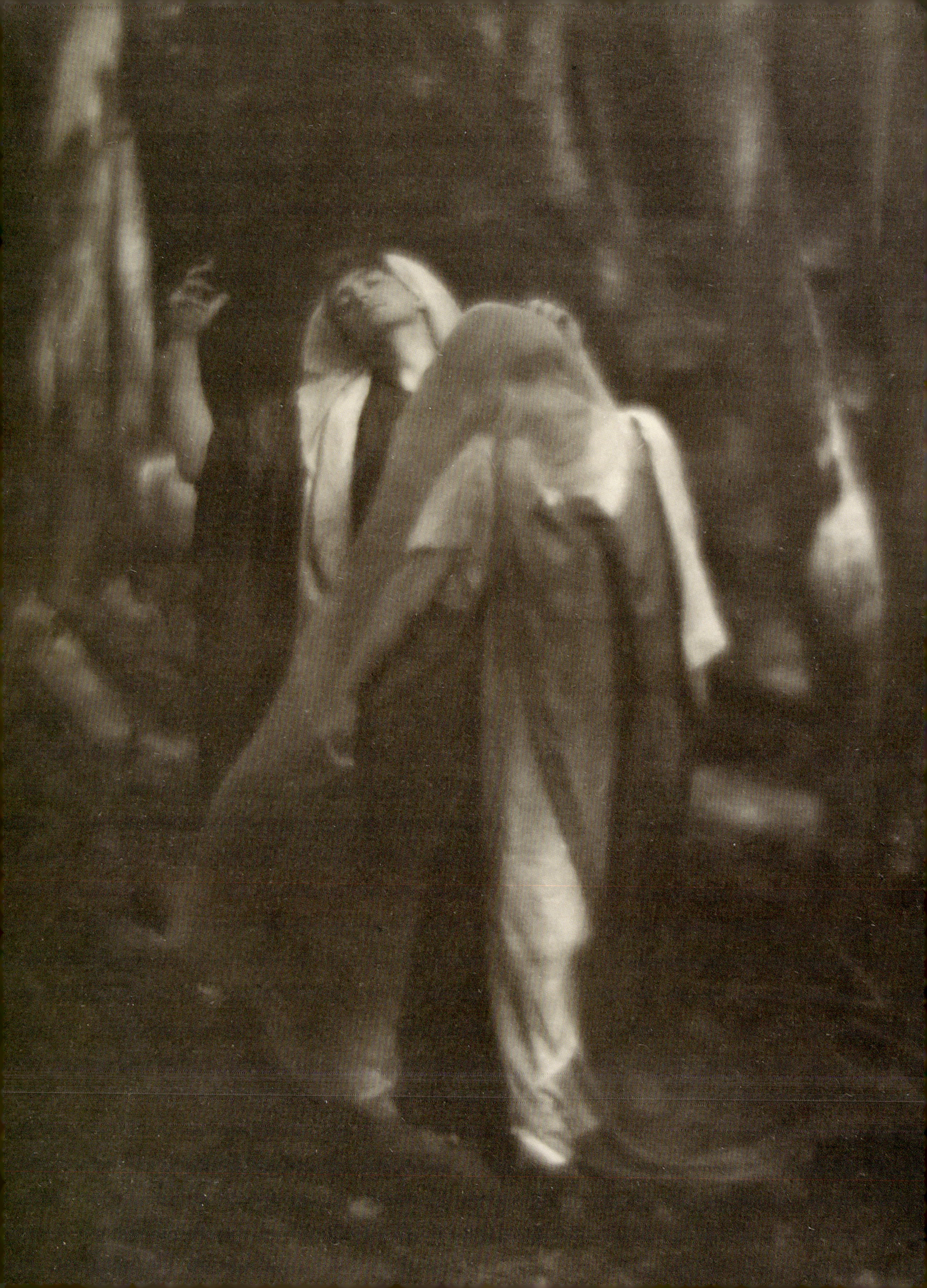

RELIGION AND SPIRITUALITY

From photography's infancy, cognoscenti have debated its scientific and spiritual ramifications. Was the ability to capture permanent images on plate and paper a discipline or little short of a miracle? Some observers expressed admiration for the controlled technical qualities of the medium, employing the language of innovation and invention to describe it as a "process . . . of great discovery."[1] One observer of Louis Daguerre's early experiments, meanwhile, described them as "drawn by the invisible pencil of Mab, the queen of the fairies."[2]

In a way, photographic practice mirrors these debates. A spiritual encounter can be both personal and mystical—an experience with the divine and otherworldly—or simply the recognition of a previously unknown form of worship. In photographic art, these encounters have often been representational, an attempt to show tales or lessons from a particular religion; they have also, however, been more abstract, meant to induce contemplation and meditation. In her early photograph *Wood beyond the World* (opposite and cat. 56), for example, Imogen Cunningham used symbolist costumes, dramatic gestures, and a soft-focus technique to evoke an imaginary, dreamlike world. To some early practitioners, however, the actual trappings of religion—cathedrals and churches, paintings and sculpture—represented a way to explore the formal possibilities of artistic photography. An image of Siena's cathedral by the Italian firm Alinari, for instance, is an exercise in line and color (cat. 55); it also, however, demonstrates the town's multilayered Catholic tradition, evoking the union of aesthetic and cultural influences that resulted in the cathedral's centuries-long creation.

Sometimes this attention to formal elements evokes religious experience in a powerful way, raising simple subjects to the level of theater. One notable example is Ara Güler's *"Allah," Old Mosque, Edirne* (cat. 62), which shows two women worshiping in front of Arabic words painted onto the facade of the Eski Cami, the old mosque in the Turkish city of Edirne. The text has an immediate appeal, offering access to both the city's residents and the viewers of the image. The two black-robed figures, captured in a moment of prayer, balance the writing on the wall and complete the visually and spiritually expressive moment even as they evoke the nature of everyday religious experience in many cultures.

In some cases, faith is a way of establishing and marking one's place in the world. The congregation in James VanDerZee's *Black Jews, Harlem* (cat. 57), for example, connects members not only to stable middle-class religious traditions but also to the African and Jewish diasporas as a way to determine and grasp their own history and identity. For other artists, work can provide an opportunity to document their own spiritual searches. Paul Strand, for instance, did not go to Mexico on a quest, but his numerous photographs of religious *santos* (cats. 59 and 60) represent a strong faith; his images are endowed with expressive immediacy through a direct connection to folk Catholicism, a subject that often put him at odds with his revolutionary colleagues in Mexico City.[3] Like Strand, Joel-Peter Witkin uses religious themes to achieve emotional intensity, but, in his case, they can be both literal and intensely private. In his *Wife of Cain* (cat. 63), for example, the artist uses a biblical figure and story, employing them in abstract, dramatic ways to achieve what he calls an "individual connection" with the "Living Christ."[4]

1. Maria Morris Hambourg, "Picturing Victorian Britain," in *The Waking Dream: Photography's First Century*, by Hambourg et al., exhibition catalog (New York: Metropolitan Museum of Art/Harry N. Abrams, 1993), 6. 2. Jules Janin, *L'artiste*, September 1, 1839, quoted in Hambourg et al., *The Waking Dream*, 42. 3. Naomi Rosenblum, "Strand/Mexico," in *México through Foreign Eyes/Visto por ojos extranjeros*, ed. Carole Naggar and Fred Ritchin (New York: W. W. Norton and Company, 1993), 370. 4. Quoted in David Levi Strauss, "An Alchemical Disturbance," sf *Camerawork* 13, no. 1 (Spring 1980): 21.

55

Alinari Brothers

Italian, firm active 1854–1920

Interior of the Cathedral of Siena, Seen from the Presbytery, c. 1865
Albumen print
Image: 19.1 × 24.9 cm (7 1/2 × 9 13/16 in); sheet: 19.7 × 24.9 cm (7 3/4 × 9 13/16 in)
Printed, lower center: *(Ed.ne Alinari) P.e I.a N.o 8954. SI-ENA—Cattedrale. L'Interno visto dal presbiterio. (Dal XII al XV Secolo.)*
University of Nebraska, gift of Jon Nelson, U-2212

The three Alinari brothers—Leopoldo (1832–65), Giuseppe (1836–90), and Romualdo (1830–90)—founded their photographic firm in Florence in 1854. Leopoldo, who trained in photography with the engraver Luigi Bardi, was largely responsible for the company's artistic direction, guiding its strategies and supervising a growing fleet of assistants; Giuseppe organized the technical aspects; and Romualdo managed the business.[1] As international travel expanded beyond the upper classes, the brothers initially capitalized on a growing demand for tourist souvenirs by purveying scenic panoramas of Italian cities (see above) and images of well-known monuments. They expanded their offerings to include portraiture and picturesque views of the Italian countryside, but they sealed their reputation with reproductions of famous works of Italian art, which increased in popularity with the advent of art criticism and history and the host of international journals devoted to these subjects.

The Alinaris' most productive years coincided with a period in which critics debated photography's status as a fine art and also questioned its suitability as a reproductive medium, especially for Old Master artworks. Michele Arcangelo Migliarini, acting director of Florence's Uffizi Gallery, summed up common late nineteenth-century anxieties: "The success of photography was deceptive and uncertain. . . . [I]ts commercialism transformed and distorted the old masters. . . . Once this field is open to all, photographic copies will take the place of the many copies produced yearly

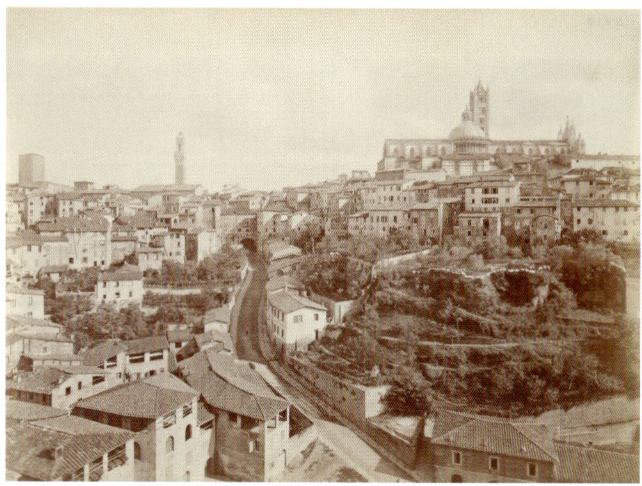

Alinari Brothers. *Panoramic View of Siena, Seen from S. Domenico*, c. 1895. Albumen print; 19.7 × 24.9 cm (7 3/4 × 9 13/16 in). University of Nebraska, gift of Jon Nelson, U-2210.

by highly skilled artists in need of work."[2] Nonetheless, the Alinaris also had their devotees, most notably, the eminent English critic John Ruskin. While no fan of the photographic medium, Ruskin commissioned and collected the brothers' pictures and encouraged his students to study their reproductions, particularly of drawings and architectural details.[3]

The Alinaris' architectural images transcend mere reproduction, however, and exist as a complex, creative mixture of carefully selected subjects, vantage points, and cropping. Here, they photographed the interior of Siena's medieval cathedral from the presbytery, an area reserved for the clergy. With their striking black-and-white stripes, the arches, columns, and ribbed vaults offer a dramatic mixture of gracious curves and stark horizontal and vertical lines. The space, which is seen looking toward the cathedral's entrance, invites the viewer to enter through the light that pours in from the side windows; both the columns and the angle of the shot, however, block any real access. The photographer's focus on Nicola Pisano's northern Gothic–inspired pulpit and the main architectural features of the church—as opposed to more overtly sacred elements such as the baptismal font, high altar, and sacristy—suggests that he meant to emphasize the cathedral's importance as a site of artistic rather than religious experience. **BKR**

1. For a brief history of the Alinari firm, see Silvia Paoli, "Alinari, Fratelli," in *Encyclopedia of Nineteenth-Century Photography*, ed. John Hannavy, vol. 2 (New York: Taylor and Francis, 2008), 25–27. **2.** Quoted in Massimo Ferretti, "The Documentation of Art," in *Alinari: Photographers of Florence, 1852–1920*, ed. Filippo Zevi (Florence: Alinari Edizioni and Idea Editions, 1978), 15. **3.** Alessandro Conti, "The Photographic Documentation of Nineteenth-Century Art," in Zevi, *Alinari*, 17.

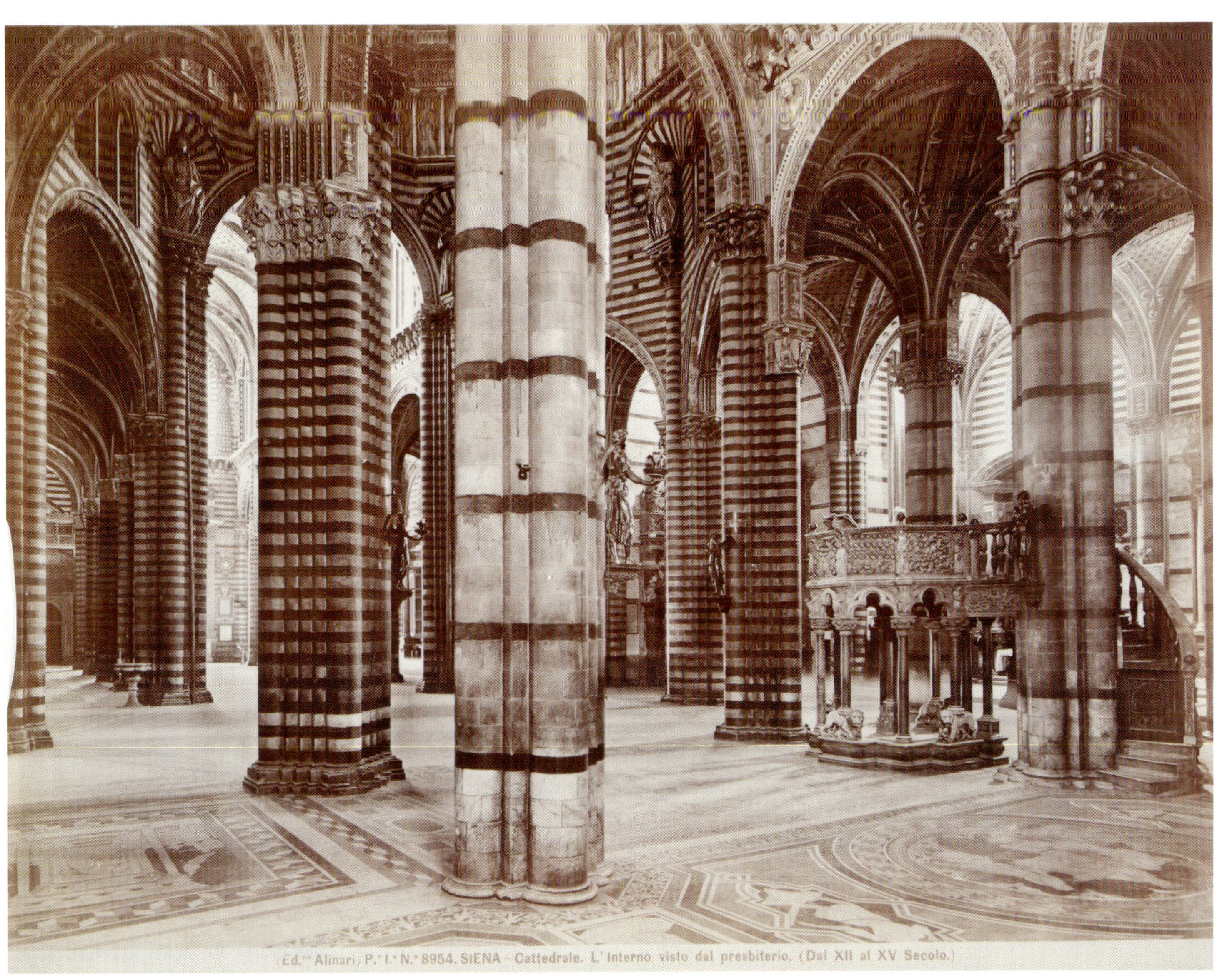

(Ed.ⁿᵉ Alinari) P.ᵉ I.ᵃ N.° 8954. SIENA – Cattedrale. L' Interno visto dal presbiterio. (Dal XII al XV Secolo.)

56

Imogen Cunningham
American, 1883–1976

Wood beyond the World, 1912
Platinum print
Image: 24 × 17.5 cm (9 7/16 × 6 7/8 in); sheet: 29.5 × 22.5 cm
(11 5/8 × 8 7/8 in)
University of Nebraska, Anna R. and Frank M. Hall
Charitable Trust, H-1170

Born in Portland, Oregon, Imogen Cunningham began to practice photography in earnest while a student at the University of Washington, exploiting her study of chemistry to enhance her photographic techniques. Shortly after graduation, she had two experiences that would determine the future direction of her career. First, she discovered an article on Gertrude Käsebier (cat. 46) in a 1907 issue of *Craftsman* magazine that extolled the emotional impact of the photographer's *Motherhood* series, claiming it possessed the "quality of world sympathy."[1] Second, she secured a job in the Seattle studio of Edward Sheriff Curtis (cat. 30), which would solidify her lifelong interest in portraiture. After a period of study in Europe, Cunningham returned to Seattle in 1910 and rented a studio in a converted farmhouse. John Butler and Clare Shepard—two of her artist neighbors—soon became friends and collaborators, modeling in classical or medieval garments for enigmatic photographs that she often set in nearby woods and based on literary precedents.[2]

The title of this image comes from William Morris's fantasy novel *Wood beyond the World,* first published by his Kelmscott Press in 1894. Cunningham admitted to being influenced by the book during her early "dream period," a moment when, she recalled, "I read William Morris and thought I understood poetry."[3] A designer, entrepreneur, and socialist agitator, Morris was one of the leaders of the British Arts and Crafts movement, which advocated joyful, autonomous labor; simple, handcrafted objects; and an intimate relationship between the fine and the decorative arts. The movement's anti-industrial philosophies and its emphasis on craftsmanship exercised considerable influence over photography during the late nineteenth and early twentieth centuries. During

this same period, practitioners allied with pictorialism and Photo-Secessionism attempted to establish the medium as a fine art, disassociating it from its mechanical origins and stressing the artistry of its practitioners through imaginative compositions, creative standards, honest labor, and spiritual understanding, principles wholly in line with the Arts and Crafts ideological agenda.[4]

Shrouded in a mysterious haze, these cloaked, veiled figures evoke the supernaturalism of Morris's book. The moment depicted may be that in which the protagonist of the novel, Golden Walter, escapes from a sorceress with a fair maiden, fleeing from primitive giants into an enchanted wood. Here, as the robed couple wander among the trees, the man throws his head and arms back in a dramatic gesture; his companion stretches to the right as she leads the pair to safety. While Cunningham printed her later photographs in gelatin silver, here she employed the platinum process, which allows for a greater tonal range and better produces the atmospheric effects she was trying to achieve in these symbolist-tinged photographs. **BKR**

1. Giles Edgerton [Mary Fanton Roberts], "Photography as an Emotional Art: A Study of the Work of Gertrude Käsebier," *Craftsman* 12, no. 1 (April 1907): 90. **2.** This identification has been made by Richard Lorenz, and Butler and Shepard may be the models here; Butler's brother Ben also occasionally posed for Cunningham and is possibly the male figure in the background; see Richard Lorenz, *Imogen Cunningham: Portraiture* (Boston: Bulfinch Press, 1997), 12. **3.** Quoted in Lorenz, *Imogen Cunningham,* 12. **4.** For more on this phenomenon, see Sarah E. Kelly, "'A New and Living Spirit': Pictorialist Principles and the Arts and Crafts Movement," in *Apostles of Beauty: Arts and Crafts from Britain to Chicago,* by Judith A. Barter et al., exhibition catalog (Chicago: Art Institute of Chicago; New Haven CT: Yale University Press, 2009), 119–50.

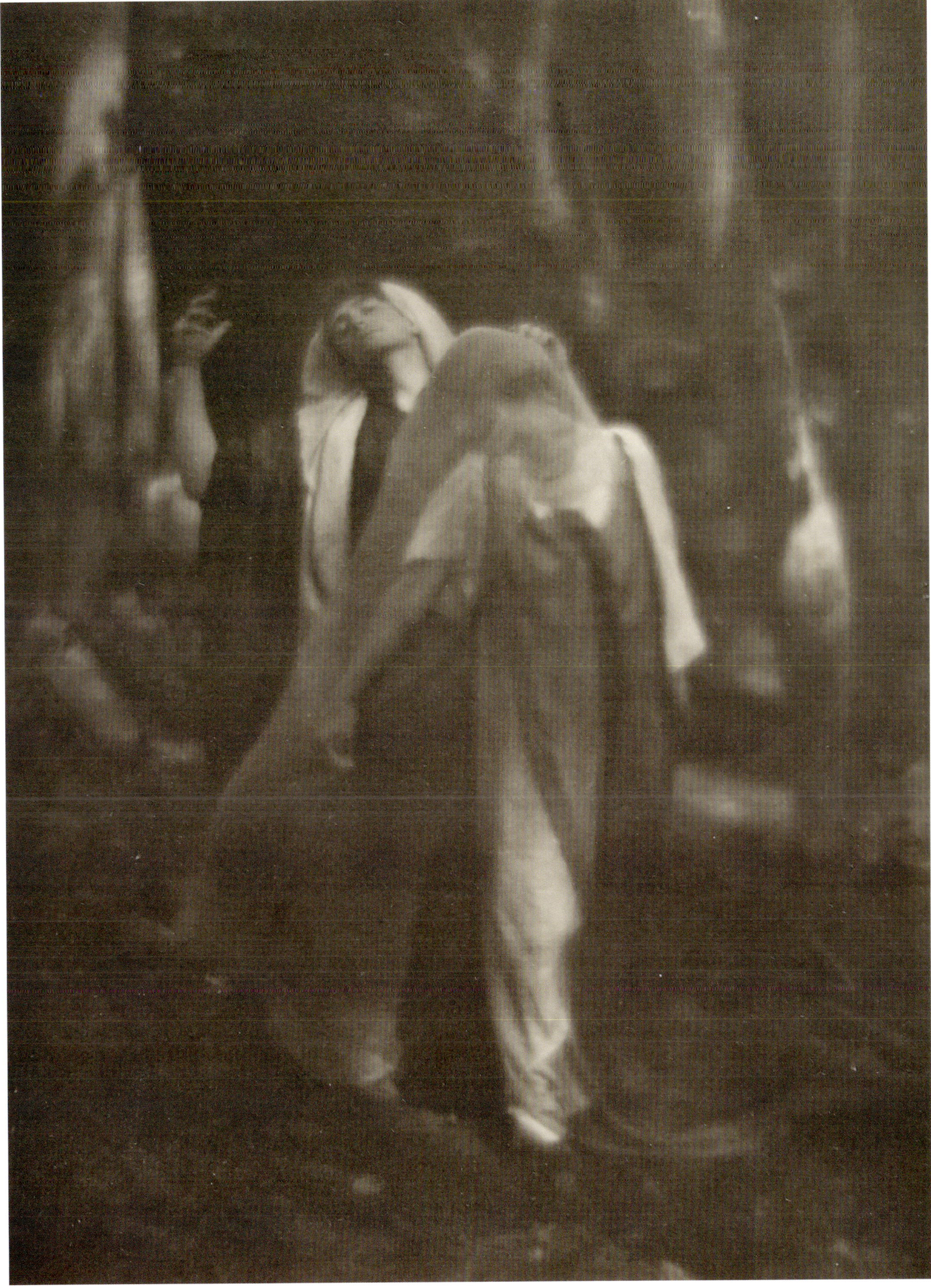

57

James VanDerZee

American, 1886–1983

Black Jews, Harlem, 1929; printed 1974
Gelatin silver print
Image: 19.1 × 23.8 cm (7 1/2 × 9 3/8 in); mount: 31.8 × 38.1 cm
(12 1/2 × 15 in)
Inscribed, on mount, lower left, in pencil: *XIII, 55/75*;
lower right: *J. VanDerZee*
Nebraska Art Association, purchased with the aid
of funds from the National Endowment for the Arts,
N-423.13

Largely self-taught, James VanDerZee first experimented with photography using mail-order cameras, which he employed to great effect as he captured the people and places of his boyhood home in Lenox, Massachusetts. After moving to New York at the beginning of the twentieth century, the artist took advantage of Harlem's booming population and artistic renaissance, opening his first studio in 1917 and becoming the photographer of record for the city's middle- and upper-class African Americans. *Black Jews, Harlem* shows the members of Beth B'nai Abraham Synagogue on the front steps of their 137th Street temple, surrounding their charismatic leader, Wentworth Arthur Matthews.[1] Larger than life, Matthews worked as a professional wrestler and boxer prior to his career as a rabbi. For this congregation—and its 1930 successor, the Commandment Keepers of the Living God—Matthews developed a doctrine that incorporated both Ethiopian Christianity and Judaism, holding that blacks were essentially Ethiopian Hebrews, descendants of King Solomon and the queen of Sheba and thus rightful heirs to Haile Selassie. The group practiced a brand of American Conservative Judaism and received most of its instruction from white Jews, with whom they were well integrated. Matthews and his followers were largely concerned with establishing their Jewish, middle-class credentials, rejecting classifications such as "Negro" and touting their community's "low rate of crime, juvenile delinquency, and shiftlessness."[2]

Their shared values are clearly on display here. VanDerZee's photographs are, in fact, assertively middle class, often self-consciously celebrating upward mobility and the established communal structures of bourgeois America: social clubs, fraternities and sororities, and political, religious, and sporting organizations. As a matter of fact, the photographer famously declared, "My first real customers were churches."[3] Here, VanDerZee reinforced Matthews's patriarchal position and spiritual leadership by placing him at the center of the composition, where he rests his left hand on a sacred text and raises his right in a pledge of faith. The rabbi's followers, clothed in formal suits and dresses, surround their spiritual guide and the scripture that unites them; children are prominently displayed as extensions of their elders' beliefs and morals.

Black Jews, Harlem offers a complex portrait of American ethnicity and religion. The sitters, for instance, announce their own allegiances by prominently displaying the U.S. flag alongside a banner emblazoned with the Star of David, the symbol of the Zionist movement. While the congregants adopt conventionally middle-class accoutrements and poses, they also subvert conventional status markers and racial distinctions by announcing, through a makeshift sign, their association with yet another culturally rich, ethnically complex group: Moors, people of North African and Middle Eastern descent, who were were expelled from Spain along with the Jews in 1492. VanDerZee's subjects destabilize predictable notions about color and race through their inventive use of history, embracing the African and Jewish diasporas as a way of navigating their own past. **BKR**

1. VanDerZee made several photographs of Matthews in the late 1920s, including ones that feature him isolated in front of the temple or framed in the window seen here at the upper right; the photographer also took pictures of the synagogue's other director, Arnold Josiah Ford. For these examples, see Deborah Willis-Braithwaite et al., *VanDerZee: Photographer, 1886–1983*, exhibition catalog (Washington DC: National Portrait Gallery; New York: Harry N. Abrams, 1994), 129; and Reginald McGhee, *The World of James Van DerZee: A Visual Record of Black Americans* (New York: Grove Press, 1969), 32–37. **2.** For this quotation, see Richard A. Davis, *The Myth of Black Ethnicity: Monophylety, Diversity, and the Dilemma of Identity* (Greenwich CT: Ablex Publishing Corporation, 1997), 113. For more information on Matthews, the Beth B'nai Abraham Synagogue, and the Commandment Keepers, see Willis-Braithwaite et al., *VanDerZee*, 129; David Levering Davis, *When Harlem Was in Vogue* (New York: Knopf, 1981), 222–23; and Joseph R. Washington Jr., *Black Sects and Cults* (Garden City NY: Anchor Books, 1973), 134. **3.** Quoted in McGhee, *The World of James VanDerZee*, 36.

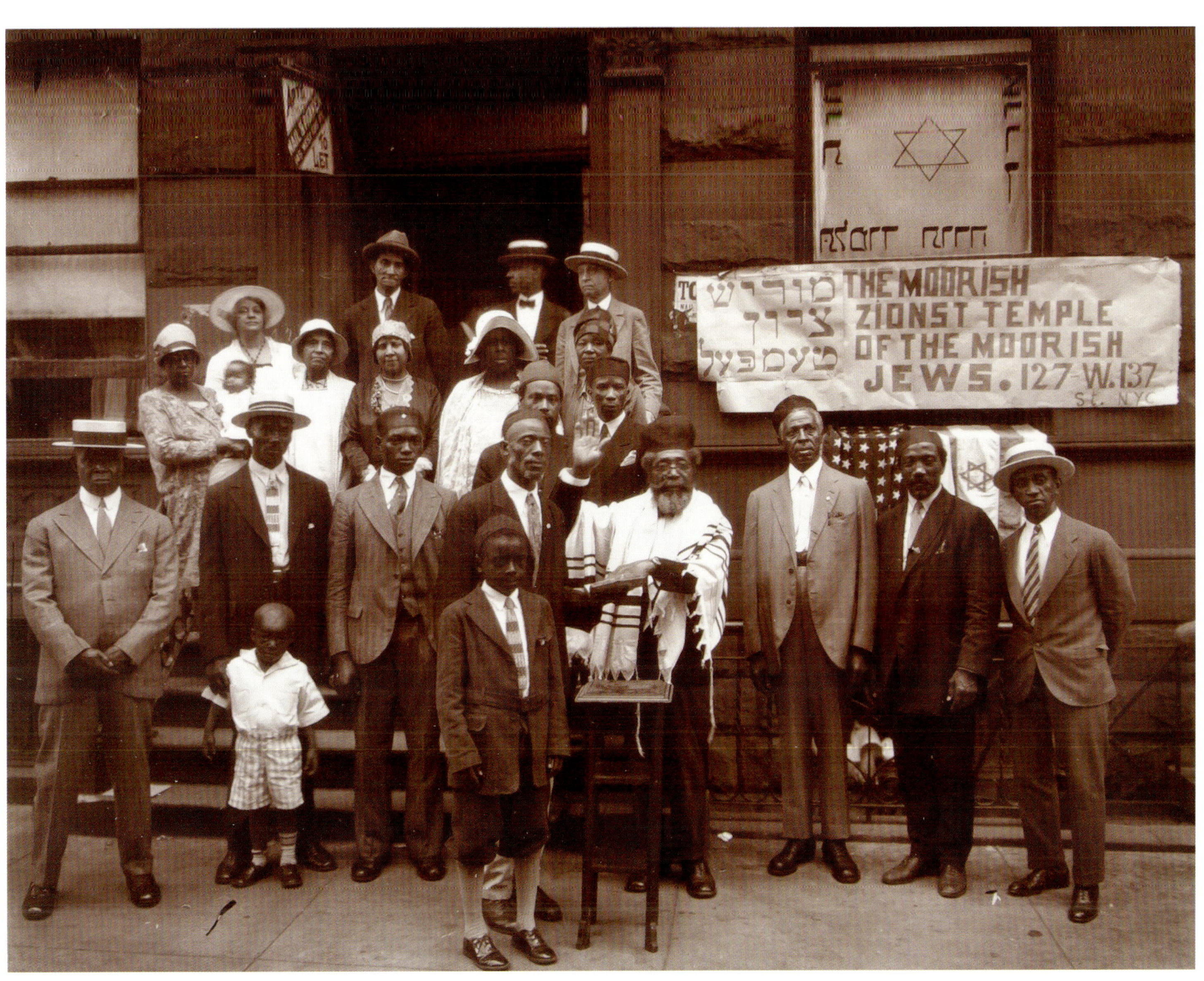
TO LET
מורישׁ
ציון
טעמפעל
THE MOORISH
ZIONST TEMPLE
OF THE MOORISH
JEWS. 127 W. 137
St. NYC

58

Edward Weston
American, 1883–1976

Church at "E" Town, New Mexico, 1933
Gelatin silver print
Image: 19.4 × 24.4 cm (7 ⅝ × 9 ⅝ in); mount: 28.2 ×
39.4 cm (11 ⅛ × 15 ½ in)
Inscribed, on mount, lower left, in pencil: *2/50*; lower
right: *Edward Weston 1933*
University of Nebraska, Anna R. and Frank M. Hall
Charitable Trust, H-512

Edward Weston is perhaps one of the most popular and recognizable photographers of the twentieth century, equally identifiable for his depictions of landscapes, nudes, portraits, and still lifes, on the one hand, and everyday objects such as egg slicers, nautilus shells, and peppers, on the other. By turning his attention to a single object or its parts, the artist created a new focus of aesthetic contemplation while also reimagining the subject itself, reducing and abstracting it. Although he had visited New York in the 1920s and made the necessary pilgrimage to the altar of Alfred Stieglitz (cat. 15), Weston created the majority of his work in southern California, outside the mainstream of artistic photography. In this regard, he—along with colleagues such as Ansel Adams (cat. 35) and Imogen Cunningham (cat. 56)—helped establish California as a major photographic center largely through the formation of f64, a collective devoted to pure, straight photography. Although the state's beaches and dunes provided a wealth of subjects, the artist also pursued other themes as he traveled to Mexico and throughout the desert Southwest in the 1920s and 1930s.

Weston toured New Mexico in June 1933 with his apprentice, filmmaker and photographer Willard Van Dyke, and his current mistress, model, and muse, Sonya Noskowiak. The trio spent a short time in Elizabethtown (the "E" Town of this image's title), a small mining settlement tucked in the mountains north of Santa Fe, close to the Colorado border.

Elizabethtown was the first incorporated town in New Mexico and, at its height, boasted a population of seven thousand due to the presence of gold mines in the area. By the time of Weston's visit, the village was largely deserted and had been a ghost town for several decades. Perhaps for this reason, the photographer was exhilarated by the landscape in and around Elizabethtown, writing in his daybook—a series of journals that he began keeping in 1915—"I knew I could go back,—it is but a day's journey. But when? It must be soon, for only at this time of year is the light at its best."[1]

The effects of light are the major focus of *Church at "E" Town*, in which Weston created strong contrasts between the light grass in the foreground, the dark mountains in the distance, the cloud-covered sky, and the architectural elements of the church. He drew additional distinctions between the building's simple rectilinear form and the gracious curves of the surrounding mountains, which resemble the abstracted nudes he began photographing a few years before. The church, with its severe cross silhouetted against the sky, stands as a symbol not only of attempts to further Christianize the West shortly after the United States accessioned the region in 1848, but also of efforts to civilize such distant, rough-and-tumble mining towns at the end of the nineteenth century. **BKR**

1. Edward Weston, daybook, July 23, 1933, in *California*, vol. 2 of *The Daybooks of Edward Weston*, ed. Nancy Newhall (New York: Aperture, 1990), 275.

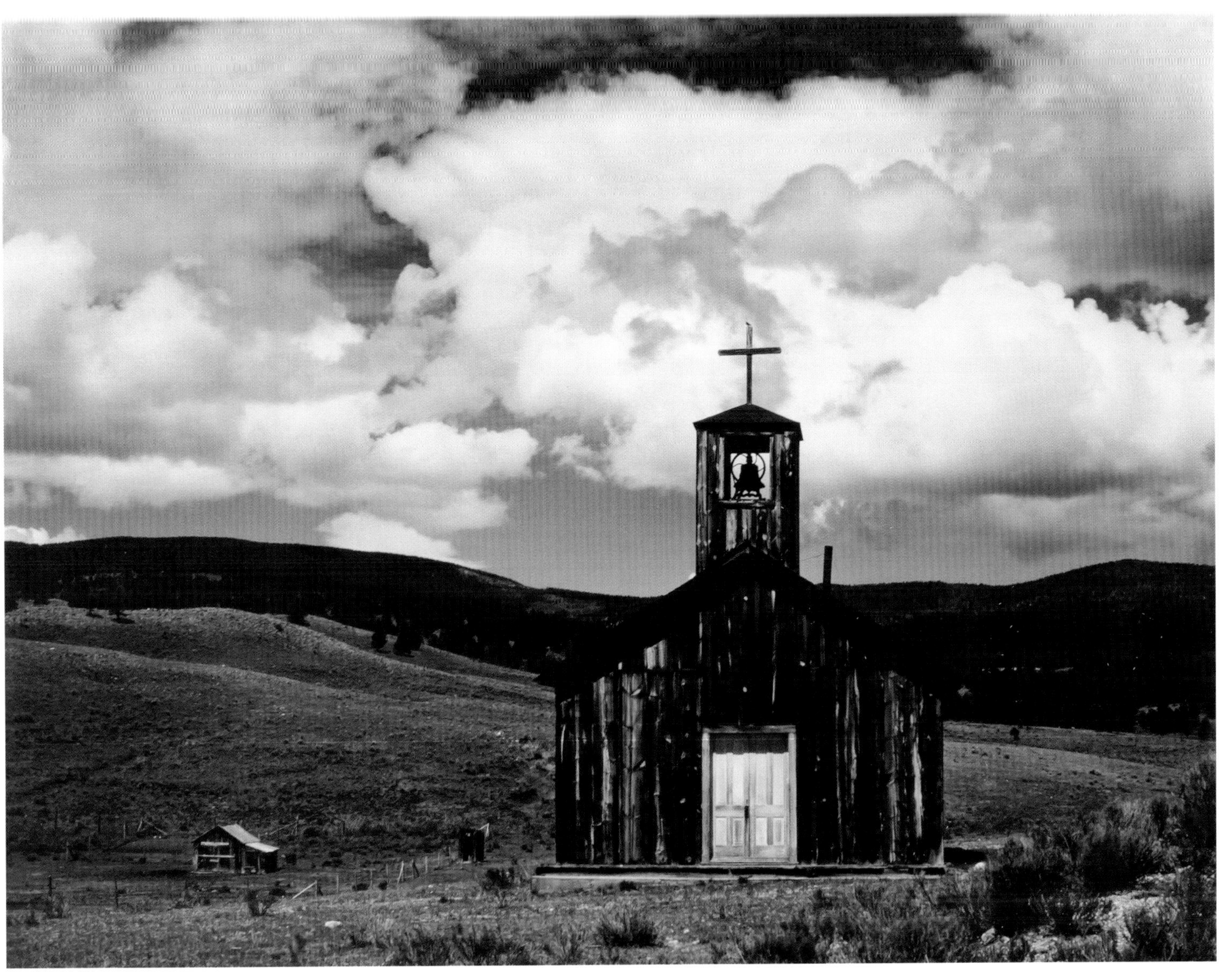

59

Paul Strand

American, 1890–1976

Church, Cuapiaxtla (from *The Mexican Portfolio*),
1932–33; published 1967
Photogravure
Image: 15.7 × 16.4 cm (6 3/16 × 6 7/16 in); sheet: 40.3 ×
31.4 cm (15 7/8 × 12 3/8 in)
University of Nebraska, University Collection, U-1745.2

Born in New York City, Paul Strand studied with celebrated documentary photographer Lewis Hine (cat. 16) at the Fieldston School for Ethical Culture, a preparatory academy originally established to provide education for the city's poor. During a class field trip, Strand visited Alfred Stieglitz's 291 gallery, an important modernist venue that helped establish photography as a fine art. Strand's encounter with Stieglitz (cat. 15) and 291's avant-garde exhibitions encouraged him to become a professional photographer, and Stieglitz later promoted his work in the gallery itself and in his publication *Camera Work*. In his early photographs, Strand experimented with formal abstractions stimulated by his urban environment, but he was also a strong advocate of using the camera as a tool for social reform; he was a founding member of the Photo League, an association that promoted political and societal change through art.

In 1932 Strand traveled to Mexico at the invitation of his friend the composer Carlos Chávez. He stayed until January 1935, receiving the support of the Mexican government, mounting successful gallery exhibitions, and directing the photography and filmmaking division of the country's Secretariat of Public Education. Although the American and European fascination with Mexico dates to the mid-nineteenth century, the 1920s and 1930s represent a climax in cultural exchange between Mexico and the United States. Several Mexican muralists—most notably, Diego Rivera and José Clemente Orozco—pursued commissions north of the border, while photographers and painters, including Josef Albers, Laura Gilpin (cat. 32), Marsden Hartley, and Edward Weston (cat. 58), all traveled south.[1] For many of these artists, direct contact with Mexico's ancient past and supposedly primitive culture served as a source of aesthetic inspiration;

for Strand specifically, the opportunity represented personal rejuvenation, allowing him to escape the dissolution of both his marriage and his sixteen-year relationship with his mentor, Stieglitz.[2] Hosting American artists and encouraging their work allowed the Mexican government to establish a national cultural identity after the brutal years of the country's revolution and subsequent dictatorships.

During his sojourn in Mexico, Strand produced 175 photographic negatives, 60 platinum prints (20 of which he issued in a 1940 and 1967 portfolio), and a critically acclaimed film, *Redes* (Waves).[3] The artist conscientiously selected and ordered the works in his Mexican portfolio so that each image establishes the context for the next one. For example, *Church, Cuapiaxtla*, taken in the east-central state of Tlaxcala, is the second photograph in the portfolio; it follows a landscape and is itself followed by a view of a statue of the Virgin of Guadalupe. Thus the series begins with a general introduction to Mexico; delves deeper in *Church, Cuapiaxtla*, whose arched gateway, doors, and second-story window represent an entry into another world; and moves on to an encounter with the Virgin, a representative expression of Mexico's cultural values. **BKR**

1. For a general history of this phenomenon, see R. Tripp Evans, *Romancing the Maya: Mexican Antiquity in the American Imagination, 1820–1915* (Austin: University of Texas Press, 2004); and James Oles et al., *South of the Border: Mexico in the American Imagination, 1914–1947*, exhibition catalog (Washington DC: Smithsonian Institution Press, 1993). **2.** For these arguments, see James Krippner, *Paul Strand in Mexico* (New York: Aperture Foundation, 2010), 9. **3.** For this information, see James Krippner, "Traces, Images, and Fictions: Paul Strand in Mexico, 1932–34," *Americas* 63, no. 3 (January 2007): 360. *Photographs of Mexico* was offered in 1940 and then rereleased in 1967 as *The Mexican Portfolio*, and it is from that edition that the two works featured in this publication come.

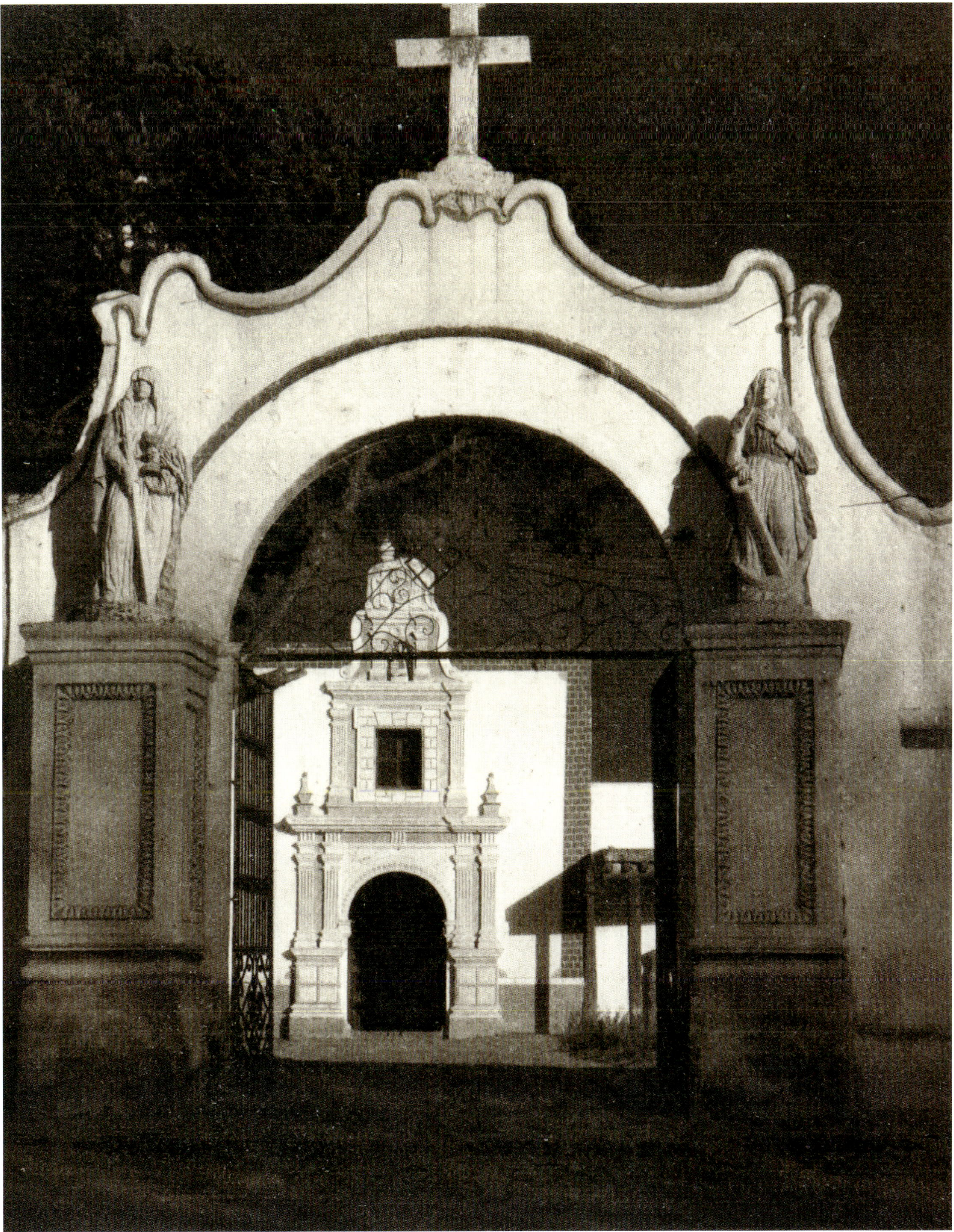

60

Paul Strand

American, 1890–1976

Crucifixion, Tlacochoaya, Oaxaca (from *The Mexican Portfolio*), 1933; published 1967
Photogravure
Image: 26 × 20.2 cm (10 ¼ × 7 ¹⁵/₁₆ in); sheet: 40.5 × 31.4 cm (15 ¹⁵/₁₆ × 12 ³/₈ in)
University of Nebraska, University Collection, U-1745.13

Between 1932 and 1933, Paul Strand took photographs of the churches, landscape, people, and religious sculpture of Mexico, which he published initially in a 1940 portfolio of twenty images, *Photographs of Mexico* (cat. 59), and then rereleased in 1967 as *The Mexican Portfolio*. Of the twenty images Strand selected for the book, the majority were portraits of men, women, and children from the various municipalities he visited during his nearly two-year stay in the country; also included were views of architecture, landscape, and religious sculptures known as *bultos*.

As an advocate of what he called "straight photography," Strand sought to document Mexico's social history, gravitating toward the rural peasantry and their folkways and excluding any sign of industrial or technological advances. According to scholar Naomi Rosenblum, the artist's emphasis on *bultos* "symbolized his 'intense faith,' which he felt the world badly needed."[1] Strand described his attraction to these objects in the following way: "Among other things I made a series of photographs in the churches, of the Christs and Madonnas, carved out of wood by the Indians. They are among the most extraordinary sculptures I have seen anywhere, and have gone apparently unnoticed. These figures [are] so alive with the intensity of the faith of those who made them."[2]

Nonetheless, as James Krippner has argued, Strand's interest in common religiosity put him at odds not only with his own non-Catholic background but also with artists and intellectuals in Mexico City, for whom such subjects were reminders of the counterrevolutionary Cristero War, a Catholic uprising against the constitution's anticlericalism.[3]

Strand endowed his photographs of *bultos* with expressive immediacy, a result of his belief that the figures were a direct connection to folk Catholicism. He achieved emotional intensity largely through a conscientious focus on the formal composition, including cropped vantage points and strong contrasts of lights and darks. In his works, he often concentrated on the figures' physical and emotional torment. In *Crucifixion, Tlacochoaya, Oaxaca*, these elements are emphasized by cloth garments, hair, and streaks of blood on the Christ figure as well as by the three-dimensionality of the carved subjects, who crowd one another in front of a framed painting. Although Strand disdained the contemporary revival of ancient Mexican crafts, claiming they had no direct parallel to the current circumstances of the rural poor, *Crucifixion* nonetheless embodies the merging of cultures that resulted from conquest and colonialism. Intense suffering, for example, is an element of Spanish religious art, as are the ornate baroque elements, which continued in Mexico into the twentieth century. Christ's kilt, meanwhile, owes a debt to Mixtec codices, which depict gods and those associated with them wearing hip cloths.[4] **BKR**

1. Naomi Rosenblum, "Strand/Mexico," in *México through Foreign Eyes/Visto por ojos extranjeros*, ed. Carole Naggar and Fred Ritchin (New York: W. W. Norton, 1993), 370. 2. Paul Strand to Irving Brown, September 29, 1934, reproduced in *Paul Strand: An American Vision*, by Sarah Greenough, exhibition catalog (Washington DC: National Gallery of Art; New York: Aperture Foundation, 1990), 96. 3. James Krippner, "Traces, Images, and Fictions: Paul Strand in Mexico, 1932–34," *Americas* 63, no. 3 (January 2007): 370. 4. Patricia Rieff Anawalt, *Before Cortes: Mesoamerican Costumes from the Codices* (Norman: University of Oklahoma Press, 1981), 106, 125.

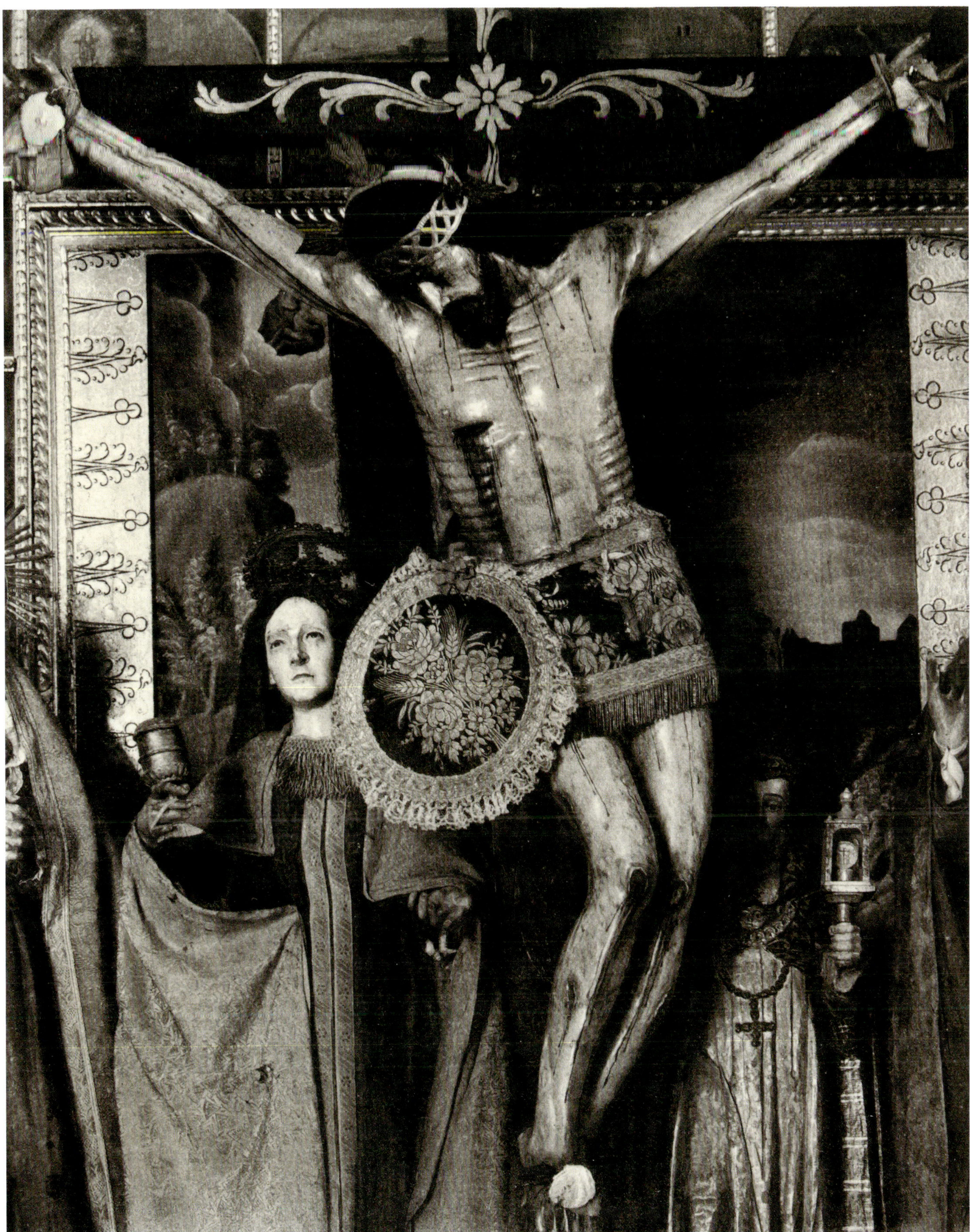

61

Erwin Blumenfeld

American, born Germany, 1897–1969

Santa Fe Christ, 1946
Gelatin silver print
Image: 43.8 × 28.6 cm (17 ¼ × 11 ¼ in); sheet: 49.5 ×
28.6 cm (19 ½ × 11 ¼ in)
Inscribed, lower left, in blue ink: *for Alex* [illegible
symbol]; lower right: *Santa Fé 1946*
University of Nebraska, gift of Alexander Liberman,
U-2991

Best known for fashion photographs that appeared on the covers and in the pages of *Harper's Bazaar* and *Vogue*, Erwin Blumenfeld also had a caustic wit and sly sense of humor that often manifested themselves in his artworks—even those of the most serious and gravest subjects. Born in Berlin, he honed his aesthetic and photographic skills in the Dadaist circles of Germany and France; after a peripatetic existence during the 1910s and 1920s, he finally settled in Paris in 1936. During his first two years there, Blumenfeld experimented with architectural photographs, portraits, and images of religious sculptures that possess the same directness and immediacy of his later pictures of fashion models.[1] An introduction to Cecil Beaton (cat. 102) in 1938 helped Blumenfeld secure employment with *Vogue*, a relationship that would continue sporadically for almost twenty years and intensify after he immigrated to the United States in 1941 to escape Nazi persecution.

Like many photographers, Blumenfeld was ambivalent about his commercial work, offering this misanthropic assessment of two of his biggest clients, cosmetic titans Elizabeth Arden and Helena Rubenstein: "Those two hideous harpies . . . only held onto life with the help of Swiss monkey glands mixed with cocaine, trying to recapture their youth."[2] At the same time, the very artificiality of the fashion industry and its focus on models—whom Blumenfeld described

as "beauties improbably daubed with paint . . . artificial light, phony shadows, real falsies, false baby teeth, artificial tears, artificial smiles"—fascinated the artist and appealed to his Dadaist sensibility, which relished cutting, pasting, and creating improbable juxtapositions and situations.[3]

The subject of this photograph is a Catholic *santo*, and it was taken when the artist began to travel extensively throughout Mexico and parts of North America. The statue perhaps attracted Blumenfeld less for its religious significance than for its associations with the type of fashion photographs he was making at the time. Indeed, scholars have described his magazine-cover portraits of women as "painted masks on which the flow of lipstick becomes an indispensable element."[4] Blumenfeld, who had an early interest in the theater and dreamed of becoming an actor, took a special interest in his models' makeup, designing and applying it himself. This heavily lacquered image of the suffering Christ, with its masklike face, thickly applied paint, and realistic clothes and hair, likely reminded him of the work that awaited back in New York. The connection with Blumenfeld's cover models is intensified by the figure's lack of context: it is isolated so that the viewer focuses completely on the face, hair, and clothes. The open-mouthed grimace may have been the artist's own commentary on the cosmetic and fashion industries, businesses he relied on for his living. **BKR**

1. For examples of Blumenfeld's work from this period—including an early photocollage of Hitler that was banned from a Berlin exhibition in 1937—see William A. Ewing and Marina Schinz, *Blumenfeld Photographs: A Passion for Beauty* (New York: Harry N. Abrams, 1989), 92, 249–50, and 114 ff. 2. From Blumenfeld's posthumous 1969 biography *Durch tausendjährige Zeit* (Frauenfeld, Switz.: Huber, 1976), quoted in Hendel Teicher, *Blumenfeld: My One Hundred Best Photos* (New York: Rizzoli, 1979), 33. 3. Teicher, *Blumenfeld*, 32. 4. Teicher, *Blumenfeld*, 33.

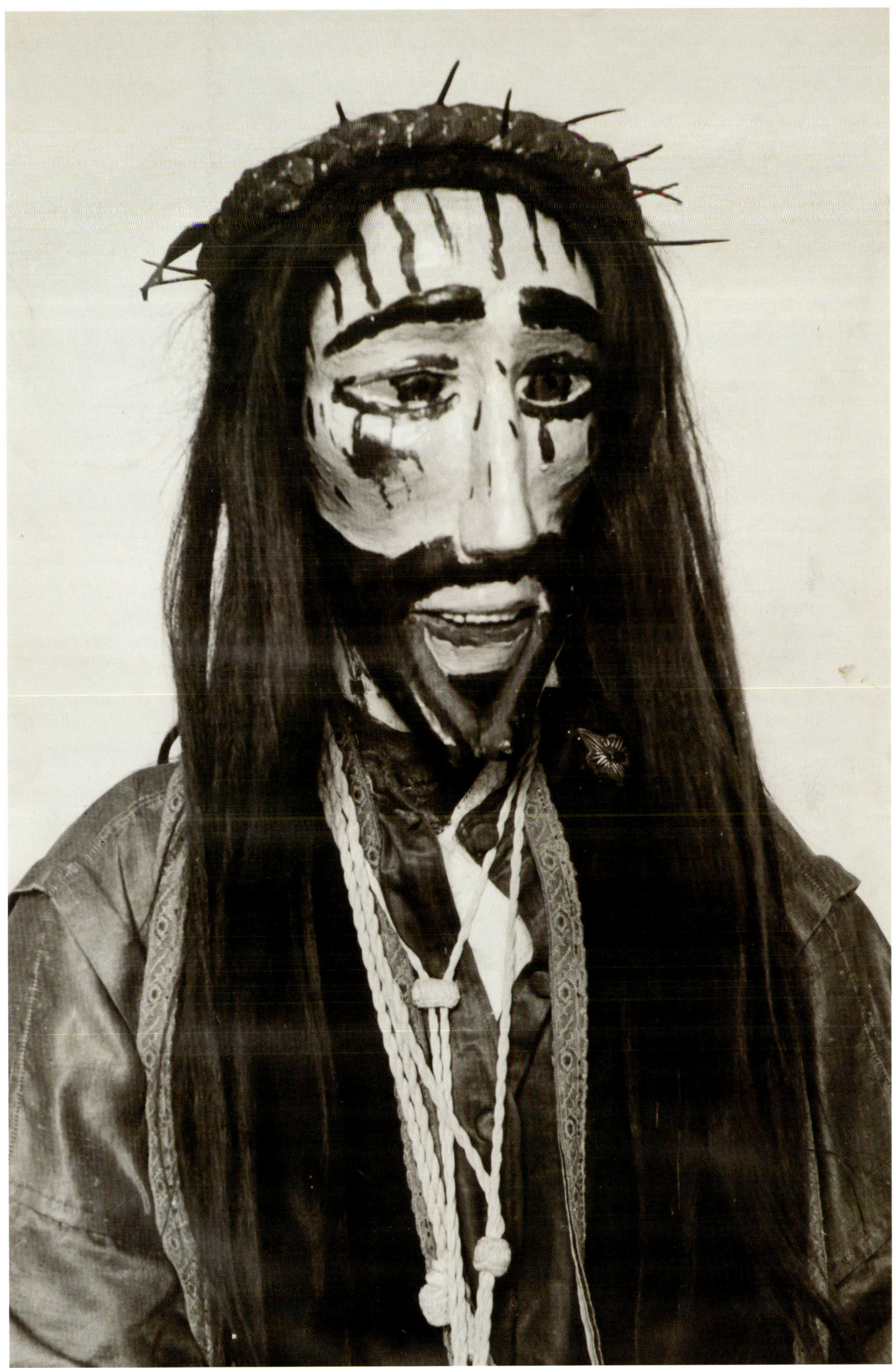

62

Ara Güler
Turkish, born 1928

"Allah," Old Mosque, Edirne, 1956
Gelatin silver print
Image and sheet: 29.5 × 24.9 cm (11 5/8 × 9 13/16 in)
Stamped, on verso, middle center: *PHOTOGRAPHED by /
ARA GULER © / BEYOGLU, GALATASARAY / TOSBAGI SOK.
10/7 / ISTANBUL, TURKEY*
University of Nebraska, University Collection, U-554

The long and productive career of Ara Güler, Turkey's most recognized photographer, extended from photojournalism to architectural surveys, and his intimate scenes of human and urban landscapes have been exhibited and published widely. Nevertheless, stemming in part from the recent nostalgia for "Old Istanbul" and a reaction to the rapid transformation of the city, Güler's work from the 1950s and 1960s has enjoyed a renewed attention during the past few years.[1] Having worked for major international agencies and periodicals, the artist was not an unknown on the international scene, but his photographs from those years were reintroduced to a much broader audience in the pages of novelist Orhan Pamuk's worldly, lyrical, and immensely popular autobiography, *Istanbul: Memories and the City*.[2] Selected by the author and the photographer, this series gave a provocative glimpse of Güler's seemingly endless archive, which stood as "the most perfect memory" of the city.[3]

Sometimes titled *"Allah"* in reference to the prominent calligraphy on the white wall and acknowledged by many critics as his best-known shot, this photograph dates from the early period of Güler's career. It does not pick an Istanbul moment but opens a window to the artist's extensive record of the entire country, its provincial cities, forgotten monuments, and invisible people. The building is Eski Cami, the old mosque, Cami-i Atik, or Ulu Cami, built between 1403 and 1414 in Edirne, the capital of the Ottoman Empire from 1356 to 1453, prior to the conquest of Constantinople. The abstracted fragment belongs to the *son cemaat yeri*, or arcaded porch, of the main façade, destined for the use of latecomers to prayers. *"Allah,"* rendered in large-scale Arabic letters, is an artistic visual code replicated on the walls of religious buildings so often that its meaning is accessible to all, regardless of whether they can decipher it or not. On the façade of Eski Cami, the calligraphy has a vernacular allure, unlike its more adorned and elaborate counterparts, including those inside the mosque.

Güler's photograph captures a simple, quotidian, but visually grand episode. Two women, entirely covered in their black robes, complement and complete the aesthetic power

of the writing on the wall. The curves and angles of their figures echo the forms of the letters while their compact solidity forms a contrast to the airiness of the rendering. Their bodies huddle together in a black mass, their individuality seeming to have disappeared against the calligraphy's impressive scale. Yet, in the issues it raises, this photograph could not be farther from the familiar colonial and Orientalist images of veiled women. Above all, it is a respectful and emotional acknowledgment of religious, conventional, and modest people going about their everyday routines. Güler maintained that his concern has always been people: "There can be no human being without love and no photography without the human being. . . . When I am taking pictures of Ayasofya what counts is the person passing by who stands for life."[4] Pamuk reflected on the relationship between Güler's people and the architectural beauty of their settings. "When they are pictured against the great Ottoman monuments, the mosques," he wrote, "these people can seem more fragile than ever."[5] It is this fragility that makes the veiled women in *"Allah"* so memorable and the photograph so powerful. **ZÇ**

1. On this topic, see Ipek Türeli, "Ara Güler's Photography of 'Old Istanbul' and Cosmopolitan Nostalgia," *History of Photography* 34, no. 3 (August 2010): 300–313. **2.** Published in Turkish as *Istanbul: Hatıralar ve Şehir* (Istanbul: Yapı Kredi Yayınları, 2003), translated into English in 2005 and subsequently into thirty-two languages. **3.** *Istanbul: Hatıralar ve Şehir*, 247. **4.** Ilker Maga, "Interview with Ara Güler," in *Ara Güler'e Saygı/Hommage à Ara Güler/Tribute to Ara Güler* (Istanbul: YGS Yayınları, 1998), 36. **5.** Orhan Pamuk, foreword to *Ara Güler's Istanbul* (New York: Thames and Hudson), 17.

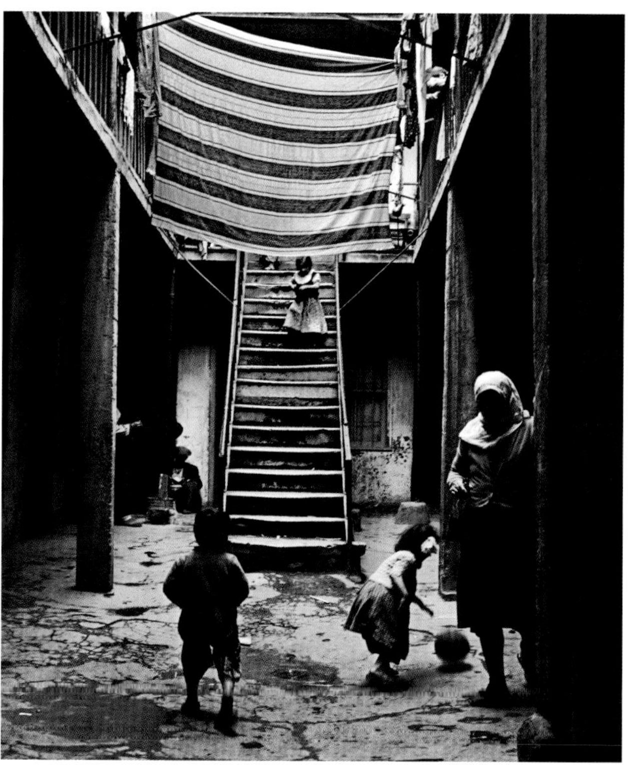

Ara Güler. *Atrium of a House, Tophane, İstanbul*, 1954. Gelatin silver print; 44.3 × 29.8 cm (17 7/16 × 11 3/4 in). University of Nebraska, University Collection, U-558.

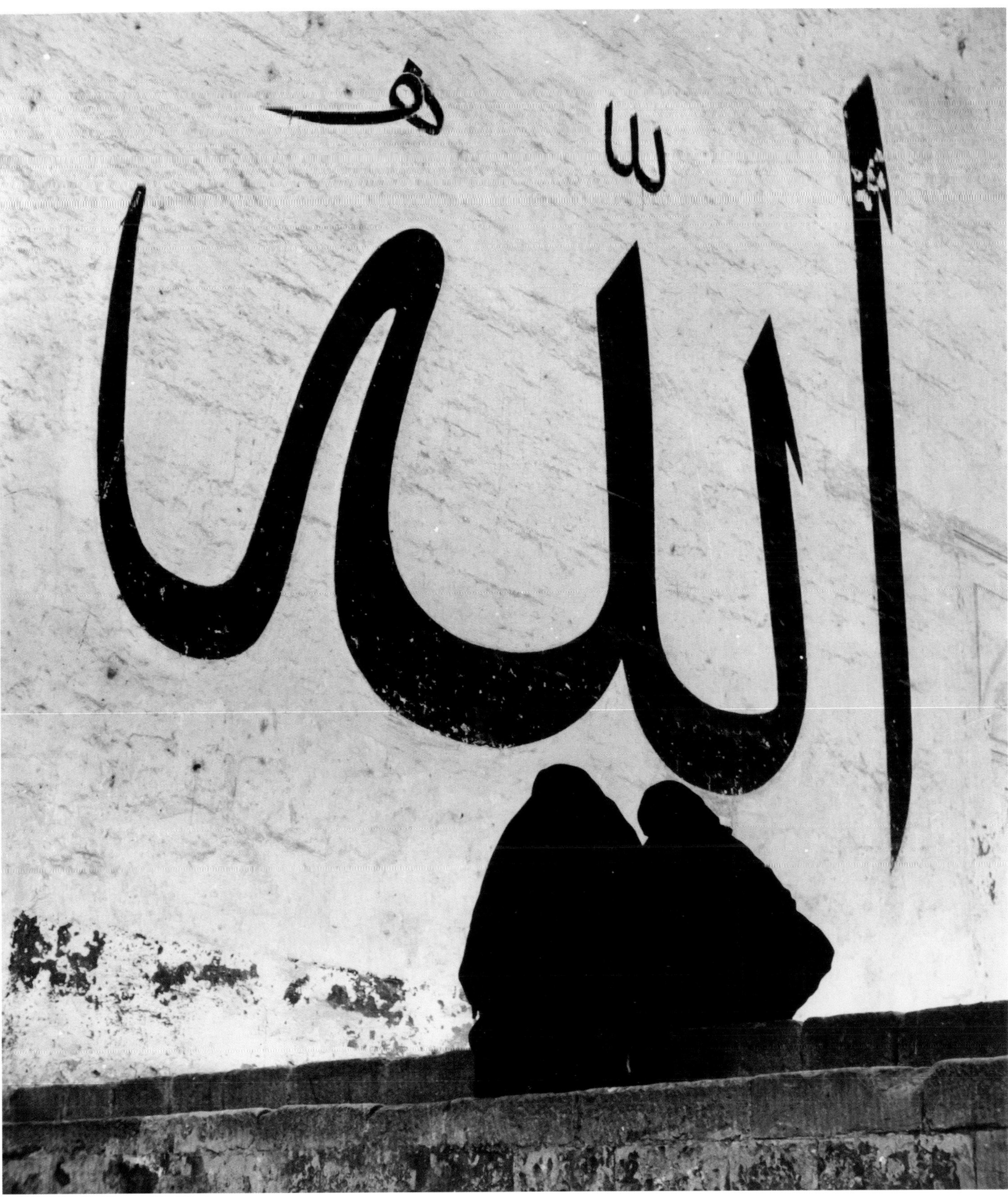

63

Joel-Peter Witkin

American, born 1939

The Wife of Cain, 1981
Gelatin silver print
Image: 36.8 × 38.1 cm (14 1/2 × 15 in); sheet: 50.5 × 40.6 cm
(19 7/8 × 16 in)
Inscribed, on verso, middle center, in pencil: *Joel Peter
Witkin* / *"The Wife of Cain"* / [illegible] *1981* / *# 9/15*
University of Nebraska, Anna R. and Frank M. Hall
Charitable Trust, H-2600

Joel-Peter Witkin describes his carefully structured, emotionally provocative tableaux as "sacred work," and while they occasionally directly address or co-opt biblical subjects and themes, they are often not literal depictions but rather the result of his prayers: "What I really want is this really humble, individual connection, not with a religious institution, but with the living Christ. Whatever it takes in a positive way to get there. The best means, it seems, of getting there is the aesthetic means of photography."[1]

The son of a Jewish father and a Roman Catholic mother, Witkin witnessed his parents' inability to resolve their religious differences, and their ultimate separation influenced his spiritual direction. But the artist's marriage of Old Master compositions and Christian subjects with unexpected elements such as severed human limbs, skeletal remains, and taxidermied animals has led critics and detractors to describe his works as "disturbing" or "exploitative," linking his vision to the photographs of societal outsiders by Diane Arbus and Weegee (cats. 49 and 106).[2] Unlike those two artists, who found their subjects in everyday life, Witkin uses what he calls "physical prodigies," which are the products of dramatic staging. His attraction to these elements is linked—like his religious experience—to his childhood biography:

It happened on a Sunday when my mother was escorting my twin brother and me down the steps of the tenement where we lived. We were going to church. While walking down the hallway to the entrance of the building, we heard an incredible crash mixed with screaming and cries for help. The accident involved three cars, all with families in them. Somehow, in the confusion, I was no longer holding my mother's hand. At the place where I stood at the curb, I could see something rolling from one of the overturned cars. It stopped at the curb where I stood. It was the head of a little girl. I bent down to touch the face, to speak to it—but before I could touch it someone carried me away.[3]

The subject of this photograph, the wife of the biblical figure Cain, is taken from the creation myth outlined in the Bible. This unnamed woman, who is the daughter of Eve and therefore Cain's own sister, bears the blemish of incest and original sin. This is suggested both by the snake wrapped around her body and by her obviously swollen belly. Indeed, her pregnancy is one of the few characteristics used to identify her in Genesis 4:16–17: "And Cain knew his wife; and she conceived." The origins of life, and the cycle of life and death itself, are repeated in the dissected baby in the upper left corner and the human skeleton that clings to the woman's back. As is his practice, Witkin scratched out elements and distressed the negative, heightening the theatricality of the bizarre, perverse composition in order to produce what he himself has described as "profound emotional dichotomies within the viewer."[4] **BKR**

1. For the first quote, see Joel-Peter Witkin, addendum to "Revolt against the Mystical," MA thesis, University of New Mexico, 1976, quoted in Geramo Celant, *Witkin* (Zurich: Scalo, 1995), 249; for the second, see David Levi Strauss, "An Alchemical Disturbance," *SF Camerawork* 13, no. 1 (Spring 1980): 21.
2. For this comparison and the author's refutation of it, see Maria Christina Villaseñor, "The Witkin Carnival," *Performing Arts Journal* 18, no. 2 (May 1996): 78. **3.** The quote is employed frequently in discussion of Witkin; I use Lance Olsen, "Lessness," in *The Inevitable: Contemporary Writers Confront Death*, ed. David Shield and Bradford Morrow (New York: W. W. Norton, 2011), 293. **4.** Quoted in Levi Strauss, "An Alchemical Disturbance," 21.

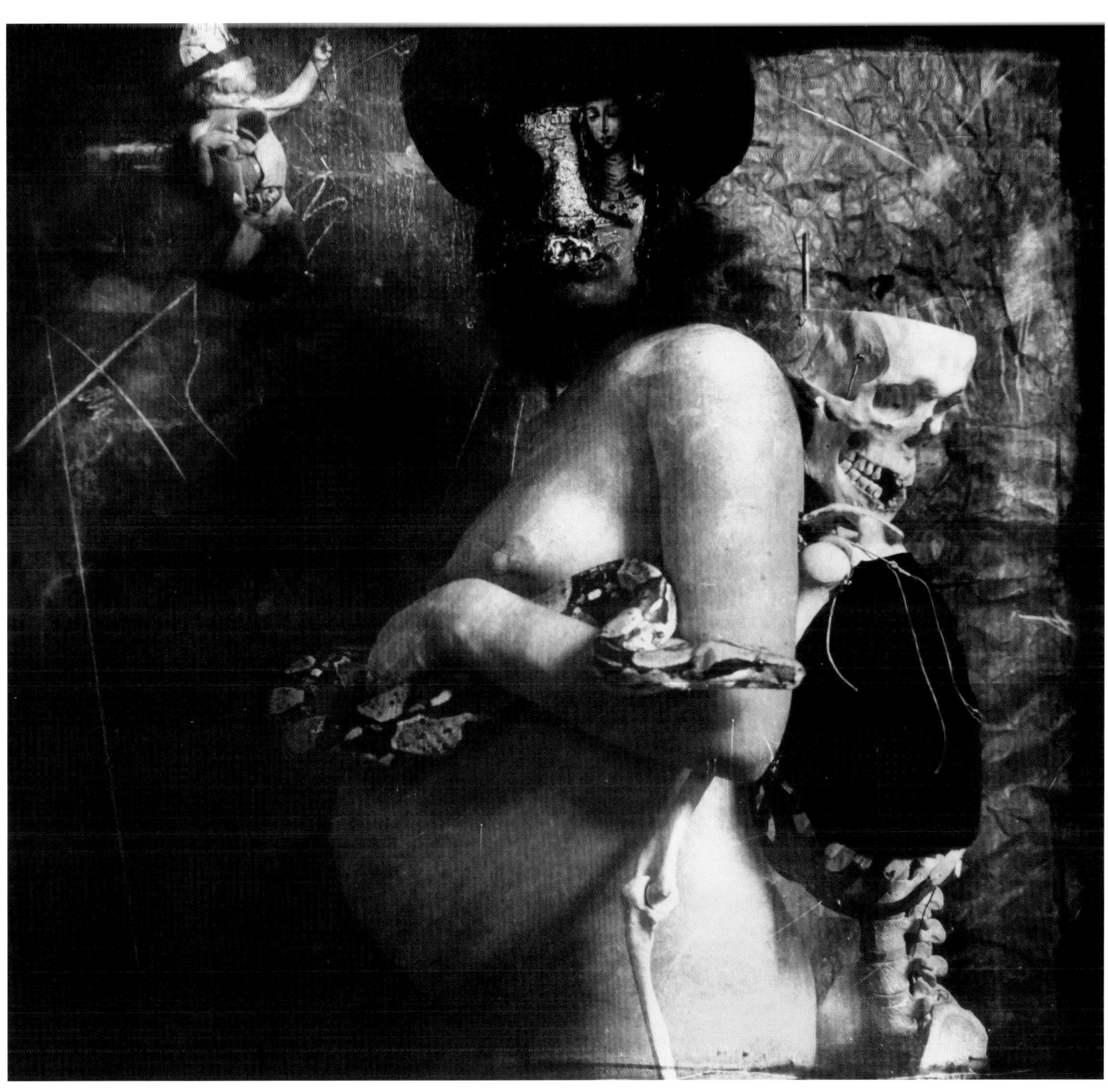

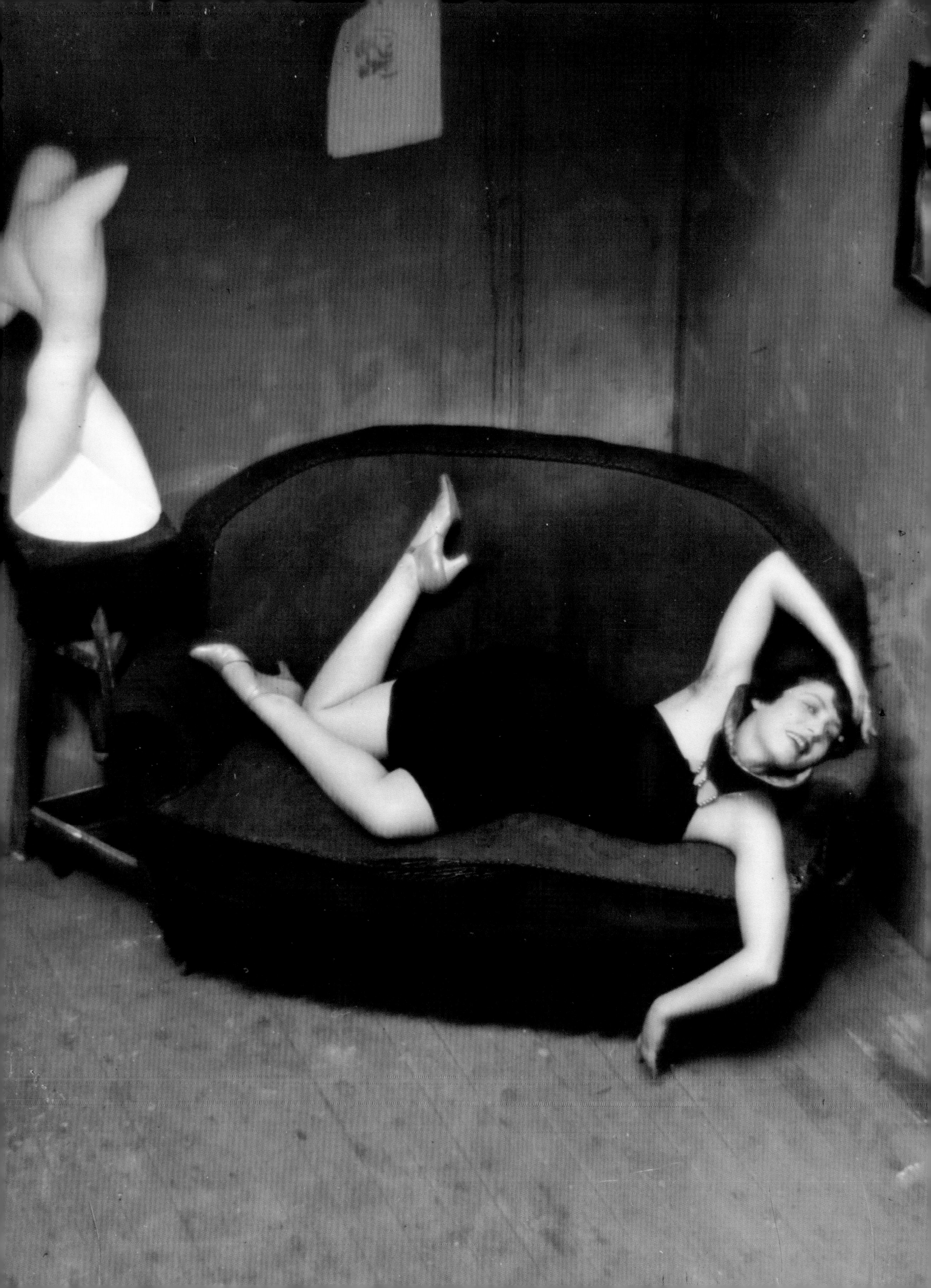

TRADITION AND MODERNITY

Beginning with the introduction of the daguerreotype in 1839, the camera became the focus of debates about its character and use: was it a machine or an artistic tool? Did it supplement or usurp the more traditional art of painting? Adding to this contention was the fact that many early photographers, Louis Daguerre and William Henry Fox Talbot among them, were entrepreneurs or gentleman-inventors who relied on their knowledge of chemistry and optics; were familiar with a range of chemical compounds, metals, and papers; and used specialized equipment and procedures. That the American painter-inventor Samuel F. B. Morse praised the daguerreotype as "one of the most beautiful discoveries of the age" only furthered these scientific and technological associations.[1]

As the nineteenth century drew to a close, debates about photography's role as an artistic medium or as a mechanical apparatus escalated. Groups of artists in America and abroad championed an effort to elevate photography and establish it as a fine art equal to painting and sculpture. Photo-Secessionists—led in America by Alfred Stieglitz (cat. 15)—formed organizations and published journals to further their agenda. In tandem with the search for craftsmanship, distinction, and simplicity undertaken by the contemporaneous Arts and Crafts movement, many of these photographers practiced pictorialism, employing soft-focus lenses, complex gradations of tone, and darkroom manipulations in a quest for individual artistic expression.

During the twentieth century, as pictorialism gave way to modernism, some artists explored traditional themes—rural landscape, for instance—in a nostalgic way, treating them as an antidote to the unprecedented advancements around them; others, meanwhile, approached such subjects as a way to explore new and different modes of modernism. Charles Sheeler (cat. 74) and Ralph Steiner (cat. 75), for example, used vernacular subjects to expand upon the modernist-traditionalist conversation, producing works firmly rooted in modernism's formal approach. Differently inclined colleagues, however, selected subjects—skyscrapers and streets, elements of commodity culture such as shop windows—that conveyed the modernity of their world. Modernism as a formal approach was itself a form of transnational encounter at the beginning of the century, a European invention that was transmitted to a supposedly backward United States. American photographers, meanwhile, visited Mexico and areas outside of the country's civilized boundaries, seeking an instinctual primitivism as inspiration for their own modernist aesthetics.

Other artists sought to harness the camera's scientific potential, creating works that expressed the medium's technological exuberance. They continued with experiments that were in themselves remarkably simple, producing startlingly modern results. Harold Edgerton's *Baton, Multiflash* (cat. 84) and Frederick Sommer's *Smoke on Glass* (cat. 85), for instance, serve as paradigms of the camera's ability to create nonobjective images, recalling the then-dominant trend of abstract expressionism in painting. In his photograms (cat. 82), Theodore Roszak utilized one of the earliest and simplest of photographic processes—securing an image on light-sensitive paper—to achieve similar results.

More recently, some practitioners have returned to experimenting with early forms of photography. Abelardo Morell, for example, uses the camera obscura, the artist's tool that inspired the invention of photography in the first place, adding a new wrinkle to the age-old conversation about the medium's modern applications (cat. 87).

1. Samuel F. B. Morse, "The Daguerreotipe," *New York Observer*, April 20, 1839, quoted in *The Daguerreotype in America*, by Beaumont Newhall, rev. ed. (Greenwich CT: New York Graphic Society, 1968), 15.

64

William Henry Fox Talbot
English, 1800–1877

Chess Players, 1842/50
Calotype
Image: 19.8 × 14.9 cm (7 13/16 × 5 7/8 in); sheet: 24.8 × 20 cm
(9 3/4 × 7 7/8 in)
University of Nebraska, Anna R. and Frank M. Hall
Charitable Trust, H-1175

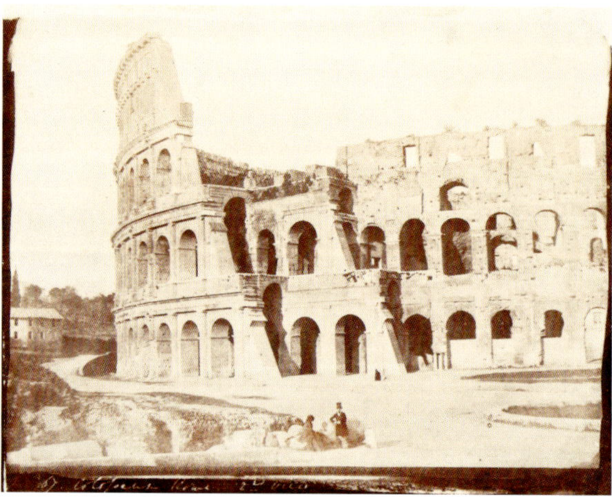

Calvert Jones. *The Coliseum, Rome, Second View*, 1846.
Calotype; 18.7 × 22.5 cm (7 3/8 × 8 7/8 in). University of Nebraska,
Anna R. and Frank M. Hall Charitable Trust, H-1172.

In 1833, as he sat on a mountainside overlooking Lake Como, William Henry Fox Talbot hit on the idea of drawing with light. Although thoroughly untalented as a conventional draftsman, he remembered the almost magical effects of the camera obscura, a long-established artist's tool that he had used on earlier travels (cat. 87). As Talbot reflected "on the inimitable beauty of the pictures of nature's painting which the glass lens of the Camera throws upon the paper in its focus," he considered "how charming it would be if it were possible to cause these natural images to imprint themselves durably, and remain fixed upon the paper."[1]

Back in his native England, Talbot figured out how to make this charming vision a reality. He was uniquely suited to the task: a talented gentleman-scholar with an independent income and time to spare, he successfully pursued a range of interests that included mathematics, optics, crystals, and colored flames.[2] Talbot drew on his abilities in experimental science and his network of contacts, using his country house, Laycock Abbey, as both a laboratory and a subject for his photographic work. In 1841 he patented the calotype process. The direct ancestor of the modern photograph, the calotype used a paper negative that could produce multiple positive prints, a characteristic Talbot sought to profit from by establishing a workshop that specialized in printing and selling his negatives and those made by other early practitioners, some of whom he taught himself.

These two calotypes suggest, in quite different ways, the business of early photography, the diversity of its subjects, and the complex relationships of its devotees. The first—one of many images Talbot made of chess players—captures two opponents deep in contemplation, with the man on the left just about to make a move. While the subject may have appealed to Talbot the scientist because it provided the opportunity to capture rational thought itself, it also provided him with a scene of, in his words, an "everyday and familiar occurrence" that had a legitimate art-historical precedent in Dutch genre painting.[3] Finally, and most simply, the poses would have been easy for the sitters to hold during the long exposure time. Talbot created many of his images outdoors on sunny days, but

he created this one in the establishment of Antoine Claudet, who appears on the right. Himself a man of science, Claudet was trained in the photographic method of Talbot's rival, Louis Daguerre (cat. 66), improving the process and opening the second daguerreotype studio in London. Impressed by his talent, Talbot persuaded Daguerre to adopt and publicize the calotype as well, but with scant commercial success.

Like the first picture, the second was almost certainly printed at Talbot's photographic workshop. It was taken by Calvert Jones, a family friend who was an early pupil.[4] Jones, a talented and imaginative photographer, made this image on a lengthy sailing trip that took him to Malta, Naples, Pompeii, and Rome. The view depicts the Coliseum, the ultimate attraction for visiting Victorians, exposing multiple layers of the structure and capturing its overgrown, romantic dilapidation.[5] Emphasizing the building's bulk are a couple of tiny, stylishly dressed tourists who look toward the camera, holding between them what appears to be a large sketch or painting, perhaps a product or keepsake of their voyage. This detail, captured as it was by Talbot's new technology, suggests the revolutionary change in image making that had occurred in the thirteen short years since his own touristic experience in Italy. **GN**

1. William Henry Fox Talbot, introductory remarks, *The Pencil of Nature* (London: Longman, Brown, Green and Longmans, 1844), n.p., quoted in Larry J. Schaaf, *The Photographic Art of William Henry Fox Talbot* (Princeton NJ: Princeton University Press, 2000), 15. **2.** The two major biographies of Talbot are H. J. P. Arnold, *William Henry Fox Talbot: Pioneer of Photography and Man of Science* (London: Hutchinson Benham, 1977); and Gail Buckland, *Fox Talbot and the Invention of Photography* (Boston: David R. Godine, 1980). **3.** William Henry Fox Talbot, caption to plate 6, *The Open Door*, in Talbot, *The Pencil of Nature*. **4.** For more on Claudet and Jones, respectively, see Arnold, *William Henry Fox Talbot*, 141–42, 149–50; and Buckland, *Fox Talbot*, 71–72, 89–94. **5.** See Andrew Szegedy-Maszak, "A Perfect Ruin: Nineteenth-Century Views of the Colosseum," *Arion*, 3rd ser., 2, no. 1 (Winter 1992): 115–42.

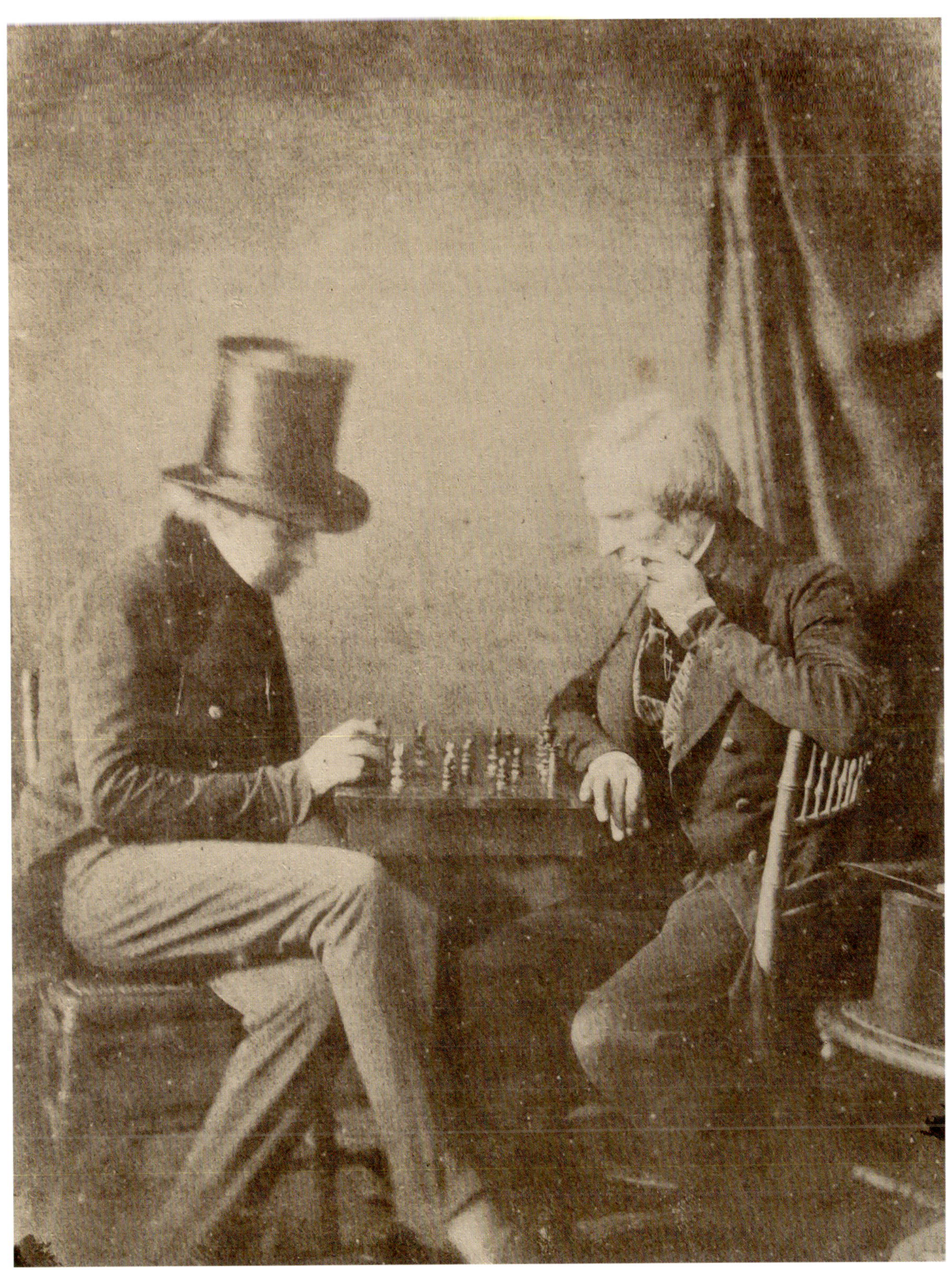

65

David Octavius Hill
Scottish, 1802–1870

Robert Adamson
Scottish, 1821–1848

Portrait of Sir Francis Grant, P.R.A.
1845, printed 1916/20
Carbon print
Image and sheet: 19.8 × 14.1 cm (7 13/16 × 5 9/16 in)
University of Nebraska, Anna R. and Frank M. Hall
Charitable Trust, H-2031

After announcing his invention of the calotype in 1841, William Henry Fox Talbot (cat. 64) set about promoting it as an alternative to the daguerreotype, which was immensely more popular (cat. 66). He frustrated his own ambitions in England by deciding to patent the technique, which meant that only comparatively wealthy individuals could pay for the right to practice it. In Scotland, however, there were no such restrictions, and Talbot's strong network of scientific contacts sparked an important episode of experimentation. His friend Sir David Brewster, a physicist at the University of Saint Andrews, began to explore the process with a chemist colleague, John Adamson; they soon taught it to the latter's younger brother, Robert, who established himself as the first calotypist in Edinburgh.

It was there that Brewster introduced Adamson to David Octavius Hill, a landscape painter and lithographer who was well connected within the city's social and cultural circles.[1] At first Hill intended to use Adamson's expertise to help him make quick portrait sketches of several hundred clergymen whom he hoped to depict in a large painting commemorating the recent founding of the Free Church of Scotland. As the partners' project progressed, however, it took on a life of its own: the calotype portraits possessed a beauty and inventiveness that seduced both their makers and the public. Over the next four and a half years, Hill and Adamson created nearly three thousand negatives that include views of Edinburgh's monuments, studies of fisher folk in the nearby village of Newhaven, and portraits of the city's notable inhabitants and visitors.

Hill and Adamson were a brilliant pair. Nineteen years older than Adamson, the engaging Hill was an experienced artist who delighted in arranging careful compositions and placing sitters at ease within them. Aesthetically astute himself, the retiring Adamson was also a consummate technician who mastered both the apparatus of the camera and the complex chemistry of the calotype process. Together they worked in the backyard of Adamson's studio, taking advantage of the available sunlight; what appear in their pictures to be furnished interior settings are pure illusions. The pair embraced improvisation, taking risks and sometimes deliberately jerking the camera to create a blurry sense of immediacy. In doing so, they adopted a practice that echoed Hill's characterization of the calotype itself as an art whose "rough and unequal texture" resembled "the imperfect work of man . . . and not the much diminished perfect work of God."[2]

In this image, we see what the calotype was capable of in their hands. Taken in September 1845, it depicts Sir Francis Grant, an aristocratic Scot who achieved fame in London as a portraitist and president of the Royal Academy. Expressive and direct, it recalls paintings by the Scottish portraitist Henry Raeburn (1756–1823), who created a powerful sense of drama by sharply illuminating the faces and hands of his sitters.[3] Hill and Adamson would have achieved this effect by using a small mirror to focus and direct the light. Most remarkable, however, is the way in which the artists managed to reduce detail and create a rich, evocative range of lights and shadows. By heightening their calotypes' resemblance to other works on paper—drawings, lithographs, mezzotints—they positioned them clearly and self-consciously as works of art.[4]

Although the partners' collaboration ended with Adamson's early death in 1848, their reputation was revived in the early twentieth century by the photographer and impresario Alfred Stieglitz, who published their images in his journal *Camera Work* (cat. 15). This exquisite carbon print, which was taken from an original negative, is a product of the moment when pictorialist photographers were rediscovering the tastes and ambitions that drove Hill and Adamson's work more than six decades earlier.[5] **GN**

1. For more on Hill and Adamson, including their relationship to Talbot, see Sara Stevenson, *The Personal Art of David Octavius Hill* (New Haven CT: Yale University Press, 2002); and Colin Ford, ed., *An Early Victorian Album: The Hill/Adamson Collection* (London: Jonathan Cape, 1974). **2.** David Octavius Hill to Henry Bicknell, January 17, 1848, archives, George Eastman House, Rochester NY, quoted in Ford, *An Early Victorian Album*, 37. **3.** For Hill's debt to Raeburn, see Roy Strong, "D. O. Hill and the Academic Tradition," in Ford, *An Early Victorian Album*, 57–61. **4.** For the resemblances between the calotype and graphic arts, see Stevenson, "The Aesthetic Character and Practice of the Calotype," in *The Personal Art*, 31–50. **5.** Between 1916 and 1920, the Edinburgh photographer and master printer Jessie Brown Bertram produced photographic carbon prints of forty-nine of Hill and Adamson's original calotype negatives. The Sheldon's print is one of these.

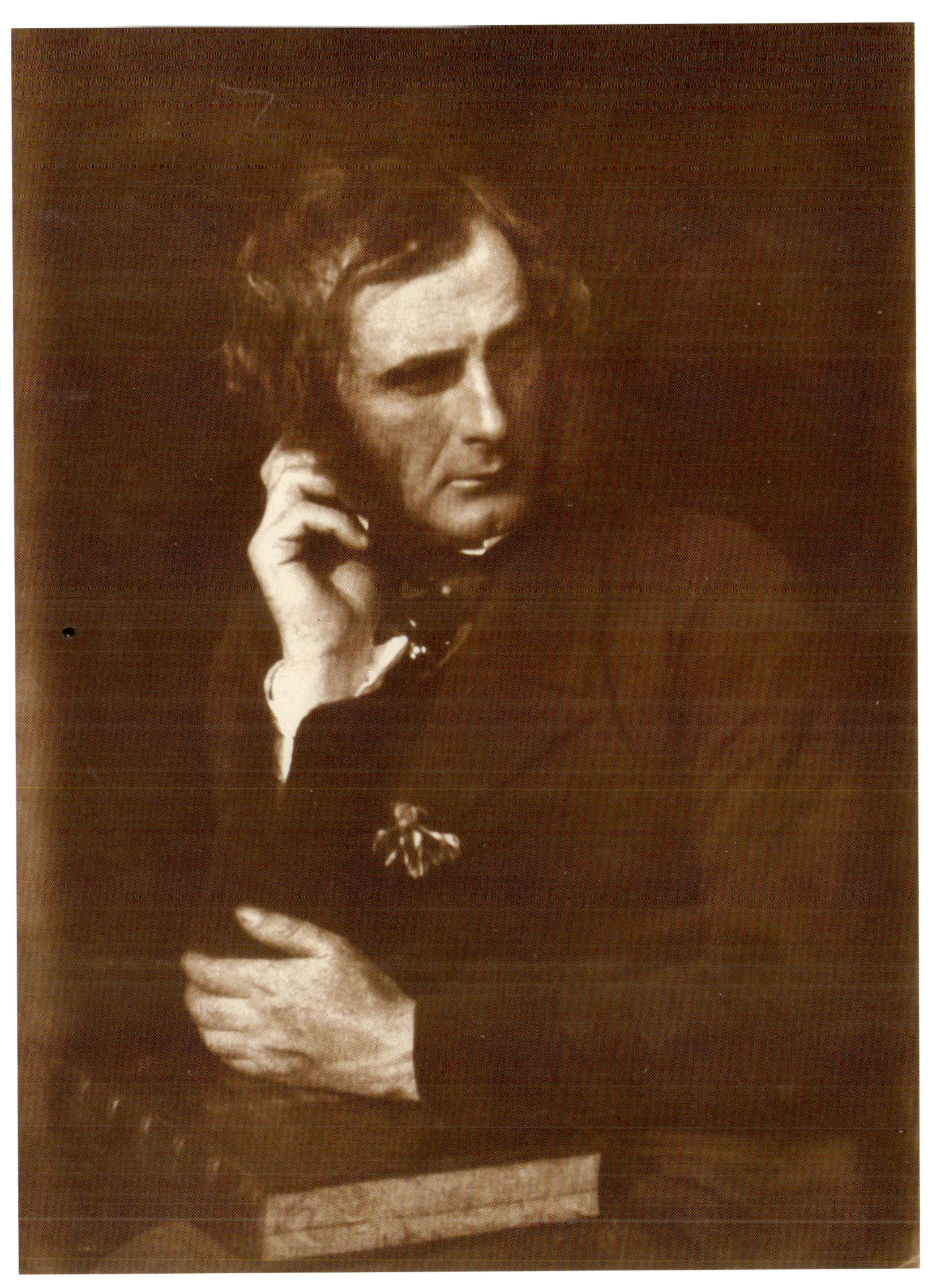

66

Artist Unknown

Portrait (Woman with Lace Gloves), 1850s
Daguerreotype with hand coloring
Image: 8.4 × 7 cm (3 5/16 × 2 3/4 in); case (open): 16.5 ×
9.5 cm (6 1/2 × 3 3/4 in)
University of Nebraska, Anna R. and Frank M. Hall
Charitable Trust, H-2568

Since the early experiments of Thomas Wedgwood and other protophotographers, artists and scientists had dreamed of discovering a way to render permanent the fleeting images of the camera obscura (cat. 87). In 1837 Louis Daguerre became the first to succeed. Originally a painter, he was the designer and proprietor of the Diorama, a popular Paris attraction that dazzled audiences with large-scale illusionistic images of Napoleon's tomb and an alpine village in a snowstorm, for example. Working by himself and with the inventor and lithographer Joseph-Nicéphore Niepce, Daguerre devoted himself to the study of chemistry and optics, developing a technique of using chemical fumes to render a highly polished, silvered copper sheet sensitive to light. Inserted into a camera, it was used to capture an image that could be immediately developed and fixed.[1] Unlike the paper-based calotypes that William Henry Fox Talbot was creating in England (cat. 64), daguerreotypes were neither easily transportable nor infinitely reproducible. Instead, they were glittering, one-of-a-kind artworks that, like the painted portrait miniatures they replaced, gained much of their power from their status as intimate, treasured objects set within protective cases of glass, gilt metal, and velvet.

The American painter and inventor Samuel F. B. Morse, in Paris promoting his new electric telegraph, learned of Daguerre's achievement even before it was unveiled to the French public. Writing in the *New York Observer*, Morse praised the daguerreotype as "one of the most beautiful discoveries of the age." "The exquisite minuteness of the delineation," Morse continued, "cannot be conceived. No painting or engraving ever approached it."[2] This enthusiasm was representative of the new technique's reception in the United States more generally. For roughly a twenty-year period beginning in the early 1840s, Americans suffered from a daguerrean fever; as early as 1851, journalist Horace Greeley was able to proclaim, "In Daguerreotypes . . . we beat the

world."[3] This was the truth: Americans brought the process to perfection, and the daguerreotype business became a major focus of invention and entrepreneurship, working its way from eastern cities to the western frontier and becoming more lucrative, experimental, and organized than anywhere else on earth.

Americans were also fascinated by the aesthetic and personal possibilities this new technology presented. To some, the camera offered the chance to break free of European artistic models and show their wide, brash country as it really was. To others, it provided individuals with the "democratic" opportunity to represent themselves as they wished, without the mediation of an artist. This was, of course, hardly the case. In addition to their artistic and technical expertise, daguerreotypists eased the process by providing their sitters with props, headrests to help them keep still, and written instructions on appropriate dress. But this impression of responsibility created a new conversation about the challenges of projecting one's essential self to the camera. While a painter could get to know a subject and assemble a portrait of a complex personality over time, the task was now seen to rest on the sitter. Speaking of this challenge, Ralph Waldo Emerson, for instance, complained that what he ended up with after all his posturing was the expression "of a mask, not a man."[4] If the young woman in this small daguerreotype feels such a burden, however, she does not show it. Gazing calmly and directly at the camera, eyes wide and intelligent, she rests her right hand against a prop that has been painted to resemble a piece of richly upholstered furniture. She has taken exquisite care with her fashionable clothing and coiffure; her lace collar, hairstyle, and dressy evening costume would have been up-to-date in the early 1850s.[5] A closer look reveals that she paid extra for just a hint of hand coloring on her cheeks and lips; her eyes are tinted a rich brown. If this is a mask, it is a charming one. **GN**

1. For more on the daguerreotype in the United States, see Beaumont Newhall, *The Daguerreotype in America*, rev. ed. (Greenwich CT: New York Graphic Society, 1968); John Wood, ed., *America and the Daguerreotype* (Iowa City: University of Iowa Press, 1991); and Merry Foresta and John Wood, *Secrets of the Dark Chamber: The Art of the American Daguerreotype*, exhibition catalog (Washington DC: National Museum of American Art and Smithsonian Institution Press, 1995). An elegant explanation of the intricacies of the daguerreotype process can be found in Matthew R. Isenburg, "Foreword: The Daguerrian Era in America, 1840–1860," in *My Likeness Taken: Daguerrian Portraits in America*, by Joan L. Severa (Kent OH: Kent State University Press, 2005), x. **2.** Samuel F. B. Morse, "The Daguerreotipe," *New York Observer*, April 20, 1839, quoted in Newhall, *The Daguerreotype in America*, 15. **3.** Horace Greeley, *Glances at Europe* (New York: Dewitt and Davenport, 1851), 26, quoted in Wood, *America and the Daguerreotype*, 11. **4.** Ralph Waldo Emerson, Journal entry, October 24, 1841, quoted in I. O. Matthiessen, *American Renaissance: Art and Expression in the Age of Emerson and Whitman*, 10th ed. (Oxford: Oxford University Press, 1966), 51. **5.** For a daguerreotype of a woman with similar garb and hairstyle, see Severa, *My Likeness Taken*, 150.

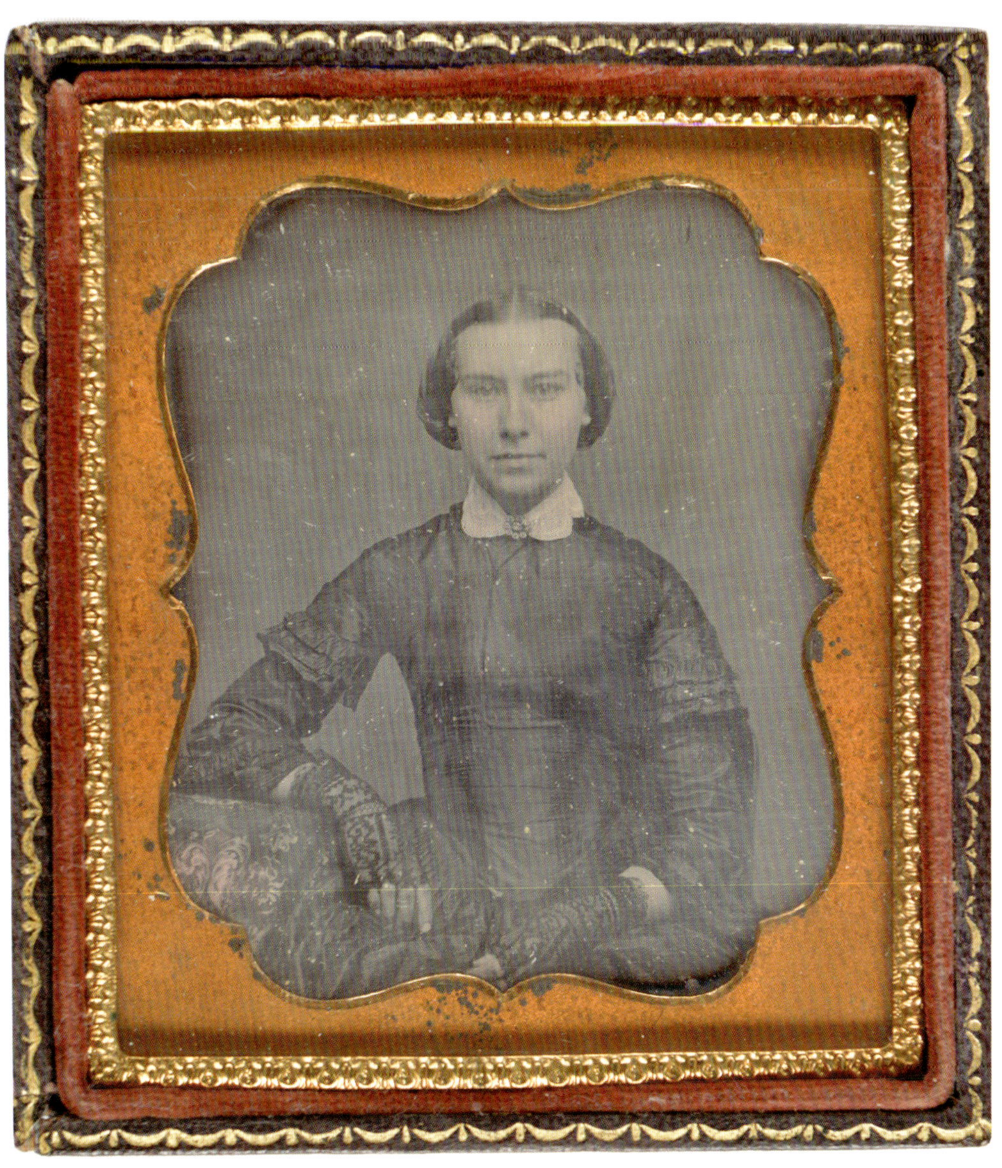

67

Jean-Baptiste-Camille Corot

French, 1796–1875

Souvenir of Ostia, 1855
Cliché-verre
Image: 27.3 × 34.3 cm (10 3/4 × 13 1/2 in); sheet: 29.7 × 36.2 cm (11 11/16 × 14 1/4 in)
Signed, lower right, in plate: COROT
University of Nebraska, Anna R. and Frank M. Hall Charitable Trust, H-1495

Although best known for his lyrical landscape paintings, Camille Corot was a master of other media as well, including drawing, etching, and lithography. Beginning in 1853, the artist began to experiment seriously with the *cliché-verre* process, a method of drawing, etching, or painting on a transparent surface and printing the resulting image on sensitized paper through exposure to light. *Cliché-verre* (in French, "glass plate") was one of the earliest techniques of reproducing images during photography's early years. Although it was costlier and more volatile than engraving or lithography, for example, it achieved popularity because it could more accurately represent an artist's original composition. While in visual terms *cliché-verre* might have had more in common with printmaking, its use of light and specialized paper led photographic pioneers to align it with photography in technical manuals: Robert Hunt's and T. H. Fielding's treatises described *cliché-verre* as "Positive Photographs from Etchings on Glass Plates" and "photogenic etchings," respectively.[1]

Corot was first introduced to the method in 1853 through his artist friend Constant Dutilleux and their like-minded colleagues, who traveled the countryside around the northern French town of Arras painting, photographing, and sketching the landscape. This view, however, is of Ostia, an ancient port at the mouth of the Tiber River. Believed to be the first Roman colony, the town was established around 354 CE, and while it was largely farmland by the nineteenth century, excavations of ruins in 1854 excited artists' imaginations. Although he had made several extended painting trips to Italy earlier in his career, Corot based this scene on memory, evoking both Ostia's ancient past and its agrarian present. A series of monumental structures dominates the far middle ground, and a small farmhouse at left leads the viewer's eye toward the foreground shepherd, whose horse carries him up the rugged outcropping.

Between 1853 and 1860, and then again from 1871 to 1874, Corot created sixty-six images in *cliché-verre*—almost two-thirds of his graphic output.[2] According to one scholar, the artist's trajectory in these works mimics that in other media, moving from crisper, more tightly detailed examples such as this one to more diffuse, atmospheric scenes later in his career.[3] Although Corot was uninterested in printing his *clichés-verre*—he left that to friends and specialized ateliers—he did test different techniques such as *tamponnage*, which involves striking the plate with the stiff bristle of a brush to create small holes and thus more atmospheric halftones. The Sheldon's example is printed in reverse from other known prints of Corot's *Souvenir of Ostia*, suggesting that it was printed by another atelier at a later date.[4] **BKR**

1. For this and a history of *cliché-verre*, see Elizabeth Glassman, "Cliché-verre in the Nineteenth Century," in *Cliché-verre: Hand-Drawn, Light Printed: A Survey of the Medium from 1839 to the Present*, by Elizabeth Glassman and Marilyn F. Symmes, exhibition catalog (Detroit: Detroit Institute of Arts, 1980), 29–44. **2.** Glassman, "Cliché-verre," 37–38. **3.** Glassman, "Cliché-verre," 39. **4.** For another example of this phenomenon, see Cabinet des estampes du Musée d'art et d'histoire, *Le cliché-verre: Corot et la gravure diaphane*, exhibition catalog (Geneva: Cabinet des estampes du Musée d'art et d'histoire/Éditions du Tricorne, 1982), 53, cats. 27–28.

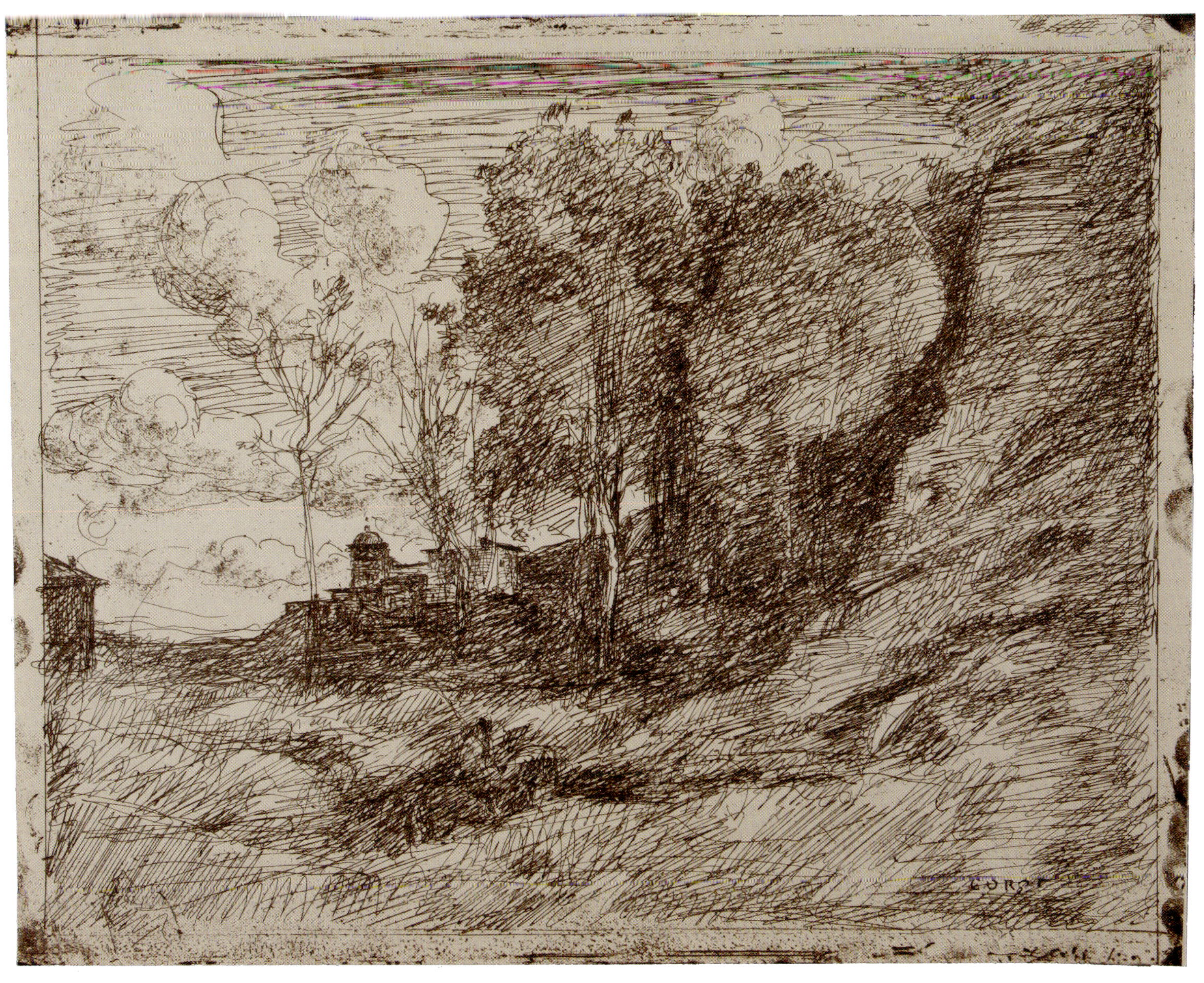

68

Eadweard Muybridge

English, 1830–1904

Lawn Tennis (plate 298 from *Animal Locomotion*), 1887
Collotype
Image: 34.9 × 50.2 cm (13 ¾ × 19 ¾ in); sheet: 48.9 ×
62.2 cm (19 ¼ × 24 ½ in)
Printed, bottom center: ANIMAL LOCOMOTION. *Plate 298 /
Copyright, 1887, by* EADWEARD MUYBRIDGE. *All rights
reserved*
University of Nebraska, Anna R. and Frank M. Hall
Charitable Trust, H-2045

Eadweard Muybridge approached his craft with entrepreneurial zeal and, as a result, is today considered one of the pioneers of photography, perhaps best known for his experiments at capturing human motion. Muybridge first came to the United States from Britain in the early 1850s, settling in San Francisco and entering the book trade. He discovered photography in the 1860s while recuperating from a head injury back in England; after returning to California in 1867, he established himself as an "artist-photographer," specializing in stereoscopic views of Yosemite Valley, the Pacific coastline, the Alaskan territories, and panoramas of San Francisco's skyline.[1]

Muybridge's interest in animal locomotion began with an introduction to former California governor and president of the Central Pacific Railroad Leland Stanford, who desired a photograph of his favorite horse at full gallop. With Stanford's patronage, for several years Muybridge investigated diverse formats and processes that would allow him to capture movement, once even resorting to fakery. Finally, in 1878, he achieved the first successful serial images of fast motion in a horse by arranging twelve cameras at twenty-one-inch

intervals, with trip wires that triggered the camera shutters. The photographer's accomplishment was greeted with wide acclaim in the press and accolades from his colleagues, some of whom were early pioneers in the process; these included painter Thomas Eakins, whose own investigations in human motion paralleled those of Muybridge. This notoriety led to a European tour in which Muybridge lectured and demonstrated his inventions. In 1883 he contracted with the University of Pennsylvania to further his experiments and went on to create an impressive body of work, accumulating some fifteen thousand negatives and producing a multivolume publication entitled *Animal Locomotion*.

Lawn Tennis is part of Muybridge's two-year research stint in Philadelphia. He constructed a large outdoor studio under the auspices of the university's veterinary department and, rather than compose a battery of cameras, used two counter-rotating discs to produce greater definition in his subjects, a device originally developed by French physiologist and photography pioneer Étienne-Jules Marey. Muybridge shot a wide range of subjects, including nude males in various positions, an astonishing array of animals from Philadelphia's Zoological Gardens (see below), and this fully clothed woman, who is seen from various angles lobbing a tennis ball.

Upon *Animal Locomotion*'s debut in 1887, the university praised Muybridge's work as contributing "to the scientific study of animal motions."[2] Critical reviews of his magnum opus went to great lengths to convince collectors that, while beautifully printed, these were not artworks but rather useful tools for the instruction of artists: "This is not an art, but it is a mine of facts of nature that no artist can afford to neglect. Here are dancing girls graceful enough to delight the soul of Raphael; athletes with heroic movement that would fire the spirit of [Michelangelo] Buonarotti; foreshortenings, and flowing contours to satisfy Tintoret. Thus to see the natural man in his own motion under nature's light is a lesson to humanity of its own glory."[3] **BKR**

1. For a history of Muybridge's early life as well as his legal and physical troubles, see Anita Ventura Mozley, "Introduction to the Dover Edition," in *Muybridge's Complete Human and Animal Locomotion*, by Eadweard Muybridge, vol. 2 (New York: Dover Publications, 1979), vii–xxxviii. **2.** Quoted in Ventura Mozley, "Introduction," xxxiii. **3.** Author unknown, New York, January 19, 1888, quoted in Robert Bartlett Haas, *Muybridge: Man in Motion* (Berkeley: University of California Press, 1976), 156.

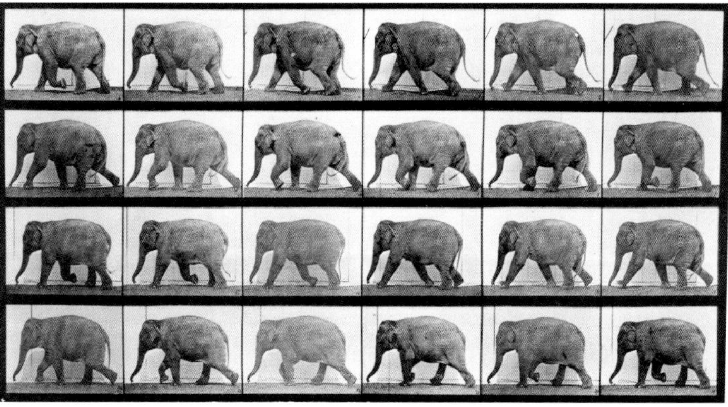

Eadweard Muybridge. *Elephant Walking*, 1887. Collotype; 20.6 × 37.8 cm (8 ⅛ × 14 ⅞ in). University of Nebraska, Anna R. and Frank M. Hall Charitable Trust, H-2046.

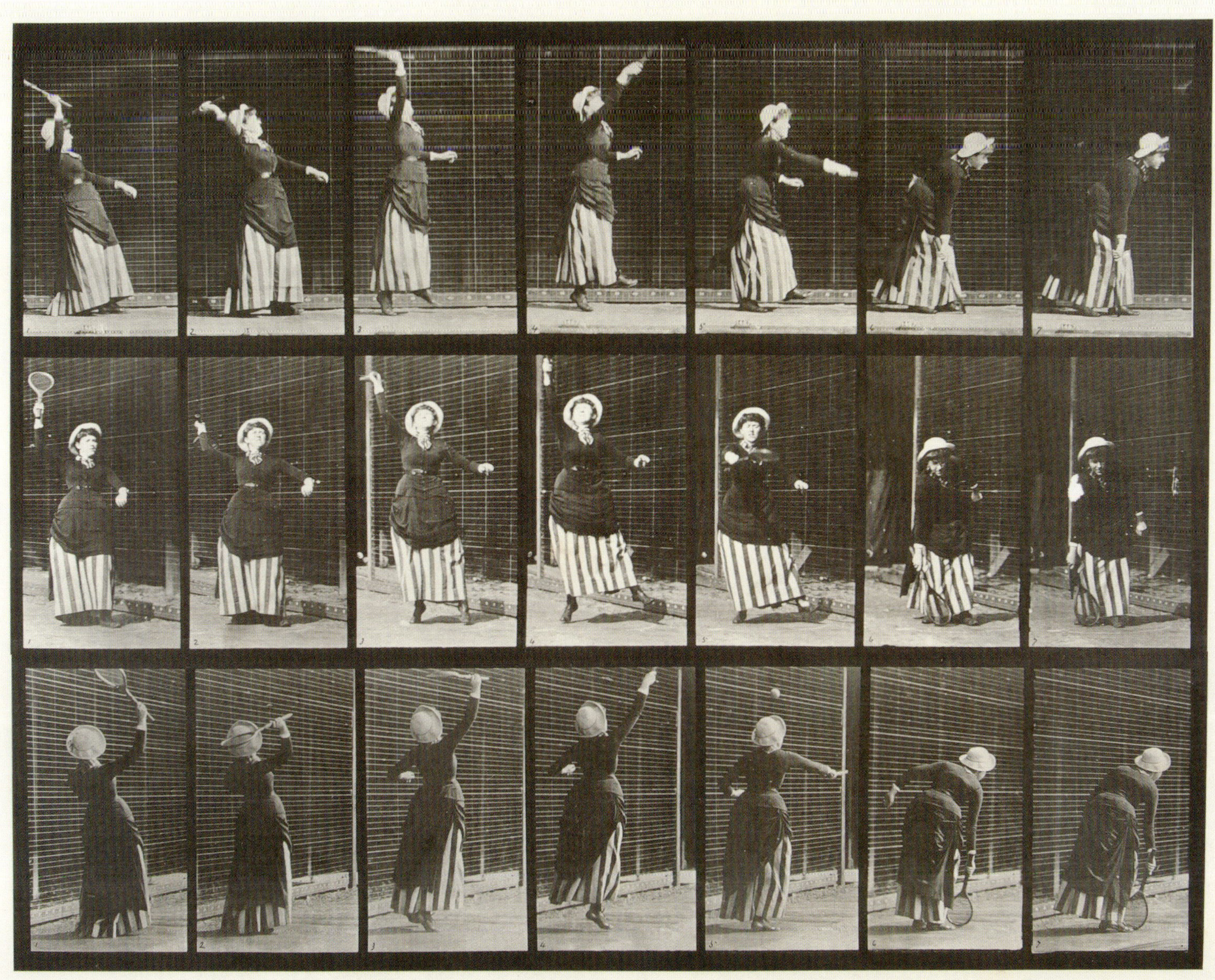

69

Clarence Hudson White

American, 1871–1925

Dewdrops (from the portfolio *Camera Work*), 1902;
published 1909
Photogravure
Image and sheet: 19.2 × 15.4 cm (7 9/16 × 6 1/16 in)
University of Nebraska, Anna R. and Frank M. Hall
Charitable Trust, H-2159.13

Trained and employed as a bookkeeper, Clarence Hudson White discovered photography on his honeymoon in Chicago, where he and his new wife attended the 1893 World's Columbian Exposition. After immersing himself through the fair's exhibitions and sales of photographic equipment, White returned to his native Ohio and took up the medium in earnest. Although completely self-taught, he garnered attention through local and then national exhibitions; by the end of the decade, he had made contact with photographic luminaries, most notably, Alfred Stieglitz (cat. 15). The two shared a close relationship for several years, and Stieglitz invited White to become one of the founding members of the Photo-Secession, an organization established to promote pictorialism and fine-art photography. Stieglitz prepared exhibitions of the groups' photographs and created a new magazine called *Camera Work* to further advance their artistic agenda and careers.

Like Stieglitz, White was a tireless promoter of photography's artistic potential. But unlike his colleague, who used galleries and publications as his forum, White directed his energies toward teaching, first at Columbia University and then at the Clarence White School of Photography, both in New York. He trained a generation of photographers that includes major talents such as Margaret Bourke-White, Laura Gilpin, Dorothea Lange, Ralph Steiner, and Doris Ulmann, all represented in this catalog (cats. 36, 32, 17, 78, 75, and 77). While White's own artistic approach and pedagogical method emphasized pictorialist practice—including nonnarrative, asymmetrical arrangements, soft-focus compositions, and a harmonious balance of tones—many of his students ultimately abandoned these methods in favor of the more straightforward documentary style that had become increasingly dominant by the 1910s. Nonetheless, White's influence is evident in much of their work.

In *Dewdrops* the artist took a completely formal approach, eliminating any narrative aspect and defying attempts at interpretation. Instead, the viewer is meant to see the objects as a series of symbols with a spiritual equivalent.[1] An elegantly translucent glass globe sits just off-center, mimicked by the delicate dewdrops on the window. White's young son emerges from the photograph's right edge, caressing the globe with his left hand. Stieglitz featured this image with a beautifully constructed, hand-tipped photogravure in the July 1908 issue of *Camera Work*. **BKR**

1. George Dimock, "Priceless Children: Child Labor and the Pictorialist Ideal," in *Priceless Children: American Photographs, 1890–1925*, exhibition catalog (Greensboro NC: Weatherspoon Art Museum; Seattle: University of Washington Press, 2001), 11.

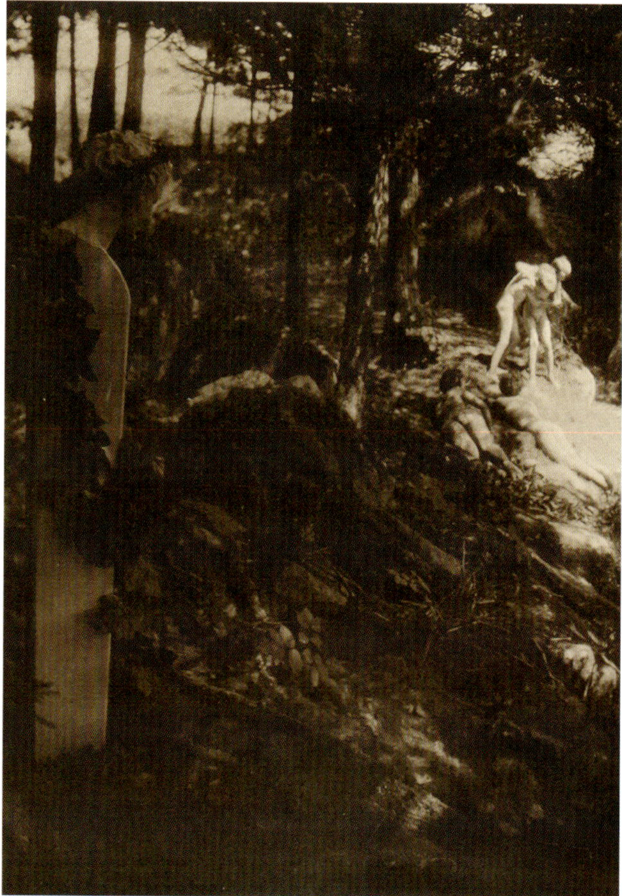

Clarence Hudson White. *Boys Wrestling* (from the portfolio *Camera Work*), 1909. Photogravure; 21.4 × 15.6 cm (8 7/16 × 6 1/8 in). University of Nebraska, Anna R. and Frank M. Hall Charitable Trust, H-2159.8.

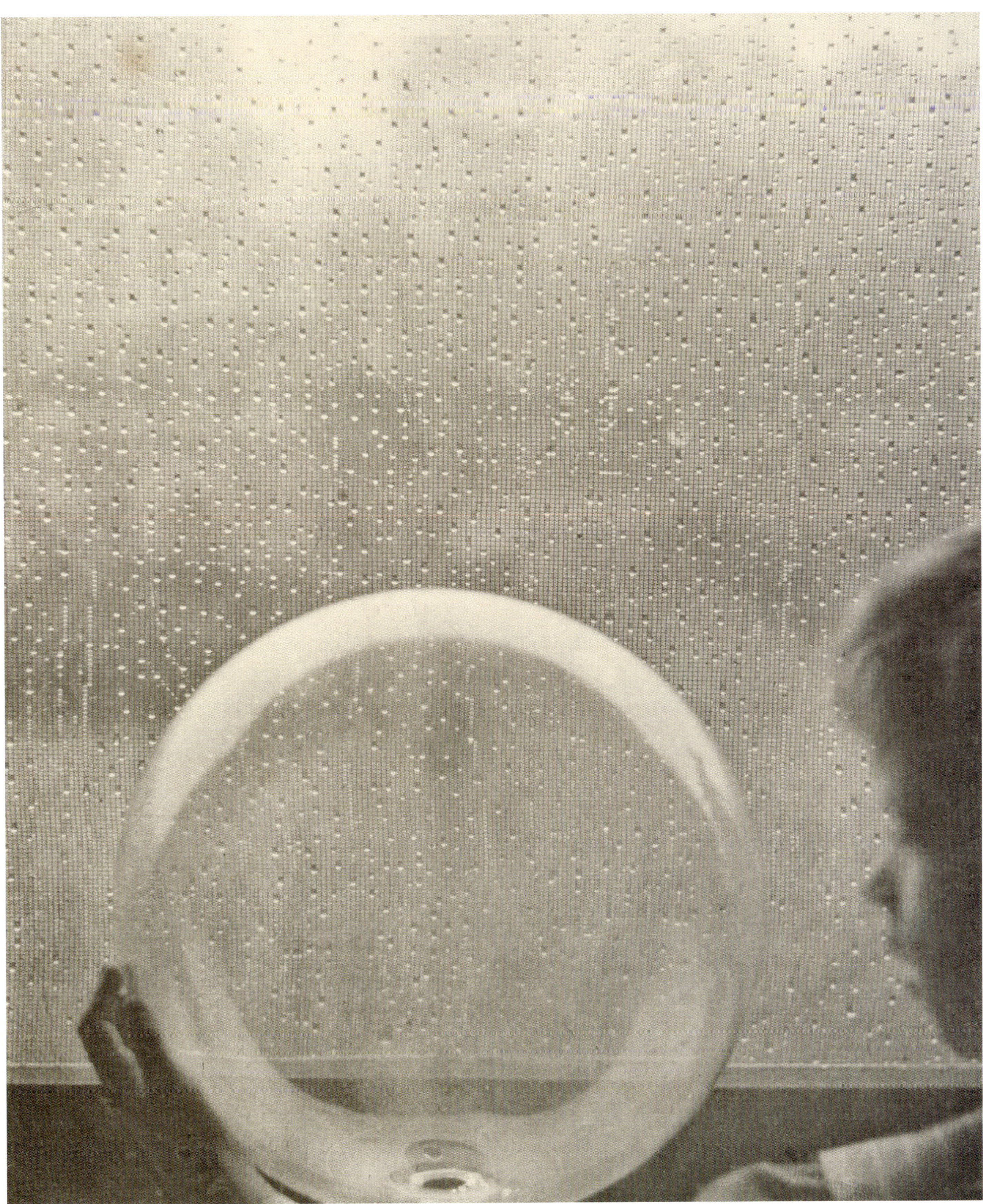

70

Jacques-Henri Lartigue
French, 1894–1986

Gaby Deslys at the Casino de Paris, 1918
Gelatin silver print
Image: 26 × 28.1 cm (10 ¼ × 11 1/16 in); sheet: 30 × 39.7 cm
(11 13/16 × 15 5/8 in)
Signed, lower right, in black ink: *J. H. Lartigue*
University of Nebraska, Anna R. and Frank M. Hall
Charitable Trust, H-2150

"The World Leaps into an Age of Innovation" screamed the headline of a November 1963 *Life* magazine spread on Jacques-Henri Lartigue, a photographer previously unknown in the United States.[1] This issue of *Life* also featured the recently assassinated John F. Kennedy on its cover, thereby ensuring the photographer's exposure to a wide audience. That same year, Lartigue received a solo exhibition at the Museum of Modern Art in New York, an event that cemented his place in the history of photography. Lartigue was hailed as an intuitive artist whose exuberant snapshots captured the technological advancements and social milieu of a French golden age.[2]

Appropriate to his later interests and subjects, Lartigue took his first photograph at the dawn of the twentieth century, in 1900 at the age of six, and two years later was given a camera of his own by his father, Henri, an amateur photographer himself. Captivated by motion and innovative machines, he portrayed the action of early aviation and automobile racing. Equally attracted to the beautiful, stylish women who strolled Paris's boulevards, Lartigue photographed their striking and elegant modern fashions, occasionally satirizing them in the process. Although World War I broke out in 1914, Lartigue rarely depicted the horrors of war, choosing instead to record the fleeting, candid moments of life. Exempt from the war because of poor health, in 1915 Lartigue enrolled in the Académie Julian and became a painter, an activity that would serve as his primary profession prior to his "discovery" as a photographer in 1963.

The wealth and status of Lartigue's family provided him the opportunity to befriend and photograph many of society's elite. The Sheldon's photograph depicts the famous entertainer Gaby Deslys—equally famed for her acting, dancing, and singing—onstage at one of France's popular music halls, the Casino de Paris.[3] The alluring Deslys was known for her romantic entanglements and stunning outfits both on- and offstage. Taken in February 1918 while she was filming *Bouclette*, a story chronicling the love affairs of a cabaret star, Lartigue's photograph embodies the joy and charisma Deslys exuded while performing. This work also illustrates the entertainer's sensational costumes and her signature feathered headdresses, echoing Lartigue's interest in women's fashion and expressing Deslys's daring modern style. The photographer's brother Maurice (nicknamed "Zissou") stares at Deslys from the wings, making this not only an image of a captivating performer but also a telling portrait of one of her admirers.

Richard Avedon noted that Lartigue's images "imply things that happened before and after the photographs were taken. They remind us of what we were never there to know."[4] Taken two years before Deslys's untimely death from a throat infection, this photograph serves as a visual record of one of her final performances. Lartigue's photograph is also a fascinating document about a society wrestling with unprecedented cultural changes: taken during the height of World War I, the image represents an escape from the horrors of modern combat while at the same time directly acknowledging phenomena like celebrity culture and popular entertainment so associated with life in the twentieth century. **AH**

1. "The World Leaps into an Age of Innovation," *Life* 55, no. 22 (November 1963): 65–72B. For a recent study of Lartigue's work, see Martine d'Astier et al., *Lartigue: Album of a Century*, exhibition catalog (Paris: Centre Georges Pompidou; New York: Harry N. Abrams, 2003). **2.** John Szarkowski, curator of Lartigue's MOMA exhibition, characterized him as a primitive genius; Szarkowski, "The Photographs of Jacques Henri Lartigue," *Bulletin of the Museum of Modern Art* 30, no. 1 (1963): 3–32. In recent years, scholars have reexamined Lartigue's role within the history of photography, positing the idea that he was acquainted with the medium's techniques and trends and was a well-equipped, gifted amateur. For an in-depth assessment of this issue, see Kevin Moore, *Jacques Henri Lartigue: The Invention of an Artist* (Princeton NJ: Princeton University Press, 2004). **3.** For a biography of Deslys, see James Gardiner, *Gaby Deslys: A Fatal Attraction* (London: Sidgwick and Jackson, 1986). **4.** Richard Avedon, afterword to *Diary of a Century*, by Jacques-Henri Lartigue (New York: Penguin Books, 1970).

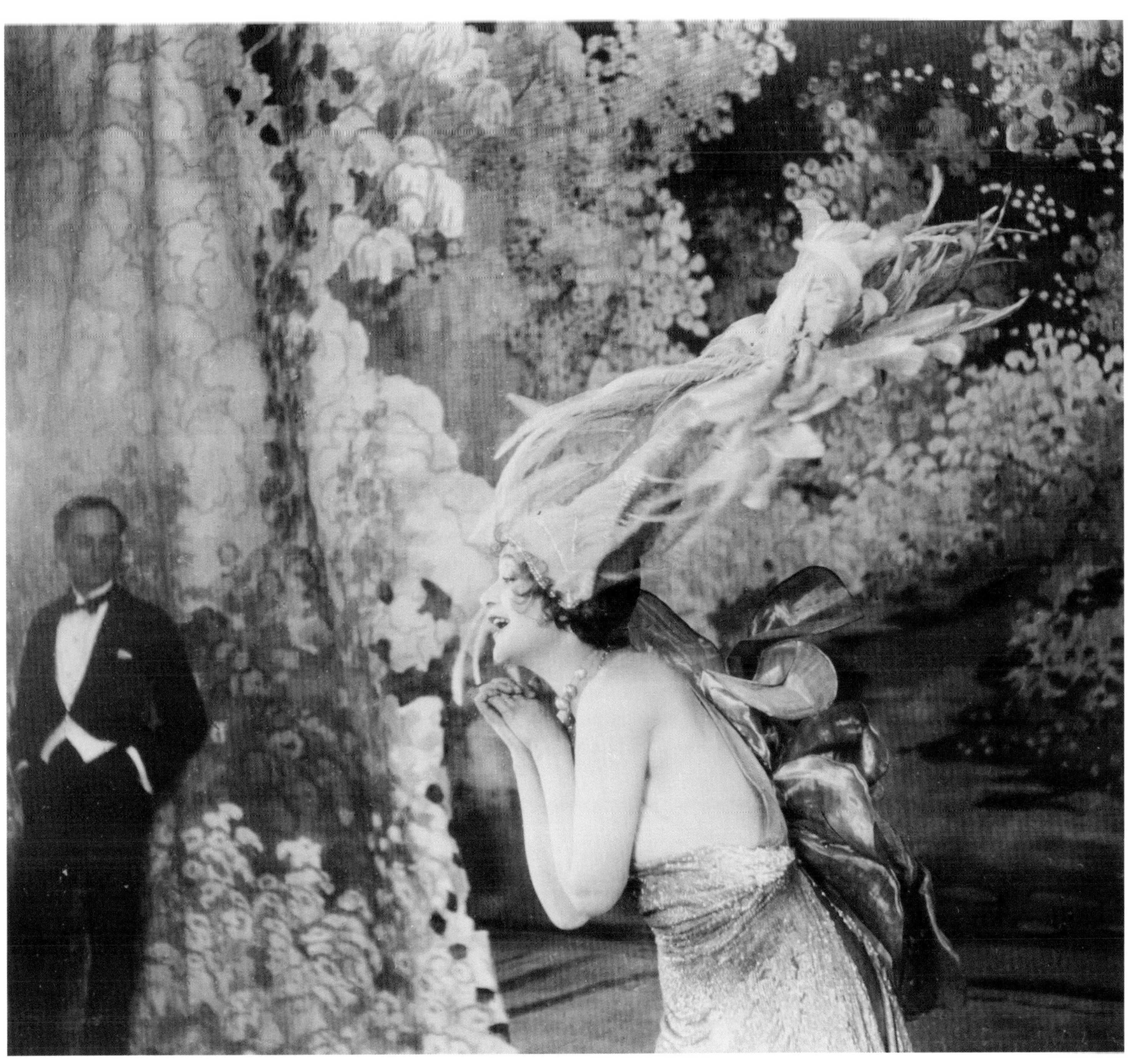

71

Constantin Brancusi

French, born Romania, 1876–1957

Brancusi at Work in the Studio, c. 1922
Gelatin silver print
Image and sheet: 40 × 29.9 cm (15 ¾ × 11 ¾ in)
Inscribed, in image, lower right, in black ink: *Q. H. P. Roché / [illegible] / C. Brancusi*; on verso, upper left, in pencil: *Brancusi [illegible] in atelier / Éve (coll. ~~H.-P. Roche~~ Guggenheim Museum) / [illegible] dans l'espace*; stamped, middle center, in red ink: *Henri Pierre Roche / 99 Boulevard Arago / Paris XIV.*
University of Nebraska, gift of Olga N. Sheldon, U-1950

One of the foremost sculptors of the twentieth century, Constantin Brancusi redefined the genre through his progressive experiments in the simplification of form, using a variety of materials to capture its essence in three dimensions. Unlike many of his contemporaries, the artist took an active approach to creating his sculptures; in fact, he carved them individually, a practice that inflected his photography.

Initially, Brancusi used photography in a purely practical way: as a document and record of his sculptures and as a marketing device for potential buyers who lived outside the environs of Paris. At first, the artist had other people photograph his work, but he became increasingly dissatisfied with the results; by the early 1920s, he began taking the pictures himself. Thereafter, he made thousands of images of his sculptures, of his studio, and of himself at work.[1] Although Brancusi was uninterested in the technical aspects of photography, he held the medium itself in high regard and knew several people associated with the cinematic and photographic vanguard working in Paris. A breakthrough came in 1921, when he was introduced to Man Ray, who advised him on the right equipment and processing techniques and helped him establish a proper studio and darkroom. Brancusi was primarily interested in photography as a way to express the simplicity of his sculptures, and his images act as a metaphor for his artistic process. Individually, they comment on his search for essential forms; collectively, they contextualize and elaborate on those forms in a way that, as Friedrich Teja Bach explained it, is akin to his "method of combining a single sculptural form into ever-new configurations."[2]

Brancusi made several self-portraits, at times self-consciously inserting his presence into a work by showing his face reflected in the polished bronze of one of his sculptures. Other photographs show the artist toiling in his studio; this gesture was an additional way of connecting himself to his artwork, establishing himself as a craftsman and sage, and acknowledging the folk art that was among his first projects and influences. Brancusi was deeply preoccupied with his studio: upon his death, he bequeathed its entire contents to the French government with the stipulation that it be reconstructed—which it was in 1997, next to the Centre Georges Pompidou in Paris.

In this photograph, the artist stoops over to finish the preparatory study for a marble sculpture; his unfinished masterpiece, the *Gallic Rooster*, stands next to him, and his face is a mask of intense concentration.[3] The studio is jammed with a number of Brancusi's works, and the harsh foreground lighting throws eerie shadows onto the walls, creating a maze of dark and light. The inscription on the bottom right of the work suggests that this particular print was a gift to his friend Henri-Pierre Roché. The avant-garde author, upon seeing photographs of the artist's bronzes for the first time in 1920, described them as "radiant."[4] **BKR**

1. For the breadth of Brancusi's photographs, see Elizabeth A. Brown, *Constantin Brancusi: Photographe* (Paris: Éditions Assouline, 1995), 76–79. **2.** Friedrich Teja Bach, "Brancusi and Photography," in *Constantin Brancusi: 1876–1957*, by Bach, Margit Rowell, and Ann Temkin, exhibition catalog (Philadelphia: Philadelphia Museum of Art; Cambridge MA: MIT Press, 1995), 316. **3.** For this identification, see Marielle Tabart and Isabelle Monod-Fontaine, *Brancusi Photographe*, exhibition catalog (Paris: Musée national d'art moderne, 1977), 119, cat. 27. **4.** Bach, "Brancusi and Photography," 312.

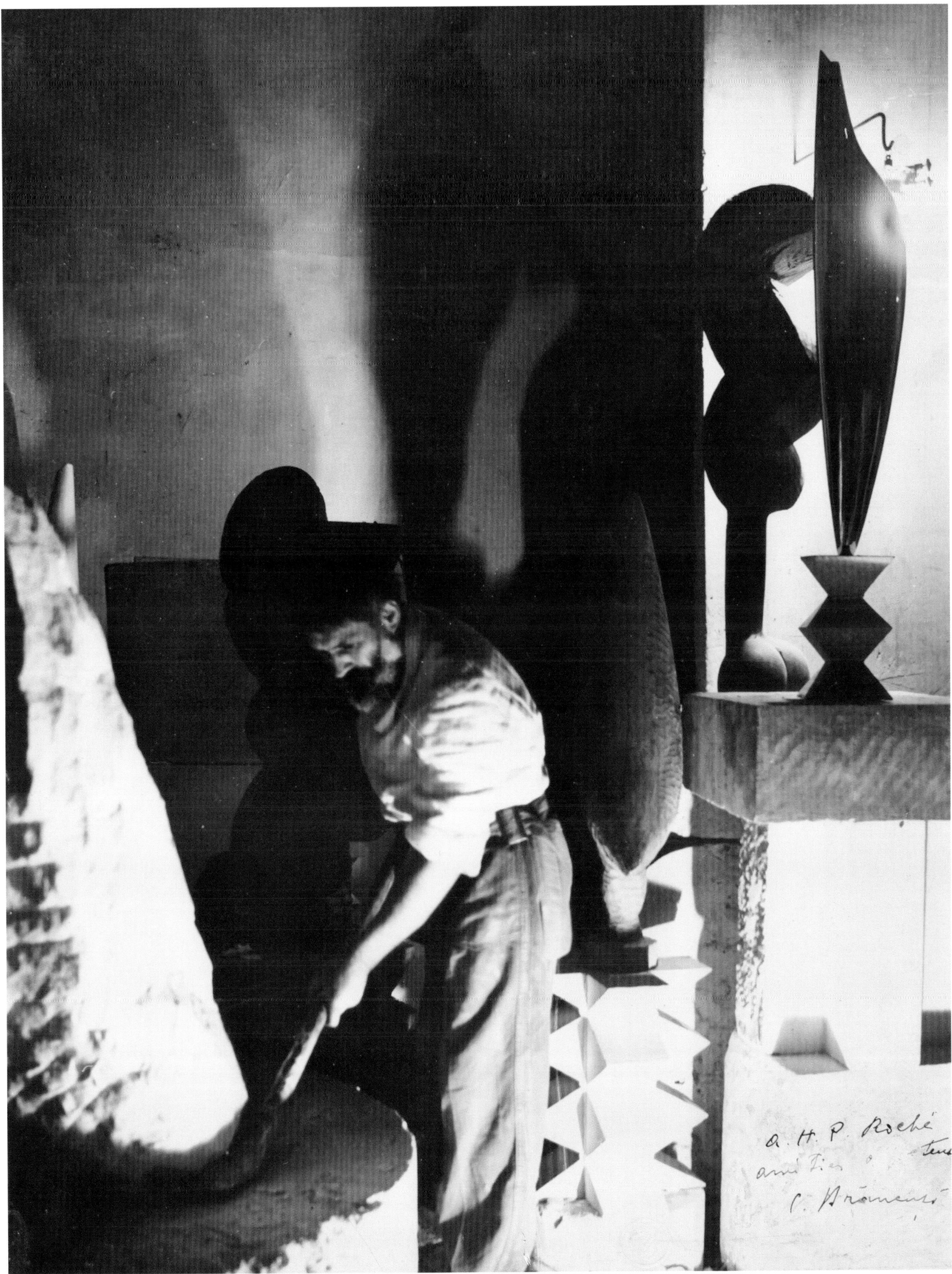

à H. P. Roché
amitiés
C. Brâncuși

72

André Kertész

American, born Hungary, 1894–1985

Satiric Dancer, 1926; printed 1967
Gelatin silver print
Image: 24.8 × 19.8 cm (9 ¾ × 7 ¹³/₁₆ in); sheet: 25.4 ×
20.3 cm (10 × 8 in)
Inscribed, on verso, upper center, in pencil: *A. Kertész
/ Paris 1926*; stamped, middle center, in blue ink: *© ANDRE
KERTESZ / This photograph may only be reproduced / for
review purposes in connection with / the photographic
exhibit* [inscription crossed out] */ Copyright © 1967*
University of Nebraska, Anna R. and Frank M. Hall
Charitable Trust, H-1426

André Kertész's vision was shaped by the uniquely vibrant culture of his birthplace, Budapest. In the years before World War I, Hungary produced an entire generation of renowned artists, musicians, poets, and writers. A prestigious group of photographers—Brassaï, Robert Capa, László Moholy-Nagy, and Martin Munkácsi—all emerged from this context. The energies of the modern age came to a particularly stimulating focus in prewar Budapest: traditional village ways intersected with urban sophistication, European high culture overlapped with indigenous folk arts. This confluence was exemplified by the music of Béla Bartók, which wove folk melodies into a high modernist idiom. Kertész, too, would unite a sensitivity to the local and the everyday with an enthusiasm for the avant-garde.

Kertész took up the camera in 1912 and learned by trial and error. Despite his shyness, he became part of the artistic community in Budapest, uniting a love for folk traditions with an excitement for the new. His breakthrough came in 1925, when he made the momentous decision to seek his fortune in Paris. In the eleven years he spent there, he came to full artistic maturity and established an international reputation. He also benefited from inclusion in a lively circle of Hungarian artists and expatriates. Kertész perfected his style in these years, combining a love for the poignant or revealing moment with an embrace of modernism. The photographic "New Vision" of the era promoted experimentation and the use of unusual vantage points in an effort to reinvent visual experience. Kertész exemplified this artistic philosophy while working in a distinctly personal, intuitive, and poetic manner.

All these traits are evident in *Satiric Dancer*. Made soon after Kertesz's arrival in Paris, this image underscores the importance of his circle of Hungarian artist friends. Here, the dancer Magda Förstner poses in the studio of painter and sculptor István Beöthy. This is a witty and exuberant work: Förstner satirizes the classic tradition of the odalisque while remaining a brazen, purely contemporary flapper. Her pose and white skin relate directly to the other key elements of the composition: Beöthy's plasters of a male torso and a female nude. Kertész frames all this carefully, using a wide-angle lens to open and flatten the volume of the room. Förstner is precisely centered, like a pinwheel or butterfly specimen.

Kertész remained in Paris until 1936, when a professional assignment drew him to New York. The job offer turned out to be disappointing, but he spent the rest of his life there—forgotten as an artist for decades and then rediscovered to universal acclaim during the "photo boom" of the 1970s. A perennial outsider, Kertész formed his sense of identity in the act of picture making. His best photographs—like this one—were cherished touchstones of his life. They were also evocations of a world that, if not perfect, was at least *his*—a realm of joy, mystery, and grace to which he fully belonged. **KFD**

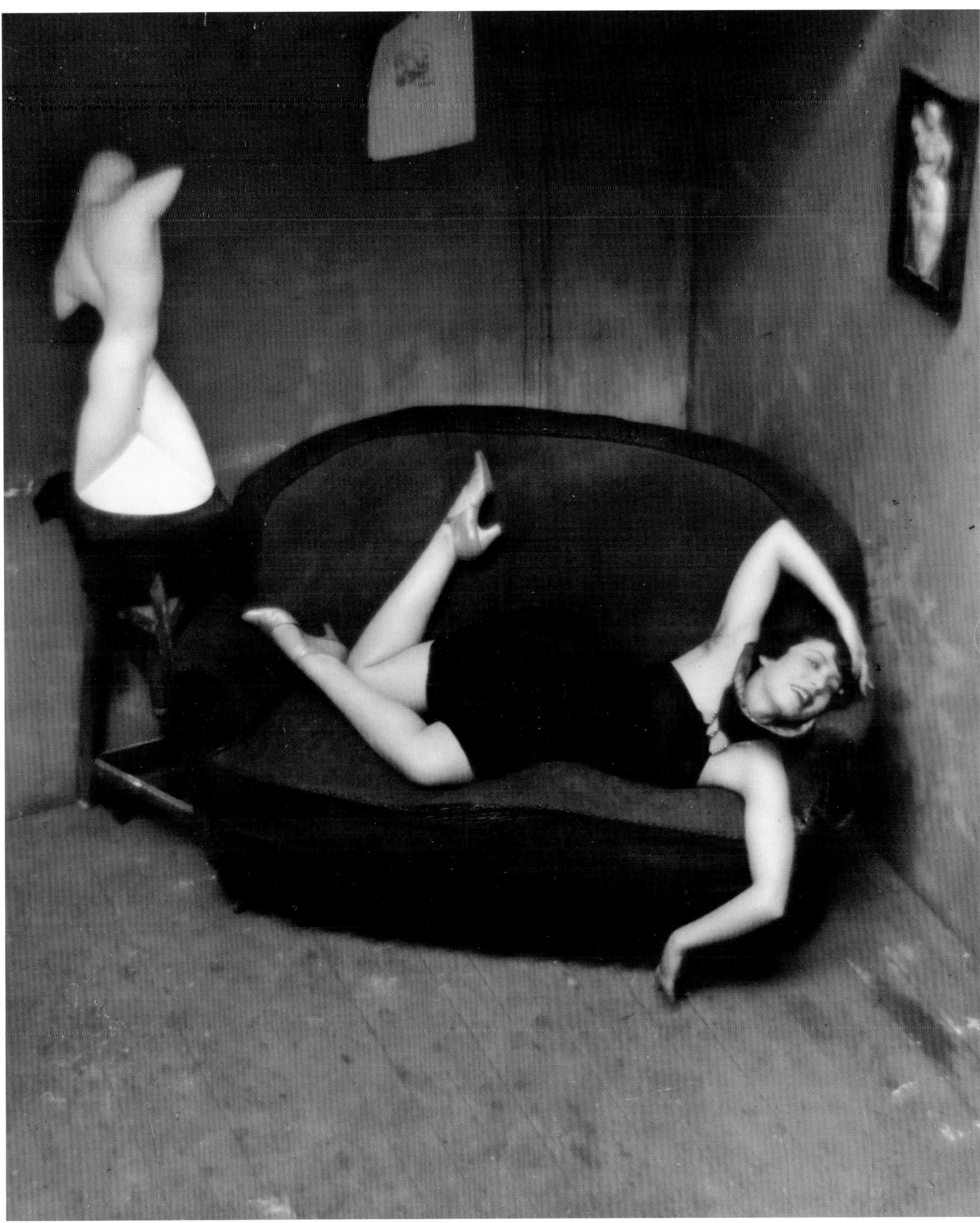

73

Henri Cartier-Bresson
French, 1908–2004

Behind the Gare St. Lazare, Paris, 1932; printed later
Gelatin silver print
Image: 36.2 × 24.4 cm (14 1/4 × 9 5/8 in); sheet: 40.6 ×
30.5 cm (16 × 12 in)
Stamped, lower left: © *Henri / Cartier / Bresson;*
signed, lower right, in black ink: *Henri Cartier-Bresson*
University of Nebraska, Anna R. and Frank M. Hall
Charitable Trust, H-2760

The originator of the famous phrase "the decisive moment," Henri Cartier-Bresson came to artistic maturity in the early 1930s and remained a revered and influential figure in the photography world for the rest of his life.[1] As a youth, he was drawn to modern literature—from Rimbaud and Mallarmé to Proust and Joyce—and then to art. In the late 1920s, he was influenced by both cubism and surrealism. From the former, he absorbed the lessons of pictorial form; from the latter, he learned the value of intuition, automatism, and the fractured or ambiguous narrative.

Cartier-Bresson began making photographs casually in 1929. His interest deepened in 1932, when he bought a 35mm Leica camera. Small, quick, and precise, the Leica became his paradigmatic tool of creative expression. In his first few years of serious effort with the camera—1932 to 1934—Cartier-Bresson created a genuinely unprecedented body of work. These pictures were made possible by the new technologies of the 35mm camera and roll film, which allowed thirty-six exposures in rapid succession. Most importantly, however, they stemmed from his own insights into the nature of picture making and the world.

The subjects of these photographs were ordinary; it was the *way* they were rendered that was new. Cartier-Bresson's decisive moment refers to an instant of perception in which the content and the form of a picture—the things recorded *and* the graphic network of relations between them—come together in a peak of resolution. Time is central to this process: each successful picture reflects a resonant sliver of duration, a split second plucked from the relentless flow of worldly experience.

Cartier-Bresson's *Behind the Gare St. Lazare, Paris,* is an iconic example of this approach.[2] In the flooded traffic circle behind the train station, the photographer captured—in a reflexive instant—a perfect conjunction of visual elements. A man leaps over water; the camera freezes his motion at the instant his foot is about to strike the glassy surface. His shape is mirrored by his reflection in the water and echoed again in the posture of the dancer on the background poster. The angle of the man's torso and lead leg is matched by the position of the hands of the station's clock. Action, reflection, representation, and time all come together in mysterious, unexpected harmony.

Cartier-Bresson was modern photography's Einstein. Instead of viewing the world mechanistically, he saw it in relativistic terms, underscoring the importance of time and the deep connectedness of things. With his little camera, he accomplished something extraordinary: he discovered a new visual world hidden in the folds of the familiar. **KFD**

1. Cartier-Bresson's most famous book carried the French title *Images à la sauvette* and, in English, *The Decisive Moment* (both editions 1952). For a recent overview of his career, see Peter Galassi, *Henri Cartier-Bresson: The Modern Century,* exhibition catalog (New York: Museum of Modern Art, 2010). **2.** It is notable, however, that this is *not* an example of Cartier-Bresson's characteristic refusal to crop his negatives. See Henri Cartier-Bresson, *Scrap Book: Photographs 1932–1946* (New York: Thames and Hudson, 2007), 86–87.

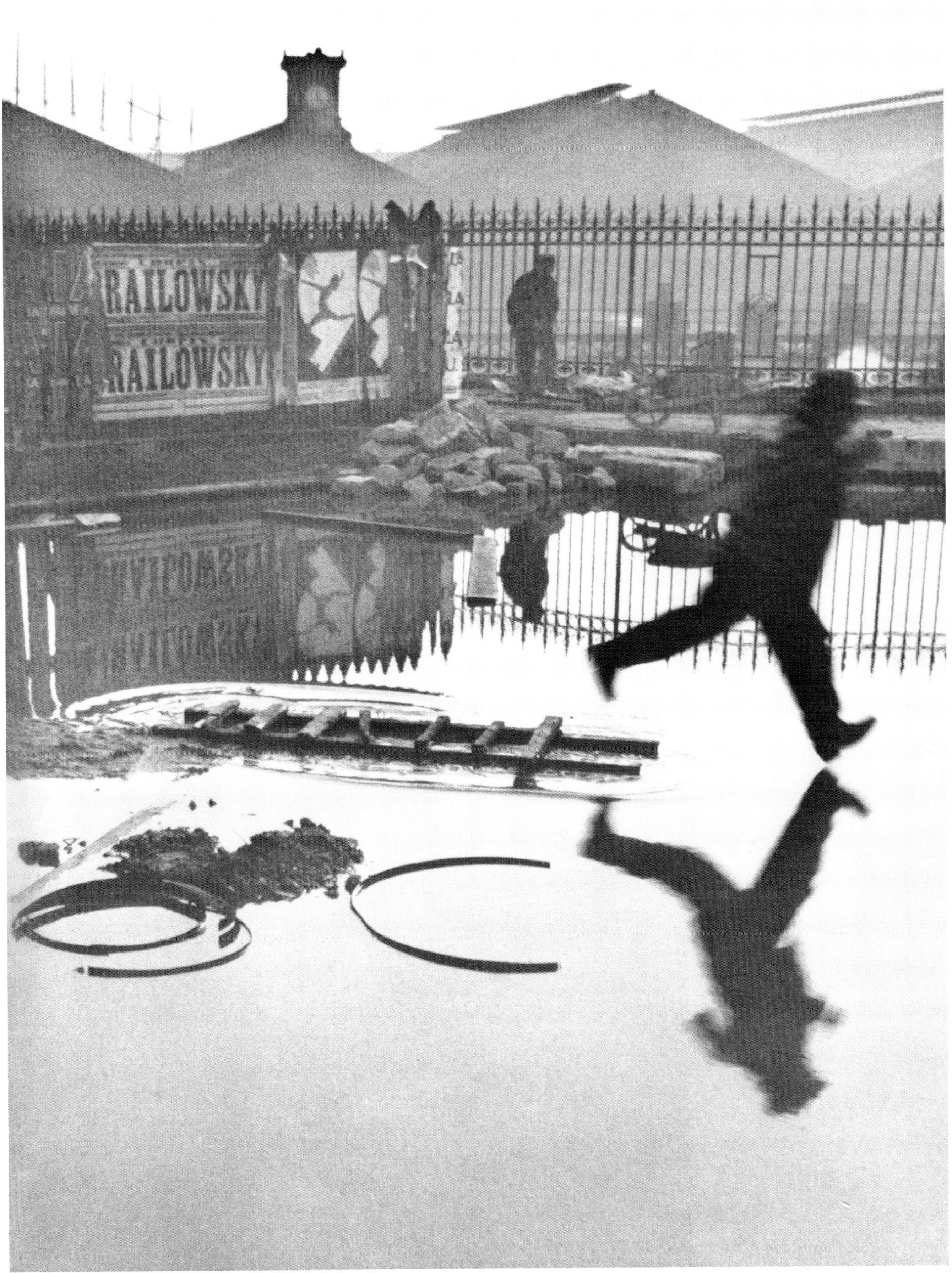

74

Charles Sheeler

American, 1883–1965

Buggy (Interior, Bucks County Barn), c. 1916
Gelatin silver print
Image: 19.7 × 24.8 cm (7 ¾ × 9 ¾ in); sheet: 20.3 ×
25.4 cm (8 × 10 in)
University of Nebraska, Anna R. and Frank M. Hall
Charitable Trust, H-2164

Perhaps best known for his paintings (see below), Charles Sheeler worked in diverse media throughout his career, including drawing, film, and photography. These served him as important adjuncts to his canvases, legitimate art forms in their own right, and significant elements in his development. Indeed, Sheeler wrote to his friend, gallerist and photographer Alfred Stieglitz: "Because of something personal which I was trying to work out in them, . . . [my photographs] were probably more akin to drawings than to my photographs of paintings and sculptures."[1] The artist routinely tested formal structures in his photographs, meticulously selecting and framing his subjects but also constructing mattes and mounts that might slightly alter the lines and patterns of a composition in order to add dramatic tension.[2]

Although Sheeler turned to photography around 1914 or 1915, he began experimenting with the medium in earnest in 1917—the year of his artistic maturity—after a successful exhibition of his photographs of African sculpture at New York's Modern Gallery.[3] *Buggy* is the result of a series of photographs that he made in and around his 1768 stone farmhouse in Doylestown, Pennsylvania, a home he had been renting since 1910 with artist Morton Schamberg, a friend and colleague.[4] Like many modernists in the first half of the twentieth century, Sheeler saw his country retreat as a vehicle for his own creative impulses—an escape from the city, a source of rejuvenation, and an opportunity to engage with the spare, rectilinear forms of vernacular architecture and art.

This barn interior was likely photographed at one of the working farms Sheeler shot in and around Doylestown. He emphasized the deep recesses of the building with theatrical backlighting, which silhouettes the buggy and provides a striking focal point in the stark brightness that penetrates the small rear window. This sense of depth invites the viewer to enter the pictorial space, while the beams and crossbeams block the entrance, producing a sense of dynamic forces in opposition. A master at framing and cropping his compositions, Sheeler deliberately shot the subject off-center, revealing farm implements on the left side; this adds to the unsettling affect of the otherwise calm, everyday subject. The artist returned to *Buggy* nearly twenty years later, creating a remarkably faithful Conté crayon drawing of the photograph; in that version, however, he explored greater contrast between light and shadow, illuminating the back of the barn even more intensely and producing even crisper detail.[5] **BKR**

1. Quoted in Theodore E. Stebbins Jr. and Norman Keyes Jr., *Charles Sheeler: The Photographs*, exhibition catalog (Boston: Museum of Fine Arts and Little, Brown, 1987), 9. **2.** Stebbins and Keyes, *Charles Sheeler*, 9, 12. **3.** Theodore E. Stebbins Jr., Gilles Mora, and Karen E. Haas, *The Photography of Charles Sheeler: American Modernist*, exhibition catalog (Boston: Museum of Fine Arts and Bulfinch Press, 2002), 9. **4.** *Buggy* has been dated to both 1915–17 and to 1917, a year when Sheeler issued three sets of twelve photographs of his Doylestown house. Although not part of this series, the image has often been associated with it. See Stebbins and Keyes, *Charles Sheeler*, 9, cat. 22; and Stebbins et al., *The Photography of Charles Sheeler*, 13, 35. For an alternate dating of 1916–17, see Karen Lucic, *Charles Sheeler in Doylestown: American Modernism and the Pennsylvania Tradition*, exhibition catalog (Allentown PA: Allentown Art Museum; Seattle: University of Washington Press, 1997), 75, cat. 26. **5.** For a reproduction of this drawing, see Lucic, *Charles Sheeler in Doylestown*, 107, cat. 48.

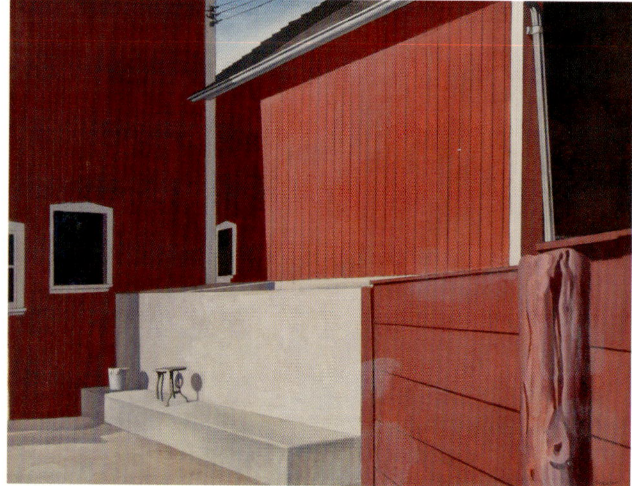

Charles Sheeler. *Barn Reds*, 1938. Egg tempera and graphite on board; 26.4 × 32.7 cm (10 ⅜ × 12 ⅞ in). University of Nebraska, Anna R. and Frank M. Hall Charitable Trust, H-200.

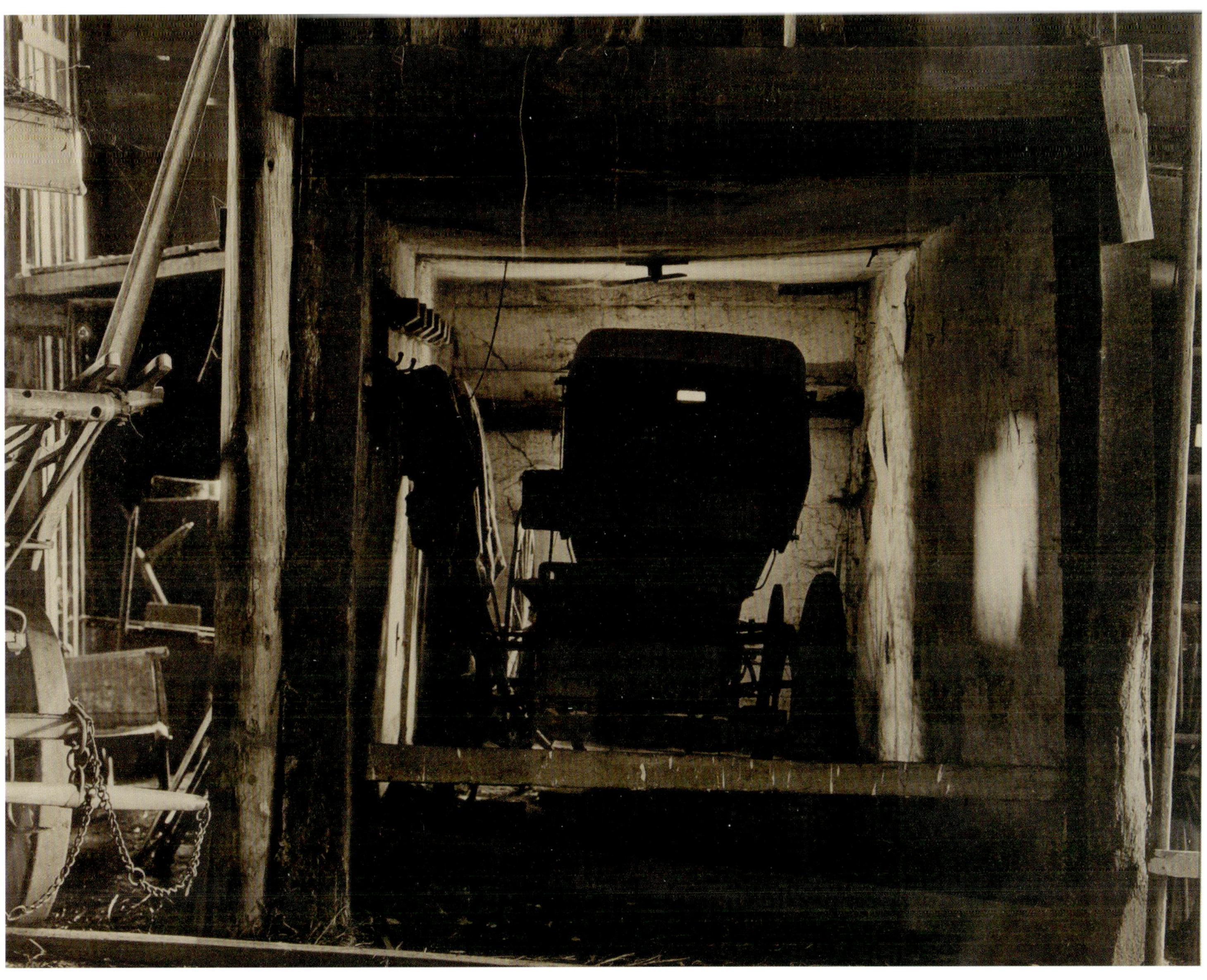

75

Ralph Steiner

American, 1899–1986

American Rural Baroque, c. 1928
Gelatin silver print
Image: 19.1 × 24.1 cm (7 1/2 × 9 1/2 in); mount: 35.6 × 43.2 cm (14 × 17 in)
Signed, on mount, lower right, in pencil: *Ralph Steiner*
University of Nebraska, Anna R. and Frank M. Hall Charitable Trust, H-2426

Ralph Steiner initially studied chemical engineering at Dartmouth College and, like Imogen Cunningham (cats. 56 and 103), employed his scientific knowledge to solve photographic problems when he took up the medium in earnest. Like many of his early twentieth-century peers, Steiner studied at the Clarence White School of Photography, and although he disagreed with the pictorialist principles still being taught when he attended from 1921 to 1922, he respected White (cat. 69), whose influence on Steiner's career is evident. It was Steiner's introduction to Paul Strand (cats. 59 and 60) in the late 1920s, however, that redirected his attention to craftsmanship and technique; he expressed admiration for Strand's ability to capture textures and create rich tonal values.

Inspired, Steiner began a series of photographs during a 1928 residency at Yaddo, the famous art colony in Saratoga Springs, New York. "All that summer," he recalled, "I photographed objects with strong textures—often waiting until the sun was at the best angle to intensify the feeling of material. But the whole summer was not spent doing technical exercises; when I saw things that amused me . . . I would stop to photograph them."[1] In *American Rural Baroque*, the artist fulfilled both of his objectives. The texture of the wicker-and-wood rocking chair is captured with crisp detail and amplified by the shadow it casts on the outside wall of the house, becoming the main focus of the viewer's attention.

The rocker on the front porch of the white clapboard home recalls the custom of sitting outdoors during warm summer months, and the scrollwork on the back of the chair—decoration more associated with elaborately ornamented baroque art—presents a deliberate contrast to the uncomplicated lines of the house and the perceived simplicity of its occupants. In that regard, it stands as an equally humorous precursor to Grant Wood's *American Gothic* (1930; Art Institute of Chicago), painted only two years later.

Like many other artists of the day, notably Charles Sheeler (cat. 74), Steiner may have seen his time in the countryside as an opportunity to engage with folk architecture, which was regarded as almost modern in its spareness. Like Sheeler, Steiner was also an experimental filmmaker, and his 1930 documentary *Modern Principles*—a ten-minute homage to mechanization—survives almost as a bookend to the contrived folksiness of *American Rural Baroque*. The photograph also demonstrates the continuing impact of Charles White's Japanese-inspired philosophies of asymmetrical composition and *notan*, the harmony of black and white: the chair sits slightly off-center, and the larger shadow weighs the composition toward the left, while the distinctive monochromatic balance leads the viewer's eye from one element to the next. **BKR**

1. Ralph Steiner, *Ralph Steiner: A Point of View* (Middletown CT: Wesleyan University Press, 1978), 48.

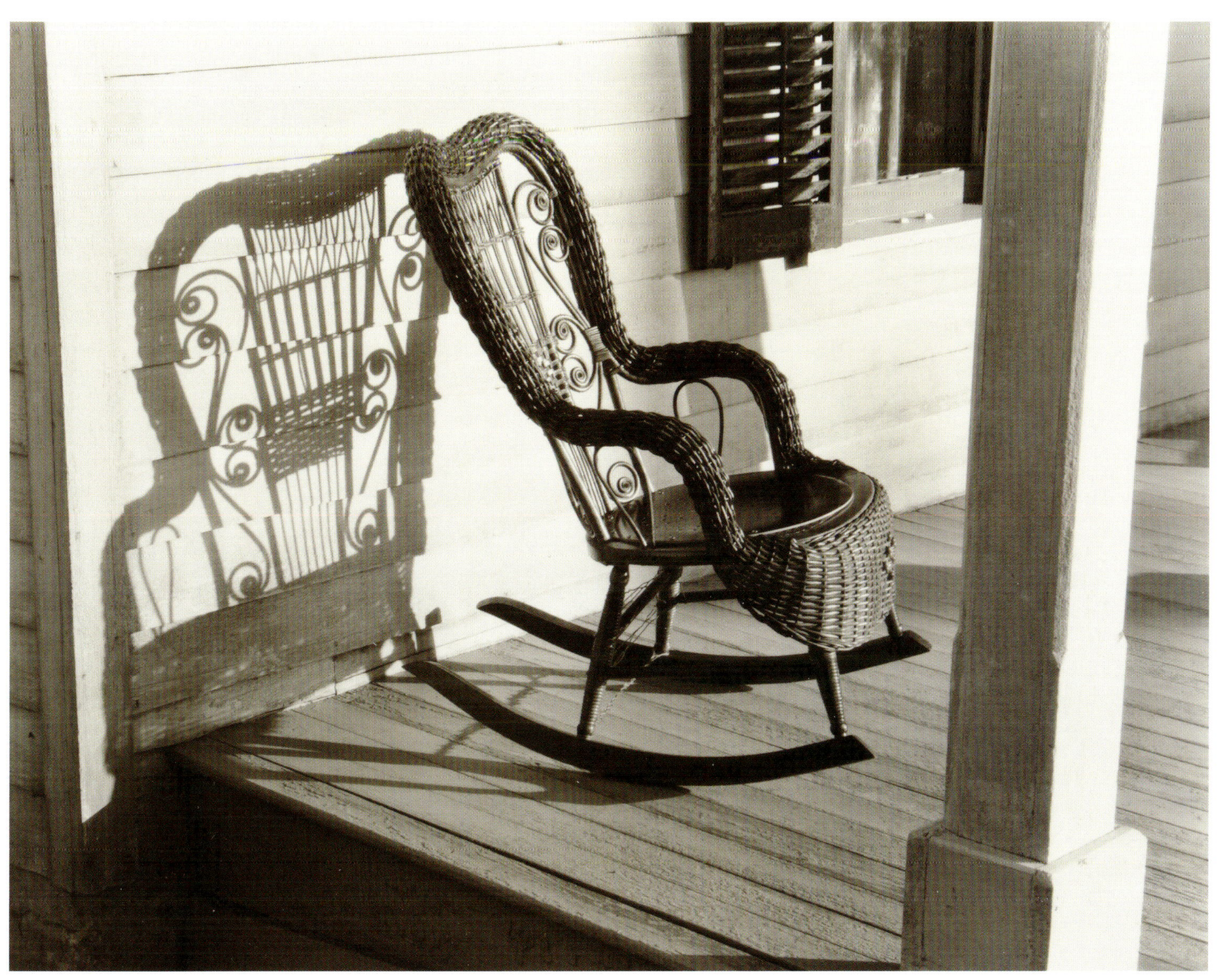

76

Eugene Buechel

American, born Germany, 1874–1954

Josephine Jumping Eagle in Airplane, 1928
Gelatin silver print
Image: 16.5 × 25.4 cm (6 1/2 × 10 in); sheet: 27.8 × 35.4 cm
(10 15/16 × 13 15/16 in)
University of Nebraska, gift of Mid-America Arts Alliance,
U-1966

A Jesuit priest, Eugene Buechel was first assigned to the Saint Francis Indian Mission on the Rosebud Reservation in 1902, two years after he immigrated to the United States. Although he left South Dakota to finish his studies in Saint Louis, Buechel returned in 1907 and stayed the rest of his life, traveling between the Rosebud and nearby Pine Ridge Reservations as an administrator, educator, and pastor. He also collected Native artifacts and botanical specimens and became an expert on the Lakota Sioux language. Beginning in 1922, Buechel taught himself photography with small view and Kodak folding cameras and began documenting the people on both reservations. While he photographed sacred rituals such as the Sun Dance, a religious ceremony practiced by many Plains people, he also focused on more quotidian aspects of reservation life, taking group portraits and candid snapshots of families and their homes; he sometimes traveled to more isolated communities as well.[1]

In the main, Buechel's photographs belie the static depictions of Native Americans that persisted even into the twentieth century. Such images show the subjects dressed in ritual clothing, performing ancient ceremonies or creating traditional crafts. Buechel, in fact, worked during a vital period of transition on the reservations, when white hegemony was nearly dominant and assimilation an expectation.[2] Indeed, his portrait of Josephine Jumping Eagle, who dons a bandanna and stares directly at the camera, juxtaposes the supposedly premodern young Indian girl with the innovative airplane, a vehicle that was often named after Native American groups. While the picture combines both a child-

ish fascination with technology and the artist's sense of playfulness, Jumping Eagle's later biography points to some of the more deleterious effects of conquest and dislocation. In the mid-1990s, her grandson, Richard Leon, was convicted of committing two murders in the Los Angeles area while on a cocaine-fueled rampage. During his trial, Leon claimed as a factor in the crime not only the systematic physical abuse inflicted by his alcoholic white father but also the suspicion instilled in him by Jumping Eagle, who taught him always to "distrust the white man" after she was forcibly relocated from South Dakota to California by the federal government.[3] **BKR**

1. For a brief biography of Buechel, see Don Doll and Jim Alinder, *Crying for a Vision: A Rosebud Sioux Trilogy, 1886–1976* (Dobbs Ferry NY: Morgan and Morgan, 1976), n.p. **2.** David Wing, introduction to *Eugene Buechel, S.J.: Rosebud and Pine Ridge Photographs, 1922–1942*, exhibition catalog (El Cajon CA: Grossmont College Development Foundation, 1974), 8. **3.** Jeannette DeSantis, "Jury Recommends Death for Murderer," *Los Angeles Daily News*, July 25, 1996.

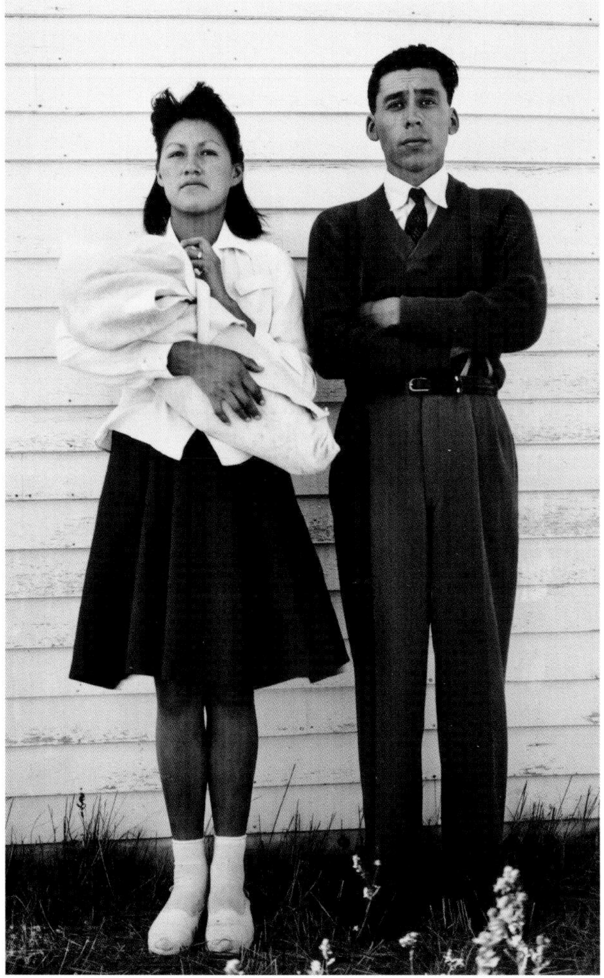

Eugene Buechel. *Theodore Bald Eagle and His Wife, Luella Williams*, 1945. Gelatin silver print; 25.6 × 15.4 cm (10 1/16 × 6 1/16 in). University of Nebraska, gift of Mid-America Arts Alliance, U-1972.

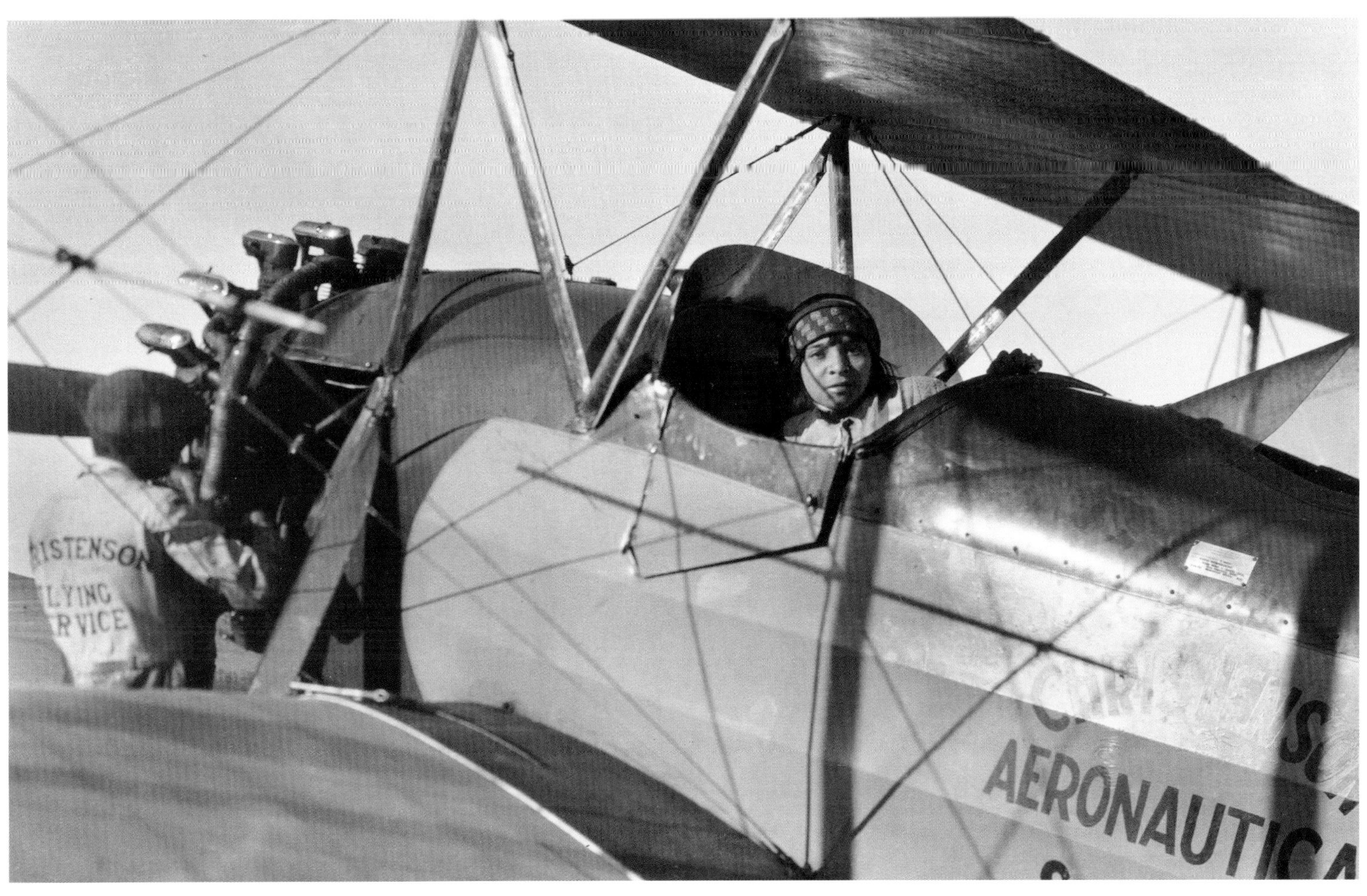
RISTENSON
FLYING
ERVICE
AERONAUTICA

77

Doris Ulmann

American, 1882–1934

Woman and Child, undated
Platinum print
Image: 20.3 × 17.3 cm (8 × 6 13/16 in); mount: 35.7 × 28.6 cm
(14 1/16 × 11 1/4 in)
Signed, on mount, lower right, in pencil: *Doris Ulmann*
University of Nebraska, Anna R. and Frank M. Hall
Charitable Trust, H-2054

Like many twentieth-century photographers, including Diane Arbus (cat. 49) and Paul Strand (cats. 59 and 60), Doris Ulmann received her early education at New York's Fieldston School for Ethical Culture. She likely had her first introduction to photography through the school's biology teacher, Lewis Hine (cat. 16), who took his students on field trips to Ellis Island to document the newly arrived immigrants. Ulmann's interest in psychology led her briefly to Columbia University before she completed her photographic studies with Clarence White (cat. 69), who served as a lifelong mentor. Hine's reformist impulses, along with White's artfully composed, carefully crafted pictorialist images, supplied Ulmann with the two influences that would remain the staples of her art. For her subjects, she often selected the poor and disenfranchised—anonymous figures most often defined by their ethnic, religious, or socioeconomic group. She shot them in the pictorialist tradition of soft focus or romantically silhouetted against their sometimes harsh, unforgiving surroundings.[1]

This image of a mother and child aptly demonstrates Ulmann's characteristic practice—employing light to its fullest effect, focusing the camera's attention on faces and hands, and concentrating on patterns and shadows. In addition, Ulmann utilized various complicated darkroom techniques to enhance the artistic nature of her prints, including oil pigment printing and, here, the platinum process. This method provides the greatest tonal range in black and white along with a softer matte surface, a stark contrast to the gelatin silver process dominant in most twentieth-century documentary photographs and prized for its greater clarity and precision. In fact, Ulmann's refusal to embrace technical advances—she remained devoted to her old equipment and traveled through the country with her tripod and glass-plate negatives—acts as a metaphor for the artist's career, registering her general disregard for the nation's industrial and technological supremacy. In addition, in capturing the often neglected folkways and people of rural America, the artist saw her aesthetic goal as picturesque rather than encouraging "social improvement," the element, in the words of one scholar, that "sets the photographs of Hine and the [contemporaneous] FSA photographers apart from those of Doris Ulmann."[2]

In search of pictorialist subject matter, by the late 1920s Ulmann had turned her attention to capturing small religious communities in New England and then to Appalachian farmers. This work led to one of her most significant series, assembling documentation of Appalachian folk arts and crafts for Allen Eaton's 1937 book, *Handicrafts of the Southern Highlands*.[3] At the invitation of Pulitzer Prize–winning novelist Julia Peterkin, Ulmann visited South Carolina in 1929 and 1930 to photograph the Gullah people working on the author's farm.

Ulmann continued to work intermittently throughout the South until her untimely death in 1934. The Sheldon's photograph likely dates from one of these periods. Here, the mother tenderly caresses the right side of her child's face; both of them droop their heads slightly and stare off into the distance. This subtle touch casts the older woman's face in shadow, adding an emotional impact to the photograph, while the contrasts of color and pattern in their clothing—along with the deliberately obscured fields in the background—add depth and texture. **BKR**

1. For more on these early, seemingly oppositional influences, see Melissa A. McEuen, *Seeing America: Women Photographers between the Wars* (Lexington: University Press of Kentucky, 2000), 11–17. **2.** David Featherstone, *Doris Ulmann: American Portraits* (Albuquerque: University of New Mexico Press, 1985), 33. **3.** For more on this and Ulmann's other itinerant projects at the time, see Featherstone, *Doris Ulmann*, 26–30, 41–50.

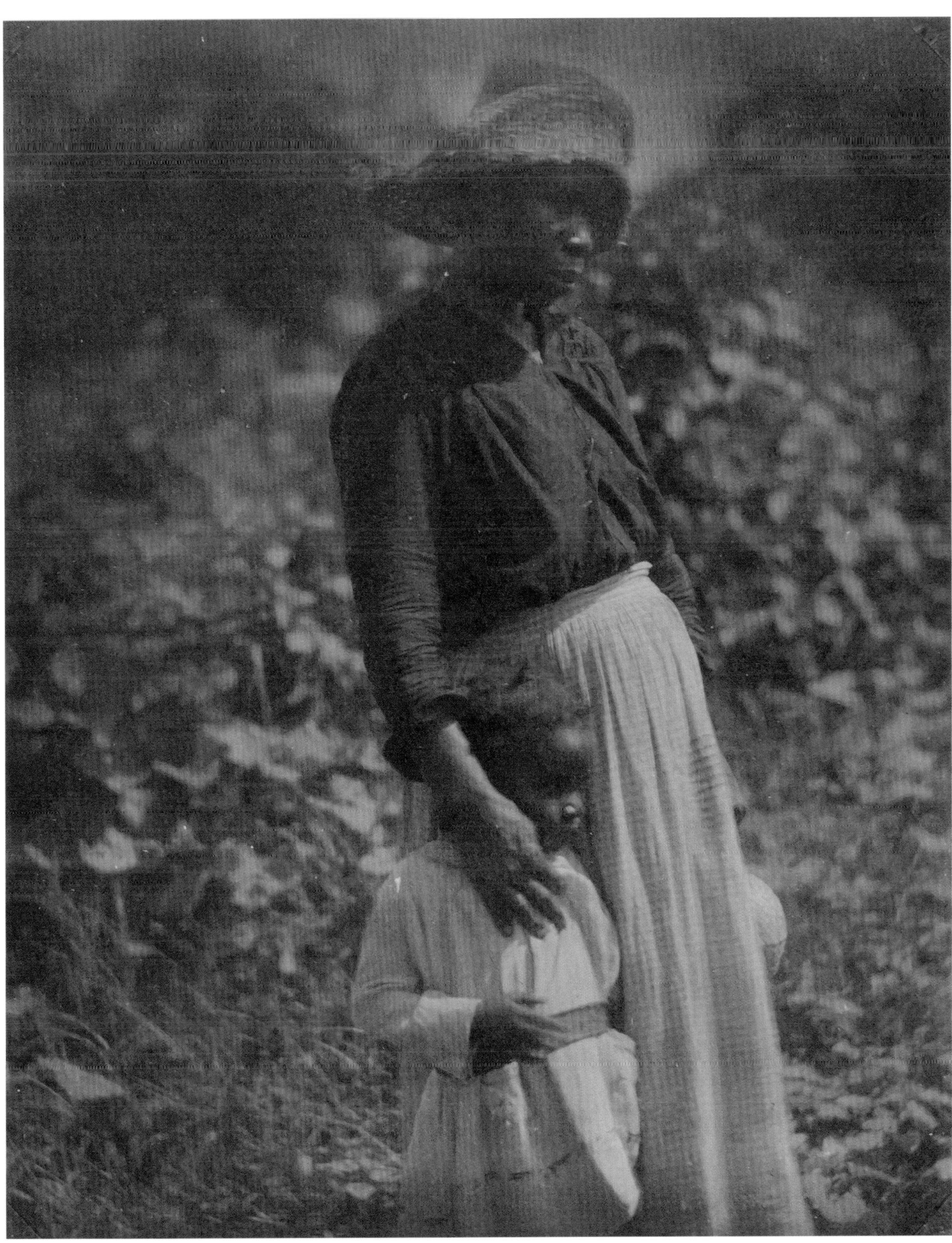

78

Dorothea Lange

American, 1895–1965

Migrant Mother, Nipomo, California, 1936; printed c. 1965
Gelatin silver print
Image and sheet: 33.7 × 26.7 cm (13 ¼ × 10 ½ in)
Signed, in image, upper right, in black ink:
Dorothea Lange 1936
University of Nebraska, Anna R. and Frank M. Hall
Charitable Trust, H-1061

After her divorce from painter Maynard Dixon and marriage to economist Paul Taylor—both in 1935—Dorothea Lange went to work for the Federal Resettlement Administration, later renamed the Farm Security Administration. (For Lange's early life and career, see cat. 17.) For the next four years, the couple traveled throughout California documenting rural poverty and the abuse of sharecroppers and migrant laborers, with Taylor collecting data and Lange taking photographs. In 1936 they visited a pea-pickers' camp in the coastal town of Nipomo north of Los Angeles. It was there that Lange fashioned *Migrant Mother*, her most famous photograph and one of the most iconic images of the twentieth century. The image has come to symbolize the hardships associated with agricultural displacement and the Great Depression, inspiring appropriations and parodies. Formally, the composition has been likened to that of a Madonna and Child, with one critic calling it an "anti–Madonna and Child," explaining, "The mother, who, we feel without reservation, wants to love and cherish her children, even as they lean on her, is severed from them by her anxiety."[1] It has also been analyzed in terms of Lange's own decision around that time to board her children at school "when family finances would not allow her to keep them."[2]

The photographer gave her account of taking this picture in a 1960 issue of *Popular Photography*:

I saw and approached the hungry and desperate mother, as if drawn by a magnet. I do not remember how I explained my presence or my camera to her, but I do remember she asked me no questions. I made five exposures, working closer and closer from the same direction. I did not ask her name or history. She told me her age, that she was 32. She said they had been living on frozen vegetables from the surrounding fields, and birds that the children killed. She had just sold the tires from her car to buy food. There she sat in that lean-to tent with her children huddled around her, and seemed to know that my pictures might help her, and so she helped me. There was a sort of equality about it.[3]

Despite her insistence that the association was one of equality, Lange's account and the very nature of the photographic process suggest otherwise. The position of subjects vis-à-vis the photographer implies that they are being "subjected to" something, and even the technical language employed for photography—"to aim," "to shoot"—suggests the power dynamic of a hunter-prey relationship. Lange's lack of curiosity about her sitter's name further indicates a preference for ideals (homeless, poor, working class) over the specifics of individuality. Like the anonymous subject in Horace Bristol's *Portrait of Tom Joad*, who was equated with a fictional character in a John Steinbeck novel (cat. 80), the family in *Migrant Mother* has become consumed by the image's myth, and their identity is secondary.

Lange's photograph depicts the family of Florence Owens Thompson (1903–1983), a Cherokee woman from Oklahoma who, like many Americans during the 1920s and 1930s, migrated westward in search of employment and stability. After her husband's death in the early 1930s, she worked as a day laborer and in restaurants to support her children; she had eight by the time Lange encountered her in Nipomo, where the family had settled briefly after experiencing car trouble.[4] Owens herself achieved no fame from the image—her identity was not uncovered until some forty years afterward—and she criticized Lange's lack of interest in her, reportedly later claiming that the photograph made her feel "ashamed."[5] **BKR**

1. George Elliott, quoted in *Seeing America: Women Photographers between the Wars*, by Melissa A. McEuen (Lexington: University Press of Kentucky, 2000), 110. **2.** McEuen, *Seeing America*. **3.** Dorothea Lange, "The Assignment I'll Never Forget: Migrant Mother," *Popular Photography* 46, no. 2 (February 1960): 42–43, 128, quoted in Milton Meltzer, *Dorothea Lange: A Photographer's Life* (Syracuse NY: Syracuse University Press, 2000), 131–32. **4.** For Owens's biography and an effective analysis of the images Lange took of her, see Judith Keller and Keith Davis, *Dorothea Lange: Photographs from the J. Paul Getty Museum* (Los Angeles: J. Paul Getty Trust, 2002), 30–33. **5.** Keller and Davis, *Dorothea Lange*, 33; and Thelma Gutierrez and Wayne Drash, "Girl from Iconic Great Depression Photo: 'We were ashamed,'" CNN *Living*, December 2, 2008, http://articles.cnn.com/2008-12-02/living/dustbowl.photo _1_migrant-mother-florence-owens-thompson-picture?_s=PM:LIVING.

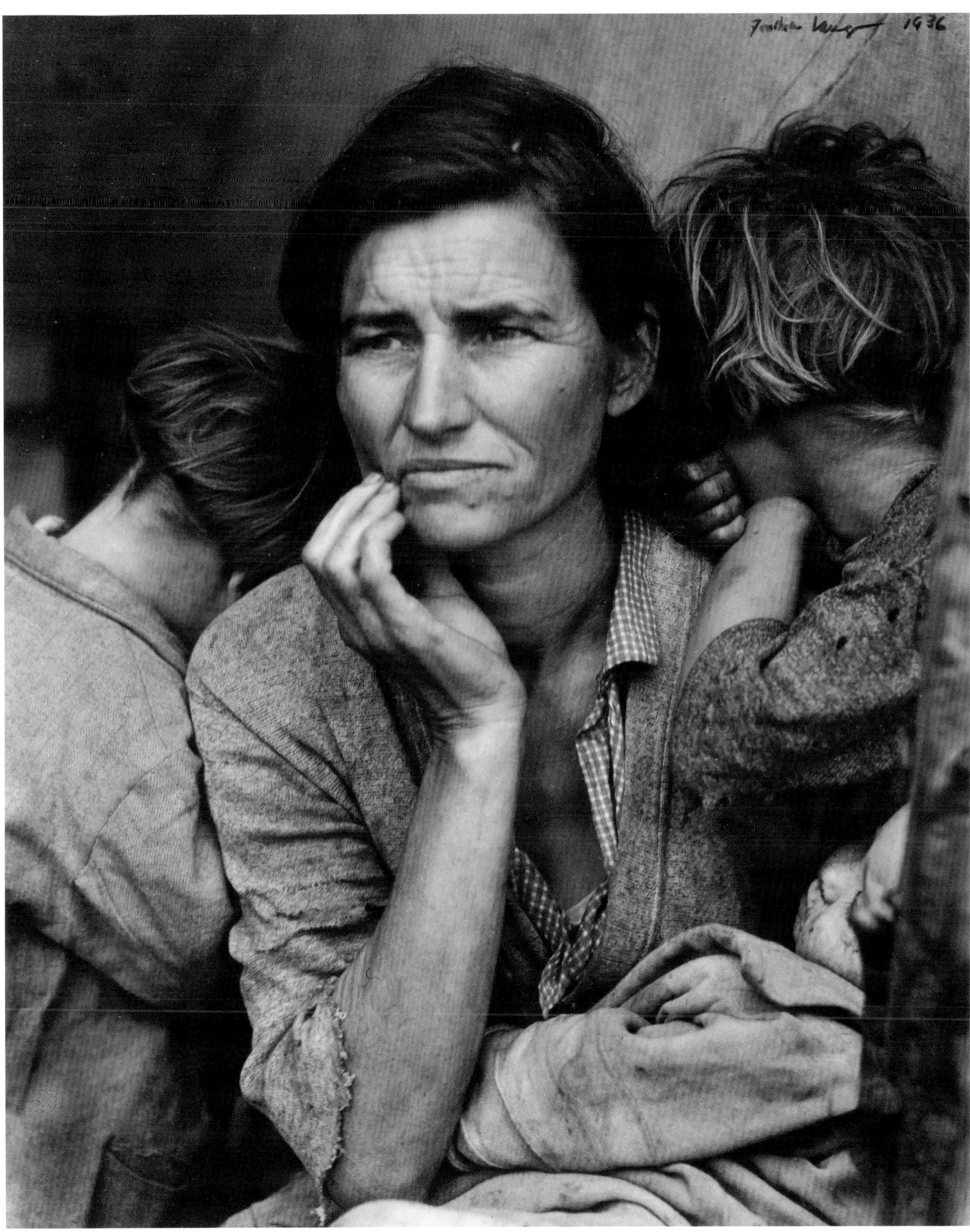
Dorothea Lange 1936

79

Manuel Álvarez Bravo

Mexican, 1902–2002

The Crouched Ones, 1934
Gelatin silver print
Image: 18.6 × 24.5 cm (7 5/16 × 9 5/8 in); mount: 35.7 ×
44.6 cm (14 1/16 × 17 9/16 in)
Signed, on mount, lower right, in pencil: *M. Alvarez
Bravo / México*
University of Nebraska, Anna R. and Frank M. Hall
Charitable Trust, H-2018

Manuel Álvarez Bravo was one of twentieth-century Mexico's foremost photographers. He drew from surrealism as he constructed his narratively ambiguous works, and his visual strategies have been compared to those of French photographer Henri Cartier-Bresson (cat. 73). During the 1930s, when he achieved his own distinctive voice, Álvarez Bravo perhaps became most respected for his ability to capture a stunning range of tonal values, particularly in his experiments with contrasts of light and dark. *The Crouched Ones* demonstrates this mastery. The photographer framed his subject—a *comedor*, or common luncheonette, open to the street—strictly, using the sides of the building, the rolling metal screen at the top, and the checkerboard floor at the bottom. The shadow thrown by the raised iron barrier, with its clearly visible sign, throws the diners' heads into darkness and anonymity, while the harsh noonday sun illuminates their backs and tattered clothes, suggesting their working-class status.

Modernist novelist and playwright Langston Hughes, who visited Mexico frequently because of family connections, wrote rhapsodically about Álvarez Bravo's exploitation of light and shadow after seeing a 1935 exhibition of his work at Mexico City's Palacio de Bellas Artes, where it was paired with that of Cartier-Bresson: "In Bravo, the sun is a quiet veil making the shadows like velvet. The shadows are endlessly deep and full, holding more—and more there—and more.

While the sun in a Bravo photo almost always has a sense of humor, one cannot be sure about the shadows."[1] Later in his life, Álvarez Bravo himself seemed to reinforce Hughes's assessment: "Light and shadow have exactly the same duality between life and death. In a certain way the shadow, the absence of light, is the negation of the light."[2] In his exhibition review, Hughes went on to humorously analyze one of this image's most distinguishing features in terms of the use of light: "Bravo's camera shows the stools in the sunshine and a row of Charlie Chaplin feet. . . . [T]he iron curtain is partly down, and the heads of the customers are in shadow—so one can laugh about the feet!"[3]

The feet of Álvarez Bravo's subjects—emphasized by the strong light and the *comedor*'s patterned tile floor—have, in fact, been the topic of frequent speculation, which may spring from the understandable desire to associate the photographer's politics with his artwork. During the period he took this picture, Álvarez Bravo was involved with the Liga de escritores y artistas revolucionarios (League of Revolutionary Writers and Artists, or LEAR), a radical organization that was established in 1933 to propagate a revolutionary mindset and agitate against government art censorship. Scholars have described the chains that lock the stools together—indistinguishable, in some cases, from the sitters' ankles—as a metaphor for the suppression of the working class, "for the tethers that fix us to our worksites."[4] Like many Mexican artists of the period, Álvarez Bravo also searched for a visual language to express an essential Mexican national identity. The photographer's portrayal of daily activities— here a group of men at their noonday meal, their single respite during the working day—may have been an attempt to document the country's attitudes, customs, and daily rituals outside the bounds of ancient visual culture and national symbols. **BKR**

1. Langston Hughes, "Pictures More than Pictures: The Work of Manuel Bravo and Cartier-Bresson," in *The Collected Works of Langston Hughes*, ed. Christopher C. De Santis, vol. 9 (Columbia: University of Missouri Press, 2002), 141. **2.** Manuel Álvarez Bravo, interviewed by Paul Hill and Thomas Cooper, March 1975, in *Dialogue with Photography* (New York: Farrar, Straus and Giroux, 1979), 234. **3.** Hughes, "Pictures More than Pictures," 141. **4.** John Mraz, *Looking for Mexico: Modern Visual Culture and National Identity* (Durham NC: Duke University Press, 2009), 89–90; see also Deborah Gribbon and Roberto Tejada, *In Focus: Manuel Alvarez Bravo: Photographs from the J. Paul Getty Museum* (Los Angeles: J. Paul Getty Museum, 2001), 40–41.

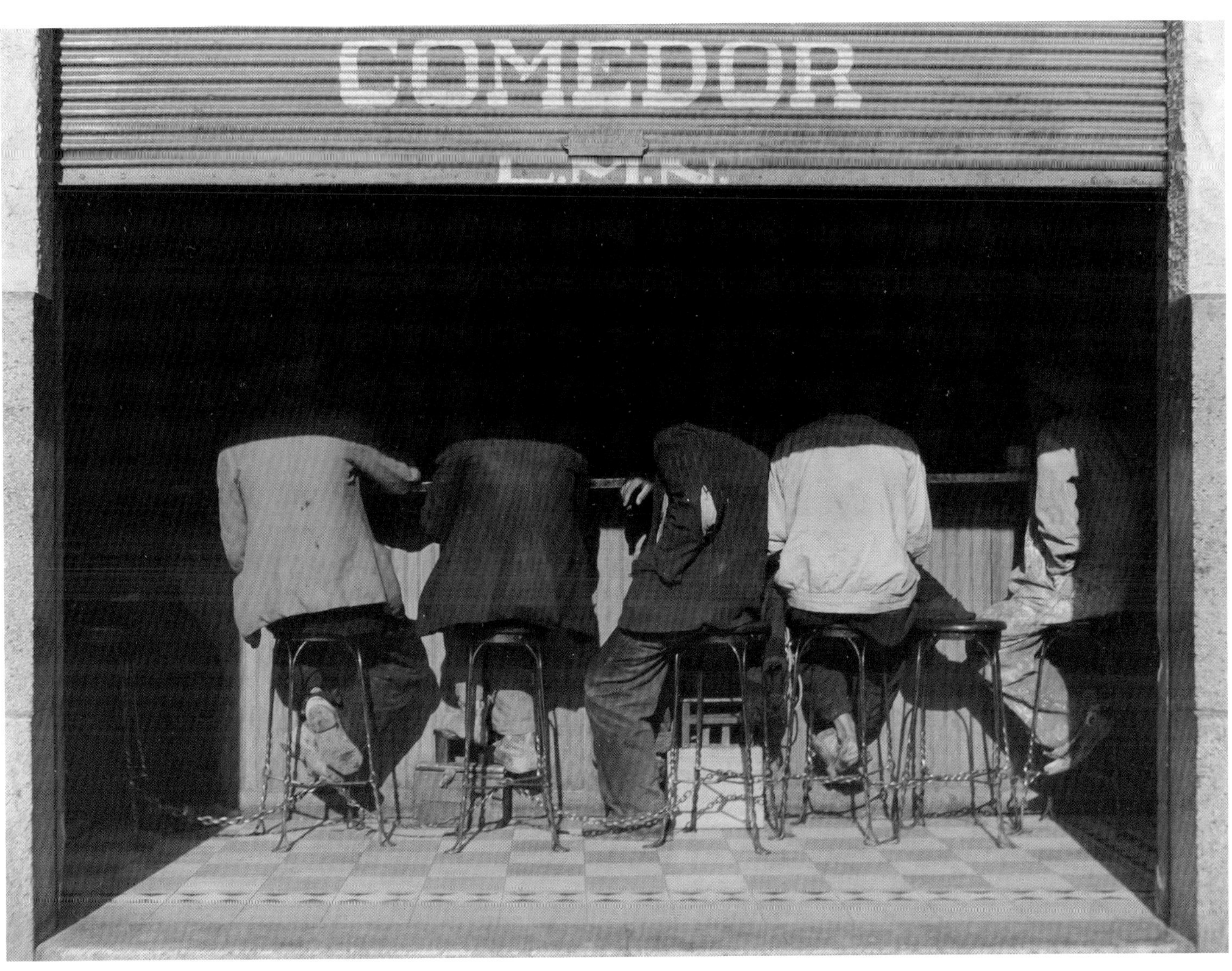

COMEDOR
F.M.N.

80

Horace Bristol

American, 1908–1997

Portrait of Tom Joad, 1938; printed 1998
Gelatin silver print
Image: 31.4 × 25.7 cm (12 3/8 × 10 1/8 in); sheet: 35.2 ×
27.9 cm (13 7/8 × 11 in)
Inscribed, on verso, lower left, in pencil: GRAPES OF
WRATH: TOM JOAD, 1938; stamped, middle center: *Horace
Bristol*; lower right: artist's estate stamp with signature
University of Nebraska, James E. M. and Helen Thomson
Acquisition Trust, U-5005

Originally trained as an architect, Horace Bristol moved to San Francisco in 1933 to work in commercial photography. There he met Ansel Adams (cat. 35) and, through him, Imogen Cunningham (cats. 56 and 103), Edward Weston (cat. 58), and other members of f64, a group that advocated a precise, straightforward approach to the medium. In 1936 Bristol became a founding photographer for the newly formed, visually driven *Life* magazine. The premier issue introduced Margaret Bourke-White's photographs of the Public Works Administration's Fort Peck Dam project (cat. 36); inspired by this work as well as by a previous photo essay Bourke-White had done on sharecroppers, Bristol developed an idea for a similar venture on California's agricultural and migrant laborers. One of the results of this ambitious project is *Portrait of Tom Joad*, named for a character in John Steinbeck's 1939 novel *The Grapes of Wrath*. Much like the figure of Joad himself, the relationship between Bristol, Steinbeck, and the creation of *The Grapes of Wrath*—and the role of Bristol's photographs in the mix—is shrouded in myth.

According to the artist's later accounts, he approached Steinbeck in 1937, proposing to collaborate on the pictorial essay on California's migrant labor camps, which were home to some three hundred thousand people displaced by the drought and dust bowl in the Great Plains.[1] The pair spent several weeks of the winter of 1937 and 1938 touring the area in and around Visalia, outside of Fresno, with Steinbeck interviewing refugees and Bristol accumulating more than one thousand images. When Bristol inquired about Steinbeck's progress some months later, however, the author backed out of the project, informing Bristol of his plans to publish the story as a novel. *The Grapes of Wrath* appeared the following year.

Upon its debut, critics questioned the veracity of Steinbeck's portrayal of life among California's migrant laborers. Although *Life* declined to publish Bristol's photographic essay when first offered it, the magazine's editors subsequently capitalized on the connection between these images and the fictional tale of the Joads to reinforce the novel's accuracy and buttress the magazine's own reputation as "a carrier of cold realism."[2] *Life* first featured Bristol's pictures in a June 1939 pictorial that coincided with *The Grapes of Wrath*'s publication, complete with accompanying text and captions that equated the photographer's subjects with Steinbeck's fictional characters: "The woman on the left-hand page might well be Ma Joad, Author Steinbeck's heroine. The man with the double-edged ax is a counterpart of his hero, Tom Joad."[3] The magazine ran another story in 1940 that juxtaposed Bristol's photographs with stills from the recently released movie version starring Henry Fonda as Tom Joad, touting Bristol's contribution to the project by stating, "Never before had the facts behind a great work of fiction been so carefully researched by the newscamera."[4] Whatever the reality behind the creation of *The Grapes of Wrath*, Bristol's photographs have become inextricably linked to it—so much so that this portrait has not only assumed the title of the novel's protagonist but also been reproduced on the cover of multiple editions of the book. **BKR**

1. Bristol began to give his account of the events upon the fiftieth anniversary of the novel's publication; see Franklin Cameron, "Horace Bristol and the Great Human Story," *Petersen's Photographic* 18, no. 10 (1990): 26–28, 30; "Horace Bristol's Grapes of Wrath," *American Photo* 5, no. 4 (1994): 75; and Sarah Boxer, "Where Fact and Fiction Intertwine," *New York Times*, November 1, 1996. **2.** The proposed collaboration between Bristol and Steinbeck, the truthfulness of the author's account, and the use of the photographer's images as a source of documentation are well analyzed in Samantha Baskind, "The 'True' Story: *Life* Magazine, Horace Bristol, and John Steinbeck's *The Grapes of Wrath*," *Steinbeck Studies* 15, no. 2 (Fall 2004): 39–74; the quote comes from 54. **3.** "The Grapes of Wrath: John Steinbeck Writes a Major Novel about Western Migration," *Life*, June 5, 1939, 67. **4.** "Speaking of Pictures: These in *Life* Prove Facts in *Grapes of Wrath*," *Life*, February 19, 1940, 11.

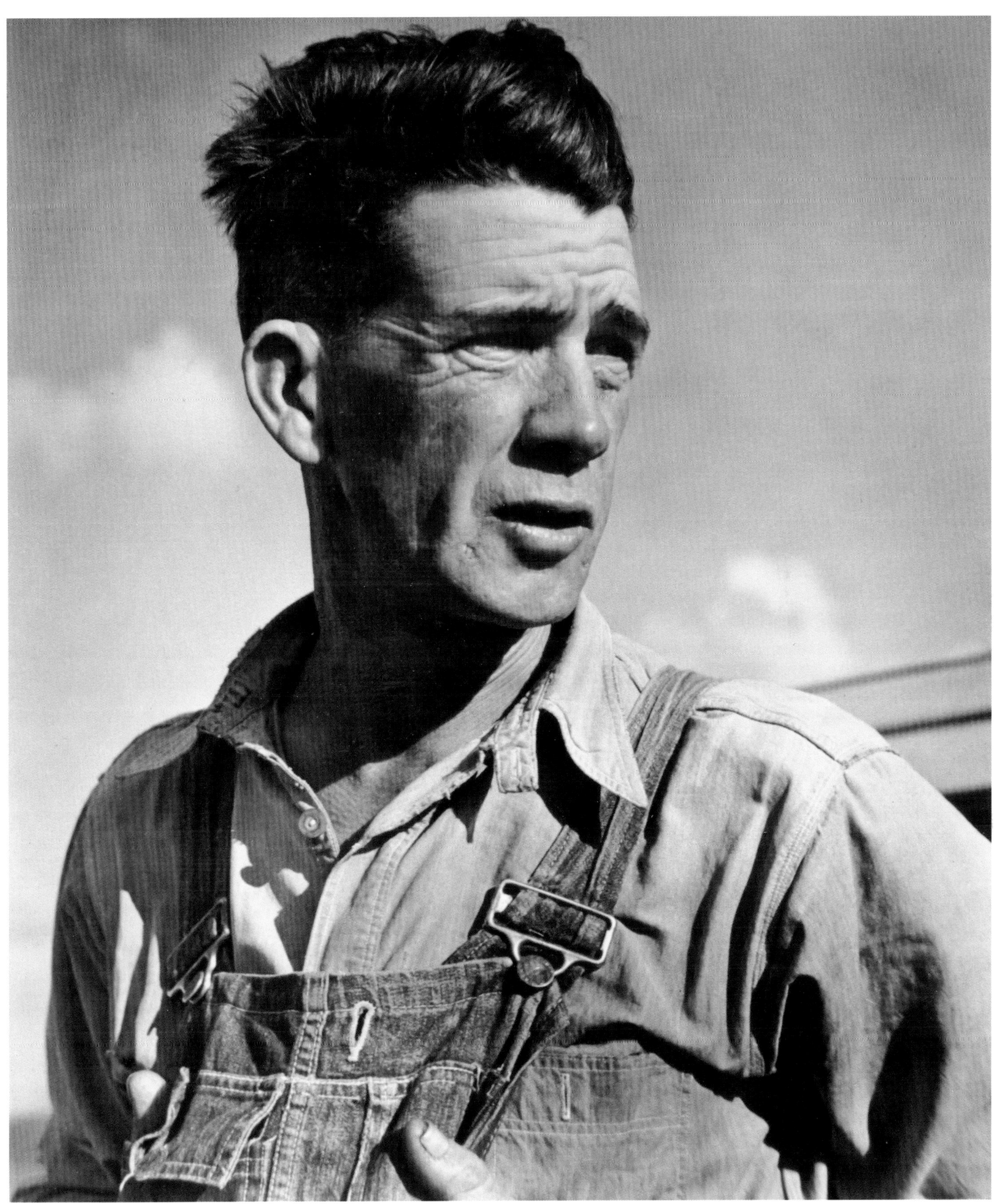

81

Wright Morris

American, 1910–1998

Bench, Cahow's Barbershop, Chapman, Nebraska, 1947
Gelatin silver print
Image: 18.9 × 24 cm (7 7/16 × 9 7/16 in); sheet: 20.2 × 25.4 cm
(7 15/16 × 10 in)
University of Nebraska, gift of Josephine Morris through
the University of Nebraska Foundation, U-5110

A native Nebraskan, Wright Morris devoted his life and career to evoking the experience of life on the Great Plains through pictures and text. In 1942 he received the first of three Guggenheim Fellowships, using the stipend to make a cross-country car trip to California, photographing sites along the way in an effort to, in his words, "[join] photographs and words." The result of Morris's artistic and personal journey was his first photographic novel, *The Inhabitants*, published in 1946 with the goal, as he described it, of resurrecting "the transient ruins of my own culture."[1] In the book, the artist juxtaposed pictures of architectural elements and unpopulated towns with accompanying fictional text meant to represent the residents. A few years later, Morris returned to Nebraska on a second Guggenheim, which allowed him to clarify and expand upon his previous work and vision in what is perhaps his most famous book, *The Home Place*.

Morris's Nebraska photographs raise the issues of memory and nostalgia that are inherent in the medium. Photography's major application is, for many, to preserve the present or, through documentation and viewing, to recapture the past. Such was the artist's experience in the town of Chapman, where he photographed Cahow's Barbershop. Chapman was a site of melancholy for Morris: it was only ten miles from his birthplace, Central City, and his mother, who was raised nearby, was buried there. According to Morris, the importance of his meeting with local barber Eddie Cahow could not be overestimated: "I knew little about my past except what I had conjured up in my fiction, most of it unpublished. Through the barber, Eddie Cahow, I reestablished old lines of communication that are still productive, almost forty years later."[2] The photographer credited this encounter with Cahow during his 1942 trip as providing the impetus for his future life's work: "The meeting with Eddie Cahow, his barber shop, and his friends, would lock me into a pact with the bygone that I had begun on the farm near Norfolk. By the time we left, early in the evening, the setting sun burning on the windshield, I was committed to the recovery of a past I had only dimly sensed that I possessed. I was blissfully ignorant of any awareness that this would prove to be the work of a lifetime."[3]

Morris took several photographs of Cahow's during his stops in Chapman. Like this one, they include what he remembered as "its chalked menu of services and prices, the tonic bottle and brushes on the chiffonier, the case of razors and towels, the postcards sent to Cahow from travelling natives . . . , the barber chair, the sink with its platter for hair massages . . . , [and] the benches with plywood seats."[4] The artist experimented with several different formats in his publications, often reversing the images or cropping them differently from text to text; he presented an expanded version of this image, for example, as an alternate version. By focusing tightly on the bench in this photograph, Morris produced a record of a particular time and place as well as a narrative of life on the plains. The printed wall calendars, for example, show that the date is May 1947, while their advertisements for corn and hybrid seed suggest a rural environment. At the same time, the five-pointed star that embellishes the back of the wood bench—a common motif in colonial architecture and woodworking that was revived at the beginning of the twentieth century—indicates early residents' efforts at refinement. A particular favorite among early Dutch colonists, the decoration hints at the many nationalities that settled the Great Plains. **BKR**

1. Wright Morris, *The Inhabitants* (New York: C. Scribner, 1946), n.p. **2.** Wright Morris, interviewed by James Alinder, September 1975, in *Wright Morris: Structures and Artifacts; Photographs, 1933–1954*, exhibition catalog (Lincoln: Sheldon Memorial Art Gallery, University of Nebraska, 1975), 113. **3.** Quoted in James Alinder, ed., *Wright Morris: Photographs and Words* (Carmel CA: Friends of Photography, 1982), 41. **4.** Morris's reminiscences of the experience are well documented in Morris, interview, 41; for the different views of Cahow's, see *Wright Morris: Structures and Artifacts*, plates 34–39.

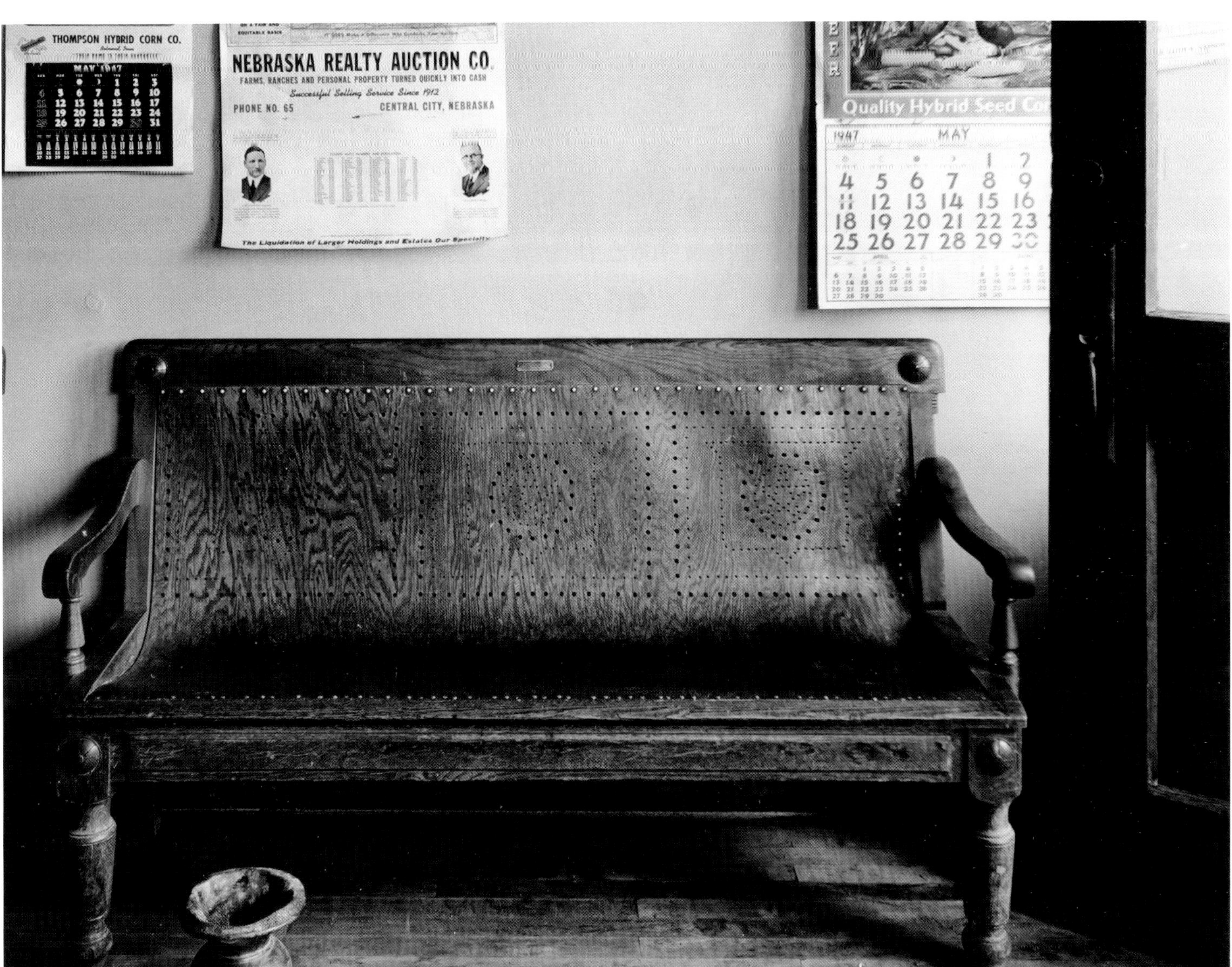

THOMPSON HYBRID CORN CO.
MAY 1947
NEBRASKA REALTY AUCTION CO.
FARMS, RANCHES AND PERSONAL PROPERTY TURNED QUICKLY INTO CASH
Successful Selling Service Since 1912
PHONE NO. 65
CENTRAL CITY, NEBRASKA
The Liquidation of Larger Holdings and Estates Our Specialty
Quality Hybrid Seed Corn
1947 MAY

82

Theodore Roszak

American, born Poland, 1907–1981

Untitled (Photogram), c. 1939
Gelatin silver print
Image and sheet: 12.5 × 10 cm (4 15/16 × 3 15/16 in)
Inscribed, on verso, middle right, in pencil: [written sideways] *13801D 65 / ROSZAK*; lower left: *TR 9828C*
University of Nebraska, gift of Don Brock, Phillip C. Johnson, and an anonymous donor by exchange, U-5082

Born in Poland, at a young age Theodore Roszak immigrated with his family to Chicago, where he attended art classes at the School of the Art Institute throughout high school and enrolled full time in 1925. Although he moved to New York to further his artistic education, he returned to Chicago to teach in 1927. A fellowship that allowed him to travel throughout Europe in the late 1920s and early 1930s, however, proved the critical factor in determining the trajectory of his career. The artist visited several countries during his stay and became familiar with the latest avant-garde trends, including cubism, purism, and surrealism, but it was his visit to the Bauhaus in Dessau, Germany, that exerted lasting influence.

Originally established in Weimar by architect Walter Gropius, the Bauhaus preached the philosophy of constructivism, which aimed at the utopian goal of merging art, science, and technology through the use of modern industrial materials and techniques. Upon his return to the United States, Roszak began to experiment with nonobjective sculpture, the medium for which he is best known. Drawing upon his newly developed skills in tool making and industrial design, he fabricated a series of metal-based constructions, biomorphic and geometric abstractions that expressed America's machine-age confidence.[1]

At the same time, Roszak was investigating similar trends in photography. However, unlike his constructions, which he exhibited widely and to great acclaim, he kept his photography fairly close to his vest. The artist began taking pictures with a camera sometime around 1931, typically concentrating on traditional subjects such as portraits and still lifes and making documents of his first sculptures. It was not until some six years later that he began experimenting with the photogram, an image fashioned by placing objects directly onto the surface of photosensitive paper and then exposing it to light. The technique fascinated Roszak, perhaps for its ability to capture the qualities of three-dimensional objects on a two-dimensional surface and for the distinct qualities of light and pattern that could be achieved by applying items with differing solidity or translucency. In this photogram, for instance, Roszak employed wire mesh, a material that appears frequently in similar works, where it adds a sense of dynamism and movement.[2] In his photograms, the artist sought to abolish content entirely, eliciting a purely retinal response from the viewer yet revealing, as he put it, "a world of geometric and amorphous structures that dispels at a glance the myth that abstract art bears no indebtedness to nature."[3]

Roszak was also likely drawn to the photogram through his connections to the Bauhaus, whose ideologues viewed photography as a natural instrument of the machine age and categorized it as one of the "productive arts," further associating it with science and technology.[4] During his travels in Europe, the artist purchased a copy of a book on the subject by Bauhaus instructor László Moholy-Nagy, an early innovator of the photogram with whom Roszak enjoyed a collegial relationship. In 1938 Roszak began teaching at the Works Progress Administration–funded Design Laboratory in New York, an alternative school modeled on the Bauhaus; Moholy-Nagy, who had moved to Chicago in 1937 to establish the New Bauhaus, acted as a consultant. **BKR**

1. For more on Roszak's sculptures and his early biography, see David Cateforis, "Theodore Roszak," in *Sculpture from the Sheldon Memorial Art Gallery*, ed. Karen O. Janovy (Lincoln: University of Nebraska Press, 2005), 76–78. **2.** For another example of one of Roszak's photograms with wire mesh, see Beth Venn and Adam D. Weinberg, eds., *Frames of Reference: Looking at American Art, 1900–1950*, exhibition catalog (New York: Whitney Museum of American Art; Berkeley: University of California Press, 1999), 99. **3.** Zabriskie Gallery, *Theodore Roszak: Photograms*, exhibition catalog (New York: Zabriskie Gallery, 1984), 9. **4.** Zabriskie Gallery, *Theodore Roszak*, 7–8.

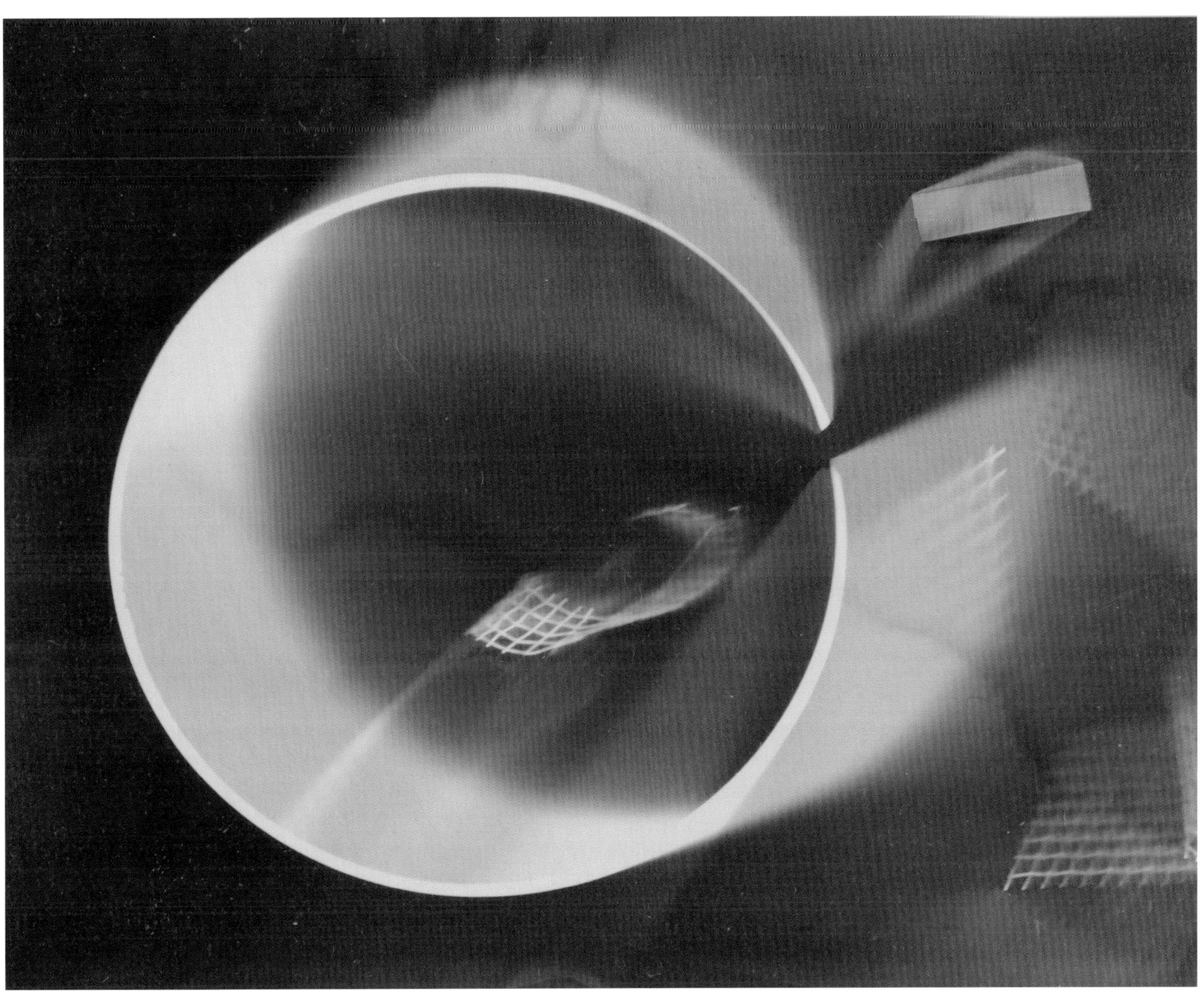

83

Harry Callahan
American, 1912–1999

Weed against Sky, Detroit (#97 from *Photographs: Harry Callahan*), 1948
Gelatin silver print
Image: 19.4 × 18.9 cm (7 5/8 × 7 7/16 in); mount: 29.8 ×
28.9 cm (11 3/4 × 11 3/8 in)
Signed, on mount, lower right, in pencil: *Harry Callahan*
University of Nebraska, Anna R. and Frank M. Hall
Charitable Trust, H-1054

Harry Callahan is known as a pioneer of twentieth-century photography. His sophisticated, elegant images synthesize two primary aesthetic approaches: the romantic, nature-based tradition of Ansel Adams and Alfred Stieglitz (cats. 35 and 15) and the experimental, abstract practice of László Moholy-Nagy. Neither Callahan's background nor his stated intentions predicted this outcome. Born and raised in and around Detroit, he reached his twenties with a job in the automotive industry and a vague yearning for self-expression. Like many young adults of his generation, he took up a hobby, joining a camera club and learning how to make picturesque landscapes and flattering portraits.

An encounter with Ansel Adams in 1941 proved revelatory. In a weekend workshop, the well-known California-based master instructed his students in what he considered the basic principles of the medium: full-frame composition, sharp focus, contact printing, and tonal range. Adams's work of that period included close-up studies of grasses, leaves, and other natural elements that were far more interesting to Callahan than the conventional landscape vistas produced by his fellow camera-club members. Of equal importance, Adams personified the artist-photographer. "That's when I first began to find myself," Callahan later recalled. "For the first time I met a serious photographer who lived, breathed and expressed himself in his work. It was through him that I first . . . became aware that a man's whole life could be spent in what I, up to this time, thought of only as a hobby."[1]

Callahan's real breakthrough came two years later, when he exposed a 4 × 5-inch negative of weed stalks peeping through snow. Overexposing and underdeveloping the film, and then overexposing in the darkroom, resulted in an extremely high-contrast print in which the weeds look like strokes of black ink against a pure white field. This idea yielded many beautiful photographs over the course of Callahan's career, of which *Weed against Sky* is one of the most extraordinary.

Weed against Sky—both landscape and still life—is radical in several respects. Callahan has eliminated all signs of texture as well as the horizon. He has also eradicated the compositional cues that establish three-dimensional space. Finally, by excluding everything other than the central motif, he gives us no sense of scale.[2] At one level, this appears to be an abstract drawing, calligraphic and two-dimensional. At another, it retains its tie to the basic elements of the natural world.

Callahan knew from very early on that the camera could satisfy his internal instinct for picture making, and he pushed his chosen medium to its limits through continual experimentation. His subjects, by contrast, were always ordinary and close at hand: a puddle rather than a waterfall, a weed rather than a rose. His achievement lies in his ability to render these conventional subjects unfamiliar. Perennially renewing his vision in the world, Callahan trusted in intuition above all. While undeniably driven and disciplined, he did not consciously pursue novel effects or innovations; he simply relied on the conviction that something would happen when he picked up his camera. *Weed against Sky* began as an impulse, based on the artist's observation and experience. The final photograph is an icon, perfectly balanced and worthy of prolonged contemplation. **BS**

1. Quoted in David Ebin, "Harry Callahan: Conventional Subjects Become Extraordinary Photographs," *Modern Photography* 21, no. 2 (February 1957): 98. **2.** Print size is another aspect of scale in photography: the artist has the option to enlarge the negative in the darkroom. The negative for *Weed against Snow* is 2¼ inches square. While Callahan sometimes made contact prints from negatives this size, he just as frequently made enlargements, as in the case of the Sheldon's print.

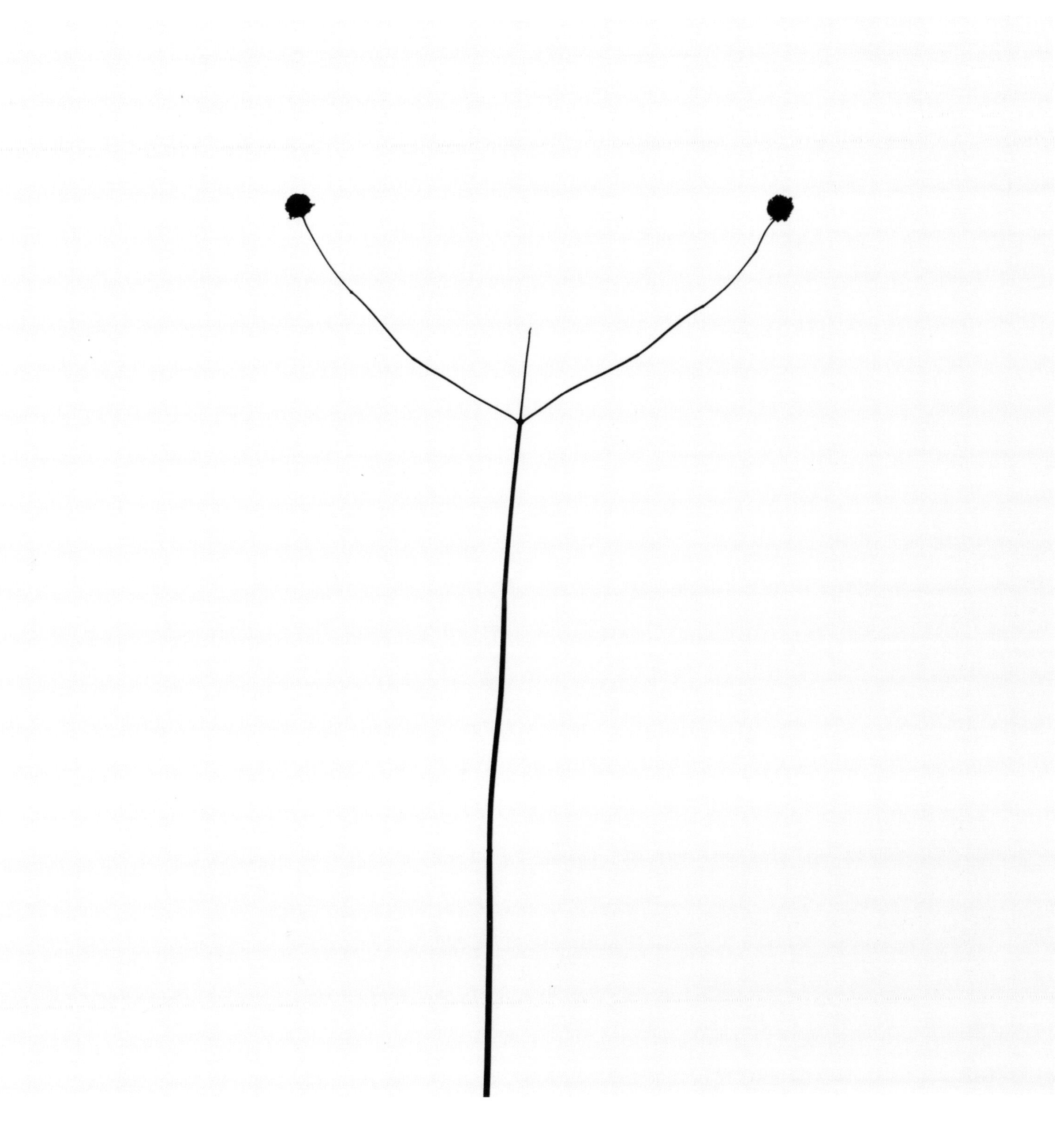

84

Harold Eugene Edgerton
American, 1903–1990

Baton, Multiflash, c. 1953
Gelatin silver print
Image: 44.3 × 36.8 cm (17 7/16 × 14 1/2 in); sheet: 50.5 ×
41 cm (19 7/8 × 16 1/8 in)
Signed, on verso, lower right, in pencil: *Harold
Edgerton / 18/50*
University of Nebraska, gift of the Harold and Esther
Edgerton Family Foundation, U-4920

The Sheldon Museum of Art's collection is particularly rich
in works by Harold Eugene Edgerton, an artist-scientist and
Nebraska native who received his bachelor's degree in electri-
cal engineering from the University of Nebraska in 1925. He
went on to further his education at the Massachusetts Institute of Technology, where he wrote his dissertation on the
use of stroboscopes on everyday objects and served as a full
professor until his retirement in 1977. Edgerton's fascination
with stroboscopic equipment increased in 1937, when he met
the Albanian American photographer Gjon Mili, who became one of his most admiring pupils. The two men formed
a lifelong collaboration, exploring the applications of Edgerton's inventions and theories to photography. Mili popu-
larized the engineer's techniques in the pages of *Life* magazine, for which he became a freelance photographer in 1939.
With two other former students, Kenneth Germeshausen
and Herbert E. Grier, Edgerton developed and perfected a
high-speed electronic flash system that he subsequently employed to capture repetitive, sequential motion. This technology enabled him to photograph a wide assortment of subjects, creating arresting, nearly abstract images of bursting
balloons, flying bullets (see below), splashing liquid, and the
kinetics of athletes, dancers, and entertainers.

Despite the visual allure of his photographs, Edgerton
nonetheless denied being an artist. "Don't make me out to
be an artist," he insisted. "I am an engineer. I am after the
facts. Only the facts."[1] He clearly saw his role as harnessing
photography in the service of science, aiding in the understanding of both motion and perception. He outlined his
agenda as follows in a 1939 publication on his photographs
and theories: "Even in the world as we normally know it, science has called our attention to the unseen and unknown,
and enabled us to see and understand by contracting and
expanding not only space but time. In doing so the scientist
and engineer have had to devise accessories for the human
eye."[2] Edgerton's theories, along with his profession, added
to the debate about the camera's function as an instrument
of art or science that emerged almost immediately after its
invention in 1839 and continued into the twentieth century.

Edgerton experimented with several versions of this subject in the early 1950s, printing different results. For this
composition, he had Muriel Sutherland, a young drum ma-
jorette, repeatedly throw her baton into the air. She is seen in
recurring profile at the bottom of the image, initially lower-
ing her arm to toss her baton skyward, then gazing up and
raising her arm as she races to catch the airborne instrument.
At first, Sutherland and her baton are unidentifiable, abstract
patterns silhouetted against a black background; they are
recognizable upon closer inspection but still almost inseparable from one another. Edgerton noted that his multiflash
fired at sixty times per second as he created this image.[3] **BKR**

1. Quoted in Estelle Jussim and Gus Kayafas, *The Photographs of Harold Edgerton* (New York: Harry N. Abrams, 1987), 18. **2.** J. R. Killian Jr., "The Meaning of Pictures: Exploring the World of Time and Motion," in *Flash! Seeing the Unseen by Ultra High-Speed Photography*, by Harold Edgerton and James R. Killian (Boston: Hale, Cushman and Flint, 1939), 9. **3.** Jussim and Kayafas, *The Photographs*, 105; for an alternate version of this photograph, see 104.

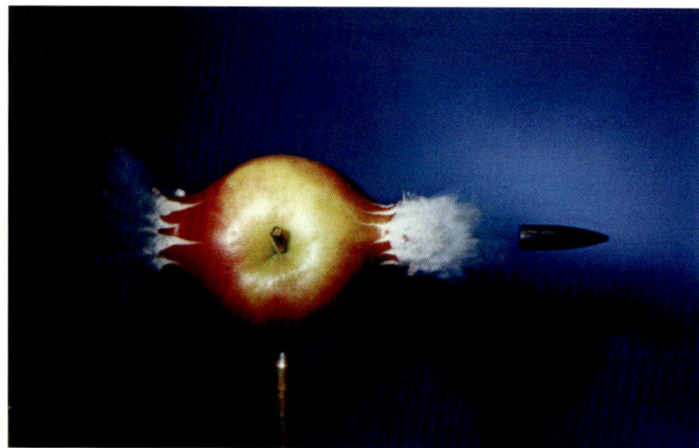

Harold Eugene Edgerton. *.30 Bullet Piercing an Apple*, 1964.
Dye transfer print; 41 × 51.4 cm (16 1/8 × 20 1/4 in). University
of Nebraska, gift of the Harold and Esther Edgerton Family
Foundation, U-4861.7.

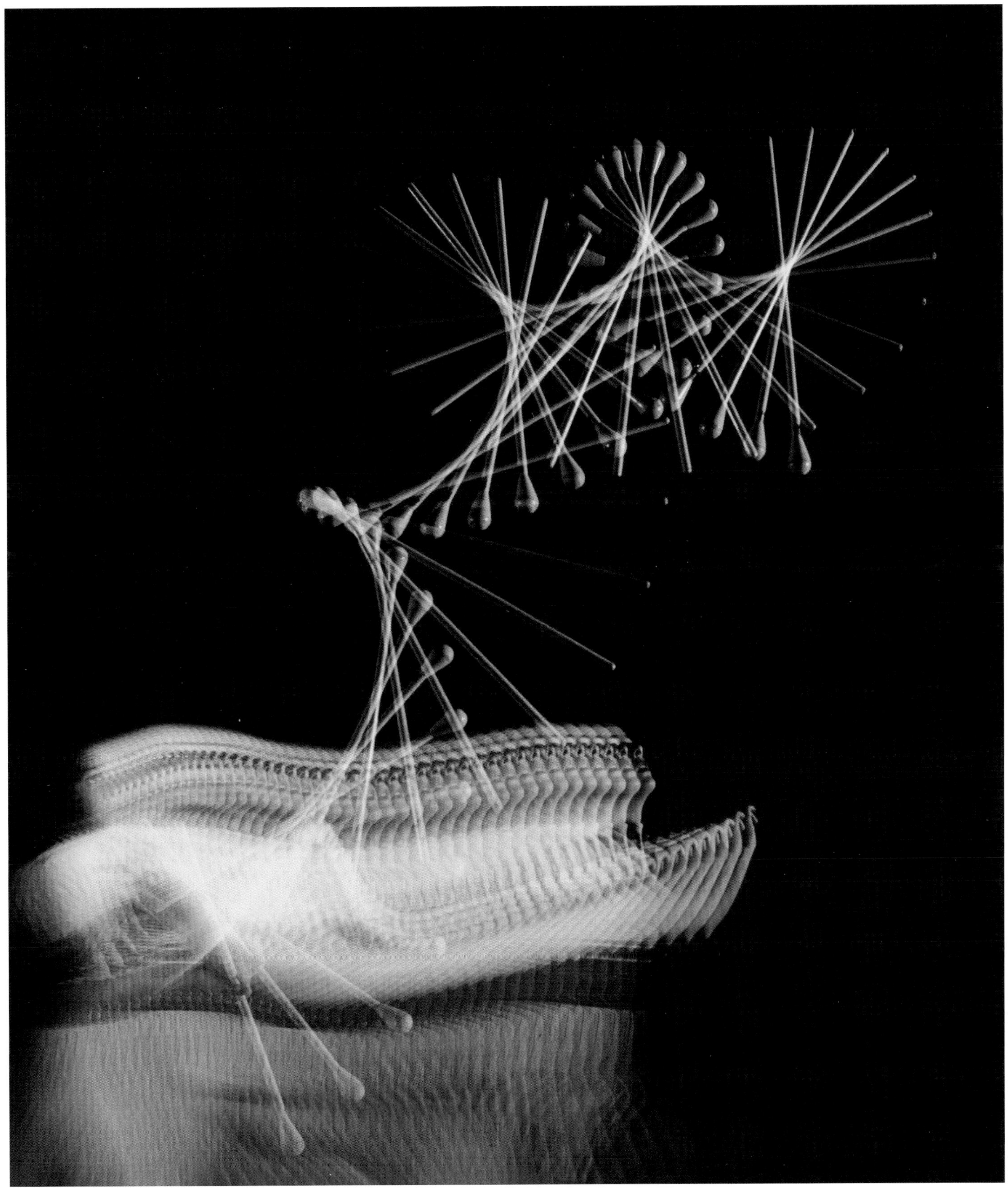

85

Frederick Sommer

American, born Italy, 1905–1999

Smoke on Glass, 1965
Gelatin silver print
Image: 34 × 26.7 cm (13 3/8 × 10 1/2 in); mount: 44.1 ×
31.8 cm (17 3/8 × 12 1/2 in)
Inscribed, on verso, on mount, upper center, in pencil:
Smoke on Glass 1965; middle center: *Frederick Sommer*
Nebraska Art Association, purchased with the aid of
funds from the National Endowment for the Arts, N-403

Frederick Sommer was a Renaissance man for a modern age, at ease in many disciplines, languages, and media. His artistic output consists of collages, drawings, landscape designs, music, and paintings, but despite his resistance to a medium-specific view, today he is best known as a photographer. Sommer came to the United States from Brazil in 1925 to work as a landscape architect. Diagnosed with tuberculosis five years later, he set aside his profession and immersed himself in travel and philosophy, becoming acquainted with European modernism. To protect his health, he settled in Arizona in 1935. At around this time, he also met Alfred Stieglitz and Edward Weston (cats. 15 and 58), leading American proponents of photography as a fine art. Stieglitz encouraged Sommer to continue drawing while Weston mentored him in the use of the large-format camera.

In the early 1940s, Sommer was photographing desert landscapes and still lifes when he met Man Ray and Max Ernst in Los Angeles. Their influence led Sommer to associate himself with surrealism. Although this affiliation was not completely comfortable from his point of view, he did find common ground with the surrealists in his employment of experimental and automatic strategies.

Sommer began to gain international recognition in the mid-1950s through publications, speaking engagements, and teaching posts, including a stint at the Bauhaus-inspired Institute of Design in Chicago. Perhaps stimulated by the experimental tenets of the institute, he began to make cameraless photographs that evolved into the *Smoke on Glass* works of the mid-1960s. These mysterious abstractions resulted from a series of operations. First the artist would make a drawing on aluminum foil, cellophane, or glass, using pigment suspended in a transparent medium. Then he would hold the matrix over a candle so that soot adhered to the drawn lines. Next, the soot-infused drawing was transferred to a piece of greased glass that could be used as a negative in the enlarger.[1] In the resulting print, the original drawing was reversed in orientation and tonality: the strokes of paint became tones of silver, resulting in a complete transfiguration of the original source drawing.

As Sommer continued to push this process, he came to accept its unpredictability and to appreciate its unique properties. The transfer added atmosphere to the drawn lines, and the enlargement of the image conferred depth of field. Perhaps most appealingly, the use of soot and glass eliminated the telltale grain of emulsion on film. Theoretically, Sommer could have used this final negative to generate multiple identical positives. But he believed in the unique fine print. The artist typically produced fewer than five prints of a negative that satisfied him, and he favored variation from print to print and over time.[2]

For Sommer, art was akin to philosophy; he considered both pursuits to be essentially engaged with problem solving. Yet at the same time, he prized mystery and equivocation, likening the *Smoke on Glass* images to the experience of "the greenhouse or the jungle."[3] While we may seek patterns and logic, we can also derive pleasure from chaos. **BS**

1. For descriptions of this process, see Sheryl Conkelton, "Seeing and Knowing the Order of Things," in *Frederick Sommer: Selected Texts and Bibliography*, ed. Sheryl Conkelton (Oxford: Clio Press, 1995), 18–19; Keith F. Davis, "Living Art: The Sources of Frederick Sommer's Work," in *The Art of Frederick Sommer: Photography, Drawing, Collage*, ed. Naomi Lyons and Jeremy Cox (Prescott AZ: Frederick and Frances Sommer Foundation, 2005), 19–20; and Frederick Sommer, "A Talk Given at the Art Institute of Chicago, October 1970, revised June 1983," in *Sommer: Words* (Tucson AZ: Center for Creative Photography, University of Arizona, 1984), 47. **2.** Sommer, "A Talk," 48. **3.** Quoted in Davis "Living Art," 20.

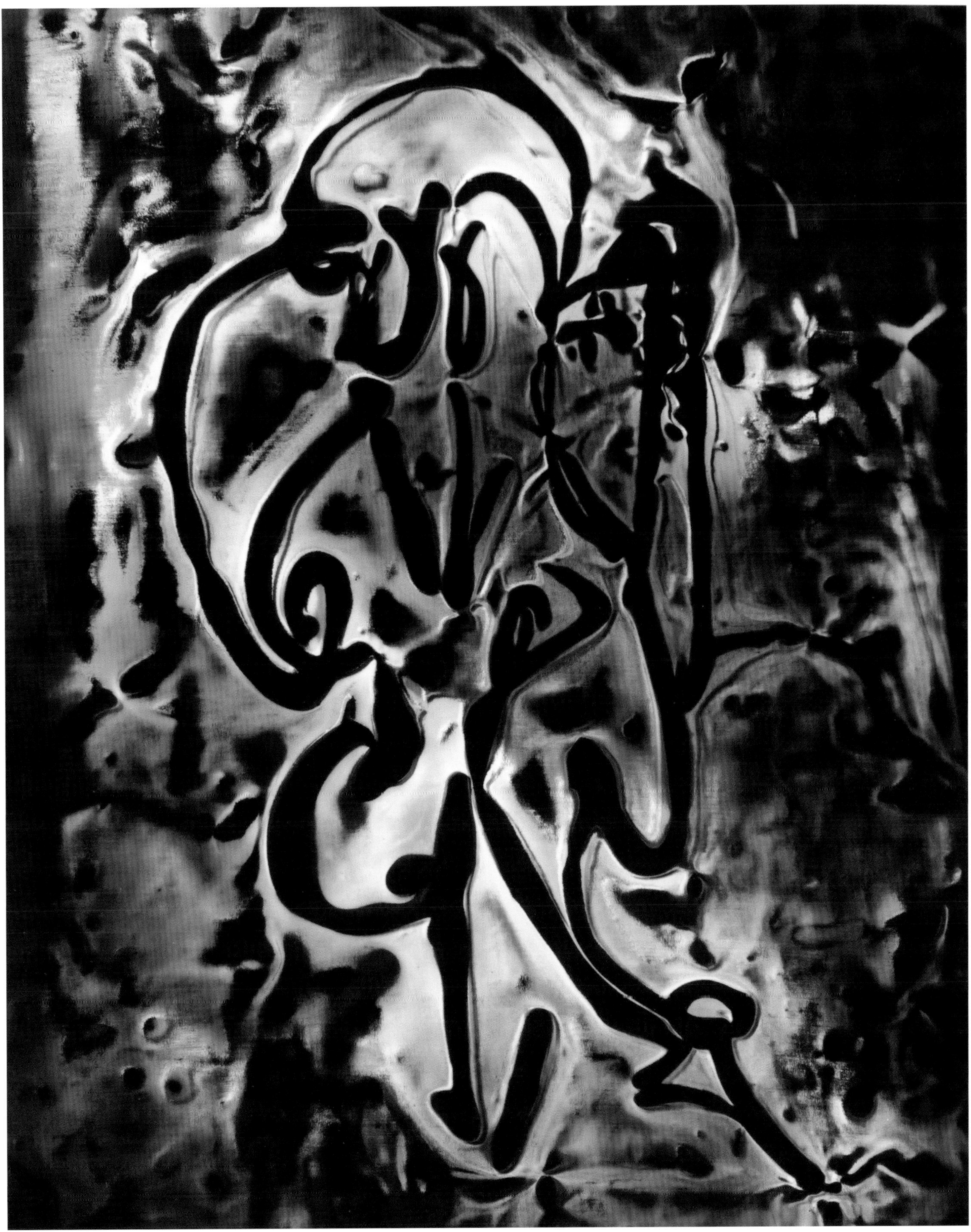

86

Han Van Nguyen
American, born Vietnam, 1956

Untitled (from the *Hominid* series), 1993
Gelatin silver print
Image: 39.3 × 35.6 cm (15 1/2 × 14 in); sheet: 50.5 × 40.5 cm
(19 7/8 × 15 15/16 in)
Inscribed, on verso, lower right, in pencil: *Hân Nguyen
1993 / Untitled. 1/25*
University of Nebraska, Anna R. and Frank M. Hall
Charitable Trust, H-3029

Born in Vietnam, San Diego–based photographer Han Nguyen immigrated to the United States in 1975. Initially aiming to study documentary street photography in the tradition of Henri Cartier-Bresson (cat. 73), Nguyen quickly realized that he lacked the "gregarious temperament" to achieve effective results in that kind of work.[1] Instead, the artist turned inward and began experimenting with enigmatic, poetic, almost dreamlike imagery in a variety of different processes and techniques. Nguyen works serially, concentrating on specific themes that have included pixilated reproductions of famous artworks, images of individual body parts, plant portraits, and highly intricate miniature reconstructions of homes and interiors. While each series has focused on a particular idea or subject, as a group they explore feelings about home, dislocation, loss of identity, and the re-creation of new selves.

In Nguyen's *Hominid* series, which he began in the early 1990s, the artist layered his photographs with negatives from seemingly disparate elements—skeletons and skulls, natural history museum dioramas and taxidermy, and reproductions of well-known European paintings, including Old Master canvases and self-portraits by Vincent van Gogh. In this untitled image, he combined taped negatives of verdant yet ruined landscapes with human artifacts such as skeletons and facial masks. The various vertical tiers, in fact, mimic the hierarchical displays in many archaeology and anthropology museums; this impression is reinforced by the seemingly endless rows of plaster masks at top and on the shelf second from bottom. While these elements seem disconnected at first glance, to the artist they represent an attempt to recover memory and history, acting as talismans of our ancestors and reminding us that the past coexists with the present. In this latter regard, Nguyen is influenced by his Buddhist faith, in which "reincarnation keeps the spirit or soul alive, while its external form changes over time."[2] These works are also explorations of the study of history. As the artist examines how both scholars and ordinary people reconstruct the past by comparing its fragmented remains, he reminds us that while time marches persistently onward in a linear fashion, human events take a more circuitous path, overlapping in a less orderly way. In his juxtaposition of the ancient past with contemporary elements and recognizable images from Western art history, Nguyen also demonstrates humanity's interconnectedness. **BKR**

1. Robert L. Pincus, "Nguyen's Exhibition Speaks to Us, Questioning Our Perceptions," *San Diego Union-Tribune*, June 1, 2006. **2.** Leah Ollman, "Han Nguyen," *Zoom Magazine* 30 (January–February 1999): 22.

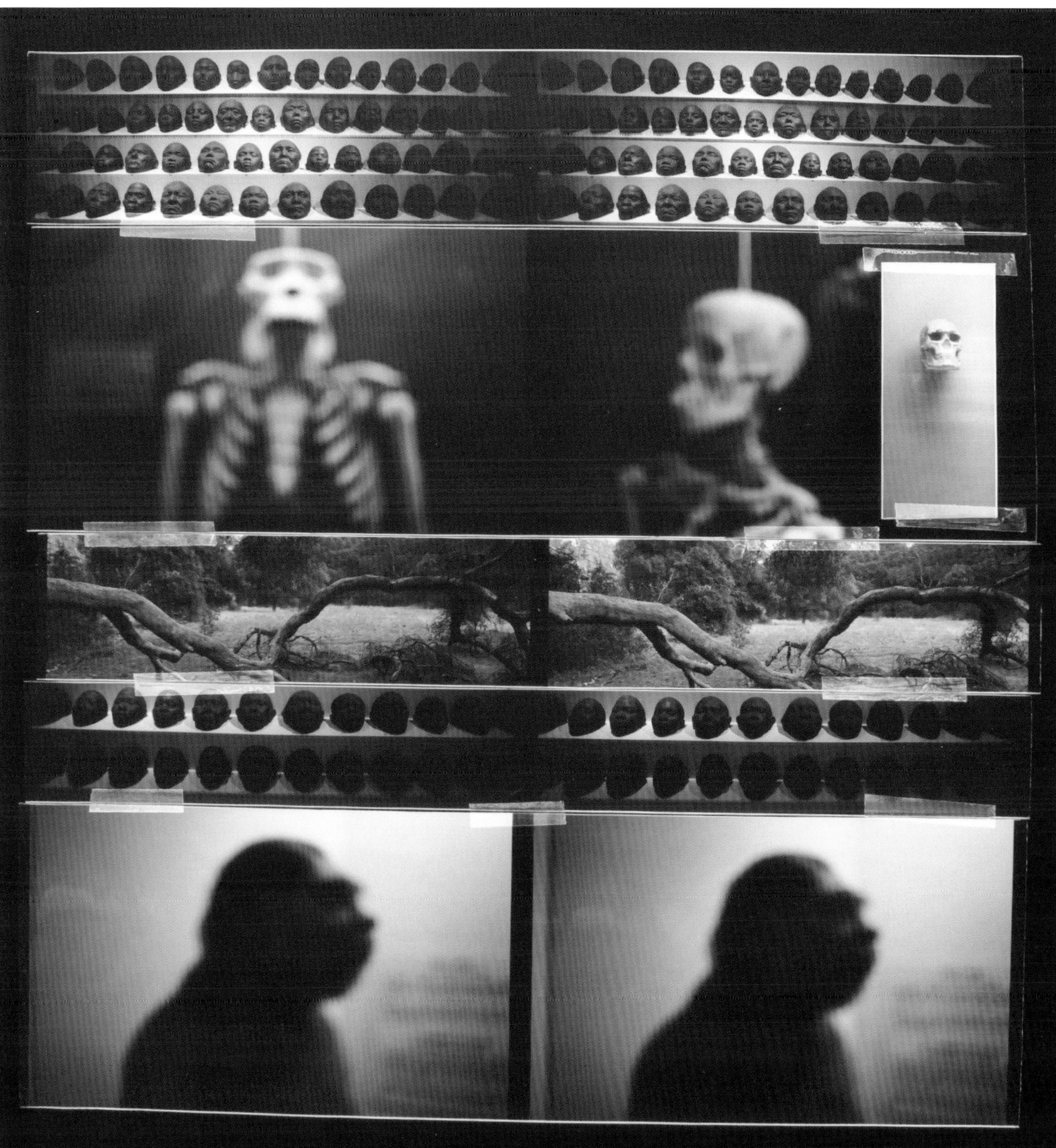

87

Abelardo Morell

American, born Cuba, 1948

Castle Courtyard in Bedroom, Umbertide, Italy, 2000
Gelatin silver print
Image: 45.9 × 56.4 cm (18 1/16 × 22 3/16 in); sheet: 50.8 × 61 cm (20 × 24 in)
Inscribed, on verso, lower left, in pencil: ABELARDO MORELL; lower right: CAMERA OBSCURA IMAGE OF CASTLE COURTYARD / IN BEDROOM, 2000
Sheldon Art Association, gift in Memory of Jean Dickinson Ames, N-777

Born in Havana, Abelardo Morell came to the United States with his family in 1962, a moment when relations between the two countries were deteriorating sharply. After a period in Miami—the gateway for Cuban immigrants—the Morells finally settled in New York, and Abelardo received a scholarship to Bowdoin College in the late 1960s. Although he majored in comparative religion, Morell took his first photography course and, as Richard Woodward described it, "gravitated toward art with a wild, spiritual dimension," finding in photography the ability to "express the alienation and turmoil—and not a little rage—that he was experiencing as a stranger in a strange land."[1] While Morrell's initial aesthetic interest was in the experimental surrealism that dominated the psychedelic 1960s and 1970s, he went on to further his studies at Yale University, whose faculty encouraged street photography. The birth of his son in the mid-1980s, however, led to greater introspection and a new interest in interiors. The artist also began to work intensively with the camera obscura, inspired by an exercise on the scientific principles of photography for his students at the Massachusetts College of Art. Since then, he has married these different strains, using a camera obscura to project images in domestic interiors and thus achieve the experimental surrealism that fascinated him in his youth.

While of ancient Asian origin, the camera obscura achieved a level of popularity in the Western world during the European Renaissance. It was used not only as a scientific device to aid in the perception of celestial phenomena but also as an instrument in the creation of highly detailed drawings and paintings; these applications eventually led to the development of photography. Despite the technical genesis of the device, its principles are actually quite simple: a small hole is punctured in a box or completely darkened room, and an outside light source passing through the hole projects the exterior image onto the surface of the box or wall upside down, with the image's clarity and perspective intact.

Morell has traveled the world experimenting with the camera obscura, ranging from Havana and Paris to London and New York. By the early 1990s, he had developed a routine that involves securing sheets of black plastic over the windows of a room, leaving a three-eighths-inch hole; the process is time-consuming, however, and subject to the vagaries of the weather. *Castle Courtyard in Bedroom* is a striking example of just how the camera obscura works on its most fundamental level and thus also a demystification of the photographic process itself. Working in a small room in the central Italian town of Umbertide, Morell darkened the space almost completely, allowing only a small amount of light to enter. The building's exterior courtyard was projected upside down on the walls of the chamber, superimposing itself on the small bed, chair, towel, and washstand. This confluence and overlapping of images unsettles both spaces, simultaneously merging and negating them, creating a dreamlike interior world freighted with new meaning.[2] Morell's use of antique methods also speaks to the revival of older equipment by contemporary photographers, raising questions about the scientific advancement supposedly ushered in with the advent of the camera. **BKR**

1. Richard B. Woodward, *Abelardo Morell* (London: Phaidon Press, 2005), 7.
2. Abelardo Morell and Luc Sante, *Camera Obscura* (New York: Bulfinch Press, 2004), 8.

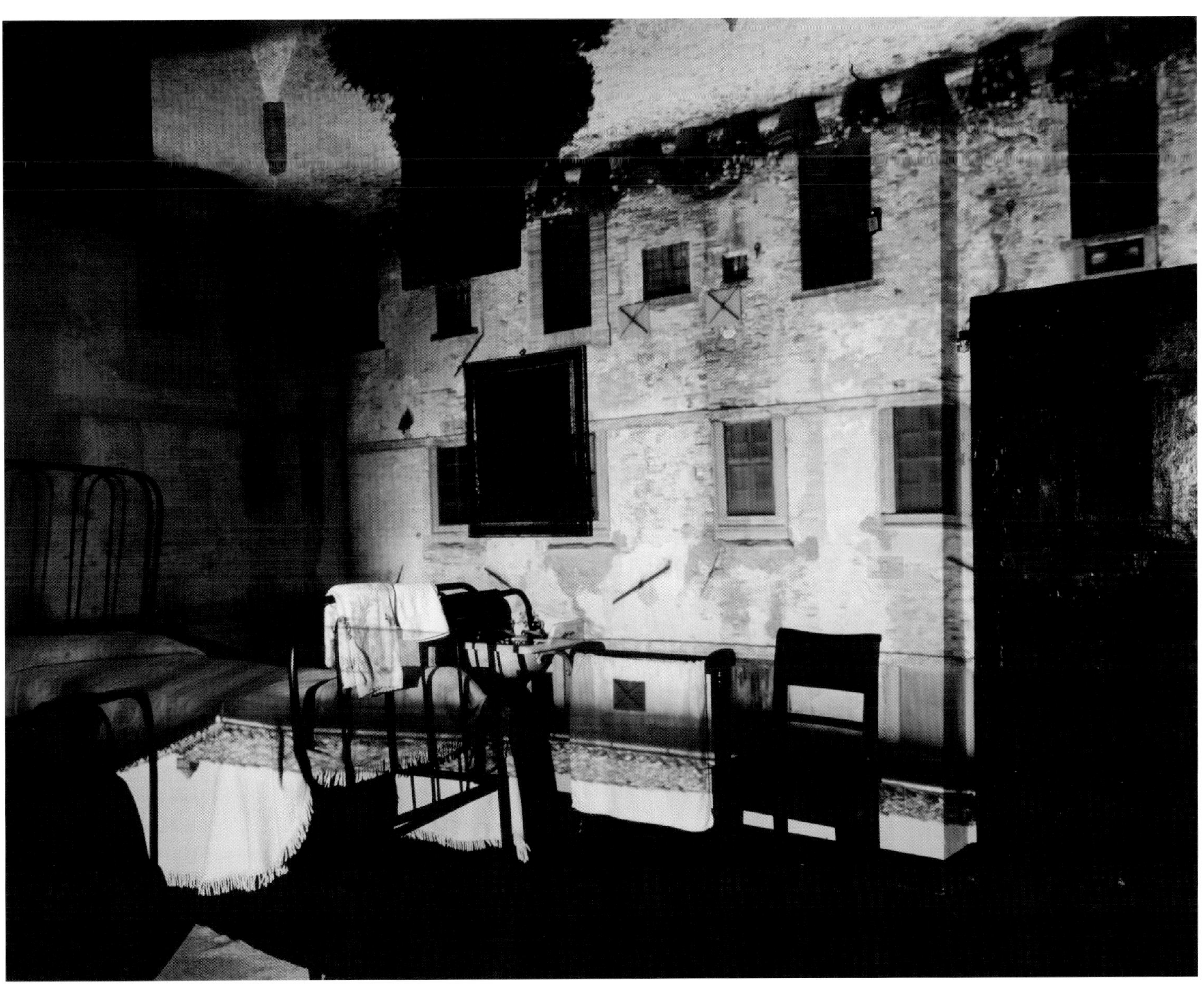

88

Vera Mercer

American, born Germany, 1936

White Goose, 2009
Inkjet print
Image and sheet: 150 × 198 cm (59 × 78 in)
University of Nebraska, Mercedes A. Augustine
Acquisition Trust, U-5598

Born in Berlin, Vera Mercer moved to Paris in 1958 with her husband, the Romanian-born Swiss artist Daniel Spoerri. There they became part of the avant-garde group Nouveaux réalistes, with closest ties to Jean Tinguely, Eva Aeppli, and Niki de Saint Phalle. Trained in modern dance, Mercer taught herself photography and turned her camera on the artists and writers of her day, including Samuel Beckett, Marcel Duchamp, Norman Mailer, Robert Rauschenberg, and Andy Warhol. According to curator Matthias Harder, Mercer's sensitivity in portraying artists reached beyond documentation to the interpretation of artistic processes.[1] For a short stint, she assisted Swiss photographer Peter Knapp, who published in *Vogue* and *Elle*. The daughter of the set designer Franz Mertz, she also photographed the German theater world, publishing in the magazine *Theater Heute*.[2]

Though all of these experiences inflect Mercer's recent still lifes in notable ways, perhaps most pivotal is her experience photographing slaughterhouse environments in the historic Parisian marketplace Les Halles (before it was demolished in 1971 to build the current underground shopping mall). From Les Halles she would bring home and photograph meat and fish, fruits and vegetables. Mercer moved to Omaha in 1970, where she and her second husband, Mark Mercer, came to develop the city's Old Market neighborhood. They stayed and eventually opened a photographic studio, exhibition gallery, and several restaurants that feature her photographs, literally combining art, food, and still life.

The Sheldon's *White Goose*, like so many of Mercer's still lifes, displays many of the accoutrements typical of the genre. Yet her photographs do more than reiterate the genre: they exceed its formal aspirations by dramatizing its elements. She incorporates theatrical lighting, permits herself to arrange elements choreographically rather than compositionally, and utilizes techniques of stagecraft such as backdrop illustrations—in this case, a detail from another of her still-life photographs.

Elements in Mercer's still-life series traditionally associated with memento mori, such as skulls, dead animals, and wilting blossoms, no longer carry their cautionary import. Instead they become mementos more redolent of art history than of death, quoting antecedent practices rather than faithfully repeating them. The moral lesson of vanitas paintings is outweighed by the sumptuousness of surface textures and the weightiness of saturated colors. In these still lifes, art offers its own lessons, including, perhaps, a meditation on death as a device of art—in the way that art frames death in visual beauty.

Mercer brings German stage design, French surrealism, slaughterhouse grit, and aristocratic bounty to her studio practice in Omaha, Nebraska. These postmodern still lifes are not only transnational, they are transhistorical, blurring discipline and genre. **JDV**

1. Matthias Harder, *Vera Mercer: Photographs and Still Lifes* (Heidelberg: Kehrer Verlag Heidelberg, 2010), 5. **2.** Harder, *Vera Mercer*, 6.

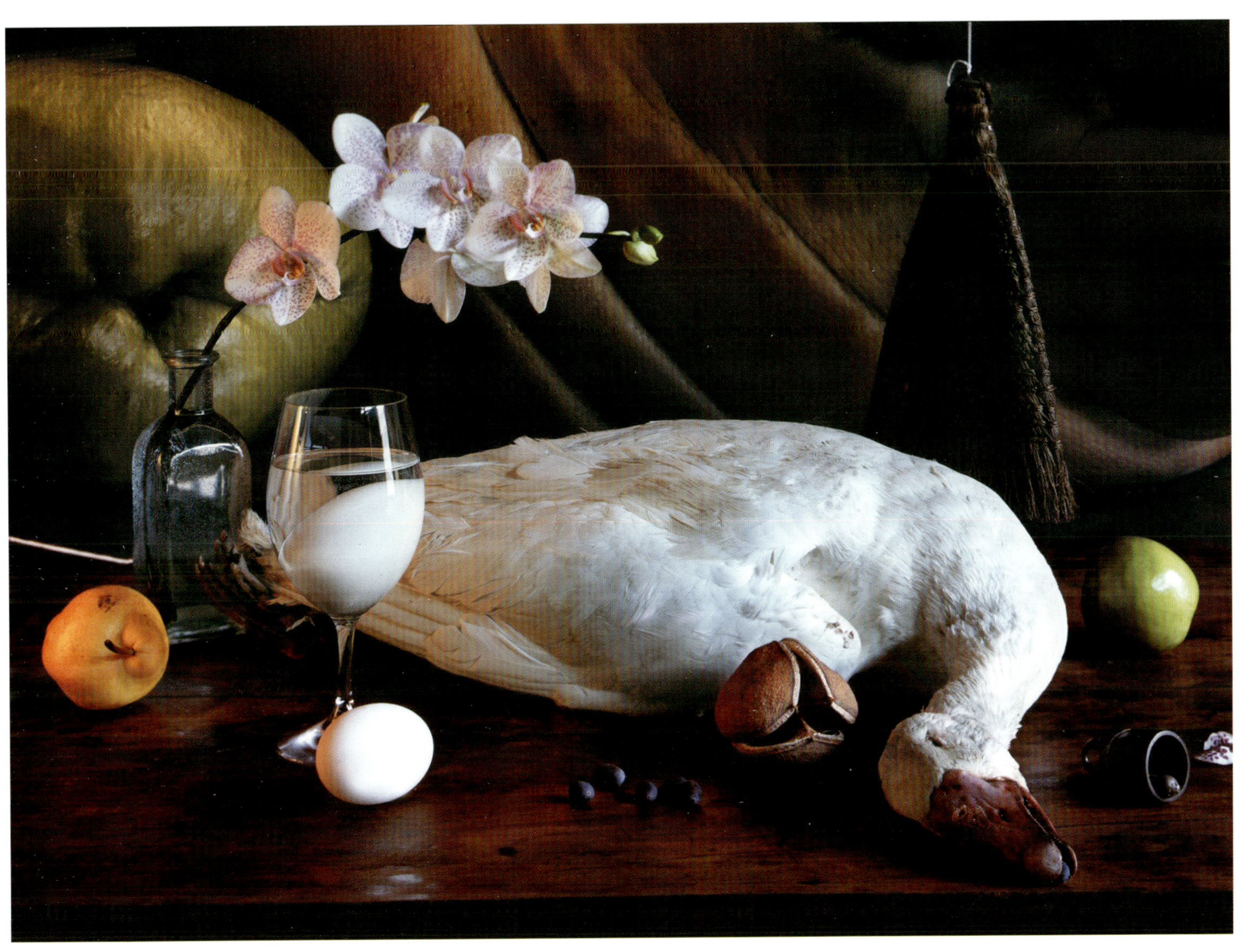

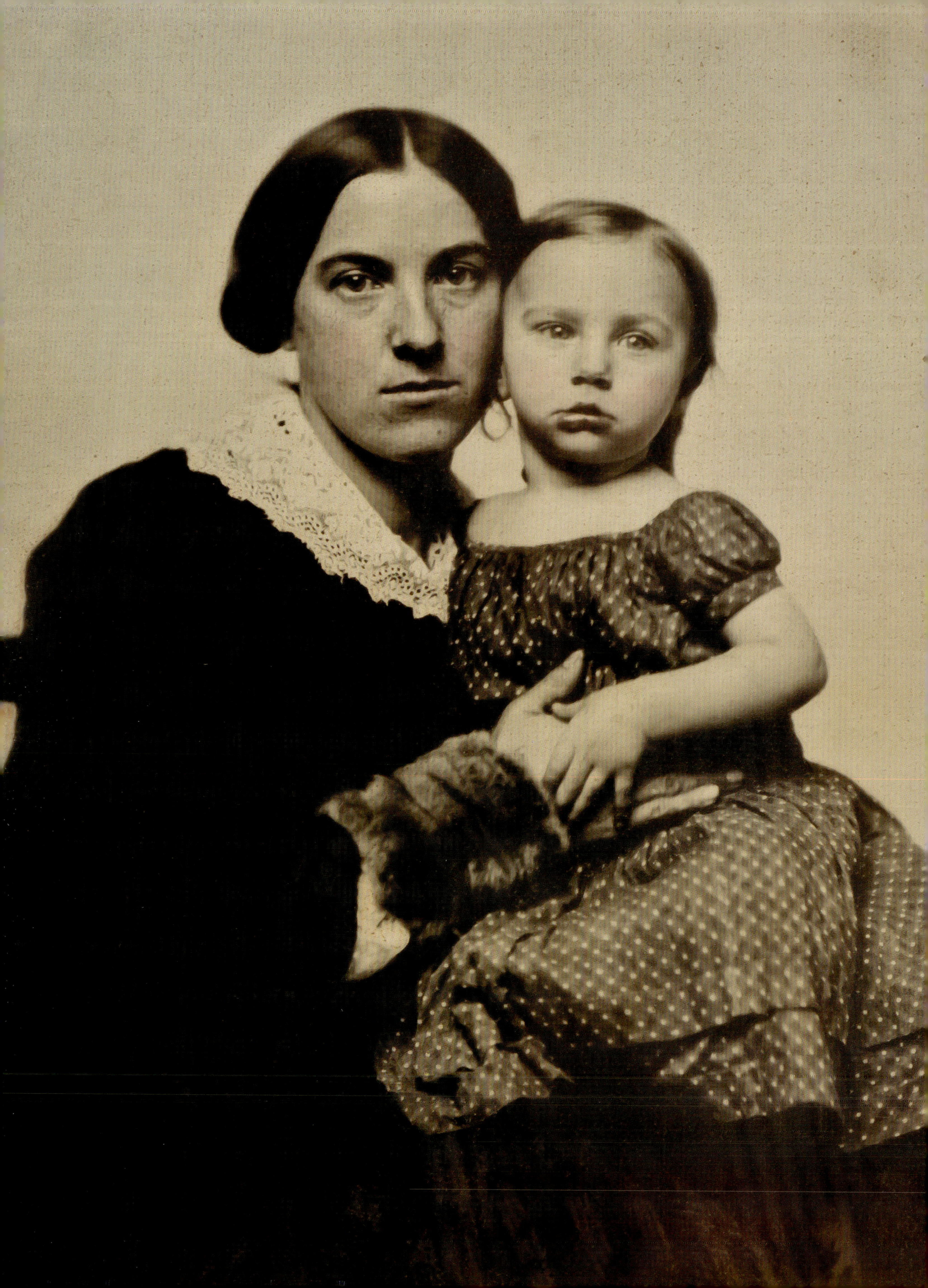

The advent of photography enabled portraits to be made and disseminated at (relatively speaking) lightning speed, creating exciting opportunities not only for commercial artists but also for thousands of consumers who could not have afforded to commission painted images of themselves. While many rushed to take advantage of this new development, early portrait photography was limited by its small range of formats and rigid modes of formal presentation. Although they were trained professionals, early practitioners could offer only a restricted repertoire of portrait sizes, a small supply of accessories, and a few studio props. Photographers did give sitters special instructions on what they should wear for their individual sessions. The limited reproducibility of early daguerreotypes, for instance, led many sitters to take special care as they presented themselves to the camera.

As unprecedented, indelible records of an individual's identity, these early photographs often reinforced gender norms, showing sitters in costume associated with exclusively male pursuits or highlighting maternal qualities (cats. 89 and 90). We can use transnational approaches to explore encounters across class and gender; such categories played important roles in photography's historical function. Male artists' fascination with female prostitutes at the beginning of the twentieth century (cats. 97, 98, and 99) is an obvious example. As a supporting instrument of imperialism, the camera also documented and disseminated images of colonized people and places, often reinforcing the essentializing characteristics and qualities of colonialist ideas. In an image of an Egyptian peasant woman made by the firm of Sébah and Joaillier (cat. 91), the (male) photographer sexualized his subject—as in the example of the reclining Turkish woman in section 1 (cat. 3). This stereotype of eroticized, exotic femininity, so popular in the Western imagination, was routinely recycled in contemporary paintings and photographs.

With the advent of cheaper, portable cameras by the end of the nineteenth century, photography turned from an elite activity reserved for amateurs and wealthy hobbyists to a more democratic one: practitioners actively sought new modes of self-representation and, in some cases, even usurped traditional approaches to representing gender. Sitters, for instance, might playfully subvert gender expectations in their activities and dress, as they did in a series of anonymous photographs showing a group of friends cross-dressing and two female voyeurs (cats. 93 and 94).

In the hands of professional photographers, whether artistic or commercial, these gender distinctions and elements of identity could be both destabilized and reinforced. Cecil Beaton's and Imogen Cunningham's portraits of Edith Sitwell and Gertrude Stein, respectively (cats. 102 and 103), subtly suggest their artistic personas and careers as poets through the careful selection of interiors, poses, and props, while Yousuf Karsh's photograph of Winston Churchill (cat. 104) only emphasizes his public character. At the same time, the emotionally direct portrait of Marsden Hartley by George Platt Lynes (cat. 105) reveals the collaborative, sympathetic possibilities between a gay artist and sitter.

Twentieth-century photographers continued this exploration of gender, identity, and sexuality, questioning distinctions and, as rigid barriers began to evaporate, treating these issues almost casually, as a simple aesthetic choice. Ruth Bernhard, for example, took advantage of her connections in San Francisco's lesbian community to create portrait nudes known for their formal explorations of line and tone (cat. 107). Robert Mapplethorpe's focus on erotic images of black men (cat. 108) was a specific attempt to address a culturally loaded subject, and Catherine Opie's depiction of Divinity Fudge (cat. 110) is not only a portrait of a like-minded performance artist but an opportunity to challenge and implode gender stereotypes.

Artist Unknown

American

Portrait in Regalia, 1850s
Ambrotype with hand coloring
Image: 14.3 × 11.1 cm (5 5/8 × 4 3/8 in); case (open): 25.4 ×
15.2 cm (10 × 6 in)
University of Nebraska, Anna R. and Frank M. Hall
Charitable Trust, H-2569

Artist Unknown

Portrait of Mother and Daughter, 1850s
Ambrotype with hand coloring
Image: 8.6 × 7.1 cm (3 3/8 × 2 13/16 in); case (open): 10.2 ×
16.5 cm (4 × 6 1/2 in)
University of Nebraska, gift of Alan Smith, U-3489

During the 1850s, the phenomenally popular daguerreotype (cat. 66) was superseded in the United States by the less expensive ambrotype. In vogue for about a decade, ambrotypes were often advertised by their makers as "daguerreotypes without reflections," which referred to the fact that they were made with glass negatives rather than highly reflective silver-coated copper plates.[1] This approach—like the related practice of producing ambrotypes in the same sizes as daguerreotypes and presenting them in similarly elaborate cases—exploited the fact that any real distinction between the two processes was lost on most consumers. Within the decade, the ambrotype was displaced by the tintype, hinting at the speedy way in which imaging technologies were being developed and discarded in the mid-nineteenth century.

The appeal of photographs at this moment was indisputable, whatever the techniques used to produce them. This was particularly the case for the expanding audience of middle-class consumers who were eager to record, as Merry Foresta put it, "the beloved child, the newest house, the promised progress of industry, the experience of loss." "Family relationships," Foresta continued, "were enacted for the camera."[2] These two ambrotypes offer a point of entry into just such areas of meaning. More precisely, they reveal important truths about the construction of gender in Victorian America, suggesting the ways in which men and women lived their lives beyond the camera's gaze.

The first image portrays a man posing stiffly with his right hand on a large Bible. What his pose begins to tell us, his costume drives home: he is a man of standing, dressed in a full complement of garments that includes a silk top hat, a vest, and an apron. Such headwear was a mark of distinction worn by senior members of fraternal orders; the apron flap is decorated with the all-seeing eye, perhaps the most easily identifiable Masonic symbol; and the lower apron features a bird, a lamb, and at center a bow and arrows. The last motif identifies the sitter as a member of the Odd Fellows, one of the many fraternal organizations that dominated nineteenth-century America. Groups like the Odd Fellows encouraged self-control and sound business practices, serving as a main vehicle for movement into and through the middle class for millions of Protestant men. Their focus on secret, highly theatrical rituals, however, may also have helped members to build meaningful relationships with one another, compensating for their increasingly marginalized status within their own families.[3] As Ann Douglas described it, "Paternal authority was a waning force" at this moment: "The middle-class American father, locked into tightening business patterns, was less and less likely to be at home."[4]

Mothers, meanwhile, had never been so powerful. The second ambrotype, which depicts a mother cheek to cheek, hand in hand with her young daughter, exemplifies the way in which nineteenth-century photographers used a simple language of gesture and touch to suggest powerful emotional intimacy.[5] It also, however, suggests the larger way in which middle-class women, even as they had lost their economic productivity to men, had claimed educational, moral, and spiritual authority within their own families. In her wildly successful *Letters to Mothers* (1838), Lydia Huntley Sigourney described the omnipotent quality of maternal influence thus: "How entire and perfect is this dominion over the unformed character of your infant. Write what you will upon the printless tablet with your wand of love. . . . The period of this influence must indeed pass away; but while it lasts, make good use of it."[6] GN

1. For more on the ambrotype, see Beaumont Newhall, *The Daguerreotype in America*, rev. ed. (Greenwich CT: New York Graphic Society, 1968), 107–8; and Thomas Feldvebel, *The Ambrotype Old and New* (Rochester NY: Graphic Arts Research Center, Rochester Institute of Technology, 1980). 2. Merry A. Foresta, "American Photographs: The First Century," in *American Photographs: The First Century*, by Merry A. Foresta, exhibition catalog (Washington DC: National Museum of American Art and Smithsonian Institution Press, 1996), 15. 3. For more on the culture of fraternalism, see Mark C. Carnes, *Secret Ritual and Manhood in Victorian America* (New Haven CT: Yale University Press, 1989); and Mary Ann Clawson, *Constructing Brotherhood: Class, Gender, and Fraternalism* (Princeton NJ: Princeton University Press, 1989). 4. Ann Douglas, *The Feminization of American Culture* (New York: Alfred A. Knopf, 1977), 74. 5. See John Wood, "The American Portrait," in *America and the Daguerreotype*, by John Wood (Iowa City: University of Iowa Press, 1991), 4. 6. Quoted in Douglas, *The Feminization*, 75.

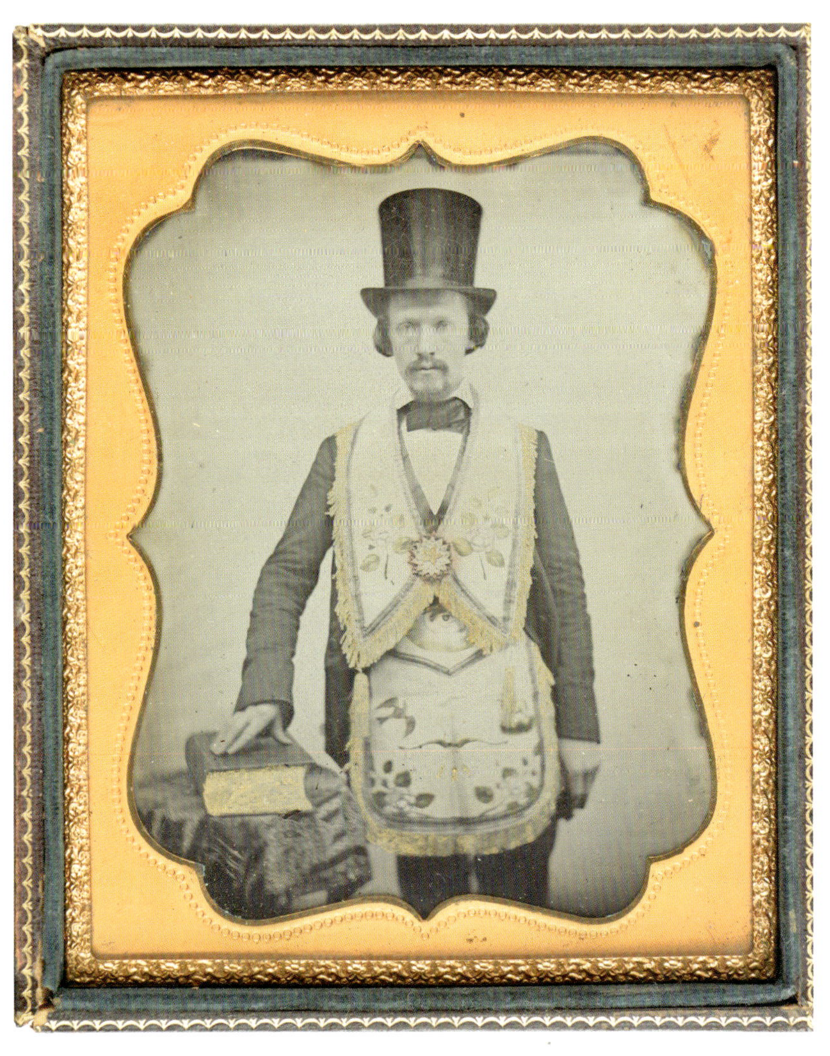

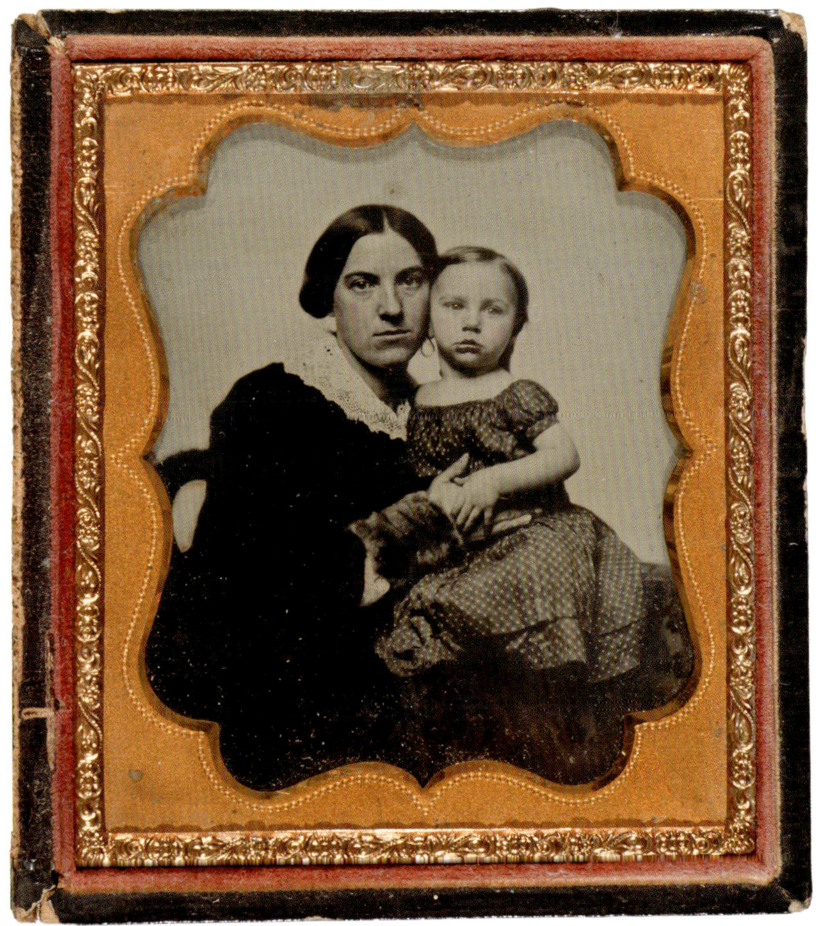

91

Jean Pascal Sébah

Turkish, 1872–1947

Policarpe Joaillier

French, active 1888–1908

Fellahine, c. 1900
Albumen print
Image and sheet: 26.5 × 21 cm (10 7/16 × 8 1/4 in)
Printed, in image, lower left: *N. 808. Fellahine.*;
lower right: *Sébah & Joaillier.*
University of Nebraska, Anna R. and Frank M. Hall
Charitable Trust, H-2257

This studio photograph, which depicts a female peasant from Upper Egypt, was most likely produced by the Cairo branch of Sébah and Joaillier (cats. 3 and 4). The image was a commercially savvy response to the demands of the tourism industry, which sought to inject a charged exoticism and otherness into the countryside as well as a rough coexistence between the temple complexes that went back thousands of years and a seemingly timeless nineteenth-century human landscape. The female figure of the *fellahine* (the feminine, French variation of the Arabic *fellah*, or "peasant") appealed to the popular imagination and existed as a familiar type that was recycled in paintings and photographs, portable *cartes de visite* and postcards. She was invariably adorned with curiously provoking headgears, costumes, and jewels; a water jug appeared frequently in her hand and sometimes on her head.

The decor behind the *fellahine* alludes to a generic Egypt and, even further, to a generic Islam. By this time, both the ornately carved wooden screen with intricate mother-of-pearl inlay and the less ornate latticework were well established architectural signs evoking the impenetrable Muslim house, commonly considered the prison of women in European Orientalist and colonial discourse. Such urban fragments did not carry ethnographic value and did not pretend to frame an authentic context for the rural houses of Lower Egypt. They did, however, serve as reductive *lieux de mémoire* with broader references constructed by nineteenth-century visual culture. The flexible studio setup allowed for variations in the background. An earlier image from the same studio featured a *fellahine* with her two children against a landscape of palm trees and pyramids in the horizon, this time pointing to a specific place.[1]

Perhaps the most striking part of the *fellahine*'s clothing is the *burguoung*, the vertical metal piece above her nose. Used to keep the veil in its place, the *burguoung* became a metonym for the women of Egypt in general. In midcentury it surfaced, for example, in many *cartes de visite* and also in the paintings of British artists such as William Holman Hunt and John Fredrick Lewis that depicted scenes in the markets of Cairo. The subject's jewelry carries some ethnographic validity: the necklace made from coins (visible beneath the head cover) and the metal bracelets and anklets are not too different from the ones described by Winifred S. Blackman in 1928.[2] In contrast, the *fellahine*'s costume, which reveals quite a bit of bare flesh, seems to fall into the category of "images of suberoticism," a term coined by Malek Alloula in his study of colonial postcards of Algerian women.[3] Nevertheless, this is not the only message conveyed by the many *fellahines* scattered throughout the world in photographs. The fully clad *fellahine*, holding onto her two children in the previously mentioned photograph by the same studio two decades earlier, stands as a counterpart to her Sheldon sister. Together, they address the two facets of the Muslim woman that titillated Western audiences for a long time: the highly sexualized and the entirely concealed. **ZÇ**

1. For this photograph, see Mounira Khemir, "The Orient in the Photographers' Mirror," in *Orientalism: Delacroix to Klee*, ed. Roger Benjamin (Sydney: Art Gallery of New South Wales, 1997), 220. **2.** Winifred S. Blackman, *The Fellahin of Upper Egypt* (1928; repr., London: Frank Cass and Company, 1968), 47-48. **3.** Malek Alloula, *The Colonial Harem* (1981; repr., Minneapolis: University of Minnesota Press, 1986), chap. 10. Even a jug, similar to the one in the Sheldon photograph, appears in cat. 115, its curvilinear shapes complementing the female body.

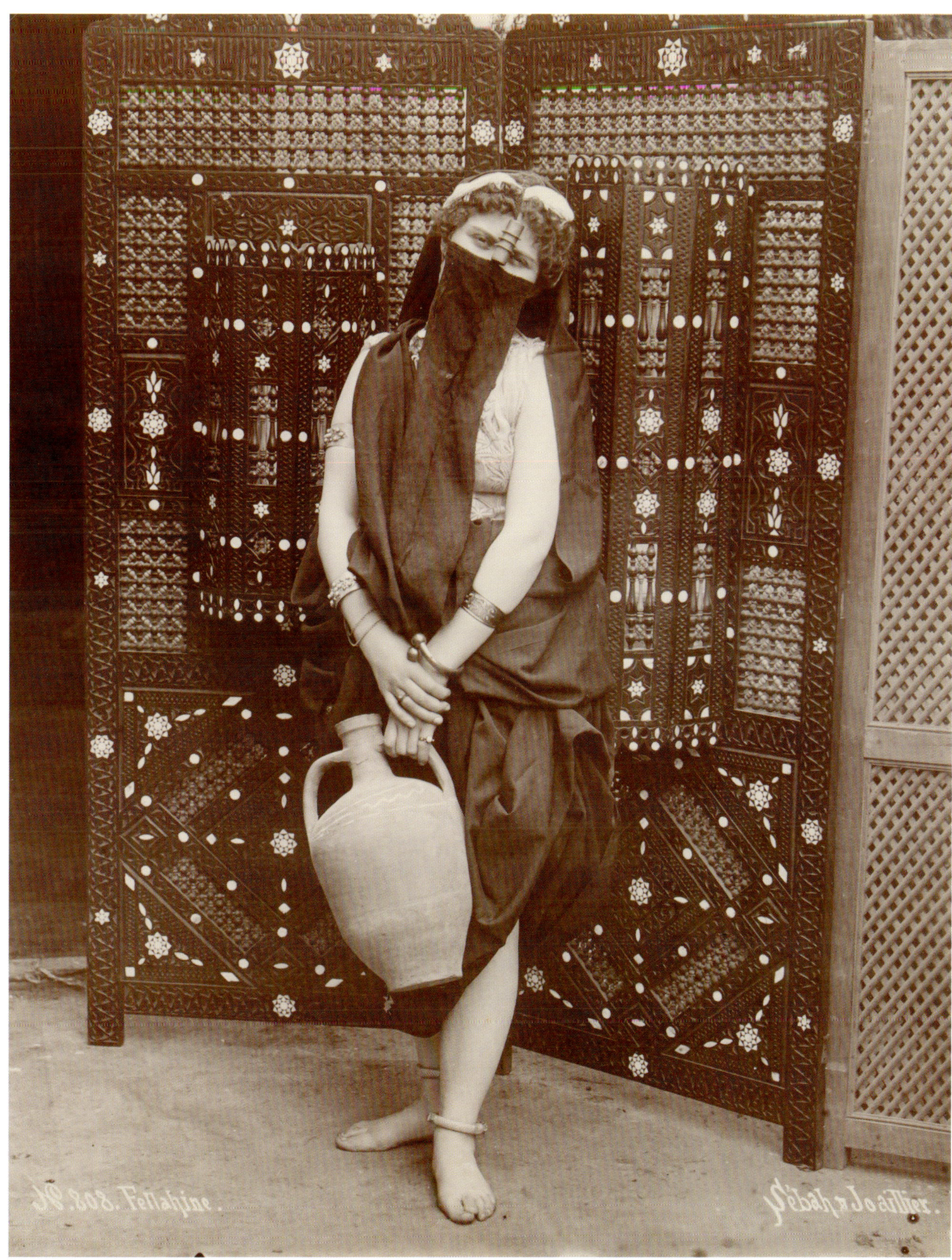

N° 208. Fellahine.
Sébah & Joaillier.

Julia Margaret Cameron
English, born India, 1815–1879

Charles Hay Cameron, 1869
Autotype
Image: 31.4 × 24.4 cm (12 3/8 × 9 5/8 in); mount: 45.9 ×
33.7 cm (18 1/16 × 13 1/4 in)
Inscribed, on mount, under image, in black ink: *Autotype
taken from the Registered Photograph from the life by
Julia Margaret Cameron*; lower center: *CHCameron /
(TAKEN BY JULIA MARGARET CAMERON)*
University of Nebraska, Anna R. and Frank M. Hall
Charitable Trust, H-1287

Born in Calcutta to an East India Company official and
a French aristocrat, Julia Margaret Pattle enjoyed a childhood rich in intellectual pursuits. Her future husband, jurist Charles Hay Cameron, introduced her to the eminent
astronomer Sir John Herschel, who became her mentor, fa-
miliarizing her with photography and its technical concepts.
Cameron's early experience with the medium, however, was
as a consumer of exhibitions and popular *cartes de visite*, inexpensive mounted portraits distributed among many mid-
dle- and upper-class families. Not until the early 1860s, after
she and her family had settled into their home on the Isle
of Wight and she was given a camera as a gift, did she begin taking photographs in earnest. Thereafter, she developed
the intimate, expressive, soft-focus portraits that became her
signature style. Cameron's goal was to counter the formal,
static portraits common to the period by creating images
that elevated photography to an art form. A contemporary
critic likened her images to the "efforts . . . of great painters,"
praising them as "characterized by very remarkable qualities—artistic and manipulative."[1]

Because of her worldly upbringing, Cameron naturally
gravitated toward the fine arts, literature, and spirituality as
sources for her compositions. This was particularly the case
in her photographs of women, whom she often posed as
classical and religious figures or in narrative scenes from
poetry and plays. Her famous image *The Mountain Nymph
Sweet Liberty*, for example, takes its title from John Milton's
"L'Allegro," a pastoral poem about a carefree, happy man first
published in 1645, while in her portrait of Alice Liddell, she
posed the sitter in the classical guise of *Alethea* (cat. 45). In
many of these depictions, the sitters have loose, flowing hair,
conforming to the carefree and spirited figures they were im-
personating while also flouting Victorian convention.

Cameron only occasionally used men as actors in her carefully constructed tableaux, and while in portraits she photographed them with the same directness and immediacy as
her women, she often surrounded them with accoutrements
of their worldly accomplishments or studies. In this photograph of her husband, however, Cameron created a tender
portrait of the man who was twenty years her senior and to
whom she had been married for just over thirty years; only
the small, wire-rimmed spectacles and Cameron's long white
beard betray his career as an eminent jurist and imperial
commissioner.

While Cameron's subjects often speak to the classical and
timeless, the process here is strictly of its moment: the autotype—often defined as a facsimile—was frequently employed
to produce multiple, long-lasting prints, further blurring the
distinction between art and copy. **BKR**

1. "Mrs. Cameron's Photographs," *Intellectual Observer* 11, no. 1 (1867): 30.

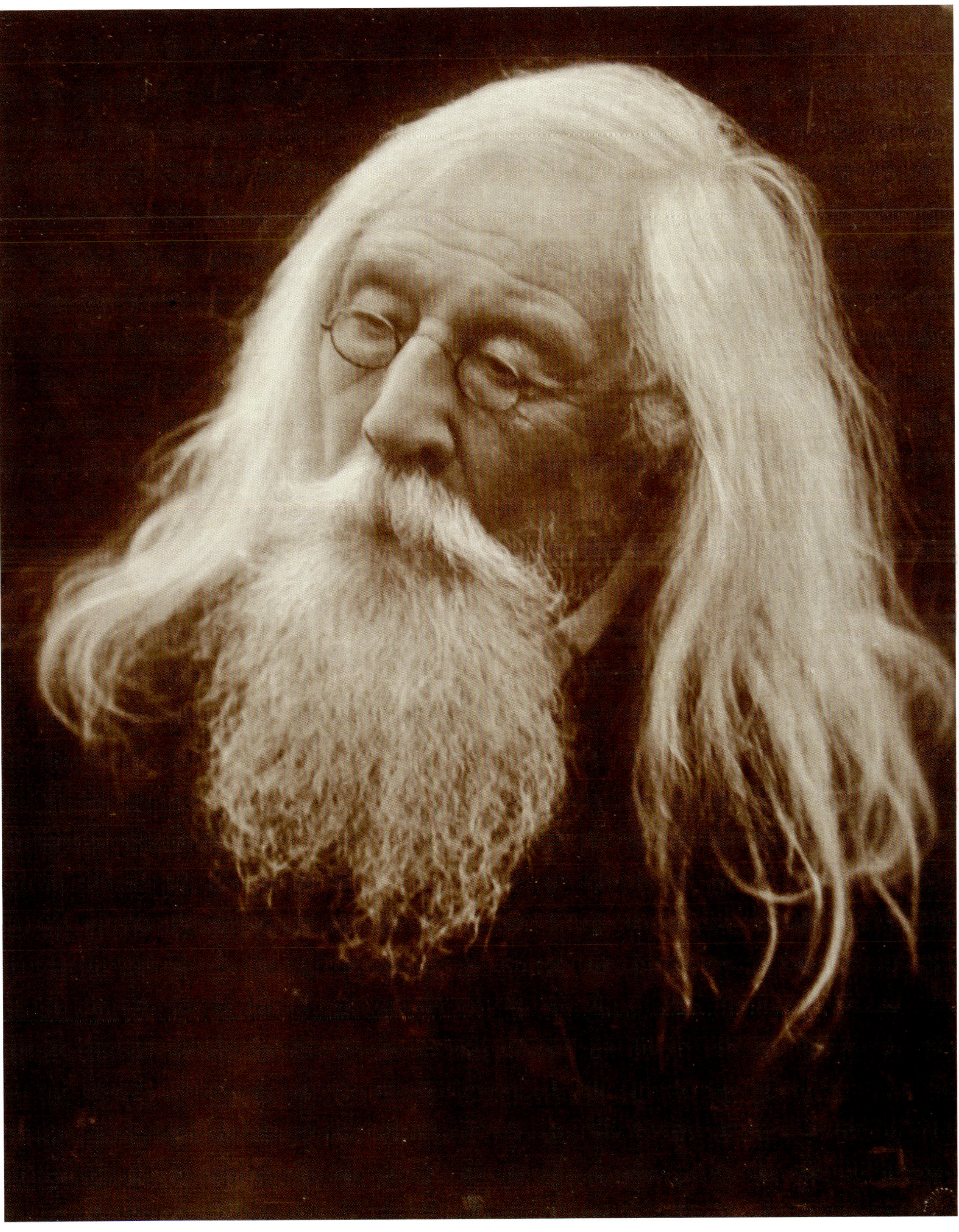

Artist Unknown

Group Portrait: Men Dressed as Women, Women Dressed as Men, c. 1890
Gelatin silver print
Image: 12.5 × 20.2 cm (4 15/16 × 7 15/16 in); mount: 15.9 × 23.5 cm (6 1/4 × 9 1/4 in)
University of Nebraska, Anna R. and Frank M. Hall Charitable Trust, H-1930

Artist Unknown

Pair of Female Peeping Toms, c. 1890
Gelatin silver print
Image: 12.7 × 20.3 cm (5 × 8 in); mount: 15.9 × 22.9 cm (6 1/4 × 9 in)
University of Nebraska, Anna R. and Frank M. Hall Charitable Trust, H-1934

These two images are from a series of works by the same photographer—and of the same group of people—that cheekily subvert contemporary expectations about gender in the Victorian era.[1] In addition, they point to the cultural and technological changes ushered in by the advent of amateur photography: inexpensive portable cameras and more convenient printing processes. The first portrait shows a group of friends cross-dressing in makeshift garments: they exchange clothes and, in the case of many of the men, wrap themselves in available linens, rugs, and shawls to complete the transformation. In the second photograph, two women slyly adjust a freestanding looking glass to spy on a young man as he removes his nightshirt, suggestively revealing his nether regions.

Toward the end of the nineteenth century, the easy and shorter dry-plate silver gelatin process superseded the more difficult and protracted wet-plate one, and convenient handheld cameras—in particular, the Kodak—transformed photography from an art reserved for specialists and wealthy amateurs to a hobby practiced by thousands. Embracing the medium's new role as a democratizing agent, these practitioners discarded conventions of portraiture and felt empowered to express themselves more freely. Perhaps surprisingly, gender reversal became part and parcel of this snapshot aesthetic, which allowed for more informal, lighthearted

portraits and gave amateur photographers greater control of their self-representation.[2] While the playful, semiprivate cross-dressing depicted in the first image does not challenge the conventions of public dress, it nonetheless shatters the boundaries between male and female character, hinting that gender is constructed.[3]

These photographic innovations also raised associated questions about public exposure, surveillance, and violation of privacy as photographers took to the streets in search of surreptitious images. The results were often manipulated, sold indiscriminately in shops, or used in advertisements without the subject's consent.[4] These two works challenge the idea of photographic voyeurism, which presupposes that subjects are unaware of being watched. In the group portrait, for example, the cross-dressers enthusiastically mug and pose for the camera, and in *Female Peeping Toms*, the composition's contrived nature suggests the subjects' active participation. Nonetheless, the act of voyeurism and the camera's ability to capture clandestine activities is here expressly acknowledged and mocked: at the end of the nineteenth century, women were more often the subjects of photographic surveillance than men, and this image shifts the dynamic from one of female victimization to one of control.[5] In addition, it humorously winks at photographs of the gruff, manly New Woman that were used to caution against the impending social disorder caused by gender reversal. **BKR**

1. Some of this photographer's other gender-bending staged images include *Apple and Popcorn Party* (H-1931), *Interrupted Proposal* (H-1932), *Evening Party, Looking at an Autograph Book* (H-1933), and *Pair of Bachelors Mending Clothes* (H-1935). **2.** See Jennifer Blessing and Judith Halberstam, *Rose Is Rose Is Rose: Gender Performance in Photography*, exhibition catalog (New York: Guggenheim Museum Publications, 1997), 53–55. **3.** Mary W. Blanchard, "The Manly New Woman," in *Off the Pedestal: New Women in the Art of Homer, Chase, and Sargent*, ed. Holly Pyne Connor, exhibition catalog (Newark NJ: Newark Museum; New Brunswick NJ: Rutgers University Press, 2006), 100, 117. **4.** For a thorough discussion of these cultural shifts and the phenomenon of voyeurism in photography, see Robert E. Mensel, "'Kodakers Lying in Wait': Amateur Photography and the Right of Privacy in New York, 1885–1915," *American Quarterly* 43, no. 1 (March 1991): 24–45; and Sandra S. Phillips, "Looking out, Looking In: Voyeurism and Its Affinities from the Beginning of Photography," in *Exposed: Voyeurism, Surveillance and the Camera since 1870*, by Sandra S. Phillips and Simon Baker, exhibition catalog (San Francisco: Museum of Modern Art; New Haven CT: Yale University Press, 2010), 11–15. **5.** See Mensel, "'Kodakers Lying in Wait,'" 34.

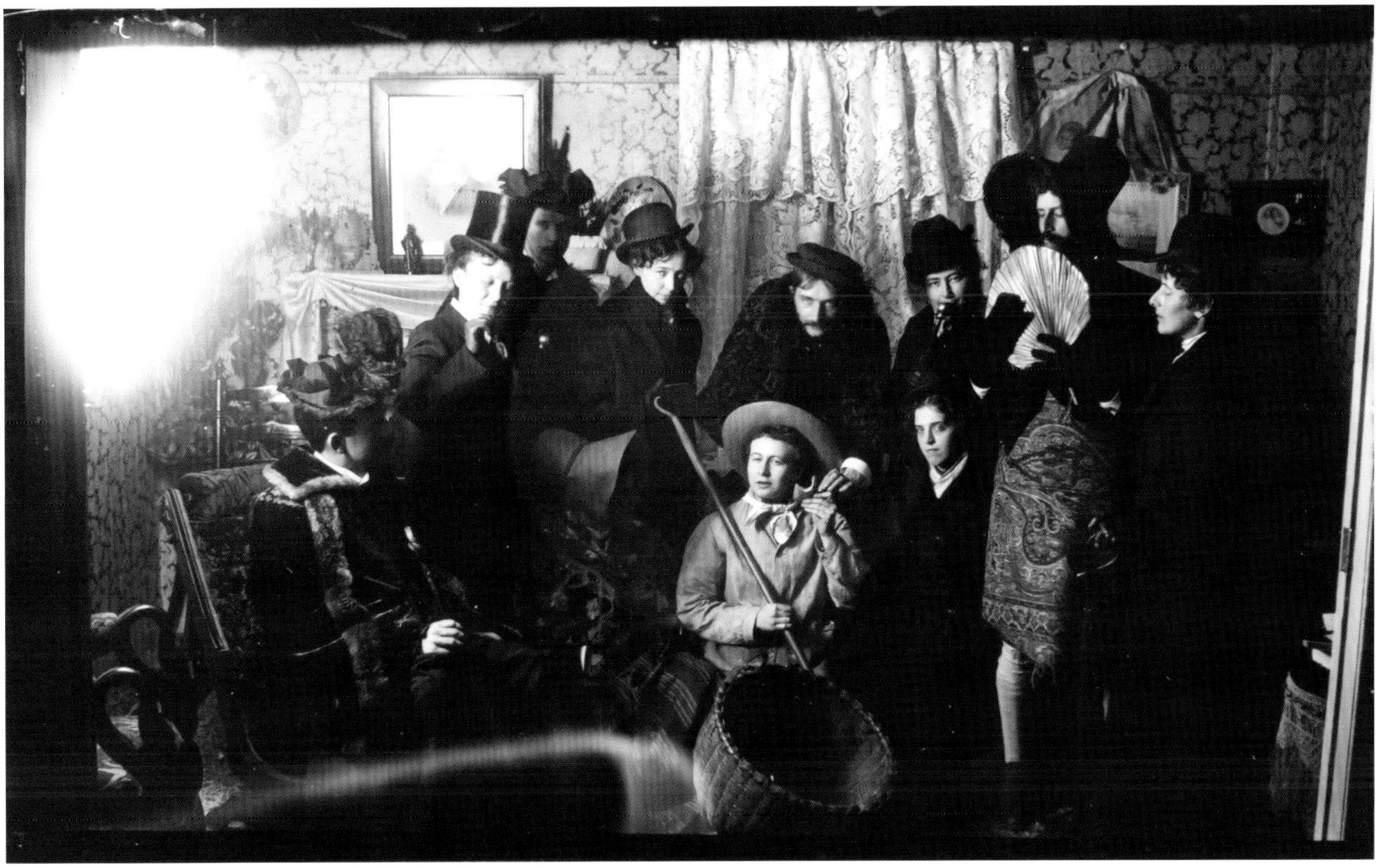

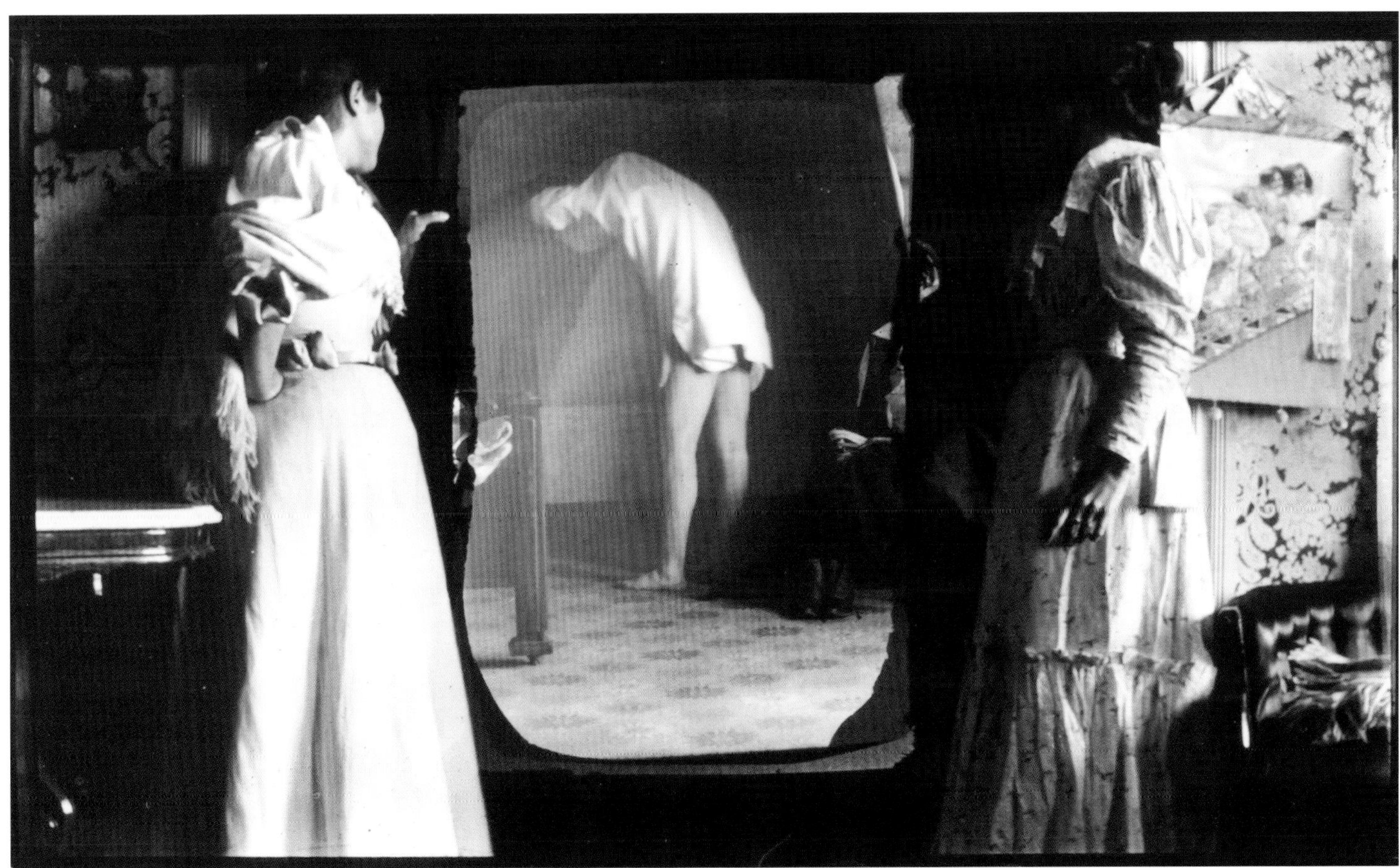

95

Edward Steichen

American, born Luxembourg, 1879–1973

Portrait of William Merritt Chase (from *Camera Work*),
c. 1906
Photogravure
Image and sheet: 20.6 × 16.5 cm (8 1/8 × 6 1/2 in)
University of Nebraska, Anna R. and Frank M. Hall
Charitable Trust, H-2053

Like many artists during the late nineteenth and early twentieth centuries, Edward Steichen came to photography after first training in other media—in his case, drawing, lithography, and painting. He taught himself with a secondhand Kodak camera alongside a group of like-minded friends in his hometown of Milwaukee. Steichen's interest in breaking down the divisions between all of these art forms attracted him to Alfred Stieglitz (cat. 15), whom he first met in New York in 1900. After that introduction, the pair produced several fruitful collaborations, including the influential journal *Camera Work*, for which Steichen created designs, and a partnership in the Little Galleries of the Photo-Secession, a space initially intended to promote the art of photography. A confirmed technician, Steichen continually tested the medium's limits throughout his career, manipulating negatives and prints through additions, omissions, and experiments with color and darkroom procedures. It was possibly his desire to connect painting and photography that first attracted him to the subject of this portrait, artist William Merritt Chase.

Chase was one of the leading American painters of the late nineteenth and early twentieth centuries and an early exponent in this country of impressionism and working directly from nature. He became known especially for his teaching: in 1896 he founded the Chase School of Art, which later became the New York School of Art, and instructed at the Pennsylvania Academy of the Fine Arts and the Art Students League. His pupils included some of the most illustrious artists of the twentieth century, including Charles Demuth, Marsden Hartley, and Georgia O'Keeffe. In a photograph taken of Chase around 1900 that appeared in the journal *International Studio*, Steichen acknowledged Chase's critical role as a teacher, showing him in profile be-

fore an empty canvas, palette in hand and right arm slightly extended as if interrupted in the middle of a lesson.[1] In his portrait photographs of men, Steichen typically favored artists over industrialists; unlike his images of women, Ronald J. Gedrim has argued, Steichen typically depicted males with their creations or with the paraphernalia of their artistic careers: chisel, paintbrush, or palette.[2]

When Chase sat for Steichen again half a decade later, he and Stieglitz included two of the portraits from that session in the April 1906 issue of *Camera Work*, an installment that featured an unprecedented twenty-six photographs by Steichen.[3] In both of these portraits, Chase appears much more like a man of leisure than a working artist. In the first, he is dressed in a top hat and overcoat, carrying a walking stick in his right hand and a pair of gloves in his left. The Sheldon's photograph is even more suggestive of the moneyed class: here, the painter's white tie is visible in the open overcoat, which is draped with a fox stole whose head is barely visible to the left of his ear. Chase carries the same walking stick in his right hand but this time raises a cigarette in his left as if in midpuff; while he turns his body in a slight three-quarter profile, his head is strictly in side view, and its subtle upturning only reinforces his imperious attitude. Chase was well known for his flamboyant dress and manners, and Steichen accentuated these qualities here, creating an indelible image of the artist as man-about-town and bon vivant, a role adopted and cultivated by many of the creative class at the turn of the century and accepted by the larger population. **BKR**

1. Ernest Knaufft, "An American Painter: William M. Chase," *International Studio* 12 (1900–1901): 151. 2. See Ronald J. Gedrim, "Peinture à la Lumière: 1898–1907," in *Edward Steichen: Lives in Photography*, by Todd Barlow and William A. Ewing, exhibition catalog (Minneapolis: Foundation for the Exhibition of Photography; New York: W. W. Norton, 2007), 88–89. 3. For these examples, see Alfred Stieglitz and Marianne Fulton Margolis, eds., *Camera Work: A Pictorial Guide* (New York: Dover Publications, 1978), 38–45; the alternate portrait of Chase appears on 38, the Sheldon's on 42. Stieglitz featured Steichen's photographs in *Camera Work* more than those of any other photographer.

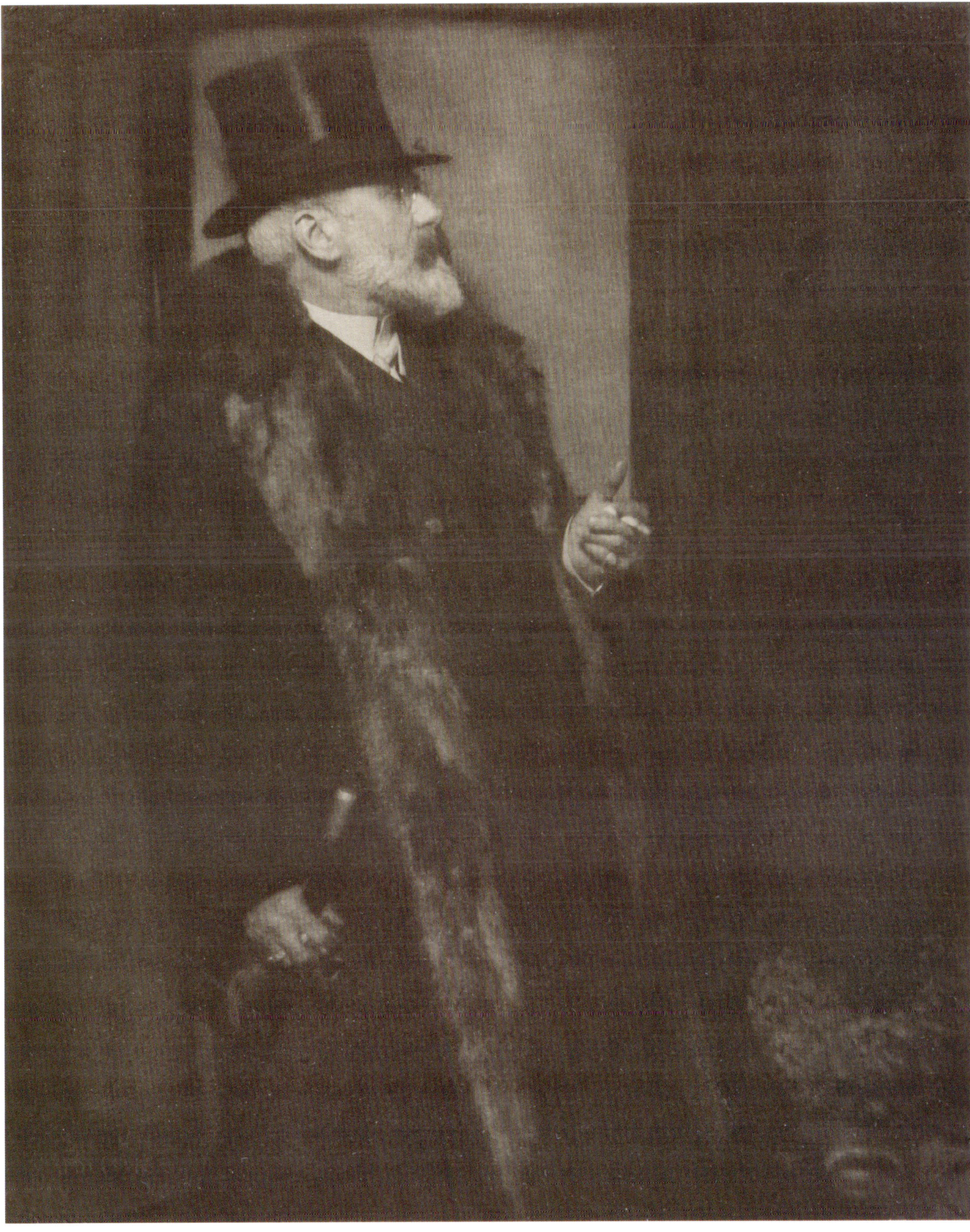

96

Arnold Genthe

American, born Germany, 1869–1942

Portrait of Horace Traubel, 1917
Gelatin silver print
Image and sheet: 28.7 × 19.1 cm (11 5/16 × 7 1/2 in)
Signed, in image, lower right, in black pen:
Arnold Genthe / N.Y.
University of Nebraska, gift of Virginia Zabriskie, U-1892

Born into a scholarly family, Arnold Genthe abandoned his desire to become a painter on the advice of a relative and instead studied classical philology, writing his doctoral dissertation in Latin. After he immigrated to San Francisco, he channeled his artistic energy into photography, which he taught himself during hours away from his tutoring position. Genthe concentrated on capturing the people of the city's Chinatown (cat. 2), creating successful images that allowed him to give up university life and pursue portrait photography as a career.[1] He established a studio, where he catered to San Francisco's elite and crafted a nationally recognized style based on sensitivity to the subject's pose, soft lighting, artistic cropping, and judicious editing. Genthe's portrait of Horace Traubel is indicative of his photographic approach at the height of his career.

Horace Traubel was lifelong companion, literary executor, and major disciple of the American poet Walt Whitman. They first became acquainted in 1873, when Whitman moved to his brother George's home in Camden, New Jersey, to convalesce from a partially paralyzing stroke and the recent death of his beloved mother. Although Traubel was not yet fifteen at the time, he soon became the poet's inseparable friend and partner in lengthy literary discussions. The young man's relationship with Whitman was a source of gossip in Camden, and Traubel later recounted that neighbors "protested against my association with the 'lecherous old man.'"[2] While no evidence exists to indicate that the pair's relationship was sexual, Michael Robertson has suggested there was "clearly an erotic charge between the two men," with Whitman bestowing kisses on his young companion not only as a sign of affection but as a form of anointment and consecration as well.[3] Traubel eventually became one of Whitman's most devoted partisans, abandoning his own clerical career to dedicate himself to maintaining and spreading his friend's literary legacy: he republished Whitman's works and produced the multivolume biography *With Walt Whitman in Camden*, based on the notes from his daily visits with the poet.

In April 1917 Genthe took several formal portrait photographs of Traubel in New York, where he had moved permanently in 1911. Some of the negatives and prints from the session demonstrate greater clarity and detail than the version in the Sheldon's collection; in two examples, Traubel leans forward, staring directly into the camera, his facial features and self-consciously bohemian flowing tie fully registered. In this image, however, Genthe employed the pictorialist standard of soft lighting to shroud his sitter's physical appearance and endow the photograph with an aura of mystery. After Whitman's death, Traubel—although celebrated for his relationship with the author—became equally well respected for his own poetry and his journal *Conservator*, a monthly magazine initially devoted to liberal religious thought. Here, Genthe paid homage to the artist rather than to the Whitman follower, creating an enigmatic, almost painterly portrait that celebrates both Traubel's achievements and Genthe's own mastery of photography. **BKR**

1. John Kuo Wei Tchen, *Genthe's Photographs of San Francisco's Old Chinatown* (New York: Dover Publications, 1984), 10. **2.** Horace Traubel, introduction to *Leaves of Grass and Democratic Vistas*, by Walt Whitman (London: Dent, 1912), 7–13. **3.** Michael Robertson, *Worshipping Walt: The Whitman Disciples* (Princeton NJ: Princeton University Press, 2008), 236.

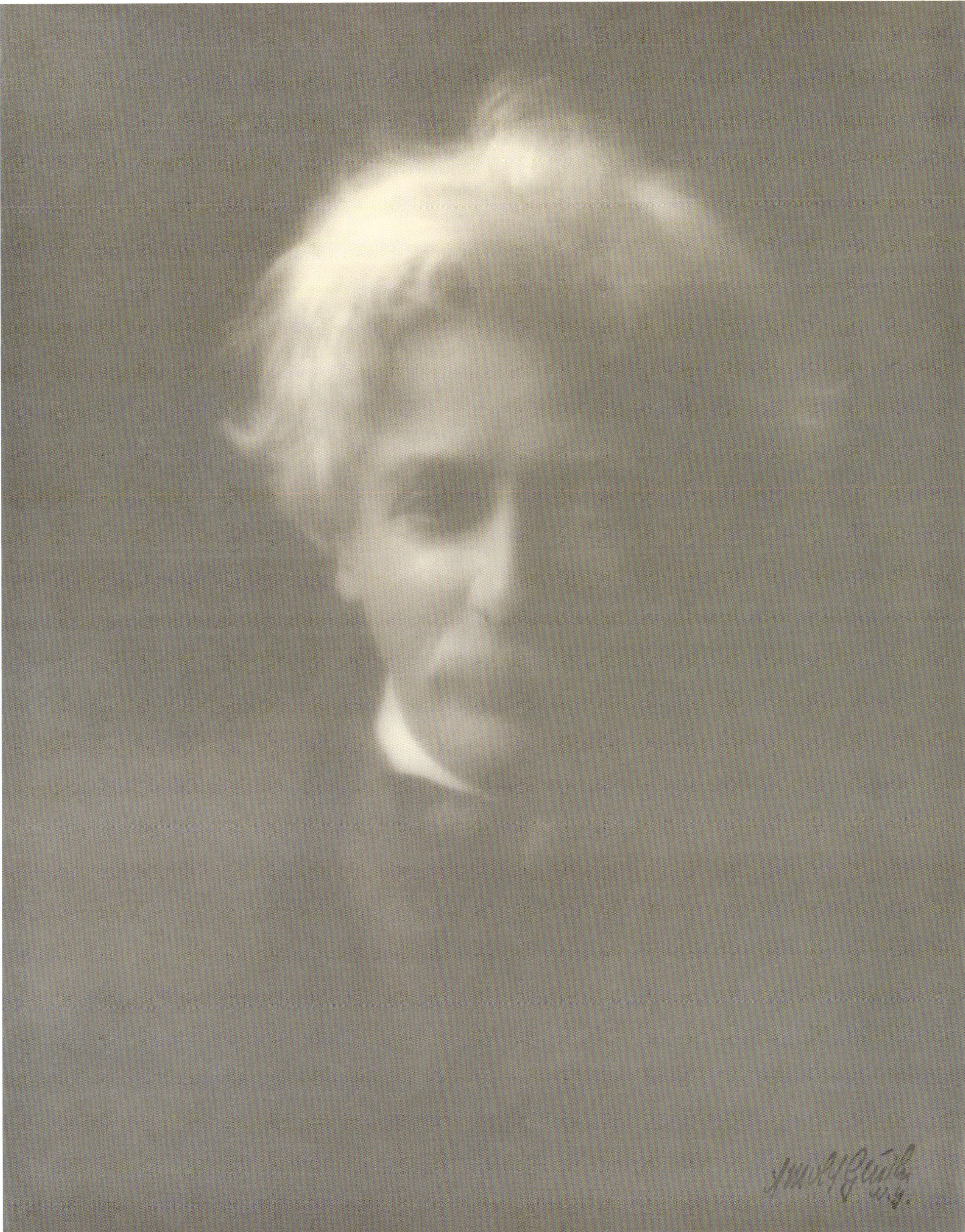

97

E. J. Bellocq

American, 1873–1949

Seated Girl (plate 7 from *Storyville Portraits*), c. 1912
Gold-chloride-toned print on printing-out paper
Image and sheet: 25.2 × 20.3 cm (9 15/16 × 8 in)
University of Nebraska, Anna R. and Frank M. Hall
Charitable Trust, H-2062

E. J. (John Ernest Joseph) Bellocq specialized in commercial photographs of machinery and ships in his native New Orleans. In his spare time, he photographed the opium dens in the city's Chinatown quarter as well as the prostitutes of the red-light district. Unpublished during his lifetime, the sometimes-damaged plates from these sessions were discovered by photographer Lee Friedlander; the prostitute portraits were printed some fifty years after they were taken, providing an invaluable snapshot of a particular time and place.[1] Bellocq's photographs were taken at a moment when conservative reformers across the United States had successfully illegalized prostitution or restricted it to specific neighborhoods of a city. In New Orleans, this area consisted of a few blocks near the waterfront that took Basin Street as its main avenue. Known as Storyville, the quarter was named after local alderman Sidney Story, who drafted the legislation establishing it. The early twentieth-century emphasis on prostitution as a vice disguised larger issues of class, race, and economic status that had been activated by rapid industrialization and modernization. As Ruth Rosen has pointed out, reformers often placed exaggerated attention on prostitution "within the context of changing gender relations"; for them, prostitution was "the most visible and dramatic form of illicit sexual relation and the most stigmatized form of female existence outside of patriarchal authority and protection."[2]

As Progressive Era reformers channeled the sex trade into controlled zones of "otherness" like Storyville, they inspired madams to walk a tightrope in which they exaggerated their establishments' perceived exoticism with promises of sexual adventure while at the same time providing a "salacious simulacrum" of decorum and homey familiarity.[3] These objectives are fully evident in Bellocq's *Seated Girl*. The boudoir interior, for example, is a parody of bourgeois respectability complete with elaborate floral wallpaper and rug, an ornate mirror atop the bureau, and the corner of a solid, curved bed visible at bottom right. Only the erotic images of nude women on the back wall hint at the promise of future sexual relations and the nature of the business in the bedroom. The young woman stares assertively at the viewer, her lips barely curling into a knowing smile; her bodice is strategically positioned to reveal her shoulders and, teasingly, the top of her breasts.

Although Bellocq's sympathy for his subjects resulted in their willingness to pose and their candid expressions, his photographs nonetheless raise interesting questions of gender and power.[4] The photographer's sitters, for example, wear clothing and strike poses no decent woman of Bellocq's own social class—he was born into a wealthy French Creole family—would have considered. In addition, the photographer's special access to Storyville's hidden world has often been credited to his own "otherness": described by contemporaries as "polite" with a "terrific" French accent, Bellocq was also short of stature and possibly hydrocephalic or encephalitic, his alternate masculinity a limited threat to his subjects.[5] **BKR**

1. Bellocq's photographs of Chinatown's opium dens have never been discovered. **2.** Ruth Rosen, *The Lost Sisterhood: Prostitution in America, 1900–1918* (Baltimore MD: Johns Hopkins University Press, 1982), 46. **3.** Mara Keire, *For Business and Pleasure: Red-Light Districts and the Regulation of Vice in the United States, 1890–1933* (Baltimore MD: Johns Hopkins University Press, 2010), 31. **4.** Susan Sontag, introduction to *Bellocq: Photographs from Storyville, the Red-Light District of New Orleans*, by Lee Friedlander, Susan Sontag, and John Szarkowski (New York: Random House, 1996), 7. **5.** Sontag, introduction; see also Jeffrey Simpson, *The Way Life Was: A Photographic Treasury from the American Past* (New York: Praeger Publishers, 1974), n.p.

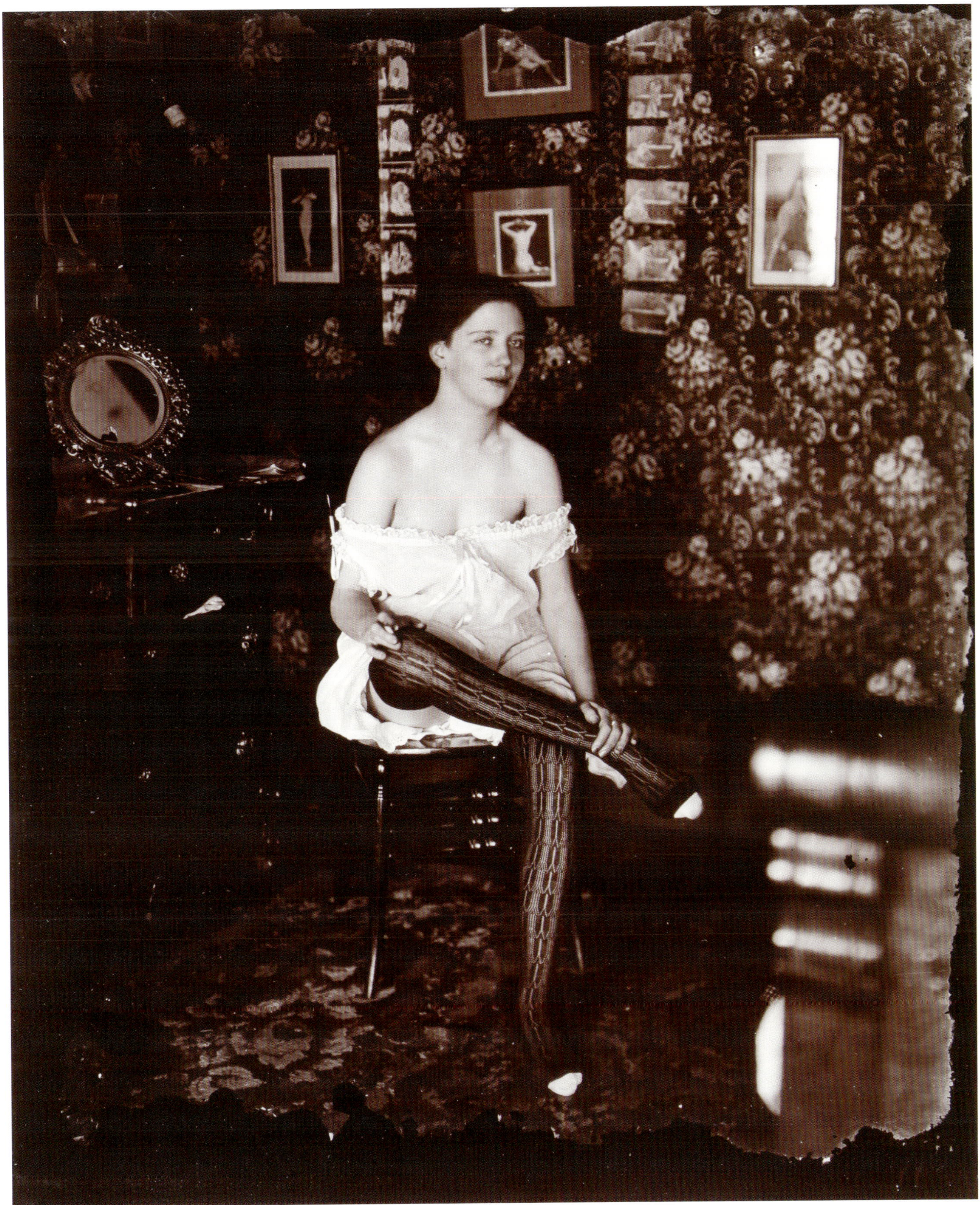

98

Brassaï (Gyula Halász)

French, born Hungary, 1899–1984

Streetwalker, near the Place d'Italie, Paris, 1932
Gelatin silver print
Image: 36.2 × 25.7 cm (14 ¼ × 10 ⅛ in); sheet: 40 × 29.8 cm (15 ¾ × 11 ¾ in)
Inscribed, lower left, in black marker: *13/30*; lower right: *Brassai*; on verso, upper center: *Tinage de l'auteur. / "Fille de joie". 1932. / Streetwalker*; stamped, middle left: *REPRODUCTION INTERDITE*; middle center: *BRASSAÏ 707-23-41 / 81, Fg St-Jacques, PARIS-14°*
University of Nebraska, Anna R. and Frank M. Hall Charitable Trust, H-1415

Gyula Halász—known as Brassaï—was one of several Hungarians to make their names in photography during the first decades of the twentieth century, a group that also included André Kertész (cat. 72). Perhaps because he had lived in Paris briefly as a child, Brassaï decided to return for good in 1924. By that time, he had completed studies at the Academy of Fine Arts, Budapest, and in Berlin, where he lived amidst the vibrant artistic and intellectual community of Weimar Germany. During his first year in the city, he eked out a living writing articles for German and Hungarian magazines and newspapers and evidenced little interest in photography. In 1925, however, Brassaï was introduced to the Parisian street scenes of Eugène Atget (cat. 99) and, the following year, to Kertész, both of whom would exercise a considerable influence on his work.[1] Four years later, Brassaï received an amateur camera as a gift and soon purchased his first professional one; from that time forward, he dedicated himself to capturing the denizens of Paris's tangled streets—people who, like himself, experienced the city mainly at night.

Around the time he shot this photograph, the artist had several personal and professional experiences that shaped his future career. First, he officially adopted the pseudonym "Brassaï" after his hometown, Brassó, a moniker he would maintain for the rest of his life. Second, in 1931 he installed a darkroom in the hotel where he lived, developing his own negatives as part of a conscious resolution to present himself as an expert craftsman. Finally, in 1933 he released a book of photographs under the title *Paris de nuit* that focused largely on the nocturnal world of the city's Montparnasse district, a bohemian enclave famed for its petty criminals and prostitutes as well as its artists.

Unlike the prostitute Atget captured a decade earlier in Versailles, this streetwalker plies her trade by the light of a street lamp in the place d'Italie, a public square that served as a bridge between Montparnasse and the Right Bank as well as a gateway to diversions on the avenue des Gobelins. According to one scholar, "darkness [was Brassaï's] best ally."[2] Here, the photographer deliberately offset the subject to the right so that the dramatic shadow she casts and the play of light and dark on the cobblestones become an equal part of the composition, leading the viewer through the image to the graffitied wall in the background. Although he resisted being identified as a photojournalist, Brassaï nonetheless admitted his own self-abnegation, deferring to a "noble desire for objectivity and faithfulness to the object."[3] This woman, with her girlish haircut and matronly clothes and purse, is both tough and vulnerable: her dangling cigarette and angled right arm denote hardness, while the glaring light itself leaves her—and her illicit trade—exposed. **BKR**

1. For Brassaï's initial lack of interest in and reservations about photography, see Paul Hill and Thomas Cooper, "Interview with Brassaï," in *Dialogue with Photography* (New York: Farrar, Straus and Giroux, 1979), 37. **2.** Alain Sayag, "The Expression of Authenticity," in *Brassaï: The Monograph*, ed. Alain Sayag and Annick Lionel-Marie, exhibition catalog (Boston: Little, Brown, 2000), 16. **3.** Sayag, "The Expression," 40.

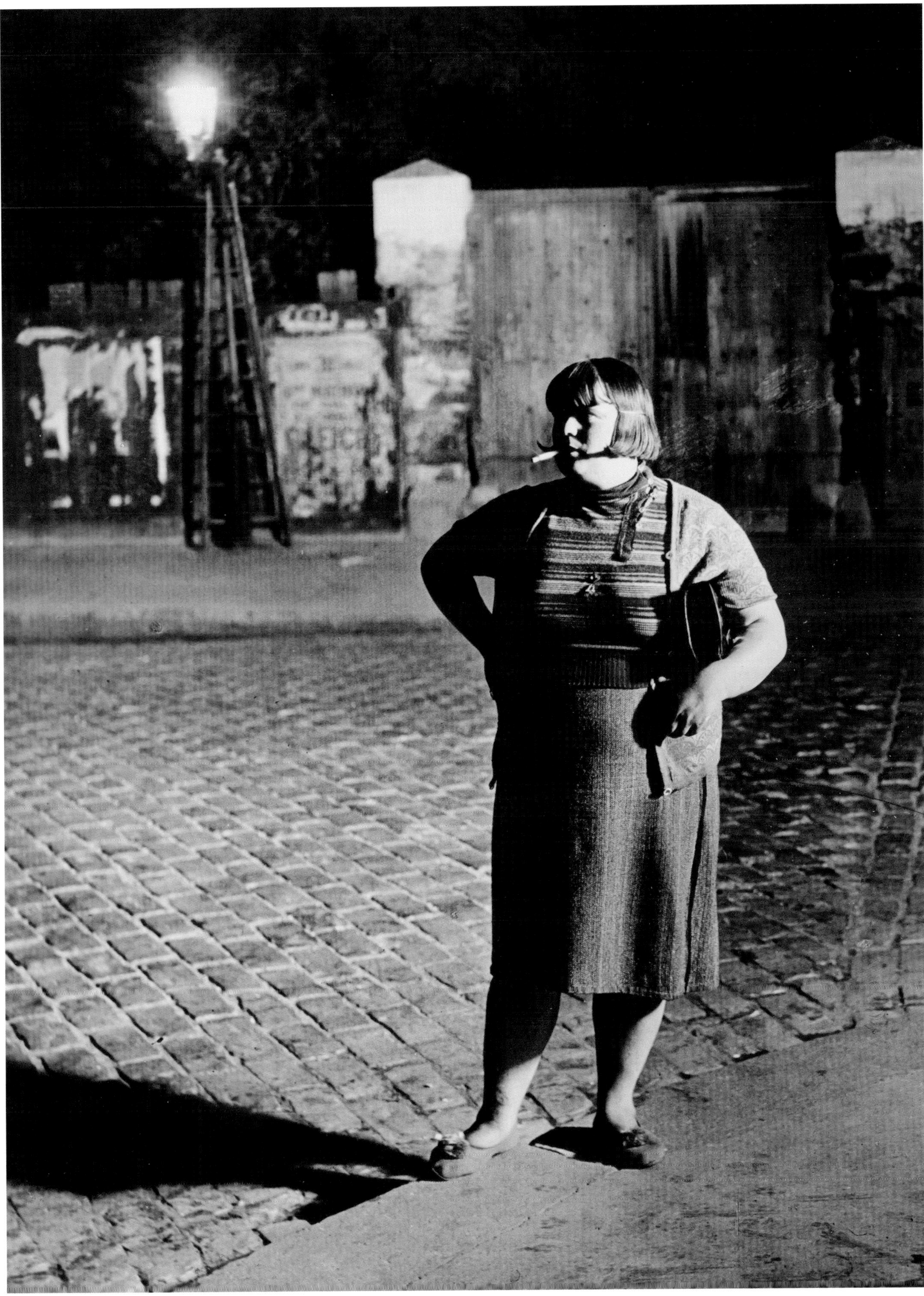

99

Eugène Atget
French, 1857–1927

Versailles, Woman and Soldier, Whorehouse (from *20 Photographs by Eugène Atget*), 1921; published 1956
Gold-toned gelatin silver print
Image: 23.2 × 17.5 cm (9 1/8 × 6 7/8 in); sheet: 33 × 25.4 cm (13 × 10 in)
University of Nebraska, Anna R. and Frank M. Hall Charitable Trust, H-837.10

During his career, which began in the mid-1890s, Eugène Atget worked primarily as a commercial photographer, achieving popular recognition only after his death. Success came for the artist in 1928, when his work was included in Paris's Premier salon indépendant de la photographie and Berenice Abbott (cat. 34) purchased his collection—including his glass negatives—after the exhibition's close. Writing the following year in the journal *Creative Art*, Abbott described Atget as "the modern forerunner in the sense that hitherto [photography] has been used as a small trade for very limited purposes."[1] Atget worked largely in trade, photographing painters' canvases and receiving public commissions to document the landmarks, monuments, and streets of Paris, creating an invaluable record that surrealist poet Robert Desnos famously described as "a dream capital from the ashes of the dead city."[2] The street, in fact, was central to Atget's aesthetic and routine, and he used his work to capture peddlers and prostitutes, parks and plazas, old stone paths and new glittering boulevards with their smart window displays (see right). The diversity of his subjects suggests the variety of urban experience that Paris offered in the first decades of the twentieth century, when the city served as an arena and playground for people of different classes and genders.

Unlike the almost humorously formal portraits of prostitutes that E. J. Bellocq created a decade earlier (cat. 97), those by Atget have been described as "mundane" and "unglamorous"—qualities that give them an element of surprise.[3] Hired by the painter André Dignimont for a book project, Atget made this photograph of two figures posed outside a brothel in the Parisian suburb of Versailles; it is one of a series of images of prostitutes, many of which were taken in front of the same establishment. Dressed in a variant of the Mother Hubbard—an unbelted, sacklike gown favored by cheap prostitutes for its ease of removal—the young woman leans against the doorframe and smiles somewhat uncomfortably. Her soldier companion, meanwhile, stands confidently outside the portal's shadow, his right arm self-consciously positioned on his hip. These two works evoke the breadth of commercial activity in 1920s Paris, where everything from suits to sex could be purchased on the street. **BKR**

1. Berenice Abbott, "Eugène Atget," in *Photography: Essays and Images*, ed. Beaumont Newhall (New York: Museum of Modern Art, 1980), 235–37. **2.** Robert Desnos, "Eugène Atget," *Le soir*, September 11, 1928, quoted in *Modern Times*, vol. 4 of *The Work of Atget*, by John Szarkowski and Maria Morris Hambourg (New York: Museum of Modern Art; Boston: New York Graphic Society, 1985), 10. **3.** Max Kozloff, *The Theatre of the Face: Portrait Photography since 1900* (London: Phaidon, 2007), 59.

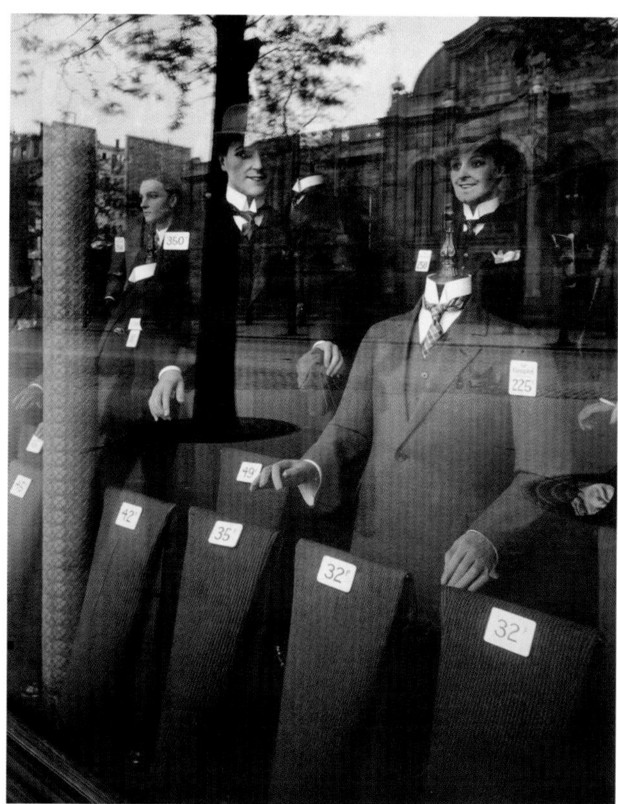

Eugène Atget. *Men's Fashions* (from *20 Photographs by Eugène Atget*), 1925, published 1956. Gold-toned gelatin silver print; 22.9 × 17.2 cm (9 × 6 3/4 in). University of Nebraska, Anna R. and Frank M. Hall Charitable Trust, H-837.3.

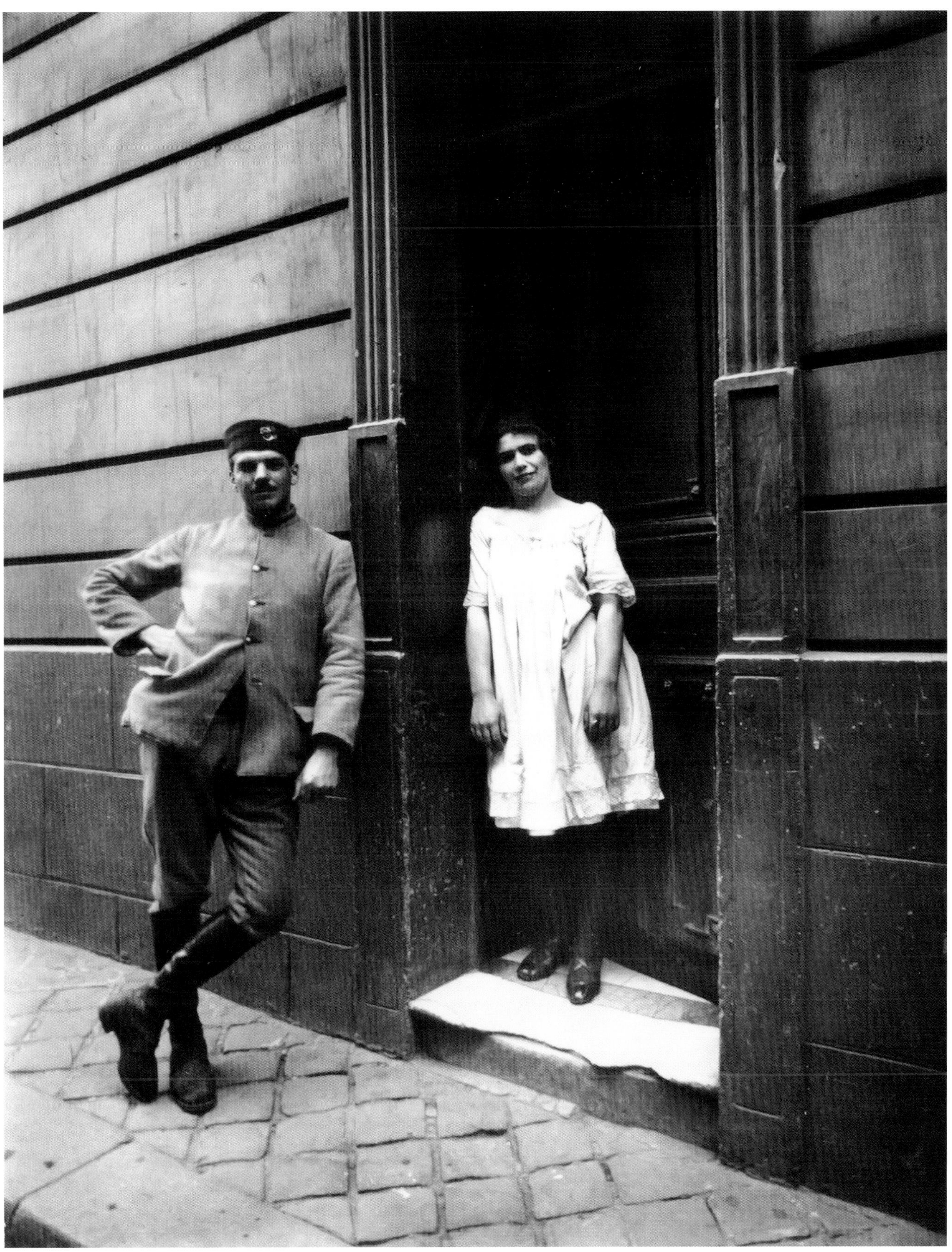

100

James VanDerZee
American, 1886–1983

Garveyite Family, Harlem, 1924; published 1974
Gelatin silver print
Image: 24.1 × 19.7 cm (9 1/2 × 7 3/4 in); mount: 31.8 × 38.1 cm (12 1/2 × 15 in)
Inscribed, on mount, lower left, in pencil: *VIII 55/75*; lower right: *J. VanDerZee*
Nebraska Art Association, purchased with the aid of funds from the National Endowment for the Arts, N-423.8

James VanDerZee moved to New York City from his native Massachusetts at the beginning of the twentieth century and quickly established himself as the photographer of choice among Harlem's middle- and upper-class African Americans, documenting the city's artistic and cultural renaissance (for another photograph by VanDerZee in the Sheldon's collection, see cat. 57).

The title of this family portrait comes from the movement founded by Marcus Garvey, a Jamaican-born journalist and orator. Garvey advanced black nationalism and Pan-Africanism with the ultimate goal of reunifying the peoples of the African diaspora into "one grand racial hierarchy" under a single national banner.[1] To support his agenda, in 1914 Garvey formed the Universal Negro Improvement Association and African Communities (Imperial) League (UNIA–ACL); three years later, he began publishing a newspaper to promote the organization's cause and philosophies.

In 1920 the UNIA–ACL staged its first convention in New York, and subsequent conferences were held there in 1922 and 1924. One of the main components of the biennial gathering was a parade, which was continued annually through the 1920s, even when the meetings ceased. The procession featured organization dignitaries and delegates, contingents from several nations, marching bands, and the extremely popular uniformed contingents from the African Legion and the Black Cross Nurses. VanDerZee photographed the 1924 event, making several group portraits of its participants as well as official images of the activities, including the parade.[2]

In this formal portrait of a Garveyite family—a name frequently bestowed on people who belonged to the UNIA–ACL or supported Garvey's views—the matriarch, clothed in an evening dress and pearls with a feathered fan in her lap, sits in an armchair flanked by two young men, both in uniform. The older of the two seems to have taken part in the parade-day events, as he proudly offers his cap to the viewer, showcasing its insignia; the young boy wears a sailor suit—characteristic children's attire of the day. The trio poses amid a motley assortment of studio props, hastily assembled to imitate a gracious home: a chest of drawers, a drooping floral arrangement, and an eerie stuffed dog appear in front of a painted backdrop that the photographer used for several of his studio portraits. The withered blooms and slightly tattered bottom of the painted screen suggest countless sessions for the many visitors who, like this family, may have visited VanDerZee while in town for the convention. **BKR**

1. Roberta A. Hill, ed., *The Marcus Garvey and Universal Negro Improvement Association Papers: Africa for the Africans, 1923–1945* (Berkeley: University of California Press, 2006), 10:320. 2. For a photograph of the 1924 parade by VanDerZee featuring Garvey in a motorcade, see Deborah Willis, *A History of Black Photographers: 1840 to the Present* (New York: W. W. Norton, 2000), 65.

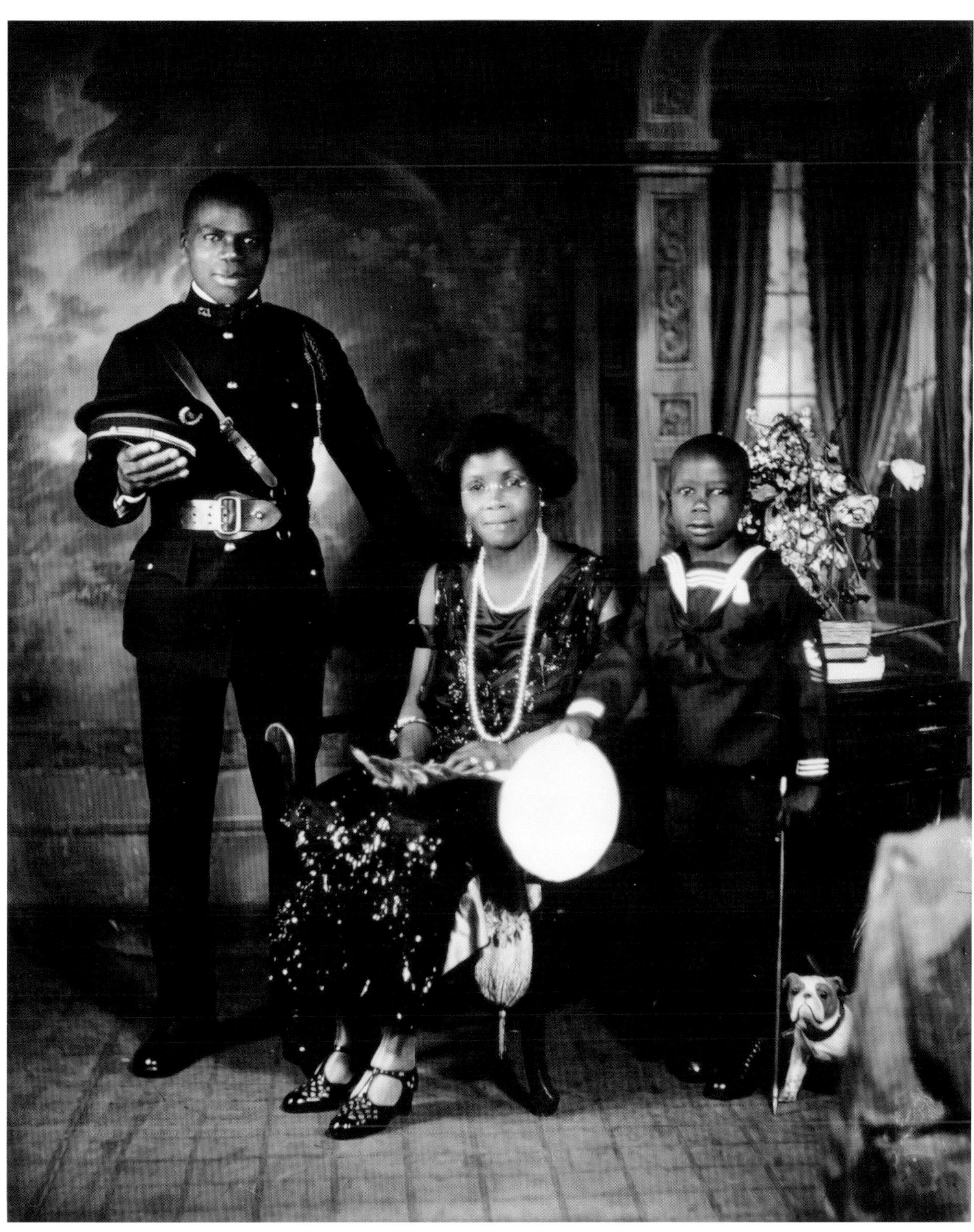

101

Walker Evans

American, 1903–1975

Penny Picture Display, Savannah, 1936
Gelatin silver print
Image: 22.2 × 17.9 cm (8 3/4 × 7 1/16 in); mount: 32.4 × 28.1
cm (12 3/4 × 11 1/16 in)
Signed, on mount, lower right, in pencil: *Walker Evans*
University of Nebraska, Anna R. and Frank M. Hall
Charitable Trust, H-2024

Considered one of the most significant figures in the history of photography, Walker Evans was known for his documentary images capturing the landscape and life of everyday America, subjects with which he became so identified that in 1938 collector and connoisseur Lincoln Kirstein described his work as "social documents."[1] Evans took up freelance photography in 1928, and throughout his career he photographed subjects as diverse as the architecture of New England and Louisiana, tenant farmers in Alabama, and New York City subways. Many of Evans's most recognizable images, however, came from his stint as photographer for the government.

Beginning in 1935, Evans worked for the Department of Agriculture's Resettlement Administration, later known as the Farm Security Administration (FSA), a program established under Franklin Roosevelt's New Deal to document and promote the government's aid to rural portions of America. Through his pictures, Evans, like other FSA photographers such as Dorothea Lange (cats. 17 and 78), chronicled the architecture, factories, farms, and people of Depression-era America.[2] Evans was assigned to photograph rural areas of Pennsylvania, Alabama, Mississippi, and Georgia, and his depictions of vernacular America soon became iconic historical records and identifiable images of the Great Depression.

While in Savannah, Georgia, in 1936, Evans discovered a photographer's temporary display in a dance studio window.[3] Aesthetically, the overlay of text on top of a gridlike pattern is reminiscent of the billboards and signs Evans enjoyed photographing. Yet *Penny Picture Display* also projects a specific socioeconomic identity of the American South.[4] This unidentified photographer carefully selected and ar-

ranged each of the 225 portraits as a representation of his work, creating a display indicative of the white middle-class clientele that would have frequented his studio. Additionally, Evans's photograph is a commentary on the nature of portrait photography, a vehicle normally utilized to highlight the individual subject. *Penny Picture Display* makes each sitter anonymous as he or she becomes lost in the framework of the larger group portrait. Evans would later comment on this photograph: "The only reason this photograph has any value is an instinct is touched in it. It's uproariously funny, and very touching and very sad and very human. All these people had composed themselves in front of the local studio camera, and I bring my camera, and they all pose again together for me. That's a fabulous fact. I look at it and think, and think, and think about all those people."[5]

Although each sitter is individually anonymous, as a whole the citizens in *Penny Picture Display* serve as a portrait of one segment of the American South. As Evans photographed them a second time, he solidified their participation in a "social document." **AH**

1. Lincoln Kirstein, "Photographs of America: Walker Evans," in *American Photographs* (New York: Museum of Modern Art, 1938), 195. 2. For more on FSA photography, see Gilles Mora and Beverly W. Brannan, *FSA: The American Vision* (New York: Abrams, 2006). 3. For a note on the scholarship surrounding the studio depicted in this photograph, see Jeff L. Rosenheim, "'The Cruel Radiance of What Is': Walker Evans and the South," in *Walker Evans*, by Maria Morris Hambourg et al. (New York: Metropolitan Museum of Art, 2000), 103n155. 4. The Library of Congress FSA/OWI collection lists this photograph as *Photographer's Window of Penny Portraits, Birmingham, Alabama*. Throughout the years, it has been published under this title and other variations. In Evans's *American Photographs*, he titles the photograph as it is listed here, and many sources place Evans in Savannah when this photograph was taken (see Rosenheim, "'The Cruel Radiance,'" 84). 5. Quoted in James R. Mellow, *Walker Evans* (New York: Basic Books, 1999), 303.

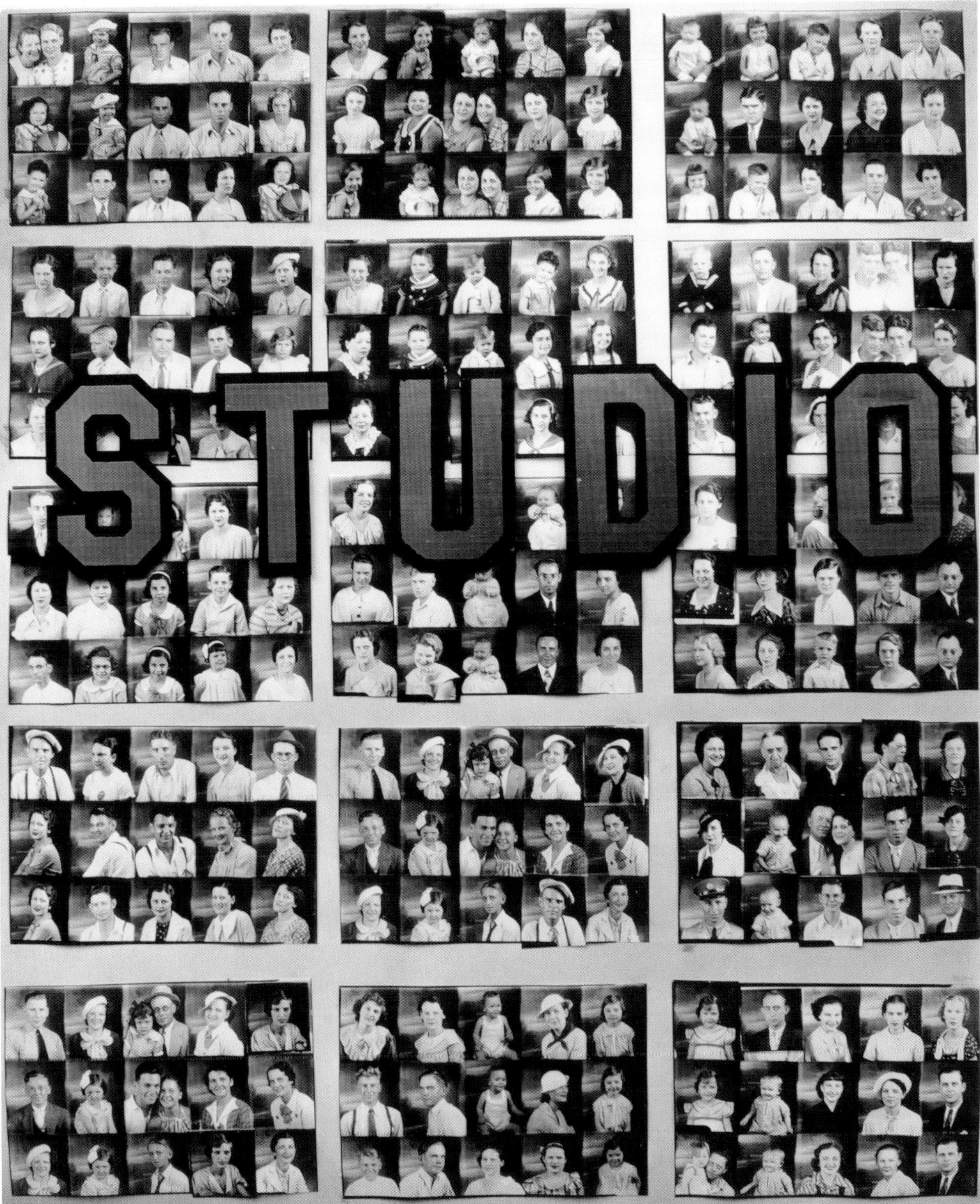

102

Cecil Beaton

English, 1904–1980

Edith Sitwell, Renishaw Hall, 1930
Gelatin silver print
Image: 45.4 × 35.9 cm (17 7/8 × 14 1/8 in); mount: 54 ×
41.9 cm (21 1/4 × 16 1/2 in)
Signed, on mount, lower right, in red crayon: *Beaton*
University of Nebraska, Anna R. and Frank M. Hall
Charitable Trust, H-2148

Originally published in British *Vogue* in October 1930, this image—oddly enough—emerged from a moment between the two world wars in which self-styled "Bright Young People" were using photography to articulate and popularize modernism and their own relationships to it. Dubbed the "Photocracy," this high bohemian circle of artists, heiresses, theater types, and writers was fascinated with the medium, in part because their own celebrity depended upon it.[1] Many found themselves pictured in *Vogue*, a magazine that epitomized the queer sensibility of the time, which entailed jettisoning Victorian sexual mores and embracing androgyny as a transgressive modernist performance. "We are discarding our prejudices," proclaimed one article. "Each month sees the disappearance of some once formidable taboo."[2]

Young, attractive, and ambitious, Cecil Beaton was perhaps the most breathless recorder of this milieu. At the time he took this picture, he was crafting an identity as a dandy, socialite, and celebrity photographer, transcending his middle-class origins by attaching himself to people whom he regarded as "smart, arty, and the set I must get in with."[3] Beaton reacted against the commercial practices of his day, deliberately positioning himself as a gentleman amateur; this enabled him not only to avoid the distasteful whiff of trade but also to define a more intimate relationship to the market and the medium. He was talented and somewhat experimental, exploring photograms and multiple exposures, but he finally settled on a fashionable, quasi-modernist approach in which he often addressed the theme of identity through doubling, mirroring his sitters in various reflective surfaces.

As he was starting out, the photographer asked a friend what he should "become in life"; the response was, "Just become a friend of the Sitwells, and wait and see what happens."[4] Edith Sitwell and her brothers, Osbert and Sacheverell, were crucial to Beaton's success due to their place at the very heart of London's bohemian world, where they assembled an alternative Bloomsbury Group filled with individuals whose work they promoted. Praising the brothers' "aristocratic looks, dignified manner, and air of lofty disdain," Beaton himself described their hyperaestheticized worldview in

the following reminiscence: "They managed to give a patina of glamour to a visit to an oculist, a bootshop, or a concert."[5] Edith was no less flamboyant, adopting an eccentric style of dress that led the novelist Elizabeth Bowen to describe her as a "high altar on the move."[6]

This haunting image of Edith at first surprises in its lack of modernity: we see her breakfasting in bed, deep in thought, reaching languidly for a tray offered by Mary Cole, her young nephew's nanny. Meant to recall the paintings of the eighteenth-century artist Johann Zoffany, whose work was rediscovered in the 1920s, the photograph hints at the love of fancy dress that Beaton and Sitwell shared with their circle, for whom the Georgian period could represent a pre-Victorian fantasy world of theatricality and relaxed sensuality. The setting is Sitwell's ancestral home, Renishaw Hall, which she described as "a world of shadow" and treated as a metaphor for her unhappy childhood.[7] More than anything else, this image exemplifies the process through which Sitwell fashioned her image as a serious poet. In 1930 she had just published a biography of Alexander Pope, whom she identified with deeply: his disgrace, she suggested, was being born with a deformed spine, and hers was to have been born an intelligent female who was unable to conform to her parents' ideal of beauty.[8] Here, she seems to impersonate Pope himself, complete with the turban they both favored. Cole, her unexpected double, makes Sitwell seem all the thinner, all the paler, all the more androgynous. **GN**

1. Beaton's and the Sitwells' extended circle included T. S. Eliot, Gertrude Stein, Violet Trefusis, William Walton, Evelyn Waugh, and Rex Whistler, to name only a few. For more on the "Photocracy" and Beaton's place within it, see David Alan Mellor, "Beaton's Beauties," in *Cecil Beaton*, by Philippe Garner and David Alan Mellor (London: Jonathan Cape, 1994), 8–44. **2.** "Paul Morand," *Vogue*, early March 1924, 86, quoted in Christopher Reed, "Design for (Queer) Living: Sexual Identity, Performance, and Décor in British *Vogue*, 1922–1926," *GLQ: A Journal of Lesbian and Gay Studies* 12, no. 3 (2006): 379. **3.** Cecil Beaton, *The Wandering Years: Diaries, 1922–1939* (Boston: Little, Brown, 1961), 86. **4.** Beaton, *The Wandering Years*, 150. For an excellent introduction to the trio, see Sarah Bradford et al., *The Sitwells and the Arts of the 1920s and 1930s*, exhibition catalog (London: National Portrait Gallery; Austin: University of Texas Press, 1996); see especially 132 for more on the precise circumstances and dating of this image. **5.** Beaton, *The Wandering Years*, 163. **6.** Quoted in Victoria Glendinning, *Edith Sitwell: A Unicorn among Lions* (New York: Knopf, 1981), 296. **7.** Edith Sitwell, *Taken Care Of: The Autobiography of Edith Sitwell* (New York: Atheneum, 1965), 179. **8.** Pope, like Sitwell, was also a brilliant manipulator of his own public image; for more on his importance to Sitwell, see Susan Hastings, "Two of the Weird Sisters: The Eccentricities of Gertrude Stein and Edith Sitwell," *Tulsa Studies in Women's Literature* 4, no. 1 (Spring 1985): 108–17.

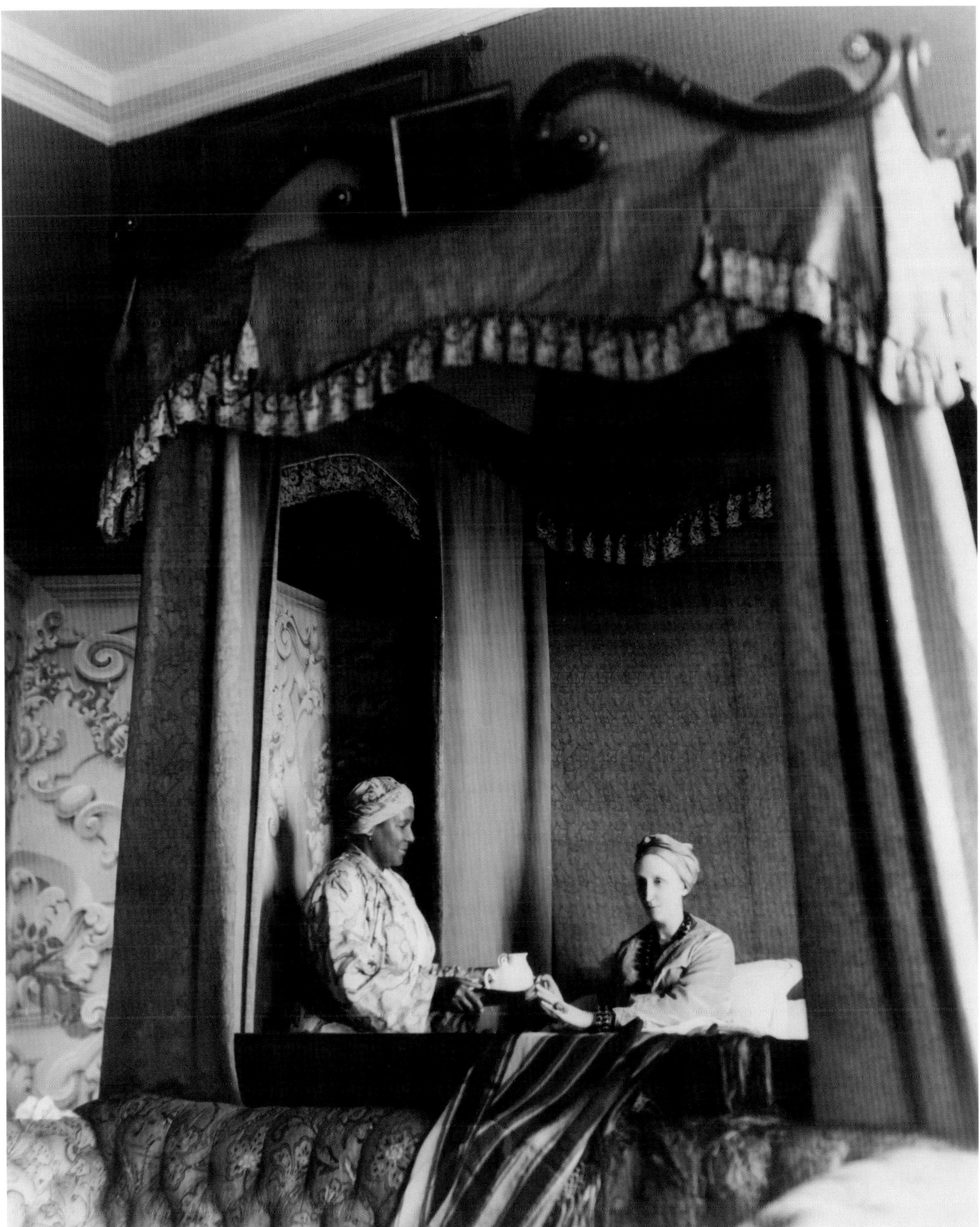

103

Imogen Cunningham
American, 1883–1976

Gertrude Stein, 1935
Gelatin silver print
Image: 17.8 × 20 cm (7 × 7 7/8 in); mount: 36.8 × 29.2 cm
(14 1/2 × 11 1/2 in)
Signed, on mount, lower right, in pencil:
Imogen Cunningham 1937
University of Nebraska, Anna R. and Frank M. Hall
Charitable Trust, H-1167

In 1917 Imogen Cunningham, along with her husband and young children, moved from Seattle to the San Francisco Bay Area.[1] This shift in location—as well as the photography world's changing styles and techniques—affected her profoundly. While pictorialist philosophies and the expressive, maternal images of Gertrude Käsebier (cat. 46) influenced Cunningham's early photographs, it was her success as a portraitist and her introduction to a new circle of artists in California that informed her later work. In 1932 she became a founding member of f64, which included Ansel Adams (cat. 35) and Edward Weston (cat. 58) and whose goal was to promote a frank, uncomplicated approach to picture making.[2] As Cunningham moved from pictorialism to modernism, her images took on greater detail and immediacy, and by the time she made this portrait of Gertrude Stein in 1935, she was displaying a greater interest in formal and documentary photography.[3]

In 1934 Stein began a tour of the United States to promote her forthcoming book, *Lectures in America*, a collection of essays on aesthetics, art, playwriting, and poetry. She arrived in California at the end of March 1935 and, after several days in the Los Angeles area, drove to San Francisco, where she settled for nearly two weeks.[4] During Stein's stay at the Mark Hopkins Hotel, Cunningham made several portraits of the famous author. In some cases, these are extremely experimental, with Cunningham producing a time-lapsed double exposure of Stein's face that captures the sitter frontally and in profile, creating an impression of dynamism and simultaneity.[5] Other images are less advanced, featuring a seated Stein holding an open copy of her book.

In the Sheldon's photograph, Stein sits with her head resting lightly on her upraised left arm, the pattern of the heavy curtain in the background mimicking the brocaded vest that became part of her signature style during the last decades of her life. Stein's expression and pose, both impatient and resigned, may be a result of what one scholar has called the "satisfying dynamic" between the artist and "willing subject."[6] For Cunningham, her interest in people was paramount: "Photography began for me with people and no matter what interest I have given [other things], I have never totally deserted the bigger significance in human life. As a document or record of personality I feel that photography isn't surpassed by any other graphic medium."[7]

Cunningham's portrait of Stein does, in fact, befit the latter's reputation as both an eccentric and a literary luminary; in its formality, it is akin to Yousuf Karsh's official portrait of Winston Churchill in this volume (cat. 104). **BKR**

1. For Cunningham's early life and career, see my entry on her 1912 *Wood beyond the World* (cat. 56). **2.** The group took its unusual name from a large-view camera's smallest aperture. See James Danziger and Barnaby Conrad III, *Interviews with Master Photographers* (New York: Paddington Press, 1977), 36. **3.** For these shifts in Cunningham's life and style, see Richard Lorenz, *Imogen Cunningham: Portraiture* (Boston: Bulfinch Press, 1997), 14–23. **4.** For a chronology of Stein's visit to America and the subjects of her lectures, see Edward Burns and Ulla E. Dydo, eds., *The Letters of Gertrude Stein and Thornton Wilder* (New Haven CT: Yale University Press, 1996), 339–51. **5.** For a reproduction of this photograph, see Richard Lorenz, *Imogen Cunningham: Ideas without End; a Life in Photographs* (San Francisco: Chronicle Books, 1993), 40, fig. 44. **6.** Lorenz, *Imogen Cunningham: Portraiture*, 9. **7.** Quoted in Lorenz, *Imogen Cunningham: Portraiture*, 9.

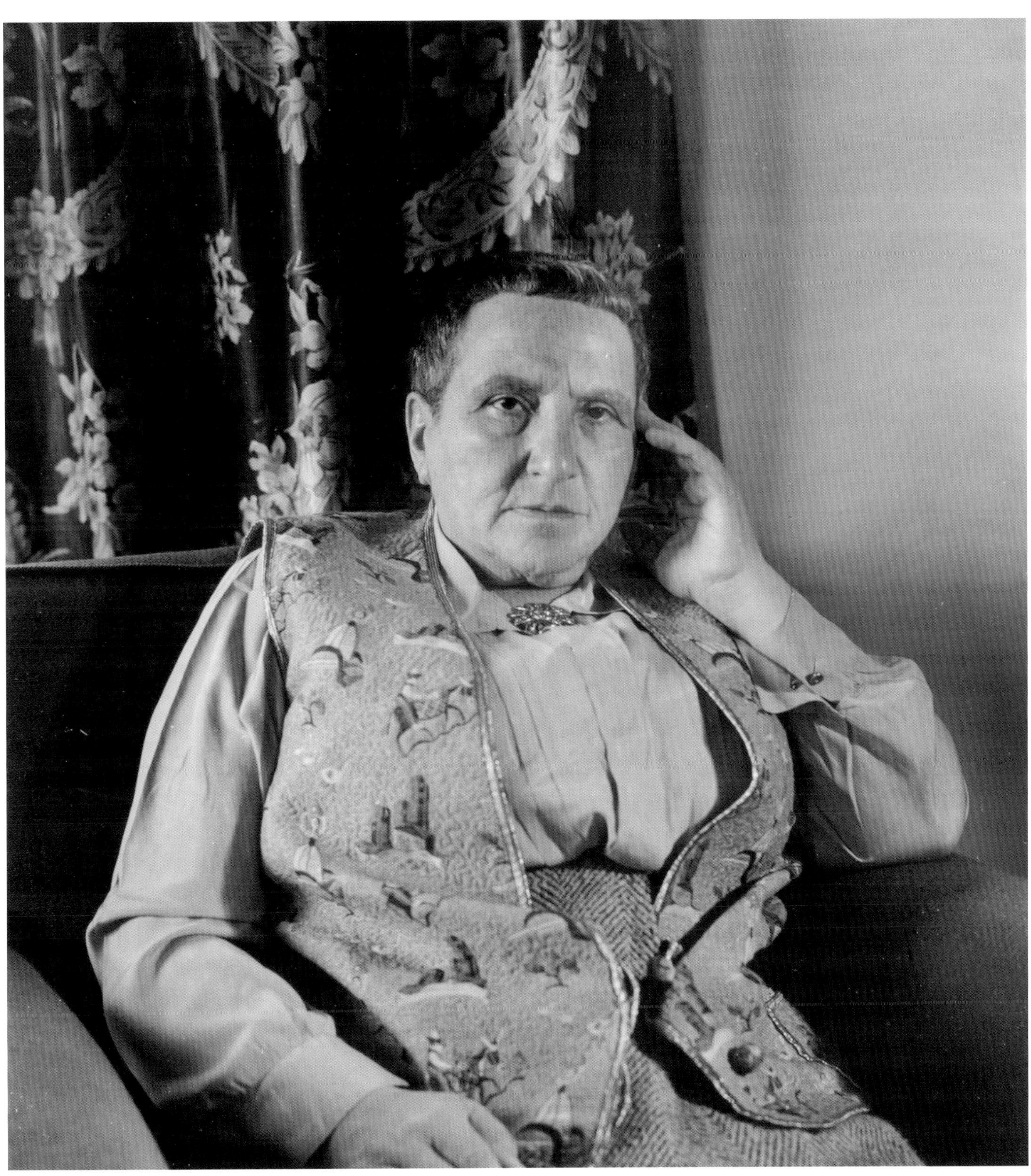

104

Yousuf Karsh

Canadian, born Turkey, 1908–2002

Winston Churchill, 1941
Gelatin silver print
Image: 49.2 × 39.4 cm (19 3/8 × 15 1/2 in); mount: 71 ×
57.8 cm (27 15/16 × 22 3/4 in)
Inscribed, in image, lower right, in white: © *Karsh /
Ottawa*
Sheldon Art Association, gift of the Lincoln Camera Club
in memory of Sten T. Anderson, FPSA, N-473

Yousuf Karsh was born in the city of Mardin in present-day Turkey to Armenian parents who, as a result of the genocide, were forced to flee from town to town. Eventually, they sent the young boy to Canada to live with his uncle Nakash, a photographer. Karsh apprenticed with his uncle while in school and then received further training from a Boston photographer for a few years before returning to Canada in 1931 to establish his own studio in Ottawa, where he dedicated himself to portraiture. The artist initially photographed amateur actors from local stages, and the experience exerted a lasting influence, introducing him to the theatrical lighting that became a mainstay of his work. A critical turn in Karsh's career, however, came in 1936, when the Canadian prime minister, Mackenzie King, invited him to photograph the visiting American president, Franklin Delano Roosevelt. Thus began a mutually beneficial relationship in which King provided several commissions for the young photographer, including perhaps his most important portrait, that of British prime minister Winston Churchill.

Karsh took Churchill's portrait on December 30, 1941, immediately after he had addressed the Canadian Parliament in Ottawa, part of a tour that included a speech in Washington DC just weeks after the attacks on Pearl Harbor and the United States' official entry into World War II. At King's request, the photographer set up a small studio in the speaker's chamber; he studied Churchill's expression and mood during the speech in anticipation of the limited time Karsh would have to spend with his subject. Karsh later described the harried and stressful photography session with the "roaring lion": "He marched in scowling, and regarded my camera as he might regard the German enemy. His expression suited me

perfectly, if I could capture it, but the cigar thrust between his teeth seemed somehow incompatible with such a solemn and formal occasion. Instinctively, I removed the cigar. At this the Churchillian scowl deepened, the head was thrust forward belligerently, and the hand placed on the hip in an attitude of anger. So he stands in my portrait in what has always seemed to me the image of England in those years."[1] Karsh snapped one additional portrait of Churchill during the brief session, in the same posture but with a smile beginning at the corners of his mouth and a surprising, mischievous twinkle in his eyes, a much more benign and personal image that "was a favorite of [Churchill's] family" for years.[2]

This portrait, however, is what sealed the artist's fame and reputation: reproduced on the cover of *Life* magazine and on the postage stamps of six nations, the photograph went on to become one of the most recognizable in the world and an iconic symbol of both the war and the "indomitable spirit of the British people."[3] The success of the image was also the result of Karsh's adept lighting, which throws many details of place and setting into shadow, including Churchill's own clothing, forcing viewers to focus on the prime minister's somber expression and tense hands, which stand out against the stark darkness. As an official portrait, it also speaks to the nature of representation, further reinforcing Churchill's public persona as the "British Bulldog" rather than revealing new, complex nuances of character during difficult times. **BKR**

1. Yousuf Karsh, *Karsh Portraits* (Toronto: University of Toronto Press, 1976), 46. Karsh later wrote that he filed the negative under the name "Roaring Lion," asserting that upon Churchill's exit from the session, he exclaimed, "Well, you can certainly make a roaring lion stand still to be photographed." The moniker "Roaring Lion" came from a quote attributed to Churchill about his wartime endeavors: "The nation had the lion's heart. I had the luck to give the roar." **2.** For this quote and a reproduction of this alternate image, see Yousuf Karsh, *Karsh: A Fifty-Year Retrospective* (Boston: Little, Brown and Company; New York: New York Graphic Society, 1983), 39. **3.** For the quote, see Karsh, *Karsh: A Fifty-Year Retrospective*, 14; for the life of the photograph, see Karsh, *Karsh Portraits*, 45.

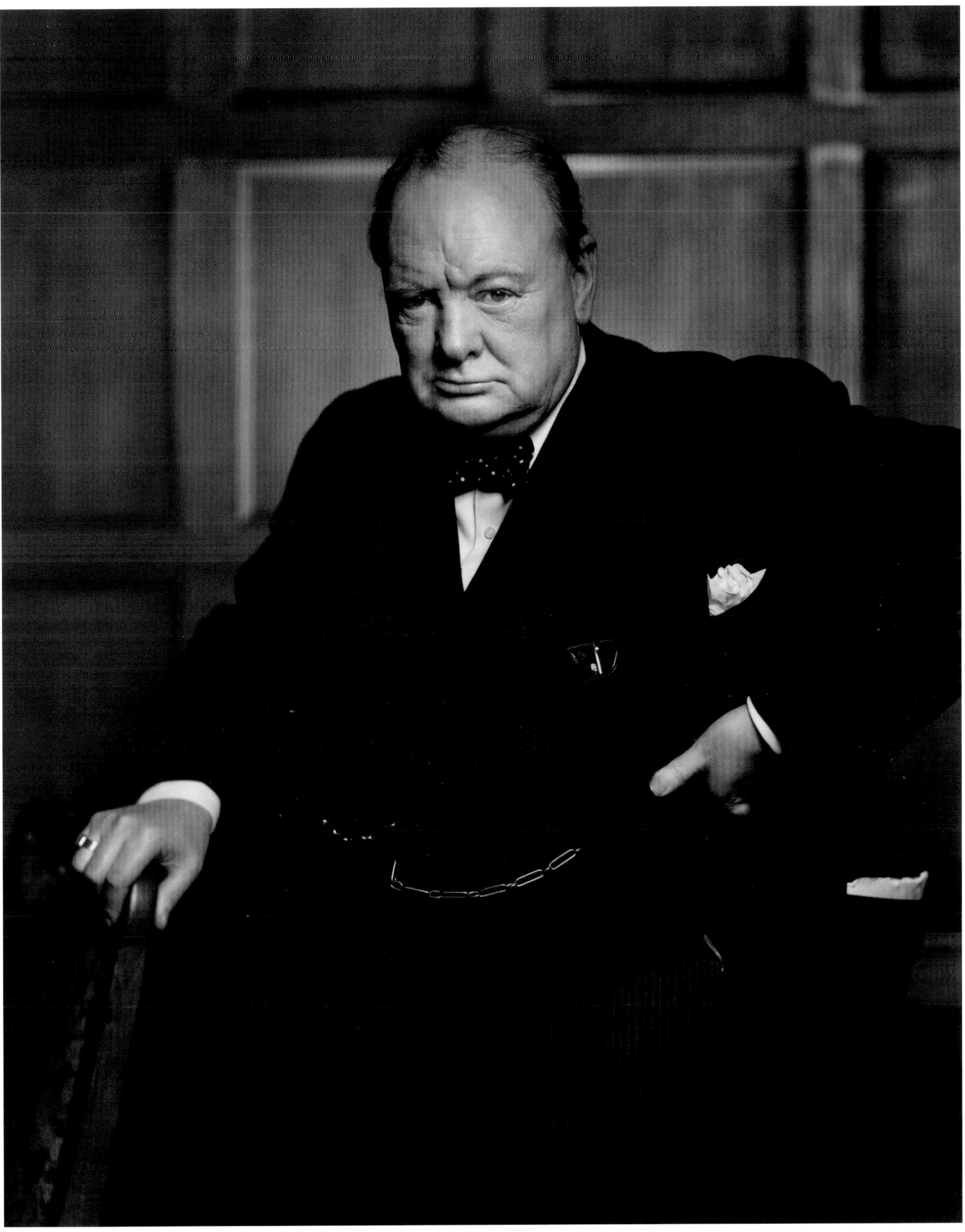

105

George Platt Lynes

American, 1907–1955

Marsden Hartley, 1943
Gelatin silver print
Image and sheet: 24.1 × 19.1 cm (9 1/2 × 7 1/2 in)
Inscribed, on verso, middle center, in black ink:
*Photograph of Marsden Hartley / by George Platt Lynes
/ Feb 4, 1943 / Return to Russell Lynes / Harper's
Magazine / 2 Park Ave / New York NY 10016*
Nebraska Art Association, gift of Lawrence Reger, N-586

Although he made his living largely from commercial and fashion photography, George Platt Lynes is perhaps best known for his intensely homoerotic images of male dancers and nudes. At the same time, he moved in cosmopolitan circles and took candid—albeit highly choreographed—portrait photographs of some of the art world's most famous personalities, including Henri Cartier-Bresson, E. M. Forster, Aldous Huxley, Gertrude Stein, and Tennessee Williams, among others. Lynes also received several portrait commissions based on his connections with a circle of artistic and sophisticated gay men in New York City, which included painters Paul Cadmus and Jared French; Lincoln Kirstein, art patron and cofounder of the American Ballet Company (now the New York City Ballet); and author Glenway Wescott and his partner, Monroe Wheeler, a curator at the Museum of Modern Art.

Lynes also photographed painter Marsden Hartley a few months before the artist's death in 1943. Although not part of the circle that included Kirstein, Wescott, and Wheeler, Hartley became acquainted with Lynes when he began using a small studio next to the photographer's. Hartley, one of America's foremost modernist artists, experimented with a variety of visual idioms during the early years of the twentieth century; he also explored his sexual orientation in his paintings, particularly those that memorialized deceased friends and loved ones. At the time he sat for this portrait, he was mourning the loss of another infatuation. The painter's demeanor is pensive and thoughtful, a reflection of his own inner anxiety; the umbrella leaning against the chair seems a reminder of dreary, gray days and associated moments of sadness. The idea of love and loss was also relevant to Lynes and alluded to in the background figures: the man facing the viewer has been identified as his studio assistant and lover, Jonathan Tichenor, whose older brother George—the photographer's former assistant and the subject of his unrequited passion—had been killed in action during World War II.[1] In the photograph, Tichenor wears his brother's military uniform, and his casual, relaxed self-presentation serves as an antidote to Hartley's tense expression and posture, while the young man who turns his back acts as a metaphor for the passing of people from the artists' lives. Although their acquaintanceship was short-lived, upon Hartley's death, Lynes expressed his sorrow in a letter to his mother: "Did I write you, or did you see in the papers, that Marsden Hartley died? The painter to whom I loaned a little room all last winter. He was sixty-six but he was at the top of his form and we were very devoted to him; it was a shock."[2]

Aside from a sense of grief, both artist and subject also shared the experience of living during a period of extreme homophobia. As a result, they self-consciously fashioned their own identities through reinvention, most notably of their names. Just before the war, Lynes began using his middle name, Platt, likely because his "fortunes were running high and he wanted a fancier name to go with his fancy new life. . . . He wanted it to have a distinguished sound."[3] Like Lynes's, Hartley's name was also a fabrication: born Edmund, he later assumed Marsden—his stepmother's last name—when he was in his early twenties, beginning his career and finding his footing as an artist. **BKR**

1. For this identification as well as other examples from the photo shoot, see David Leddick, *Intimate Companions: A Triography of George Platt Lynes, Paul Cadmus, Lincoln Kirstein, and Their Circle* (New York: St. Martin's Press, 2000), 167–68; Leddick, *George Platt Lynes: 1907–1955* (Cologne: Benedikt Taschen Verlag, 2000), 34–36; and Jonathan D. Katz and David C. Ward, *Hide/Seek: Difference and Desire in American Portraiture*, exhibition catalog (Washington DC: Smithsonian Books, 2010), 138–39. **2.** Quoted in Leddick, *Intimate Companions*, 168. **3.** Leddick, *Intimate Companions*, 159.

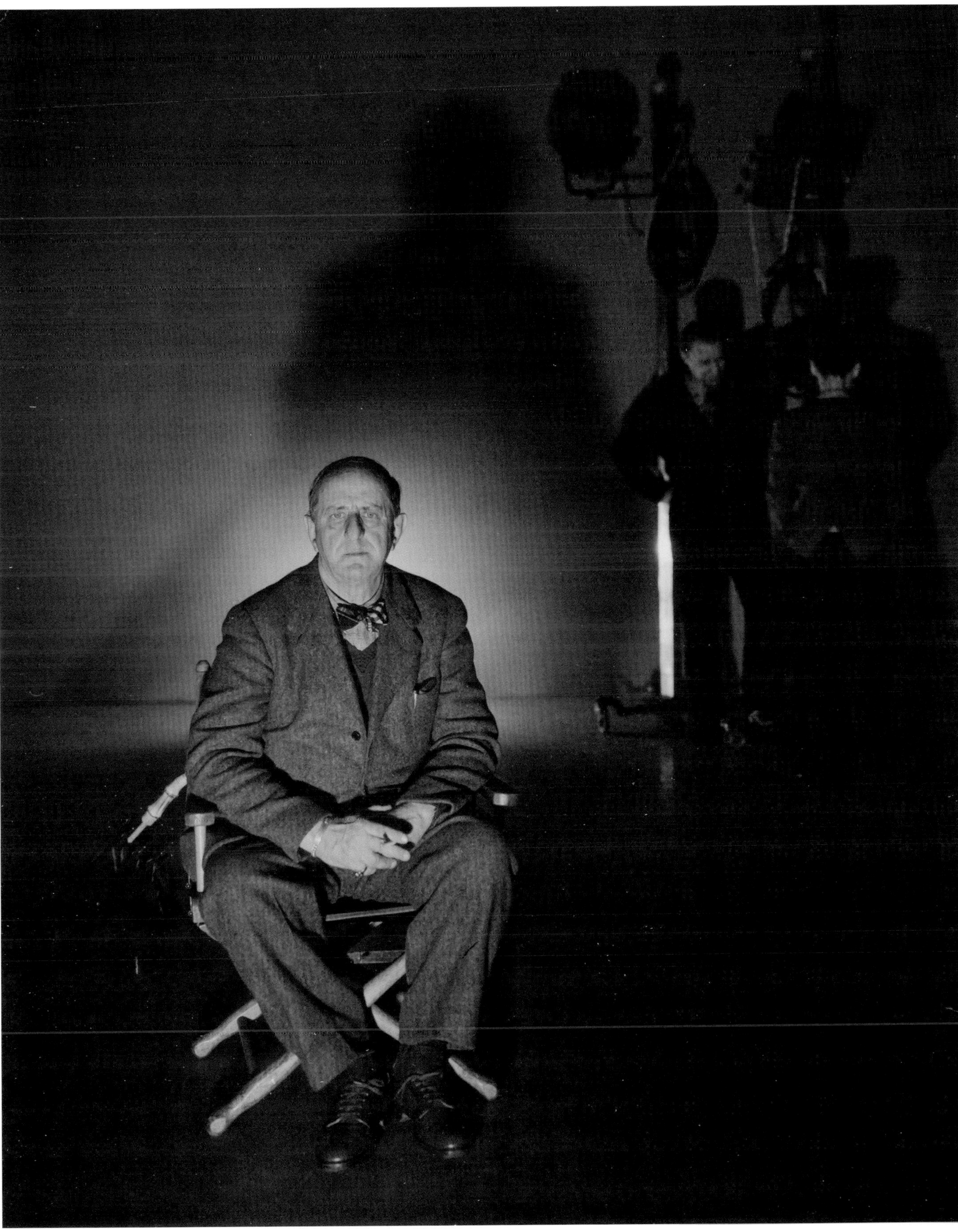

106

Weegee (Arthur Fellig)
American, born Poland, 1899–1968

Policeman and Buttonman, c. 1930
Gelatin silver print
Image: 15.1 × 11.8 cm (5 15/16 × 4 5/8 in); sheet: 17.8 × 12.9 cm
(7 × 5 1/16 in)
University of Nebraska, Anna R. and Frank M. Hall
Charitable Trust, H-2895

Rising from the ranks of anonymous stock photographers, Arthur Fellig—nicknamed Weegee—became one of the most sought after and controversial photojournalists of the 1930s and 1940s.[1] Working in the darkroom of the *New York Times* and Acme Newspictures before striking out on his own, he created images that appeared in many of the major newspapers of the day. Successful books, including *Naked City* and *Weegee by Weegee*, helped cement the photographer and his pictures in the public imagination.[2]

An immigrant to the United States, Weegee grew up on Manhattan's Lower East Side and represented the people and neighborhoods of his youth throughout his career. His mise-en-scènes appealed to a popular audience, who often saw themselves represented in his photographs. Unlike much of 1930s New Deal photography, which was meant to inspire social reform, Weegee's images of New York's crime, nightlife, and tenements offered a blunt, sometimes humorous, often dramatic narrative of an evening's events as splashed across tabloid pages. Taking pictures of Coney Island, Harlem, the Lower East Side, Times Square, and Greenwich Village, Weegee documented the working class of the city. Central to his success was the installation of a police radio in his car, which enabled him to be one of the first photographers on the scene, sometimes arriving at an accident or murder site before the police.

Again and again, Weegee's ambulance chasing allowed him to capture moments of high tension and drama in his images. *Policeman and Buttonman* encompasses many of the photographer's familiar themes.[3] The picture juxtaposes a straitlaced, skeptical police officer with an unknown figure who wears an odd assortment of items, including an array of buttons, a dress, and a flowered hat with feathers. The scene is made more uncomfortable by the buttonman's steadfast refusal to acknowledge the presence of the policeman; instead, he stares blankly out at the viewer. Although it is not clear why he is in custody, his unconventional appearance commands our attention, and our need to stare back at him is mirrored in the officer's steady gaze. Many of Weegee's photographs highlight the crowds who have gathered to gawk at the unfolding dramas being documented; here, both we and the policeman serve that function.

The modernist photographer Paul Strand (cats. 59 and 60) described Weegee as "the photographer of all that teeming, violent, human life that goes on in New York below the impersonal surface of more or less orderly work-a-day living."[4] He is best known as an artist who blurred the lines between documentation and art, journalism and sensationalism. **SF**

1. There are two popular stories of how Fellig adopted the name Weegee. The first explains it as a variation of "Squeegee Boy," a nickname he had while working at the *New York Times*. The second relates it to the then-popular Ouija board game that Fellig was known to have played. For a detailed account of Weegee's early career, see Miles Barth, ed., *Weegee's World* (Boston: Bulfinch Press, 1997), 11–33. **2.** When it was first published in 1945, *Naked City* went through six printings in its first year. See Anthony Lee, *Weegee and the Naked City* (Berkeley: University of California Press, 2008), 1. **3.** The image is given the alternate title *Arrestation* in *Weegee dans la collection Berinson*, exhibition catalog (Paris: Gallimard, 2007), 84. **4.** Paul Strand, "Weegee Gives Journalism a Shot of Creative Photography," *PM*, July 22, 1945, quoted in *Unknown Weegee*, ed. Cynthia Young, exhibition catalog (New York: International Center of Photography; Göttingen: Steidl, 2006), 19.

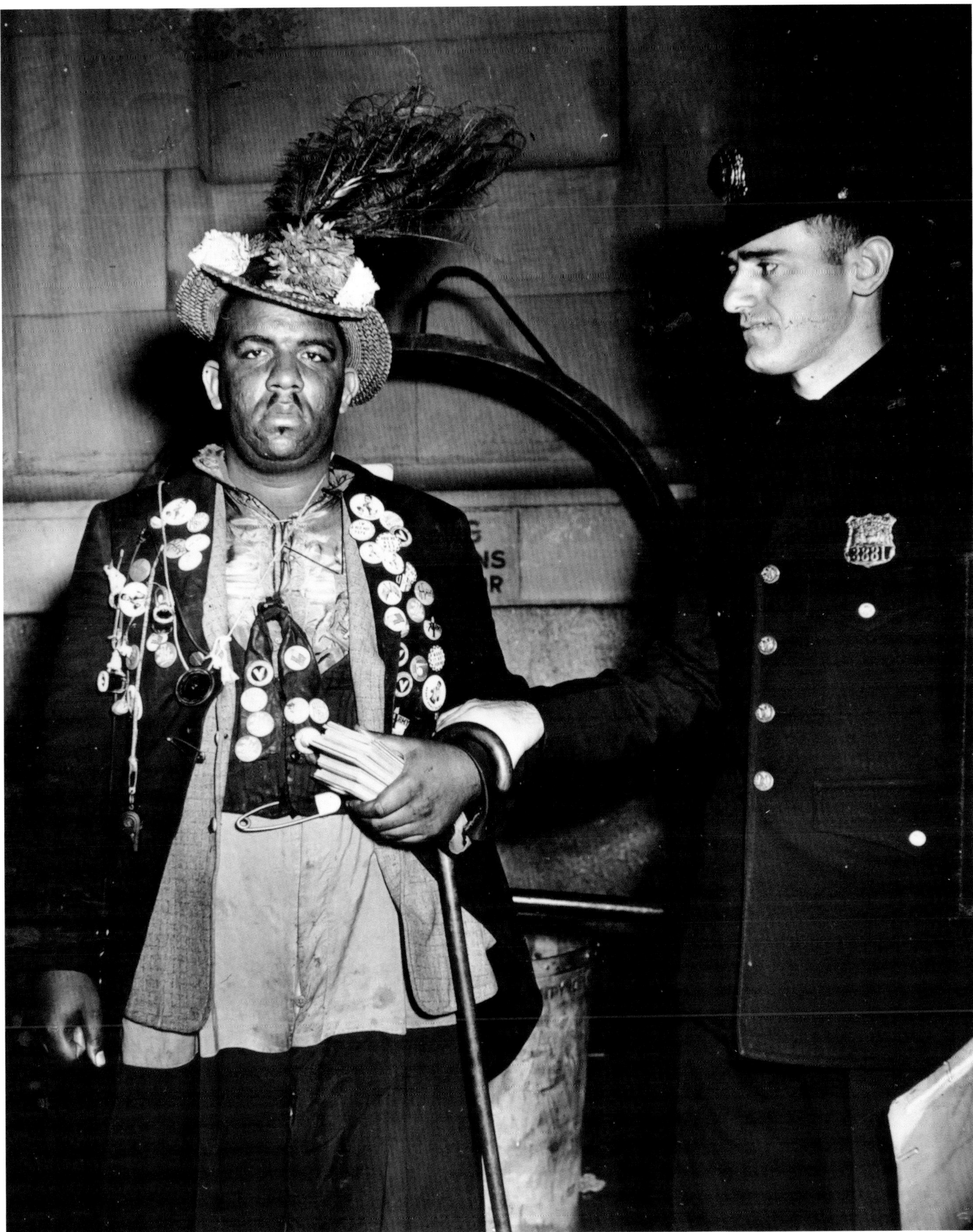

107

Ruth Bernhard

American, born Germany, 1905–2006

Two Forms (#10 from *The Eternal Body*), 1965
Gelatin silver print
Image: 24 × 17.8 cm (9 7/16 × 7 in); mount: 41.3 × 31.4 cm
(16 1/4 × 12 3/8 in)
Signed, on mount, lower right, in pencil: *Ruth Bernhard*
Nebraska Art Association, purchased with the aid of
funds from the National Endowment for the Arts, N-389

Born in Berlin and trained at that city's Academy of Art, Ruth Bernhard moved to New York in the late 1920s to join her father, a prominent typographical designer who already lived there. Initially, she assisted Ralph Steiner (cat. 75) and used that experience to purchase her own camera equipment and start her fledgling photography career. Bernhard quickly fell in with the circle of bohemian artists centered around Greenwich Village and became involved in Manhattan's lesbian subculture through photographer Berenice Abbott (cat. 34) and her partner, art critic Elizabeth McCausland. As a result, Bernhard fashioned a bisexual identity, and from the 1930s onward, she made nudes—often of lesbian couples— her primary subject and was one of the few photographers to concentrate on the theme during this period.[1]

During the 1930s and 1940s, Bernhard traveled between New York and California, where she first encountered Edward Weston (cat. 58) and became involved with f64, a collective whose goal was to promote a straightforward, purist approach to photography. In 1953 Bernhard moved to San Francisco with her partner, Eveline Phimster, and began a series of portrait nudes, releasing a portfolio of fifty in the mid-1960s under the title *The Eternal Body*. Among these was one of her most famous, *Two Forms*, in which a black woman and a white woman press their bare bodies against one another, creating a near abstraction and a subtle study of the contrasts of light and dark. The artist later described the creation of the photograph as one of serendipity. On her lunch break with a friend, a sometime model stopped by Bernhard's apartment, and both offered to pose: "I was unprepared, but I got my camera and put film in it. As they took off their clothes I noticed that the black woman had crease marks on her stomach and the white woman had no muscle tone, so I asked them to face each other."[2]

Bernhard acknowledged a debt to Weston in her choice of subject and adopted many of her friend and mentor's formal approaches, including abstracting elements and subjects in-spired by nature. Unlike Weston, however, she did not rely on natural light to express a sense of flesh's tactility but instead employed studio lighting and darkroom techniques to refine the intricacies of light and create an idealized nude figure. The artist later explained her attraction to this subject—and her aesthetic goals in depicting it—in the following terms: "In photographing the nude, it is my aim to transform the complexities of the figure into harmonies of simplified form. The underlying variety of nature's designs and shapes amaze and thrill me. I have approached my work with the nude much as I create a still life—with patience and reverence. My quest, through the magic of light and shadow, is to isolate, to simplify and to give emphasis to form with the greatest clarity."[3]

As Bernhard suggested, these "harmonies of simplified form" applied both to her still lifes and her portrait subjects, and these two images exhibit parallels in their cropping, framing, lighting, and, most relevantly, positioning. By selecting nontraditional nude subjects and treating them like her natural ones, Bernhard at once liberated and objectified them. **BKR**

1. Margaretta Mitchell, *Ruth Bernhard: Between Art and Life* (San Francisco: Chronicle Books, 2000), 54–58. **2.** Quoted in Mitchell, *Ruth Bernhard*, 101. **3.** Ruth Bernhard, *The Eternal Body* (San Francisco: Chronicle Books, 1986), n.p.

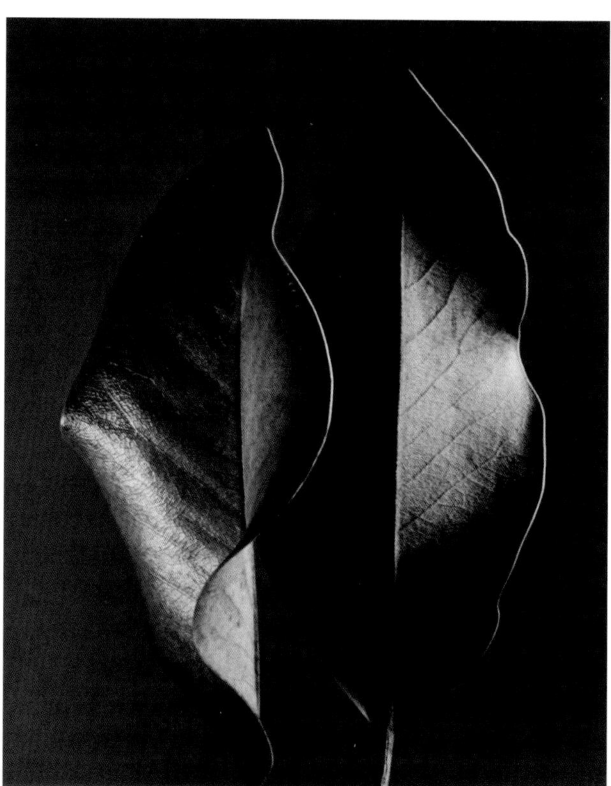

Ruth Bernhard. *Two Leaves* (#7 from *The Gift of the Commonplace*), 1953. Gelatin silver print; 24.8 × 18.9 cm (9 3/4 × 7 7/16 in). Nebraska Art Association, purchased with the aid of funds from the National Endowment for the Arts, N-390.

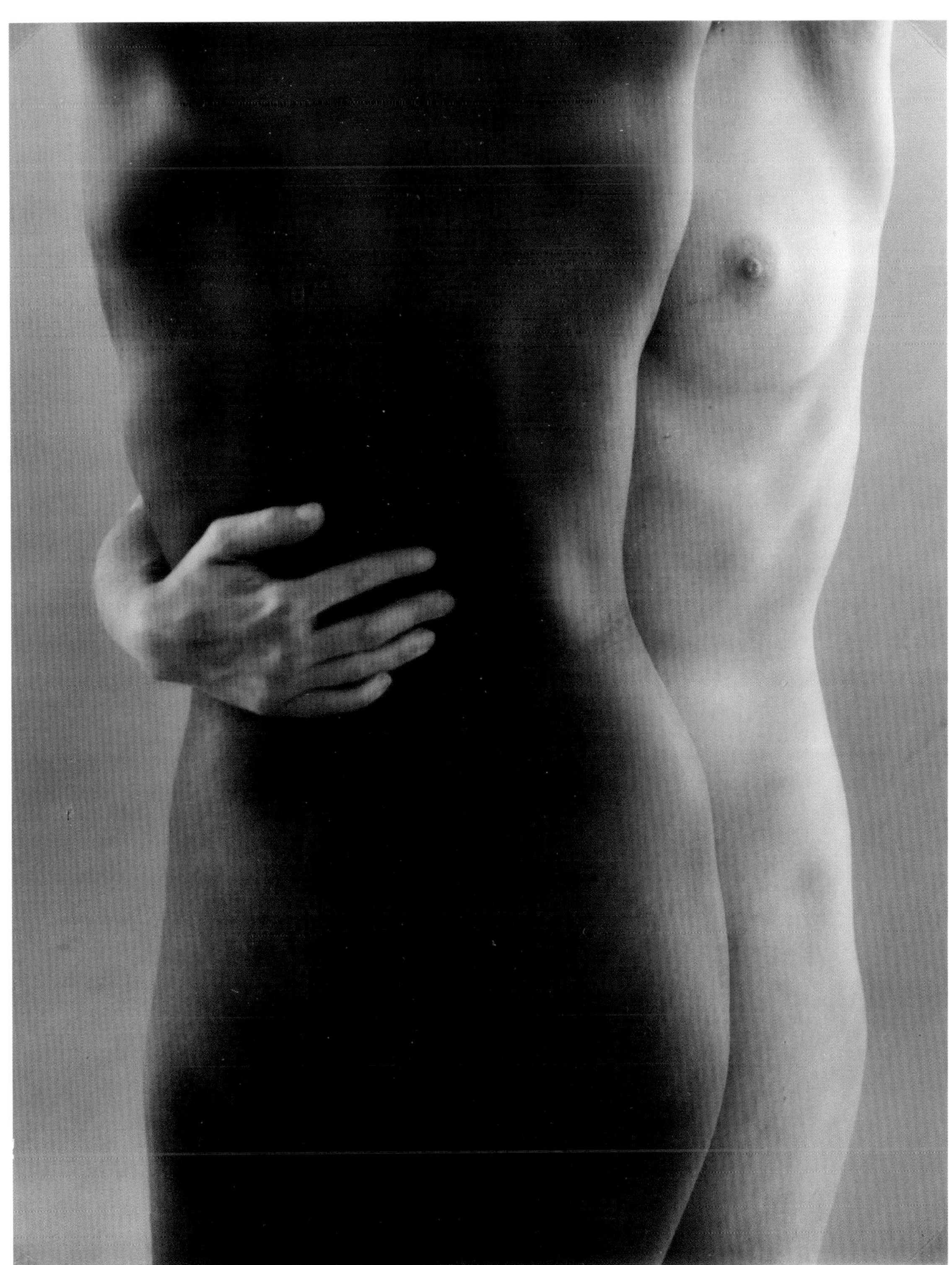

108

Robert Mapplethorpe

American, 1946–1989

Ken Moody, 1983
Gelatin silver print
Image: 48.6 × 38.7 cm (19 1/8 × 15 1/4 in); sheet: 50.2 ×
40 cm (19 3/4 × 15 3/4 in)
Inscribed, on verso, lower left, in black ink: *1280 1/10
Ken 1983*; lower center: artist's stamp with handwritten
inscriptions
University of Nebraska, Anna R. and Frank M. Hall
Charitable Trust, H-2606

Robert Mapplethorpe decided to pursue a career as an artist in the late 1960s. In his early works—collages and constructions—he incorporated magazine photographs and other mass-produced imagery. By the mid-1970s he had taken up the camera himself, mentored by curator Sam Wagstaff, who was also his lover for a time.[1] Very quickly, Mapplethorpe attained mastery not only of his chosen medium but also of his preferred themes: still life, portraiture, and the human body. These are traditional art-historical genres, and the artist aspired to the perfection and beauty he saw in classical statuary. "If I had been born one hundred or two hundred years ago," he remarked, "I might have been a sculptor, but photography is a very quick way to see, to make sculpture."[2]

For all its references to the art of the past, Mapplethorpe's photography remains rooted in his own obsessions and, by extension, in the pressing social concerns of the 1980s. He set his parameters with a trio of portfolios, each containing thirteen prints: *X* and *Y* (both 1978) were followed by *Z* (1981). *X* depicts sadomasochistic scenarios, *Y* features floral still lifes, and *Z* focuses on black male nudes. Part of the appeal of this third subject was its social transgression. As Mapplethorpe explained, he began to make erotically inflected photographs of black men because he "hadn't seen pictures like that before. . . . It was a subject that nobody had used because it was loaded."[3]

With rare exceptions, Mapplethorpe worked in the studio rather than in the street, preferring to maintain total control over gesture, lighting, movement, and setting. As indicated by his frequent self-portraits, he asserted himself as a participant in the image-making scenario. In the case of black male subjects, this intensified the power relationship, whether calibrated in terms of class, race, or sexuality. Many of Mapplethorpe's models were also his lovers, but this was not the case with Ken Moody, the subject of this photograph and a regular sitter between 1983 and 1985.

Although Mapplethorpe frequently photographed Moody's face and profile, here he concentrated on his body, seen from behind, with his left shoulder slightly angled toward the camera to catch the light. A white background contrasts with dark skin. Wearing only a black thong, Moody portrays the archetypal athlete, pausing between physical exertions. Beyond this basic classical allusion, the picture's true subject is tonality, specifically, the lustrous range from black through gray to white that can be achieved in the gelatin silver process.

Mapplethorpe was always concerned with the photograph as a material art object. Not only did he choreograph the exposure of the film, he had distinct preferences for printing style and sometimes designed custom frames. However, he did not carry out the darkroom work himself, instead delegating this task to Tom Baril, a fellow photographer and master printer.[4] Here Baril skillfully rendered the effect of cool, soft illumination.

Mapplethorpe died of AIDS-related complications in 1989, shortly before the eruption of controversy around his retrospective exhibition *The Perfect Moment*, organized by the Institute of Contemporary Art, Philadelphia. Still today, his work is seen as both polished and provocative. **BS**

1. Wagstaff, whose collection is now housed at the J. Paul Getty Museum, Los Angeles, was a voracious collector of photographs from the vernacular to the canonical. **2.** Janet Kardon, "Robert Mapplethorpe Interview," in *Robert Mapplethorpe: The Perfect Moment*, by Janet Kardon, David Joselit, and Kay Larson, exhibition catalog (Philadelphia: Institute of Contemporary Art, University of Pennsylvania, 1988), 27. **3.** Kardon, "Robert Mapplethorpe Interview," 28. **4.** Gordon Baldwin, "In the Studio," in *Robert Mapplethorpe: Portraits*, by Gordon Baldwin, exhibition catalog (Palm Springs CA: Palm Springs Art Museum, 2009), 17.

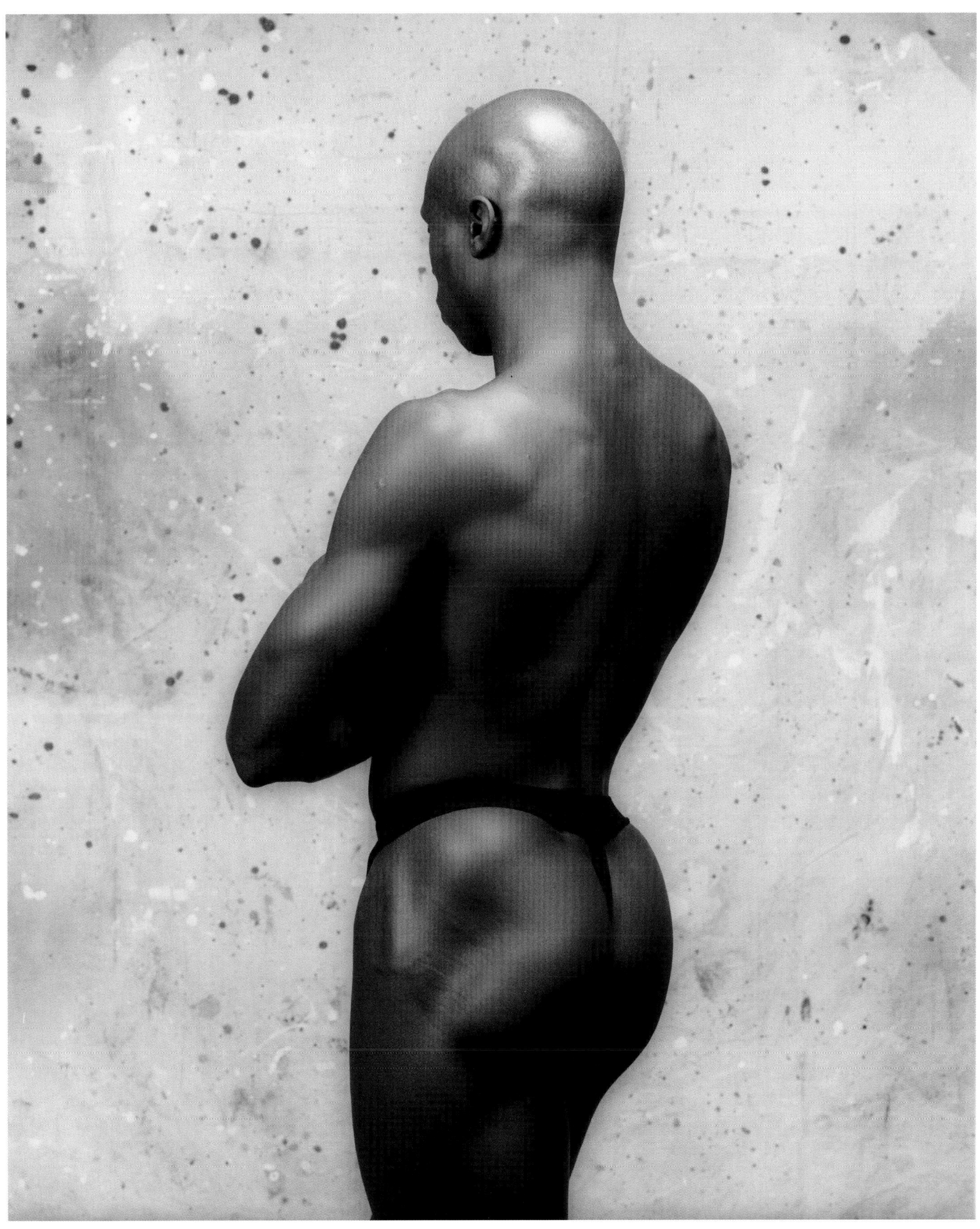

109

Frank Stewart

American, born 1949

Smoke and the Lovers, 1992
Gelatin silver print
Image: 30.8 × 46 cm (12 1/8 × 18 1/8 in); sheet: 40.6 ×
50.8 cm (16 × 20 in)
Signed, lower right, in ink: *Frank Stewart*
University of Nebraska, Robert E. Schweser and
Fern Beardsley Schweser Acquisition Fund, through
the University of Nebraska Foundation, U-5615

The setting for this photograph is Hawkins Grill in Memphis, Tennessee, where Frank Stewart grew up. As a teenager, the photographer was a regular at the place and knew to order the smoked shoulder sandwich, which grew in his imagination into the standard against which barbecue all over America (and sometimes beyond) was to be judged.

Stewart's book on barbecue, *Smokestack Lightning: Adventures in the Heart of Barbecue Country*, was inspired by Hawkins Grill. Back in Memphis for the project, the photographer took Lolis Eric Elie, who was writing the text for the book, directly to Hawkins Grill. Naturally, they ordered the smoked shoulder with hot sauce. Elie recalled that you could taste the smoke through the crunch of the fresh bread and slow-flavored meat. "It is the sort of sandwich," he wrote, "that makes you begin debating halfway through it, whether you should order a second immediately so that it will be ready the moment you finish the first."[1]

So it is quite by intention that *Smoke and the Lovers*—a spare, understated work of art—is thick with personal meanings for the photographer. The jukebox, seen at left and in the mirror at right, announces this as a place where customers came not only to eat but also to hear music and to dance, a local place of ritual play and drama. The lines of the jukebox match those of the veneered walls, the mirror, the seats and tables: midcentury modern with room to jitterbug.

No liquor was served at Hawkins, said Stewart. So along with the barbecue, the lovers have ordered soft drinks and a "setup": a bucket of ice and glasses for the bottles they've brought with them. The sign above their heads, which reads *Under Age*, spells out the rules of the house: no service for people too young to drink. Stewart recalls taking this photograph at 3:00 or 3:30 in the morning. The manager had just snapped all the lights on, signaling that it was time to go home. So the dark privacy of the smoker and the lovers was suddenly uncovered by the glaring light. And yet for all the specificity of these back-in-the-day details, the photograph—taken, we remember, not in the 1950s or 1960s but in 1992—has an eerie, timeless quality. Certainly the looks and leans of the back-table lovers transcend time. These two have been enjoying a private party in the corner: music, food, drink, perhaps a dance, and now a moment of low-voiced love talk. "The man in the hat is laying down the red-hot game," says Stewart.[2]

The bright lights have made the man in the foreground close his eyes while he enjoys a last cigarette, the smoke drifting above his head like musings in his mind. True to Stewart's aesthetic, the photograph retains its sense of mystery: What is the meaning of the age or the solitariness of the lone man? Does Stewart include him as a next stage in the photograph's narration? Is he an ironic comment on the smoke and mirrors of the romance at his back?

Elie felt Hawkins Grill had a party's-over quality about it: "It is this feeling of the dying embers of a once-blazing party that you get on a Sunday night at Hawkins—this feeling except also with it the feeling that the party probably last blazed many years ago."[3] And yet perhaps because of its spare but highly ritualized setting, *Smoke and the Lovers* burns into our imagination today. Telling an American story of its era, it also is a story of the black diaspora. It is a timeless tale of every man and woman, of smoke rising to heaven, a man alone, a couple, a prelude to a kiss. The party's over, and yet—as the lovers' closeness suggests—the party continues elsewhere. **RGO**

1. Lolis Eric Elie and Frank Stewart, *Smokestack Lightning: Adventures in the Heart of Barbecue Country* (Berkeley CA: 10 Speed Press, 2005), 4. **2.** Elie and Stewart, *Smokestack Lightning*. **3.** Elie and Stewart, *Smokestack Lightning*, 4.

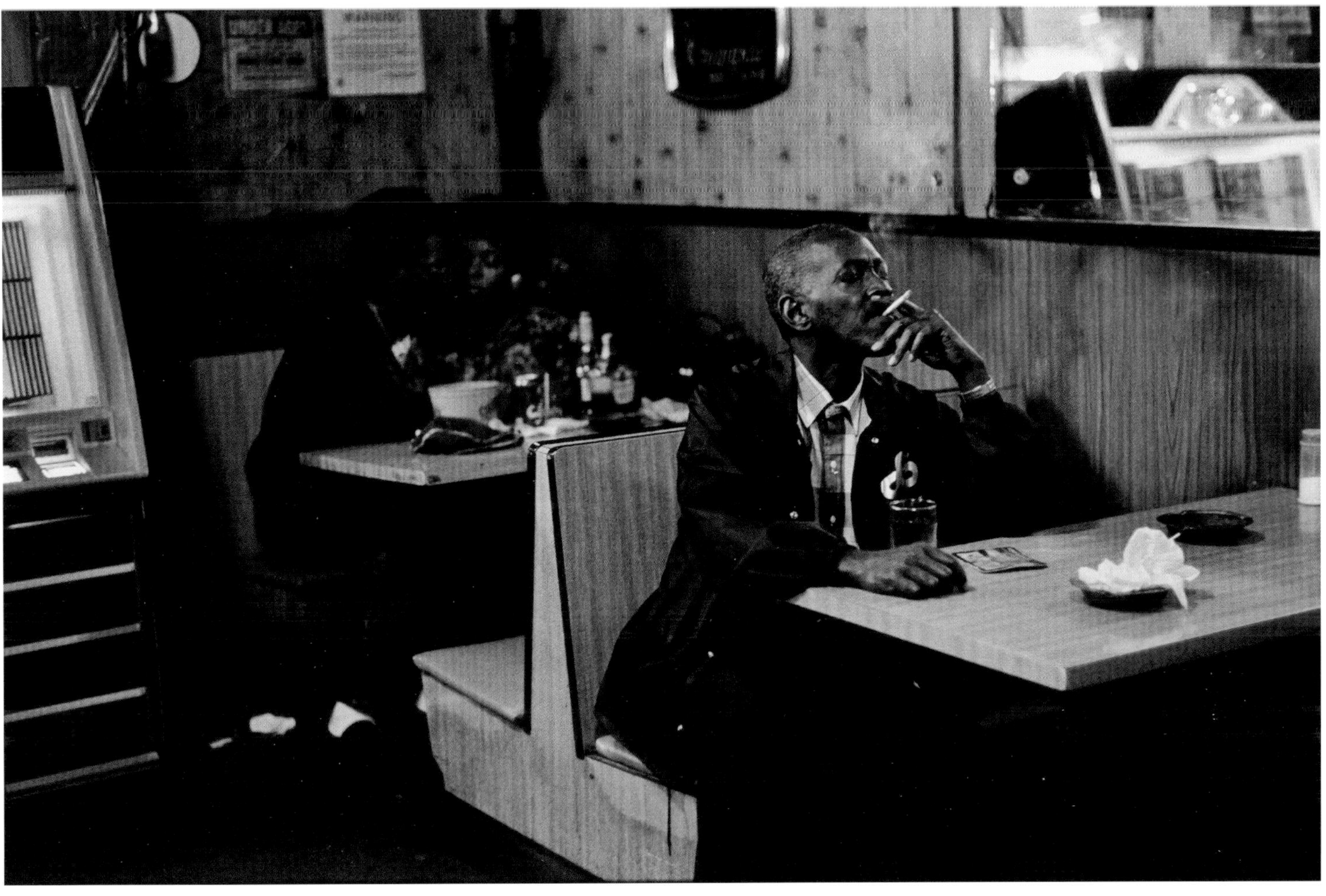

110

Catherine Opie
American, born 1961

Divinity Fudge, 1997
Chromogenic print
Image and sheet: 152.4 × 76.2 cm (60 × 30 in)
University of Nebraska, Olga N. Sheldon Acquisition
Trust, U-5589

Growing up in Sandusky, Ohio, Catherine Opie discovered her calling as a photographer an early age. In the early 1980s she entered the BFA program at the San Francisco Art Institute, where she studied under noted social-documentary photographers Larry Sultan and Henry Wessel. She also came out fully as a lesbian, participating in the city's sadomasochistic leather subculture. The members of this community became the subjects of her first important body of work, a series entitled *Being and Having* (1991), which focuses on gender-bending lesbians. In the artist's words, she was "inspired by all these people who were giving themselves the freedom to image themselves however they saw fit."[1]

In her photographs, Opie takes over the imaging to a large extent, although a strong collaborative element remains. While a believer in the documentary tradition, she is also interested in the iconic, and her visual sources come from the history of painting as much as photography. For example, the colored backgrounds in her portraits of the 1990s refer directly to sixteenth-century Dutch master Hans Holbein, an affinity brought to her attention by fellow artist Richard Hawkins. The device serves a specific purpose, as the artist has explained: "It's about separating the subject from their world, but still representing their world through their body."[2]

Divinity Fudge is one of a series of portraits made between 1993 and 1997. By then settled in Los Angeles, Opie pushed the two central impulses in her work—the documentary and the aesthetic—by embracing the rich detail afforded by the 4 × 5-inch camera and emphasizing the figure's isolation against a colored background. The deliberate restrictions of her studio setup enhance, rather than suppress, the subject's individuality. Eschewing the furnishings and accoutrements of traditional portraiture, the artist looks for signs of identity, lifestyle, and character marked on the body. The sitter in turn manifests these signs through gaze, gesture, and posture.

The charismatic subject of this photograph, performance artist Divinity Fudge (Darryl Carlton), immediately commands our attention. Opie's choice of yellow for the background highlights Divinity's dark skin tone, amplifies the leopard-print garments, and silhouettes the defiant stance. Although the performer's clothing hints at a Tarzan/Jane parody and her name brings to mind an old-fashioned sugary candy, Opie does not permit the image to slide into absurdity. She knows Divinity as a serious artist who in 1994 participated in one of the most scandalous episodes in the so-called culture wars. During a performance of *Four Scenes in a Harsh Life* at the Walker Art Center in Minneapolis, Ron Athey—another frequent Opie subject—cut Divinity's back and then lifted the blood-soaked paper towels over the audience, triggering public anxiety about AIDS and alternative lifestyles.[3] Here, Opie, who famously made self-portraits with messages cut into her own flesh, depicts a fellow artist with respect and admiration. **BS**

1. Quoted in Harmony Hammond, *Lesbian Art in America: A Contemporary History* (New York: Rizzoli, 2000), 150. **2.** Quoted in Jennifer Blessing, *Catherine Opie: American Photographer*, exhibition catalog (New York: Solomon R. Guggenheim Museum, 2009), 52. **3.** Jennifer Doyle, "Blood Work and 'Art Criminals,'" *Art:21 blog*, December 10, 2008, http://blog.art21.org/2008/12/10/blood-work-art-criminals/. Opie made portraits of Carlton again in 2000. The series *Large Format Polaroids* includes an image of Athey and Carlton restaging the performance (*Ron Cutting Divinity*) as well as the portrait *Darryl Carlton/Back*; see Blessing, *Catherine Opie*, 160–61, 164.

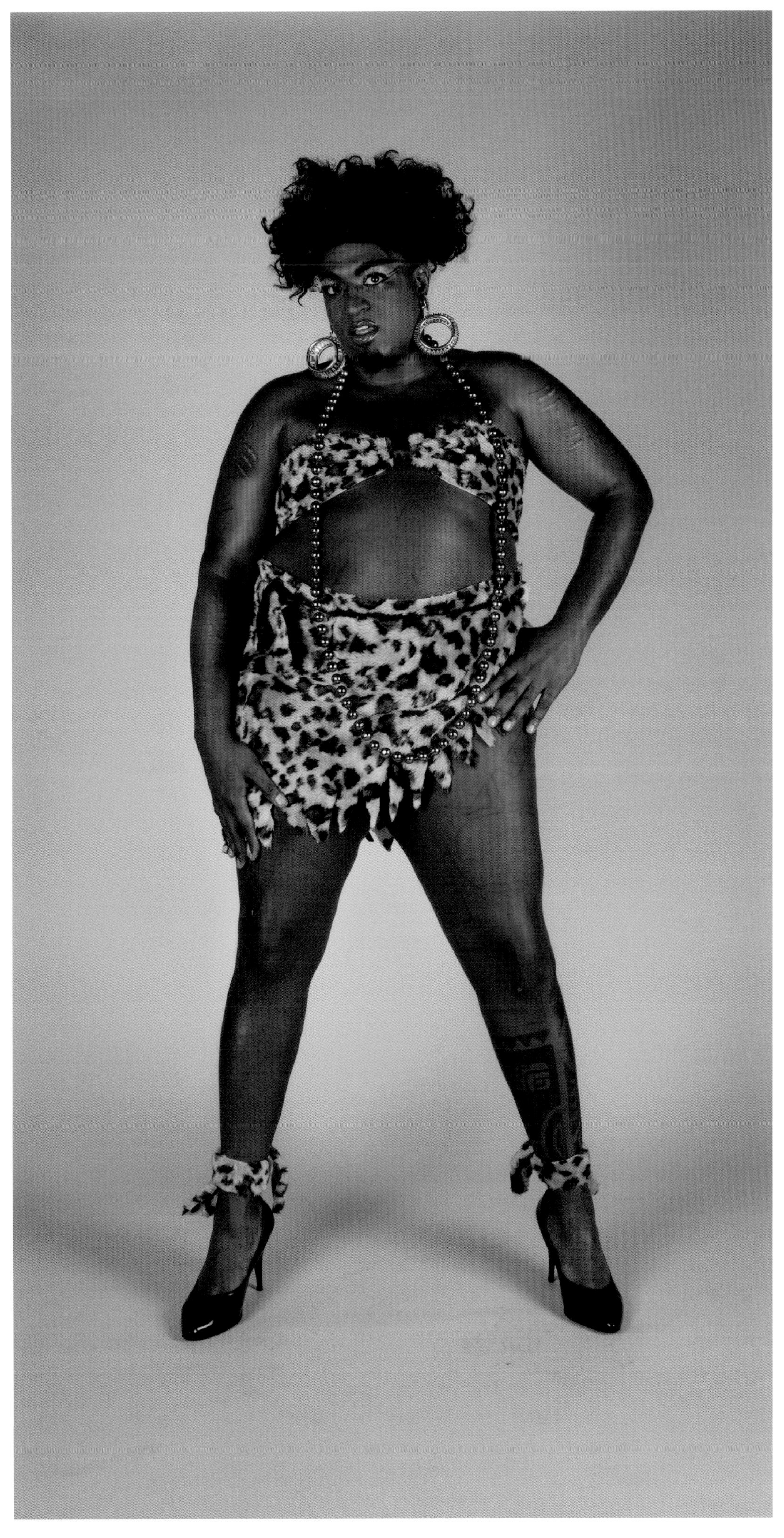

111

Delilah Montoya

American, born 1955

Doreen Hilton (from the series *Women Boxers: The New Warriors*), 2006
Epson pigment print
Image: 75.9 × 55.7 cm (29 7/8 × 21 15/16 in); sheet: 87.6 × 66 cm (34 1/2 × 26 in)
Inscribed, lower left, in pencil: *Doreen*; lower right: 1/3 *Delilah Montoya 06*
University of Nebraska, Olga N. Sheldon Acquisition Trust, U-5590

In the photographs and digital prints of Delilah Montoya, identity is a construct of fact and fiction, past and present. Born in Texas and raised in Omaha, the artist studied at the University of New Mexico and is now associate professor at the University of Houston. Her work is centered primarily on her experience of the Southwest, exploring her Chicana identity through the filter of American, Mexican, Native American, and Spanish perspectives. Montoya's undertakings include documenting the detritus along border-crossing

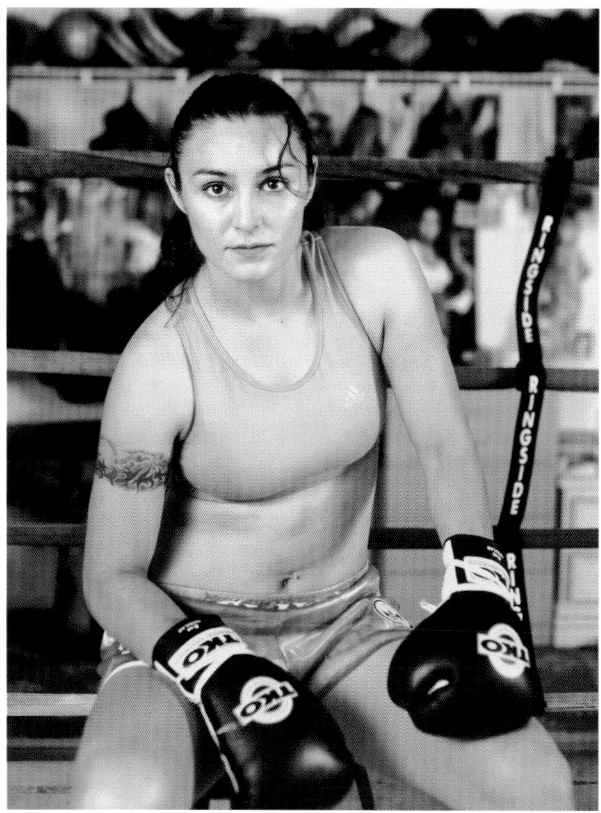

Delilah Montoya. *Jackie Chavez* (from the series *Women Boxers: The New Warriors*), 2006, printed 2010. Gelatin silver print; 89 × 66 cm (35 × 26 in). University of Nebraska, Olga N. Sheldon Acquisition Trust, U-5591.

trails, recording the significance of the Sacred Heart icon in the Albuquerque community, and inventing narratives of the pilgrimage of a Chicana female hero. Collectively, her artworks express a personal ideology that bridges numerous cultural, emotional, historical, political, and religious discourses.

In 2005, when Montoya was drawn into the nascent world of professional women's boxing, she discovered it was laced with incredibly rich, interconnecting threads of class, ethnicity, gender, and race. There, women found a physical outlet for their competitive and combative natures. They came to the sport from homemaking, the military, and business professions, putting in long hours training and traveling rough regional fight circuits for a few minutes of brutal athletic rivalry in the ring.

Historically, women were not supposed to be the sugar in the "sweet science" but were sidelined as a supporting cast of raucous broads and buxom ring card girls. Or they participated in exhibition sports such as kickboxing, mud wrestling, and roller derby, where sexuality was objectified over athleticism. The women that Montoya met were gym rats who loved the sport—its dance, muscles, sweat, and impact. They were not wanton women but *malcriadas*, bad girls who did not conform to society's dictates. And in their own ways, each fought battles to earn the respect of family and communities uncomfortable with women as full-on gladiators.

Montoya's investigations became the 2006 publication and exhibition *Women Boxers: The New Warriors*. In it she documented female pugilists in training and competition, back halls and private moments. The artist's grainy, black-and-white images not only drown out the distracting details of poorly lit halls but also situate the viewer within a traditional visual framework of classic prizefighting.

Adopting a guarded stance with poised fists, subject Doreen Hilton provided Montoya with the paradigmatic visage of the boxer: confident, confrontational, at the ready. A twenty-five-year-old super flyweight, Hilton is fresh from battle, having quickly lost her bout to newcomer Jodie Esquibel; her eyes subtly reveal the wounding that her face is only beginning to betray. Since that time, Hilton does not seem to have furthered her career, recording instead an ignominious public comparison to all-time loser by knockout, Omaha's own Bruce "The Mouse" Strauss.[1] Women's boxing, however, has achieved a new status as a first-time medal competition sport in the 2012 Olympics. **JLF**

1. Mike Hall, "Boxing: Winner Could Go Places," *Albuquerque Journal*, October 28, 2005.

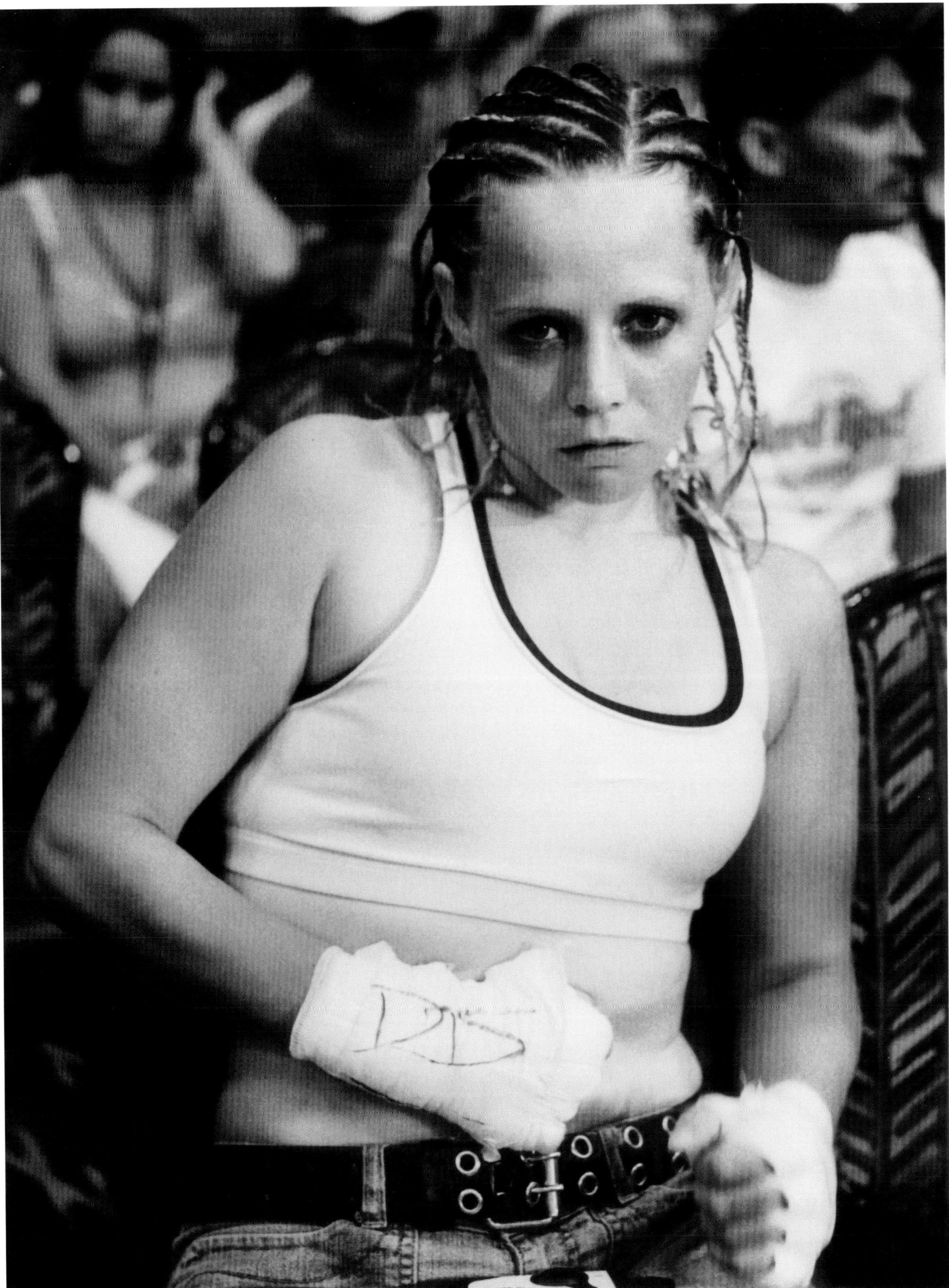

112

ORLAN
French, born 1947

Painting Portrait of Ru-Ton-Ye-Wee-Ma, Strutting Pigeon, Wife of White Cloud, with ORLAN's Photographic Portrait (#6 from *American Indian Self-Hybridization*), 2005
Inkjet print on photorag
Image: 152.4 × 129.5 cm (60 × 51 in); sheet: 170.2 × 152.4 cm (67 × 60 in)
University of Nebraska, promised gift of Rhonda Garelick and Jorge Daniel Veneciano, L-1-2012

This hauntingly strange and alternately facetious portrait trifles with our senses. The harmony we should feel upon seeing a mother and child embrace is rattled by the uncannily adult visage of the child staring back at us—discomfiting and amusing at the same time. We don't know what to feel.

ORLAN's work has long been about the impossibility of an integral self. For her, the self is pieced together through multiple performances—the self is "hybridized," to use the artist's term. One's inability to know how to feel upon seeing this image, for example, supports ORLAN's point. Our haplessness before the image, strangely hybridized as it is, reflexively exposes the fissures of our own sutured integrity. The image appeals and repels. We are tossed. Neither here nor there, we experience affective dissonance, a form of fracture at the seams of selfhood. Nothing serious, though—we simply avert our gaze to recompose ourselves.

Painting Portrait of Ru-Ton-Ye-Wee-Ma, Strutting Pigeon resonates with several photographic series in which the artist explored the re-creation of the self, often through performance. In fact, the portrait alludes to one of her earliest works: a photograph of herself giving birth to an androgynous mannequin, titled *Orlan accouche d'elle m'aime* (1964), which translates (via a homophone in French) as both "Orlan Gives Birth to Herself" and "Orlan Loves Herself."[1] In *Strutting Pigeon*, we register a comparable effect: artist as both mother and embracing daughter.

The *American Indian Self-Hybridization* series digitally fuses photographic images of the artist's face with portraits painted by George Catlin in the mid-nineteenth century. Two prior self-hybridization series incorporated images from pre-Columbian statuary and African sculpture and masks, respectively. What, we might ask, is French artist ORLAN's relationship with these portraits of Native Americans? Does she play at being Indian, or does she question the playing of any identity? We note first that many of her Catlin portraits are of Great Plains Indians and that this region was acquired by the U.S. government from France in the Louisiana

Purchase. The area we call Nebraska, for instance, was once French territory. French fur traders intermingled with indigenous peoples, creating what one scholar calls a "cultural and biological hybridization"—the very terms of ORLAN's visual intervention.[2]

French Indians were inducted into Catholic society, though intermarriages were not sanctioned.[3] Catholic iconography offers another core precedent for *Strutting Pigeon*: the paintings of Giotto and Duccio in the late Middle Ages, which depict the Christ Child as a mini-adult. Here, ORLAN casts herself as both Madonna and Child, continuing her ongoing critique of Catholicism, even among the American Indian portraits.

Finally, Strutting Pigeon was one of fourteen Iowa who toured Europe with Catlin's Indian Gallery, in which Native peoples were to perform their identity—in London's Vauxhall Gardens, for instance—by dressing in full regalia, reenacting ritual dances, constructing teepees, riding, shooting, and singing songs.[4] They performed Native Americanness, which reconstructs the identity on display. Strutting Pigeon's portrait was painted in London, while the Iowa back home were relocated to reservations along the Kansas-Nebraska border.[5]

ORLAN's self-hybridization may be seen as the play of self from a French-American postcolonial point of view. The image's English-French-American-Iowa valences yield themselves to transnational perspectives. From this view, the hybridized self is but a microcosm of the hybridized nation—which all nations are. If ORLAN's work seems to lend itself effortlessly to transnational study, it is because the artist herself already inhabits its critique of singularity. **JDV**

1. C. Jill O'Bryan, *Carnal Art: Orlan's Refacing* (Minneapolis: University of Minnesota Press, 2005), 1. **2.** Tanis C. Thorne, *The Many Hands of My Relations: French and Indians on the Lower Missouri* (Columbia: University of Missouri Press, 1996), 65. **3.** Thorne, *The Many Hands*, 82. **4.** *Ru-Ton-Ye-Wee-Ma, Strutting Pigeon, Wife of White Cloud*, Smithsonian American Art Museum, accessed January 24, 2012, http://americanart.si.edu/collections/ search/artwork/?id=4398. The Iowa story is told in George Catlin, *The Adventures of the Ojibbeway and Ioway Indians in England, France, and Belgium*, vol. 2 (London, 1852). **5.** The Iowa had settled along the Platte River before their relocation to reservations in Kansas, Nebraska, and Oklahoma. For a history of the Iowa in the Nebraska region, see Martha Royce Blaine, *The Ioway Indians* (Norman: University of Oklahoma Press, 1979).

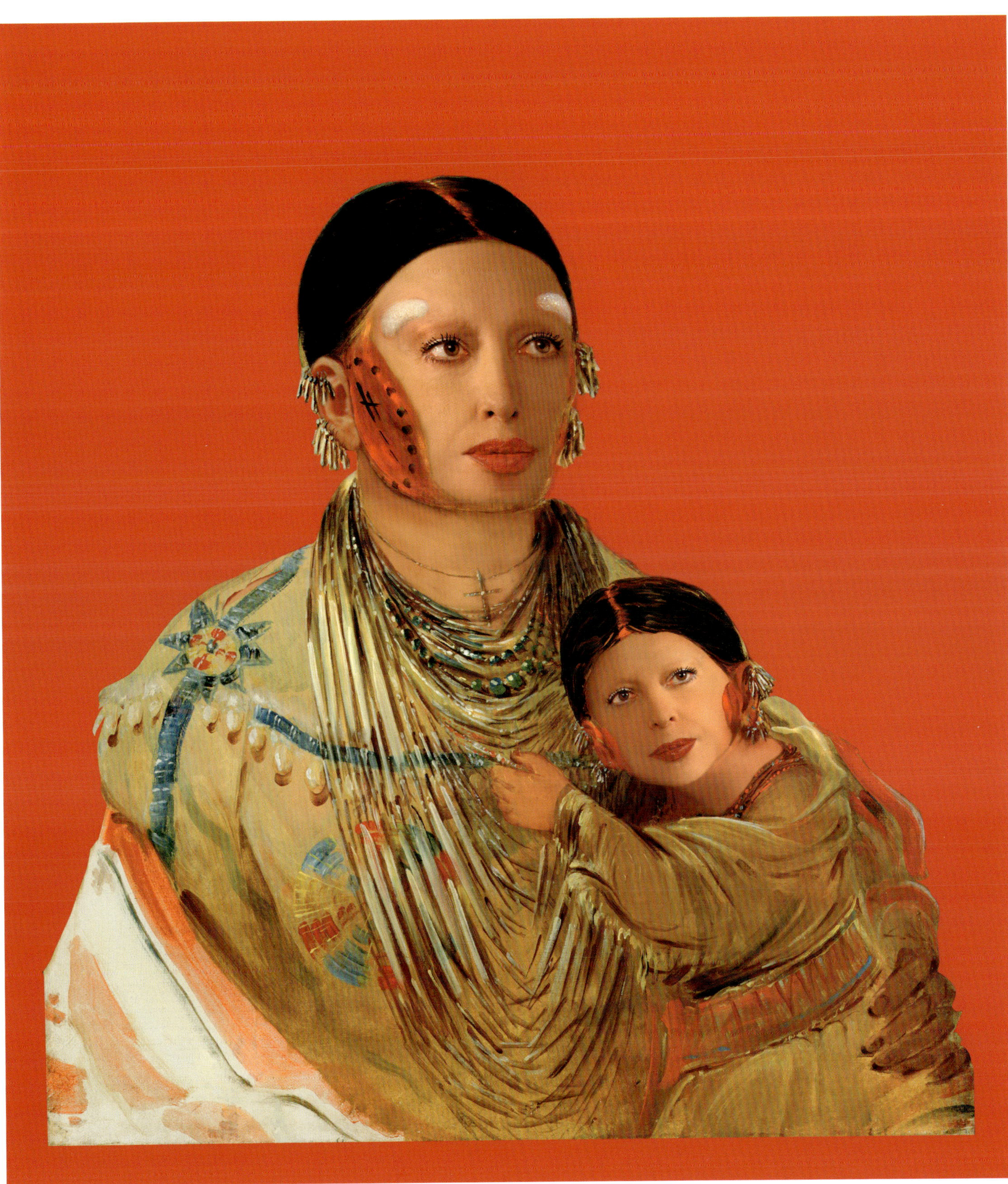

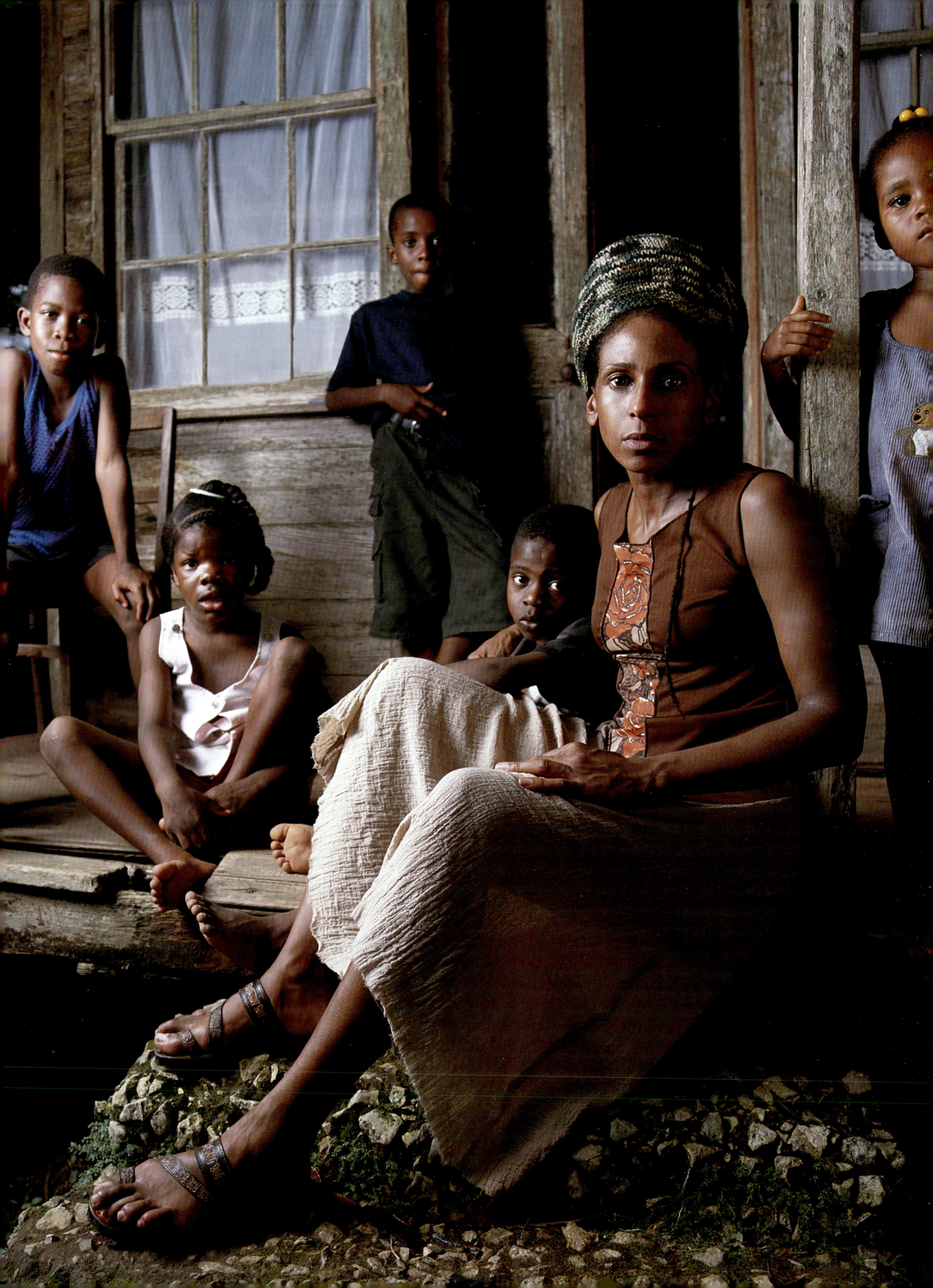

ILLUSTRATION CREDITS

Every effort has been made to contact and acknowledge copyright holders for all reproductions; additional rights holders are encouraged to contact the Sheldon Museum of Art.

Cat. 6: © Lalla Essaydi/Courtesy Edwynn Houk Gallery, New York. **Cat. 11 and p. 24:** © reserved; Sheldon Museum of Art. **Cat. 15:** © 2011 Artists Rights Society (ARS), New York. **Cat. 17:** © The Dorothea Lange Collection, Oakland Museum of California, City of Oakland. Gift of Paul S. Taylor. **Cat. 18:** Aaron Siskind Foundation. **Cat. 19:** Courtesy Graciela Iturbide. **Cat. 20:** © Muna Tseng Dance Projects Inc., New York. **Cat. 21:** Courtesy of the artist and Jack Shainman Gallery, New York. **Cats. 22, 44, and p. 94:** © Sheldon Museum of Art. **Cat. 23:** © Renée Cox. **Cat. 24:** Courtesy of Binh Danh. **Cat. 25:** © Yinka Shonibare, MBE/Courtesy James Cohan Gallery, New York/Shanghai. **Cat. 32:** © Amon Carter Museum of American Art, Fort Worth TX. **p. 70:** © 1979 Amon Carter Museum of American Art, Fort Worth TX. **Cat. 34:** Berenice Abbott/Commerce Graphics. **Cat. 35:** © 2011 The Ansel Adams Publishing Rights Trust. **p. 76:** © 2012 The Ansel Adams Publishing Rights Trust. **Cat. 36:** Margaret Bourke-White/Time & Life Pictures/Getty Images. **Cat. 37:** Terry Evans. **Cat. 38:** Copyright The Estate of Harry Callahan, Courtesy Pace/MacGill Gallery, New York. **Cat. 39:** © Winston Conway Link. **Cat. 40:** Reproduced with the permission of the Minor White Archive, Princeton University Art Museum. © Trustees of Princeton University. **Cat. 41 and p. 88:** Mark Klett. **Cat. 42:** © John Pfahl. **Cat. 43:** © Richard Misrach, courtesy Fraenkel Gallery, San Francisco; Marc Selwyn Fine Art, Los Angeles; and Pace/MacGill Gallery, New York. **Cat. 44 and p. 94:** © Sheldon Museum of Art. **Cat. 48:** Image © Sherry Turner DeCarava, courtesy The DeCarava Archives 2011. **Cat. 49:** © The Estate of Diane Arbus. **Cat. 50:** Danny Lyon, Magnum Photos. **Cat. 51:** © Starr Ockenga. **Cat. 52:** Lauren Greenfield/INSTITUTE. **Cat. 53:** © Sally Mann. Courtesy Gagosian Gallery. **Cat. 54:** Courtesy of Alec Soth. **Cat. 55 and p. 120:** Alinari/Art Resource, New York. **Cat. 56:** © 1910, 2011 The Imogen Cunningham Trust. **Cats. 57 and 100:** © Donna Mussenden VanDerZee. **Cat. 58:** © 1981 Center for Creative Photography, Arizona Board of Regents. **Cats. 59 and 60:** Copyright © Aperture Foundation, Inc., Paul Strand Archive. **Cat. 61:** © The Estate of Erwin Blumenfeld. **Cat. 62 and p. 134:** © Ara Güler—Istanbul—Turkey. **Cat. 63:** Courtesy Joel-Peter Witkin. **Cat. 70:** Photograph by Jacques-Henri Lartigue © Ministère de la Culture—France/AAJHL. **Cat. 71:** © 2011 Artists Rights Society (ARS), New York/ADAGP, Paris. **Cat. 72:** © Estate of André Kertész/Higher Pictures. **Cat. 73:** Henri Cartier-Bresson, Magnum Photos. **Cat. 74:** The Lane Collection. **Cat. 75:** Courtesy of the Estate. **Cat. 76 and p. 164:** Buechel Memorial Lakota Museum, St. Francis Mission. **Cat. 79:** © Asociación Manuel Álvarez Bravo. **Cat. 80:** © Horace Bristol/CORBIS. **Cat. 81:** © 2003 Center for Creative Photography, Arizona Board of Regents. **Cat. 82:** Photo © Estate of Theodore Roszak/Licensed by VAGA, New York NY. **Cat. 83:** Copyright The Estate of Harry Callahan, Courtesy Pace/MacGill Gallery, New York. **Cat. 84 and p. 180:** © Harold & Esther Edgerton Foundation, 2013, courtesy of Palm Press, Inc. **Cat. 85:** © Frederick & Frances Sommer Foundation. **Cat. 86:** Courtesy of Han Van Nguyen. **Cat. 87:** Courtesy of Abelardo Morell and Bonni Benrubi Gallery. **Cat. 88:** © Vera Mercer. **Cat. 95:** Permission of the Estate of Edward Steichen. **Cat. 97:** Image by E. J. Bellocq © Lee Friedlander, courtesy Fraenkel Gallery, San Francisco. **Cat. 98:** © Estate Brassaï—RMN-Grand Palais. **Cat. 100:** © Donna Mussenden VanDerZee. **Cat. 102:** Cecil Beaton/Vogue © The Condé Nast Publications Ltd. **Cat. 103:** © 1935, 2011 The Imogen Cunningham Trust. **Cat. 104:** © Yousuf Karsh. **Cat. 105:** © Estate of George Platt Lynes. **Cat. 106:** Weegee (Arthur Fellig)/International Center of Photography/Getty Images. **Cat. 107 and p. 224:** Reproduced with permission of the Ruth Bernhard Archive, Princeton University Art Museum. © Trustees of Princeton University. **Cat. 108:** Ken Moody © Copyright The Robert Mapplethorpe Foundation. Courtesy Art + Commerce. **Cat. 109:** © Frank Stewart. **Cat. 110:** Courtesy Regen Projects, Los Angeles © Catherine Opie. **Cat. 111 and p. 232:** © Delilah Montoya. **Cat. 112:** Courtesy of ORLAN and Galerie Michel Rein.

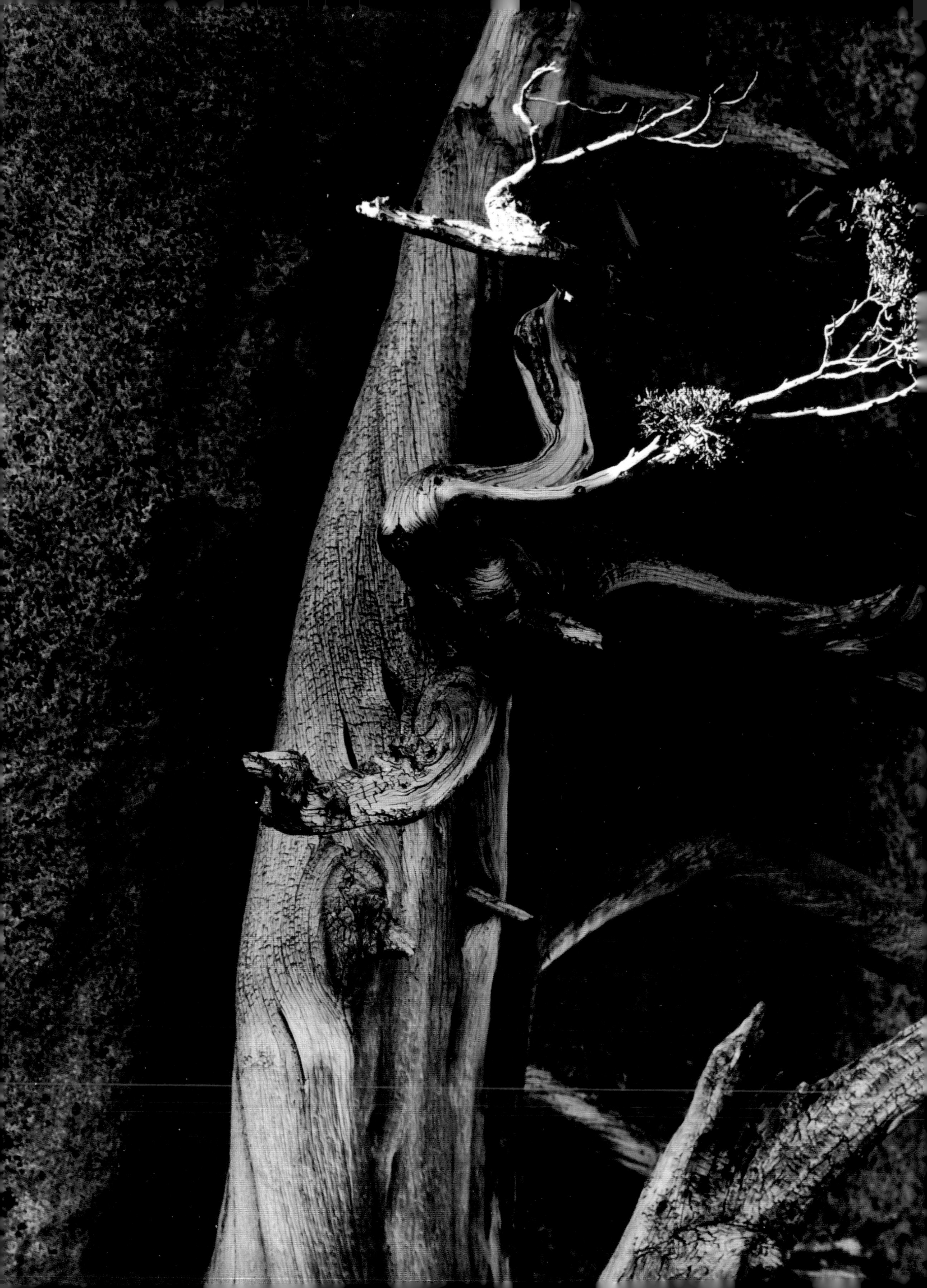

Abbott, Berenice, *Cliff and Ferry Streets*, 74–75

Adams, Ansel, *Moonrise over Hernandez, New Mexico*, 76; *Zabriskie Point, Death Valley National Monument, California*, 76 77

Adamson, Robert, *Portrait of Sir Francis Grant, P.R.A.*, 142–43. *See also* Hill, David Octavius

Alinari Brothers, *Interior of the Cathedral of Siena, Seen from the Presbytery*, 120–21; *Panoramic View of Siena, Seen from S. Domenico*, 120

Álvarez Bravo, Manuel, *The Crouched Ones*, 170–71

Amero, Emilio, *Bride Dancing the Zandunga*, 102–3

Anderson, John A., *Jordan's Trading Post*, 30–31; *Yellow Hair and His Wife, Plenty Horse*, 30

Arbus, Diane, *Child with a Toy Hand Grenade in Central Park, N.Y.C.*, 106–7

Artist Unknown, *Aix-les-Bains–La Place des Bains*, 62

Artist Unknown, *Basket and Broom Peddler*, 2–3

Artist Unknown, *Group Portrait: Men Dressed as Women, Women Dressed as Men*, 198–99

Artist Unknown, *Pair of Female Peeping Toms*, 198–99

Artist Unknown, *Portrait (Woman with Lace Gloves)*, 144–45

Artist Unknown, *Portrait in Regalia*, 192–93

Artist Unknown, *Portrait of Mother and Daughter*, 190, 192–93

Artist Unknown, *Untitled (Street Scene in Kyoto)*, 2

Artist Unknown, *View of the Corinth Canal*, 62–63

Atget, Eugène, *Men's Fashions*, 208, 238; *Versailles, Woman and Soldier, Whorehouse*, 208–9

Bailey, Dix and Mead, *Steps*, 28–29. *See also* Cross, William R.

Beato, Felice (Felix), *Constantinople*, 20–21. *See also* Robertson, James

Beaton, Cecil, *Edith Sitwell, Renishaw Hall*, 214–15

Bedford, Francis, *Ludlow Castle from the River*, 60–61

Bellocq, E. J., *Seated Girl*, 204–5

Bernhard, Ruth, *Two Forms, x*, 224–25; *Two Leaves*, 224

Blumenfeld, Erwin, *Santa Fe Christ*, 132–33

Bonfils, Félix, *Cairo Seen from Mokkatam*, 22–23; *Egyptian Women in Street Costume*, 10–11

Bourke-White, Margaret, *Steel Lines, Fort Peck, Montana*, 78–79

Brancusi, Constantin, *Brancusi at Work in the Studio*, 154–55

Brassaï (Gyula Halász), *Streetwalker, near the Place d'Italie, Paris*, 206–7

Bristol, Horace, *Portrait of Tom Joad*, 172–73

Buechel, Eugene, *Josephine Jumping Eagle in Airplane*, 164–65; *Theodore Bald Eagle and His Wife, Luella Williams*, 164

Callahan, Harry, *Chicago*, 82–83; *Weed against Sky, Detroit*, 178–79

Cameron, Julia Margaret, *Alethea*, 98–99; *Charles Hay Cameron*, 196–97

Cartier-Bresson, Henri, *Behind the Gare St. Lazare, Paris*, 158–59

Coburn, Alvin Langdon, *The Sphinx, London Embankment*, 24–25; *The Water Carrier*, 24

Corot, Jean-Baptiste-Camille, *Souvenir of Ostia*, 146–47

Cox, Renée, *Mother of Us All*, 50–51, 236

Cross, William R., *Steps*, 28–29. *See also* Bailey, Dix and Mead

Cunningham, Imogen, *Gertrude Stein*, 216–17; *Wood beyond the World*, 118, 122–23

Curtis, Edward Sheriff, *Beaver Totem, Deserted Village*, 66; *Part of Columbia Glacier, Prince William Sound*, 66–67

Danh, Binh, *Vivian Nguyen, Environmental Studies, UNL, Class of 2014*, 52–53

DeCarava, Roy, *Graduation*, 104–5

Edgerton, Harold Eugene, *.30 Bullet Piercing an Apple*, 180; *Baton, Multiflash*, 180–81

Essaydi, Lalla, *Les femmes du Maroc, #25, A and B*, 12–15

Evans, Terry, *Dam near Hyderabad*, 80–81

Evans, Walker, *Penny Picture Display, Savannah*, 212–13

Francis Frith and Company, *George Meredith's House at Boxhill, Surrey*, 58; *Village 1906, Alfington*, 58–59

Fritz, Dana, *Humid Tropics, Eden Project*, 94; *Painted Leaves and Dripping Moss, Lied Jungle*, 94–95

Genthe, Arnold, *Paying New Year's Calls, Chinatown, San Francisco,* 4–5; *Portrait of Horace Traubel,* 202–3

Gilpin, Laura, *Sunrise at the Grand Canyon,* 70; *The White House, Canyon de Chelly,* 70–71

González Palma, Luis, *Milagros, ii,* 48–49

Greenfield, Lauren, *Lindsey at a Fourth of July Party Three Days after Her Surgery, Calabasas,* 112–13

Güler, Ara, *"Allah," Old Mosque, Edirne,* 134–35; *Atrium of a House, Tophane, İstanbul,* 134

Hill, David Octavius, *Portrait of Sir Francis Grant, P.R.A.,* 142–43. See also Adamson, Robert

Hine, Lewis, *Slovak Mother—Ellis Island,* 34–35; *Sullivan's Delivery Boy, South Carolina,* 34

Iturbide, Graciela, *El gallo, Juchitán,* 40–41

Jackson, William Henry, *Pike's Peak from the Garden of the Gods,* 64–65

Joaillier, Policarpe, *Fellahine,* 194–95; *A Turkish Woman in Street Dress,* xii, 6–7; *Yuksek-Kaldirim,* 8–9. See also Sébah, Jean Pascal

Jones, Calvert, *The Coliseum, Rome, Second View,* 140

Karsh, Yousuf, *Winston Churchill,* 218–19

Käsebier, Gertrude, *Portrait (Miss N.),* 100; *Sunshine in the House (The Clarence White Family in Maine),* 100–101

Kertész, André, *Satiric Dancer,* 138, 156–57

Klett, Mark, *Looking through the Snow Tunnel above Goat Lake, Sawtooth Range, Idaho,* 88–89; *Storm Clouds over Eastern Idaho: Near Craters of the Moon,* 88

Lange, Dorothea, *The General Strike, San Francisco,* 36–37; *Migrant Mother, Nipomo, California,* 168–69

Lartigue, Jacques-Henri, *Gaby Deslys at the Casino de Paris,* 152–53

Link, O. Winston, *Bringing in the Cows on the Norvel Ryan Farm, as Train No. 3 Passes [Cow 13, Shawsville, Virginia],* 84–85

Lummis, Charles Fletcher, *Pueblo of Taos, Old Church and North House,* 26–27; *Pueblo Santo Domingo, Corn Dance,* 26

Lynes, George Platt, *Marsden Hartley,* 220–21

Lyon, Danny, *Uptown, Chicago, July 1965,* 96, 108–9

Mann, Sally, *Candy Cigarette,* 114–15

Mapplethorpe, Robert, *Ken Moody, 1983,* 226–27

Mercer, Vera, *White Goose,* 188–89

Misrach, Richard, *Desert Fire #1, Burning Palms,* 56, 92–93

Montoya, Delilah, *Doreen Hilton,* 232–33; *Jackie Chavez,* 232

Morell, Abelardo, *Castle Courtyard in Bedroom, Umbertide, Italy,* 186–87

Morris, Wright, *Bench, Cahow's Barbershop, Chapman, Nebraska,* 174–75

Muybridge, Eadweard, *Elephant Walking,* 148; *Lawn Tennis,* 148–49

Nguyen, Han Van, *Untitled,* 184–85

Ockenga, Starr, *Mother and Daughter,* 110–11

Opie, Catherine, *Divinity Fudge,* 230–31

ORLAN, *Painting Portrait of Ru-Ton-Ye-Wee-Ma, Strutting Pigeon, Wife of White Cloud, with ORLAN's Photographic Portrait,* 234–35

Pfahl, John, *Four Corners Power Plant (morning), Farmington, New Mexico,* 90–91

Robertson, James, *Constantinople,* 20–21. See also Beato, Felice (Felix)

Roszak, Theodore, *Untitled (Photogram),* 176–77

Sébah, Jean Pascal, *Fellahine* 194–95; *A Turkish Woman in Street Dress,* xii, 6–7; *Yuksek-Kaldirim,* 8–9. See also Joaillier, Policarpe

Seligmann, Herbert J., *New York, Skyline,* 72–73

Señán y González, *Granada, Alhambra, Door of Justice,* 18–19

Sheeler, Charles, *Barn Reds,* 160; *Buggy (Interior, Bucks County Barn),* 160–61

Shonibare, Yinka, *The Sleep of Reason Produces Monsters (America),* viii, 54–55

Siskind, Aaron, *Uruapan 11, Mexico,* 38–39

Sommer, Frederick, *Smoke on Glass,* xi, 182–83

Soth, Alec, *The Flechs,* 116–17

Steichen, Edward, *Portrait of William Merritt Chase,* 200–201

Steiner, Ralph, *American Rural Baroque,* 162–63

Stewart, Frank, *Smoke and the Lovers,* 228–29

Stieglitz, Alfred, *The Steerage,* 32–33

Strand, Paul, *Church, Cuapiaxtla,* 128–29; *Crucifixion, Tlacochoaya, Oaxaca,* 130–31

Taber, Isaiah West, *Sentinel Rock and Sentinel Falls,* 68–69; *Three Brothers, Yosemite Valley,* 68

Talbot, William Henry Fox, *Chess Players,* 140–41

Tseng Kwong Chi, *New York, New York,* 42–43

Ulmann, Doris, *Woman and Child,* 166–67

VanDerZee, James, *Black Jews, Harlem,* 124–25; *Garveyite Family, Harlem,* 210–11

Weegee (Arthur Fellig), *Policeman and Buttonman,* 222–23

Weems, Carrie Mae, *Grabbing Snatching Blink and You Be Gone,* 44–47

Weston, Edward, *Church at "E" Town, New Mexico,* 126–27

White, Clarence Hudson, *Boys Wrestling,* 150; *Dewdrops,* 150–51

White, Minor, *Juniper, Lake Tenaya, California,* 86–87, 238

Witkin, Joel-Peter, *The Wife of Cain,* 136–37

Zangaki, Adelphoi, *Fantasia d'un mariage,* 16; *Femme turque,* 16–17